The Celtic Story

The Will to Win

ALLAN CANNING

TOMMY CANNING

PATRICK CANNING

MAINSTREAM
PUBLISHING

EDINBURGH AND LONDON

First published in Great Britain in 1988 by
MAINSTREAM PUBLISHING COMPANY
(EDINBURGH) LTD
7 Albany Street
Edinburgh EH1 3UG

ISBN 9781845964016

A catalogue record for this book is available
from the British Library

Printed in Great Britain by
Butler, Tanner & Dennis Ltd, Frome, Somerset

Dedicated to:

Our Blessed Lady. Our thanks to her not only because Celtic came into being in St Mary's hall in the Calton but also because all the best things in our lives have come through her.

Our late father, John Canning: a true Celtic man until his untimely death in 1974. As a young man in the 1950s, he was involved in the running of the New Stevenston Lanarkshire branch of the Celtic Supporters Club. Understandably, he instilled in his five sons a love of Celtic, and we are forever grateful to him for handing on 'the faith' to us. We miss you even more each day.

The memory of Tommy Burns and all the deceased members of the Celtic family, both players and supporters, who are the reason we fans have dreams and songs to sing. Thank you. *Requiescat in Pace*. Amen.

ACKNOWLEDGEMENTS

Our thanks to Billy McNeill for contributing the foreword to this edition of the book. Billy McNeill's association with the book goes back to the original publication in the centenary year when, as manager of Celtic, he along with captain Roy Aitken came along to promote the book at its launch one cold autumn day in St Mary's hall in the Calton. A few days later, they led Celtic to victory over Rangers at Celtic Park, winning three goals to one.

Our thanks also to Jack McGinn, chairman of Celtic in 1988, who along with then editor of the *Celtic View* Kevin McKenna suggested we try having the idea published as a book rather than feature as a comic strip in the *Celtic View*. Jack McGinn also kindly wrote the foreword for the original publication as well as commissioning us to paint a portrait of Jock Stein for the newly dedicated lounge in Celtic Park. This was followed shortly after by a portrait of Brother Walfrid that was commissioned as a gift to the Celtic Supporters Club named after him in Co. Sligo.

Our gratitude is due to Pat Woods for use of his extensive collection of Celtic imagery from a long way back, as well as insights, facts and figures that were so crucial in the research for the original publication. To our friend and retired postmaster in Clynder, Douglas Nicholson, an ardent Celtic fan who gave us use of every *Celtic View* that had been published since 1967. To our friend Kevin Gallagher, whose photographic memory and total recall about Celtic is legendary, a man with the holiness of Pope Pius XII and the charisma of Charlie Tully all rolled into one. The Gallagher family are steeped in the history of Celtic, and Kevin was a reliable source for some of the apocryphal tales and quotes that appear, especially the humorous ones involving Celtic fans. To another friend Gerry McGrane for his assistance with photography used in the cover art. To Father Dominic Mary of the Franciscans of the Eternal Word in Alabama, USA, for his promise of prayers and encouragement for the work we undertook in the new edition. To John Cassidy and Geraldine Reid of Quigley's Point for the kind permission to use their inspirational music for promotion of the book on the website. Also to Bob Halligan Jnr of Ceili Rain for permission to use his amazing music for the website video clips. To Tony Hamilton at Celtic Media and Margot McCuaig at Celtic TV for their kind assistance with our research and photography of Celtic Park on match days. Our thanks also to Bill Campbell and Peter Mackenzie, along with all the staff at Mainstream Publishing who made this book a reality.

To all our family and friends who have supported us through the work on the book with their cheerful encouragement and good wishes. To Patrick's wife Marilyn for all her labours on the Internet informing Celtic Supporters Clubs worldwide. And last but not least to our mother, Mary Canning, whose idea it was back in 1987 to produce the book in the first place and whose presence in our lives continues to be a source of inspiration.

FOREWORD

Every now and again, more frequently than I can count, someone will ask me what my most vivid memory of Celtic is. Usually, I'm asked by a supporter who wants to know about my playing career. The most obvious and expected reply would be lifting the European Cup in Lisbon 1967. But sometimes other experiences come back to me, almost more memorable and vivid, as if they only just happened the other day.

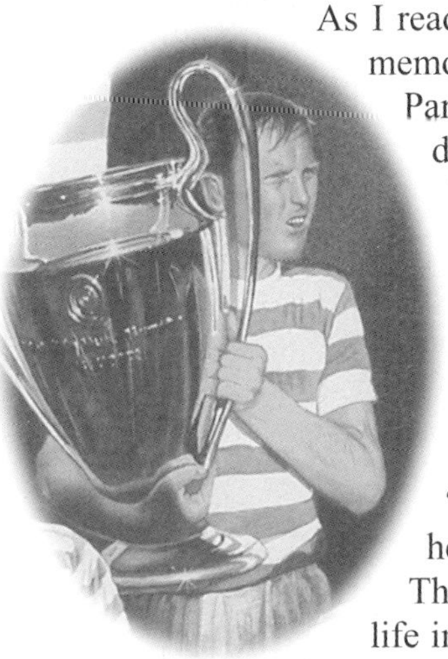

As I read through *The Celtic Story: The Will to Win,* I was overwhelmed by the memories that came flooding back, including one of my very first visit to Celtic Park and taking my place in the Jungle with my auntie Grace. In those far-off days, there were no seats in the Jungle; in fact, conditions were quite basic by today's standards – just a series of broad steps with no barriers to hold on to. Once a packed Jungle started to sway, there was no way you could keep your feet. On this particular occasion, if I remember right, the game with Rangers was tied at 1–1 with only a few minutes left to play when Charlie Tully – the least likely player on the park to do so – headed in the winner for Celtic. As you can imagine, the Celtic support went wild, and the Jungle especially. All I could hear from my aunt was, 'Help, Billy, I've lost my shoe!' To this day, I still laugh when I think of her limping back to the bus stop wearing the one shoe.

This is what's so special about this book – the expertly drawn pages bring to life in a unique way the story of Celtic and will prompt memories of their own in the reader.

Over the years, the many players who have come from abroad to play for Celtic usually say the familiar words: 'Celtic are such a big club, the chance to play here is too good to pass up.' But I would say that, true though these sentiments are, this is still a huge understatement. Celtic is much more than just a big football club; the supporters and club together make one family and, as in every family, they are united through the good times as well as the bad.

As the players will all testify, even many years after pulling on the green and white hoops of Celtic they are still regarded as part of the family and are welcomed and honoured with love and affection in even the most far-flung corners of the world. I am always, as I'm sure they are, genuinely surprised and moved by the depth of this affection.

Over the years, we can recall the grief at the loss of some of the famous names from the family: wee Jimmy, Bobby Murdoch, Ronnie Simpson – my fellow Lisbon Lions; in more recent days, former players like Phil O'Donnell and Tommy Burns. The latter died as I was sitting down to pen these words. I am sure that when Tommy died, the universal outpouring of grief was merited, as Tommy was in many ways a genuine Celtic man. He fully embodied what is really meant by the term. Always the Celtic fan, he knew how the fans felt about the club and the players. Both as a player and manager, he would always make himself available to the supporters. Tommy had his priorities in the right order: faith, family, then football; but you'd be hard pushed to separate them. His contribution both to the game and to society was immense and widespread, as we saw with the reaction from every sphere following his death.

One thing I am certain of is that no one will be unmoved when reading this book – I know I wasn't – and it will become a treasured part of every Celtic fan's, and indeed any football supporter's, library.

Billy McNeill MBE

INTRODUCTION

*T**he Celtic Story: The Will to Win* was first published by Mainstream 20 years ago during Celtic's centenary year. We held the book launch appropriately in the very same hall of St Mary's in the Calton where Celtic were founded.

We all have very vivid and emotional memories of that first publication. We waded through an enormous amount of material while researching and compiling the book, and even though we were all much younger (Tommy was just 18 years old), the workload was overwhelming at times as we toiled around the clock for over eight months, trying to complete the artwork and story at the same time as Celtic were winning the double in that memorable season 1987–88.

In the years following the first publication, we discovered that the book was particularly treasured by older fans, who enjoyed reading it as a bedtime story to their children and grandchildren. Reminiscing about games or players they remembered would usually lead them to elaborate on a particular episode or character. One father confessed that he was moved to tears when he read to his young son the episode regarding the death of John Thomson. The dramatic recreation in the book really brought home to him the sadness and tragedy of Thomson's untimely death. It brought tears to his eyes and made a deep impression on his young child, too.

We heard through letters to fanzines or through speaking to fans themselves that some people were desperately searching for another new copy, as their own book had become tattered and worn. It had become a rare collector's item. Gradually, the idea to do a new revised edition with additional material became a reality, and so here it is. This edition contains the material from the original book plus new images and accounts of events over the last 20 years. The new material includes some of the highlights as well as the humour, triumphs and tragedies of these past two decades.

When we first had the idea to re-visit *The Celtic Story*, we thought it would be a straightforward matter once we had dug out the old artwork. Little did we realise that we would be creating almost a complete second book, such have been the achievements of the club over the last 20-year period. Once again, we found ourselves working into the wee small hours and rising early in the morning as we toiled to meet the publishing deadline. There were other similarities, as season 2007–08 turned out to be as eventful as that of 20 years earlier. There were many unexpected twists and turns, but Celtic duly obliged by winning the Championship in dramatic fashion, giving us the perfect ending to our story. Gordon Strachan, being only the third manager in Celtic's history to win three League titles in succession, has reached an important milestone and joins Willie Maley and Jock Stein in the history books.

We believed 20 years ago and still do today that this is a novel and unique way to tell the story of Celtic, making it more accessible to young readers and introducing them to the history of the club in a way that may be less intimidating than a written tome or even a DVD with the same footage that they might have seen before. The format was to be that of a comic book. *Roy of the Rovers* immediately sprang to mind, and Celtic fans would argue that the fictional stories and exploits of comic-book footballers are quite tame in comparison with the events, folklore and characters in the colourful 'fairytale' history of Celtic. An example of the challenge we faced, however, can be seen when it came to recreating visually the goal of Patsy Gallacher in the 1925 Scottish Cup final against Dundee. Patsy took on half of the opposing team and ended his run by somersaulting over the goalkeeper into the net with the ball between his feet. Who would have believed such a goal was scored? Extraordinary, and yet it's true, but previously the only record of it was in the written or verbal accounts from players and people who were there. It is now lovingly recreated in this book for all to see and imagine how it might have looked.

When considering where to begin with the new artwork and more recent events, being admirers of Tommy Burns, both as a player and as a person, he came to mind immediately. So the very first drawings for the new edition were some images of Tommy Burns in action. This was back in January of 2008 and, at that time, we had no idea that Tommy would no longer be with us by the end of the football season in May. It seemed fitting to begin this version of the book with him and to let him be a starting point for the whole story of Celtic.

From the front cover to the last page in the book, we hope this telling of Celtic's history brings a smile, a laugh and a tear, and above all hope, as it celebrates the club's humble origins and remarkable achievements thus far. We certainly had a lot of fun putting it together, and we hope it will bring to life the events in Celtic's history and become a collector's item for a whole new generation of fans as well as some of the older fans who wanted a new updated version. This is for them.

When all is said and done, the three of us feel honoured and privileged to have been involved in the creation of such a book — with its combination of excellent illustrations by Tommy, some words by Patrick and the backgrounds and layouts by Allan — which invokes heart-warming memories of Celtic's finest players and fans. It's a unique club with a unique history, but of course you already knew that.

As part of the Celtic family, we hope other members of the family will appreciate what we have tried to do in the re-telling of Celtic's story. All that remains now is to sit back, read and enjoy. Hail, hail!

Patrick, Tommy and Allan Canning

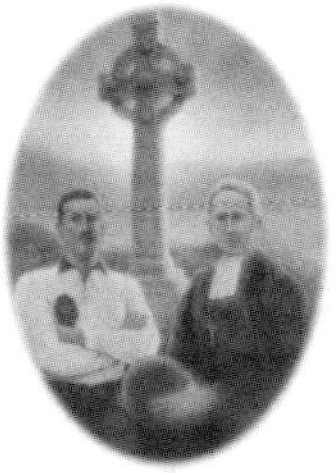

PROLOGUE

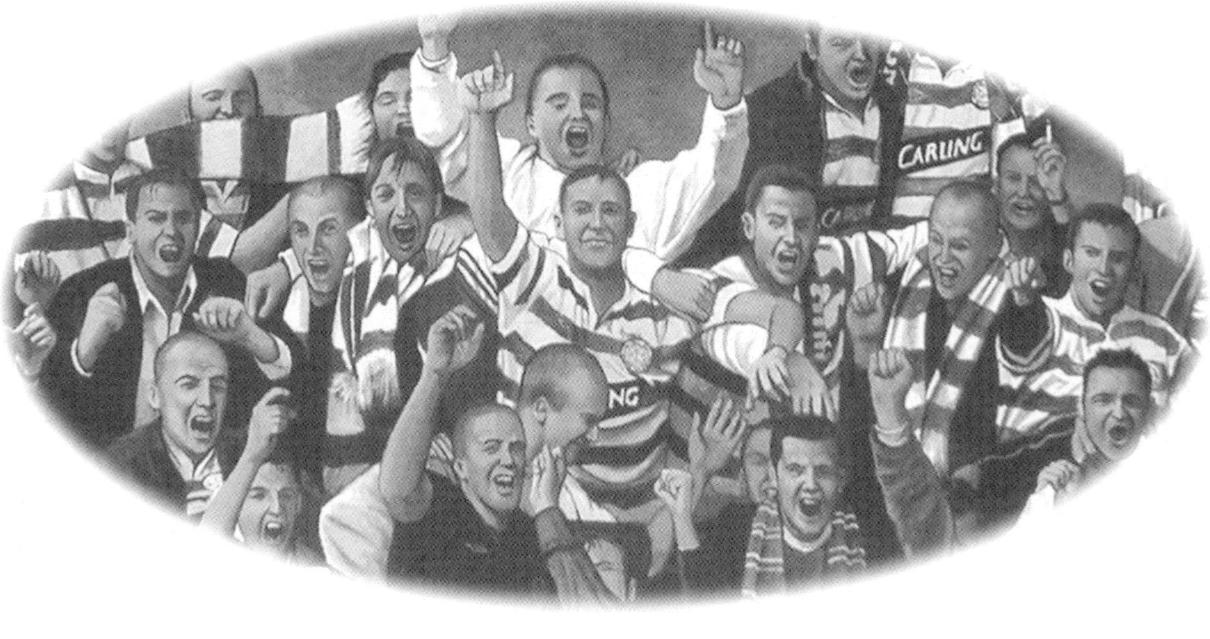
CARLING

perpetual light

'with hope in your heart'

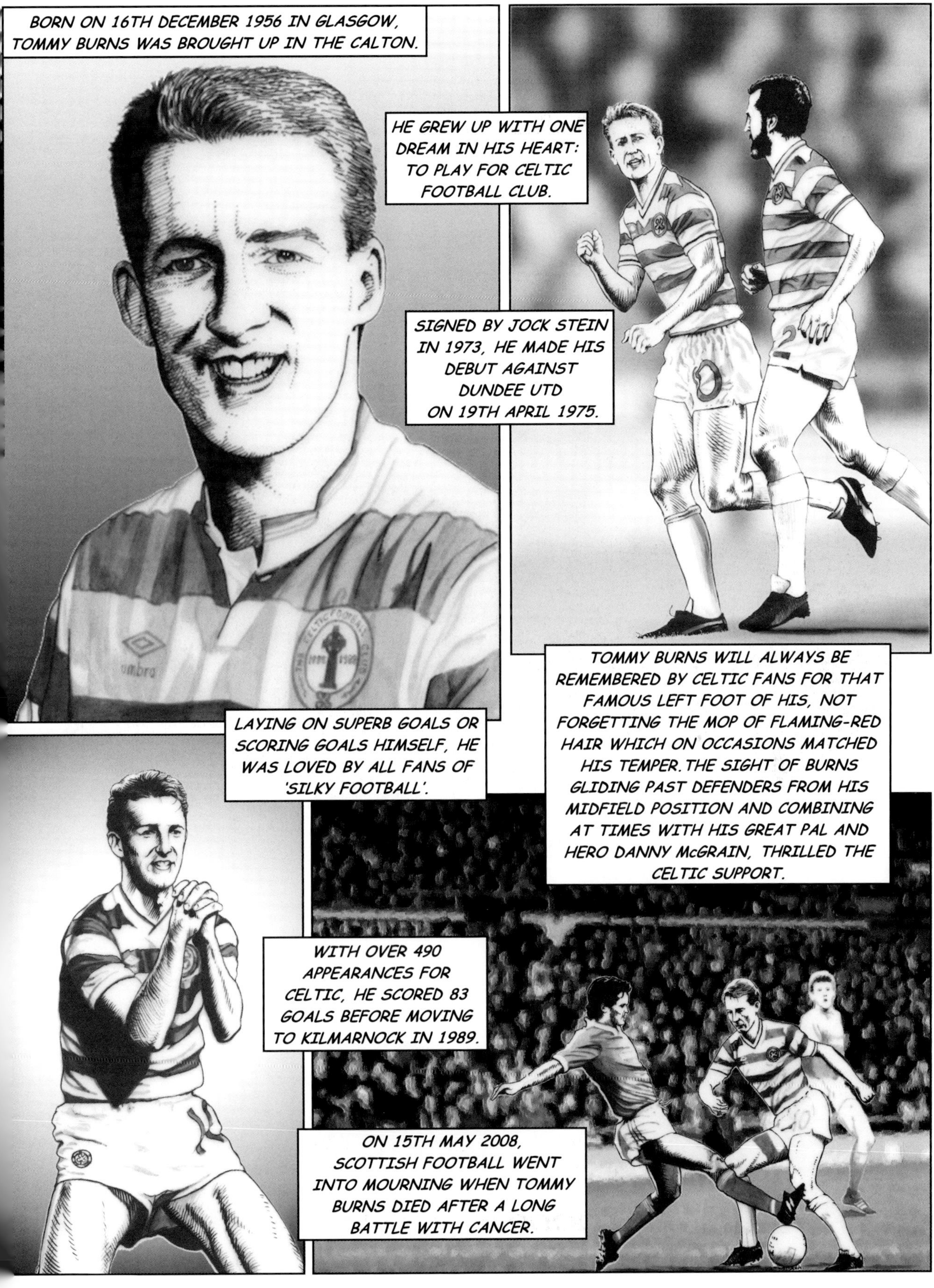
BORN ON 16TH DECEMBER 1956 IN GLASGOW, TOMMY BURNS WAS BROUGHT UP IN THE CALTON.
HE GREW UP WITH ONE DREAM IN HIS HEART: TO PLAY FOR CELTIC FOOTBALL CLUB.
SIGNED BY JOCK STEIN IN 1973, HE MADE HIS DEBUT AGAINST DUNDEE UTD ON 19TH APRIL 1975.
TOMMY BURNS WILL ALWAYS BE REMEMBERED BY CELTIC FANS FOR THAT FAMOUS LEFT FOOT OF HIS, NOT FORGETTING THE MOP OF FLAMING-RED HAIR WHICH ON OCCASIONS MATCHED HIS TEMPER. THE SIGHT OF BURNS GLIDING PAST DEFENDERS FROM HIS MIDFIELD POSITION AND COMBINING AT TIMES WITH HIS GREAT PAL AND HERO DANNY McGRAIN, THRILLED THE CELTIC SUPPORT.
LAYING ON SUPERB GOALS OR SCORING GOALS HIMSELF, HE WAS LOVED BY ALL FANS OF 'SILKY FOOTBALL'.
WITH OVER 490 APPEARANCES FOR CELTIC, HE SCORED 83 GOALS BEFORE MOVING TO KILMARNOCK IN 1989.
ON 15TH MAY 2008, SCOTTISH FOOTBALL WENT INTO MOURNING WHEN TOMMY BURNS DIED AFTER A LONG BATTLE WITH CANCER.

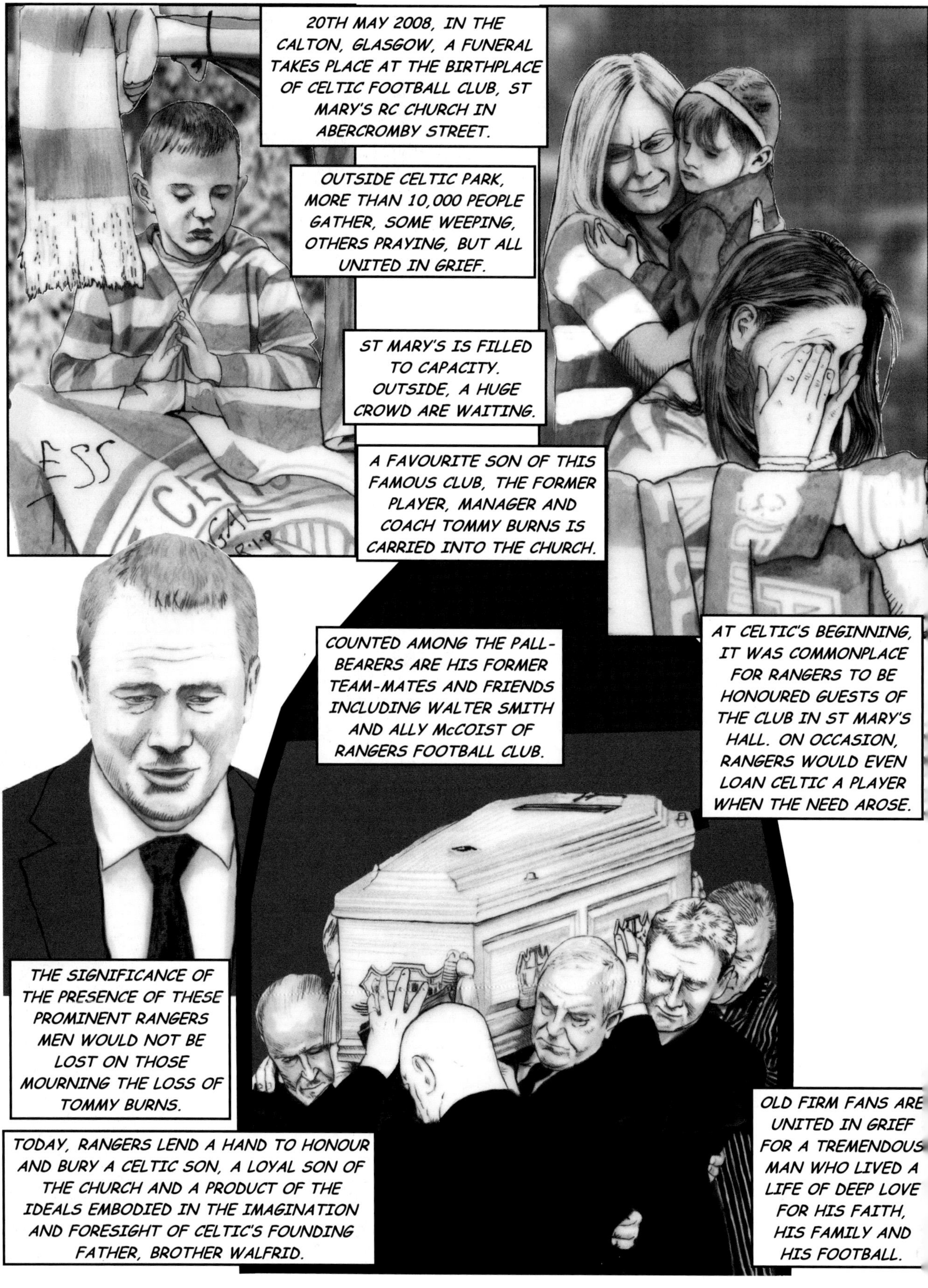
20TH MAY 2008, IN THE CALTON, GLASGOW, A FUNERAL TAKES PLACE AT THE BIRTHPLACE OF CELTIC FOOTBALL CLUB, ST MARY'S RC CHURCH IN ABERCROMBY STREET.
OUTSIDE CELTIC PARK, MORE THAN 10,000 PEOPLE GATHER, SOME WEEPING, OTHERS PRAYING, BUT ALL UNITED IN GRIEF.
ST MARY'S IS FILLED TO CAPACITY. OUTSIDE, A HUGE CROWD ARE WAITING.
A FAVOURITE SON OF THIS FAMOUS CLUB, THE FORMER PLAYER, MANAGER AND COACH TOMMY BURNS IS CARRIED INTO THE CHURCH.
AT CELTIC'S BEGINNING, IT WAS COMMONPLACE FOR RANGERS TO BE HONOURED GUESTS OF THE CLUB IN ST MARY'S HALL. ON OCCASION, RANGERS WOULD EVEN LOAN CELTIC A PLAYER WHEN THE NEED AROSE.
COUNTED AMONG THE PALL-BEARERS ARE HIS FORMER TEAM-MATES AND FRIENDS INCLUDING WALTER SMITH AND ALLY McCOIST OF RANGERS FOOTBALL CLUB.
THE SIGNIFICANCE OF THE PRESENCE OF THESE PROMINENT RANGERS MEN WOULD NOT BE LOST ON THOSE MOURNING THE LOSS OF TOMMY BURNS.
TODAY, RANGERS LEND A HAND TO HONOUR AND BURY A CELTIC SON, A LOYAL SON OF THE CHURCH AND A PRODUCT OF THE IDEALS EMBODIED IN THE IMAGINATION AND FORESIGHT OF CELTIC'S FOUNDING FATHER, BROTHER WALFRID.
OLD FIRM FANS ARE UNITED IN GRIEF FOR A TREMENDOUS MAN WHO LIVED A LIFE OF DEEP LOVE FOR HIS FAITH, HIS FAMILY AND HIS FOOTBALL.

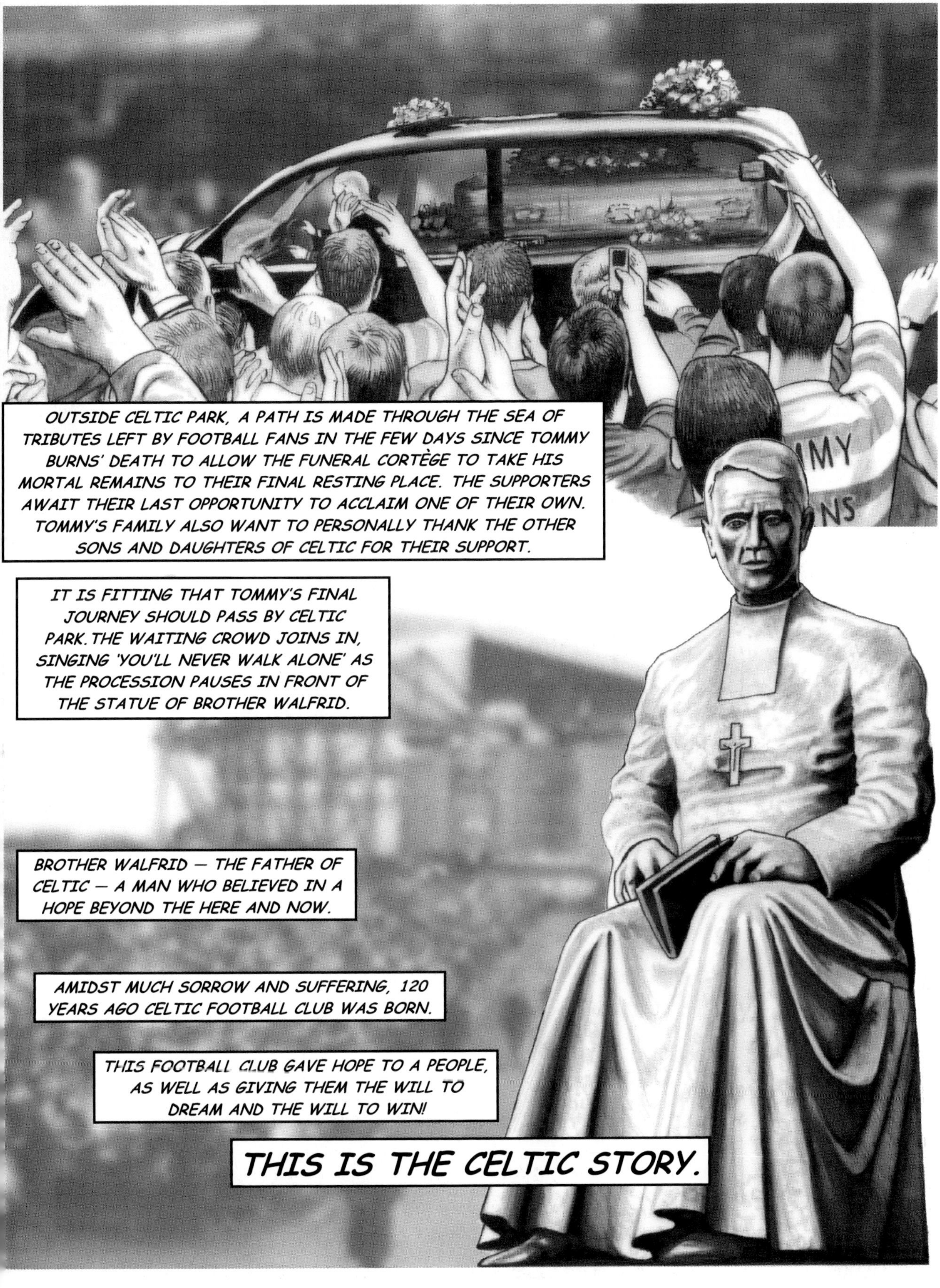
OUTSIDE CELTIC PARK, A PATH IS MADE THROUGH THE SEA OF TRIBUTES LEFT BY FOOTBALL FANS IN THE FEW DAYS SINCE TOMMY BURNS' DEATH TO ALLOW THE FUNERAL CORTÈGE TO TAKE HIS MORTAL REMAINS TO THEIR FINAL RESTING PLACE. THE SUPPORTERS AWAIT THEIR LAST OPPORTUNITY TO ACCLAIM ONE OF THEIR OWN. TOMMY'S FAMILY ALSO WANT TO PERSONALLY THANK THE OTHER SONS AND DAUGHTERS OF CELTIC FOR THEIR SUPPORT.
IT IS FITTING THAT TOMMY'S FINAL JOURNEY SHOULD PASS BY CELTIC PARK.THE WAITING CROWD JOINS IN, SINGING 'YOU'LL NEVER WALK ALONE' AS THE PROCESSION PAUSES IN FRONT OF THE STATUE OF BROTHER WALFRID.
BROTHER WALFRID — THE FATHER OF CELTIC — A MAN WHO BELIEVED IN A HOPE BEYOND THE HERE AND NOW.
AMIDST MUCH SORROW AND SUFFERING, 120 YEARS AGO CELTIC FOOTBALL CLUB WAS BORN.
THIS FOOTBALL CLUB GAVE HOPE TO A PEOPLE, AS WELL AS GIVING THEM THE WILL TO DREAM AND THE WILL TO WIN!
THIS IS THE CELTIC STORY.

chapter 1

Beginnings

'when you walk'

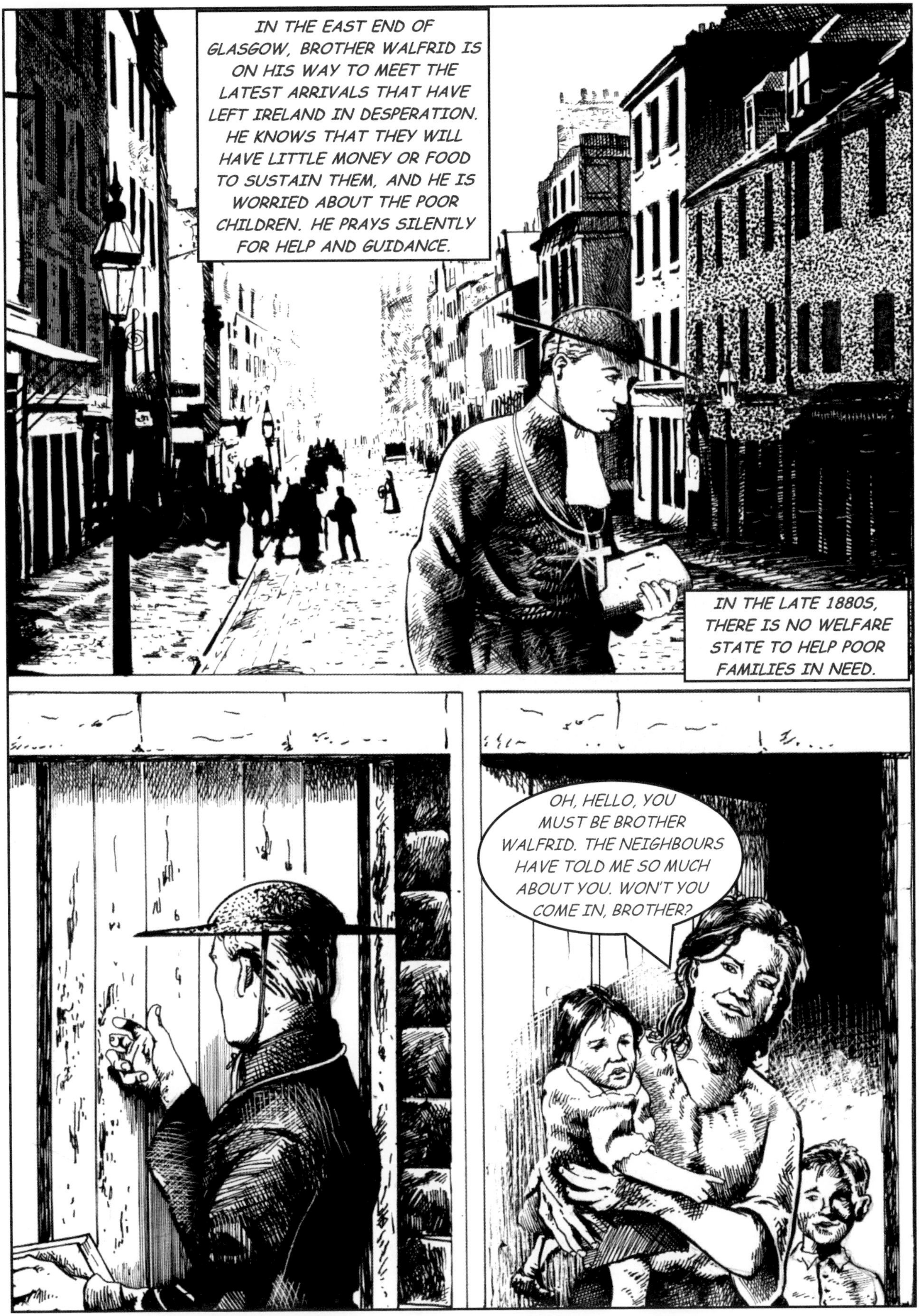
IN THE EAST END OF GLASGOW, BROTHER WALFRID IS ON HIS WAY TO MEET THE LATEST ARRIVALS THAT HAVE LEFT IRELAND IN DESPERATION. HE KNOWS THAT THEY WILL HAVE LITTLE MONEY OR FOOD TO SUSTAIN THEM, AND HE IS WORRIED ABOUT THE POOR CHILDREN. HE PRAYS SILENTLY FOR HELP AND GUIDANCE.
IN THE LATE 1880S, THERE IS NO WELFARE STATE TO HELP POOR FAMILIES IN NEED.
OH, HELLO, YOU MUST BE BROTHER WALFRID. THE NEIGHBOURS HAVE TOLD ME SO MUCH ABOUT YOU. WON'T YOU COME IN, BROTHER?

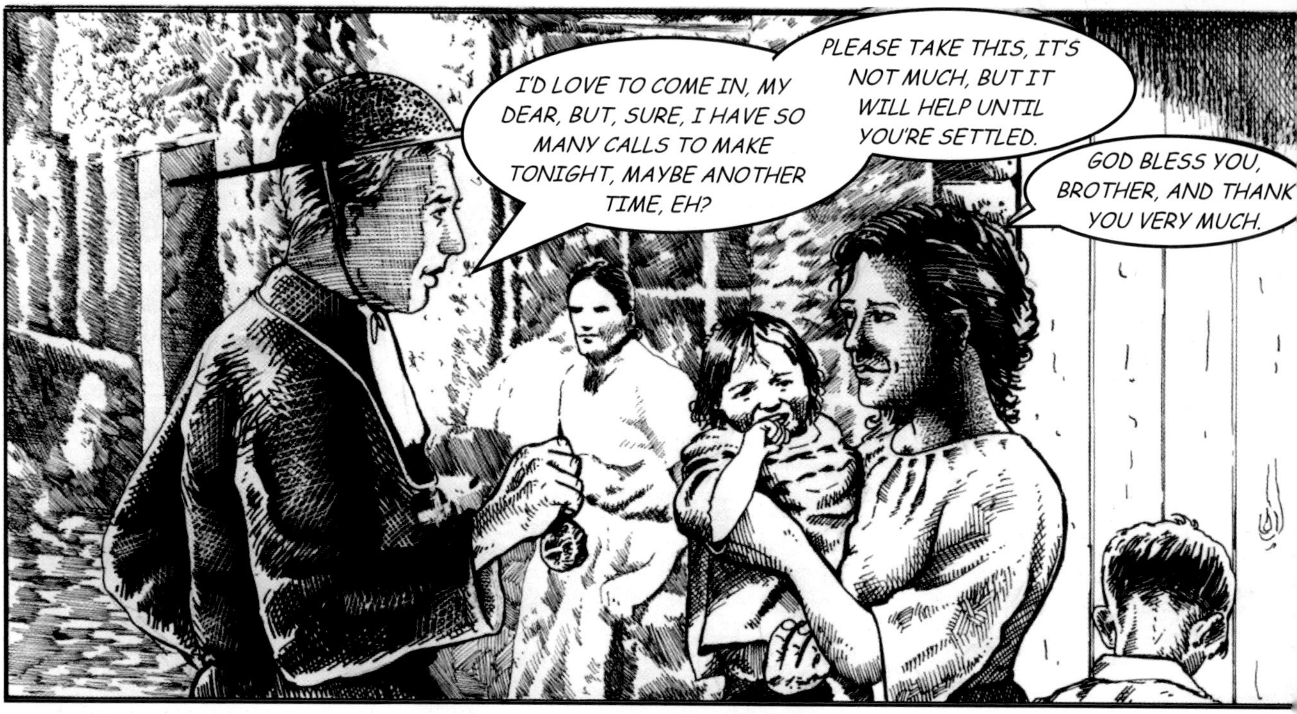
I'D LOVE TO COME IN, MY DEAR, BUT, SURE, I HAVE SO MANY CALLS TO MAKE TONIGHT, MAYBE ANOTHER TIME, EH?
PLEASE TAKE THIS, IT'S NOT MUCH, BUT IT WILL HELP UNTIL YOU'RE SETTLED.
GOD BLESS YOU, BROTHER, AND THANK YOU VERY MUCH.

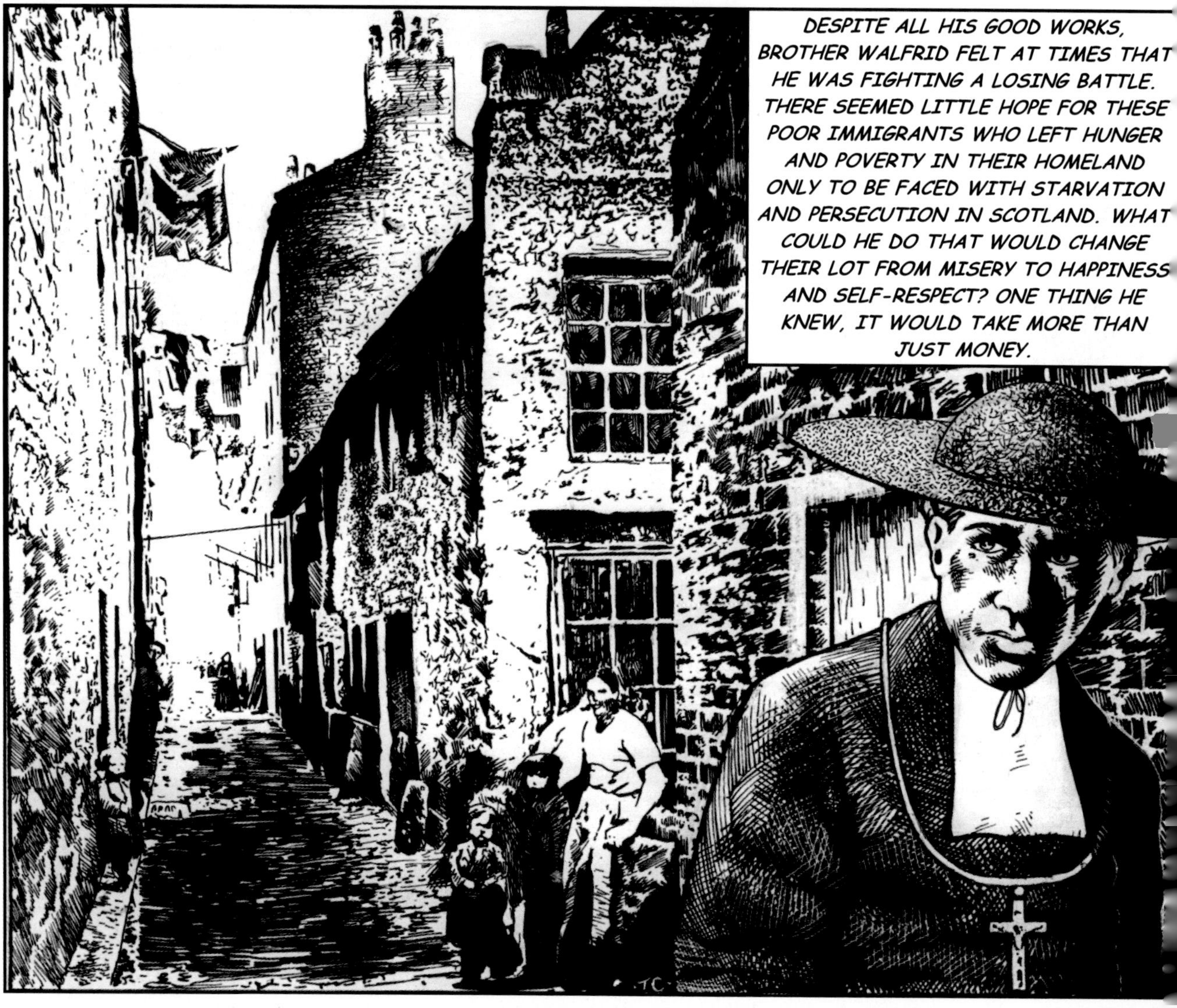
DESPITE ALL HIS GOOD WORKS, BROTHER WALFRID FELT AT TIMES THAT HE WAS FIGHTING A LOSING BATTLE. THERE SEEMED LITTLE HOPE FOR THESE POOR IMMIGRANTS WHO LEFT HUNGER AND POVERTY IN THEIR HOMELAND ONLY TO BE FACED WITH STARVATION AND PERSECUTION IN SCOTLAND. WHAT COULD HE DO THAT WOULD CHANGE THEIR LOT FROM MISERY TO HAPPINESS AND SELF-RESPECT? ONE THING HE KNEW, IT WOULD TAKE MORE THAN JUST MONEY.

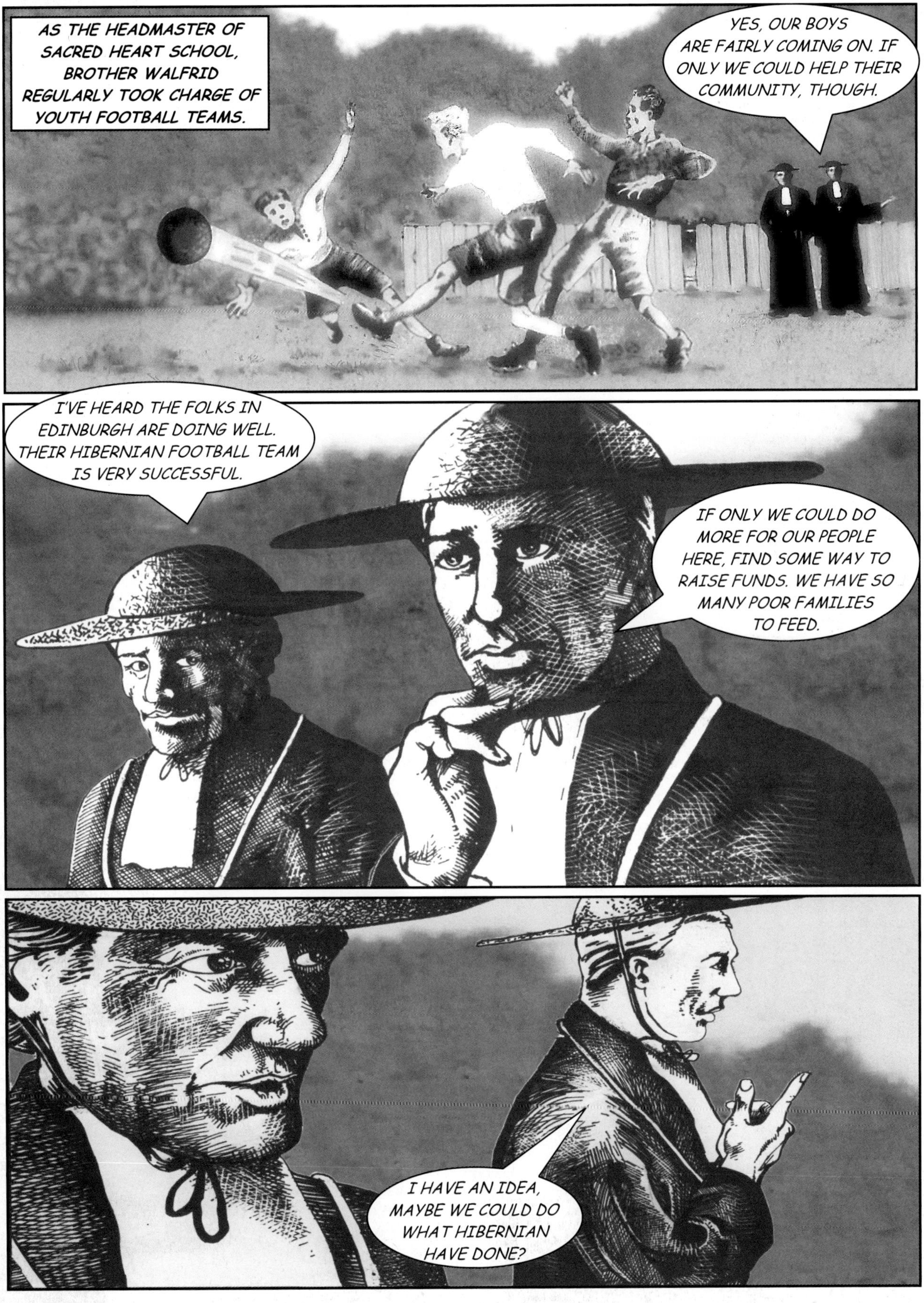
AS THE HEADMASTER OF SACRED HEART SCHOOL, BROTHER WALFRID REGULARLY TOOK CHARGE OF YOUTH FOOTBALL TEAMS.
YES, OUR BOYS ARE FAIRLY COMING ON. IF ONLY WE COULD HELP THEIR COMMUNITY, THOUGH.
I'VE HEARD THE FOLKS IN EDINBURGH ARE DOING WELL. THEIR HIBERNIAN FOOTBALL TEAM IS VERY SUCCESSFUL.
IF ONLY WE COULD DO MORE FOR OUR PEOPLE HERE, FIND SOME WAY TO RAISE FUNDS. WE HAVE SO MANY POOR FAMILIES TO FEED.
I HAVE AN IDEA, MAYBE WE COULD DO WHAT HIBERNIAN HAVE DONE?

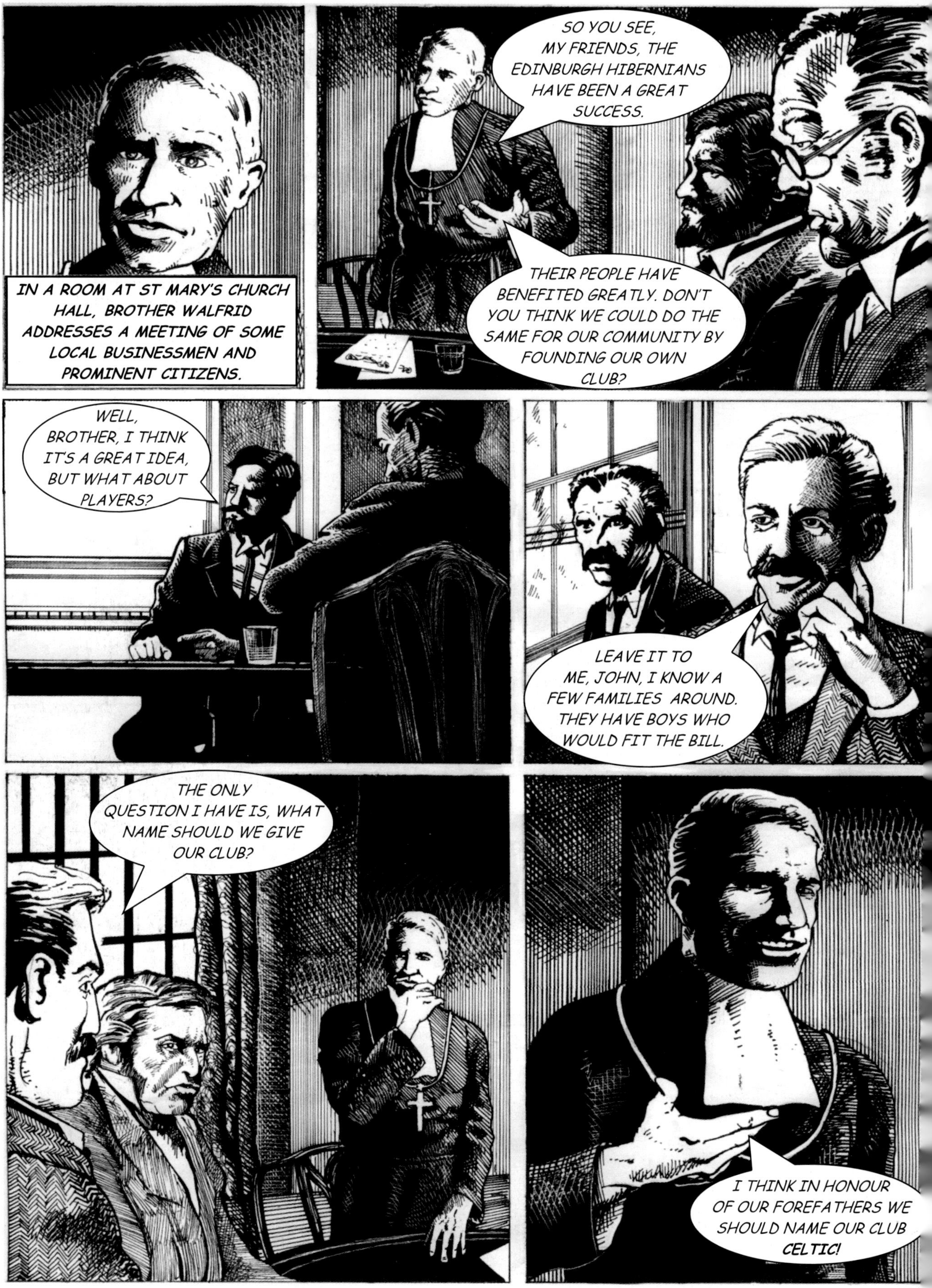
IN A ROOM AT ST MARY'S CHURCH HALL, BROTHER WALFRID ADDRESSES A MEETING OF SOME LOCAL BUSINESSMEN AND PROMINENT CITIZENS.
SO YOU SEE, MY FRIENDS, THE EDINBURGH HIBERNIANS HAVE BEEN A GREAT SUCCESS.
THEIR PEOPLE HAVE BENEFITED GREATLY. DON'T YOU THINK WE COULD DO THE SAME FOR OUR COMMUNITY BY FOUNDING OUR OWN CLUB?
WELL, BROTHER, I THINK IT'S A GREAT IDEA, BUT WHAT ABOUT PLAYERS?
LEAVE IT TO ME, JOHN, I KNOW A FEW FAMILIES AROUND. THEY HAVE BOYS WHO WOULD FIT THE BILL.
THE ONLY QUESTION I HAVE IS, WHAT NAME SHOULD WE GIVE OUR CLUB?
I THINK IN HONOUR OF OUR FOREFATHERS WE SHOULD NAME OUR CLUB CELTIC!

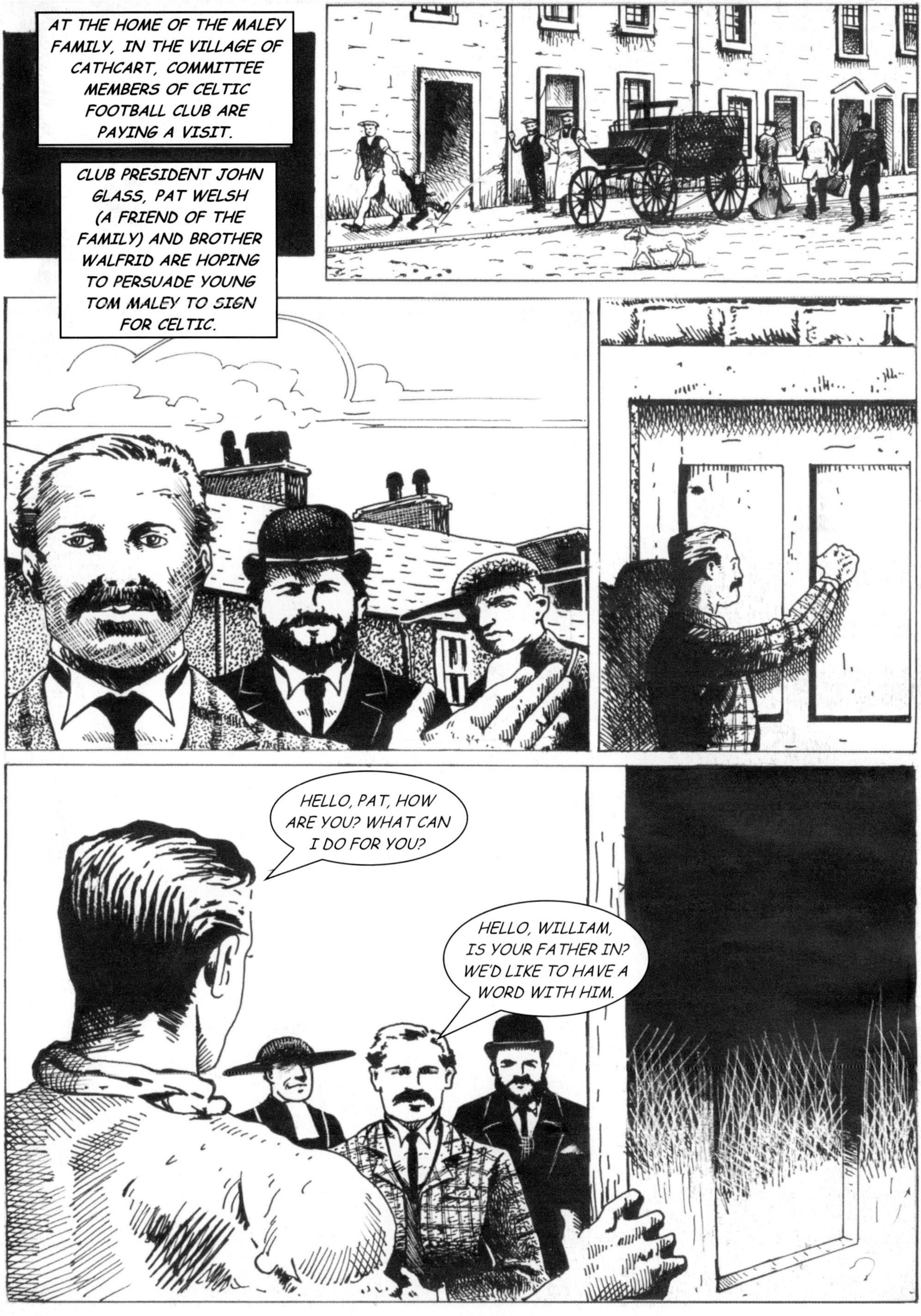
AT THE HOME OF THE MALEY FAMILY, IN THE VILLAGE OF CATHCART, COMMITTEE MEMBERS OF CELTIC FOOTBALL CLUB ARE PAYING A VISIT.
CLUB PRESIDENT JOHN GLASS, PAT WELSH (A FRIEND OF THE FAMILY) AND BROTHER WALFRID ARE HOPING TO PERSUADE YOUNG TOM MALEY TO SIGN FOR CELTIC.
HELLO, PAT, HOW ARE YOU? WHAT CAN I DO FOR YOU?
HELLO, WILLIAM, IS YOUR FATHER IN? WE'D LIKE TO HAVE A WORD WITH HIM.

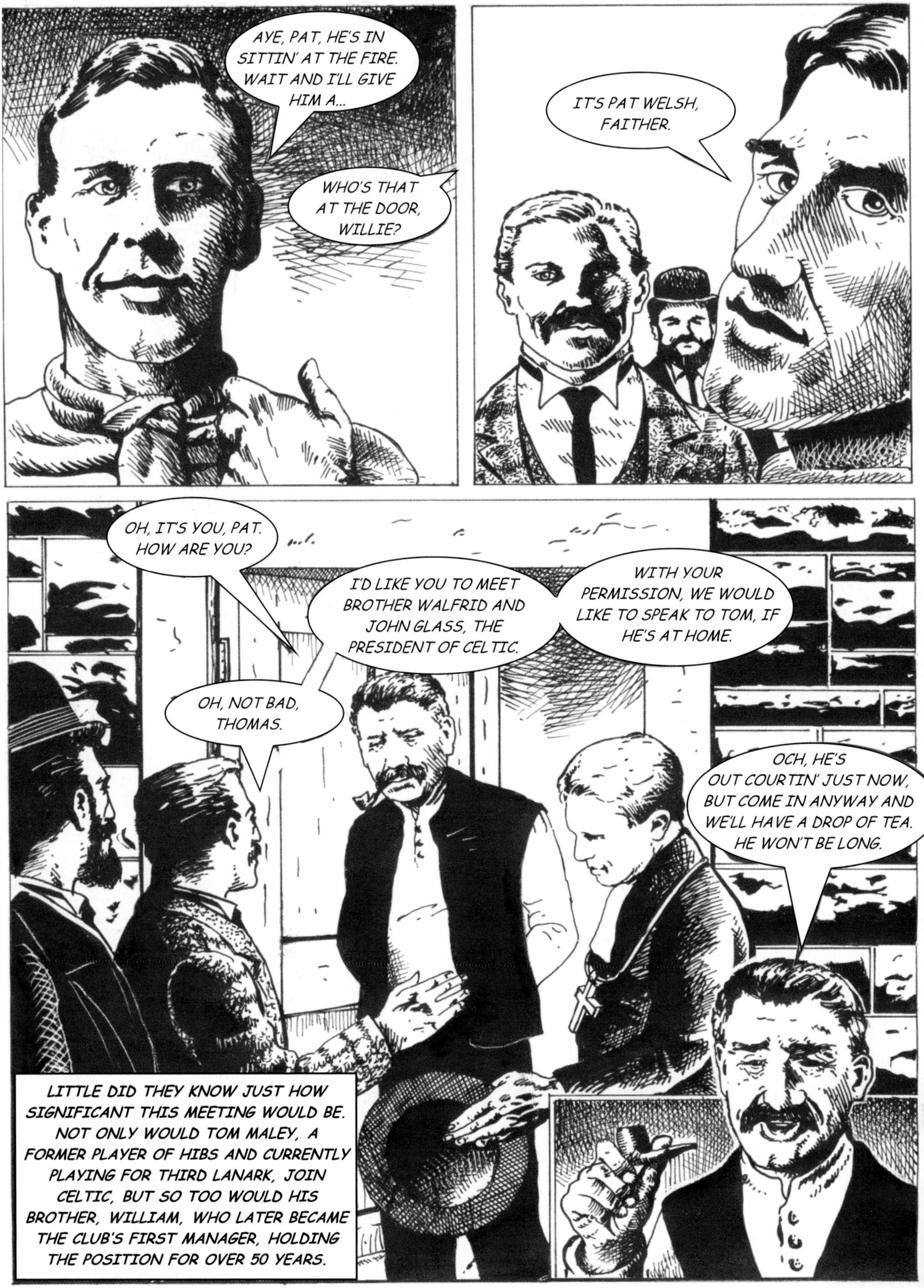
AYE, PAT, HE'S IN SITTIN' AT THE FIRE. WAIT AND I'LL GIVE HIM A...
WHO'S THAT AT THE DOOR, WILLIE?
IT'S PAT WELSH, FAITHER.
OH, IT'S YOU, PAT. HOW ARE YOU?
OH, NOT BAD, THOMAS.
I'D LIKE YOU TO MEET BROTHER WALFRID AND JOHN GLASS, THE PRESIDENT OF CELTIC.
WITH YOUR PERMISSION, WE WOULD LIKE TO SPEAK TO TOM, IF HE'S AT HOME.
OCH, HE'S OUT COURTIN' JUST NOW, BUT COME IN ANYWAY AND WE'LL HAVE A DROP OF TEA. HE WON'T BE LONG.
LITTLE DID THEY KNOW JUST HOW SIGNIFICANT THIS MEETING WOULD BE. NOT ONLY WOULD TOM MALEY, A FORMER PLAYER OF HIBS AND CURRENTLY PLAYING FOR THIRD LANARK, JOIN CELTIC, BUT SO TOO WOULD HIS BROTHER, WILLIAM, WHO LATER BECAME THE CLUB'S FIRST MANAGER, HOLDING THE POSITION FOR OVER 50 YEARS.

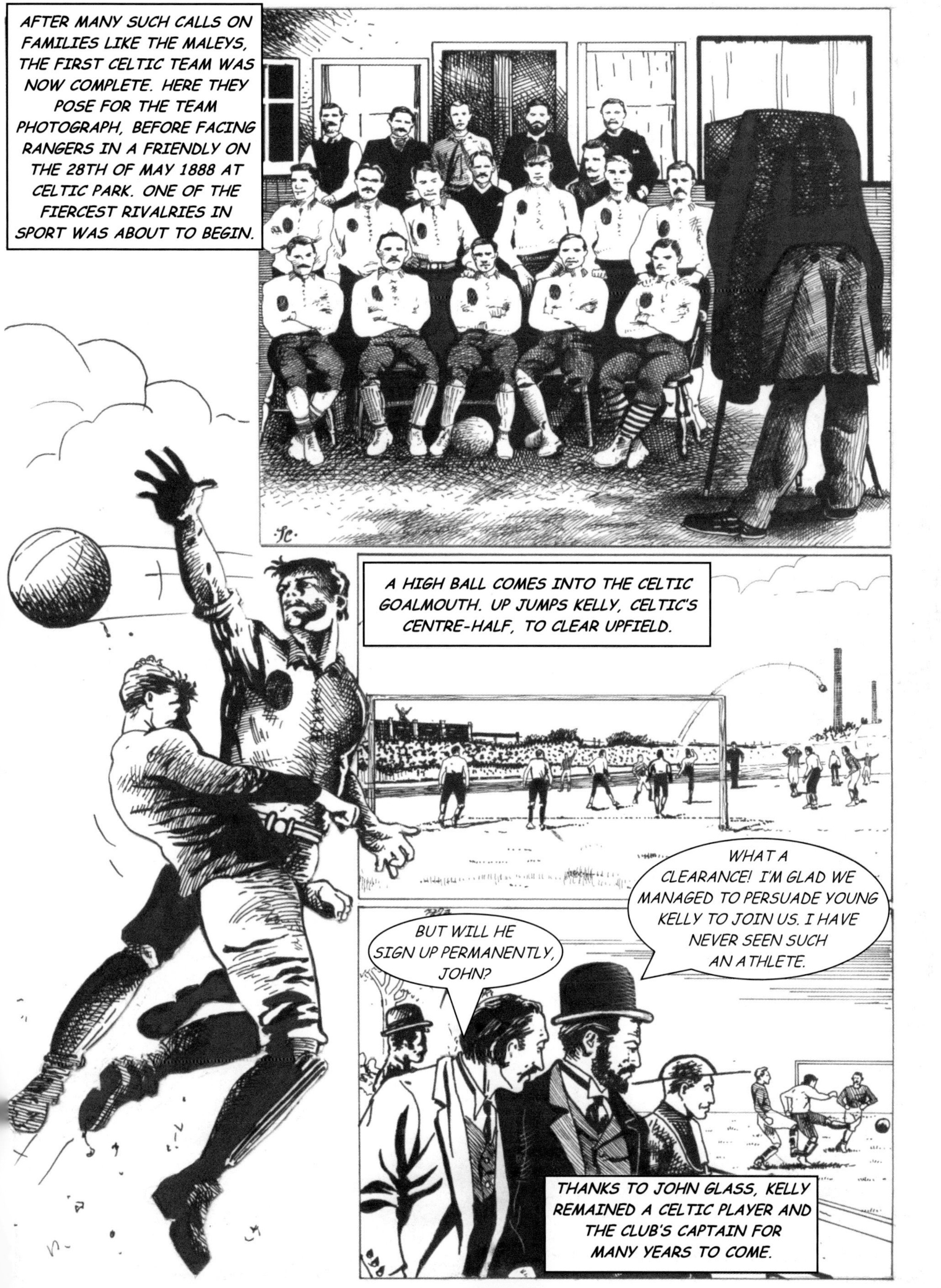
AFTER MANY SUCH CALLS ON FAMILIES LIKE THE MALEYS, THE FIRST CELTIC TEAM WAS NOW COMPLETE. HERE THEY POSE FOR THE TEAM PHOTOGRAPH, BEFORE FACING RANGERS IN A FRIENDLY ON THE 28TH OF MAY 1888 AT CELTIC PARK. ONE OF THE FIERCEST RIVALRIES IN SPORT WAS ABOUT TO BEGIN.
A HIGH BALL COMES INTO THE CELTIC GOALMOUTH. UP JUMPS KELLY, CELTIC'S CENTRE-HALF, TO CLEAR UPFIELD.
WHAT A CLEARANCE! I'M GLAD WE MANAGED TO PERSUADE YOUNG KELLY TO JOIN US. I HAVE NEVER SEEN SUCH AN ATHLETE.
BUT WILL HE SIGN UP PERMANENTLY, JOHN?
THANKS TO JOHN GLASS, KELLY REMAINED A CELTIC PLAYER AND THE CLUB'S CAPTAIN FOR MANY YEARS TO COME.

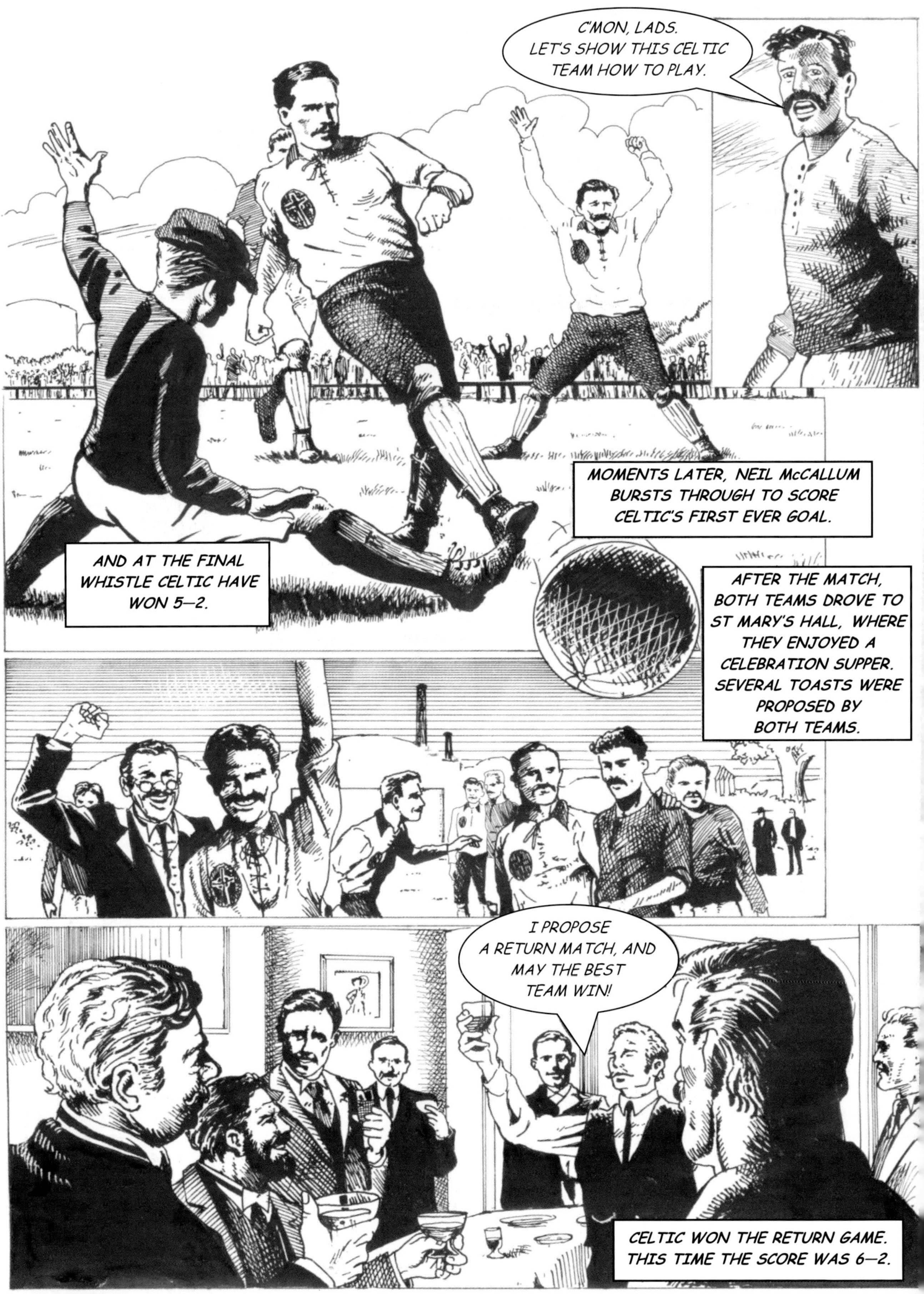
C'MON, LADS. LET'S SHOW THIS CELTIC TEAM HOW TO PLAY.
MOMENTS LATER, NEIL McCALLUM BURSTS THROUGH TO SCORE CELTIC'S FIRST EVER GOAL.
AND AT THE FINAL WHISTLE CELTIC HAVE WON 5—2.
AFTER THE MATCH, BOTH TEAMS DROVE TO ST MARY'S HALL, WHERE THEY ENJOYED A CELEBRATION SUPPER. SEVERAL TOASTS WERE PROPOSED BY BOTH TEAMS.
I PROPOSE A RETURN MATCH, AND MAY THE BEST TEAM WIN!
CELTIC WON THE RETURN GAME. THIS TIME THE SCORE WAS 6—2.

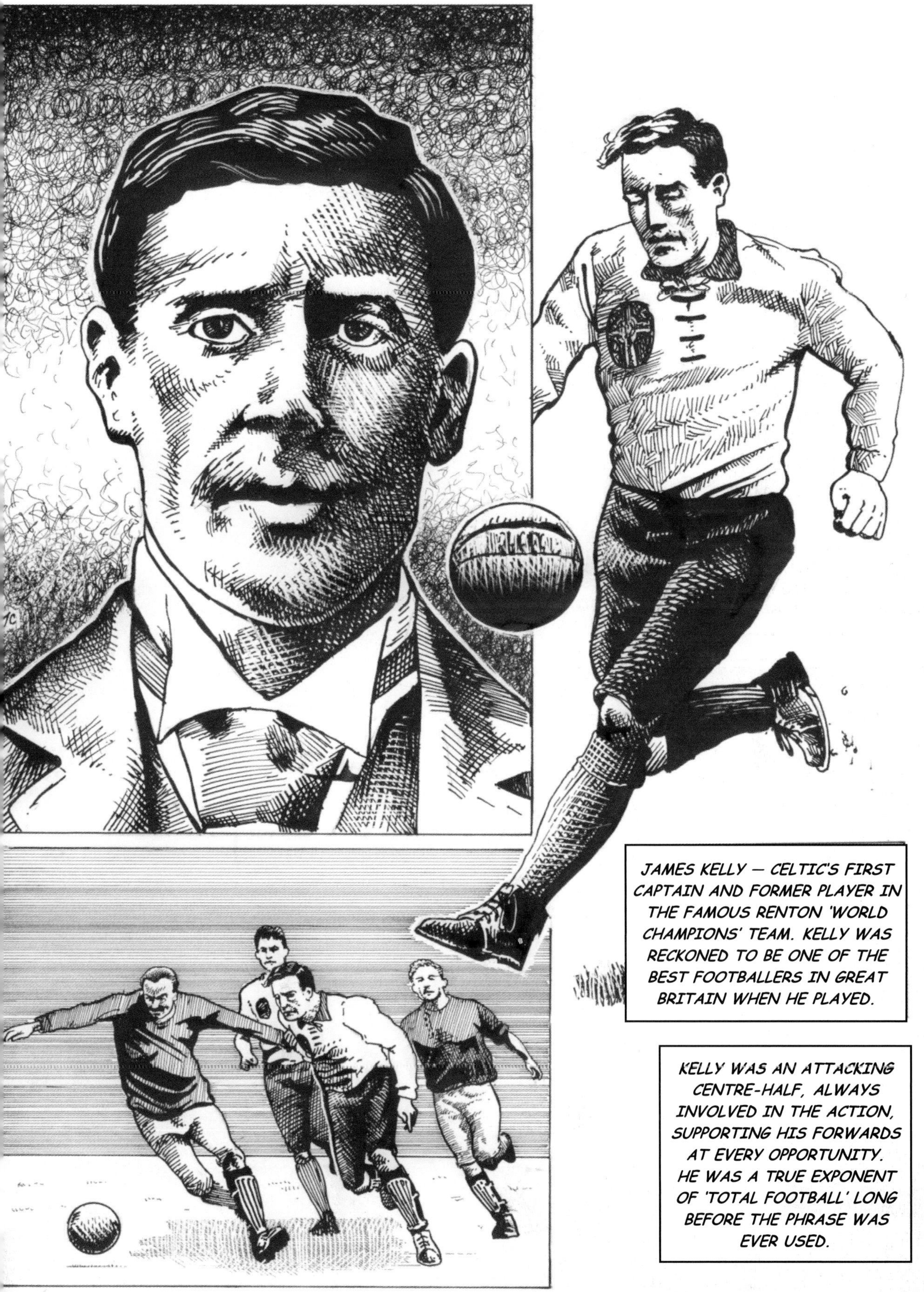
JAMES KELLY — CELTIC'S FIRST CAPTAIN AND FORMER PLAYER IN THE FAMOUS RENTON 'WORLD CHAMPIONS' TEAM. KELLY WAS RECKONED TO BE ONE OF THE BEST FOOTBALLERS IN GREAT BRITAIN WHEN HE PLAYED.
KELLY WAS AN ATTACKING CENTRE-HALF, ALWAYS INVOLVED IN THE ACTION, SUPPORTING HIS FORWARDS AT EVERY OPPORTUNITY. HE WAS A TRUE EXPONENT OF 'TOTAL FOOTBALL' LONG BEFORE THE PHRASE WAS EVER USED.

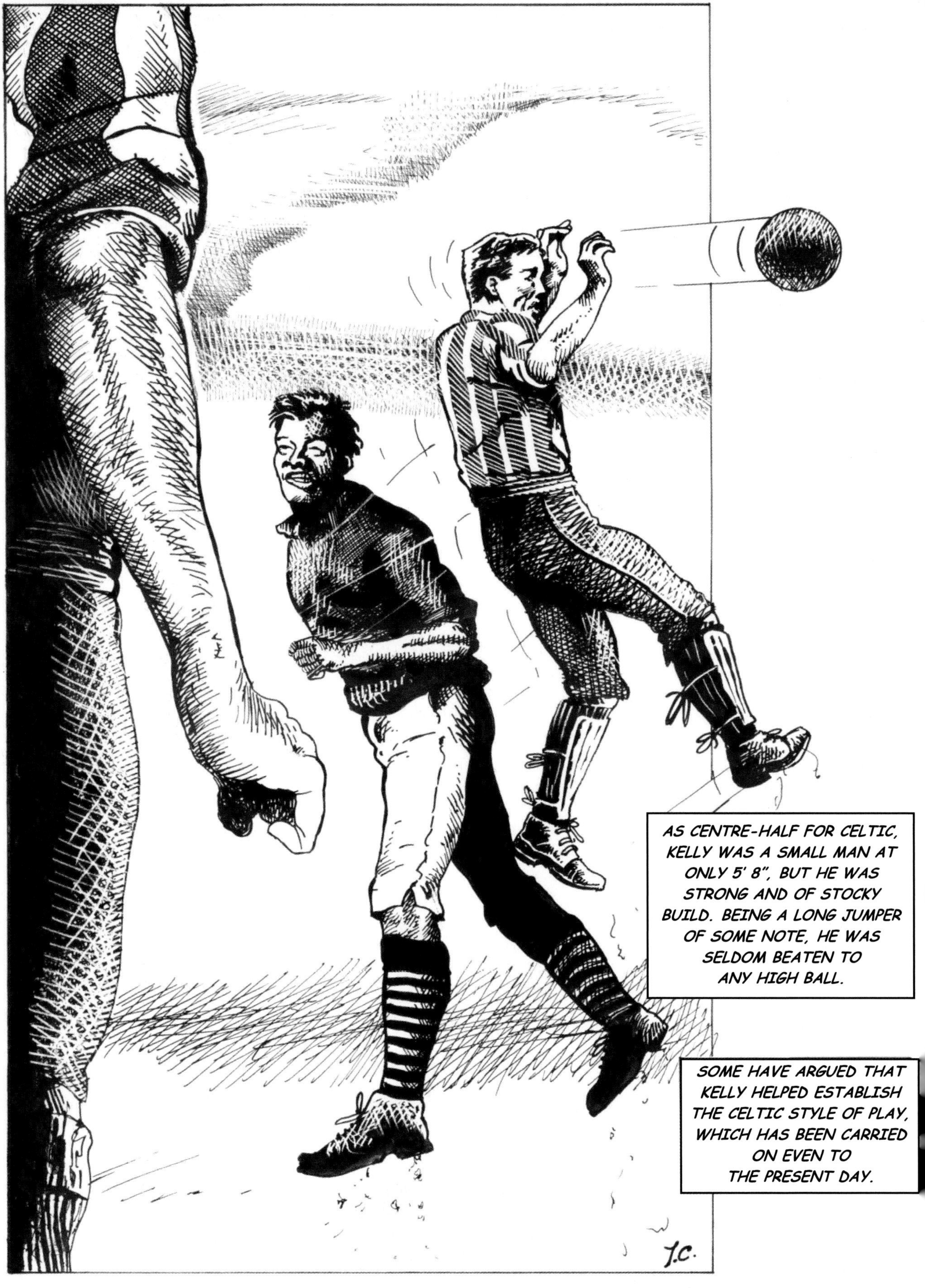
AS CENTRE-HALF FOR CELTIC, KELLY WAS A SMALL MAN AT ONLY 5' 8", BUT HE WAS STRONG AND OF STOCKY BUILD. BEING A LONG JUMPER OF SOME NOTE, HE WAS SELDOM BEATEN TO ANY HIGH BALL.
SOME HAVE ARGUED THAT KELLY HELPED ESTABLISH THE CELTIC STYLE OF PLAY, WHICH HAS BEEN CARRIED ON EVEN TO THE PRESENT DAY.

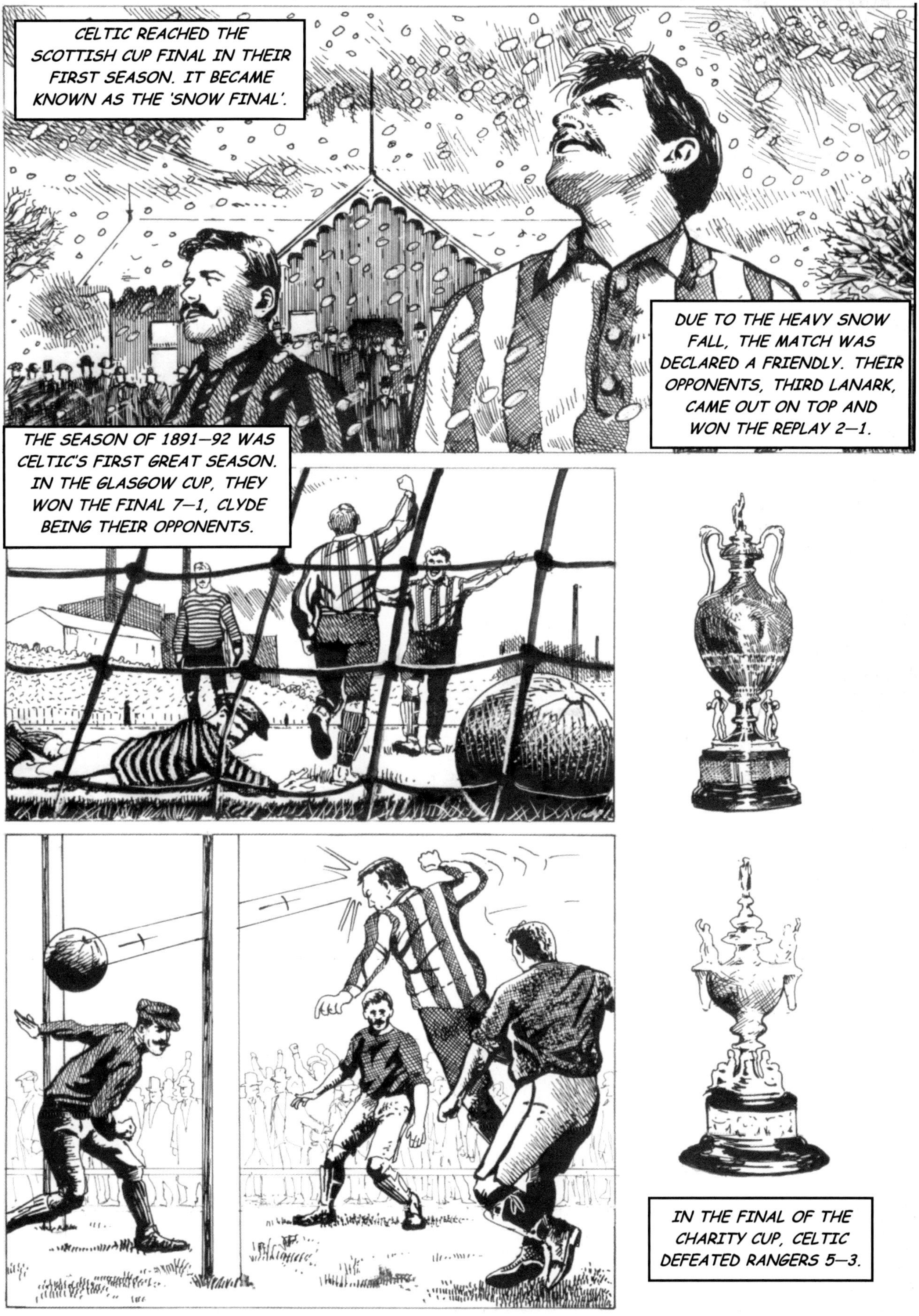
CELTIC REACHED THE SCOTTISH CUP FINAL IN THEIR FIRST SEASON. IT BECAME KNOWN AS THE 'SNOW FINAL'.
DUE TO THE HEAVY SNOW FALL, THE MATCH WAS DECLARED A FRIENDLY. THEIR OPPONENTS, THIRD LANARK, CAME OUT ON TOP AND WON THE REPLAY 2–1.
THE SEASON OF 1891–92 WAS CELTIC'S FIRST GREAT SEASON. IN THE GLASGOW CUP, THEY WON THE FINAL 7–1, CLYDE BEING THEIR OPPONENTS.
IN THE FINAL OF THE CHARITY CUP, CELTIC DEFEATED RANGERS 5–3.

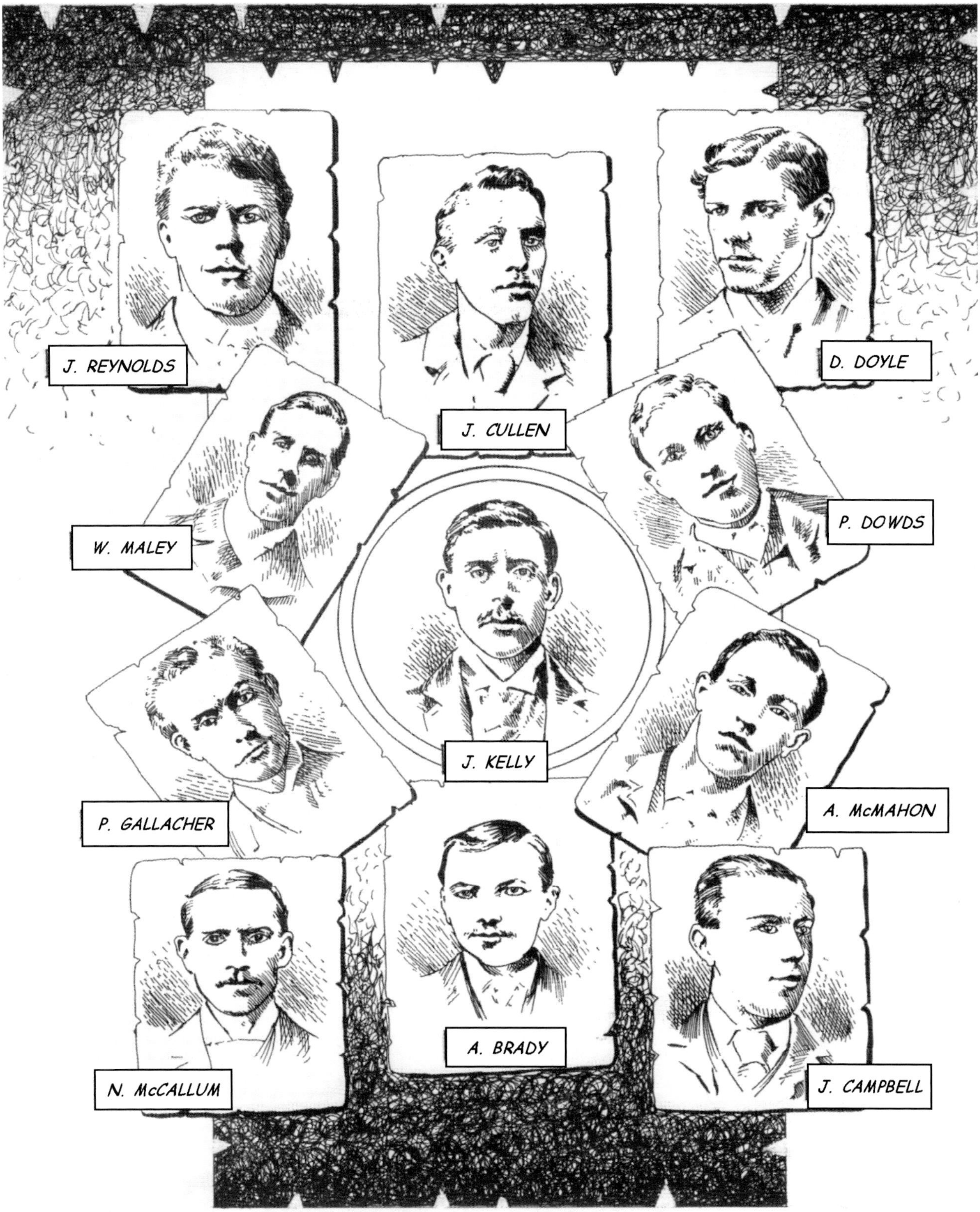
J. REYNOLDS
J. CULLEN
D. DOYLE
W. MALEY
P. DOWDS
J. KELLY
P. GALLACHER
A. McMAHON
N. McCALLUM
A. BRADY
J. CAMPBELL

THE CELTIC TEAM FOR
THE SCOTTISH CUP
FINAL OF 1892.

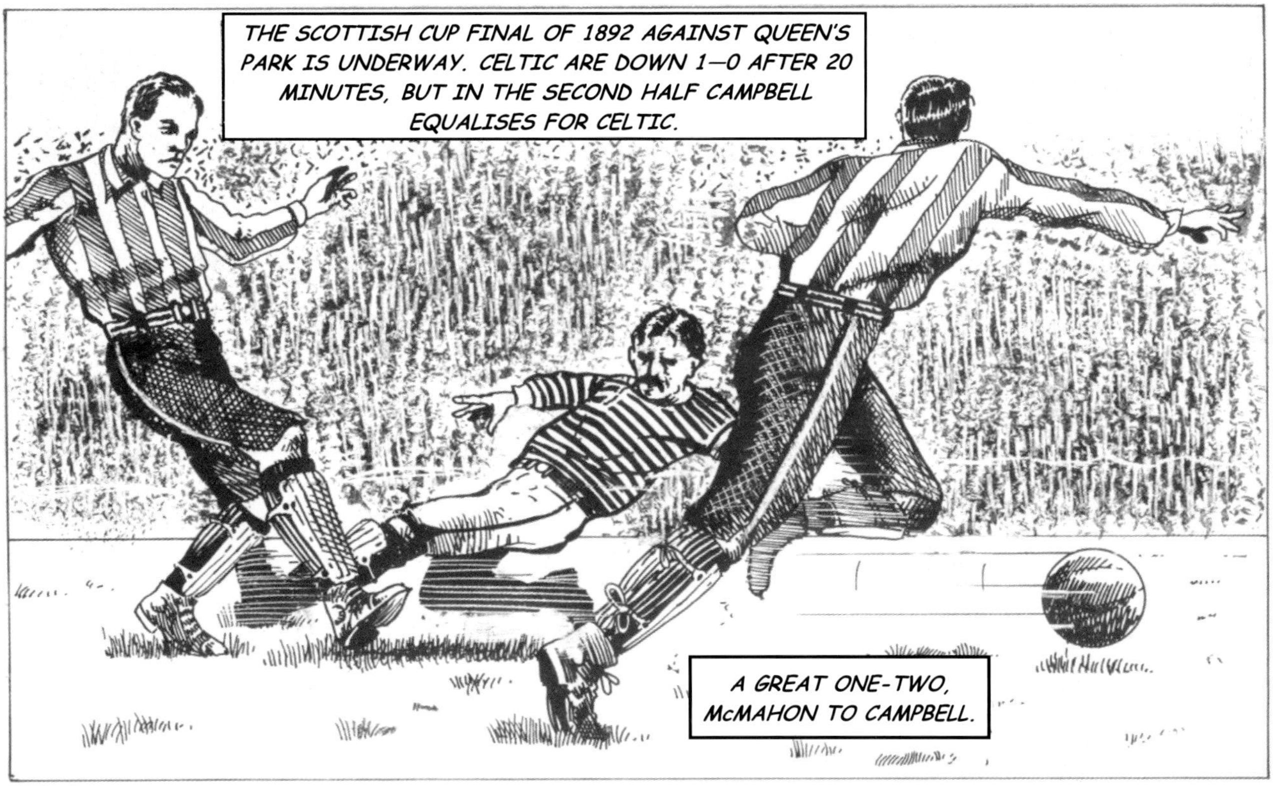
THE SCOTTISH CUP FINAL OF 1892 AGAINST QUEEN'S PARK IS UNDERWAY. CELTIC ARE DOWN 1—0 AFTER 20 MINUTES, BUT IN THE SECOND HALF CAMPBELL EQUALISES FOR CELTIC.
A GREAT ONE-TWO, McMAHON TO CAMPBELL.

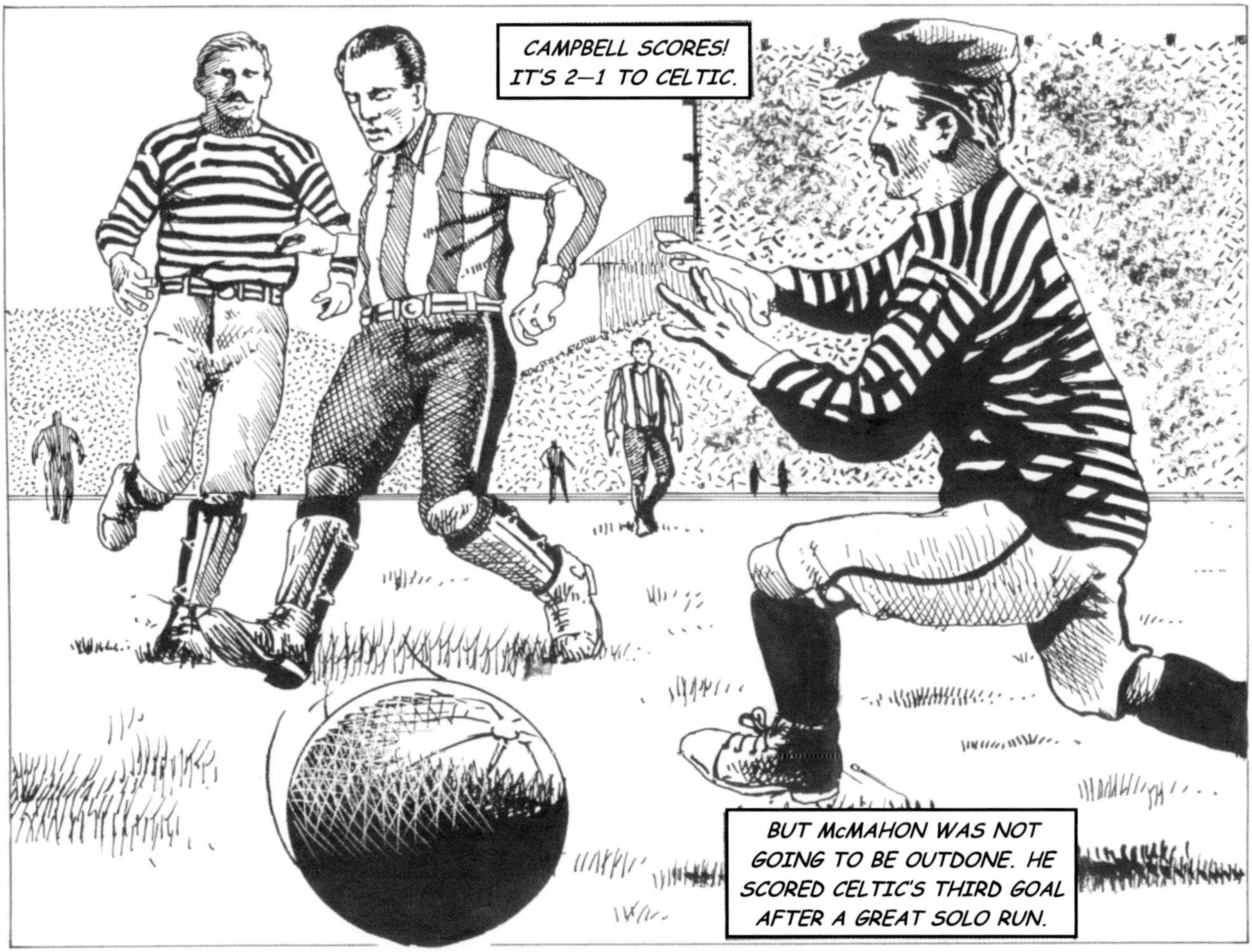
CAMPBELL SCORES! IT'S 2—1 TO CELTIC.
BUT McMAHON WAS NOT GOING TO BE OUTDONE. HE SCORED CELTIC'S THIRD GOAL AFTER A GREAT SOLO RUN.

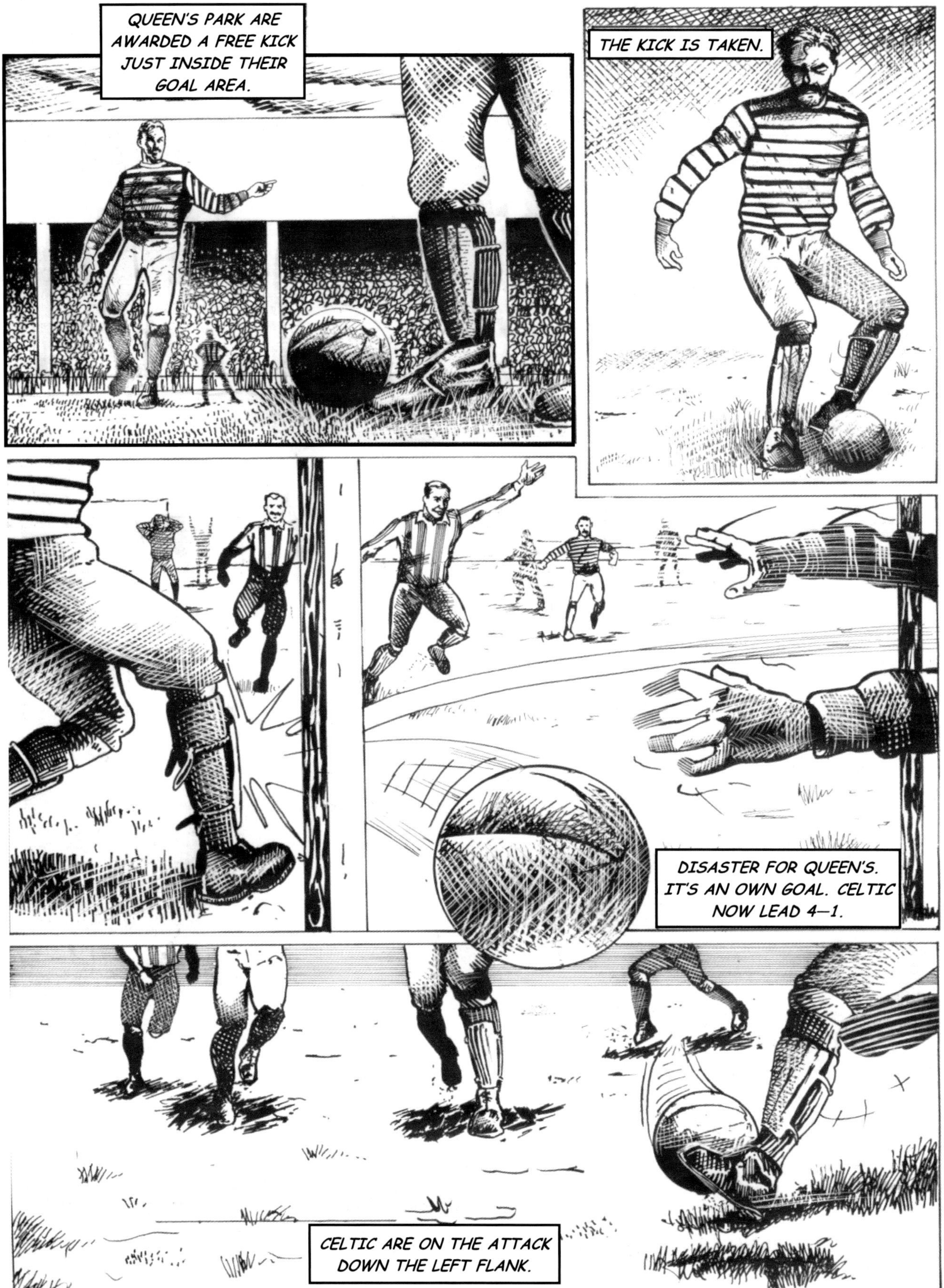
QUEEN'S PARK ARE AWARDED A FREE KICK JUST INSIDE THEIR GOAL AREA.
THE KICK IS TAKEN.
DISASTER FOR QUEEN'S. IT'S AN OWN GOAL. CELTIC NOW LEAD 4—1.
CELTIC ARE ON THE ATTACK DOWN THE LEFT FLANK.

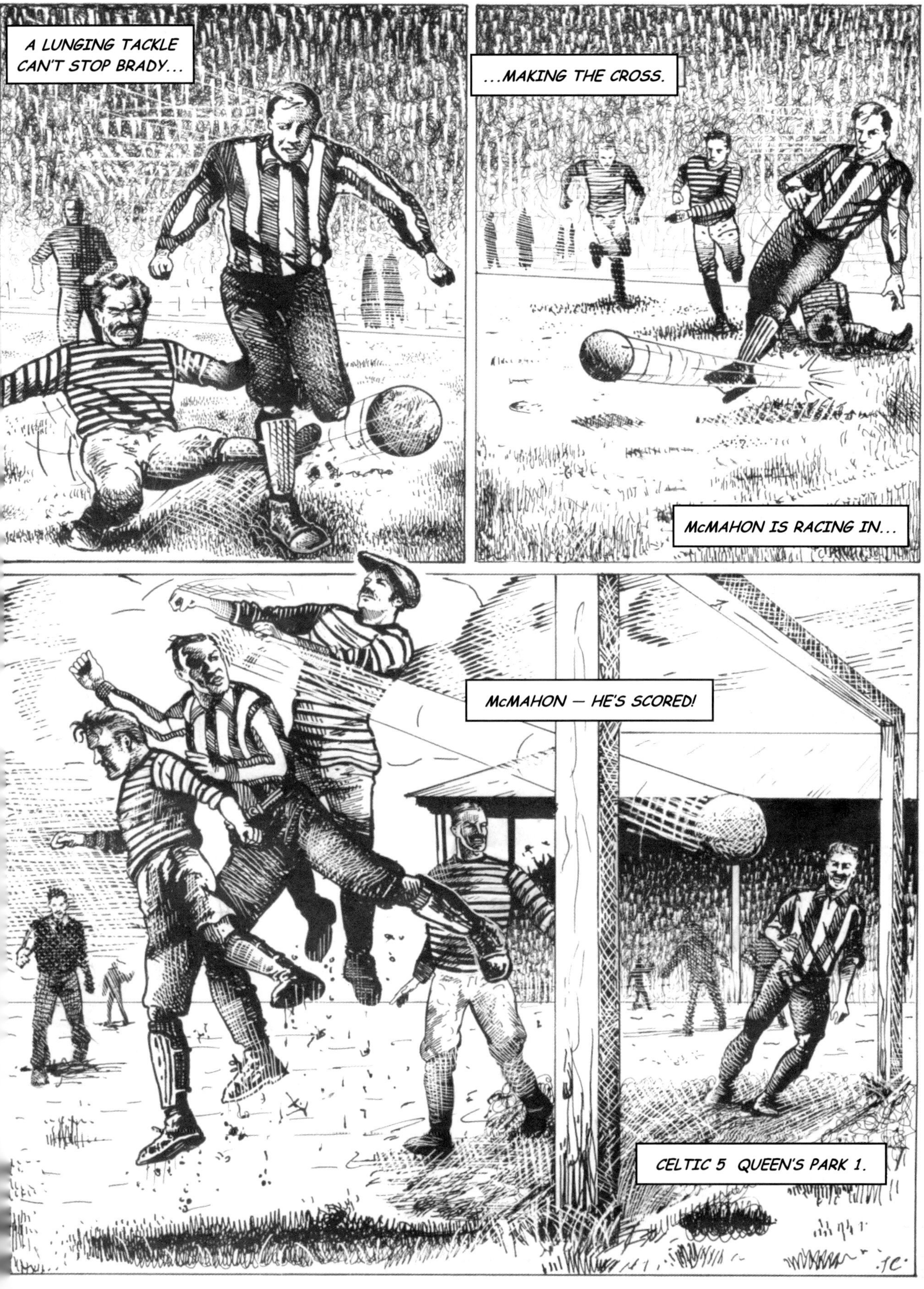
A LUNGING TACKLE CAN'T STOP BRADY...
...MAKING THE CROSS.
McMAHON IS RACING IN...
McMAHON — HE'S SCORED!
CELTIC 5 QUEEN'S PARK 1.

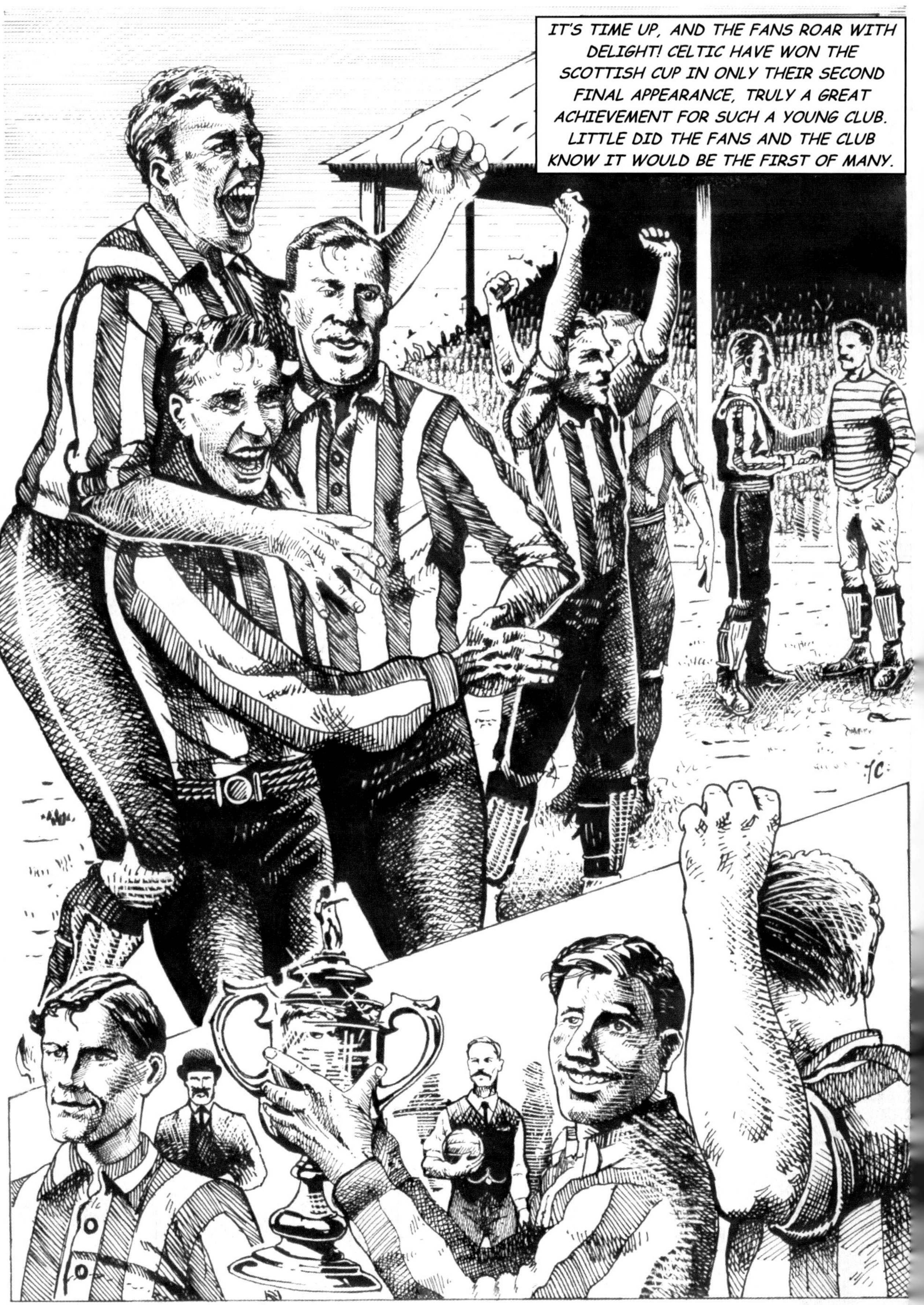
IT'S TIME UP, AND THE FANS ROAR WITH DELIGHT! CELTIC HAVE WON THE SCOTTISH CUP IN ONLY THEIR SECOND FINAL APPEARANCE, TRULY A GREAT ACHIEVEMENT FOR SUCH A YOUNG CLUB. LITTLE DID THE FANS AND THE CLUB KNOW IT WOULD BE THE FIRST OF MANY.

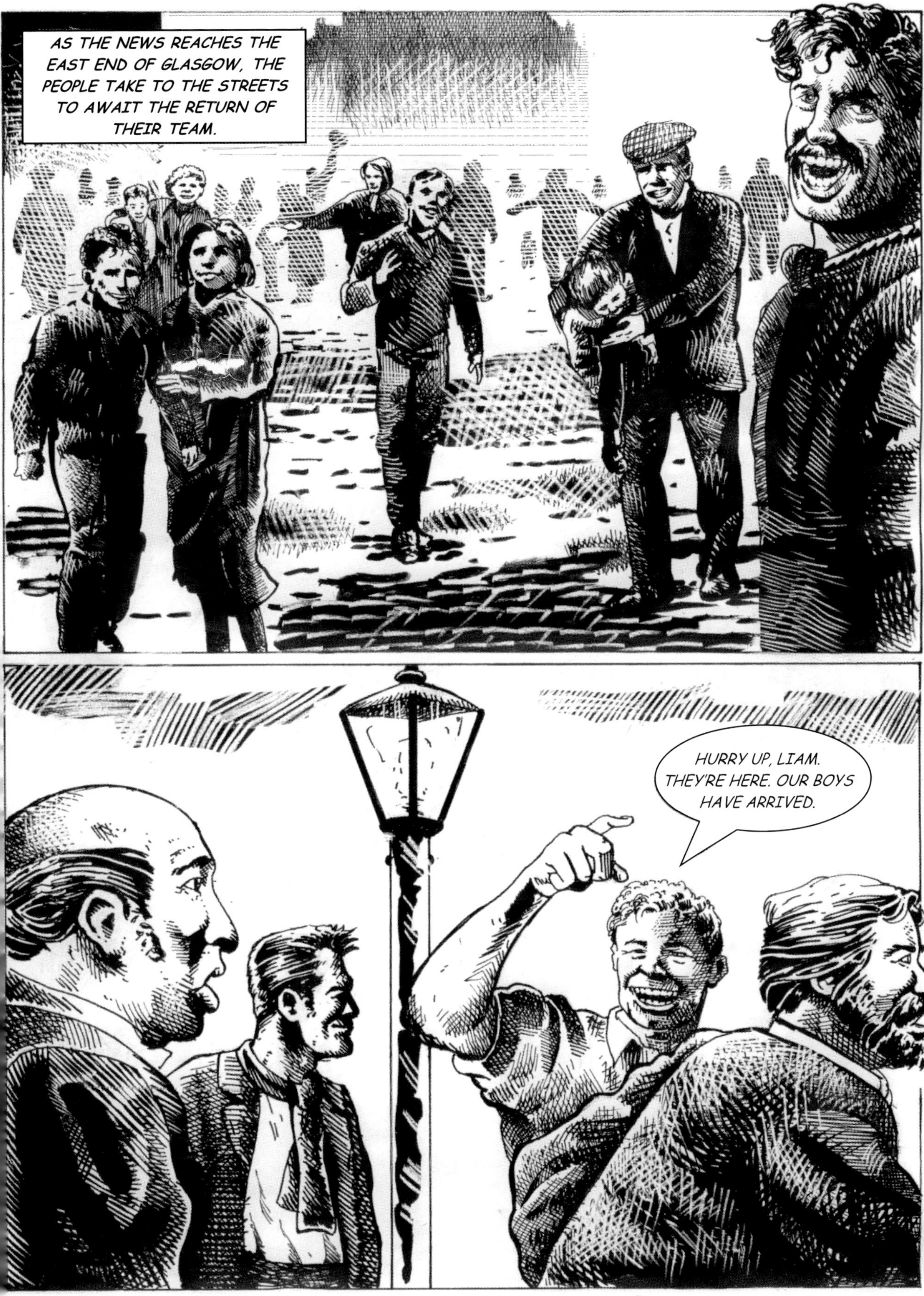
AS THE NEWS REACHES THE EAST END OF GLASGOW, THE PEOPLE TAKE TO THE STREETS TO AWAIT THE RETURN OF THEIR TEAM.
HURRY UP, LIAM. THEY'RE HERE. OUR BOYS HAVE ARRIVED.

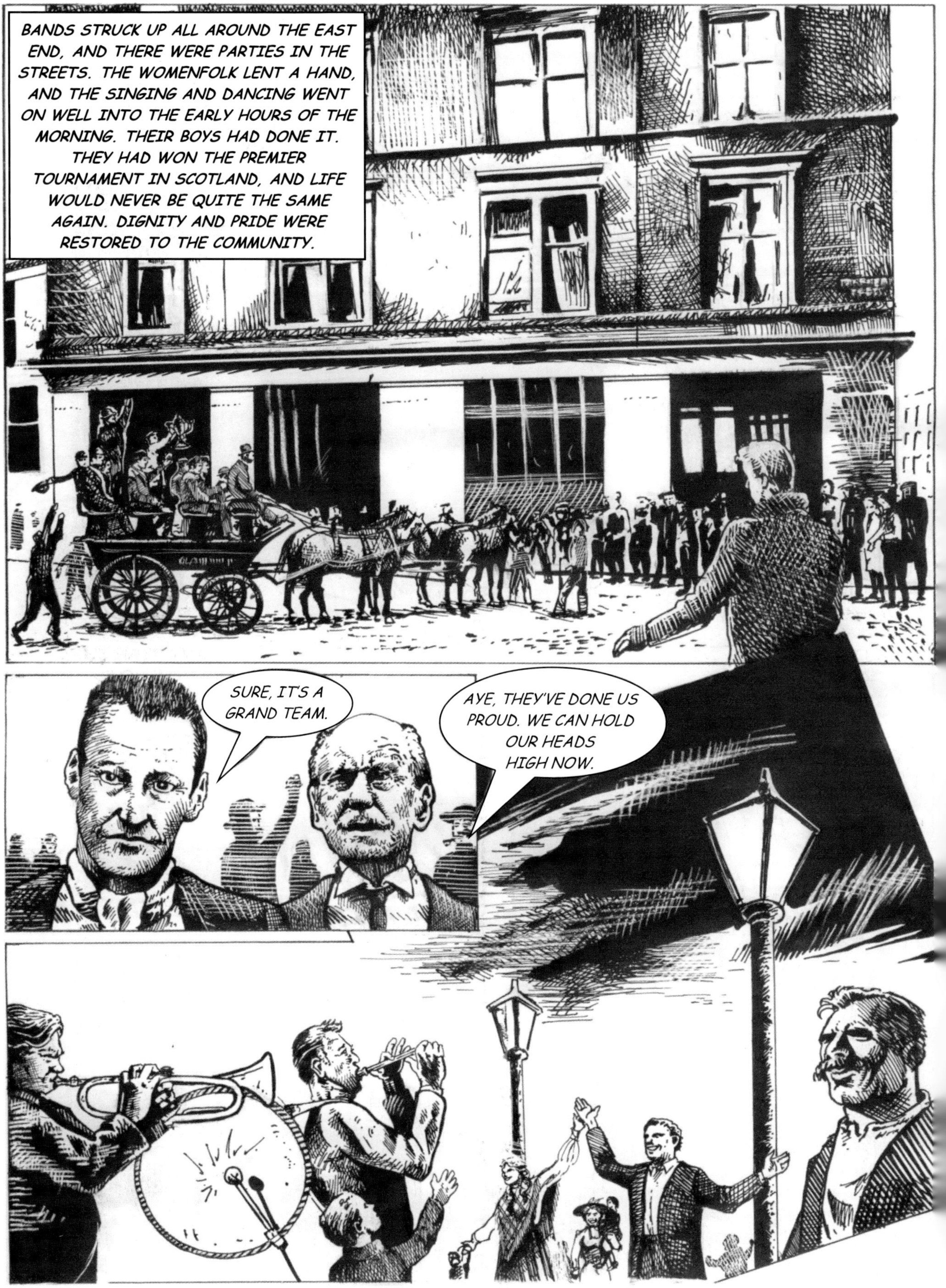
BANDS STRUCK UP ALL AROUND THE EAST END, AND THERE WERE PARTIES IN THE STREETS. THE WOMENFOLK LENT A HAND, AND THE SINGING AND DANCING WENT ON WELL INTO THE EARLY HOURS OF THE MORNING. THEIR BOYS HAD DONE IT. THEY HAD WON THE PREMIER TOURNAMENT IN SCOTLAND, AND LIFE WOULD NEVER BE QUITE THE SAME AGAIN. DIGNITY AND PRIDE WERE RESTORED TO THE COMMUNITY.
SURE, IT'S A GRAND TEAM.
AYE, THEY'VE DONE US PROUD. WE CAN HOLD OUR HEADS HIGH NOW.

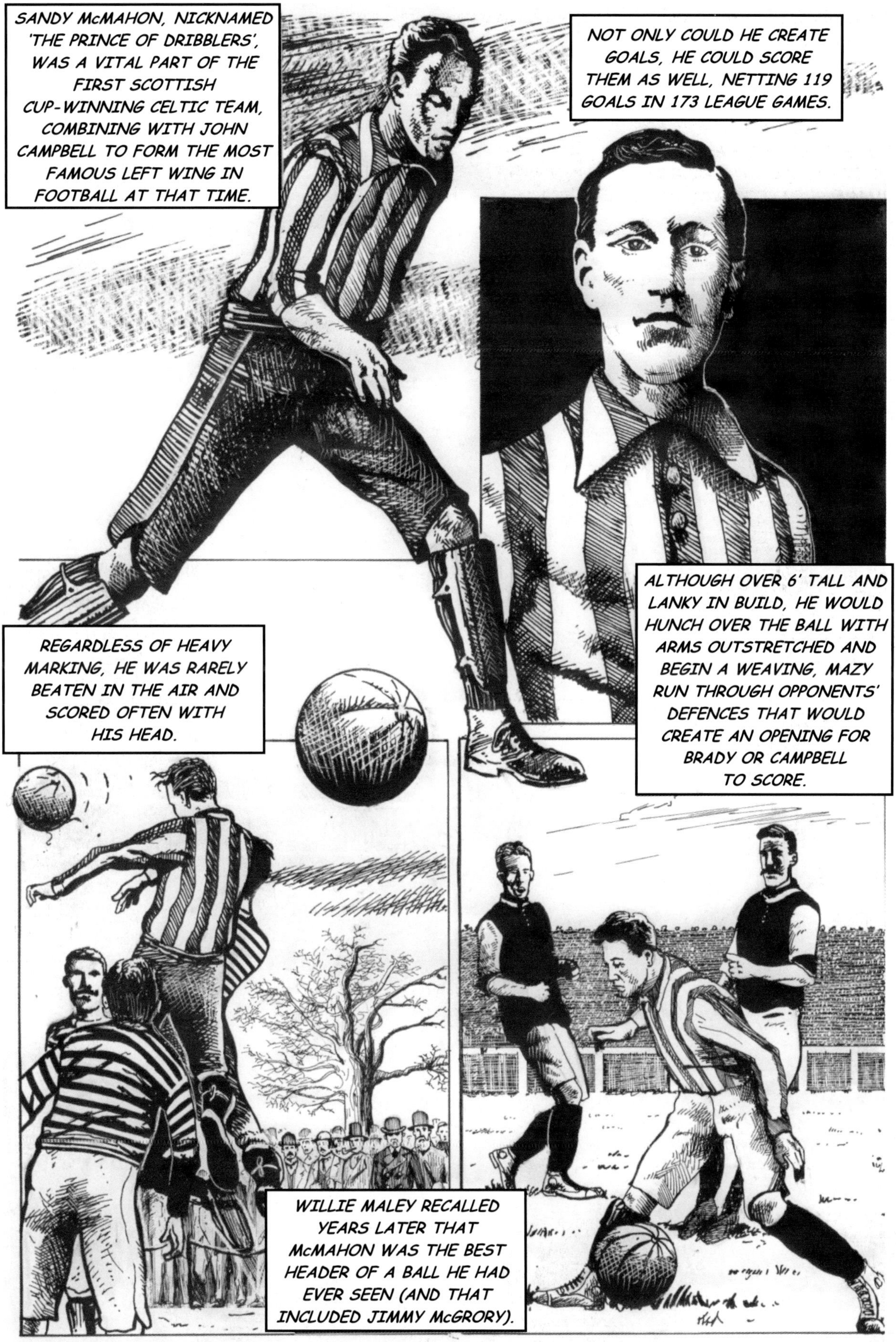
SANDY McMAHON, NICKNAMED 'THE PRINCE OF DRIBBLERS', WAS A VITAL PART OF THE FIRST SCOTTISH CUP-WINNING CELTIC TEAM, COMBINING WITH JOHN CAMPBELL TO FORM THE MOST FAMOUS LEFT WING IN FOOTBALL AT THAT TIME.
NOT ONLY COULD HE CREATE GOALS, HE COULD SCORE THEM AS WELL, NETTING 119 GOALS IN 173 LEAGUE GAMES.
ALTHOUGH OVER 6' TALL AND LANKY IN BUILD, HE WOULD HUNCH OVER THE BALL WITH ARMS OUTSTRETCHED AND BEGIN A WEAVING, MAZY RUN THROUGH OPPONENTS' DEFENCES THAT WOULD CREATE AN OPENING FOR BRADY OR CAMPBELL TO SCORE.
REGARDLESS OF HEAVY MARKING, HE WAS RARELY BEATEN IN THE AIR AND SCORED OFTEN WITH HIS HEAD.
WILLIE MALEY RECALLED YEARS LATER THAT McMAHON WAS THE BEST HEADER OF A BALL HE HAD EVER SEEN (AND THAT INCLUDED JIMMY McGRORY).

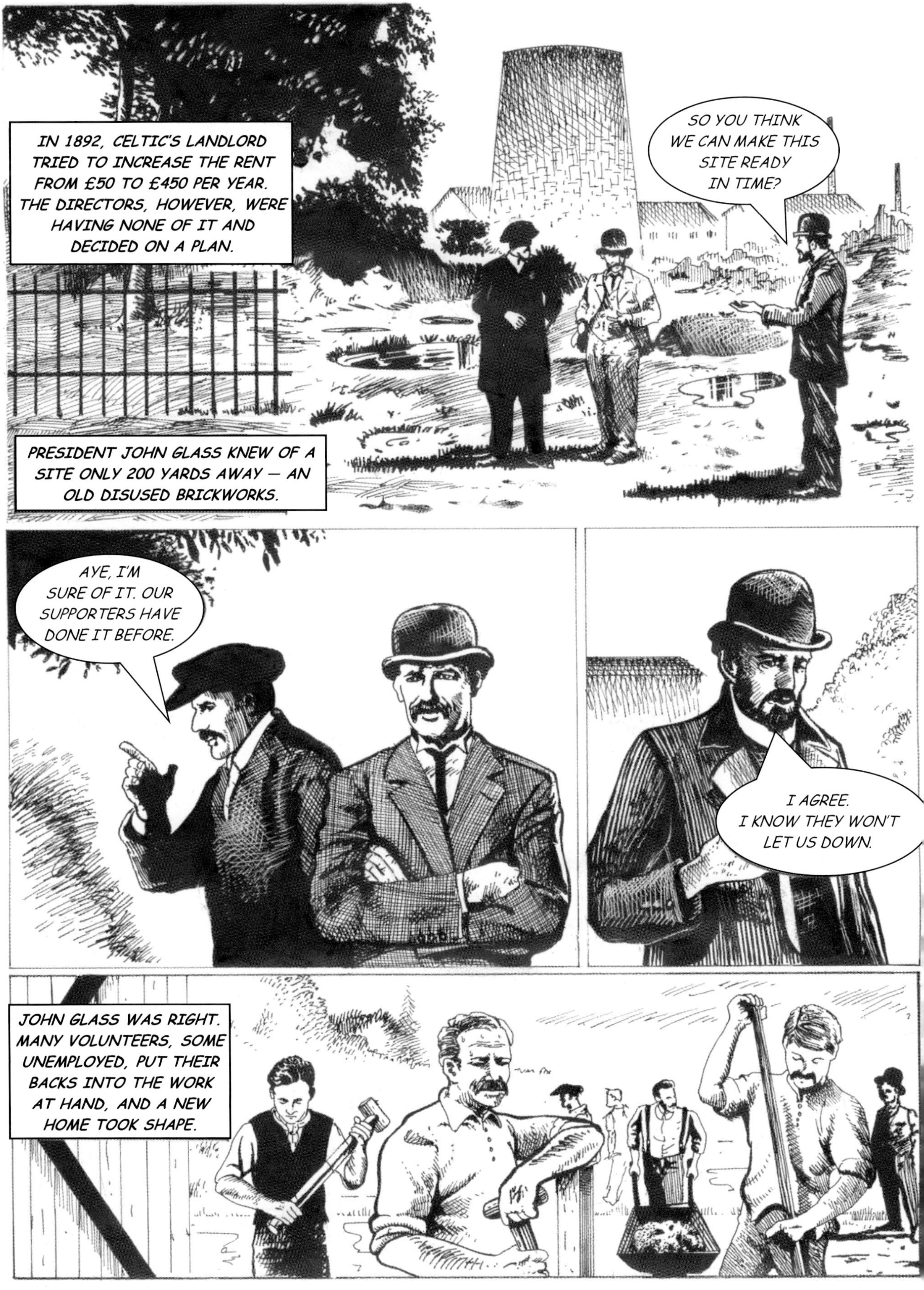
IN 1892, CELTIC'S LANDLORD TRIED TO INCREASE THE RENT FROM £50 TO £450 PER YEAR. THE DIRECTORS, HOWEVER, WERE HAVING NONE OF IT AND DECIDED ON A PLAN.
PRESIDENT JOHN GLASS KNEW OF A SITE ONLY 200 YARDS AWAY — AN OLD DISUSED BRICKWORKS.
SO YOU THINK WE CAN MAKE THIS SITE READY IN TIME?
AYE, I'M SURE OF IT. OUR SUPPORTERS HAVE DONE IT BEFORE.
I AGREE. I KNOW THEY WON'T LET US DOWN.
JOHN GLASS WAS RIGHT. MANY VOLUNTEERS, SOME UNEMPLOYED, PUT THEIR BACKS INTO THE WORK AT HAND, AND A NEW HOME TOOK SHAPE.

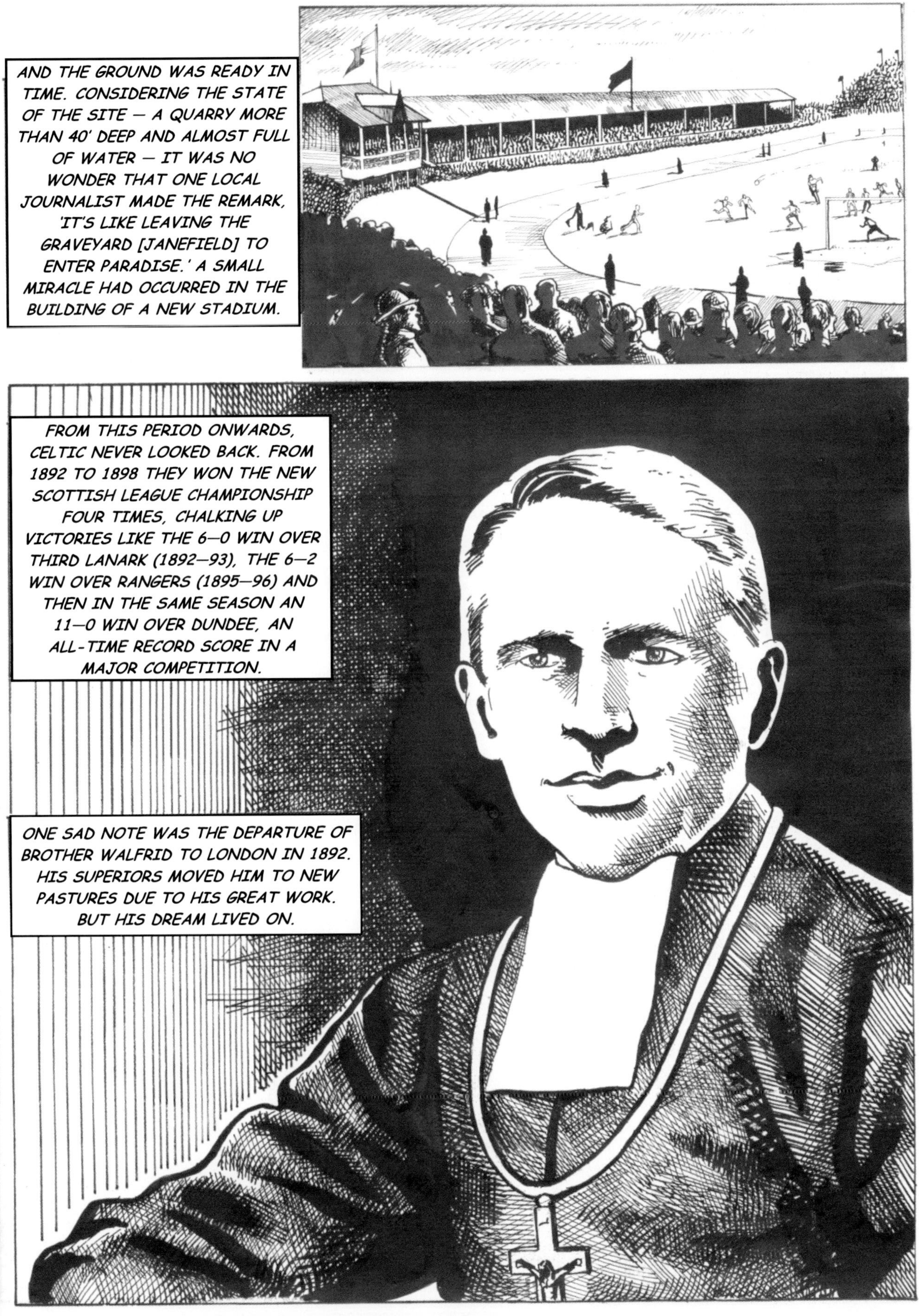
AND THE GROUND WAS READY IN TIME. CONSIDERING THE STATE OF THE SITE — A QUARRY MORE THAN 40' DEEP AND ALMOST FULL OF WATER — IT WAS NO WONDER THAT ONE LOCAL JOURNALIST MADE THE REMARK, 'IT'S LIKE LEAVING THE GRAVEYARD [JANEFIELD] TO ENTER PARADISE.' A SMALL MIRACLE HAD OCCURRED IN THE BUILDING OF A NEW STADIUM.
FROM THIS PERIOD ONWARDS, CELTIC NEVER LOOKED BACK. FROM 1892 TO 1898 THEY WON THE NEW SCOTTISH LEAGUE CHAMPIONSHIP FOUR TIMES, CHALKING UP VICTORIES LIKE THE 6—0 WIN OVER THIRD LANARK (1892—93), THE 6—2 WIN OVER RANGERS (1895—96) AND THEN IN THE SAME SEASON AN 11—0 WIN OVER DUNDEE, AN ALL-TIME RECORD SCORE IN A MAJOR COMPETITION.
ONE SAD NOTE WAS THE DEPARTURE OF BROTHER WALFRID TO LONDON IN 1892. HIS SUPERIORS MOVED HIM TO NEW PASTURES DUE TO HIS GREAT WORK. BUT HIS DREAM LIVED ON.

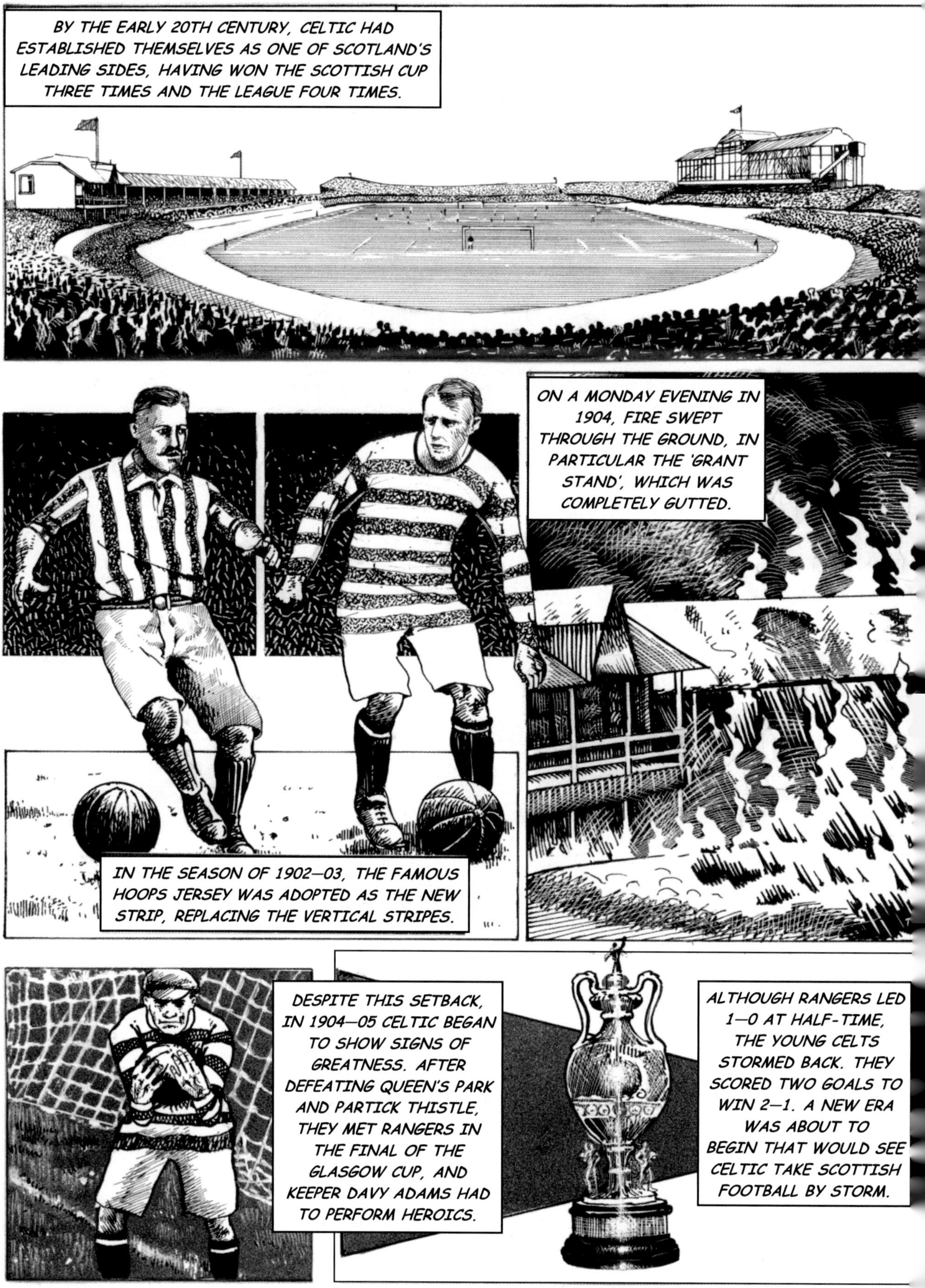
BY THE EARLY 20TH CENTURY, CELTIC HAD ESTABLISHED THEMSELVES AS ONE OF SCOTLAND'S LEADING SIDES, HAVING WON THE SCOTTISH CUP THREE TIMES AND THE LEAGUE FOUR TIMES.
IN THE SEASON OF 1902–03, THE FAMOUS HOOPS JERSEY WAS ADOPTED AS THE NEW STRIP, REPLACING THE VERTICAL STRIPES.
ON A MONDAY EVENING IN 1904, FIRE SWEPT THROUGH THE GROUND, IN PARTICULAR THE 'GRANT STAND', WHICH WAS COMPLETELY GUTTED.
DESPITE THIS SETBACK, IN 1904–05 CELTIC BEGAN TO SHOW SIGNS OF GREATNESS. AFTER DEFEATING QUEEN'S PARK AND PARTICK THISTLE, THEY MET RANGERS IN THE FINAL OF THE GLASGOW CUP, AND KEEPER DAVY ADAMS HAD TO PERFORM HEROICS.
ALTHOUGH RANGERS LED 1–0 AT HALF-TIME, THE YOUNG CELTS STORMED BACK. THEY SCORED TWO GOALS TO WIN 2–1. A NEW ERA WAS ABOUT TO BEGIN THAT WOULD SEE CELTIC TAKE SCOTTISH FOOTBALL BY STORM.

chapter 2

early legends

'through a storm'

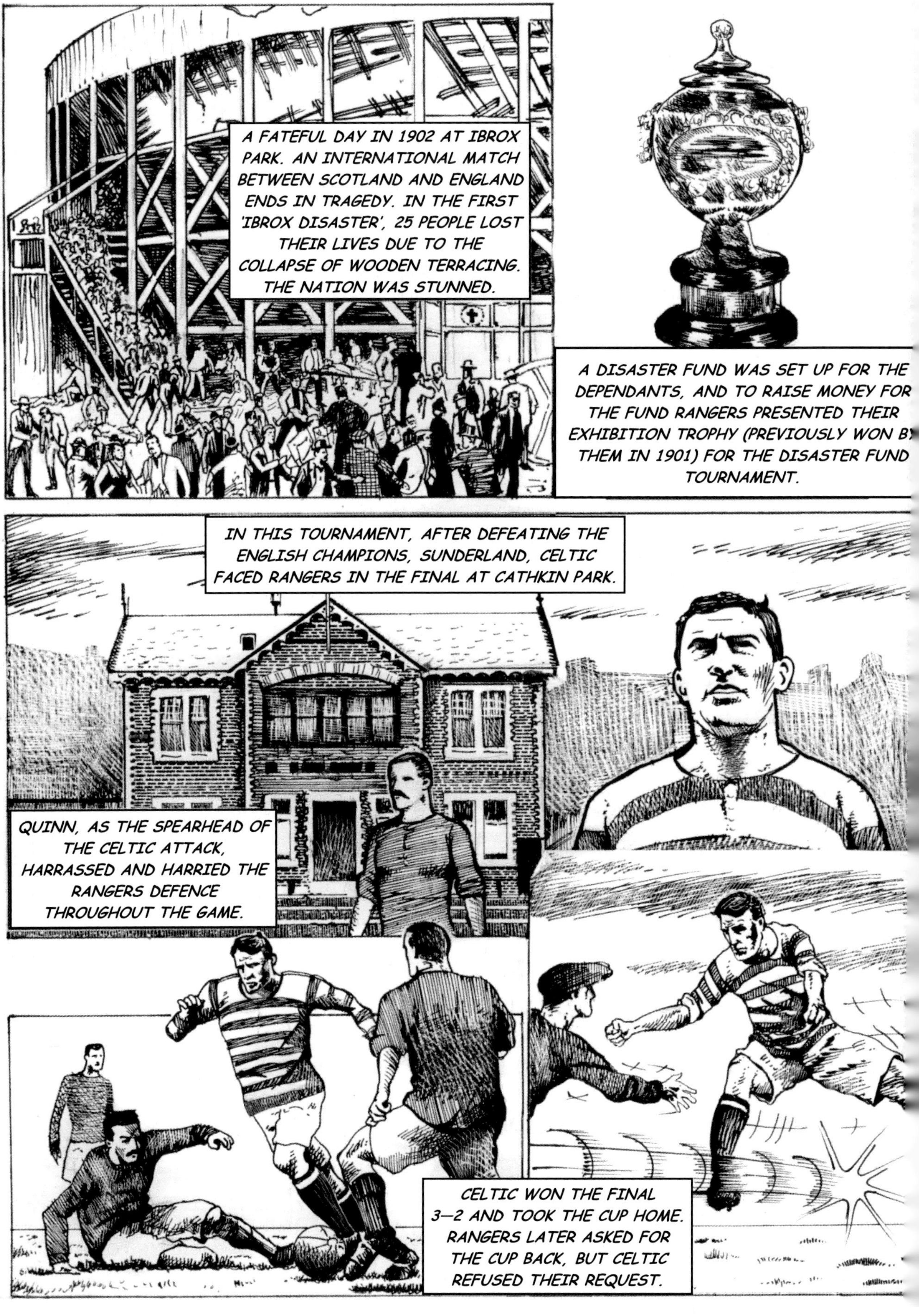
A FATEFUL DAY IN 1902 AT IBROX PARK. AN INTERNATIONAL MATCH BETWEEN SCOTLAND AND ENGLAND ENDS IN TRAGEDY. IN THE FIRST 'IBROX DISASTER', 25 PEOPLE LOST THEIR LIVES DUE TO THE COLLAPSE OF WOODEN TERRACING. THE NATION WAS STUNNED.
A DISASTER FUND WAS SET UP FOR THE DEPENDANTS, AND TO RAISE MONEY FOR THE FUND RANGERS PRESENTED THEIR EXHIBITION TROPHY (PREVIOUSLY WON BY THEM IN 1901) FOR THE DISASTER FUND TOURNAMENT.
IN THIS TOURNAMENT, AFTER DEFEATING THE ENGLISH CHAMPIONS, SUNDERLAND, CELTIC FACED RANGERS IN THE FINAL AT CATHKIN PARK.
QUINN, AS THE SPEARHEAD OF THE CELTIC ATTACK, HARRASSED AND HARRIED THE RANGERS DEFENCE THROUGHOUT THE GAME.
CELTIC WON THE FINAL 3—2 AND TOOK THE CUP HOME. RANGERS LATER ASKED FOR THE CUP BACK, BUT CELTIC REFUSED THEIR REQUEST.

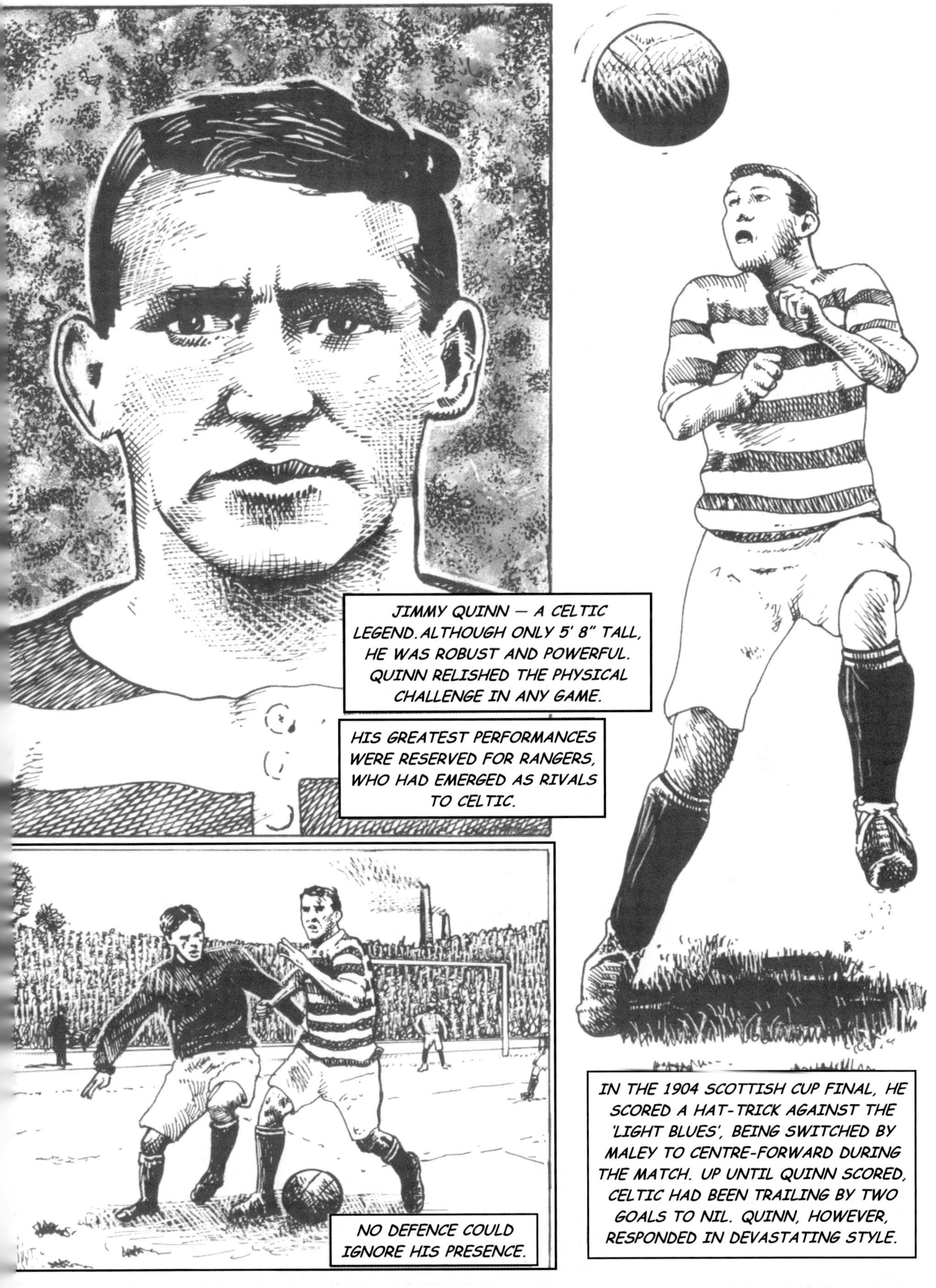
JIMMY QUINN — A CELTIC LEGEND. ALTHOUGH ONLY 5' 8" TALL, HE WAS ROBUST AND POWERFUL. QUINN RELISHED THE PHYSICAL CHALLENGE IN ANY GAME.
HIS GREATEST PERFORMANCES WERE RESERVED FOR RANGERS, WHO HAD EMERGED AS RIVALS TO CELTIC.
IN THE 1904 SCOTTISH CUP FINAL, HE SCORED A HAT-TRICK AGAINST THE 'LIGHT BLUES', BEING SWITCHED BY MALEY TO CENTRE-FORWARD DURING THE MATCH. UP UNTIL QUINN SCORED, CELTIC HAD BEEN TRAILING BY TWO GOALS TO NIL. QUINN, HOWEVER, RESPONDED IN DEVASTATING STYLE.
NO DEFENCE COULD IGNORE HIS PRESENCE.

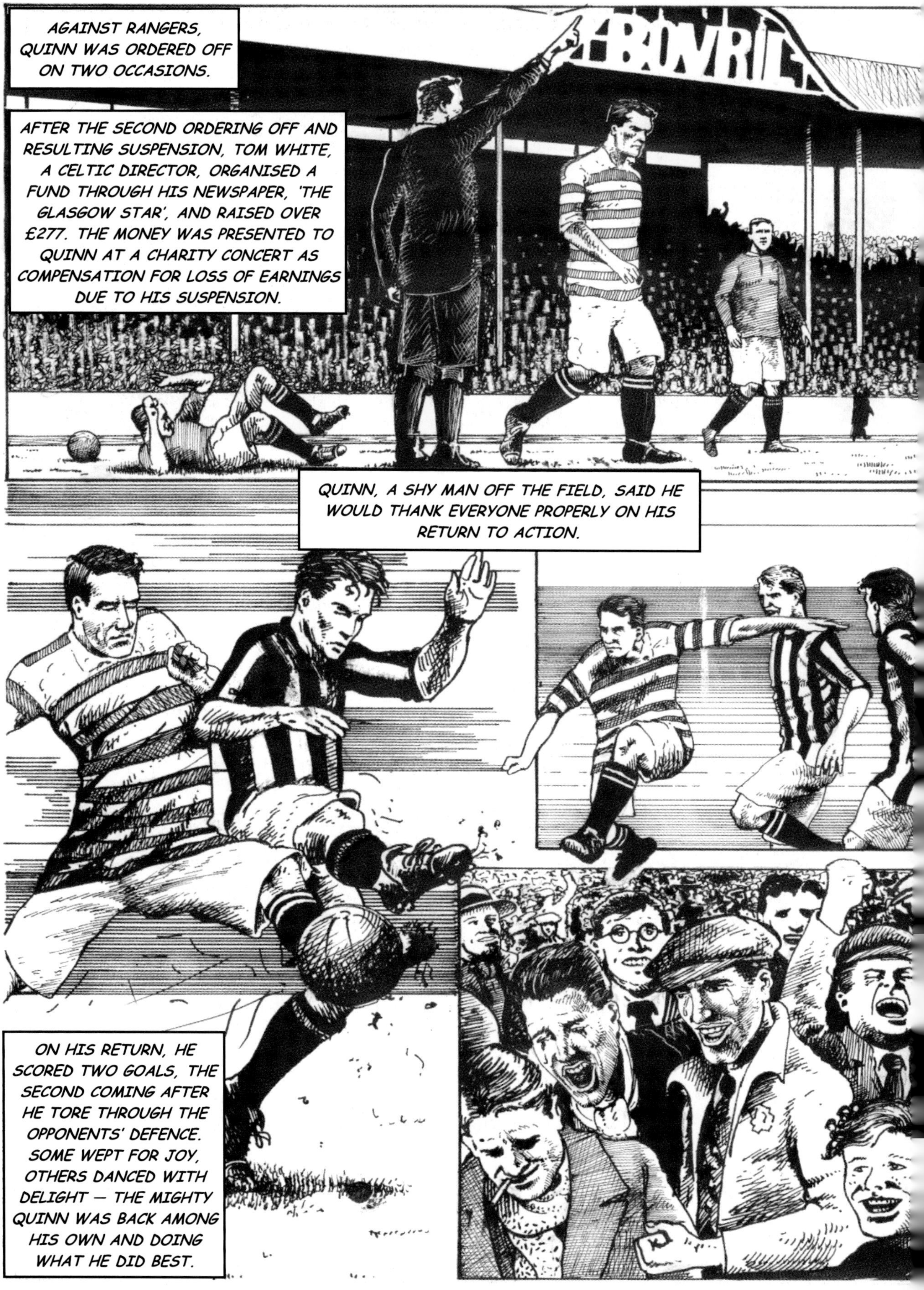
AGAINST RANGERS, QUINN WAS ORDERED OFF ON TWO OCCASIONS.
AFTER THE SECOND ORDERING OFF AND RESULTING SUSPENSION, TOM WHITE, A CELTIC DIRECTOR, ORGANISED A FUND THROUGH HIS NEWSPAPER, 'THE GLASGOW STAR', AND RAISED OVER £277. THE MONEY WAS PRESENTED TO QUINN AT A CHARITY CONCERT AS COMPENSATION FOR LOSS OF EARNINGS DUE TO HIS SUSPENSION.
QUINN, A SHY MAN OFF THE FIELD, SAID HE WOULD THANK EVERYONE PROPERLY ON HIS RETURN TO ACTION.
ON HIS RETURN, HE SCORED TWO GOALS, THE SECOND COMING AFTER HE TORE THROUGH THE OPPONENTS' DEFENCE. SOME WEPT FOR JOY, OTHERS DANCED WITH DELIGHT — THE MIGHTY QUINN WAS BACK AMONG HIS OWN AND DOING WHAT HE DID BEST.

CELTIC TEAM 1905–06: BACK ROW, L–R: R.DAVIS (TRAINER), R.CAMPBELL, D.McLEOD, H.WATSON, D.HAMILTON, A.McNAIR, A.WILSON, E.GARRY, J.McCOURT, D.ADAMS. FRONT ROW: J.YOUNG, J.HAY, A.BENNET, J.McMENEMY, W.LONEY, J.QUINN, P.SOMMERS, W.McNAIR.

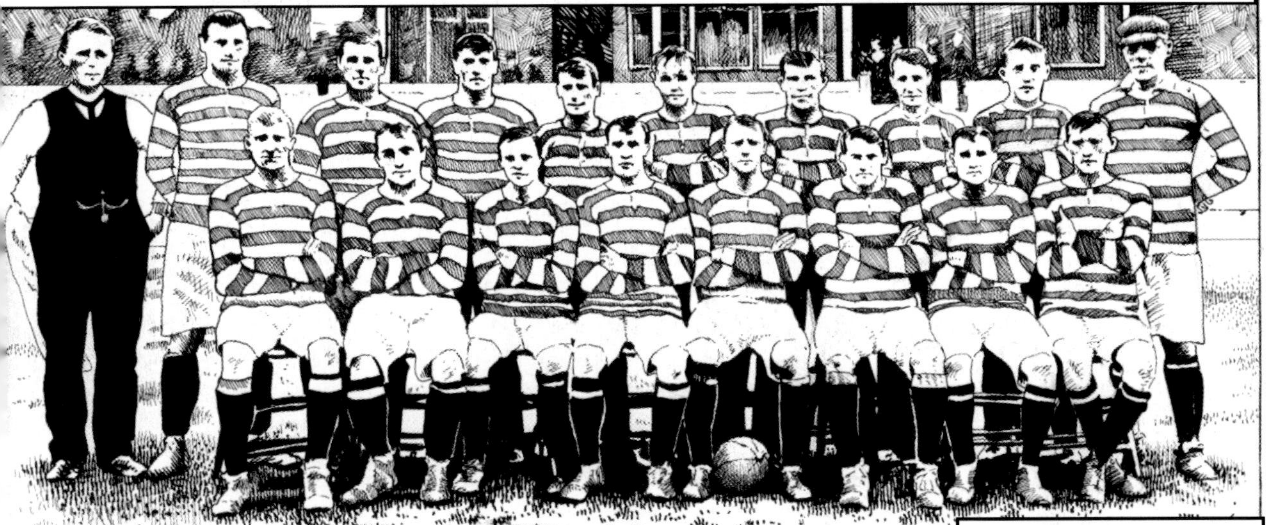

BETWEEN 1904 AND 1910, CELTIC WON THE LEAGUE SIX TIMES IN A ROW, A FEAT NOT EQUALLED UNTIL 1972 BY A TEAM CALLED CELTIC!

SCOTTISH CUP

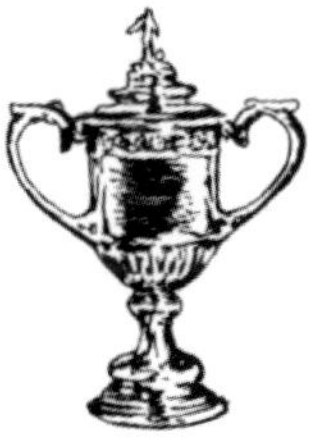

LEAGUE CHAMPIONSHIP TROPHY

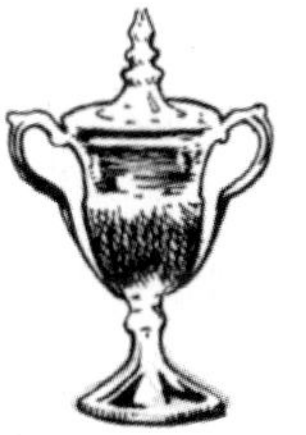

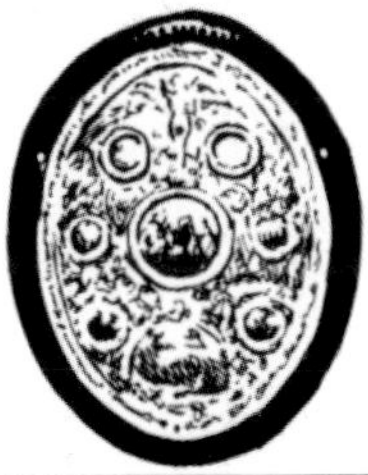

THE SCOTTISH LEAGUE SHIELD

THE SCOTTISH LEAGUE PRESENTED A SPECIAL SHIELD TO CELTIC IN RECOGNITION OF THEIR RECORD SIX-IN-A-ROW TITLES. THE CELTIC TEAM OF 1908 WAS THE FIRST SCOTTISH TEAM TO WIN FOUR TROPHIES IN ONE SEASON; CHARITY CUP, SCOTTISH CUP, GLASGOW CUP AND LEAGUE TROPHY.

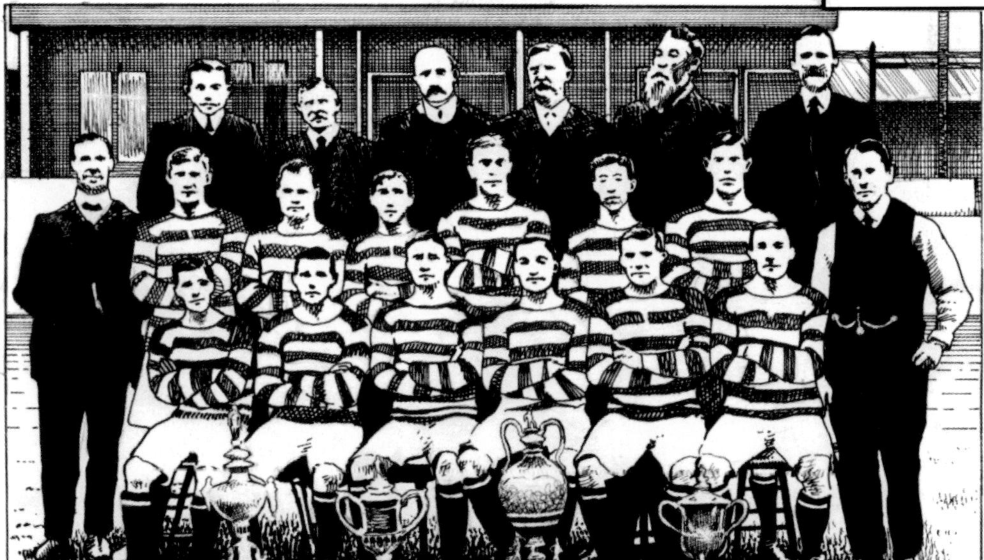

CELTIC TEAM 1908–09: BACK ROW, L–R: DIRECTORS T.WHITE, J.KELLY, T.COLGAN, J.McKILLOP, J.GRANT, M.DUNBAR. MIDDLE ROW: W.MALEY (SECRETARY), J.YOUNG, P.SOMMERS, J.McMENEMY, D.ADAMS, J.MITCHELL, J.WEIR, R.DAVIS (TRAINER). FRONT ROW: D.HAMILTON, D.McLEOD, W.LONEY, J.HAY, J.QUINN, W.McNAIR

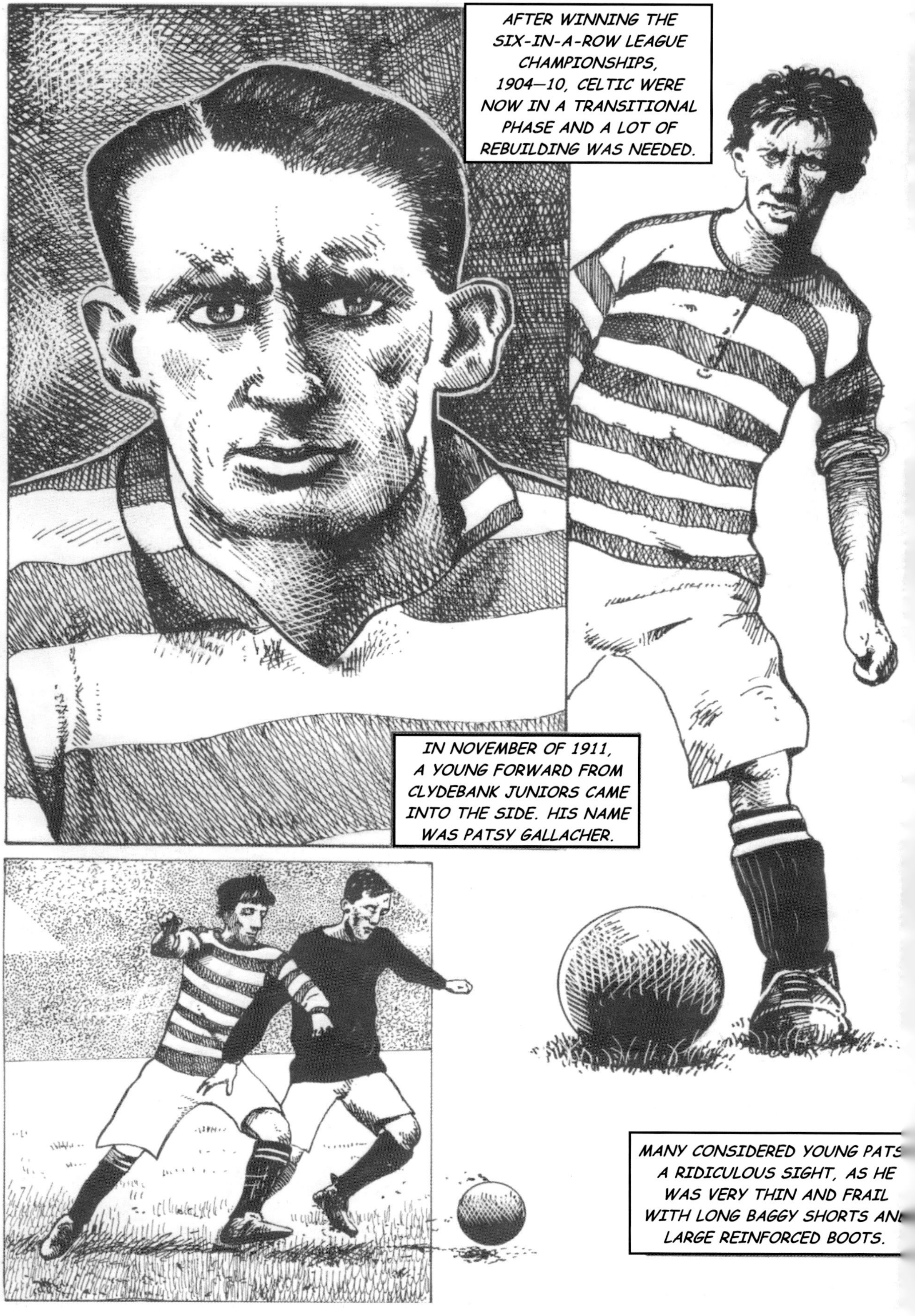
AFTER WINNING THE SIX-IN-A-ROW LEAGUE CHAMPIONSHIPS, 1904—10, CELTIC WERE NOW IN A TRANSITIONAL PHASE AND A LOT OF REBUILDING WAS NEEDED.
IN NOVEMBER OF 1911, A YOUNG FORWARD FROM CLYDEBANK JUNIORS CAME INTO THE SIDE. HIS NAME WAS PATSY GALLACHER.
MANY CONSIDERED YOUNG PATS A RIDICULOUS SIGHT, AS HE WAS VERY THIN AND FRAIL WITH LONG BAGGY SHORTS AN LARGE REINFORCED BOOTS.

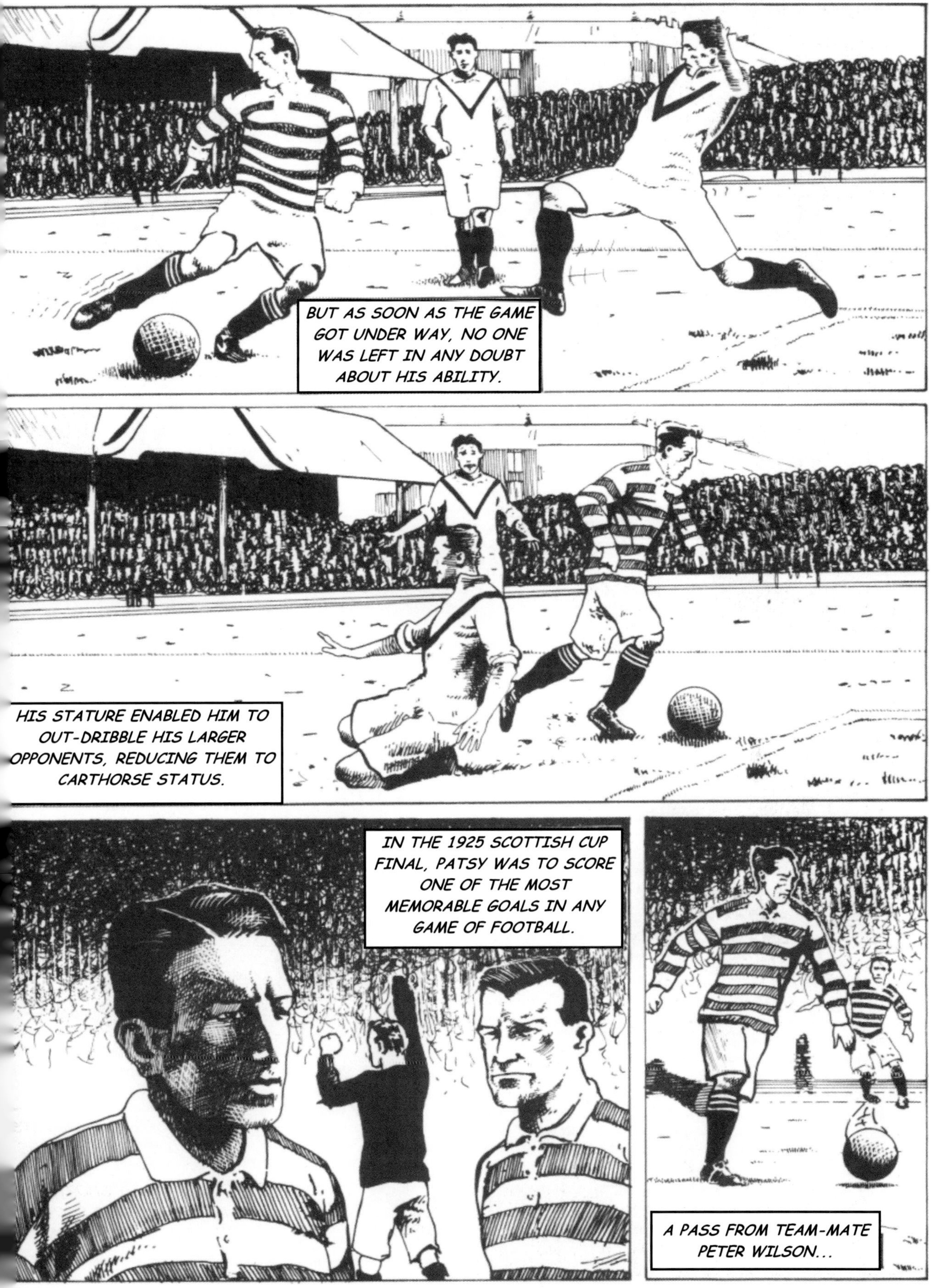
BUT AS SOON AS THE GAME GOT UNDER WAY, NO ONE WAS LEFT IN ANY DOUBT ABOUT HIS ABILITY.
HIS STATURE ENABLED HIM TO OUT-DRIBBLE HIS LARGER OPPONENTS, REDUCING THEM TO CARTHORSE STATUS.
IN THE 1925 SCOTTISH CUP FINAL, PATSY WAS TO SCORE ONE OF THE MOST MEMORABLE GOALS IN ANY GAME OF FOOTBALL.
A PASS FROM TEAM-MATE PETER WILSON...

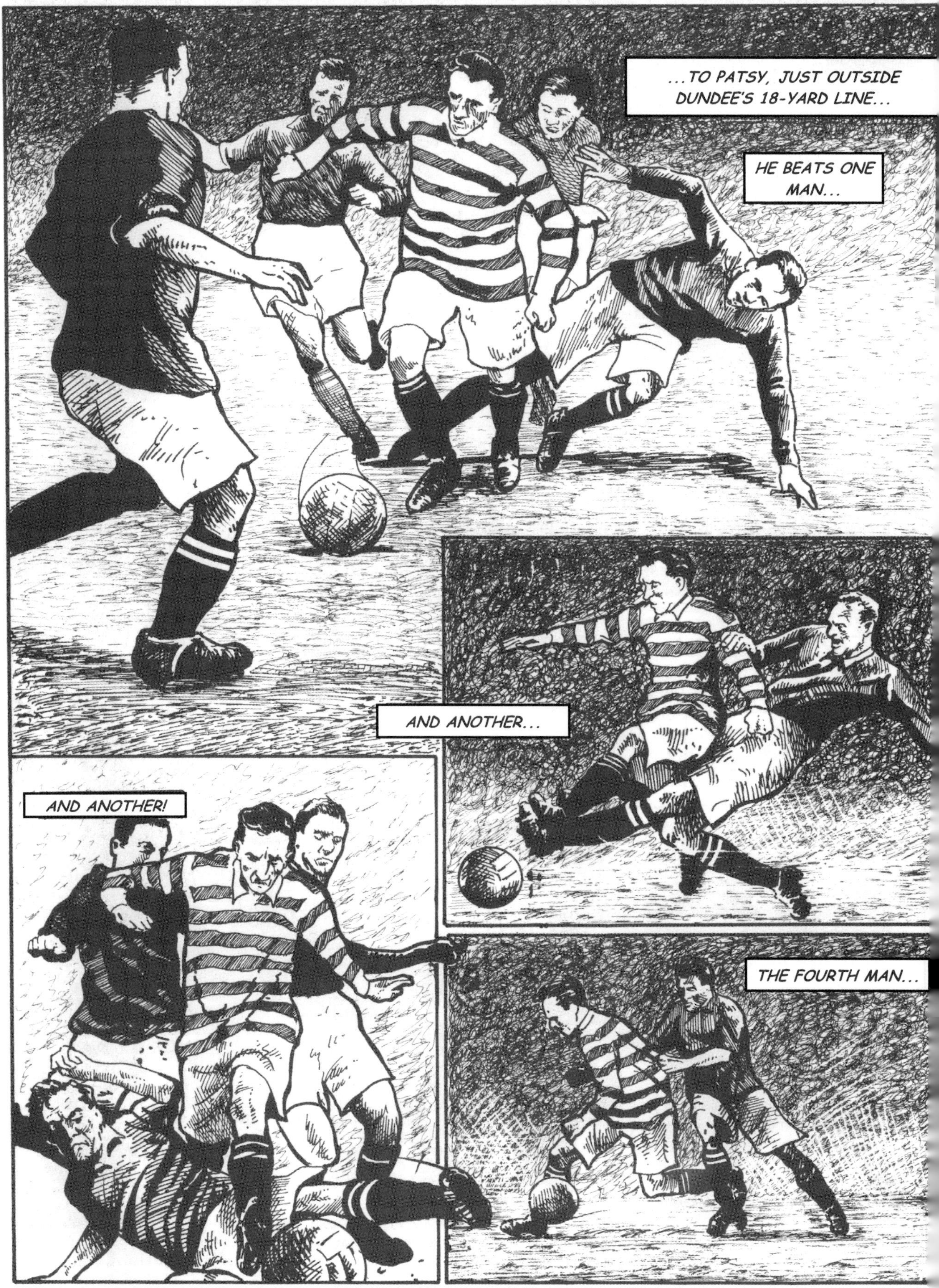
...TO PATSY, JUST OUTSIDE DUNDEE'S 18-YARD LINE...
HE BEATS ONE MAN...
AND ANOTHER...
AND ANOTHER!
THE FOURTH MAN...

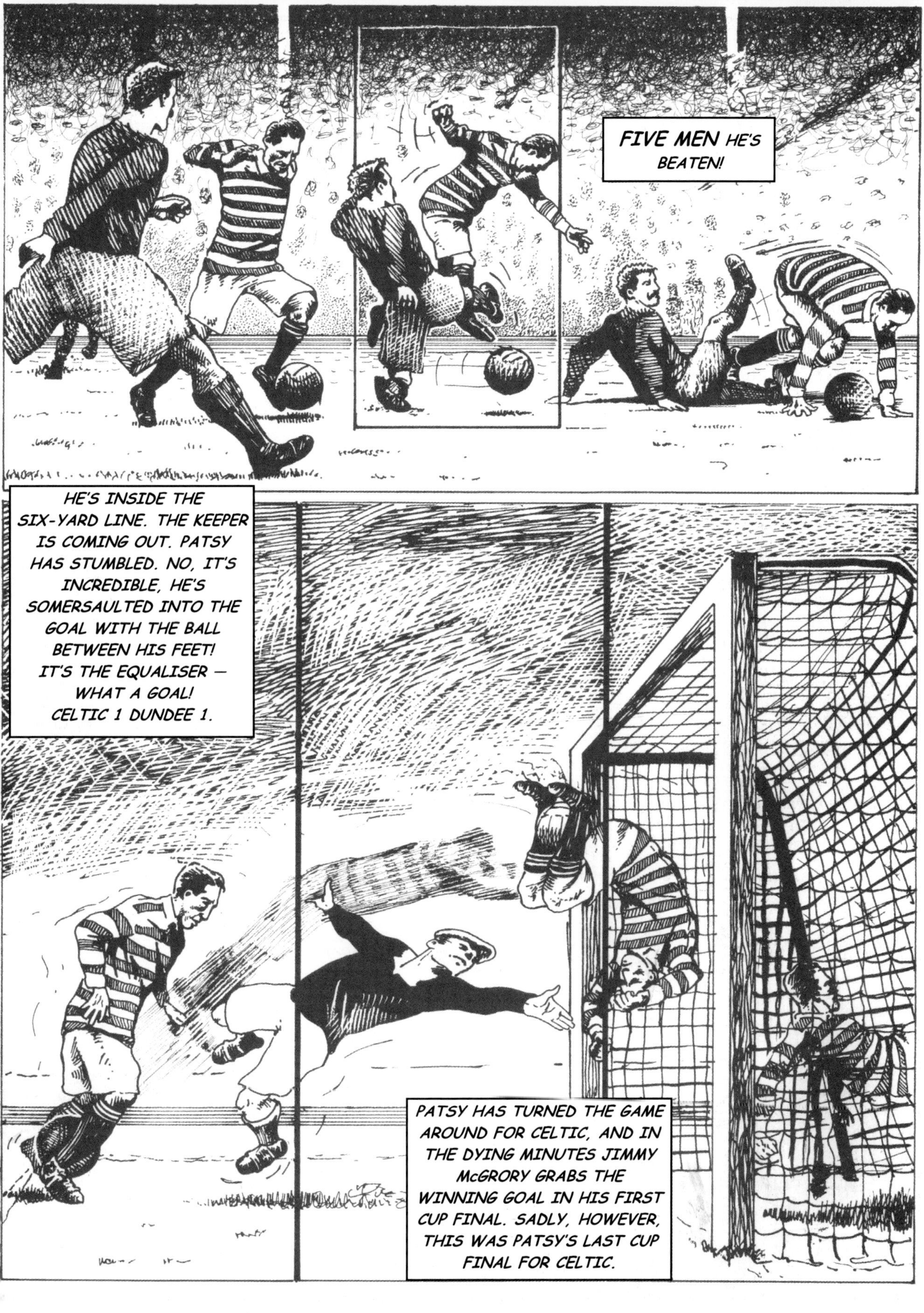
FIVE MEN HE'S BEATEN!
HE'S INSIDE THE SIX-YARD LINE. THE KEEPER IS COMING OUT. PATSY HAS STUMBLED. NO, IT'S INCREDIBLE, HE'S SOMERSAULTED INTO THE GOAL WITH THE BALL BETWEEN HIS FEET! IT'S THE EQUALISER — WHAT A GOAL! CELTIC 1 DUNDEE 1.
PATSY HAS TURNED THE GAME AROUND FOR CELTIC, AND IN THE DYING MINUTES JIMMY McGRORY GRABS THE WINNING GOAL IN HIS FIRST CUP FINAL. SADLY, HOWEVER, THIS WAS PATSY'S LAST CUP FINAL FOR CELTIC.

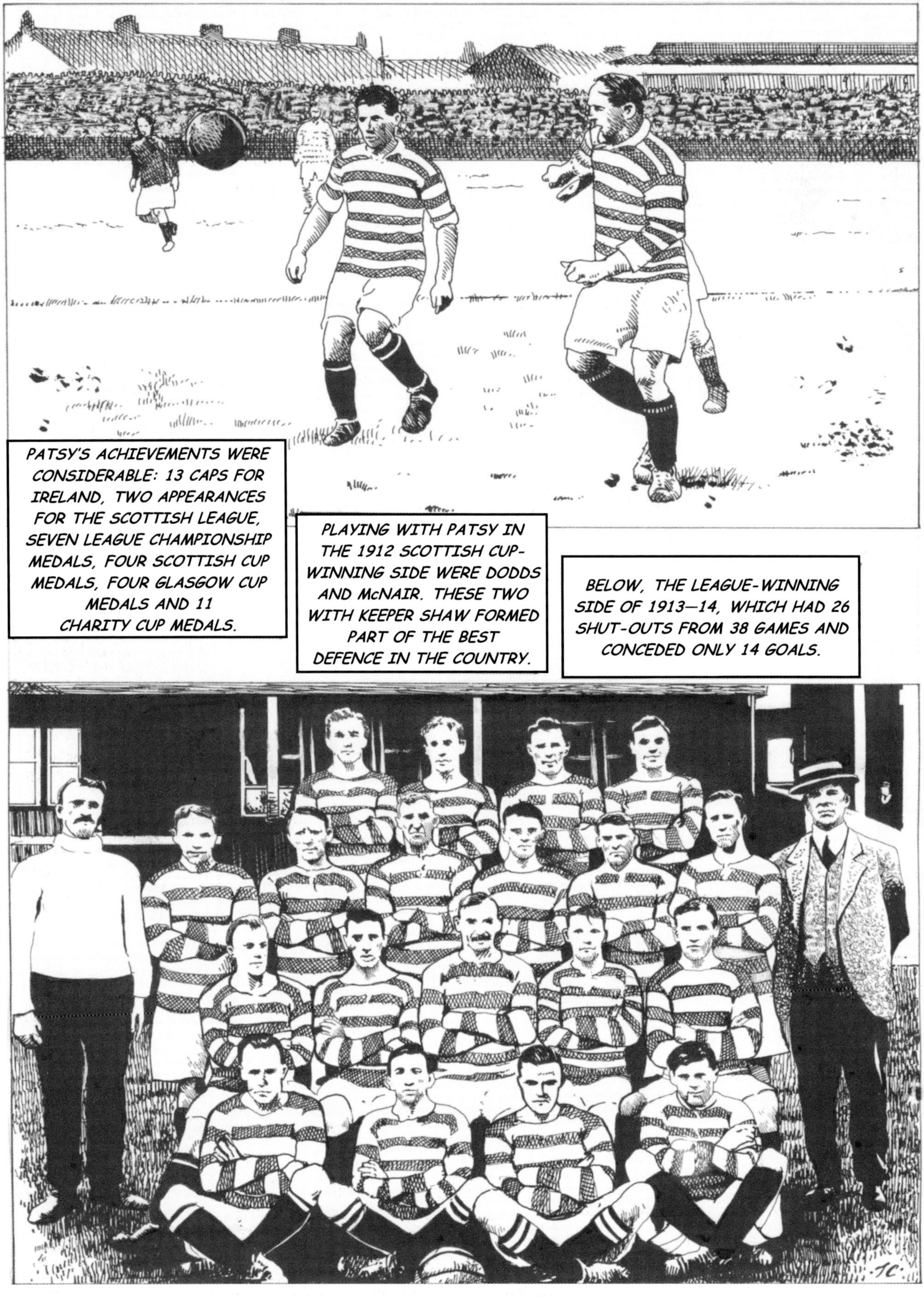
PATSY'S ACHIEVEMENTS WERE CONSIDERABLE: 13 CAPS FOR IRELAND, TWO APPEARANCES FOR THE SCOTTISH LEAGUE, SEVEN LEAGUE CHAMPIONSHIP MEDALS, FOUR SCOTTISH CUP MEDALS, FOUR GLASGOW CUP MEDALS AND 11 CHARITY CUP MEDALS.
PLAYING WITH PATSY IN THE 1912 SCOTTISH CUP-WINNING SIDE WERE DODDS AND McNAIR. THESE TWO WITH KEEPER SHAW FORMED PART OF THE BEST DEFENCE IN THE COUNTRY.
BELOW, THE LEAGUE-WINNING SIDE OF 1913—14, WHICH HAD 26 SHUT-OUTS FROM 38 GAMES AND CONCEDED ONLY 14 GOALS.
TC

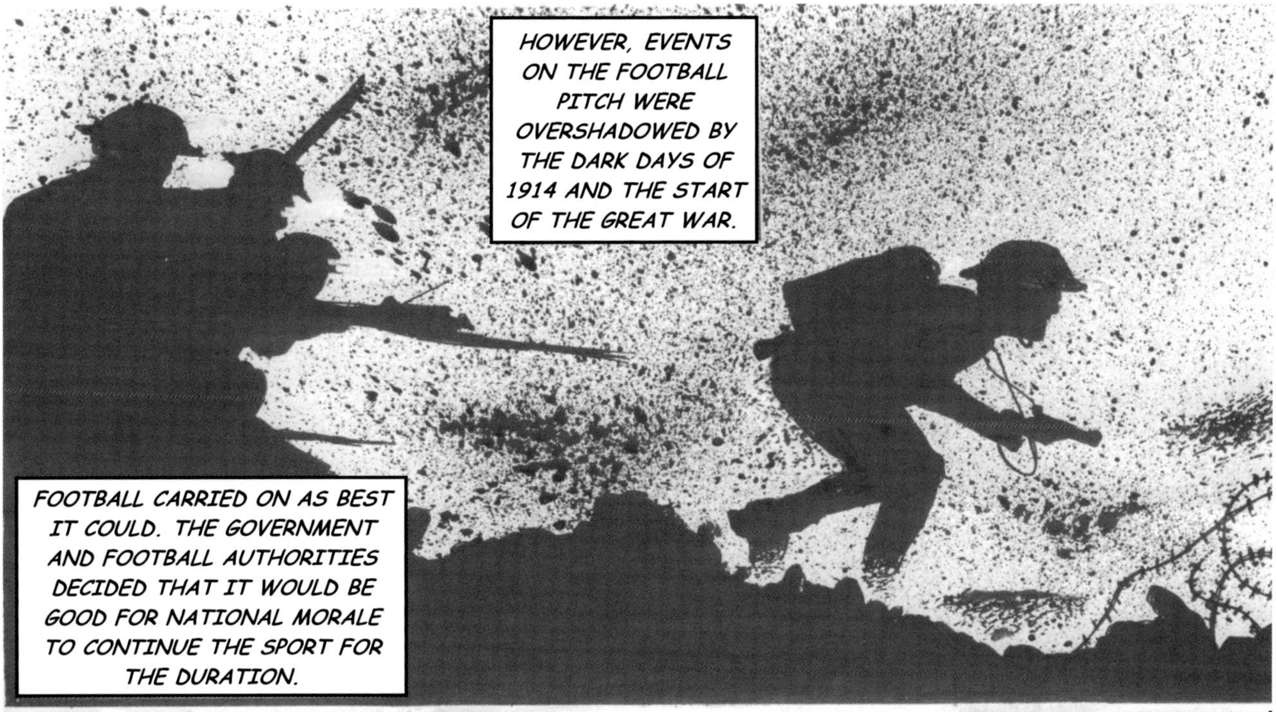
HOWEVER, EVENTS ON THE FOOTBALL PITCH WERE OVERSHADOWED BY THE DARK DAYS OF 1914 AND THE START OF THE GREAT WAR.
FOOTBALL CARRIED ON AS BEST IT COULD. THE GOVERNMENT AND FOOTBALL AUTHORITIES DECIDED THAT IT WOULD BE GOOD FOR NATIONAL MORALE TO CONTINUE THE SPORT FOR THE DURATION.

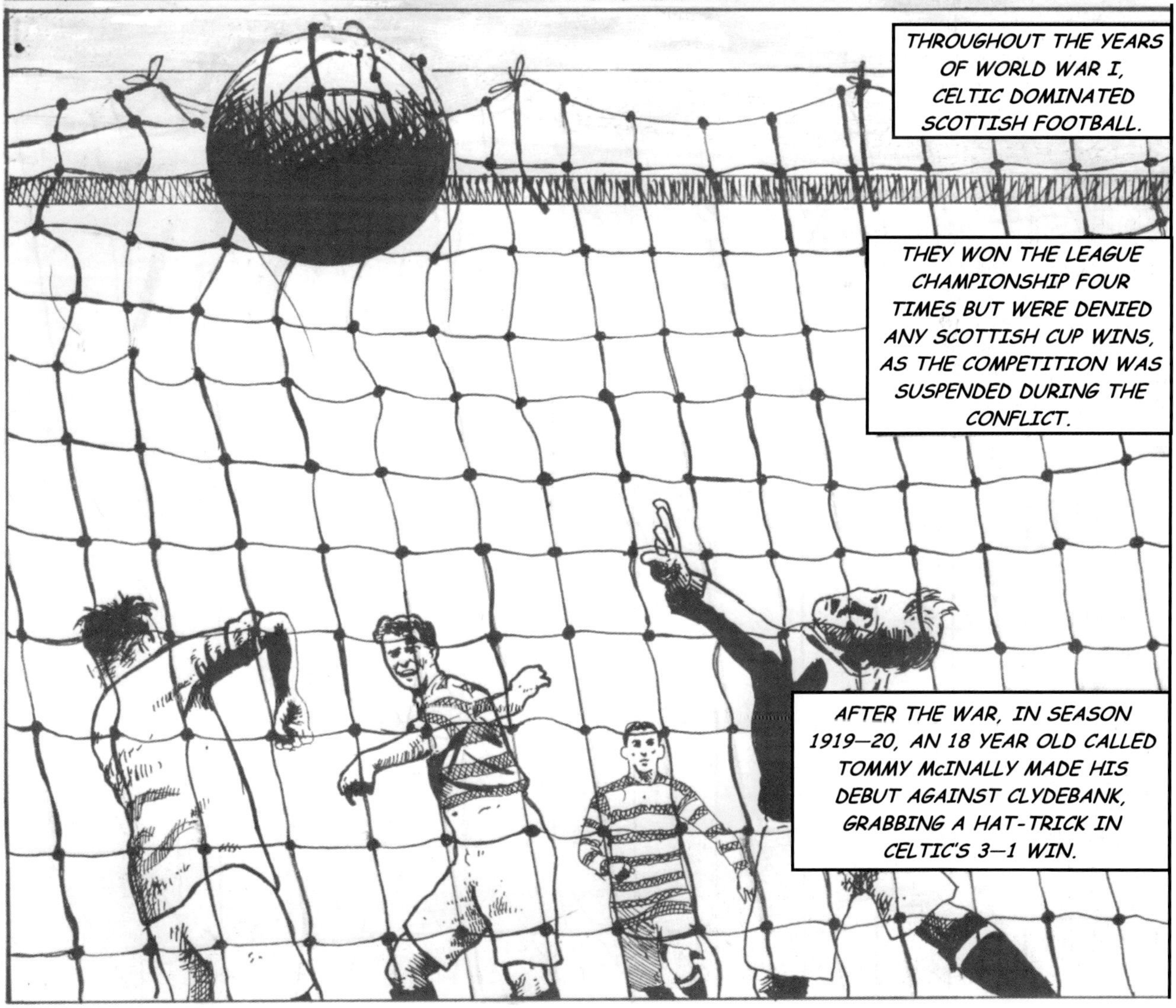
THROUGHOUT THE YEARS OF WORLD WAR I, CELTIC DOMINATED SCOTTISH FOOTBALL.
THEY WON THE LEAGUE CHAMPIONSHIP FOUR TIMES BUT WERE DENIED ANY SCOTTISH CUP WINS, AS THE COMPETITION WAS SUSPENDED DURING THE CONFLICT.
AFTER THE WAR, IN SEASON 1919–20, AN 18 YEAR OLD CALLED TOMMY McINALLY MADE HIS DEBUT AGAINST CLYDEBANK, GRABBING A HAT-TRICK IN CELTIC'S 3–1 WIN.

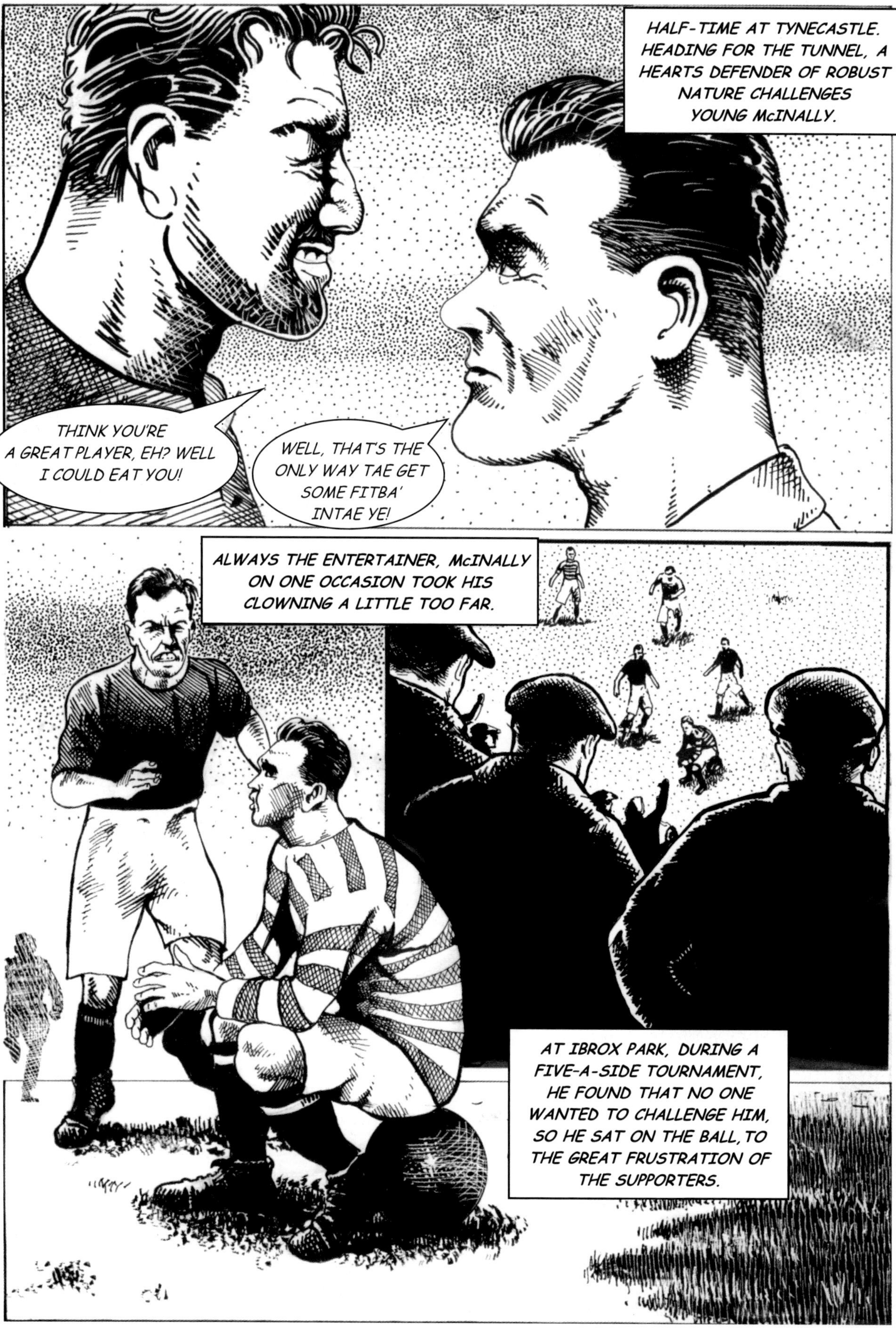
HALF-TIME AT TYNECASTLE. HEADING FOR THE TUNNEL, A HEARTS DEFENDER OF ROBUST NATURE CHALLENGES YOUNG McINALLY.
THINK YOU'RE A GREAT PLAYER, EH? WELL I COULD EAT YOU!
WELL, THAT'S THE ONLY WAY TAE GET SOME FITBA' INTAE YE!
ALWAYS THE ENTERTAINER, McINALLY ON ONE OCCASION TOOK HIS CLOWNING A LITTLE TOO FAR.
AT IBROX PARK, DURING A FIVE-A-SIDE TOURNAMENT, HE FOUND THAT NO ONE WANTED TO CHALLENGE HIM, SO HE SAT ON THE BALL, TO THE GREAT FRUSTRATION OF THE SUPPORTERS.

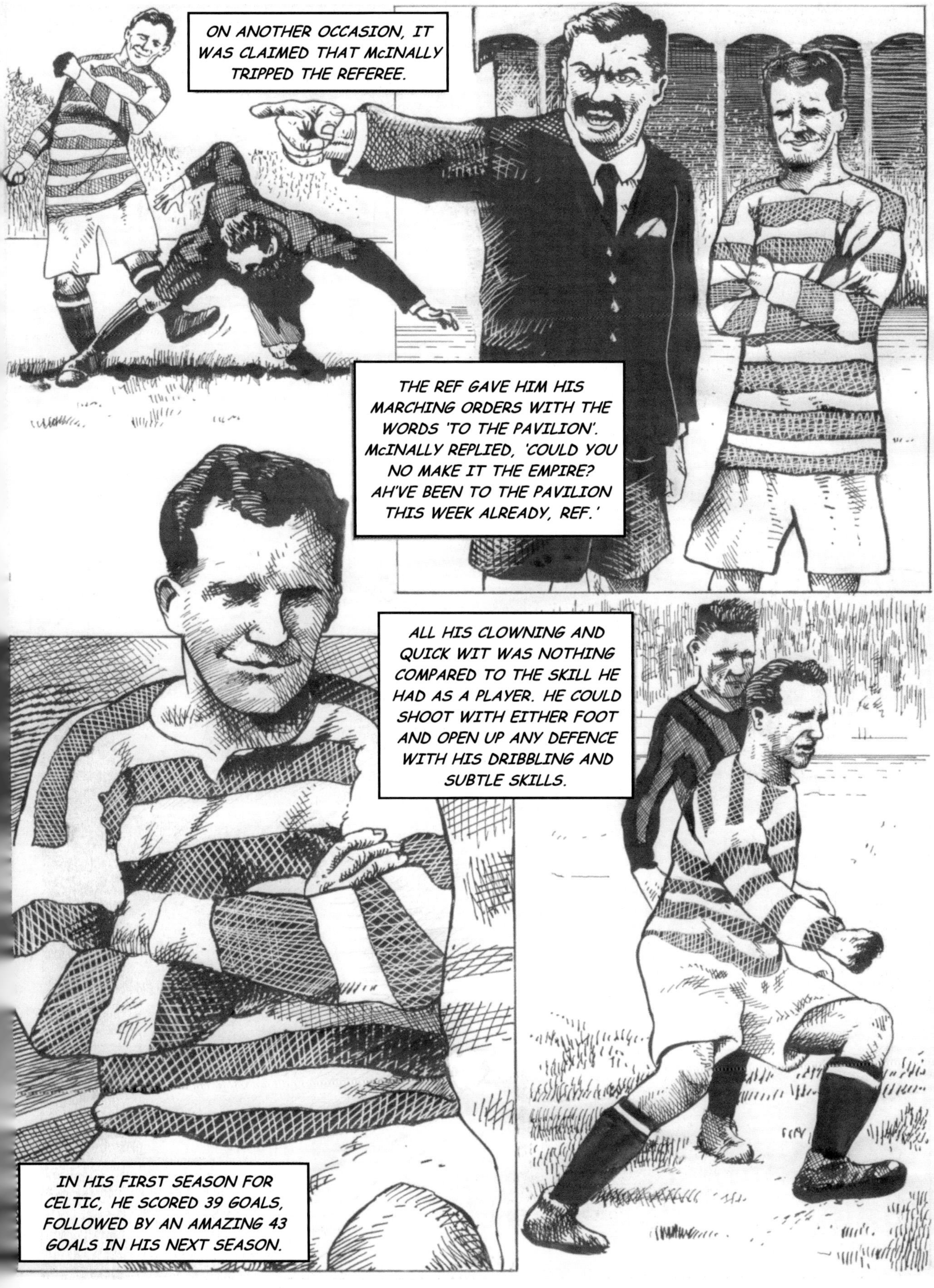
ON ANOTHER OCCASION, IT WAS CLAIMED THAT McINALLY TRIPPED THE REFEREE.
THE REF GAVE HIM HIS MARCHING ORDERS WITH THE WORDS 'TO THE PAVILION'. McINALLY REPLIED, 'COULD YOU NO MAKE IT THE EMPIRE? AH'VE BEEN TO THE PAVILION THIS WEEK ALREADY, REF.'
ALL HIS CLOWNING AND QUICK WIT WAS NOTHING COMPARED TO THE SKILL HE HAD AS A PLAYER. HE COULD SHOOT WITH EITHER FOOT AND OPEN UP ANY DEFENCE WITH HIS DRIBBLING AND SUBTLE SKILLS.
IN HIS FIRST SEASON FOR CELTIC, HE SCORED 39 GOALS, FOLLOWED BY AN AMAZING 43 GOALS IN HIS NEXT SEASON.

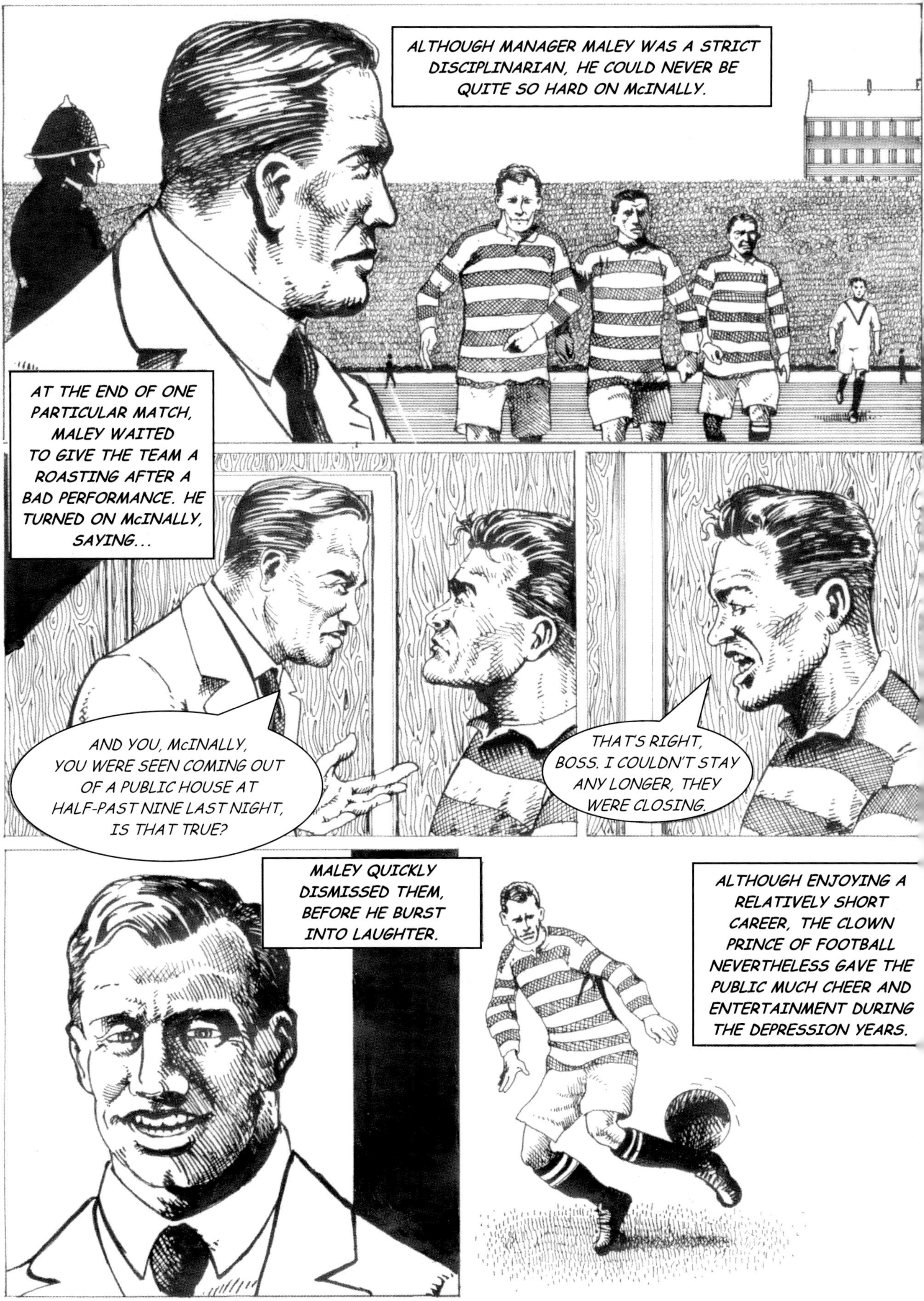
ALTHOUGH MANAGER MALEY WAS A STRICT DISCIPLINARIAN, HE COULD NEVER BE QUITE SO HARD ON McINALLY.
AT THE END OF ONE PARTICULAR MATCH, MALEY WAITED TO GIVE THE TEAM A ROASTING AFTER A BAD PERFORMANCE. HE TURNED ON McINALLY, SAYING...
AND YOU, McINALLY, YOU WERE SEEN COMING OUT OF A PUBLIC HOUSE AT HALF-PAST NINE LAST NIGHT, IS THAT TRUE?
THAT'S RIGHT, BOSS. I COULDN'T STAY ANY LONGER, THEY WERE CLOSING.
MALEY QUICKLY DISMISSED THEM, BEFORE HE BURST INTO LAUGHTER.
ALTHOUGH ENJOYING A RELATIVELY SHORT CAREER, THE CLOWN PRINCE OF FOOTBALL NEVERTHELESS GAVE THE PUBLIC MUCH CHEER AND ENTERTAINMENT DURING THE DEPRESSION YEARS.

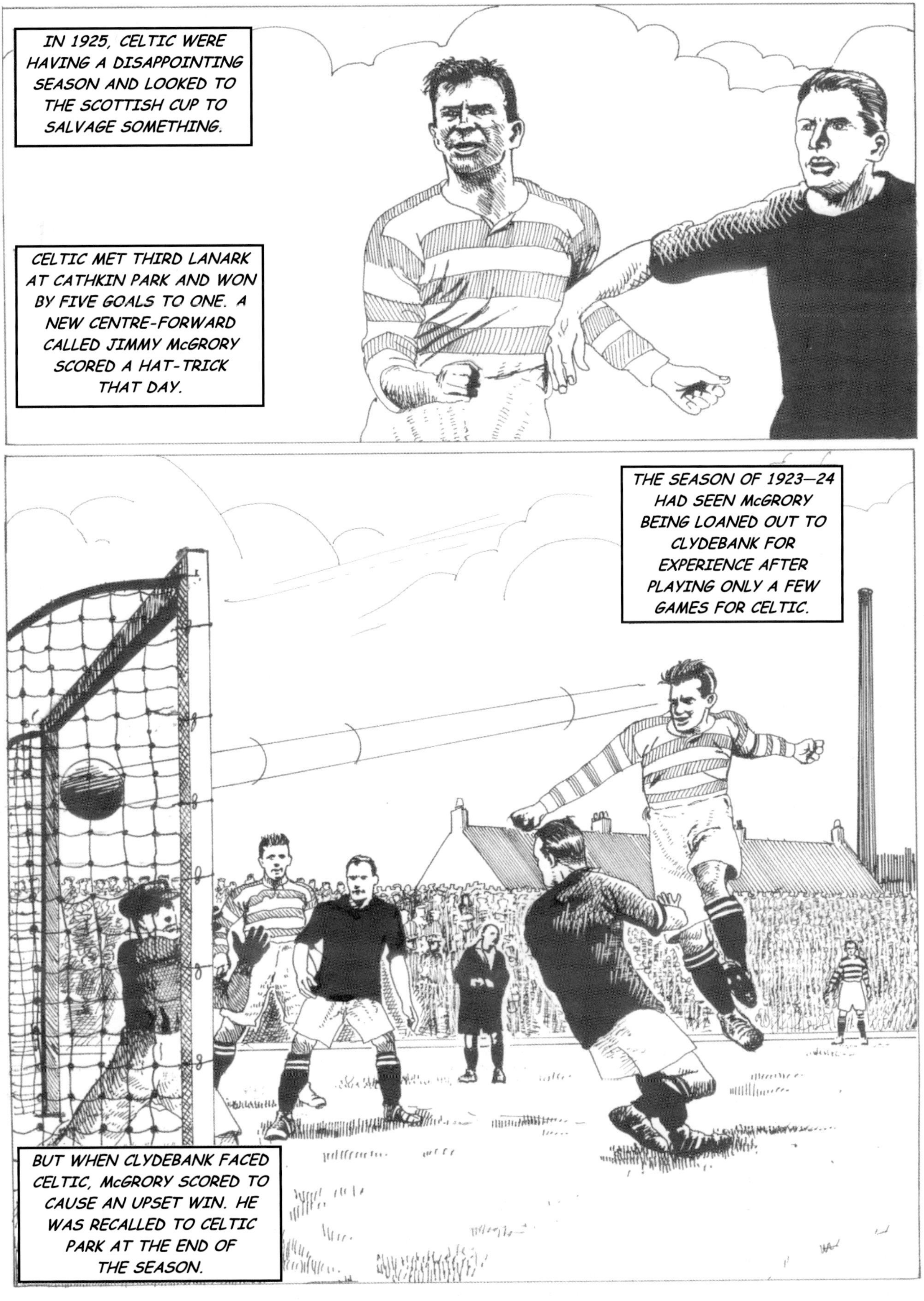
IN 1925, CELTIC WERE HAVING A DISAPPOINTING SEASON AND LOOKED TO THE SCOTTISH CUP TO SALVAGE SOMETHING.
CELTIC MET THIRD LANARK AT CATHKIN PARK AND WON BY FIVE GOALS TO ONE. A NEW CENTRE-FORWARD CALLED JIMMY McGRORY SCORED A HAT-TRICK THAT DAY.
THE SEASON OF 1923—24 HAD SEEN McGRORY BEING LOANED OUT TO CLYDEBANK FOR EXPERIENCE AFTER PLAYING ONLY A FEW GAMES FOR CELTIC.
BUT WHEN CLYDEBANK FACED CELTIC, McGRORY SCORED TO CAUSE AN UPSET WIN. HE WAS RECALLED TO CELTIC PARK AT THE END OF THE SEASON.

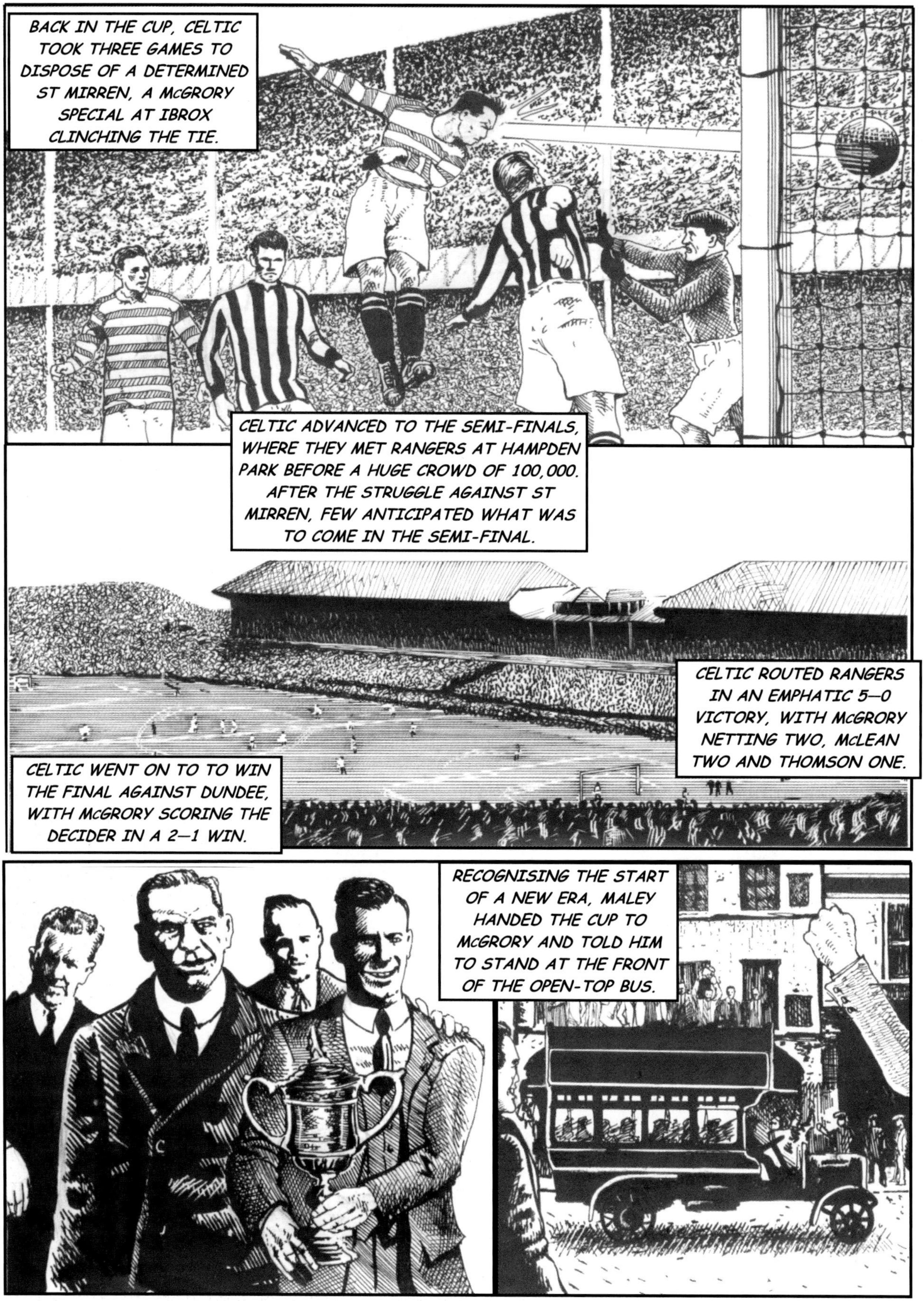
BACK IN THE CUP, CELTIC TOOK THREE GAMES TO DISPOSE OF A DETERMINED ST MIRREN, A McGRORY SPECIAL AT IBROX CLINCHING THE TIE.
CELTIC ADVANCED TO THE SEMI-FINALS, WHERE THEY MET RANGERS AT HAMPDEN PARK BEFORE A HUGE CROWD OF 100,000. AFTER THE STRUGGLE AGAINST ST MIRREN, FEW ANTICIPATED WHAT WAS TO COME IN THE SEMI-FINAL.
CELTIC ROUTED RANGERS IN AN EMPHATIC 5—0 VICTORY, WITH McGRORY NETTING TWO, McLEAN TWO AND THOMSON ONE.
CELTIC WENT ON TO TO WIN THE FINAL AGAINST DUNDEE, WITH McGRORY SCORING THE DECIDER IN A 2—1 WIN.
RECOGNISING THE START OF A NEW ERA, MALEY HANDED THE CUP TO McGRORY AND TOLD HIM TO STAND AT THE FRONT OF THE OPEN-TOP BUS.

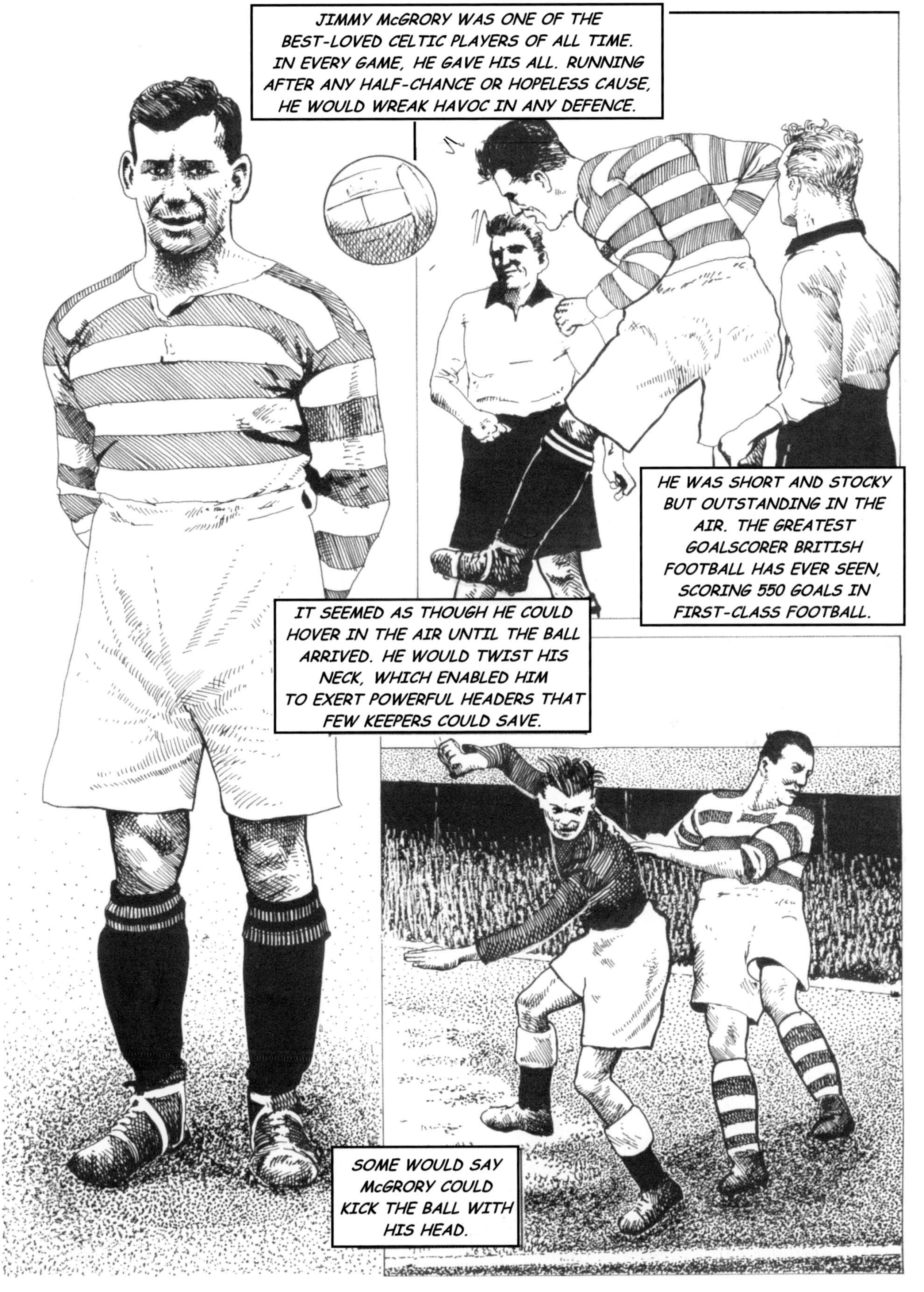
JIMMY McGRORY WAS ONE OF THE BEST-LOVED CELTIC PLAYERS OF ALL TIME. IN EVERY GAME, HE GAVE HIS ALL. RUNNING AFTER ANY HALF-CHANCE OR HOPELESS CAUSE, HE WOULD WREAK HAVOC IN ANY DEFENCE.
HE WAS SHORT AND STOCKY BUT OUTSTANDING IN THE AIR. THE GREATEST GOALSCORER BRITISH FOOTBALL HAS EVER SEEN, SCORING 550 GOALS IN FIRST-CLASS FOOTBALL.
IT SEEMED AS THOUGH HE COULD HOVER IN THE AIR UNTIL THE BALL ARRIVED. HE WOULD TWIST HIS NECK, WHICH ENABLED HIM TO EXERT POWERFUL HEADERS THAT FEW KEEPERS COULD SAVE.
SOME WOULD SAY McGRORY COULD KICK THE BALL WITH HIS HEAD.

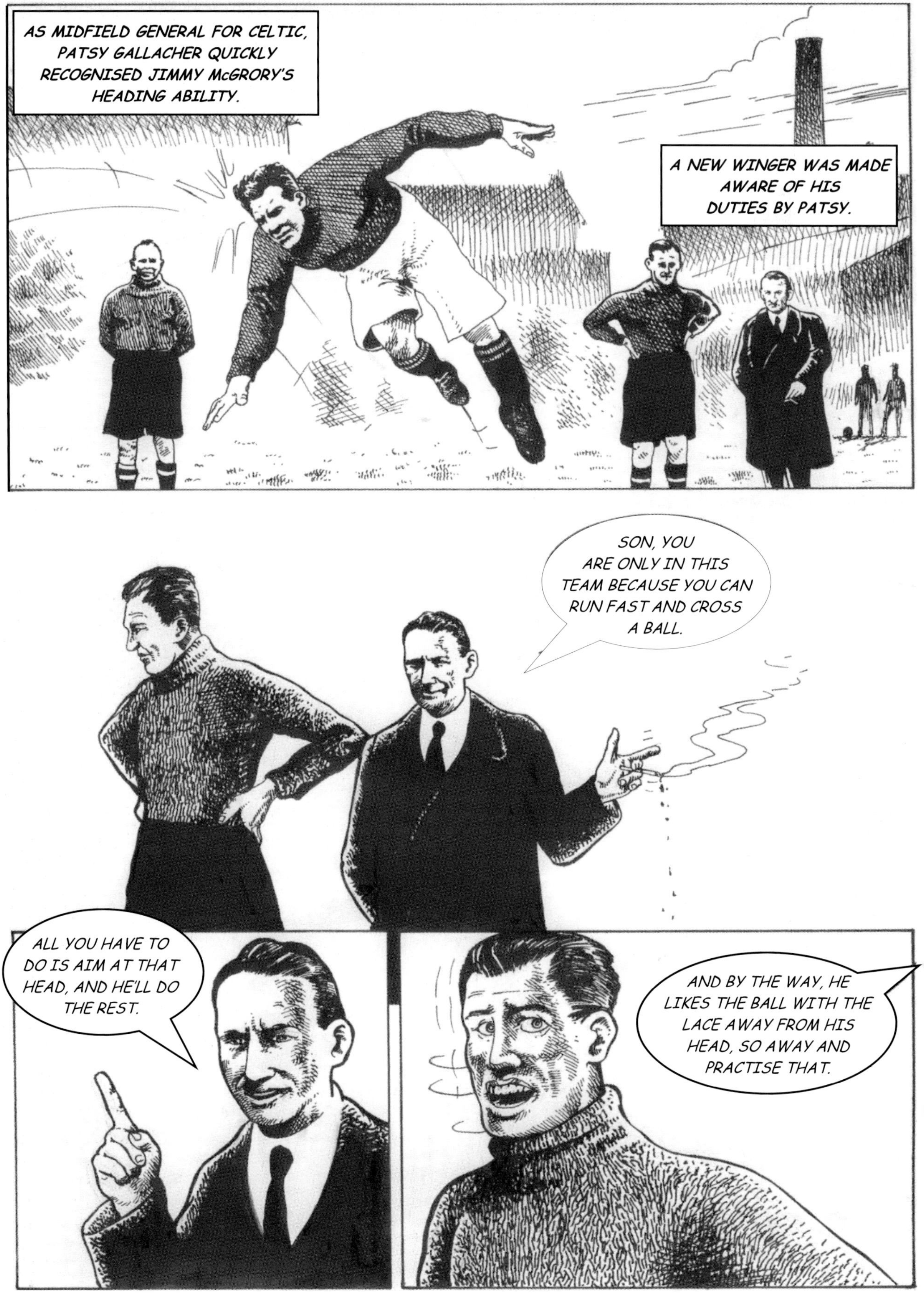
AS MIDFIELD GENERAL FOR CELTIC, PATSY GALLACHER QUICKLY RECOGNISED JIMMY McGRORY'S HEADING ABILITY.
A NEW WINGER WAS MADE AWARE OF HIS DUTIES BY PATSY.
SON, YOU ARE ONLY IN THIS TEAM BECAUSE YOU CAN RUN FAST AND CROSS A BALL.
ALL YOU HAVE TO DO IS AIM AT THAT HEAD, AND HE'LL DO THE REST.
AND BY THE WAY, HE LIKES THE BALL WITH THE LACE AWAY FROM HIS HEAD, SO AWAY AND PRACTISE THAT.

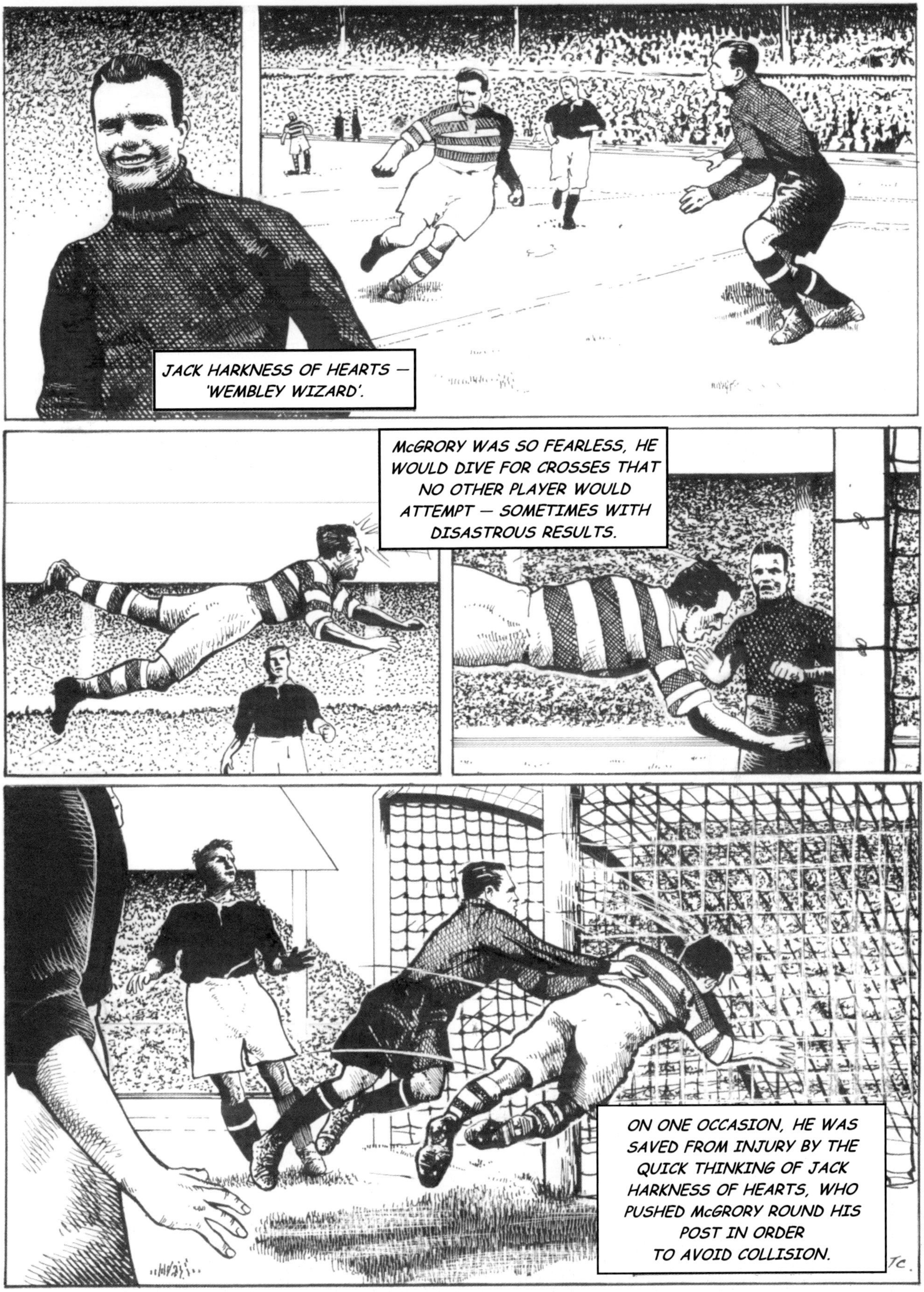
JACK HARKNESS OF HEARTS — 'WEMBLEY WIZARD'.
McGRORY WAS SO FEARLESS, HE WOULD DIVE FOR CROSSES THAT NO OTHER PLAYER WOULD ATTEMPT — SOMETIMES WITH DISASTROUS RESULTS.
ON ONE OCCASION, HE WAS SAVED FROM INJURY BY THE QUICK THINKING OF JACK HARKNESS OF HEARTS, WHO PUSHED McGRORY ROUND HIS POST IN ORDER TO AVOID COLLISION.
TC.

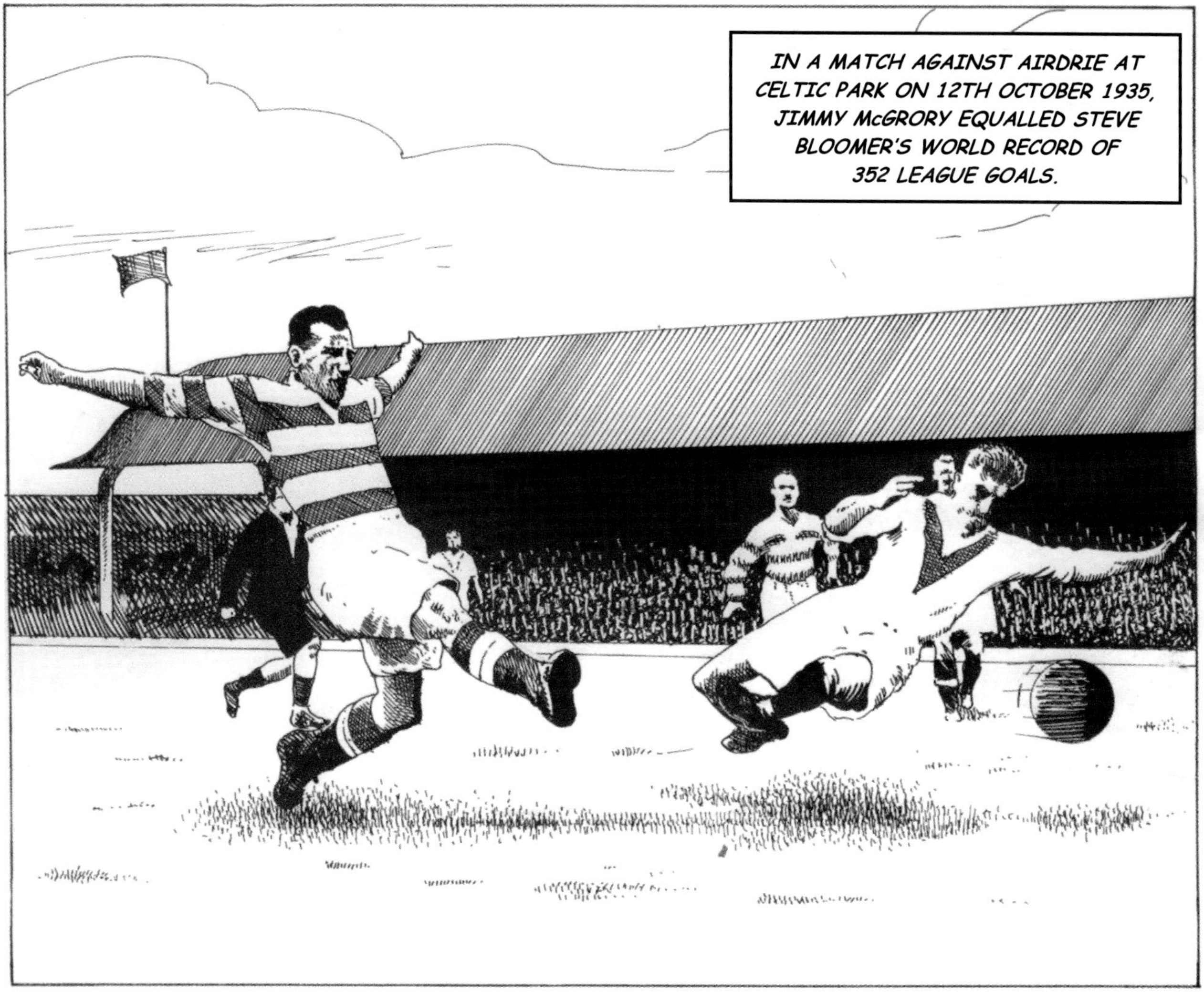
IN A MATCH AGAINST AIRDRIE AT CELTIC PARK ON 12TH OCTOBER 1935, JIMMY McGRORY EQUALLED STEVE BLOOMER'S WORLD RECORD OF 352 LEAGUE GOALS.

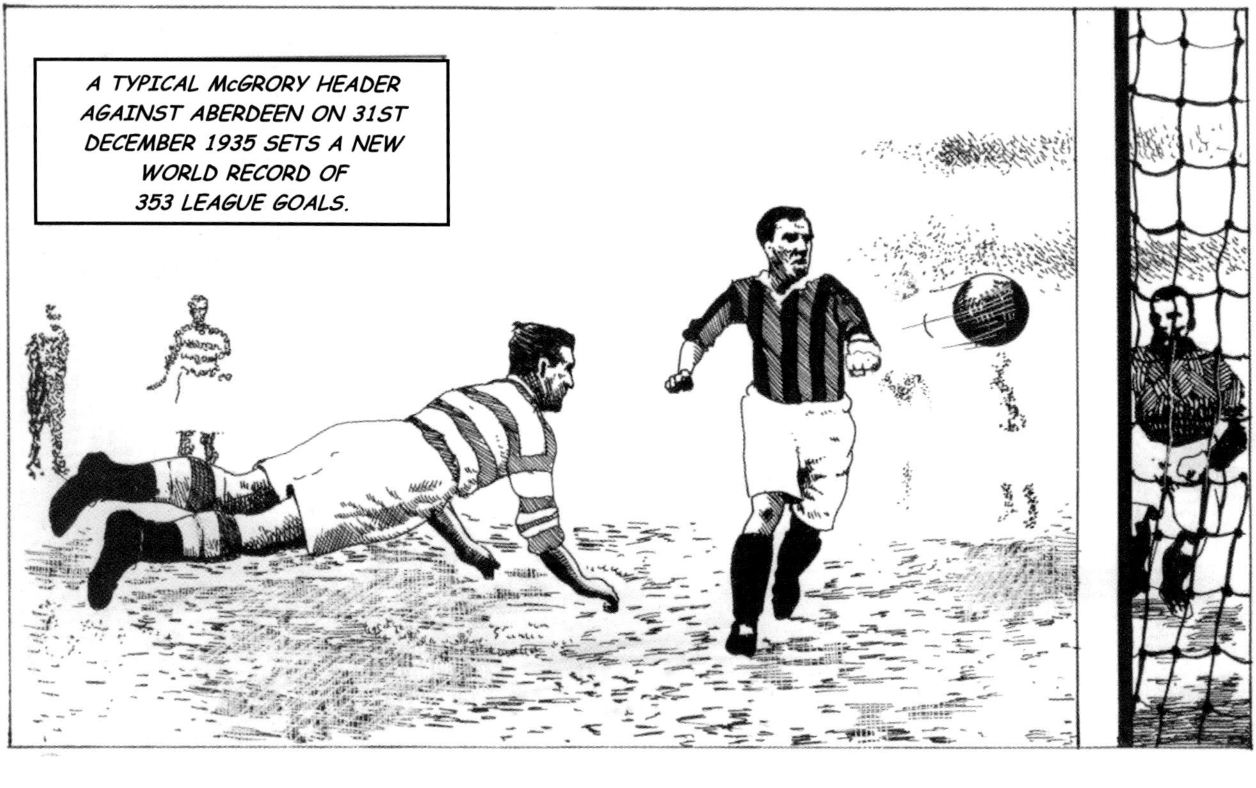
A TYPICAL McGRORY HEADER AGAINST ABERDEEN ON 31ST DECEMBER 1935 SETS A NEW WORLD RECORD OF 353 LEAGUE GOALS.

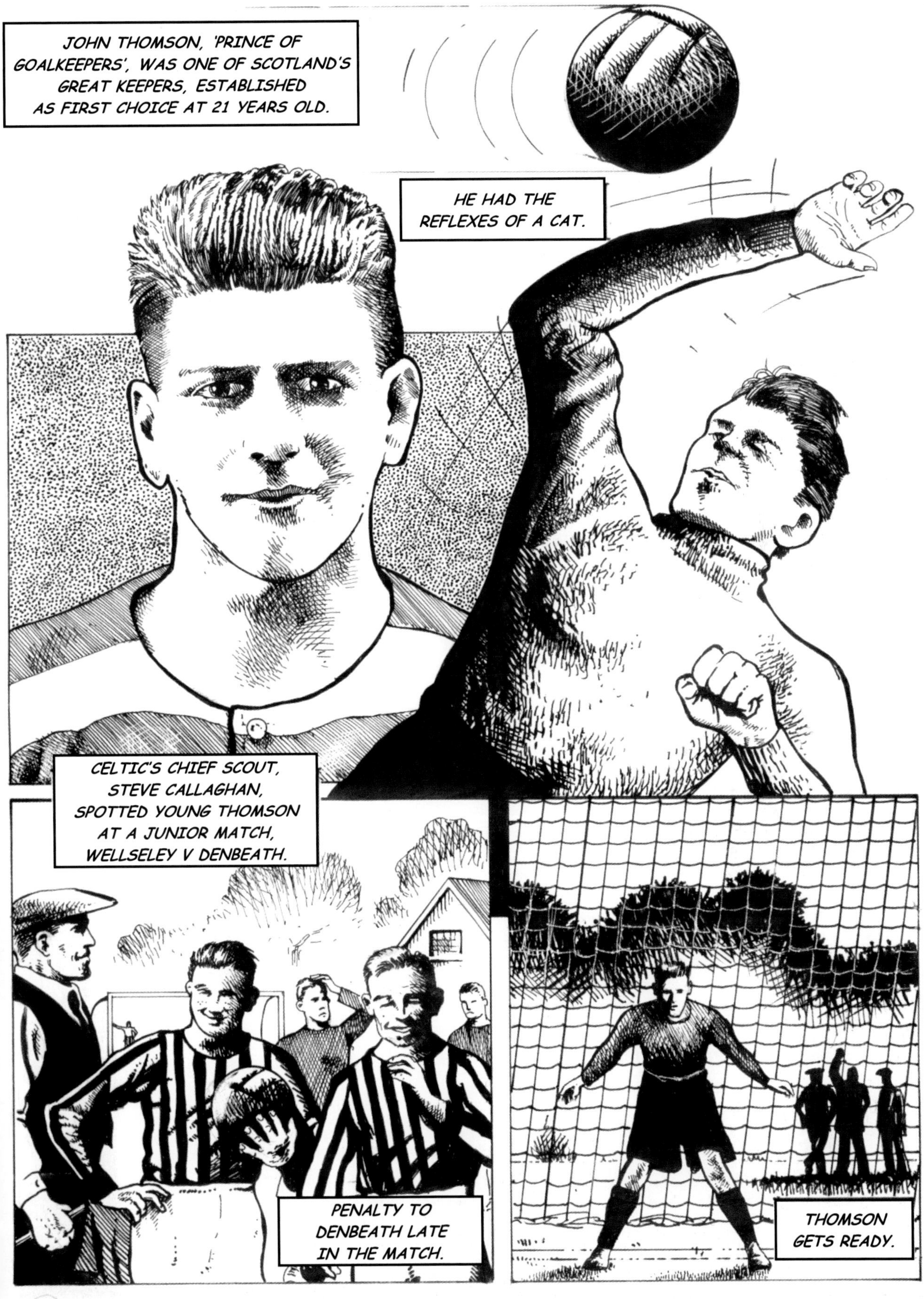
JOHN THOMSON, 'PRINCE OF GOALKEEPERS', WAS ONE OF SCOTLAND'S GREAT KEEPERS, ESTABLISHED AS FIRST CHOICE AT 21 YEARS OLD.
HE HAD THE REFLEXES OF A CAT.
CELTIC'S CHIEF SCOUT, STEVE CALLAGHAN, SPOTTED YOUNG THOMSON AT A JUNIOR MATCH, WELLSELEY V DENBEATH.
PENALTY TO DENBEATH LATE IN THE MATCH.
THOMSON GETS READY.

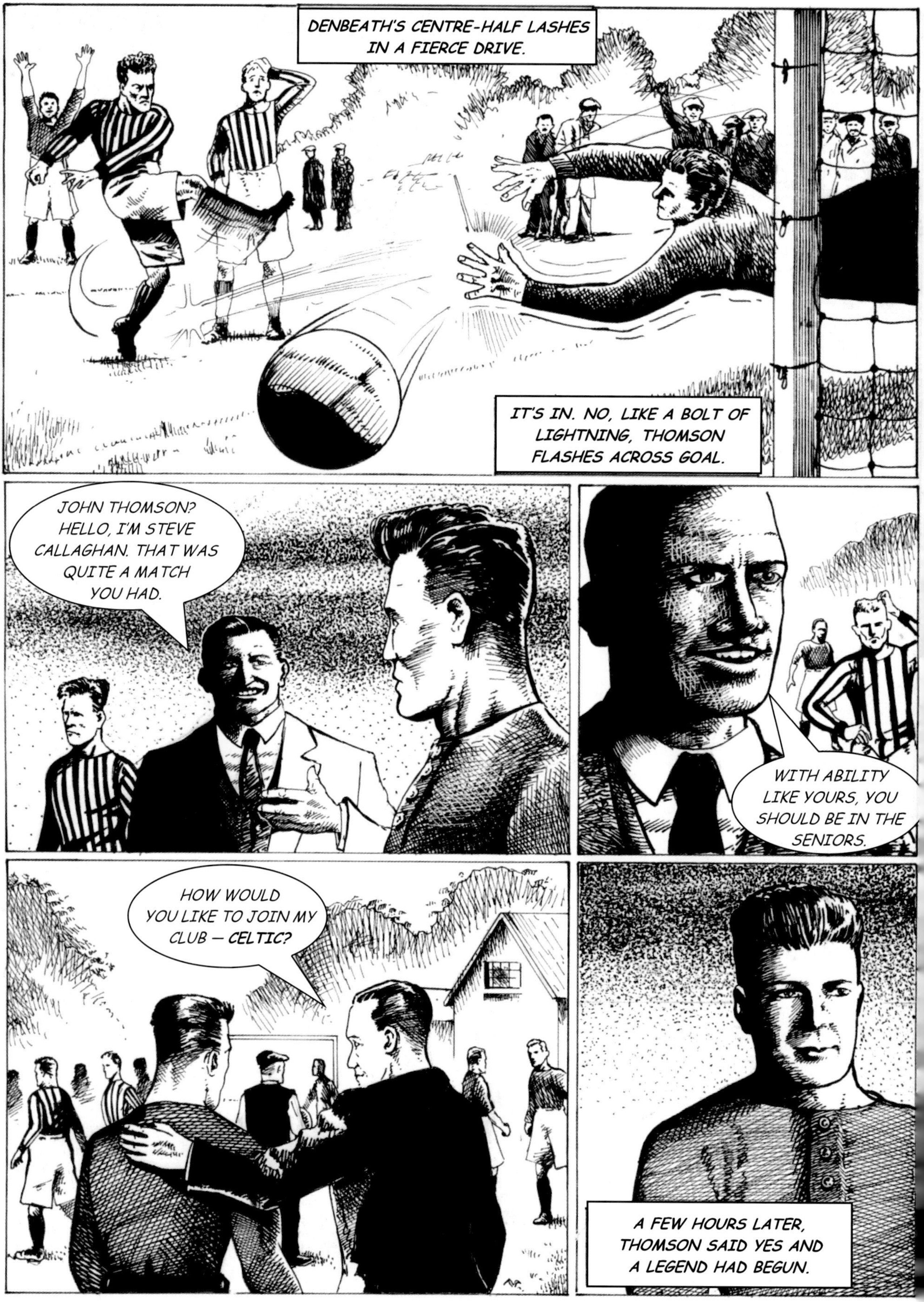
DENBEATH'S CENTRE-HALF LASHES IN A FIERCE DRIVE.
IT'S IN. NO, LIKE A BOLT OF LIGHTNING, THOMSON FLASHES ACROSS GOAL.
JOHN THOMSON? HELLO, I'M STEVE CALLAGHAN. THAT WAS QUITE A MATCH YOU HAD.
WITH ABILITY LIKE YOURS, YOU SHOULD BE IN THE SENIORS.
HOW WOULD YOU LIKE TO JOIN MY CLUB — CELTIC?
A FEW HOURS LATER, THOMSON SAID YES AND A LEGEND HAD BEGUN.

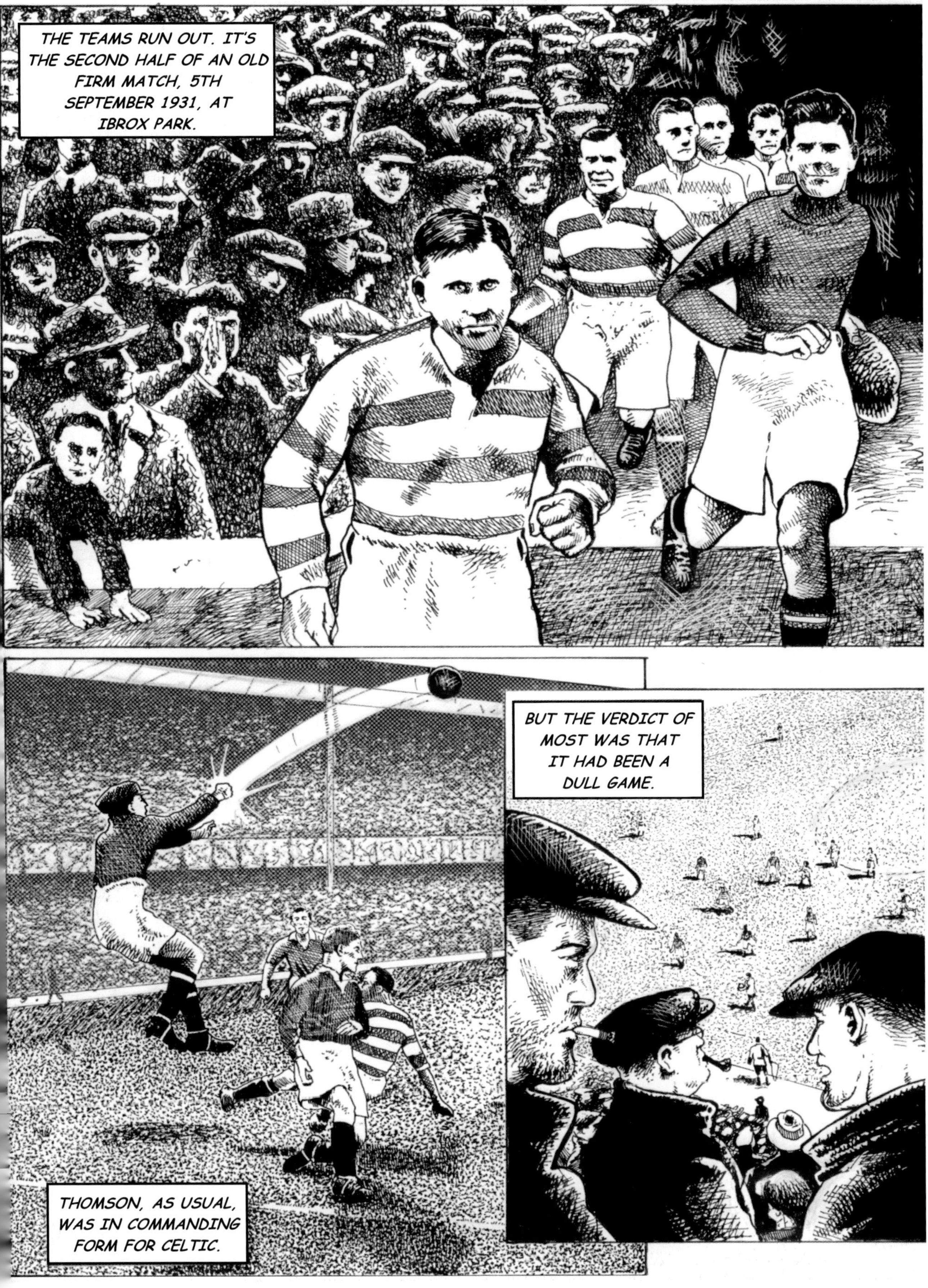
THE TEAMS RUN OUT. IT'S THE SECOND HALF OF AN OLD FIRM MATCH, 5TH SEPTEMBER 1931, AT IBROX PARK.
THOMSON, AS USUAL, WAS IN COMMANDING FORM FOR CELTIC.
BUT THE VERDICT OF MOST WAS THAT IT HAD BEEN A DULL GAME.

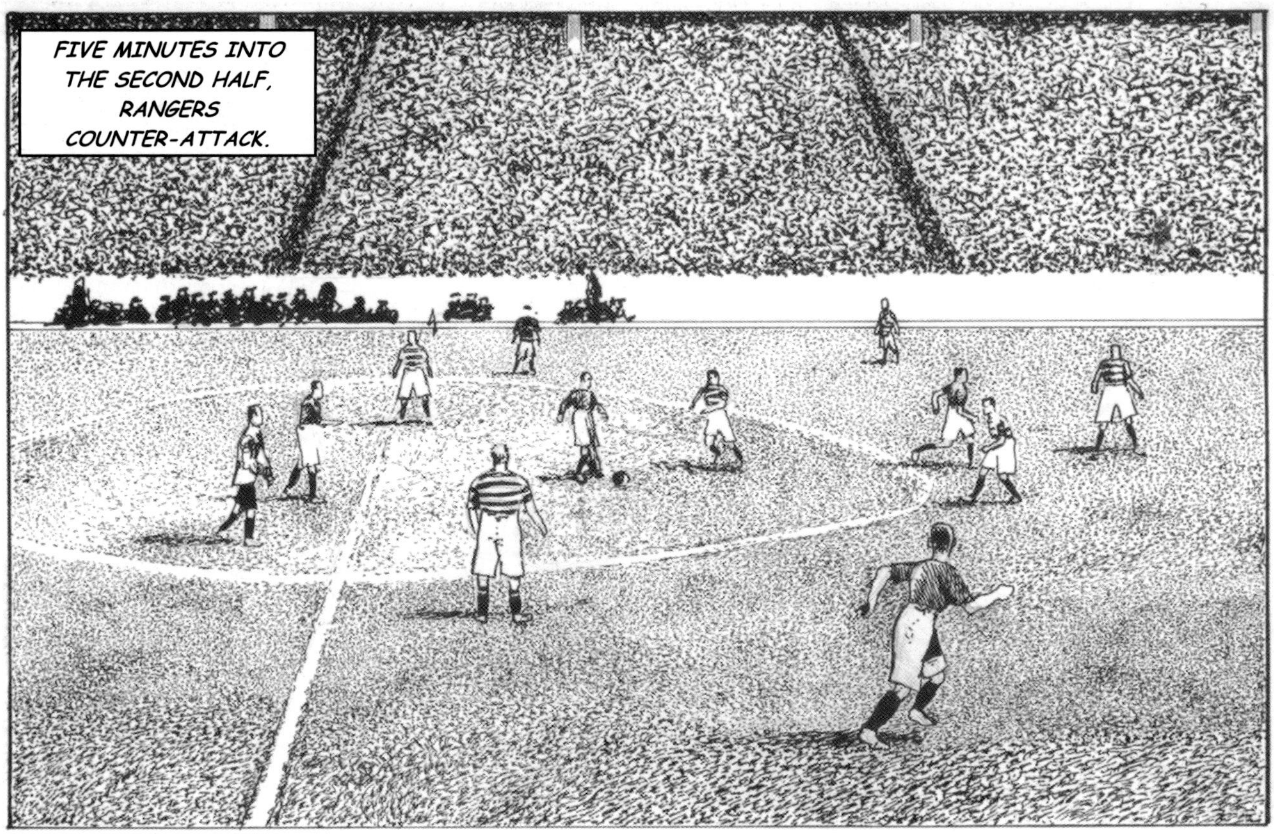
FIVE MINUTES INTO THE SECOND HALF, RANGERS COUNTER-ATTACK.

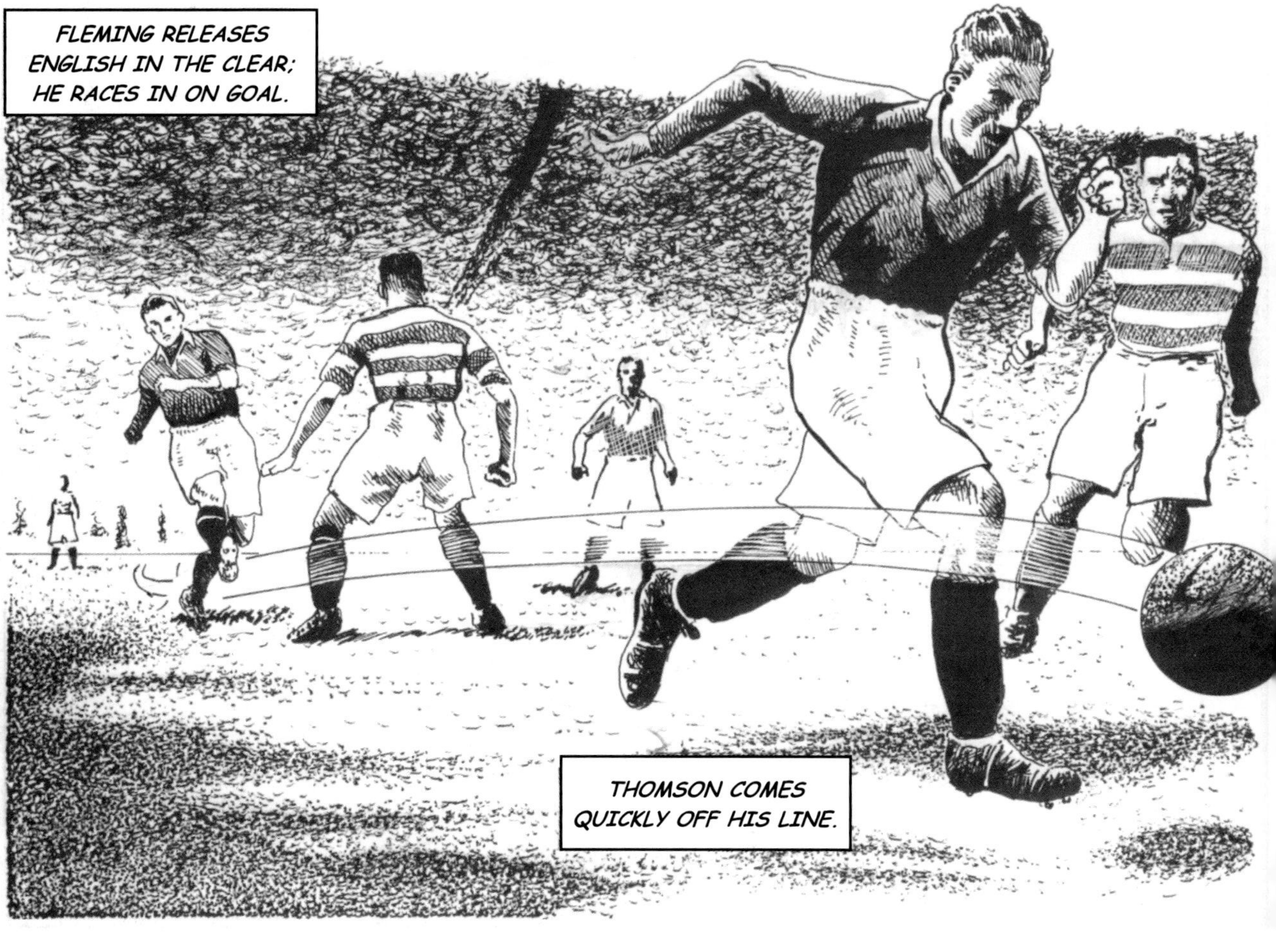
FLEMING RELEASES ENGLISH IN THE CLEAR; HE RACES IN ON GOAL.
THOMSON COMES QUICKLY OFF HIS LINE.

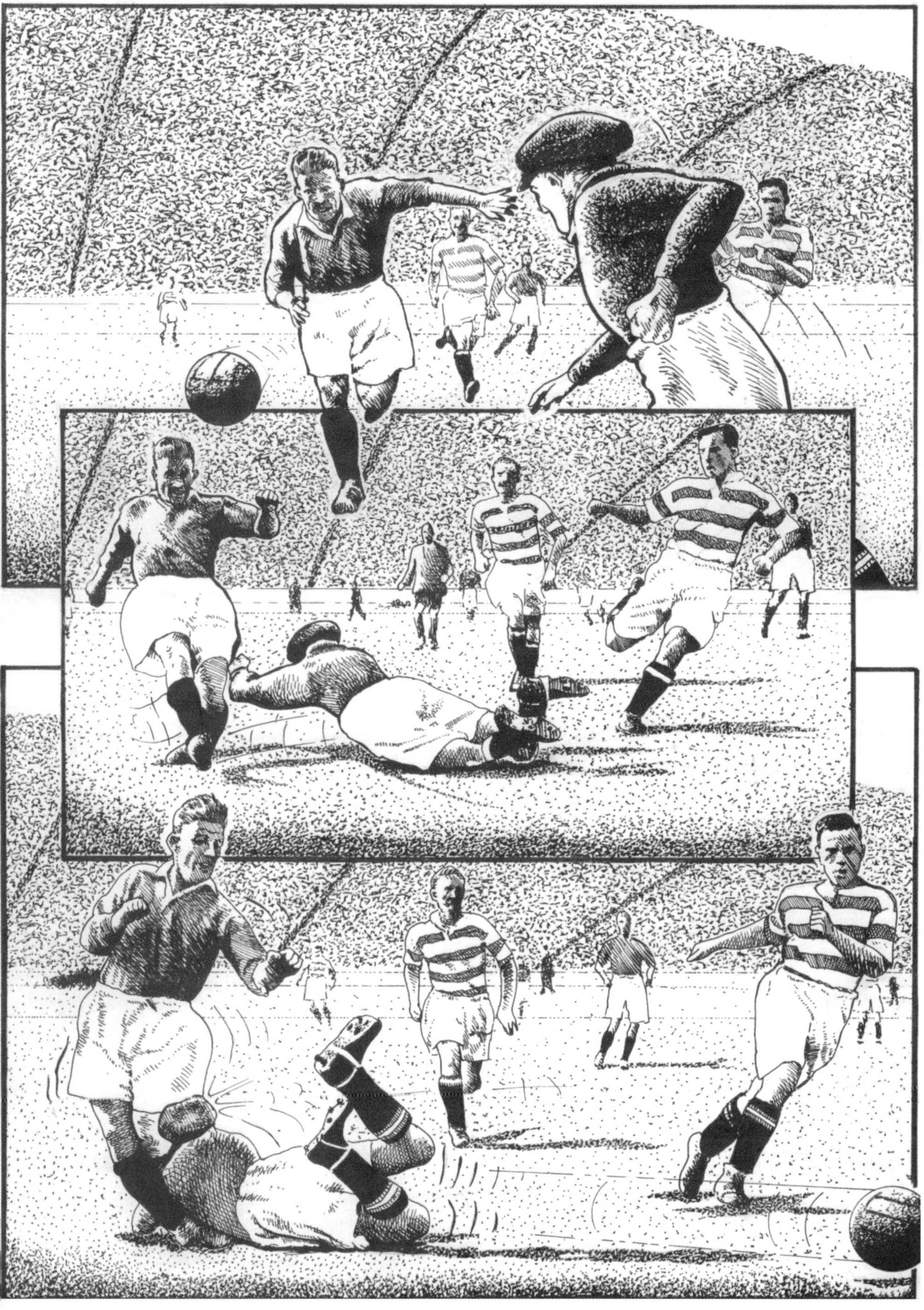

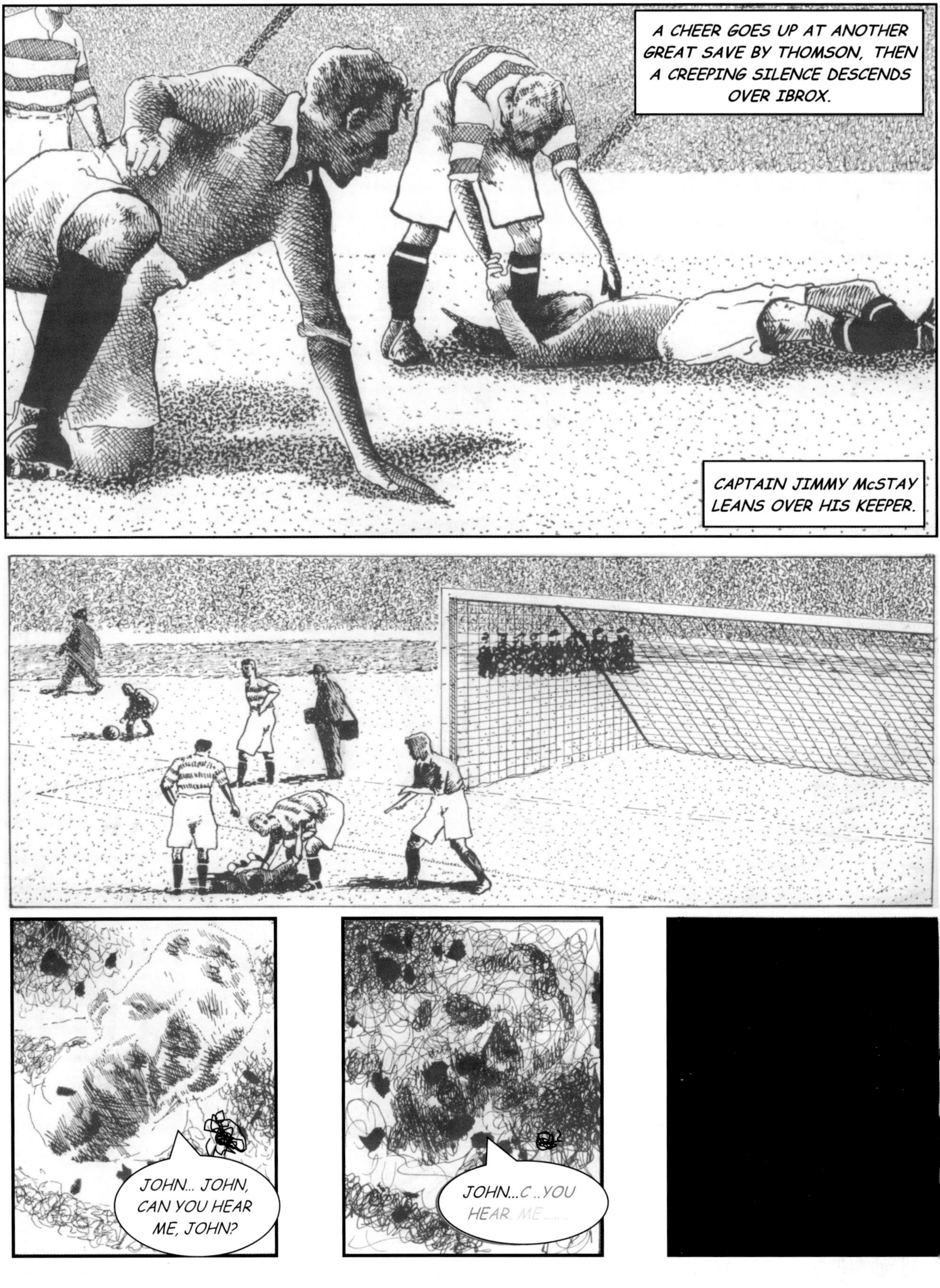
A CHEER GOES UP AT ANOTHER GREAT SAVE BY THOMSON, THEN A CREEPING SILENCE DESCENDS OVER IBROX.
CAPTAIN JIMMY McSTAY LEANS OVER HIS KEEPER.
JOHN... JOHN, CAN YOU HEAR ME, JOHN?
JOHN...C ..YOU HEAR. ME.......

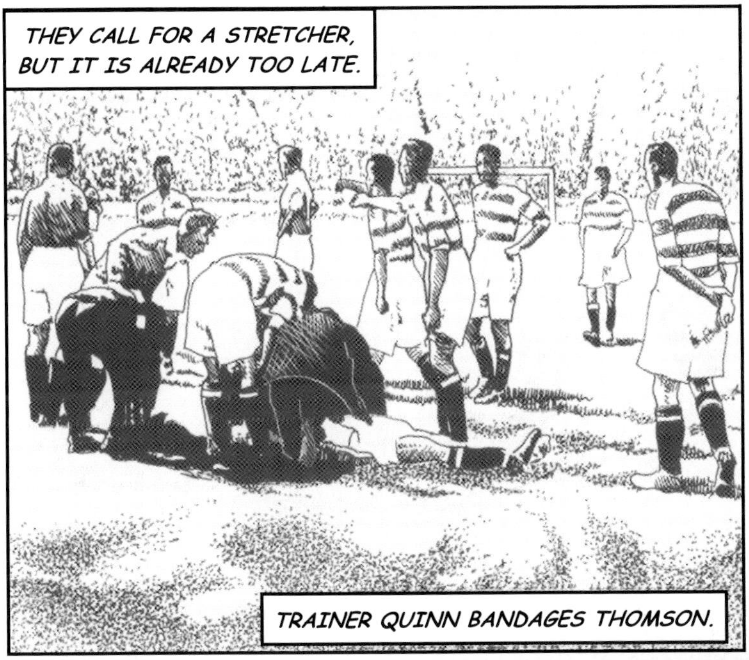
THEY CALL FOR A STRETCHER, BUT IT IS ALREADY TOO LATE.
TRAINER QUINN BANDAGES THOMSON.

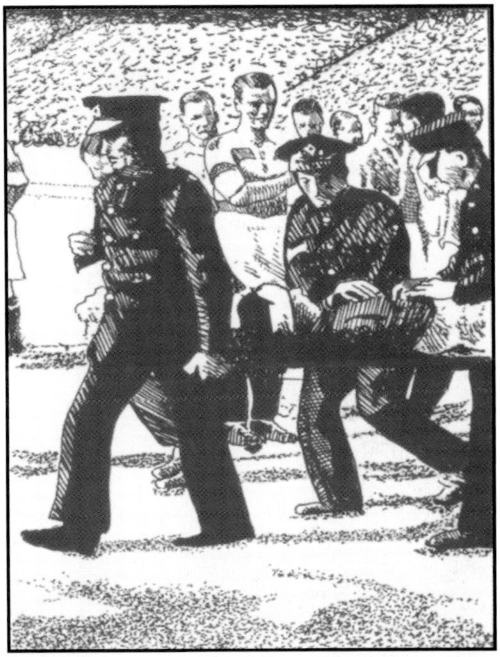

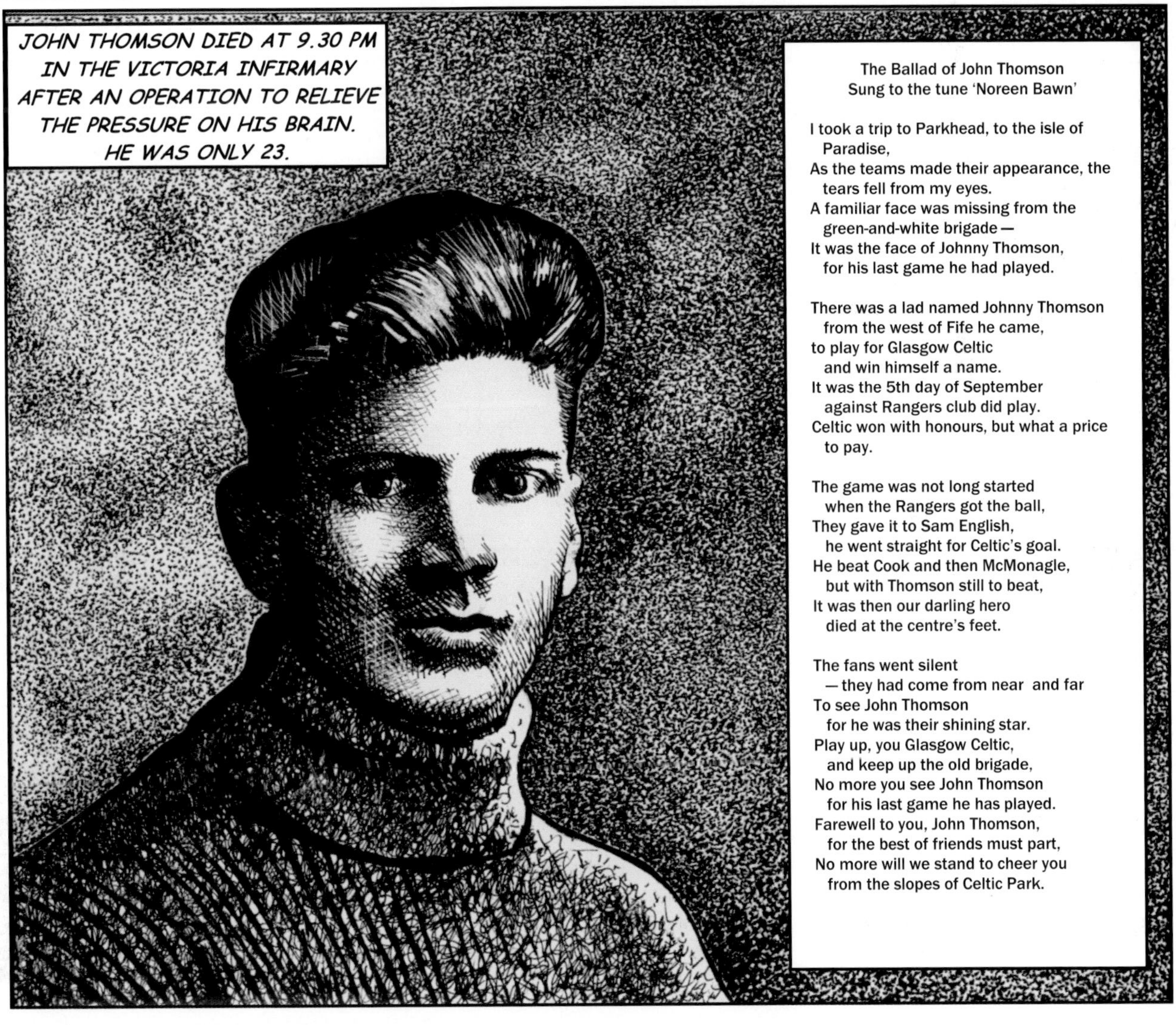
JOHN THOMSON DIED AT 9.30 PM IN THE VICTORIA INFIRMARY AFTER AN OPERATION TO RELIEVE THE PRESSURE ON HIS BRAIN. HE WAS ONLY 23.
The Ballad of John Thomson
Sung to the tune 'Noreen Bawn'
I took a trip to Parkhead, to the isle of Paradise,
As the teams made their appearance, the tears fell from my eyes.
A familiar face was missing from the green-and-white brigade —
It was the face of Johnny Thomson, for his last game he had played.
There was a lad named Johnny Thomson from the west of Fife he came,
to play for Glasgow Celtic and win himself a name.
It was the 5th day of September against Rangers club did play.
Celtic won with honours, but what a price to pay.
The game was not long started when the Rangers got the ball,
They gave it to Sam English, he went straight for Celtic's goal.
He beat Cook and then McMonagle, but with Thomson still to beat,
It was then our darling hero died at the centre's feet.
The fans went silent — they had come from near and far
To see John Thomson for he was their shining star.
Play up, you Glasgow Celtic, and keep up the old brigade,
No more you see John Thomson for his last game he has played.
Farewell to you, John Thomson, for the best of friends must part,
No more will we stand to cheer you from the slopes of Celtic Park.

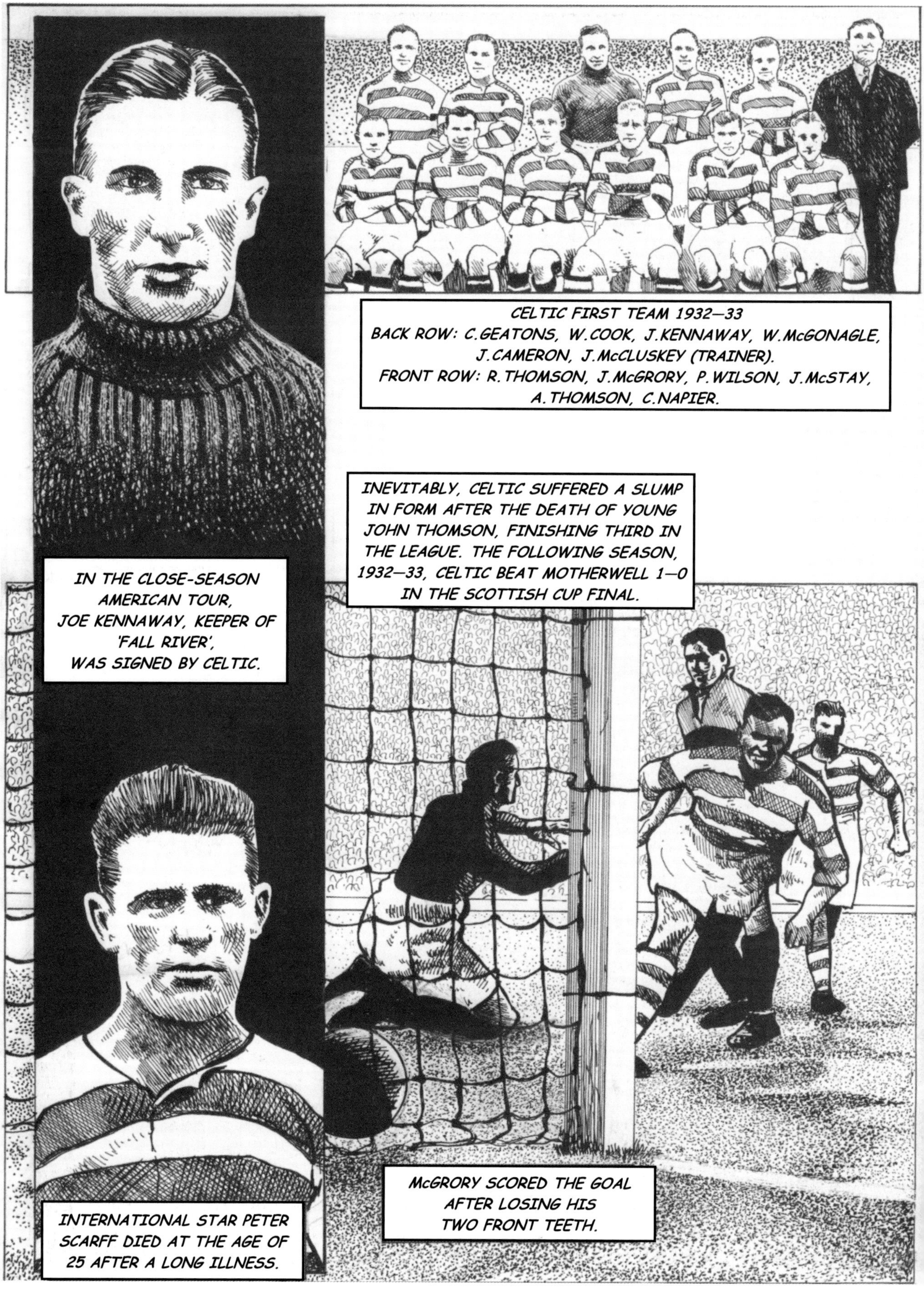
CELTIC FIRST TEAM 1932–33
BACK ROW: C.GEATONS, W.COOK, J.KENNAWAY, W.McGONAGLE, J.CAMERON, J.McCLUSKEY (TRAINER).
FRONT ROW: R.THOMSON, J.McGRORY, P.WILSON, J.McSTAY, A.THOMSON, C.NAPIER.
INEVITABLY, CELTIC SUFFERED A SLUMP IN FORM AFTER THE DEATH OF YOUNG JOHN THOMSON, FINISHING THIRD IN THE LEAGUE. THE FOLLOWING SEASON, 1932–33, CELTIC BEAT MOTHERWELL 1–0 IN THE SCOTTISH CUP FINAL.
IN THE CLOSE-SEASON AMERICAN TOUR, JOE KENNAWAY, KEEPER OF 'FALL RIVER', WAS SIGNED BY CELTIC.
McGRORY SCORED THE GOAL AFTER LOSING HIS TWO FRONT TEETH.
INTERNATIONAL STAR PETER SCARFF DIED AT THE AGE OF 25 AFTER A LONG ILLNESS.

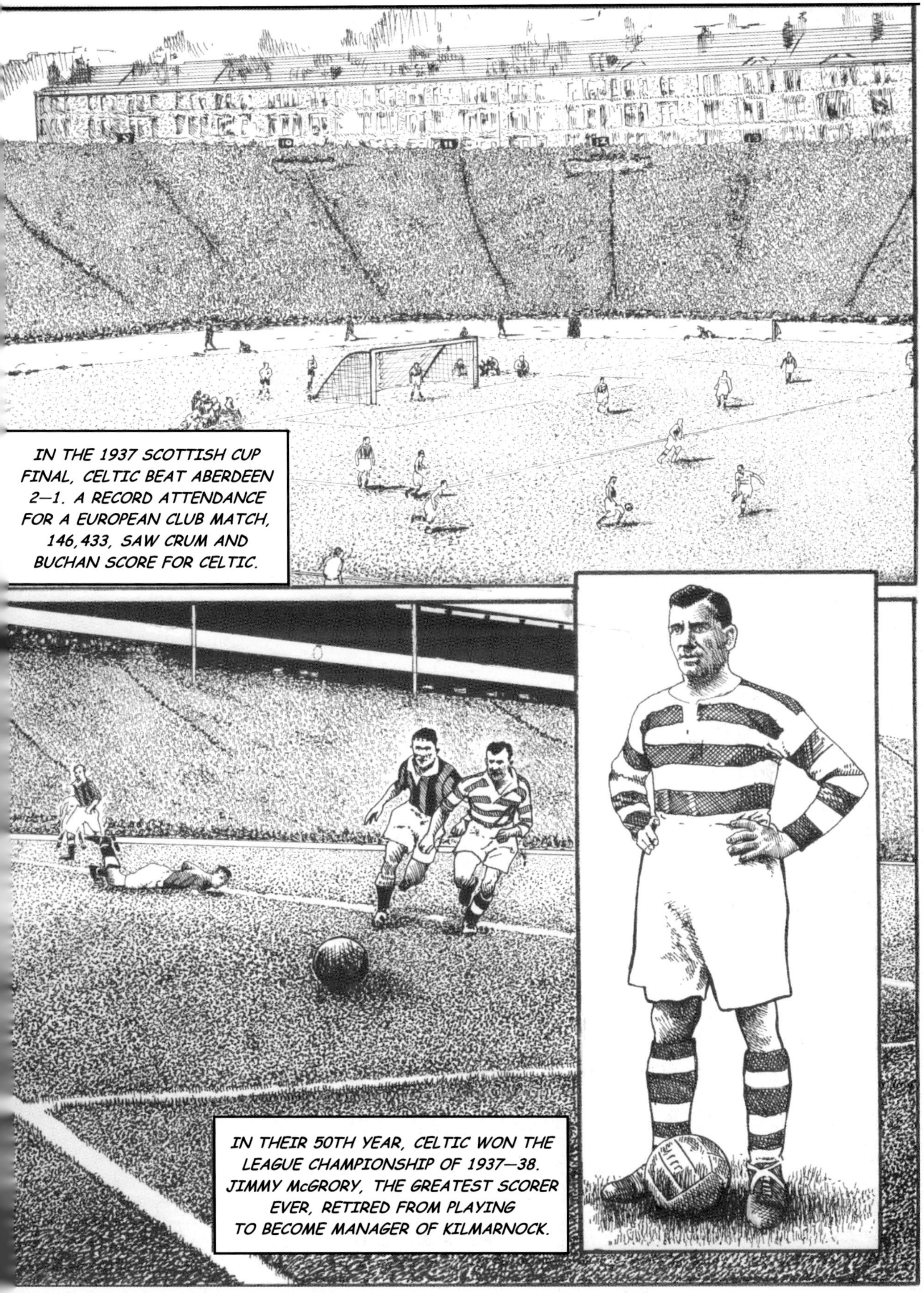
IN THE 1937 SCOTTISH CUP FINAL, CELTIC BEAT ABERDEEN 2—1. A RECORD ATTENDANCE FOR A EUROPEAN CLUB MATCH, 146,433, SAW CRUM AND BUCHAN SCORE FOR CELTIC.
IN THEIR 50TH YEAR, CELTIC WON THE LEAGUE CHAMPIONSHIP OF 1937—38. JIMMY McGRORY, THE GREATEST SCORER EVER, RETIRED FROM PLAYING TO BECOME MANAGER OF KILMARNOCK.

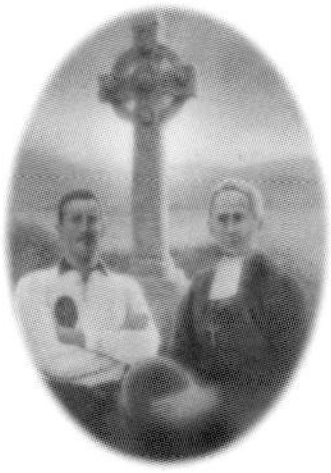

chapter 3

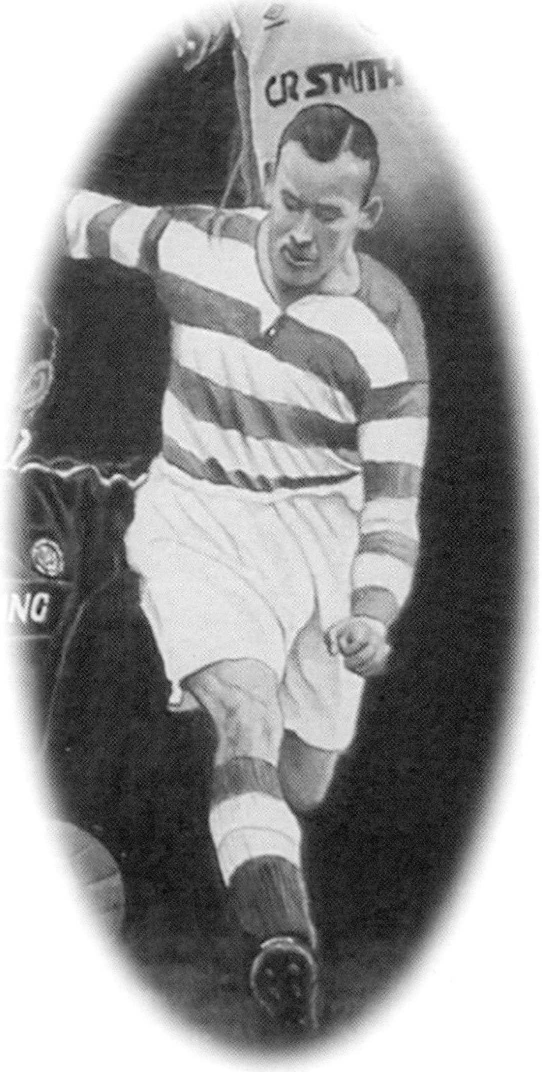
CR SMITH

the interregnum

'hold your head up high'

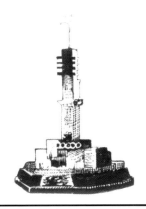

AT IBROX PARK IN 1938, CELTIC WON THE EMPIRE EXHIBITION TROPHY. IN A BEST OF BRITISH TOURNAMENT, THEY DEFEATED EVERTON IN THE FINAL 1—0 AFTER EXTRA TIME.

THE RISE OF THE THIRD REICH IN GERMANY SAW THE OUTBREAK OF WORLD WAR II. AS A RESULT, ALL LEAGUE AND CUP COMPETITIONS WERE SUSPENDED. UNOFFICIAL REGIONAL LEAGUES WERE ESTABLISHED DURING THIS TIME.

IN 1940, EX-CAPTAIN JIMMY McSTAY TOOK OVER FROM MANAGER WILLIE MALEY, WHO RETIRED AFTER 52 YEARS OF SERVICE TO THE CLUB.

MANY YEARS WOULD PASS BEFORE HIS ACHIEVEMENTS WOULD BE EQUALLED.

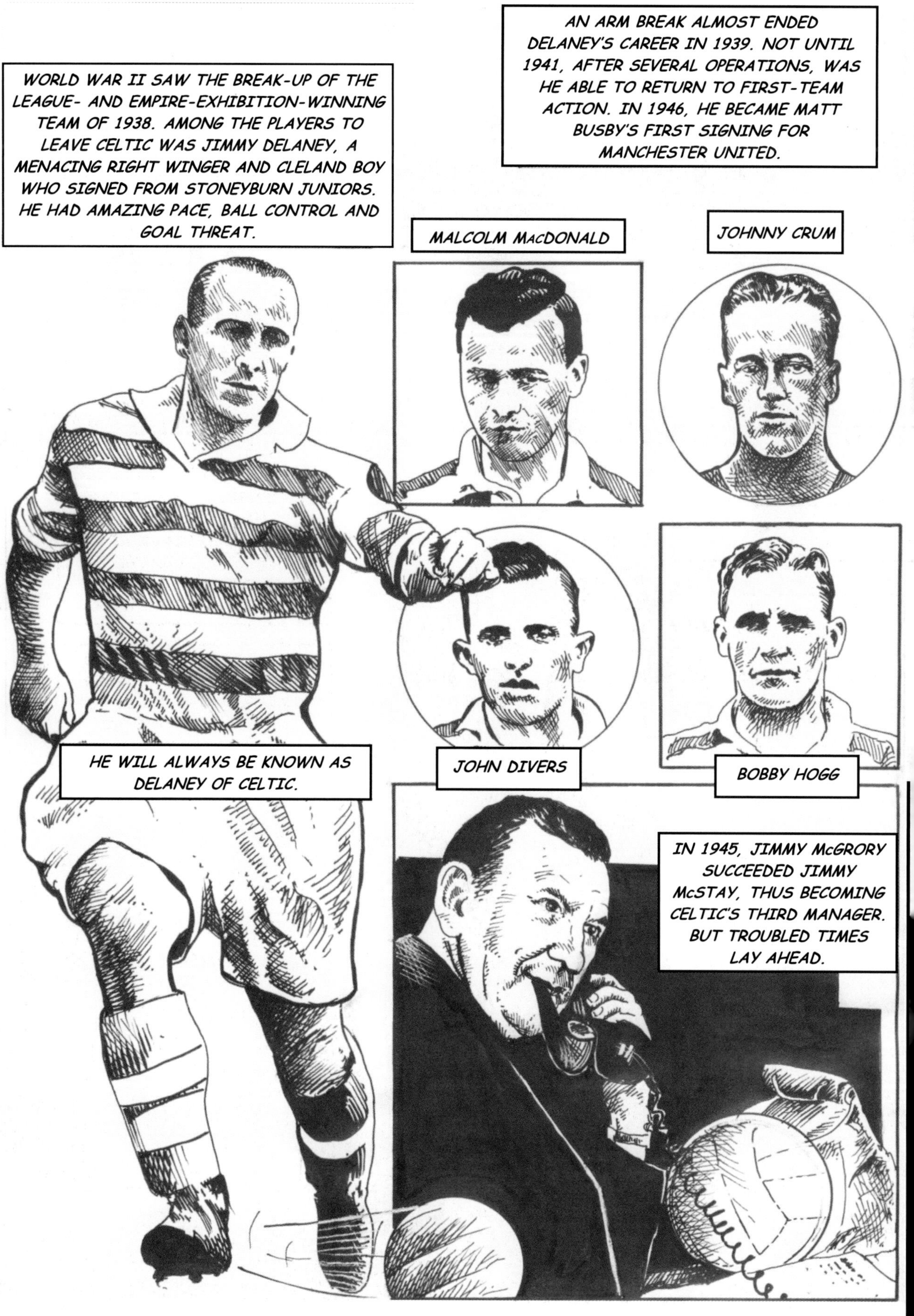
WORLD WAR II SAW THE BREAK-UP OF THE LEAGUE- AND EMPIRE-EXHIBITION-WINNING TEAM OF 1938. AMONG THE PLAYERS TO LEAVE CELTIC WAS JIMMY DELANEY, A MENACING RIGHT WINGER AND CLELAND BOY WHO SIGNED FROM STONEYBURN JUNIORS. HE HAD AMAZING PACE, BALL CONTROL AND GOAL THREAT.
AN ARM BREAK ALMOST ENDED DELANEY'S CAREER IN 1939. NOT UNTIL 1941, AFTER SEVERAL OPERATIONS, WAS HE ABLE TO RETURN TO FIRST-TEAM ACTION. IN 1946, HE BECAME MATT BUSBY'S FIRST SIGNING FOR MANCHESTER UNITED.
MALCOLM MACDONALD
JOHNNY CRUM
HE WILL ALWAYS BE KNOWN AS DELANEY OF CELTIC.
JOHN DIVERS
BOBBY HOGG
IN 1945, JIMMY McGRORY SUCCEEDED JIMMY McSTAY, THUS BECOMING CELTIC'S THIRD MANAGER. BUT TROUBLED TIMES LAY AHEAD.

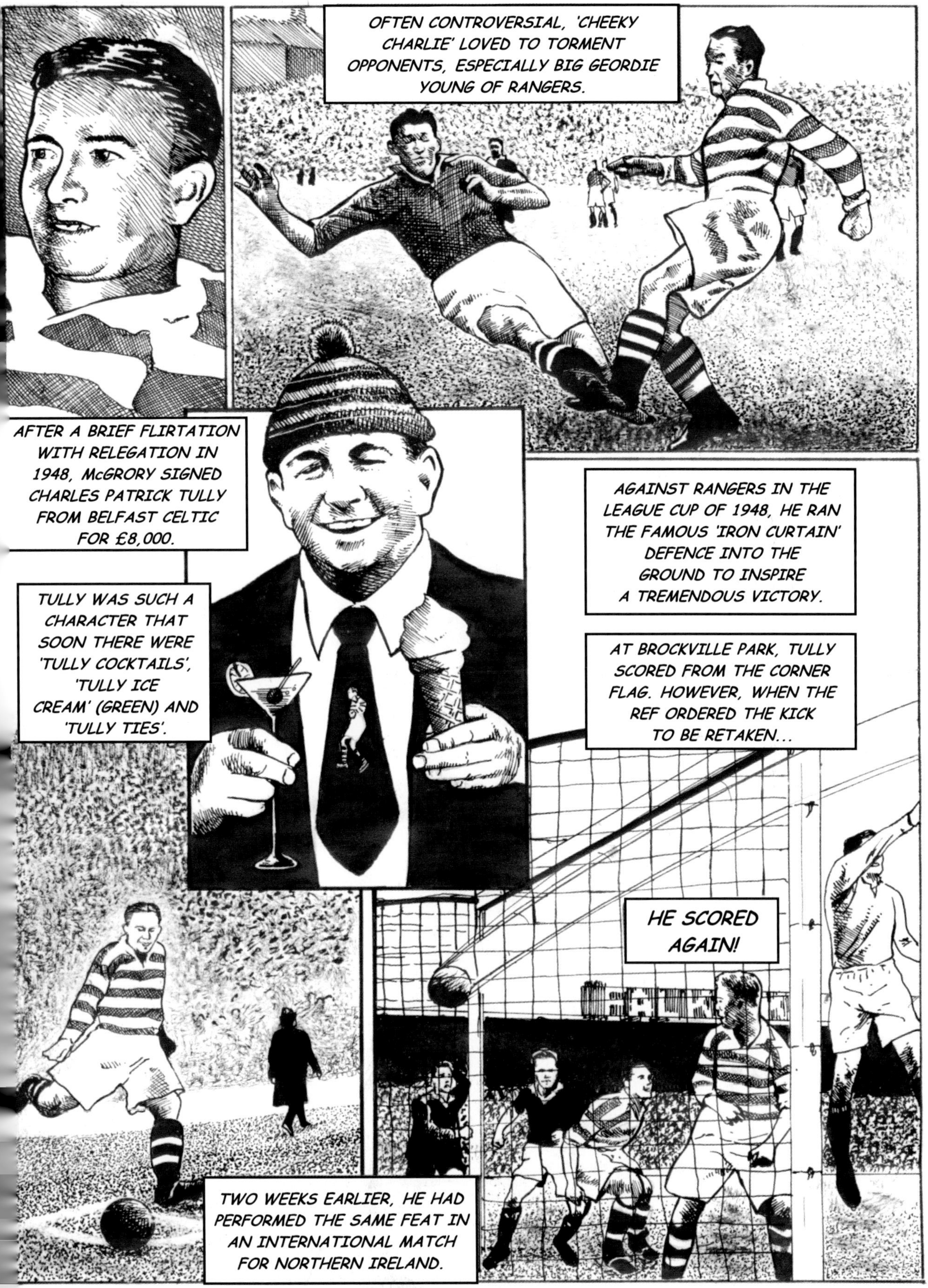
AFTER A BRIEF FLIRTATION WITH RELEGATION IN 1948, McGRORY SIGNED CHARLES PATRICK TULLY FROM BELFAST CELTIC FOR £8,000.
OFTEN CONTROVERSIAL, 'CHEEKY CHARLIE' LOVED TO TORMENT OPPONENTS, ESPECIALLY BIG GEORDIE YOUNG OF RANGERS.
TULLY WAS SUCH A CHARACTER THAT SOON THERE WERE 'TULLY COCKTAILS', 'TULLY ICE CREAM' (GREEN) AND 'TULLY TIES'.
AGAINST RANGERS IN THE LEAGUE CUP OF 1948, HE RAN THE FAMOUS 'IRON CURTAIN' DEFENCE INTO THE GROUND TO INSPIRE A TREMENDOUS VICTORY.
AT BROCKVILLE PARK, TULLY SCORED FROM THE CORNER FLAG. HOWEVER, WHEN THE REF ORDERED THE KICK TO BE RETAKEN...
HE SCORED AGAIN!
TWO WEEKS EARLIER, HE HAD PERFORMED THE SAME FEAT IN AN INTERNATIONAL MATCH FOR NORTHERN IRELAND.

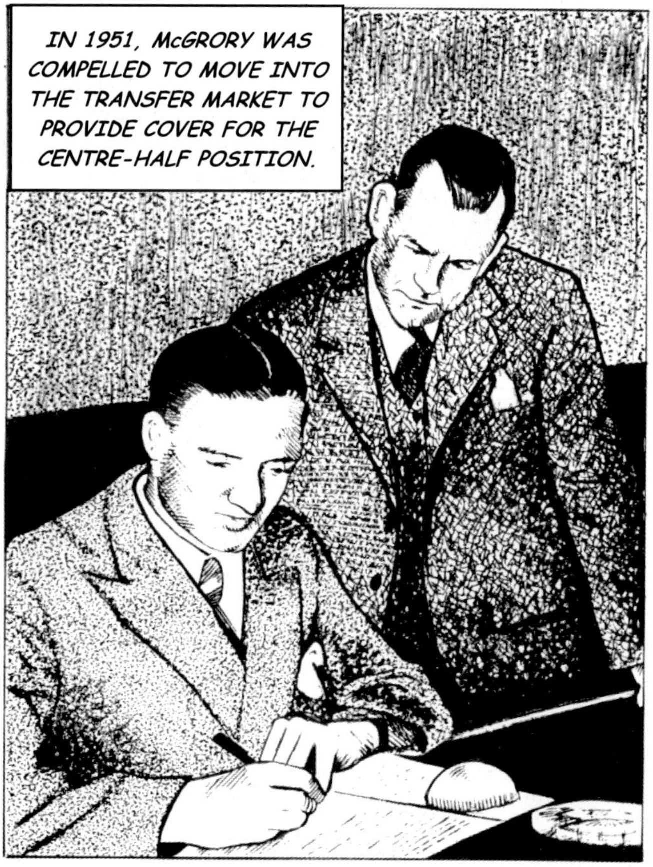
IN 1951, McGRORY WAS COMPELLED TO MOVE INTO THE TRANSFER MARKET TO PROVIDE COVER FOR THE CENTRE-HALF POSITION.

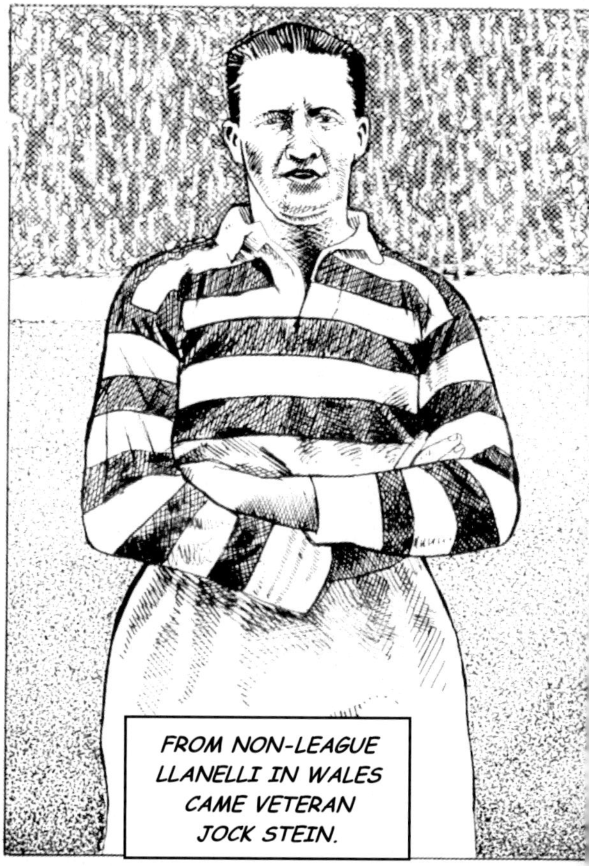
FROM NON-LEAGUE LLANELLI IN WALES CAME VETERAN JOCK STEIN.

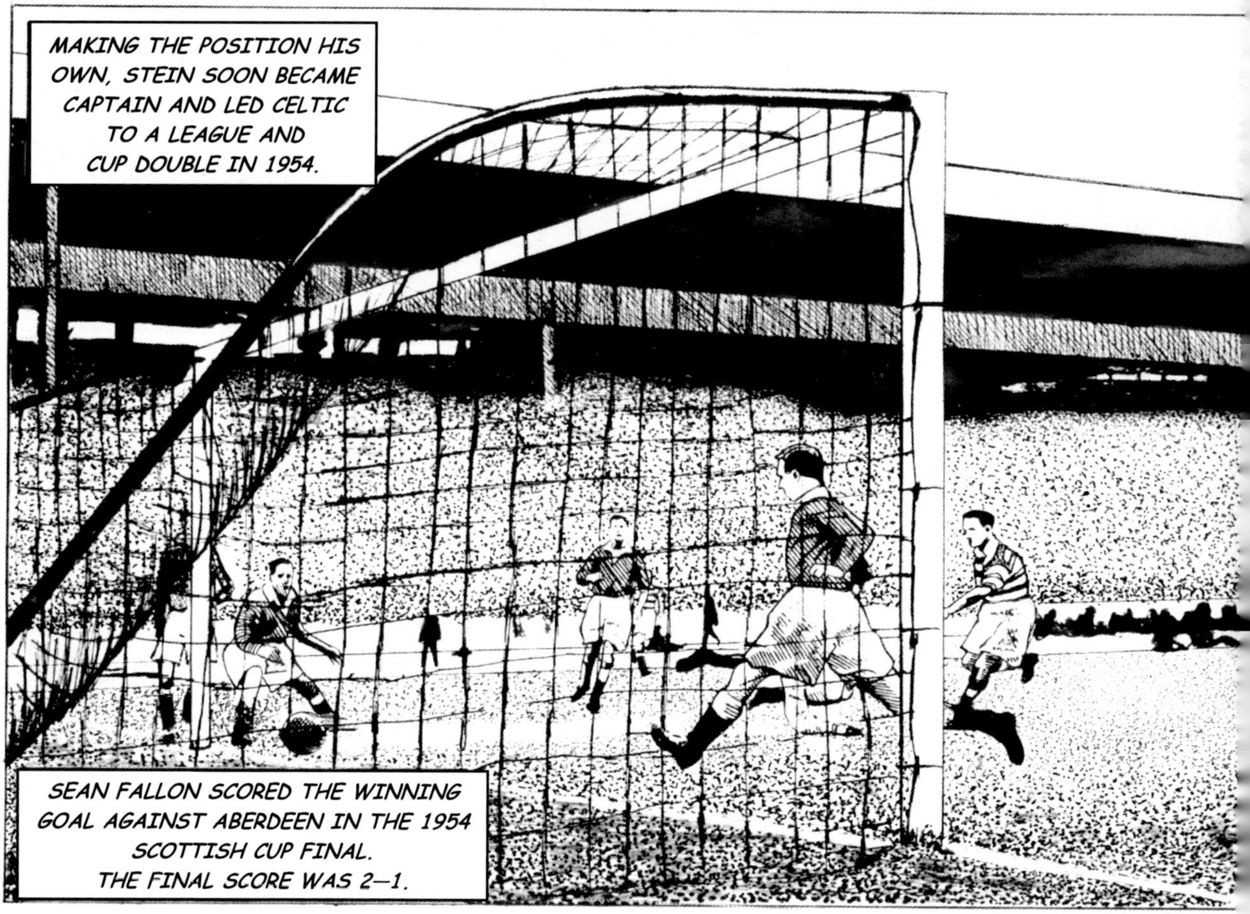
MAKING THE POSITION HIS OWN, STEIN SOON BECAME CAPTAIN AND LED CELTIC TO A LEAGUE AND CUP DOUBLE IN 1954.
SEAN FALLON SCORED THE WINNING GOAL AGAINST ABERDEEN IN THE 1954 SCOTTISH CUP FINAL.
THE FINAL SCORE WAS 2–1.

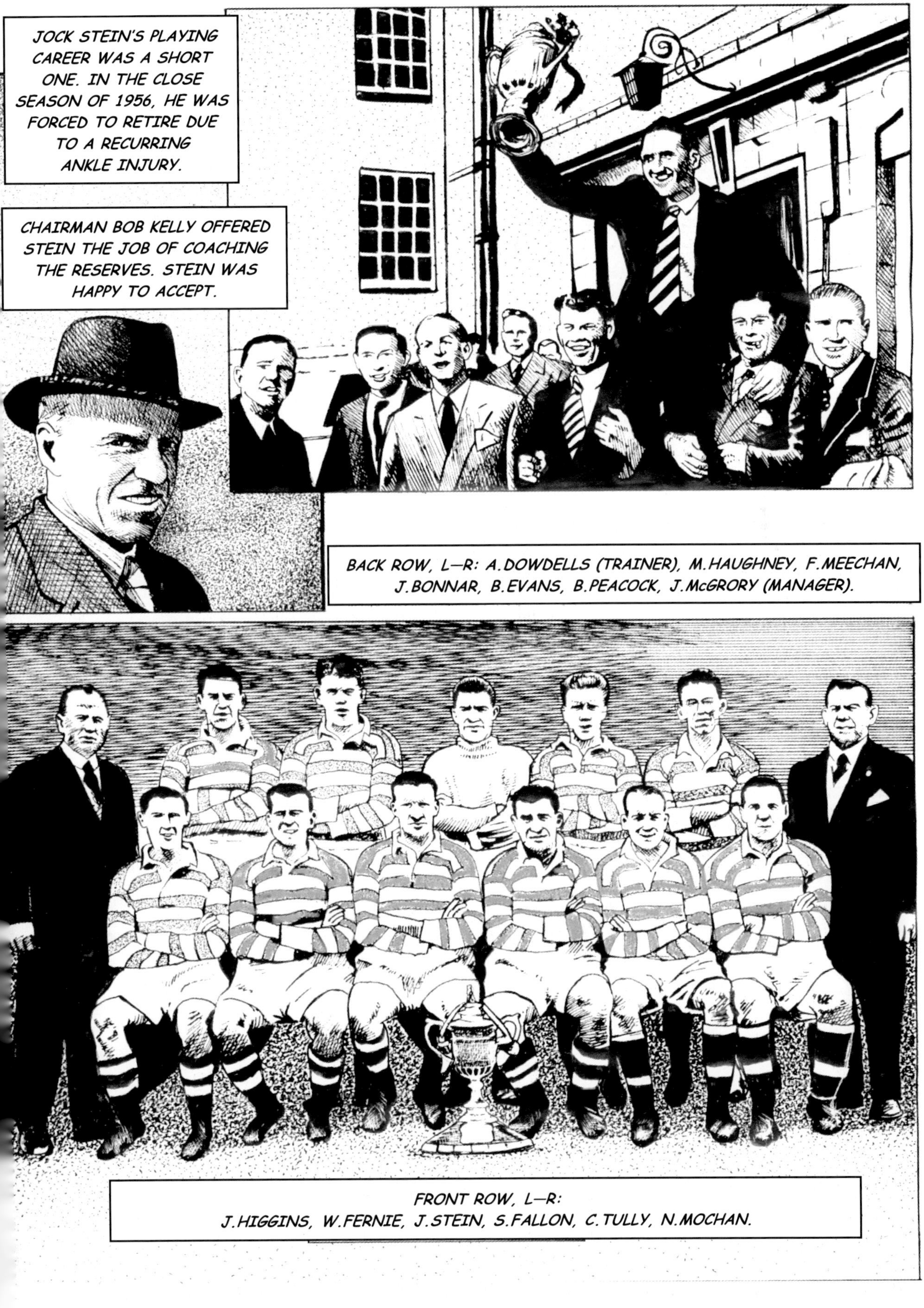
JOCK STEIN'S PLAYING CAREER WAS A SHORT ONE. IN THE CLOSE SEASON OF 1956, HE WAS FORCED TO RETIRE DUE TO A RECURRING ANKLE INJURY.
CHAIRMAN BOB KELLY OFFERED STEIN THE JOB OF COACHING THE RESERVES. STEIN WAS HAPPY TO ACCEPT.
BACK ROW, L–R: A.DOWDELLS (TRAINER), M.HAUGHNEY, F.MEECHAN, J.BONNAR, B.EVANS, B.PEACOCK, J.McGRORY (MANAGER).
FRONT ROW, L–R: J.HIGGINS, W.FERNIE, J.STEIN, S.FALLON, C.TULLY, N.MOCHAN.

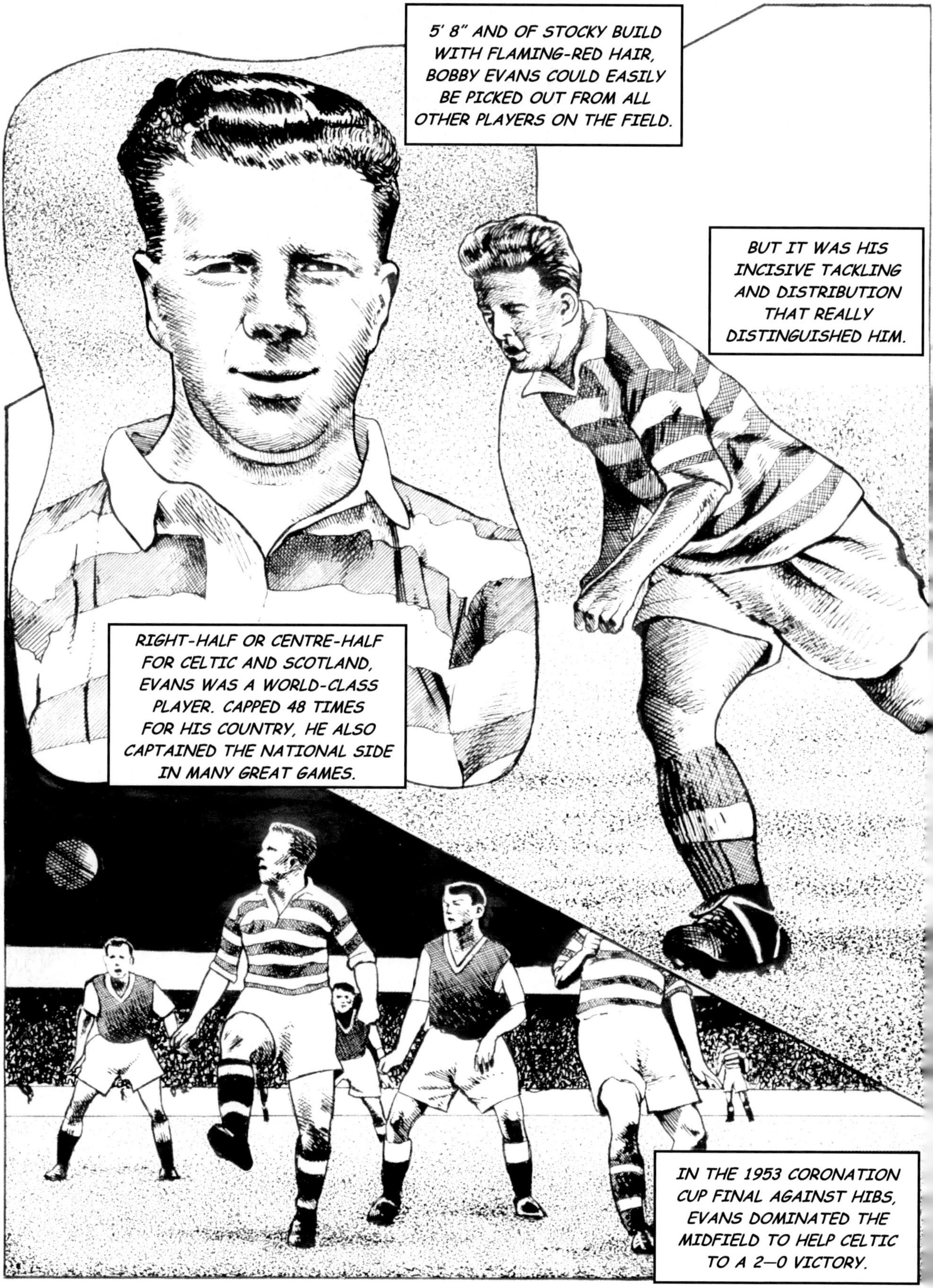
5' 8" AND OF STOCKY BUILD WITH FLAMING-RED HAIR, BOBBY EVANS COULD EASILY BE PICKED OUT FROM ALL OTHER PLAYERS ON THE FIELD.
BUT IT WAS HIS INCISIVE TACKLING AND DISTRIBUTION THAT REALLY DISTINGUISHED HIM.
RIGHT-HALF OR CENTRE-HALF FOR CELTIC AND SCOTLAND, EVANS WAS A WORLD-CLASS PLAYER. CAPPED 48 TIMES FOR HIS COUNTRY, HE ALSO CAPTAINED THE NATIONAL SIDE IN MANY GREAT GAMES.
IN THE 1953 CORONATION CUP FINAL AGAINST HIBS, EVANS DOMINATED THE MIDFIELD TO HELP CELTIC TO A 2—0 VICTORY.

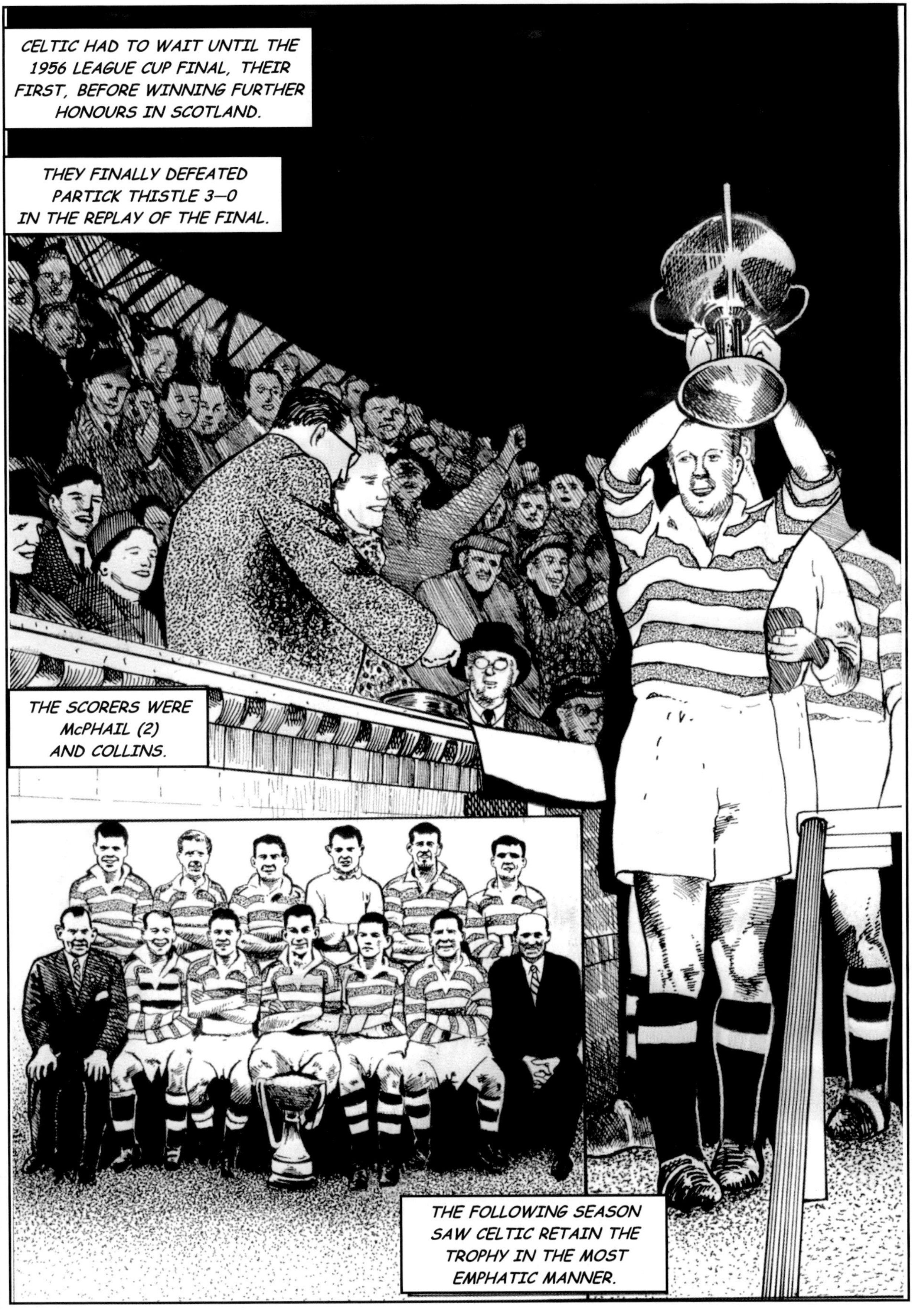
CELTIC HAD TO WAIT UNTIL THE 1956 LEAGUE CUP FINAL, THEIR FIRST, BEFORE WINNING FURTHER HONOURS IN SCOTLAND.
THEY FINALLY DEFEATED PARTICK THISTLE 3—0 IN THE REPLAY OF THE FINAL.
THE SCORERS WERE McPHAIL (2) AND COLLINS.
THE FOLLOWING SEASON SAW CELTIC RETAIN THE TROPHY IN THE MOST EMPHATIC MANNER.

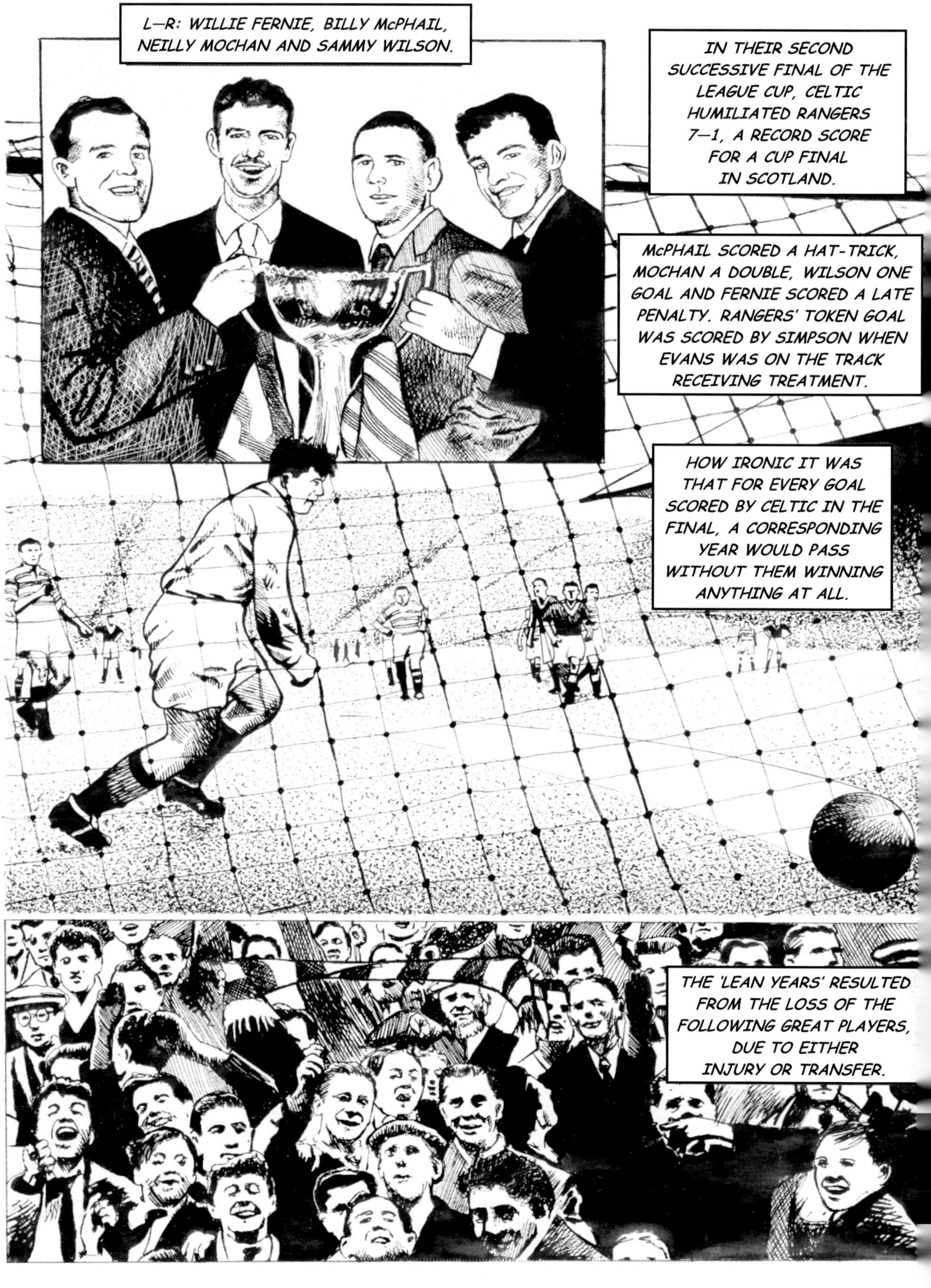
L–R: WILLIE FERNIE, BILLY McPHAIL, NEILLY MOCHAN AND SAMMY WILSON.
IN THEIR SECOND SUCCESSIVE FINAL OF THE LEAGUE CUP, CELTIC HUMILIATED RANGERS 7–1, A RECORD SCORE FOR A CUP FINAL IN SCOTLAND.
McPHAIL SCORED A HAT-TRICK, MOCHAN A DOUBLE, WILSON ONE GOAL AND FERNIE SCORED A LATE PENALTY. RANGERS' TOKEN GOAL WAS SCORED BY SIMPSON WHEN EVANS WAS ON THE TRACK RECEIVING TREATMENT.
HOW IRONIC IT WAS THAT FOR EVERY GOAL SCORED BY CELTIC IN THE FINAL, A CORRESPONDING YEAR WOULD PASS WITHOUT THEM WINNING ANYTHING AT ALL.
THE 'LEAN YEARS' RESULTED FROM THE LOSS OF THE FOLLOWING GREAT PLAYERS, DUE TO EITHER INJURY OR TRANSFER.

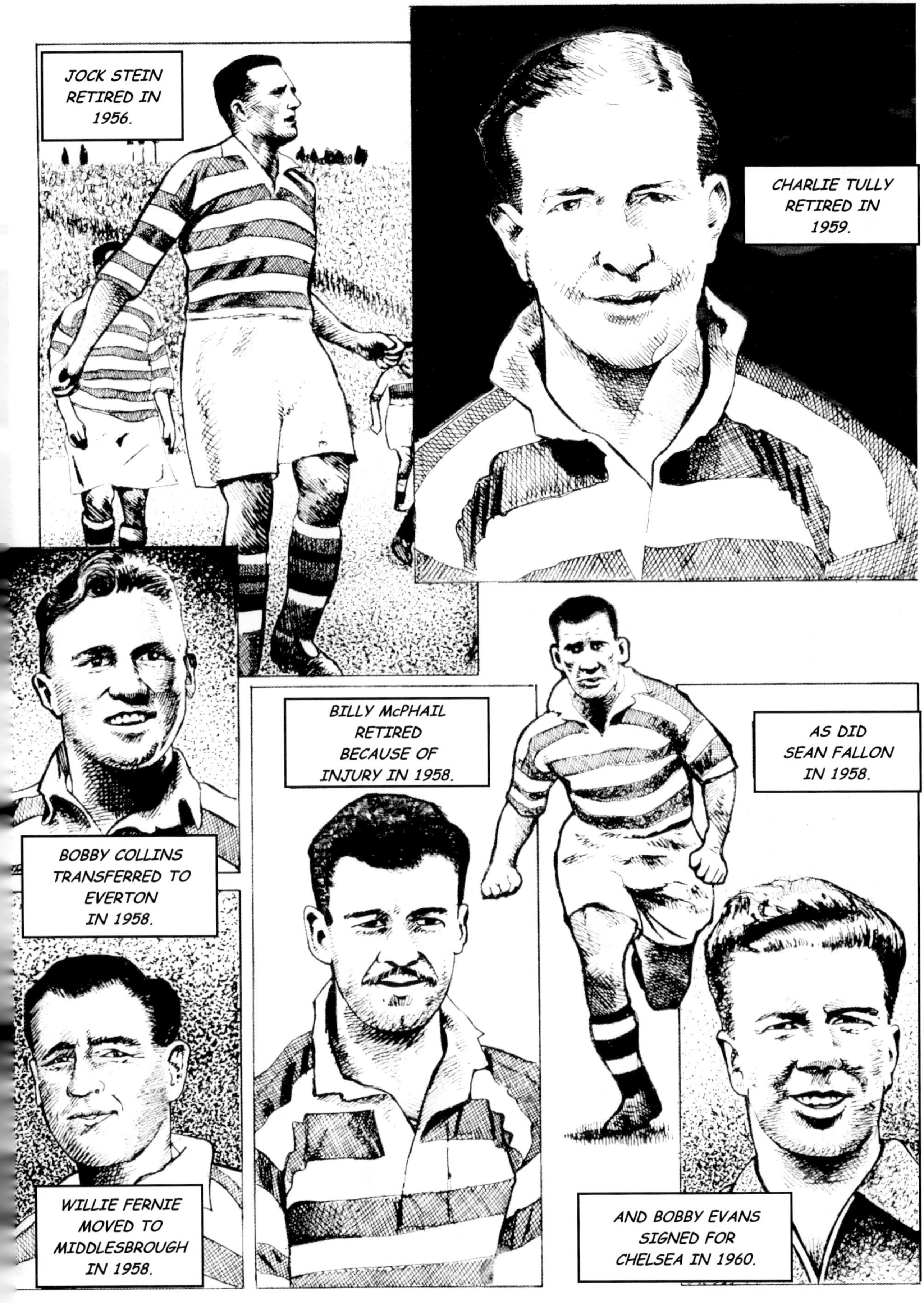
JOCK STEIN RETIRED IN 1956.
CHARLIE TULLY RETIRED IN 1959.
BOBBY COLLINS TRANSFERRED TO EVERTON IN 1958.
WILLIE FERNIE MOVED TO MIDDLESBROUGH IN 1958.
BILLY McPHAIL RETIRED BECAUSE OF INJURY IN 1958.
AS DID SEAN FALLON IN 1958.
AND BOBBY EVANS SIGNED FOR CHELSEA IN 1960.

chapter 4

stein's revolution

'and don't be afraid of the dark'

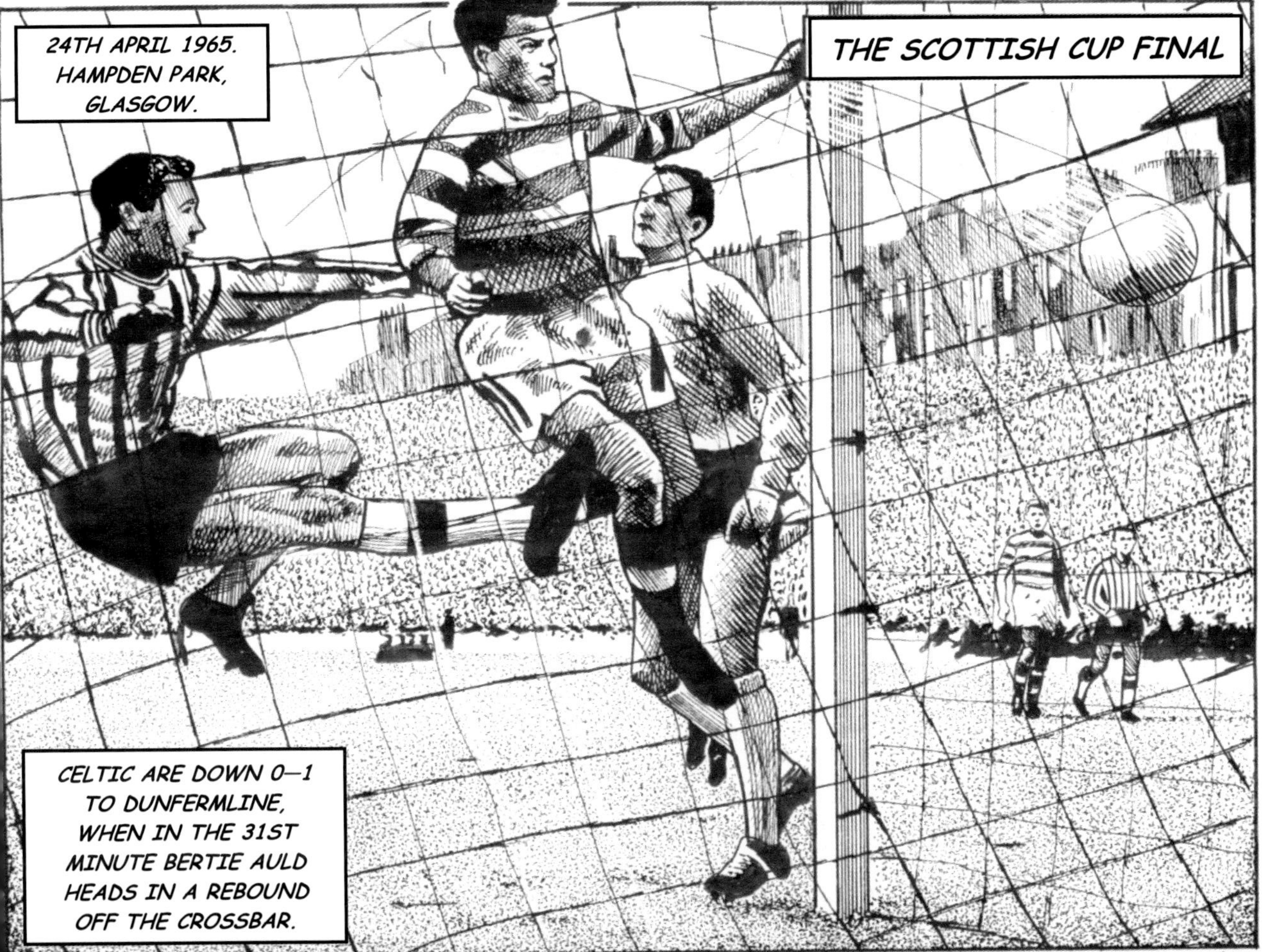
24TH APRIL 1965. HAMPDEN PARK, GLASGOW.
THE SCOTTISH CUP FINAL
CELTIC ARE DOWN 0—1 TO DUNFERMLINE, WHEN IN THE 31ST MINUTE BERTIE AULD HEADS IN A REBOUND OFF THE CROSSBAR.

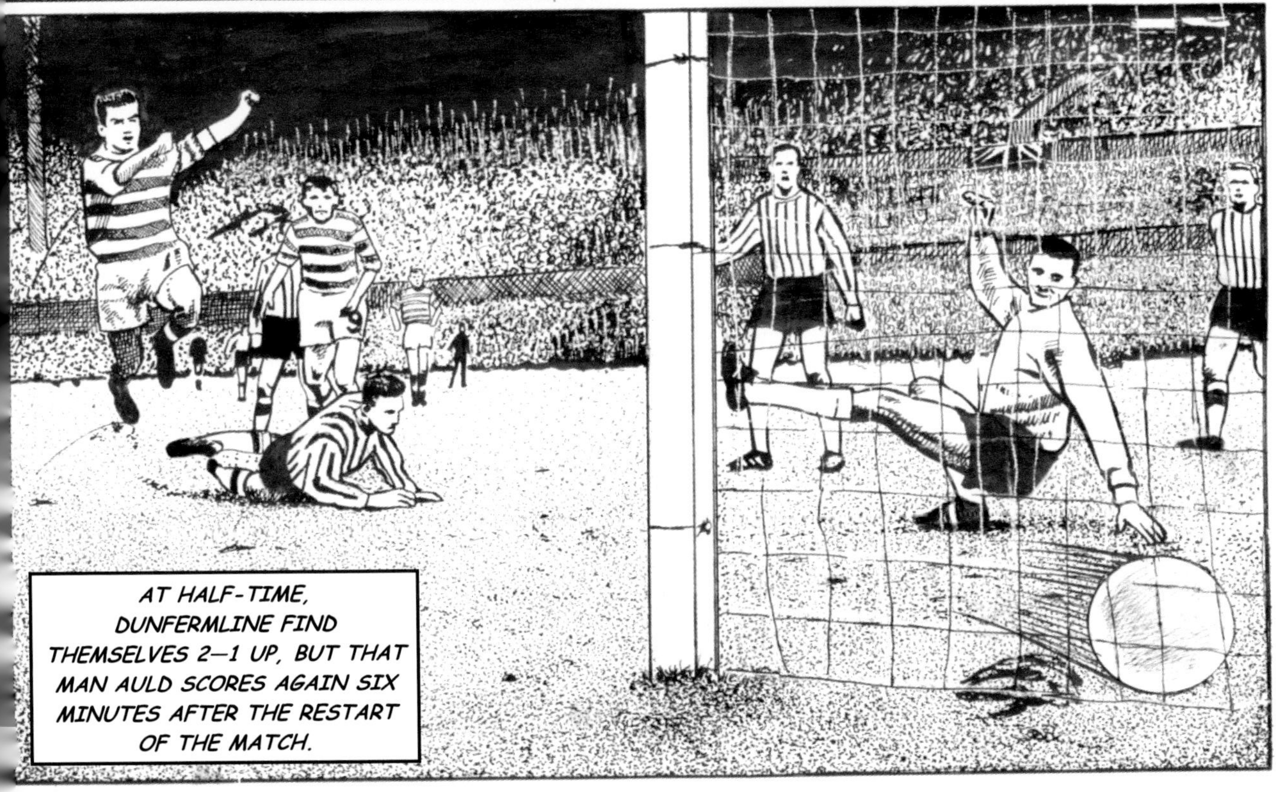
AT HALF-TIME, DUNFERMLINE FIND THEMSELVES 2—1 UP, BUT THAT MAN AULD SCORES AGAIN SIX MINUTES AFTER THE RESTART OF THE MATCH.

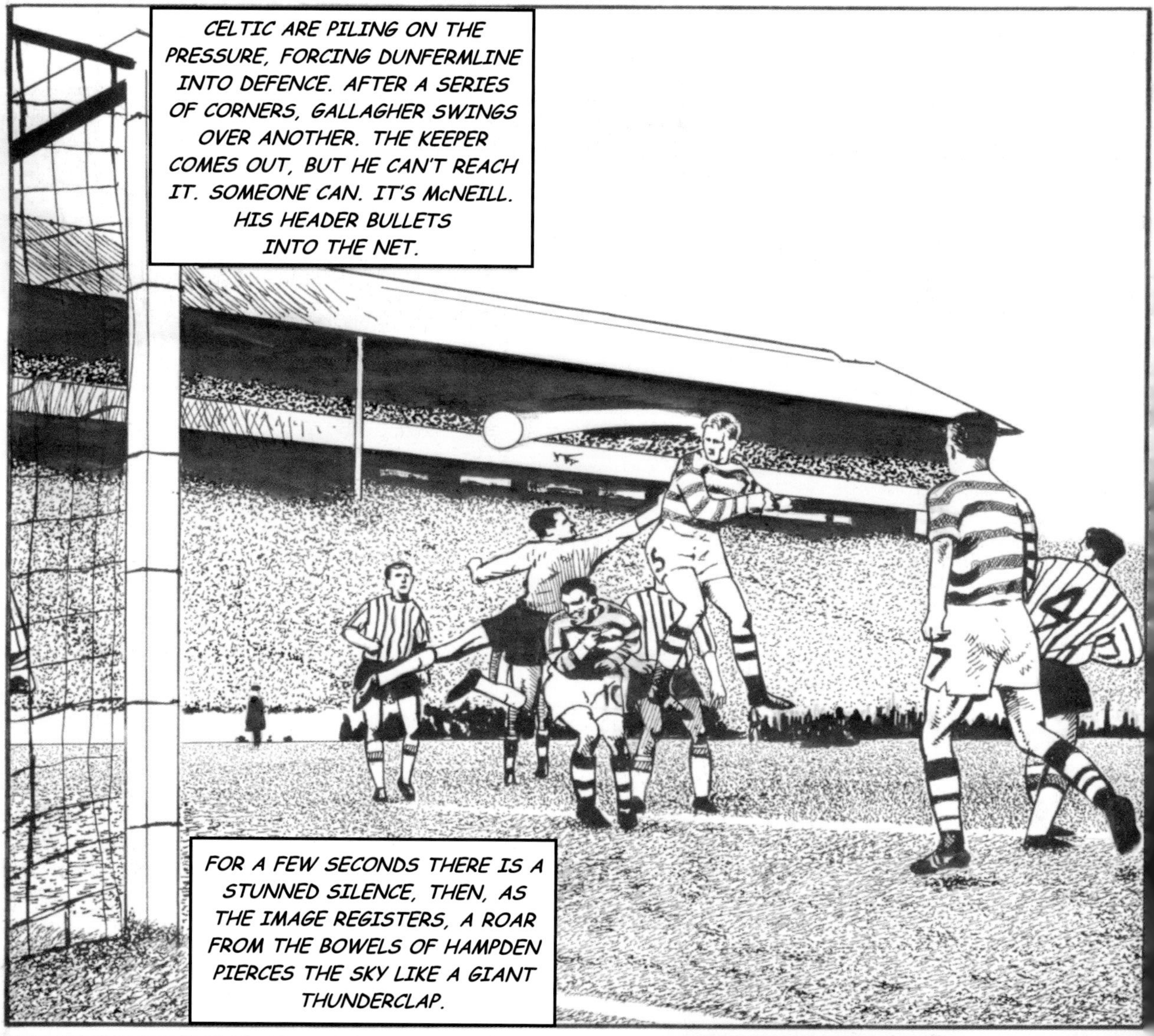
CELTIC ARE PILING ON THE PRESSURE, FORCING DUNFERMLINE INTO DEFENCE. AFTER A SERIES OF CORNERS, GALLAGHER SWINGS OVER ANOTHER. THE KEEPER COMES OUT, BUT HE CAN'T REACH IT. SOMEONE CAN. IT'S McNEILL. HIS HEADER BULLETS INTO THE NET.
FOR A FEW SECONDS THERE IS A STUNNED SILENCE, THEN, AS THE IMAGE REGISTERS, A ROAR FROM THE BOWELS OF HAMPDEN PIERCES THE SKY LIKE A GIANT THUNDERCLAP.

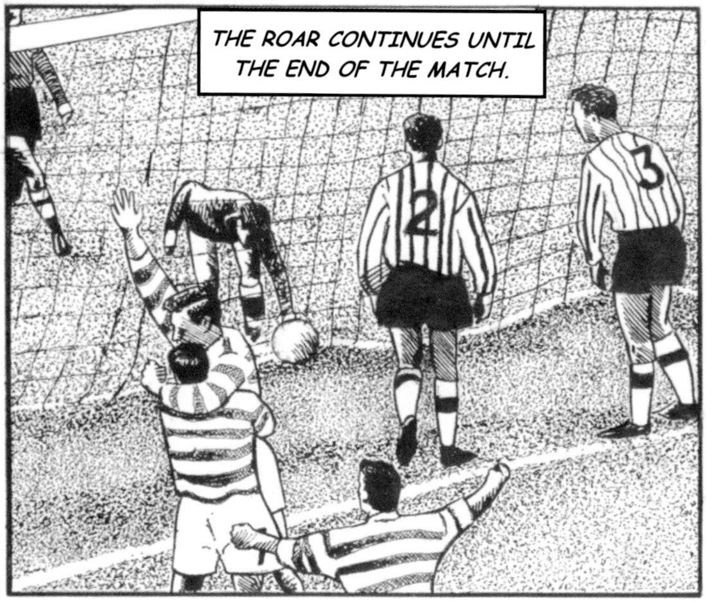
THE ROAR CONTINUES UNTIL THE END OF THE MATCH.

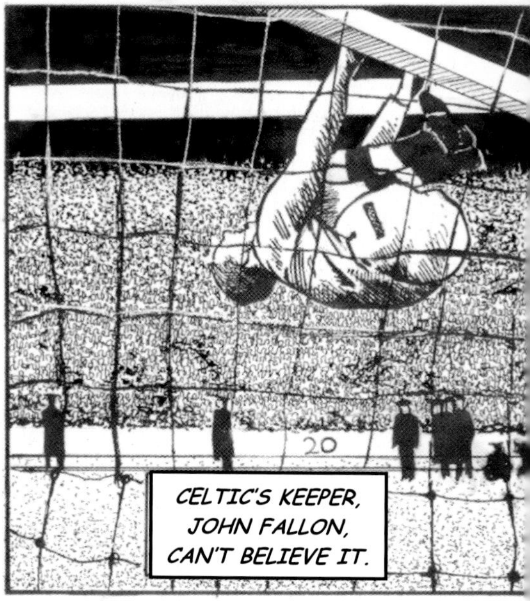
CELTIC'S KEEPER, JOHN FALLON, CAN'T BELIEVE IT.

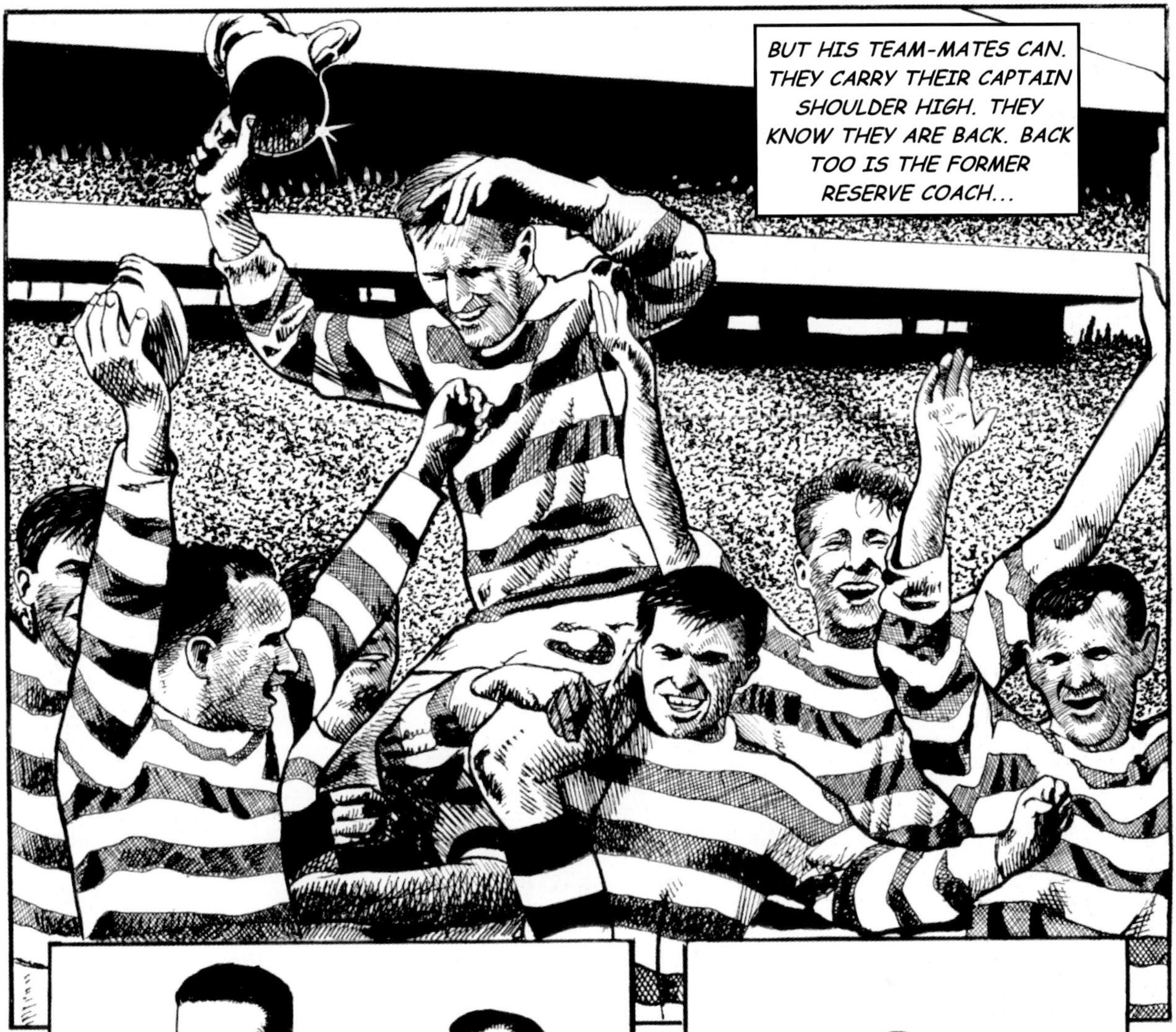
BUT HIS TEAM-MATES CAN. THEY CARRY THEIR CAPTAIN SHOULDER HIGH. THEY KNOW THEY ARE BACK. BACK TOO IS THE FORMER RESERVE COACH...

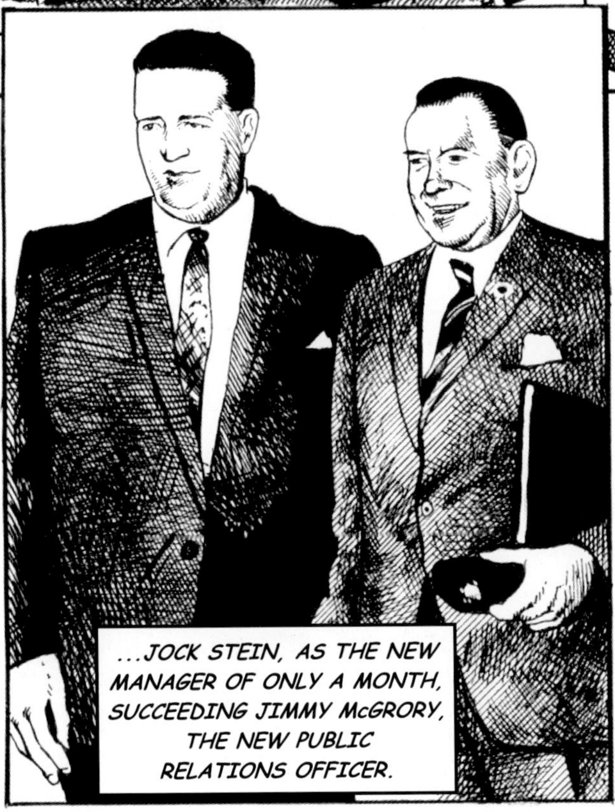
...JOCK STEIN, AS THE NEW MANAGER OF ONLY A MONTH, SUCCEEDING JIMMY McGRORY, THE NEW PUBLIC RELATIONS OFFICER.

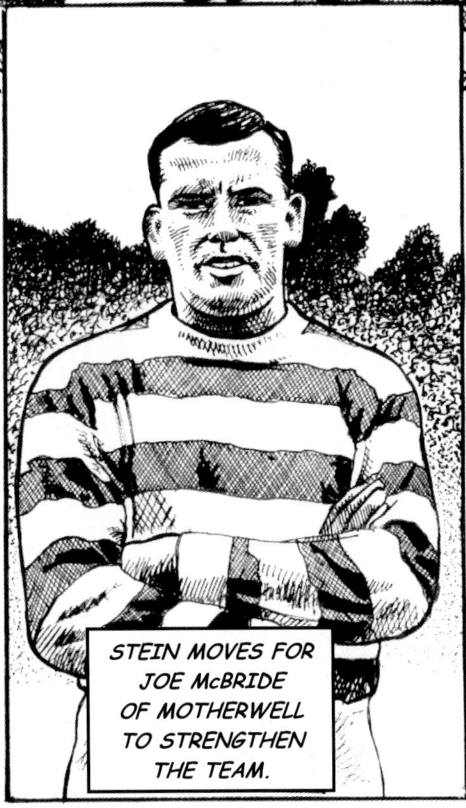
STEIN MOVES FOR JOE McBRIDE OF MOTHERWELL TO STRENGTHEN THE TEAM.

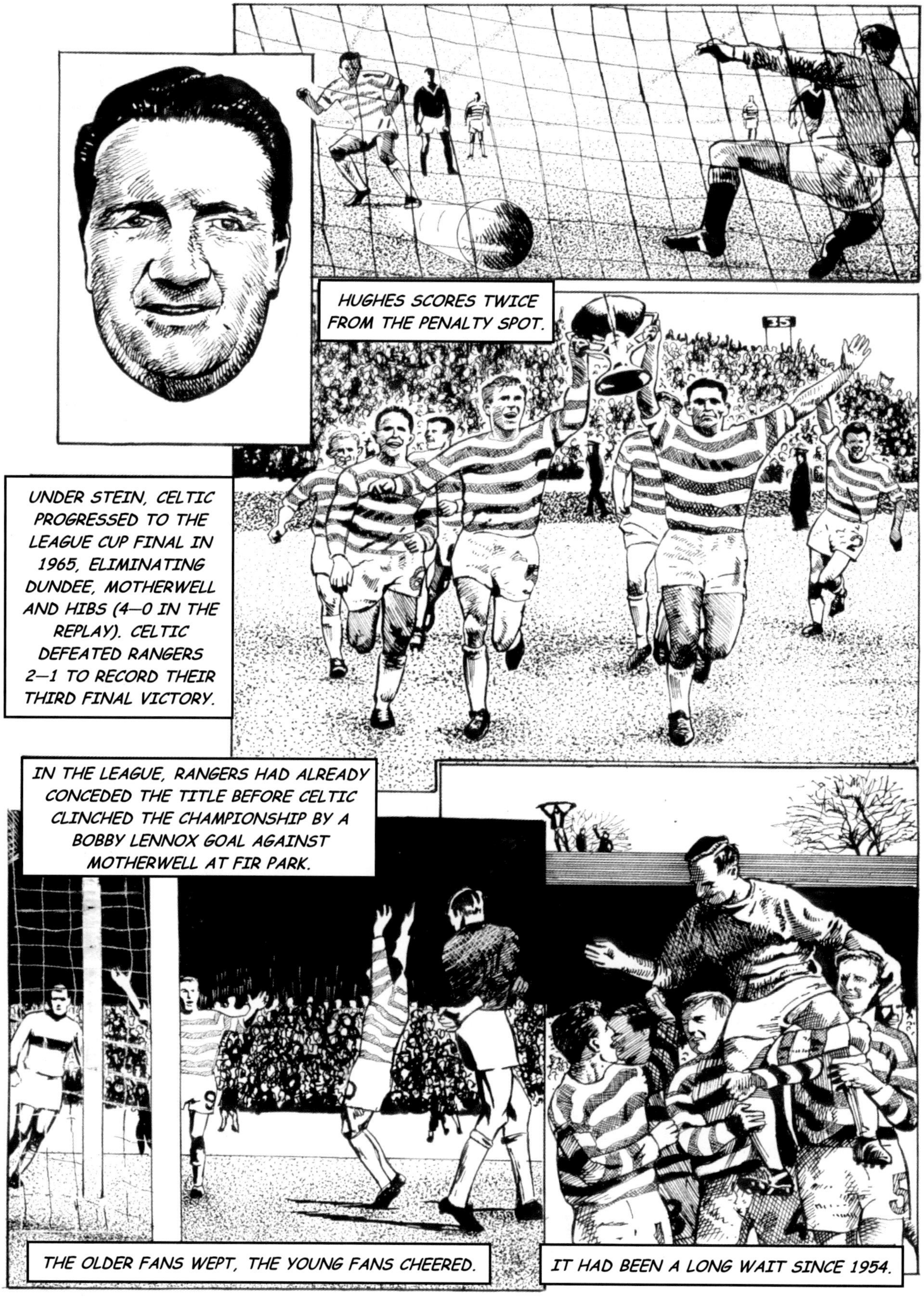
HUGHES SCORES TWICE FROM THE PENALTY SPOT.
UNDER STEIN, CELTIC PROGRESSED TO THE LEAGUE CUP FINAL IN 1965, ELIMINATING DUNDEE, MOTHERWELL AND HIBS (4–0 IN THE REPLAY). CELTIC DEFEATED RANGERS 2–1 TO RECORD THEIR THIRD FINAL VICTORY.
IN THE LEAGUE, RANGERS HAD ALREADY CONCEDED THE TITLE BEFORE CELTIC CLINCHED THE CHAMPIONSHIP BY A BOBBY LENNOX GOAL AGAINST MOTHERWELL AT FIR PARK.
THE OLDER FANS WEPT, THE YOUNG FANS CHEERED.
IT HAD BEEN A LONG WAIT SINCE 1954.

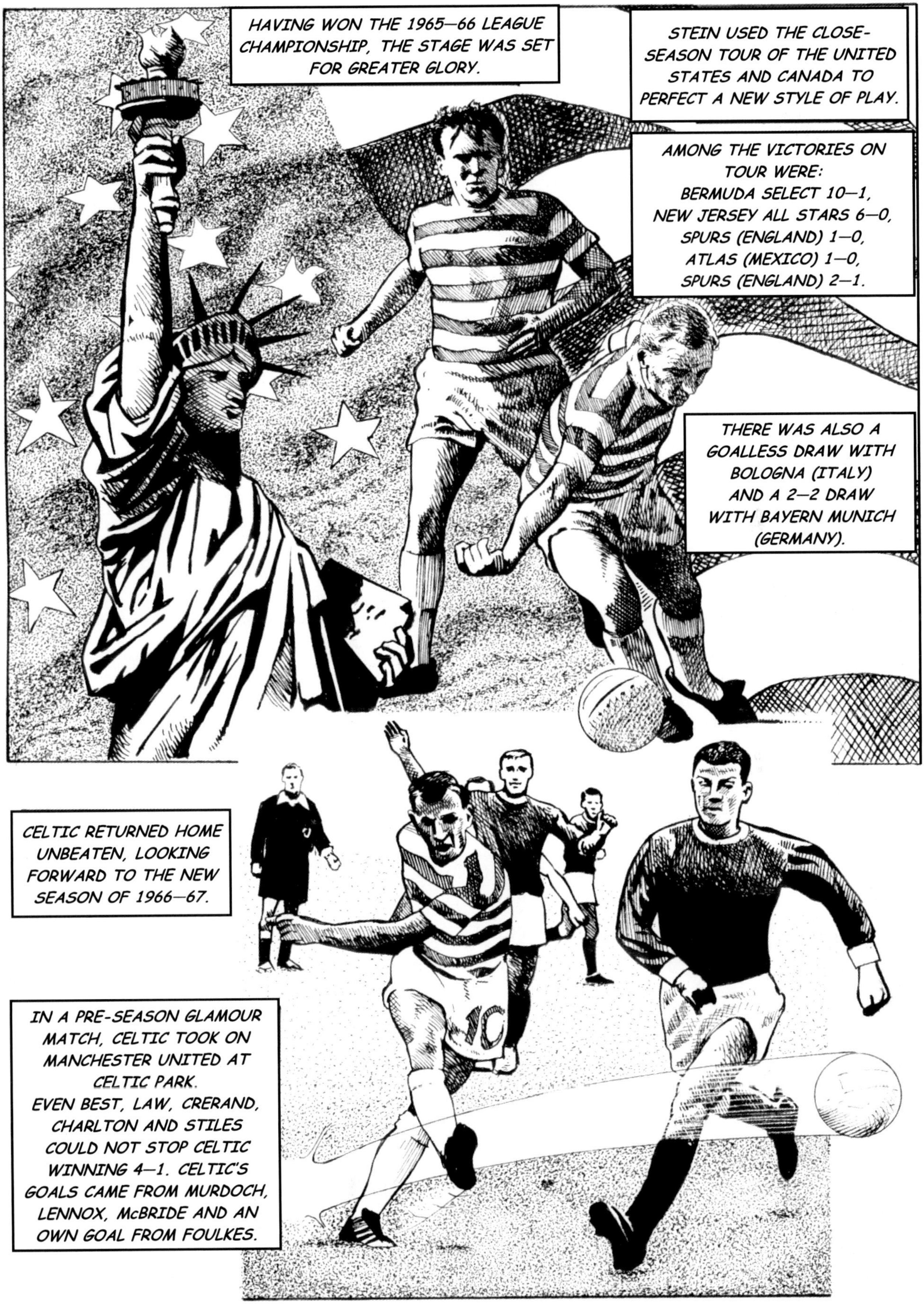
HAVING WON THE 1965–66 LEAGUE CHAMPIONSHIP, THE STAGE WAS SET FOR GREATER GLORY.
STEIN USED THE CLOSE-SEASON TOUR OF THE UNITED STATES AND CANADA TO PERFECT A NEW STYLE OF PLAY.
AMONG THE VICTORIES ON TOUR WERE: BERMUDA SELECT 10–1, NEW JERSEY ALL STARS 6–0, SPURS (ENGLAND) 1–0, ATLAS (MEXICO) 1–0, SPURS (ENGLAND) 2–1.
THERE WAS ALSO A GOALLESS DRAW WITH BOLOGNA (ITALY) AND A 2–2 DRAW WITH BAYERN MUNICH (GERMANY).
CELTIC RETURNED HOME UNBEATEN, LOOKING FORWARD TO THE NEW SEASON OF 1966–67.
IN A PRE-SEASON GLAMOUR MATCH, CELTIC TOOK ON MANCHESTER UNITED AT CELTIC PARK. EVEN BEST, LAW, CRERAND, CHARLTON AND STILES COULD NOT STOP CELTIC WINNING 4–1. CELTIC'S GOALS CAME FROM MURDOCH, LENNOX, McBRIDE AND AN OWN GOAL FROM FOULKES.

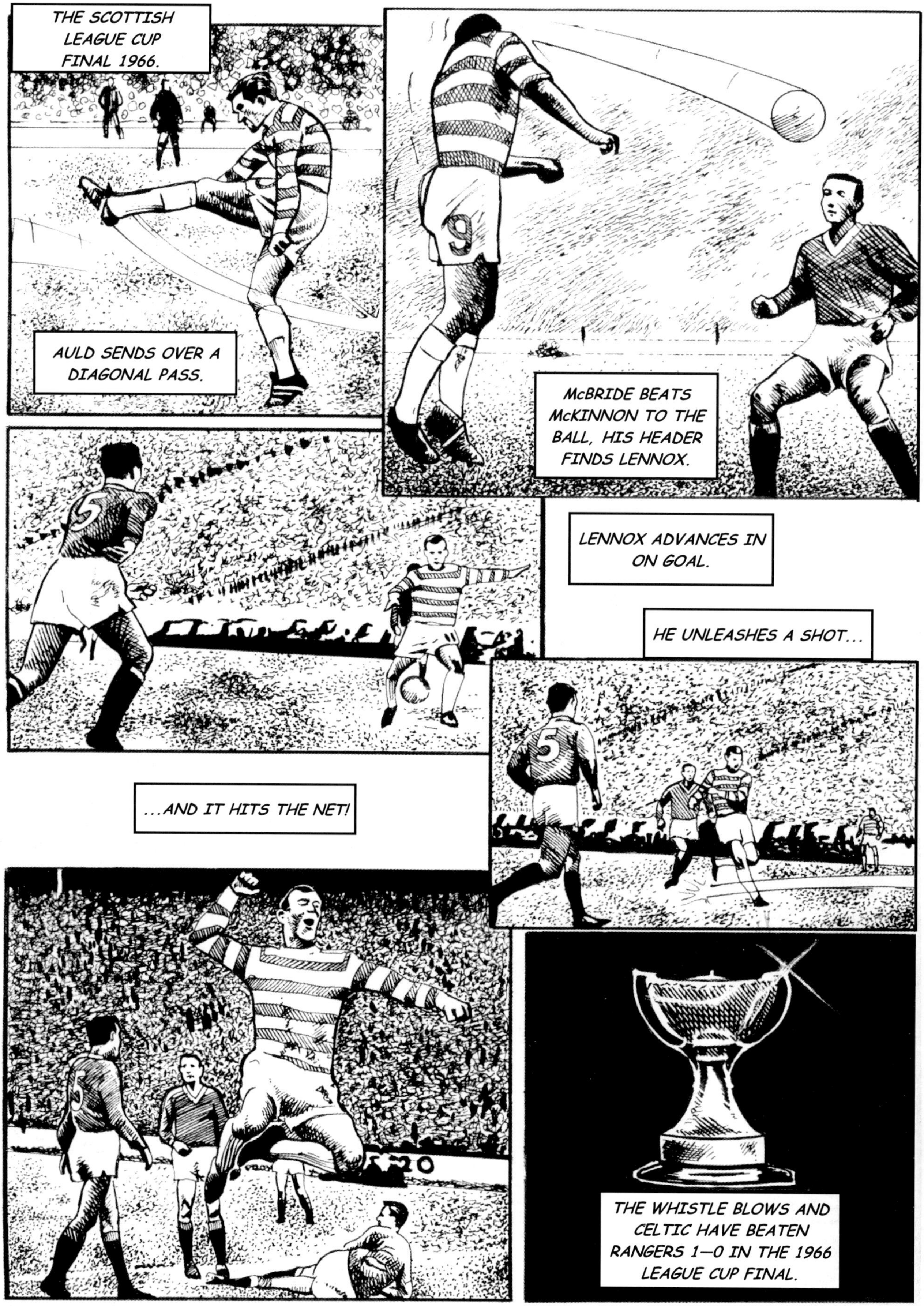
THE SCOTTISH LEAGUE CUP FINAL 1966.
AULD SENDS OVER A DIAGONAL PASS.
McBRIDE BEATS McKINNON TO THE BALL, HIS HEADER FINDS LENNOX.
LENNOX ADVANCES IN ON GOAL.
HE UNLEASHES A SHOT...
...AND IT HITS THE NET!
THE WHISTLE BLOWS AND CELTIC HAVE BEATEN RANGERS 1–0 IN THE 1966 LEAGUE CUP FINAL.

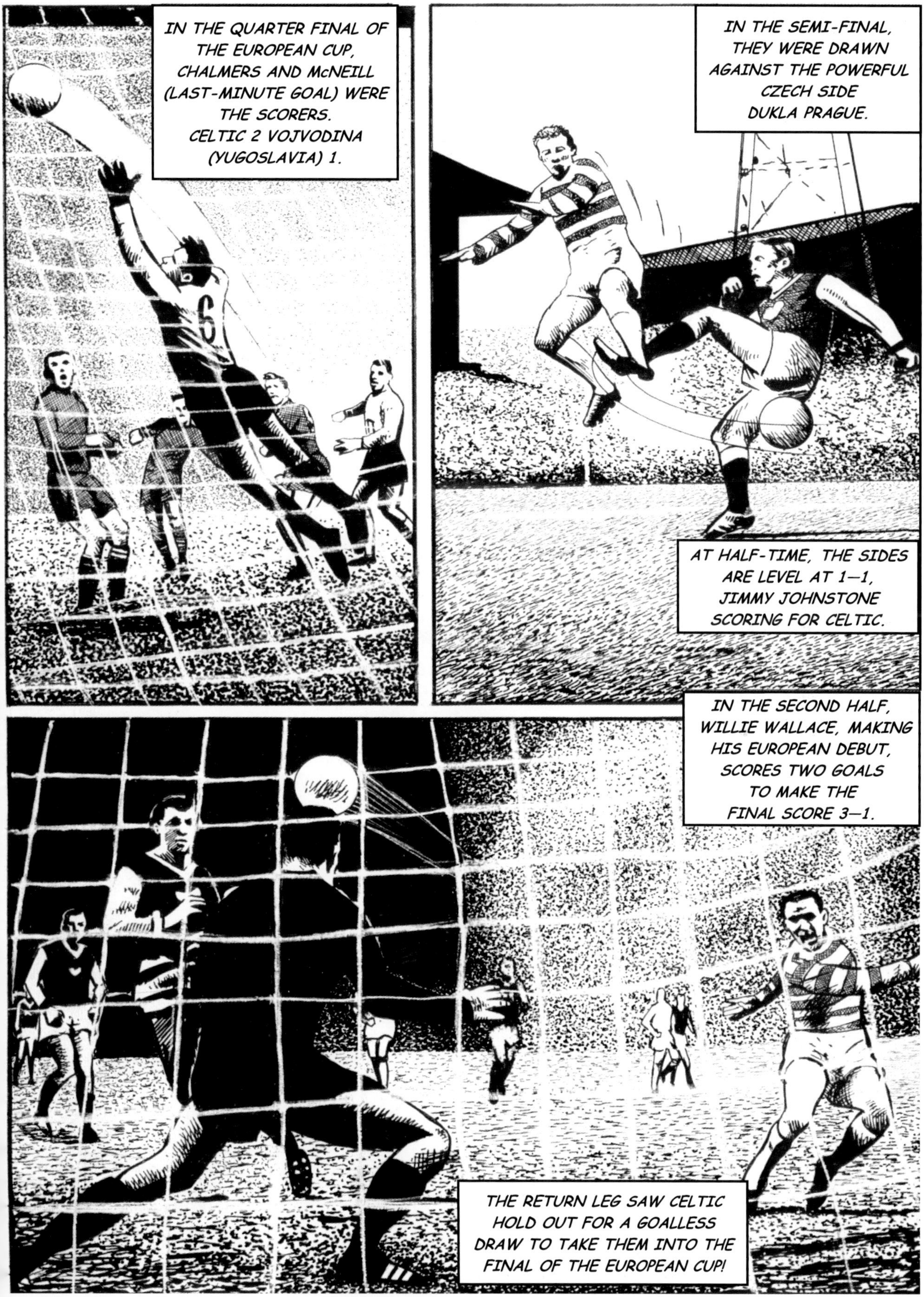
IN THE QUARTER FINAL OF THE EUROPEAN CUP, CHALMERS AND McNEILL (LAST-MINUTE GOAL) WERE THE SCORERS. CELTIC 2 VOJVODINA (YUGOSLAVIA) 1.
IN THE SEMI-FINAL, THEY WERE DRAWN AGAINST THE POWERFUL CZECH SIDE DUKLA PRAGUE.
AT HALF-TIME, THE SIDES ARE LEVEL AT 1—1, JIMMY JOHNSTONE SCORING FOR CELTIC.
IN THE SECOND HALF, WILLIE WALLACE, MAKING HIS EUROPEAN DEBUT, SCORES TWO GOALS TO MAKE THE FINAL SCORE 3—1.
THE RETURN LEG SAW CELTIC HOLD OUT FOR A GOALLESS DRAW TO TAKE THEM INTO THE FINAL OF THE EUROPEAN CUP!

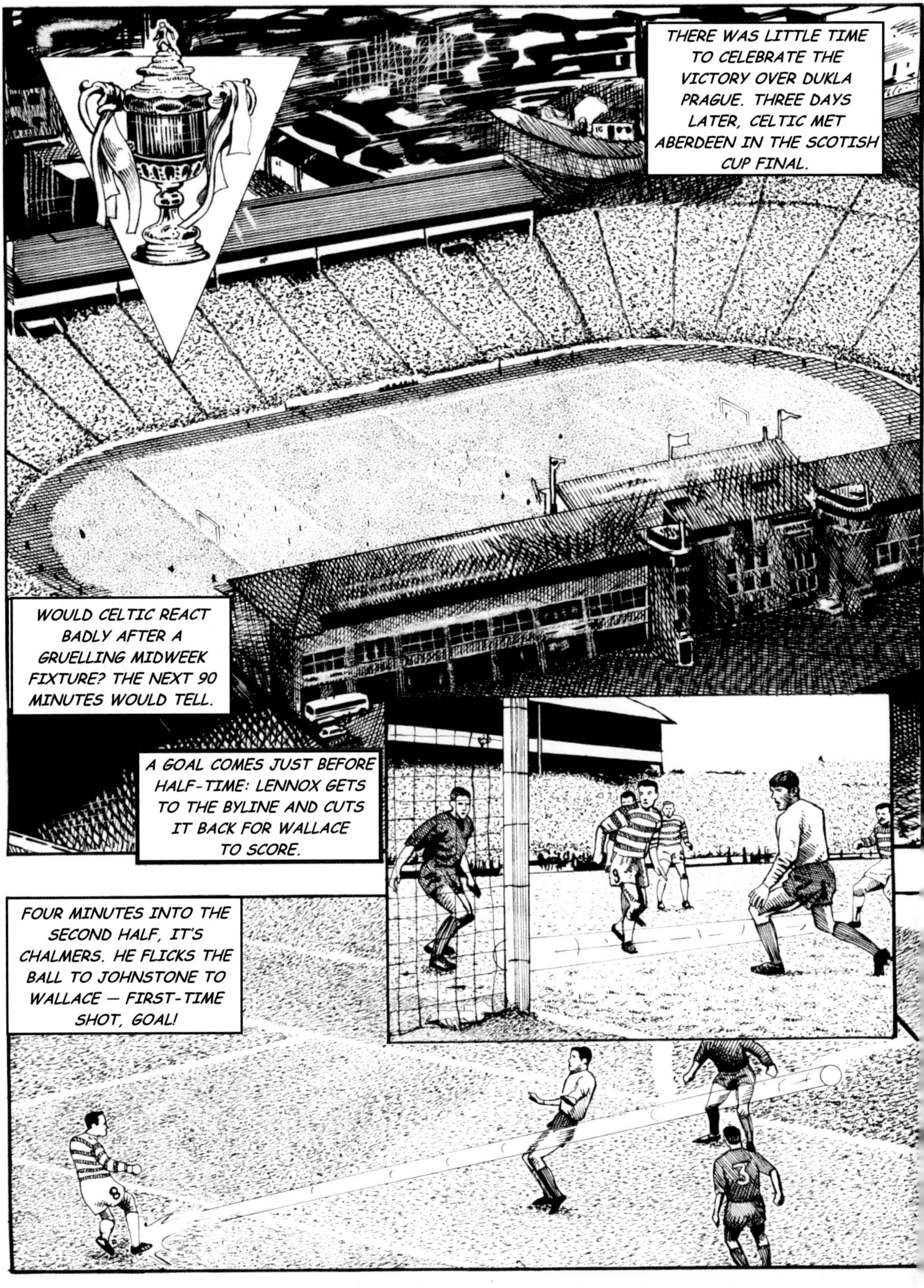
THERE WAS LITTLE TIME TO CELEBRATE THE VICTORY OVER DUKLA PRAGUE. THREE DAYS LATER, CELTIC MET ABERDEEN IN THE SCOTISH CUP FINAL.
WOULD CELTIC REACT BADLY AFTER A GRUELLING MIDWEEK FIXTURE? THE NEXT 90 MINUTES WOULD TELL.
A GOAL COMES JUST BEFORE HALF-TIME: LENNOX GETS TO THE BYLINE AND CUTS IT BACK FOR WALLACE TO SCORE.
FOUR MINUTES INTO THE SECOND HALF, IT'S CHALMERS. HE FLICKS THE BALL TO JOHNSTONE TO WALLACE — FIRST-TIME SHOT, GOAL!

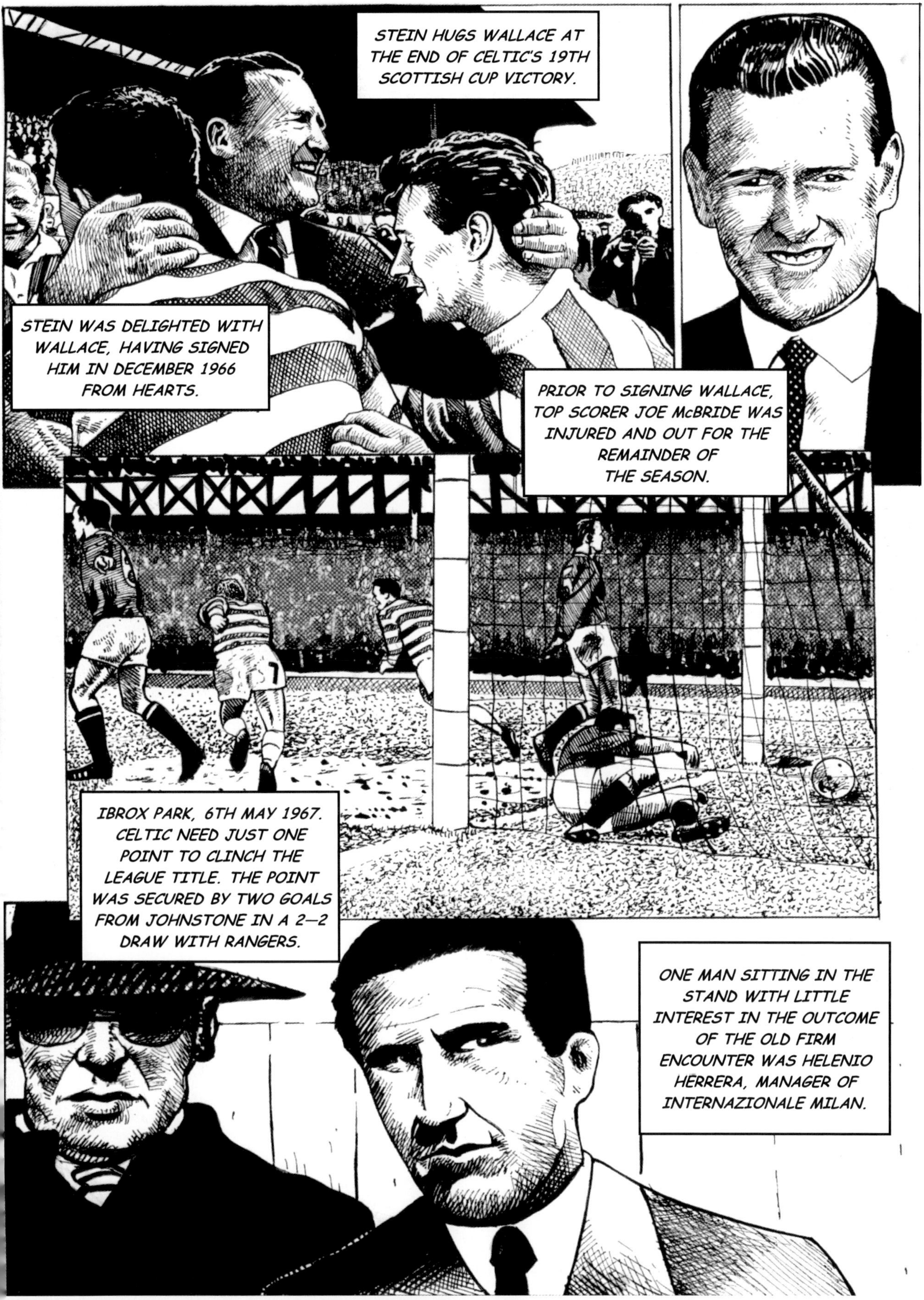
STEIN HUGS WALLACE AT THE END OF CELTIC'S 19TH SCOTTISH CUP VICTORY.
STEIN WAS DELIGHTED WITH WALLACE, HAVING SIGNED HIM IN DECEMBER 1966 FROM HEARTS.
PRIOR TO SIGNING WALLACE, TOP SCORER JOE McBRIDE WAS INJURED AND OUT FOR THE REMAINDER OF THE SEASON.
IBROX PARK, 6TH MAY 1967. CELTIC NEED JUST ONE POINT TO CLINCH THE LEAGUE TITLE. THE POINT WAS SECURED BY TWO GOALS FROM JOHNSTONE IN A 2—2 DRAW WITH RANGERS.
ONE MAN SITTING IN THE STAND WITH LITTLE INTEREST IN THE OUTCOME OF THE OLD FIRM ENCOUNTER WAS HELENIO HERRERA, MANAGER OF INTERNAZIONALE MILAN.

chapter 5

nos venit. nos vidi. nos vincit!

'at the end of the storm'

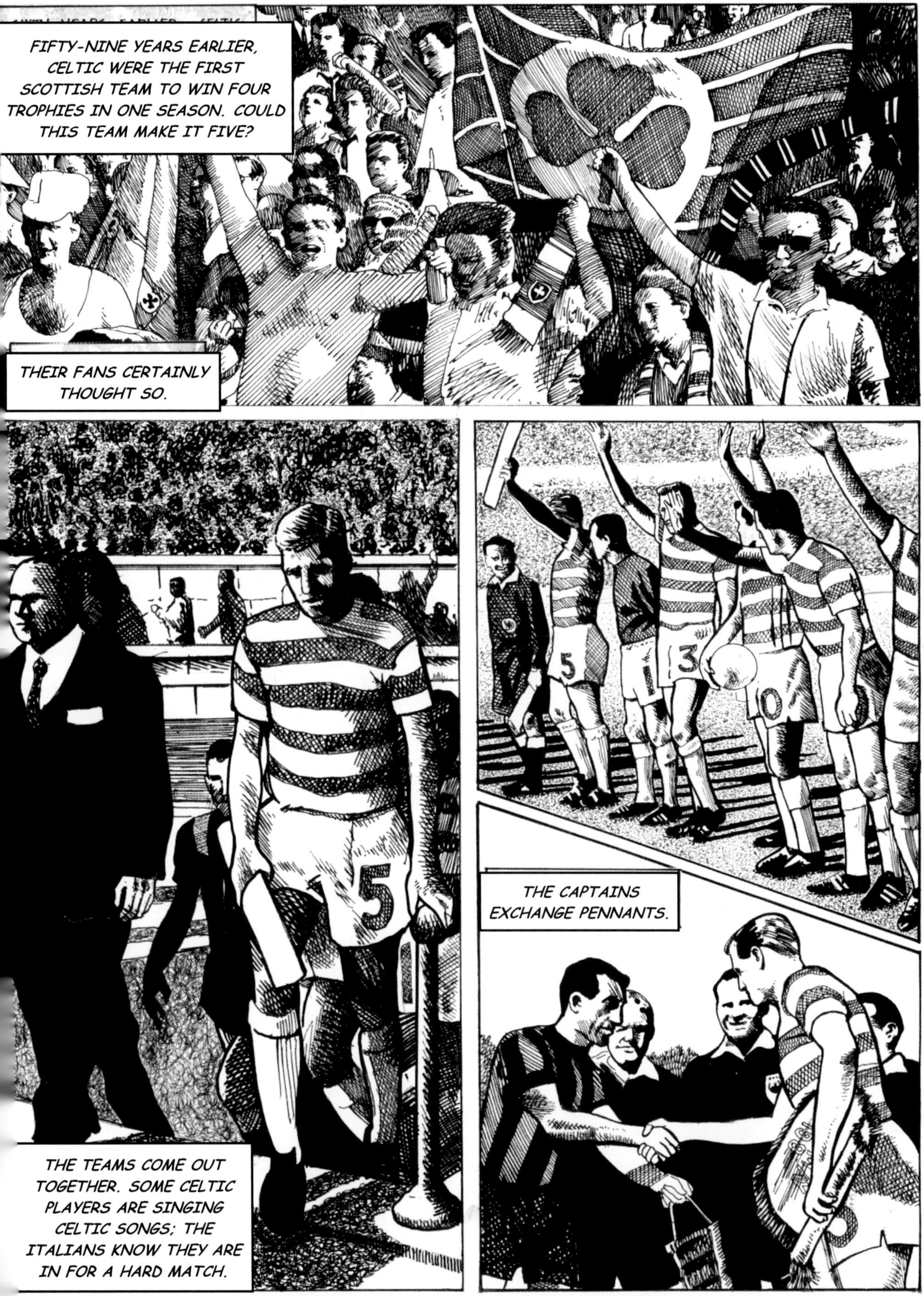
FIFTY-NINE YEARS EARLIER, CELTIC WERE THE FIRST SCOTTISH TEAM TO WIN FOUR TROPHIES IN ONE SEASON. COULD THIS TEAM MAKE IT FIVE?
THEIR FANS CERTAINLY THOUGHT SO.
THE TEAMS COME OUT TOGETHER. SOME CELTIC PLAYERS ARE SINGING CELTIC SONGS; THE ITALIANS KNOW THEY ARE IN FOR A HARD MATCH.
THE CAPTAINS EXCHANGE PENNANTS.

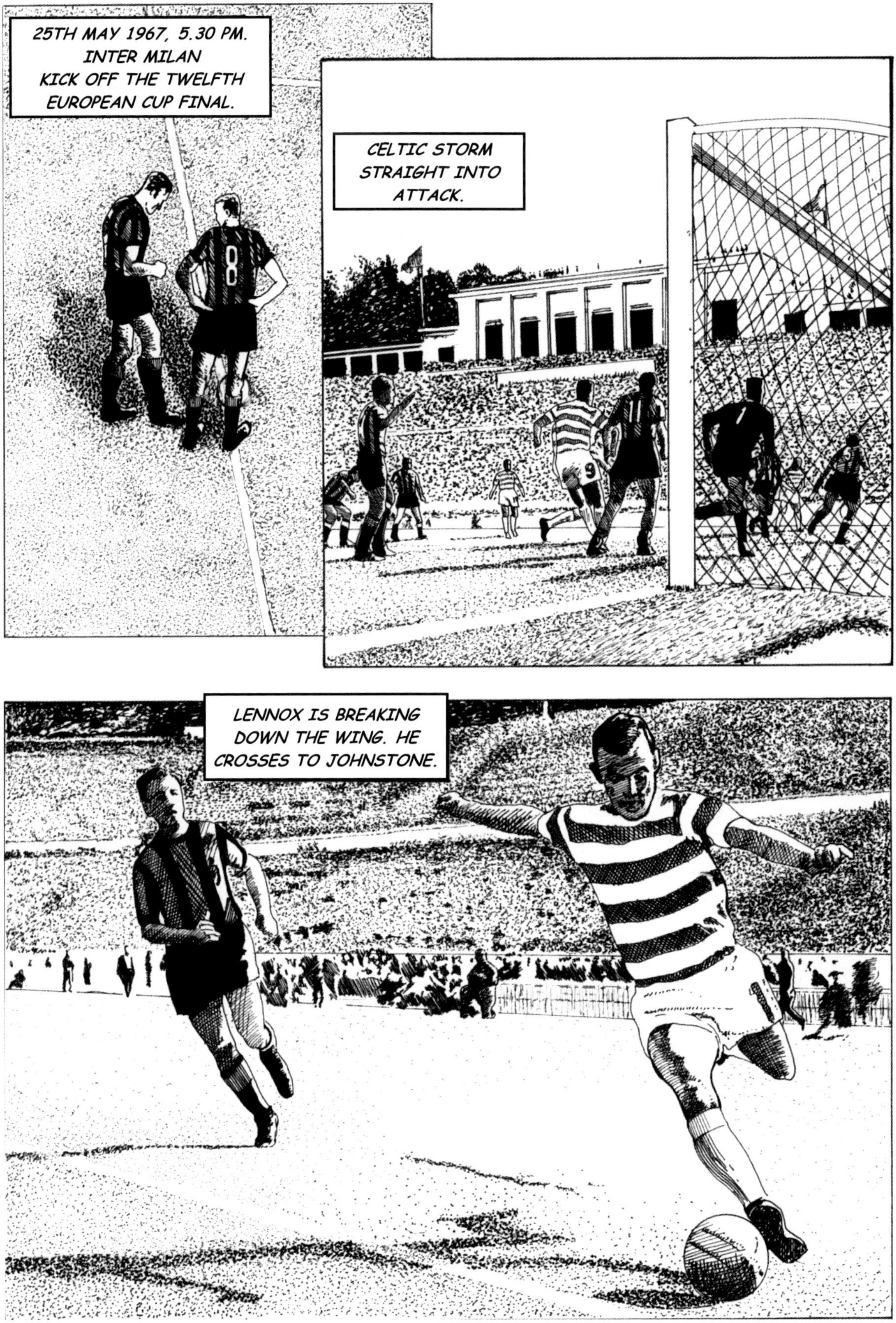
25TH MAY 1967, 5.30 PM.
INTER MILAN
KICK OFF THE TWELFTH
EUROPEAN CUP FINAL.
CELTIC STORM
STRAIGHT INTO
ATTACK.
LENNOX IS BREAKING
DOWN THE WING. HE
CROSSES TO JOHNSTONE.

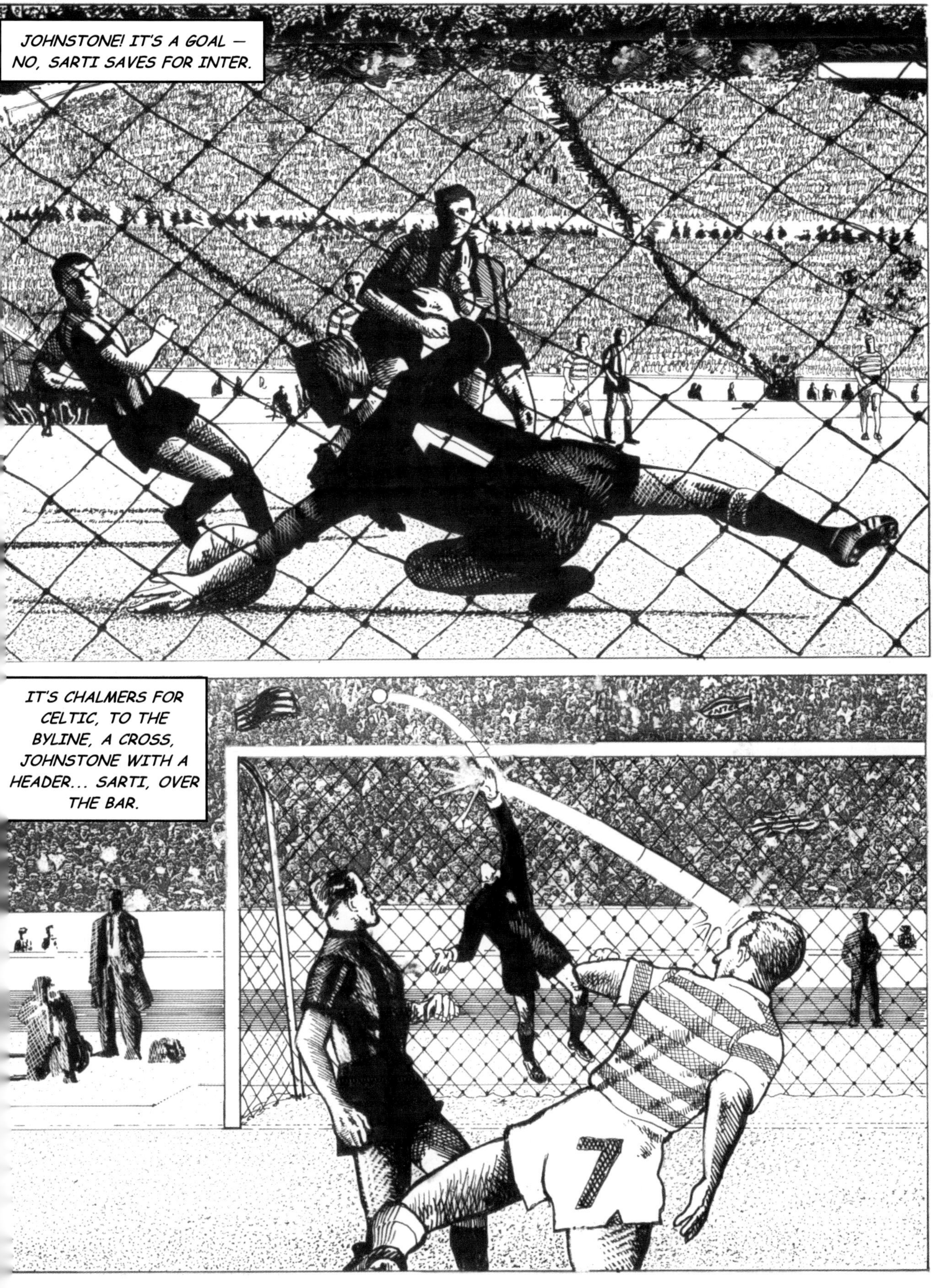
JOHNSTONE! IT'S A GOAL — NO, SARTI SAVES FOR INTER.
IT'S CHALMERS FOR CELTIC, TO THE BYLINE, A CROSS, JOHNSTONE WITH A HEADER... SARTI, OVER THE BAR.

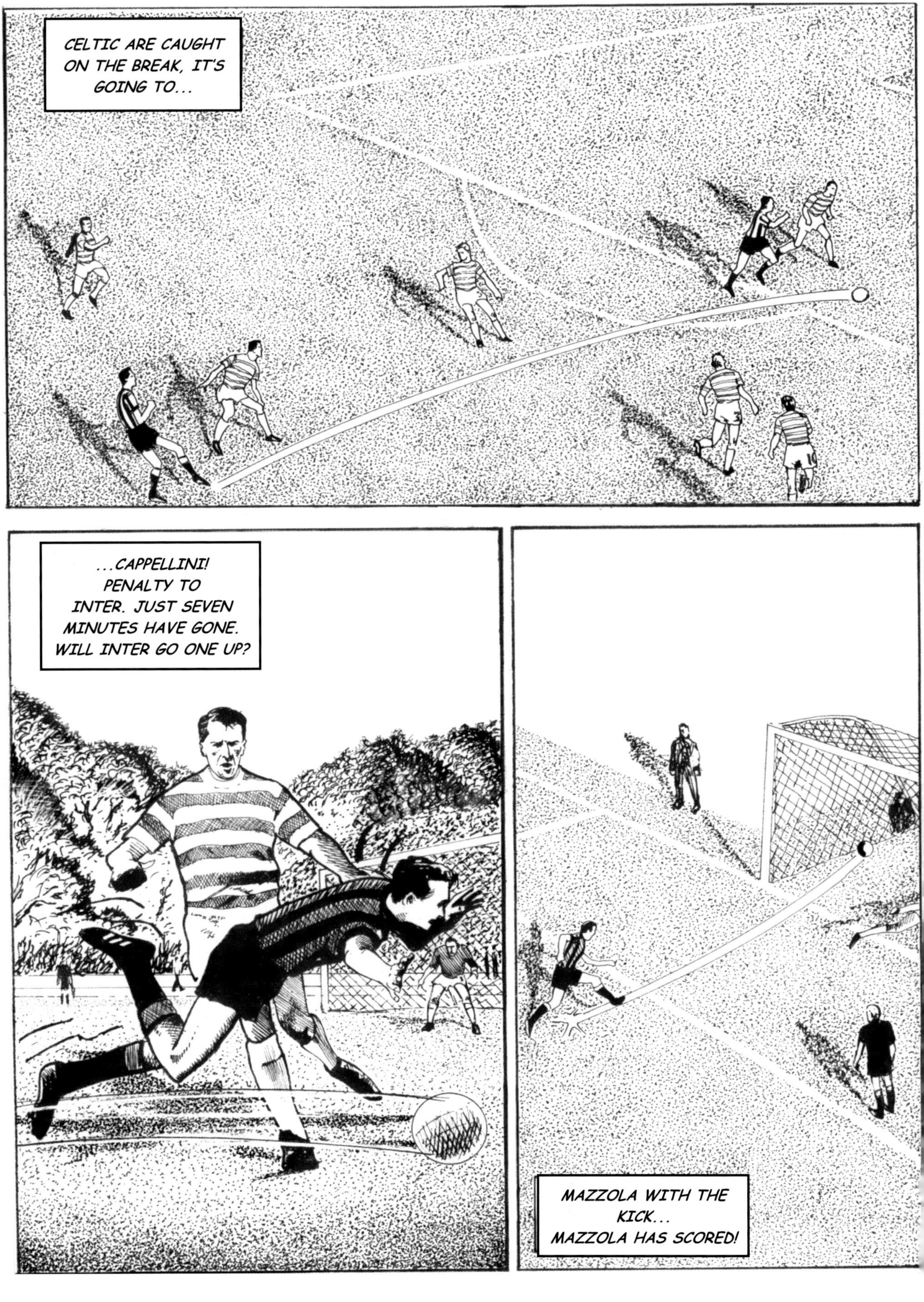
CELTIC ARE CAUGHT ON THE BREAK, IT'S GOING TO...
...CAPPELLINI! PENALTY TO INTER. JUST SEVEN MINUTES HAVE GONE. WILL INTER GO ONE UP?
MAZZOLA WITH THE KICK... MAZZOLA HAS SCORED!

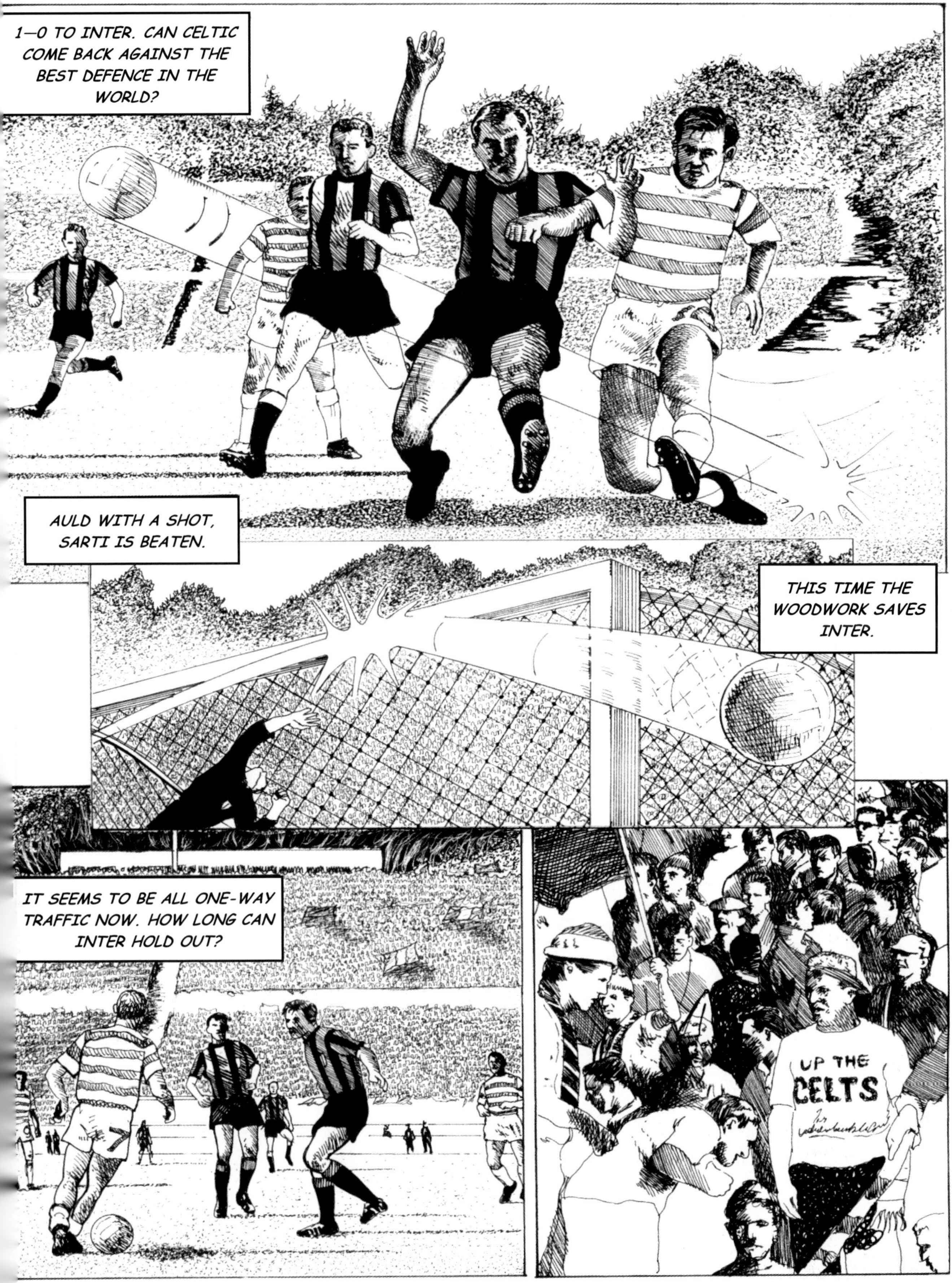
1—0 TO INTER. CAN CELTIC COME BACK AGAINST THE BEST DEFENCE IN THE WORLD?
AULD WITH A SHOT, SARTI IS BEATEN.
THIS TIME THE WOODWORK SAVES INTER.
IT SEEMS TO BE ALL ONE-WAY TRAFFIC NOW. HOW LONG CAN INTER HOLD OUT?
UP THE CELTS

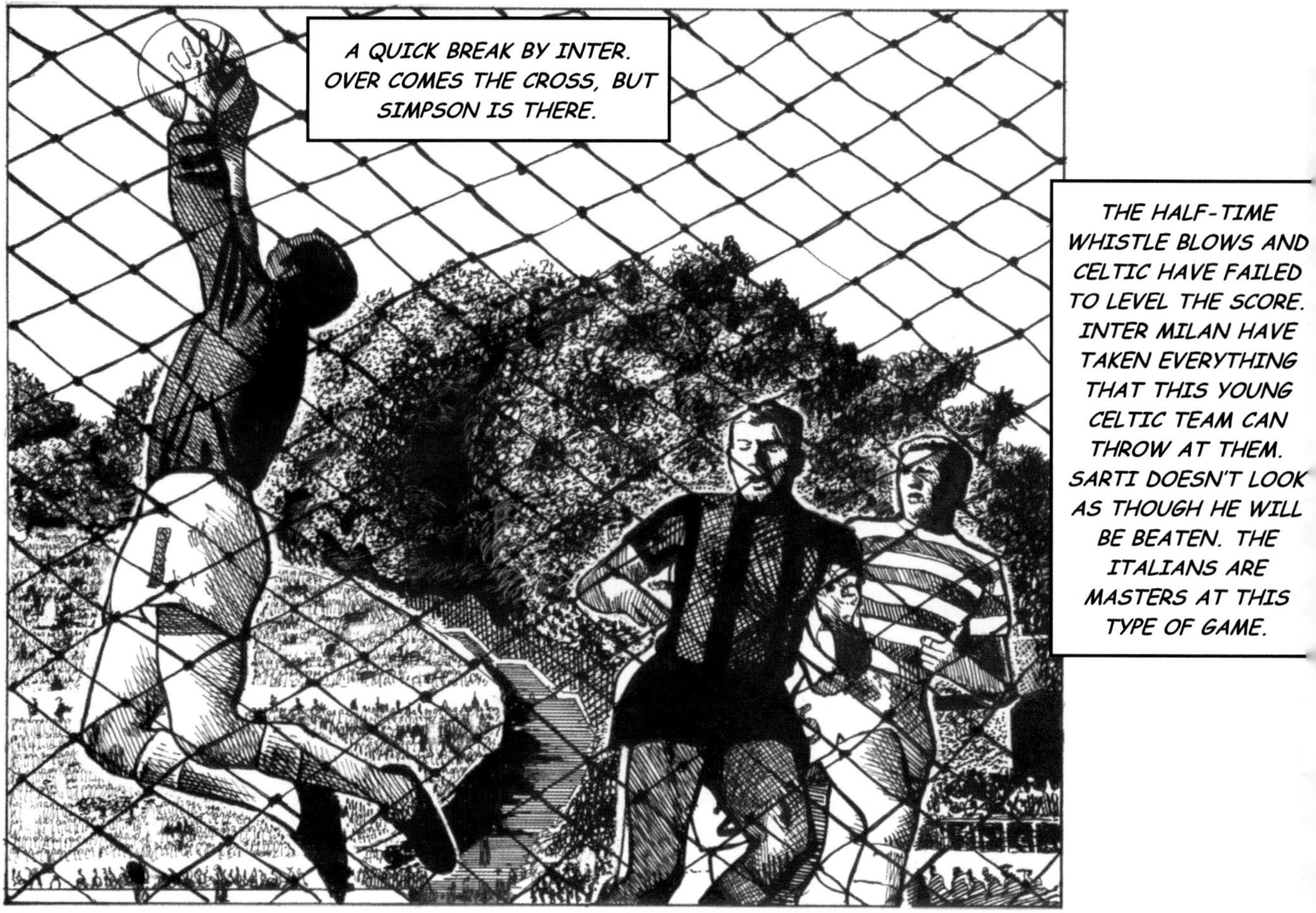
A QUICK BREAK BY INTER. OVER COMES THE CROSS, BUT SIMPSON IS THERE.
THE HALF-TIME WHISTLE BLOWS AND CELTIC HAVE FAILED TO LEVEL THE SCORE. INTER MILAN HAVE TAKEN EVERYTHING THAT THIS YOUNG CELTIC TEAM CAN THROW AT THEM. SARTI DOESN'T LOOK AS THOUGH HE WILL BE BEATEN. THE ITALIANS ARE MASTERS AT THIS TYPE OF GAME.

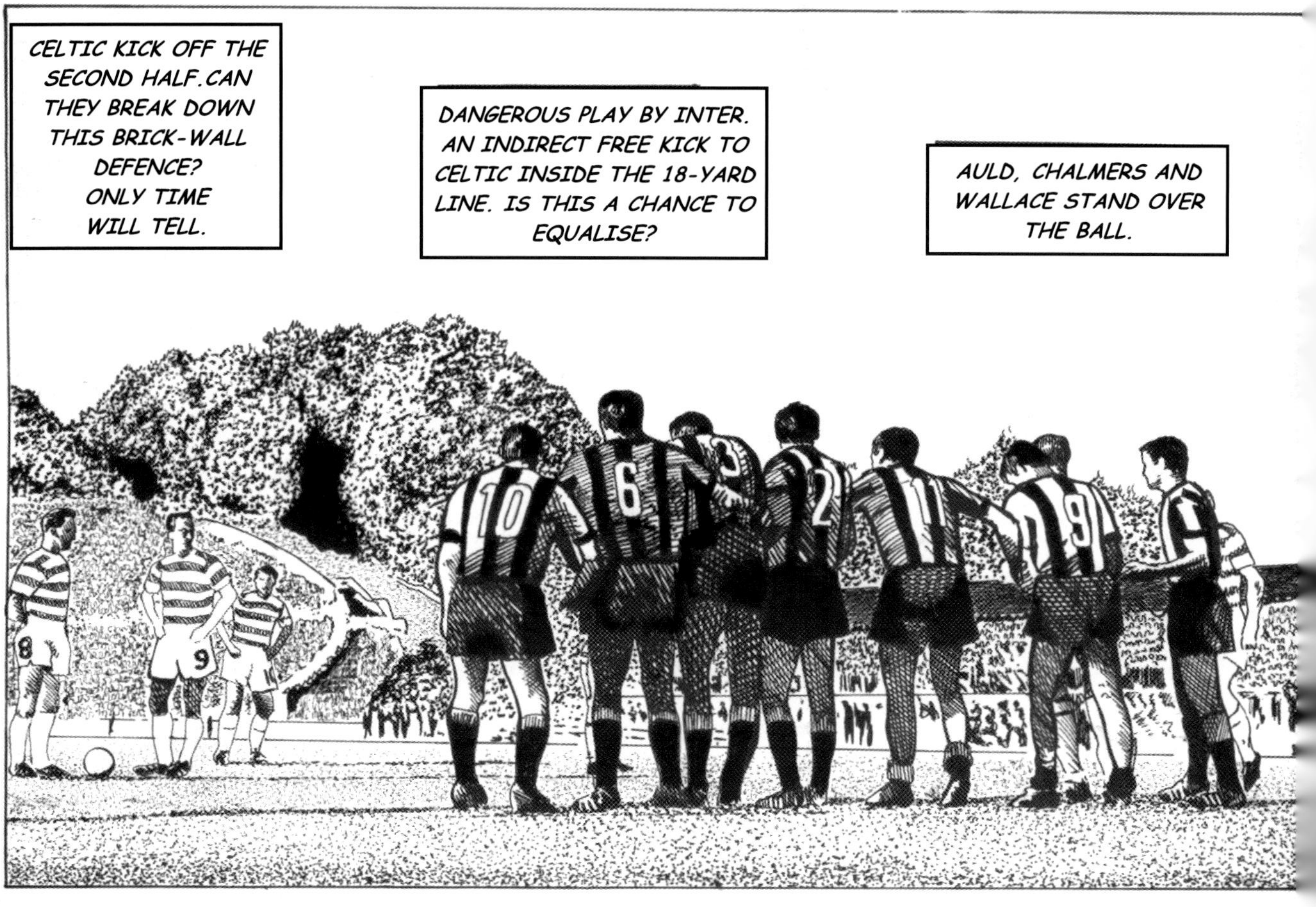
CELTIC KICK OFF THE SECOND HALF.CAN THEY BREAK DOWN THIS BRICK-WALL DEFENCE? ONLY TIME WILL TELL.
DANGEROUS PLAY BY INTER. AN INDIRECT FREE KICK TO CELTIC INSIDE THE 18-YARD LINE. IS THIS A CHANCE TO EQUALISE?
AULD, CHALMERS AND WALLACE STAND OVER THE BALL.

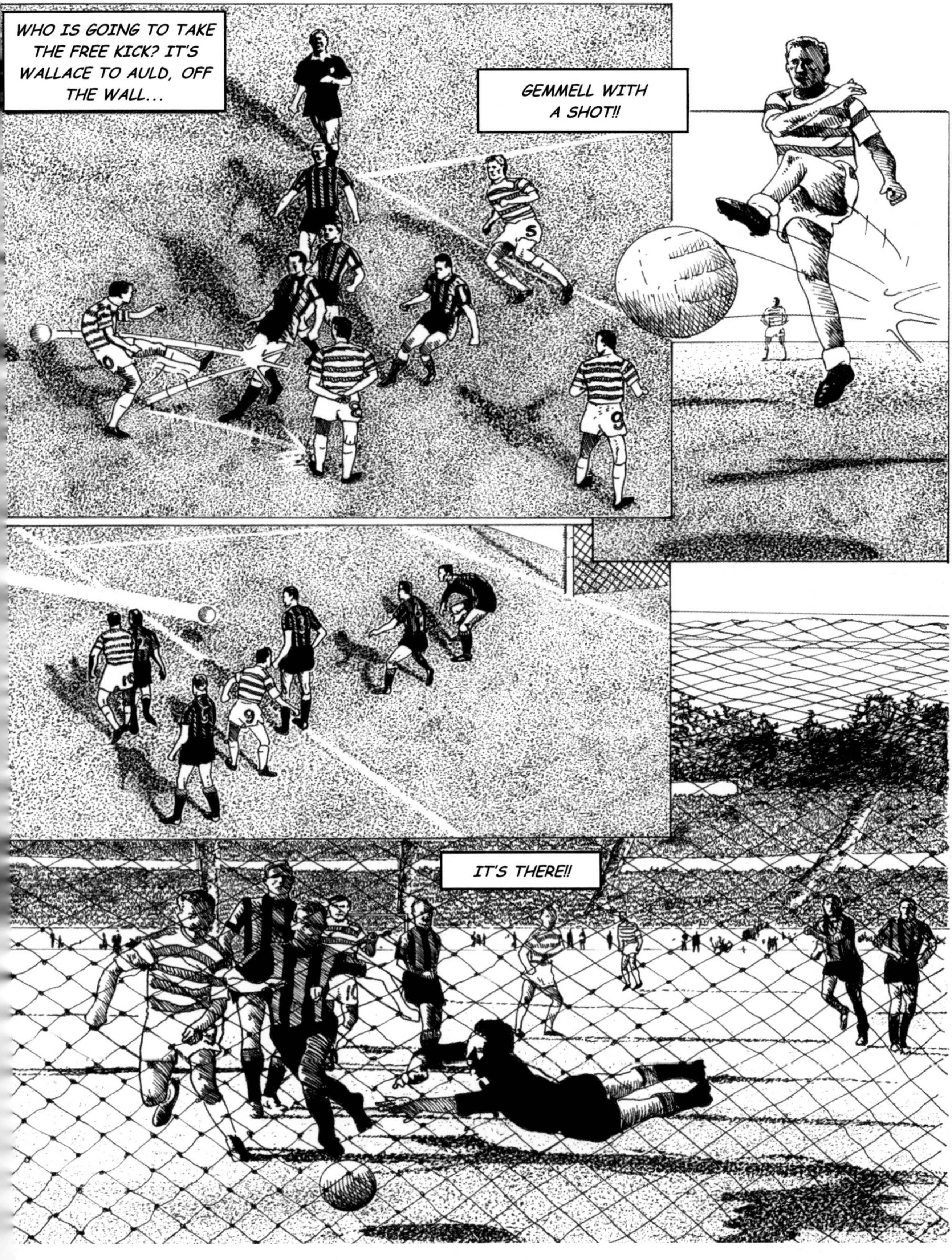
WHO IS GOING TO TAKE THE FREE KICK? IT'S WALLACE TO AULD, OFF THE WALL...
GEMMELL WITH A SHOT!!
IT'S THERE!!

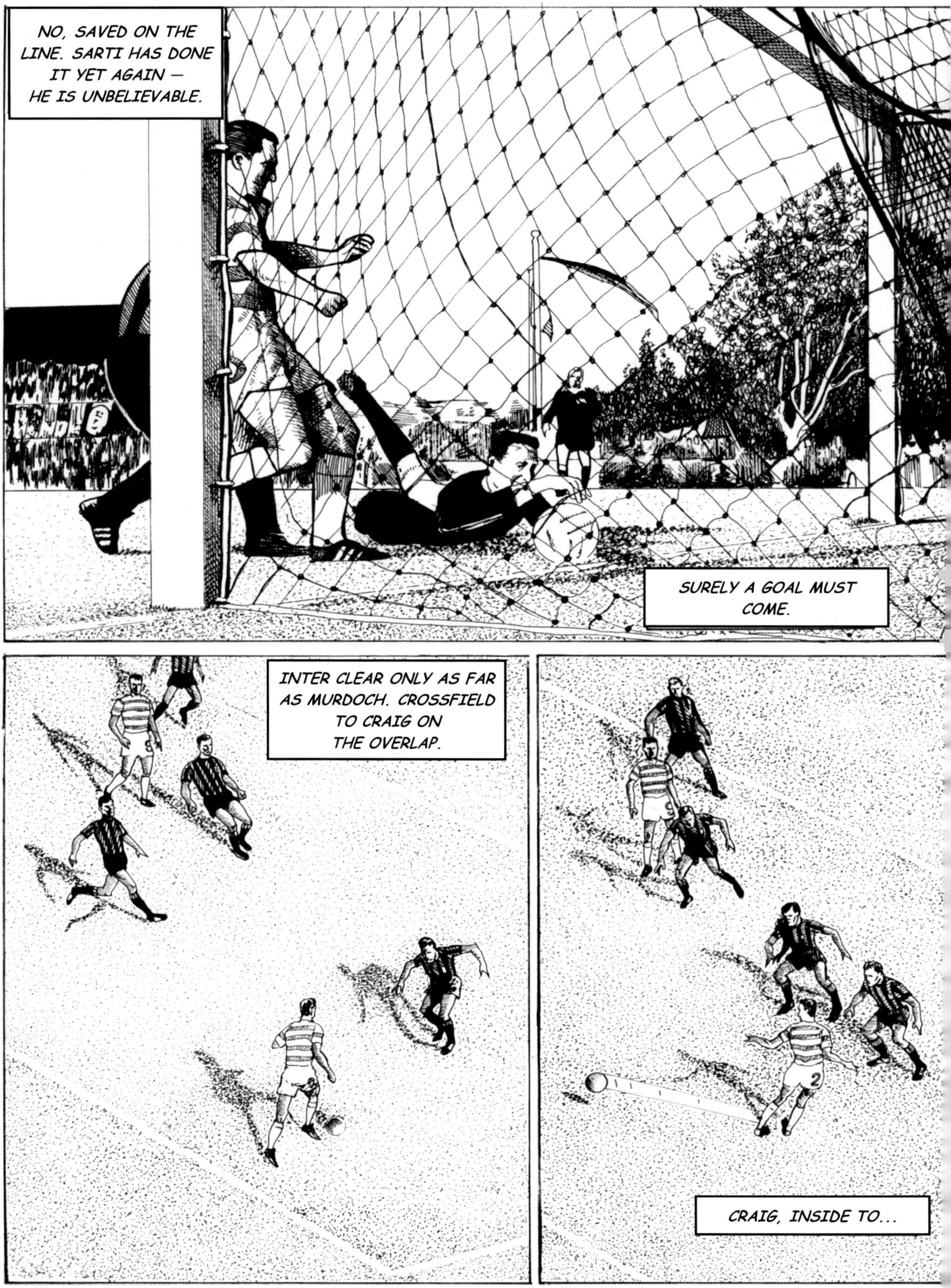
NO, SAVED ON THE LINE. SARTI HAS DONE IT YET AGAIN — HE IS UNBELIEVABLE.
SURELY A GOAL MUST COME.
INTER CLEAR ONLY AS FAR AS MURDOCH. CROSSFIELD TO CRAIG ON THE OVERLAP.
CRAIG, INSIDE TO...

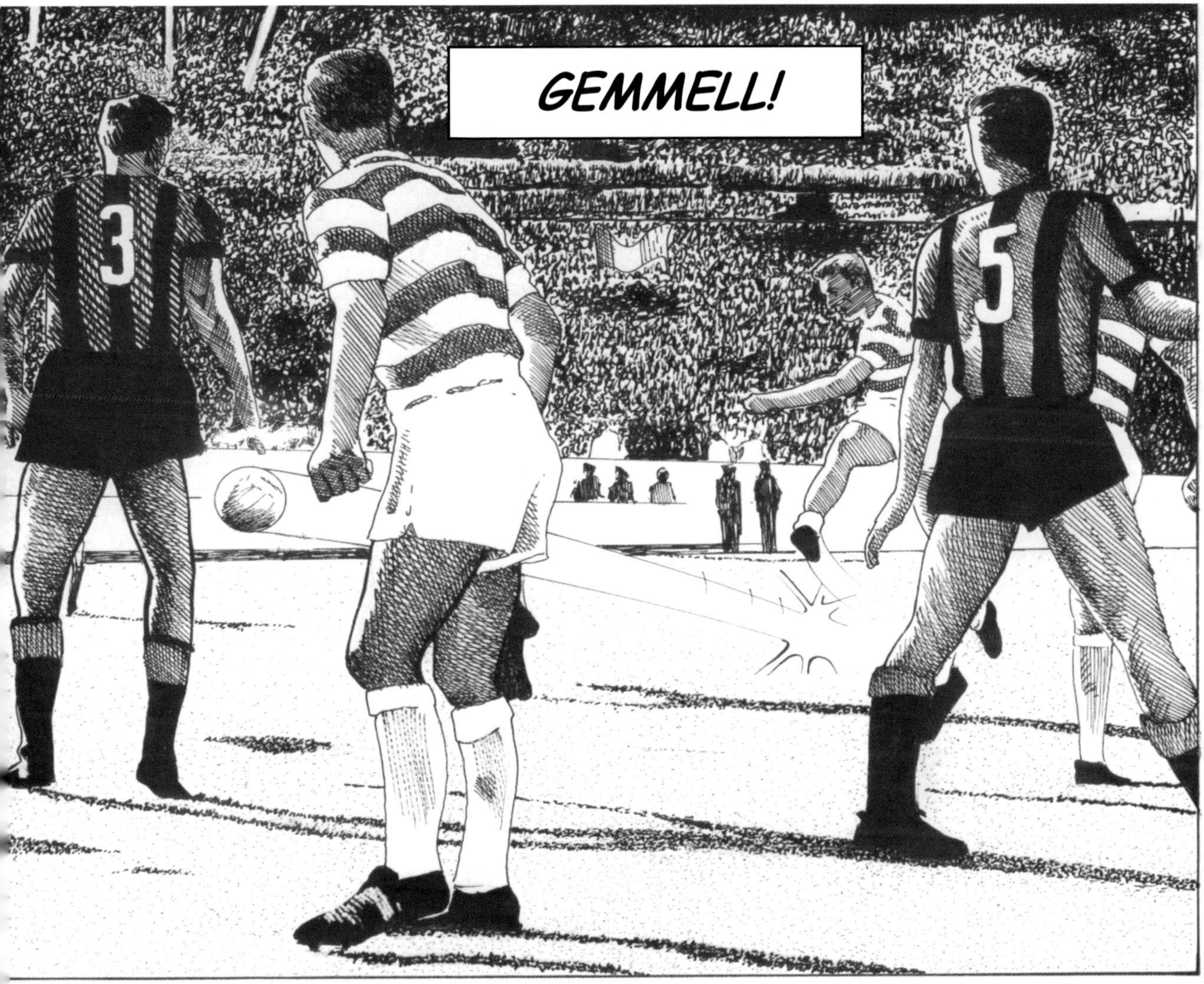
GEMMELL!

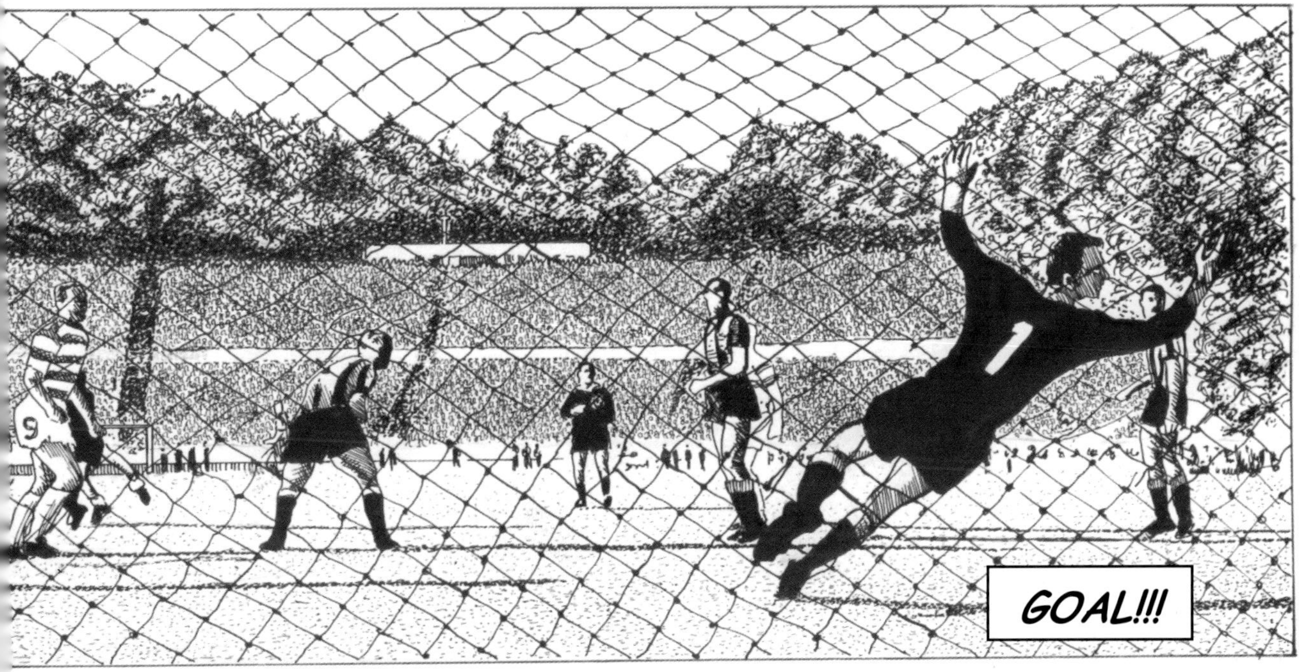
GOAL!!!

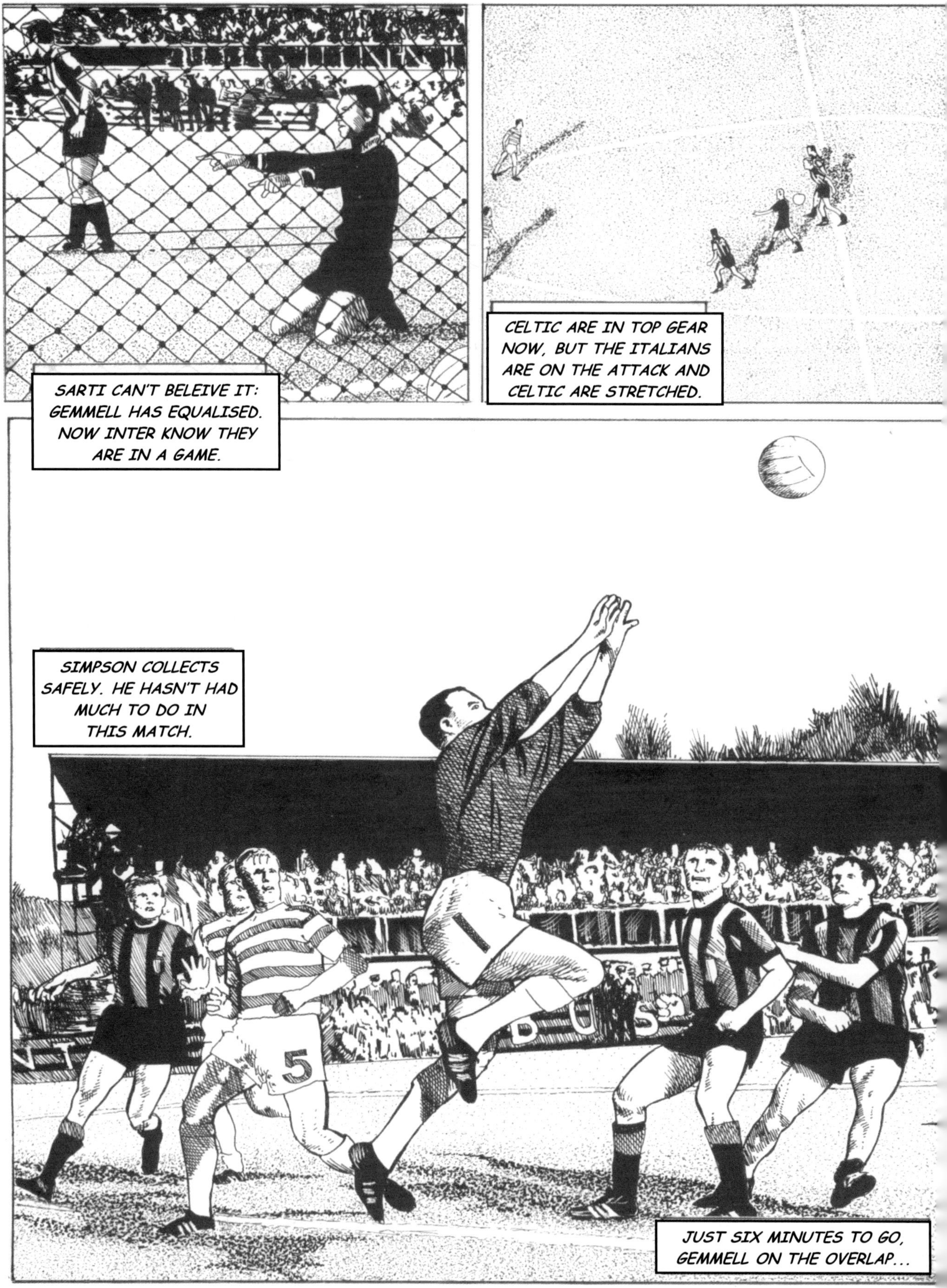
SARTI CAN'T BELEIVE IT: GEMMELL HAS EQUALISED. NOW INTER KNOW THEY ARE IN A GAME.
CELTIC ARE IN TOP GEAR NOW, BUT THE ITALIANS ARE ON THE ATTACK AND CELTIC ARE STRETCHED.
SIMPSON COLLECTS SAFELY. HE HASN'T HAD MUCH TO DO IN THIS MATCH.
JUST SIX MINUTES TO GO, GEMMELL ON THE OVERLAP...

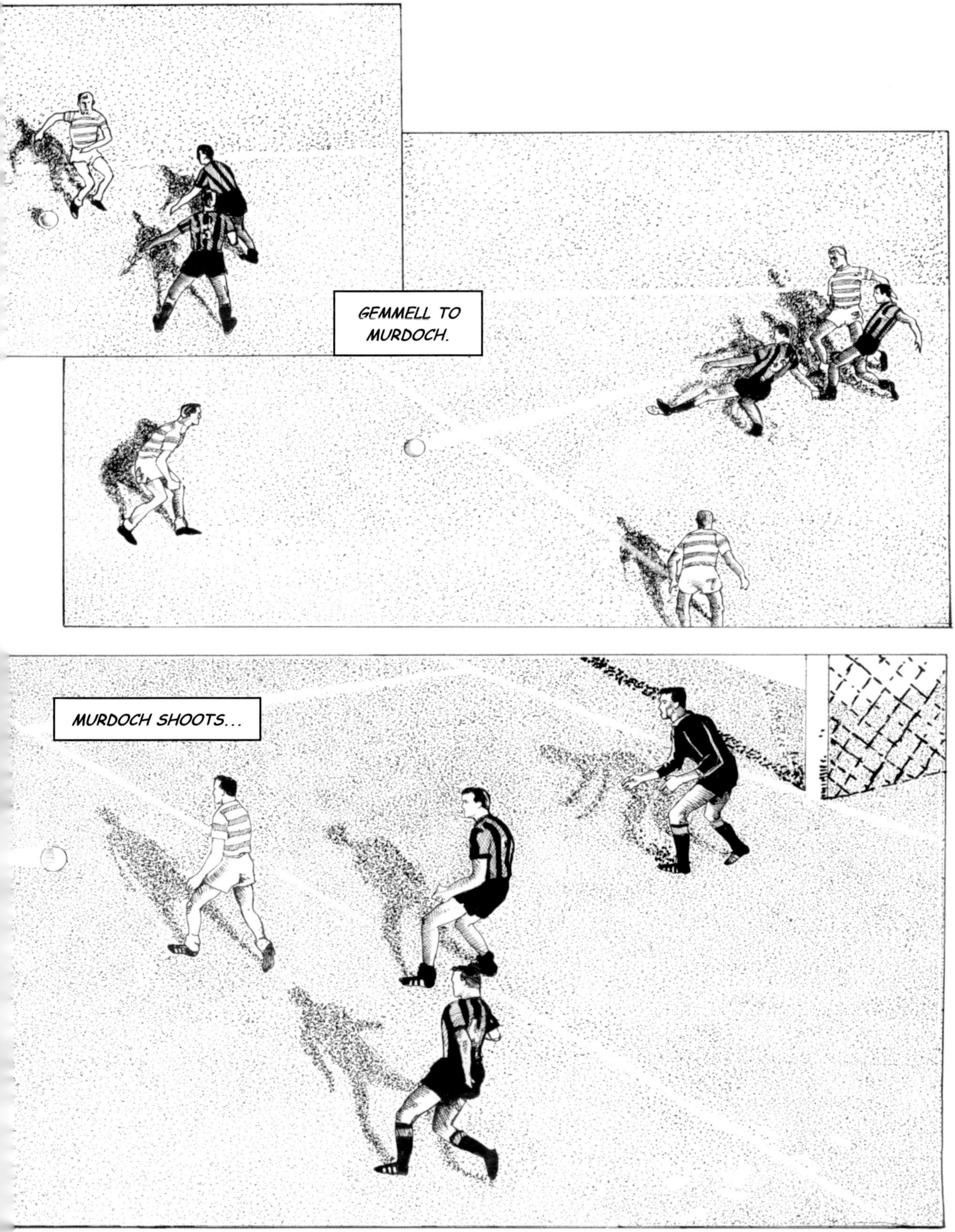
GEMMELL TO
MURDOCH.
MURDOCH SHOOTS...

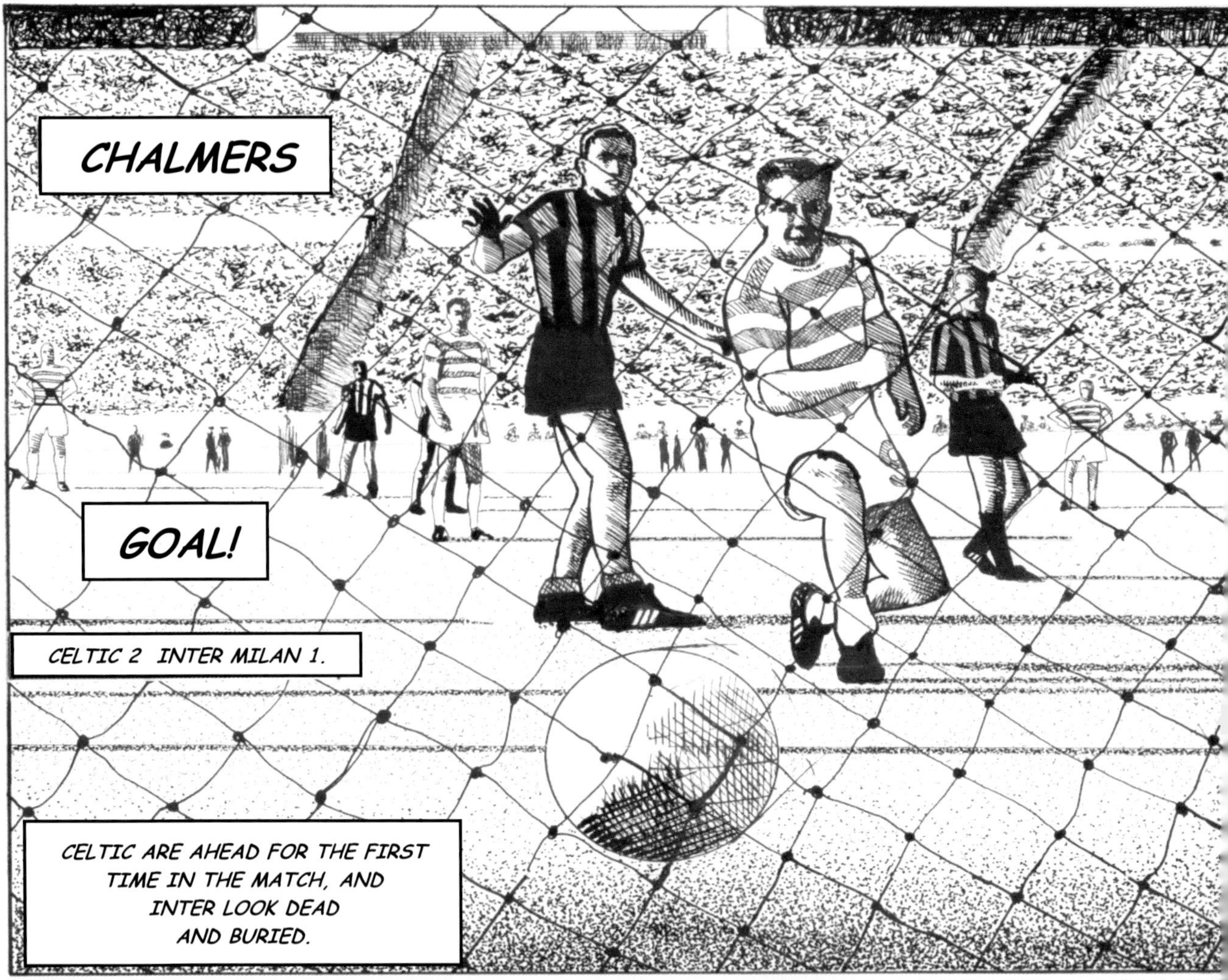
CHALMERS
GOAL!
CELTIC 2 INTER MILAN 1.
CELTIC ARE AHEAD FOR THE FIRST TIME IN THE MATCH, AND INTER LOOK DEAD AND BURIED.

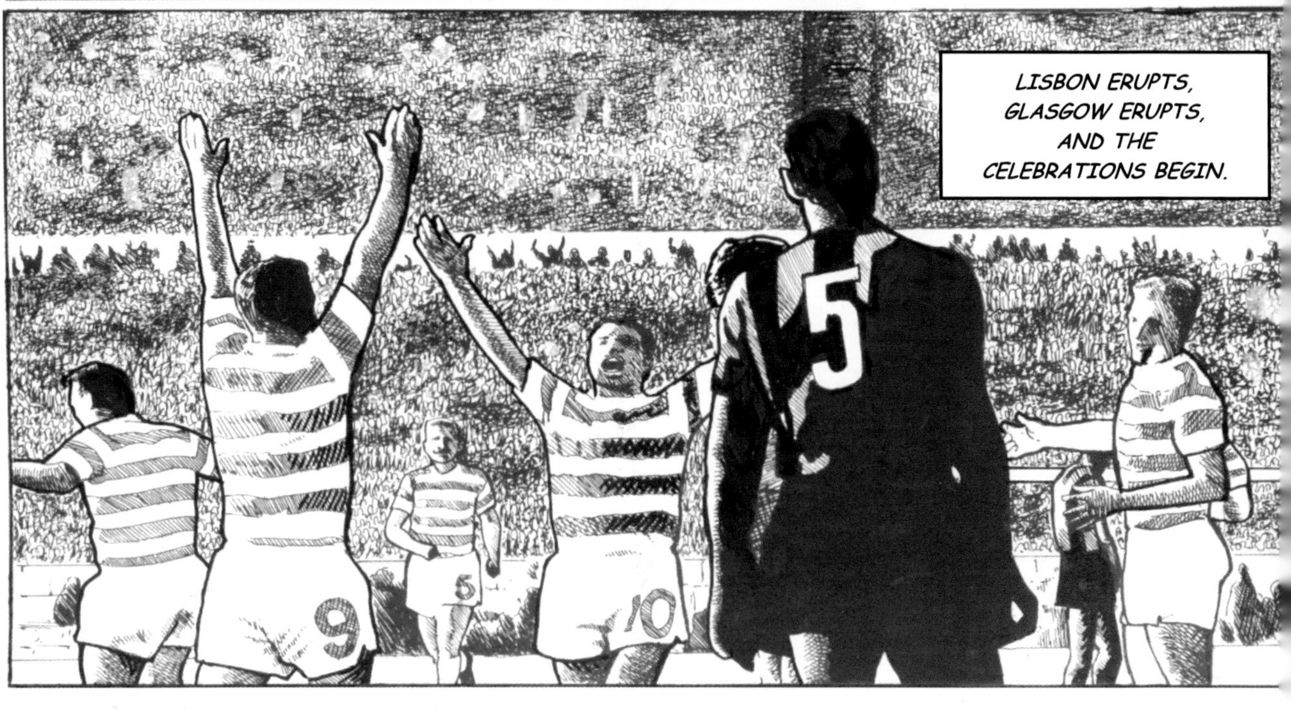
LISBON ERUPTS, GLASGOW ERUPTS, AND THE CELEBRATIONS BEGIN.

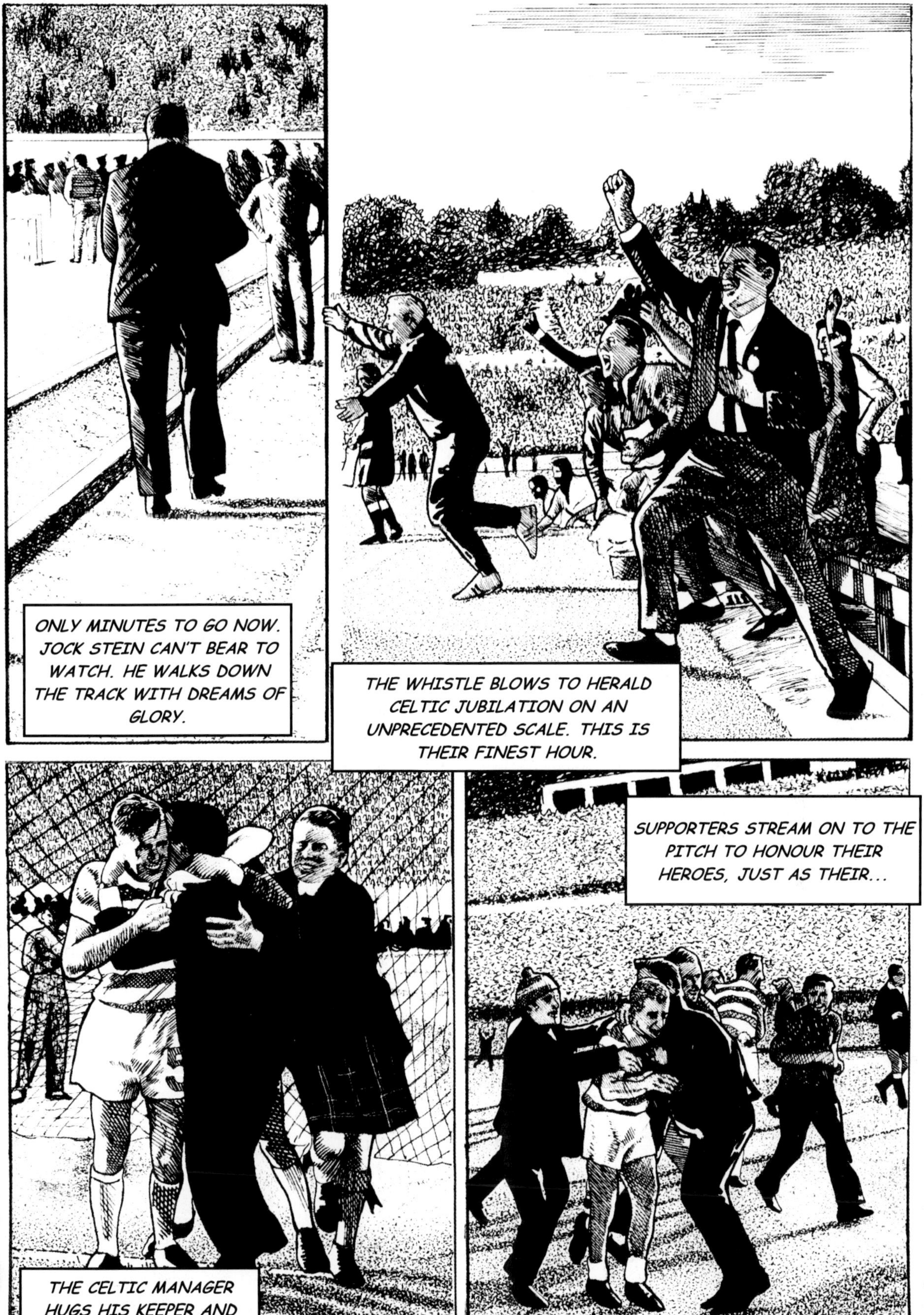
ONLY MINUTES TO GO NOW. JOCK STEIN CAN'T BEAR TO WATCH. HE WALKS DOWN THE TRACK WITH DREAMS OF GLORY.
THE WHISTLE BLOWS TO HERALD CELTIC JUBILATION ON AN UNPRECEDENTED SCALE. THIS IS THEIR FINEST HOUR.
THE CELTIC MANAGER HUGS HIS KEEPER AND CAPTAIN.
SUPPORTERS STREAM ON TO THE PITCH TO HONOUR THEIR HEROES, JUST AS THEIR...

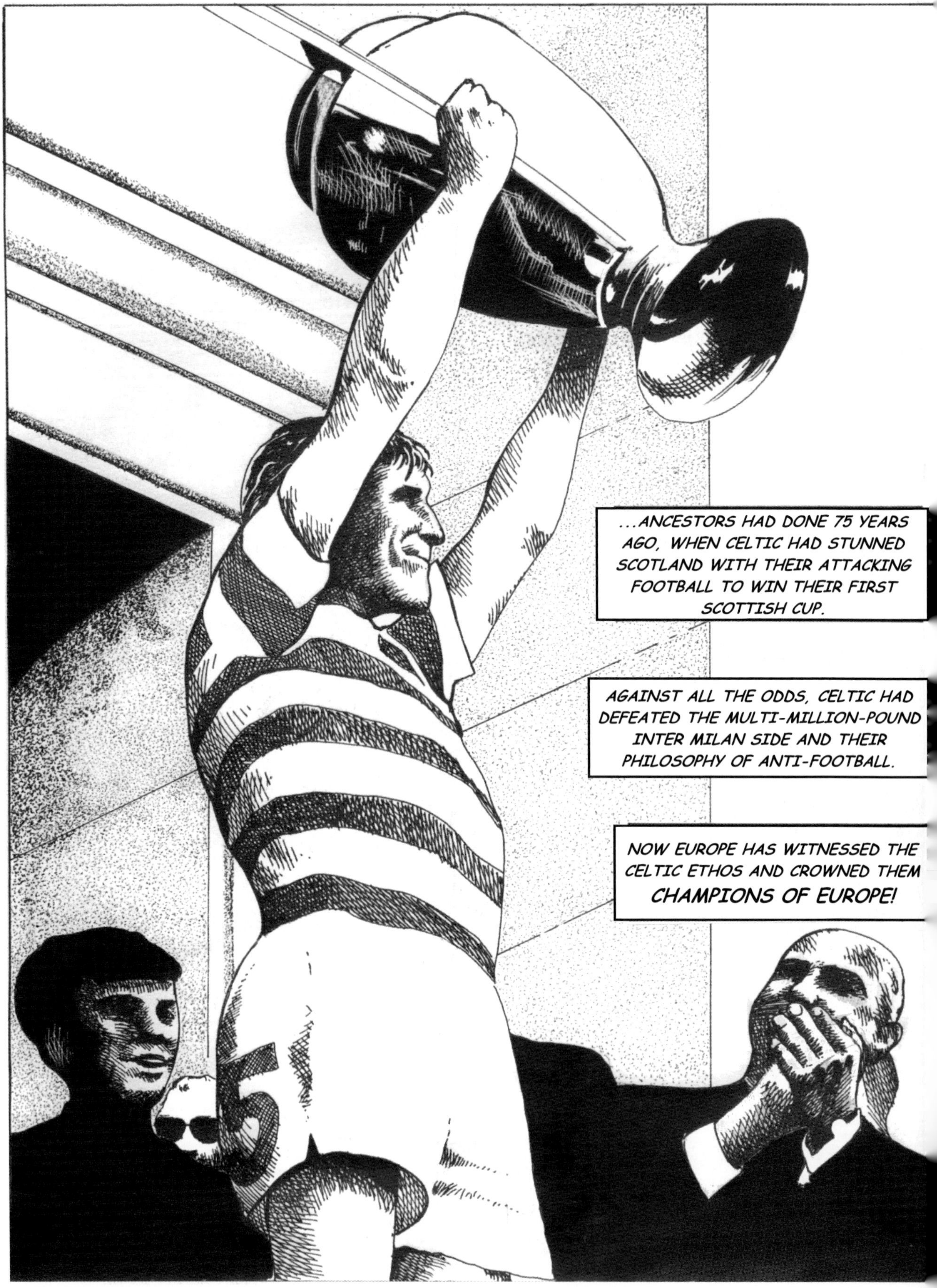
...ANCESTORS HAD DONE 75 YEARS AGO, WHEN CELTIC HAD STUNNED SCOTLAND WITH THEIR ATTACKING FOOTBALL TO WIN THEIR FIRST SCOTTISH CUP.
AGAINST ALL THE ODDS, CELTIC HAD DEFEATED THE MULTI-MILLION-POUND INTER MILAN SIDE AND THEIR PHILOSOPHY OF ANTI-FOOTBALL.
NOW EUROPE HAS WITNESSED THE CELTIC ETHOS AND CROWNED THEM CHAMPIONS OF EUROPE!

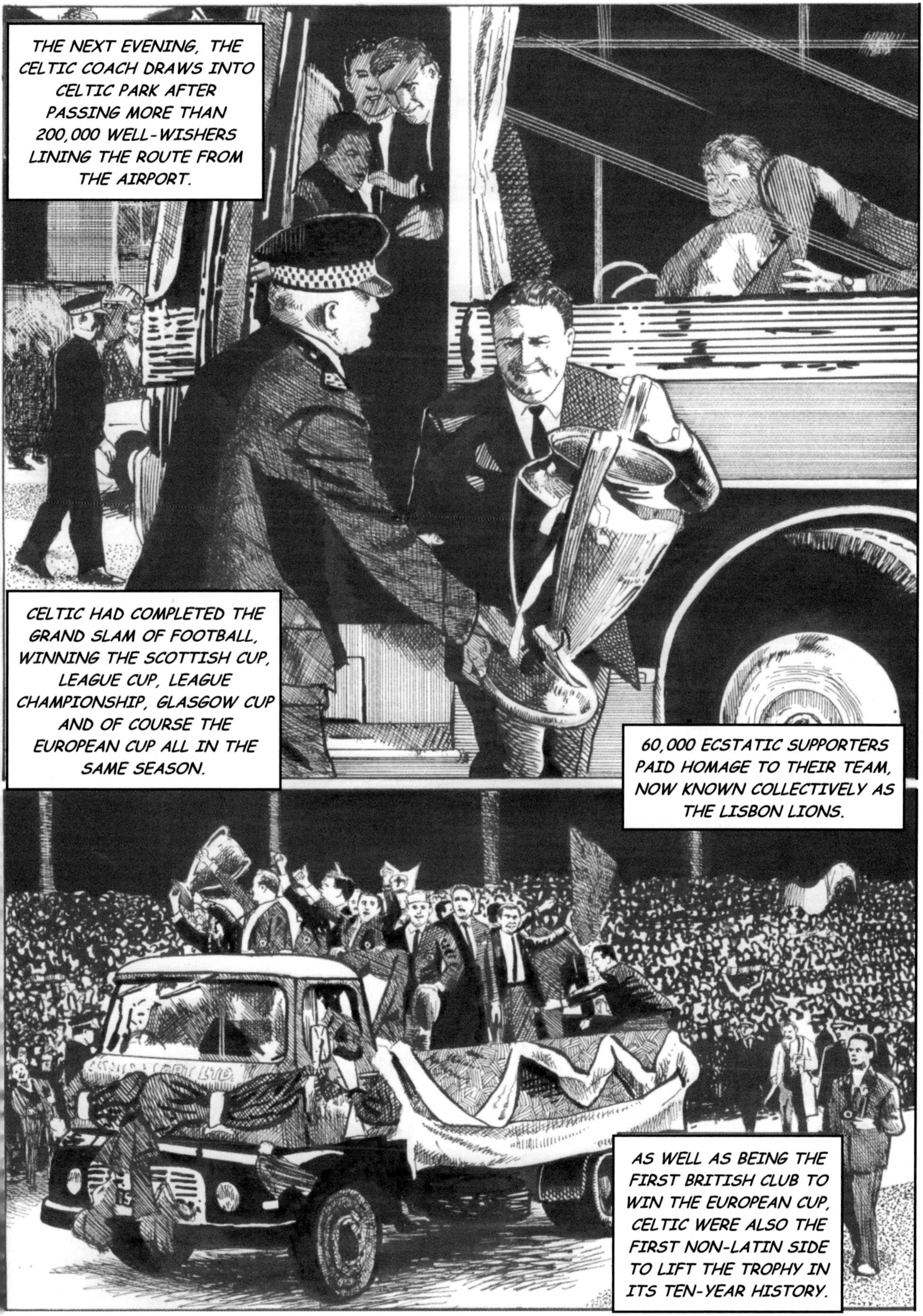
THE NEXT EVENING, THE CELTIC COACH DRAWS INTO CELTIC PARK AFTER PASSING MORE THAN 200,000 WELL-WISHERS LINING THE ROUTE FROM THE AIRPORT.
CELTIC HAD COMPLETED THE GRAND SLAM OF FOOTBALL, WINNING THE SCOTTISH CUP, LEAGUE CUP, LEAGUE CHAMPIONSHIP, GLASGOW CUP AND OF COURSE THE EUROPEAN CUP ALL IN THE SAME SEASON.
60,000 ECSTATIC SUPPORTERS PAID HOMAGE TO THEIR TEAM, NOW KNOWN COLLECTIVELY AS THE LISBON LIONS.
AS WELL AS BEING THE FIRST BRITISH CLUB TO WIN THE EUROPEAN CUP, CELTIC WERE ALSO THE FIRST NON-LATIN SIDE TO LIFT THE TROPHY IN ITS TEN-YEAR HISTORY.

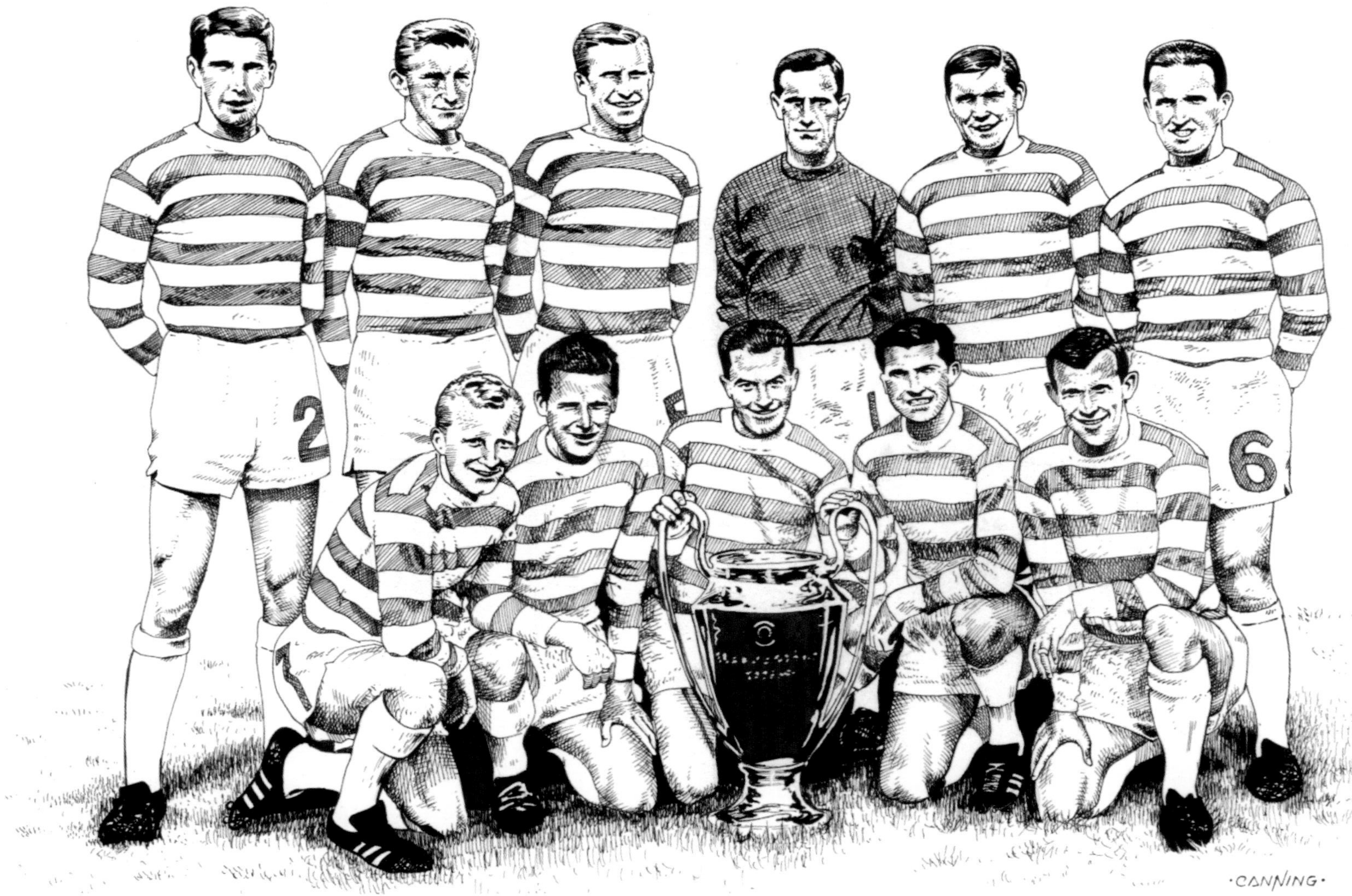
2
6
·CANNING·

THE LISBON LIONS

BACK ROW, L—R:

JIM CRAIG, TOMMY GEMMELL, BILLY McNEILL (CAPT), RONNIE SIMPSON, BOBBY MURDOCH, JOHN CLARK.

FRONT ROW, L—R:

JIMMY JOHNSTONE, WILLIE WALLACE, STEVIE CHALMERS, BERTIE AULD, BOBBY LENNOX.

chapter 6

another tilt at glory

'there's a golden sky'

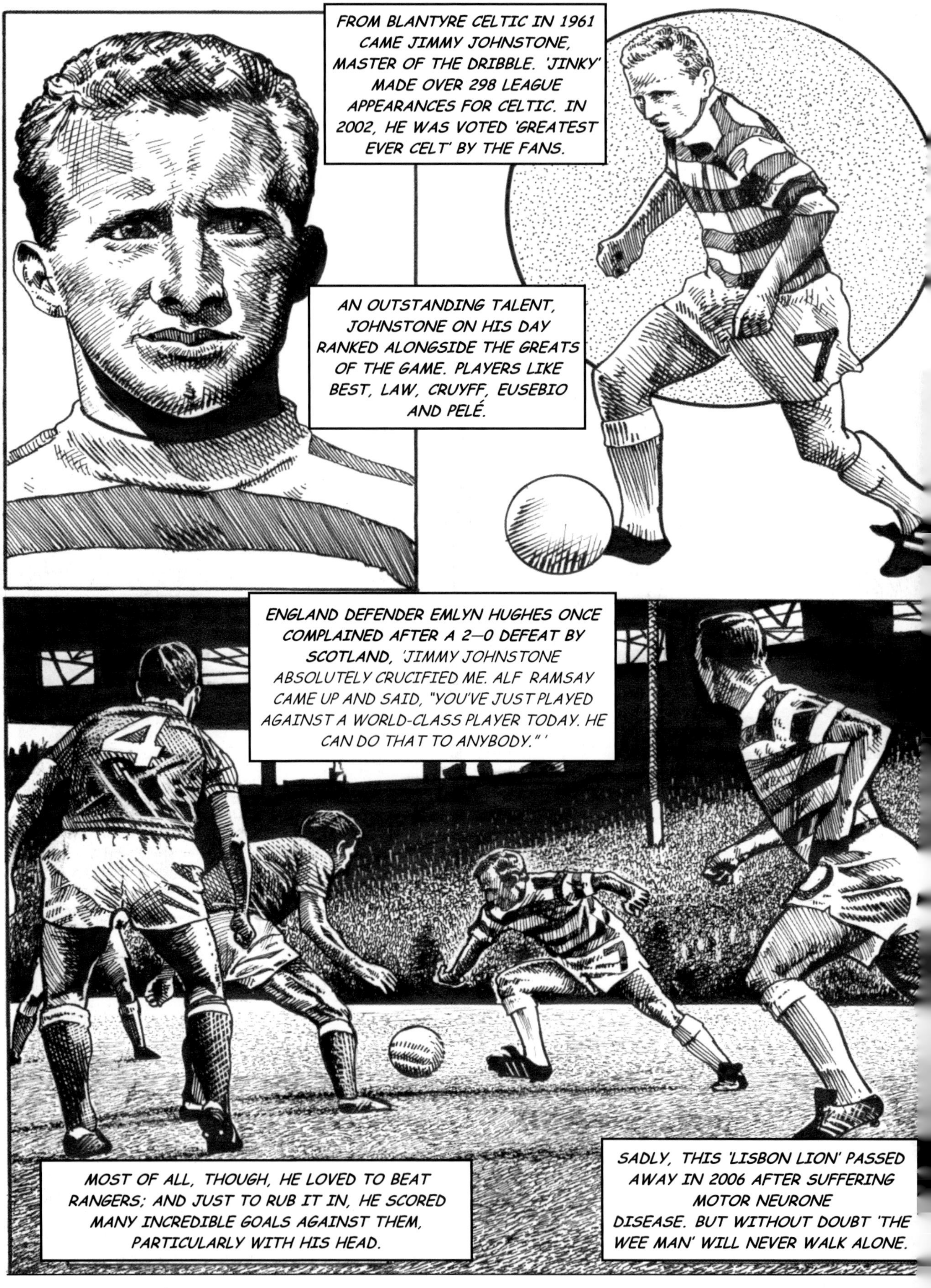
FROM BLANTYRE CELTIC IN 1961 CAME JIMMY JOHNSTONE, MASTER OF THE DRIBBLE. 'JINKY' MADE OVER 298 LEAGUE APPEARANCES FOR CELTIC. IN 2002, HE WAS VOTED 'GREATEST EVER CELT' BY THE FANS.
AN OUTSTANDING TALENT, JOHNSTONE ON HIS DAY RANKED ALONGSIDE THE GREATS OF THE GAME. PLAYERS LIKE BEST, LAW, CRUYFF, EUSEBIO AND PELÉ.
7
ENGLAND DEFENDER EMLYN HUGHES ONCE COMPLAINED AFTER A 2—0 DEFEAT BY SCOTLAND, 'JIMMY JOHNSTONE ABSOLUTELY CRUCIFIED ME. ALF RAMSAY CAME UP AND SAID, "YOU'VE JUST PLAYED AGAINST A WORLD-CLASS PLAYER TODAY. HE CAN DO THAT TO ANYBODY." '
4
7
MOST OF ALL, THOUGH, HE LOVED TO BEAT RANGERS; AND JUST TO RUB IT IN, HE SCORED MANY INCREDIBLE GOALS AGAINST THEM, PARTICULARLY WITH HIS HEAD.
SADLY, THIS 'LISBON LION' PASSED AWAY IN 2006 AFTER SUFFERING MOTOR NEURONE DISEASE. BUT WITHOUT DOUBT 'THE WEE MAN' WILL NEVER WALK ALONE.

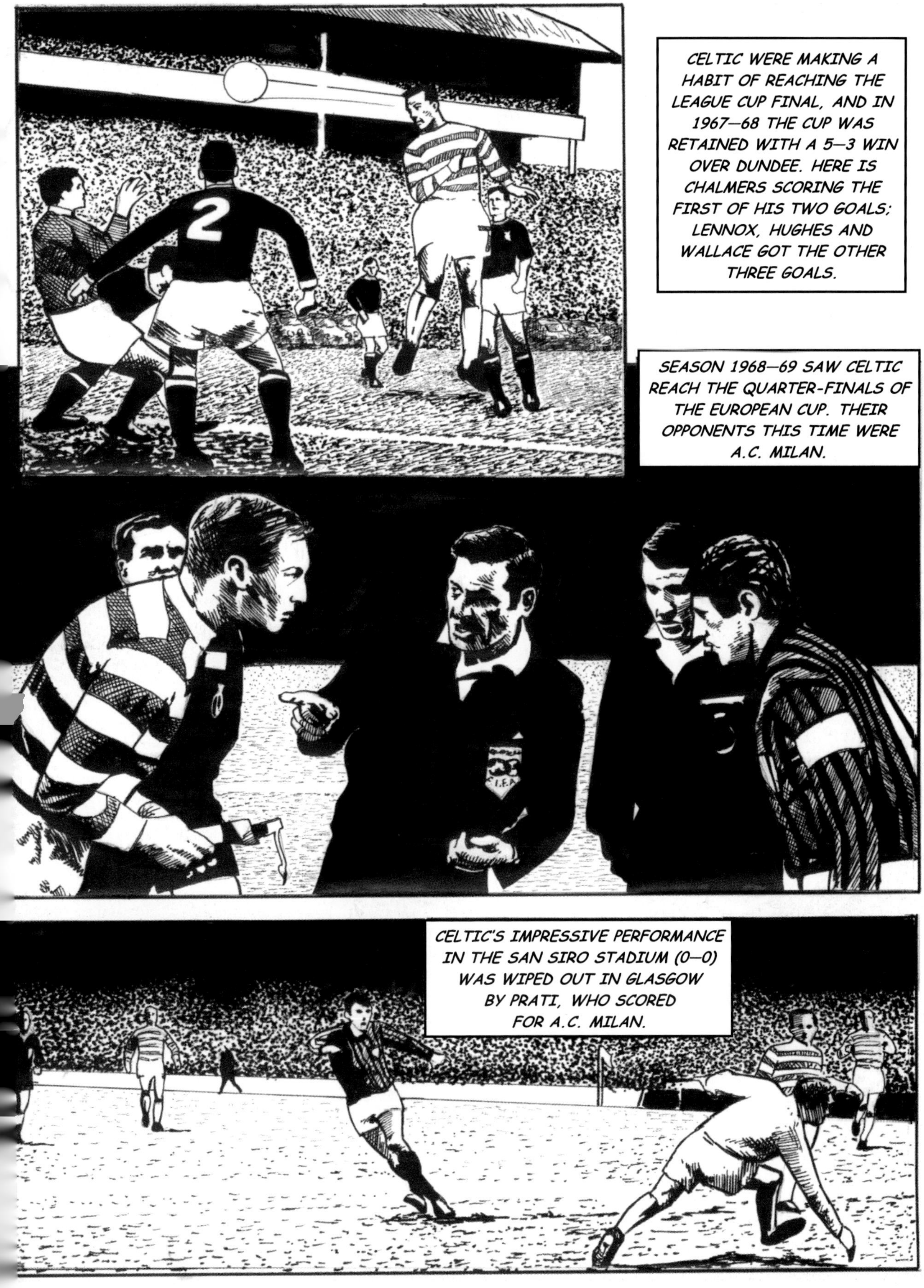
CELTIC WERE MAKING A HABIT OF REACHING THE LEAGUE CUP FINAL, AND IN 1967–68 THE CUP WAS RETAINED WITH A 5–3 WIN OVER DUNDEE. HERE IS CHALMERS SCORING THE FIRST OF HIS TWO GOALS; LENNOX, HUGHES AND WALLACE GOT THE OTHER THREE GOALS.
SEASON 1968–69 SAW CELTIC REACH THE QUARTER-FINALS OF THE EUROPEAN CUP. THEIR OPPONENTS THIS TIME WERE A.C. MILAN.
CELTIC'S IMPRESSIVE PERFORMANCE IN THE SAN SIRO STADIUM (0–0) WAS WIPED OUT IN GLASGOW BY PRATI, WHO SCORED FOR A.C. MILAN.

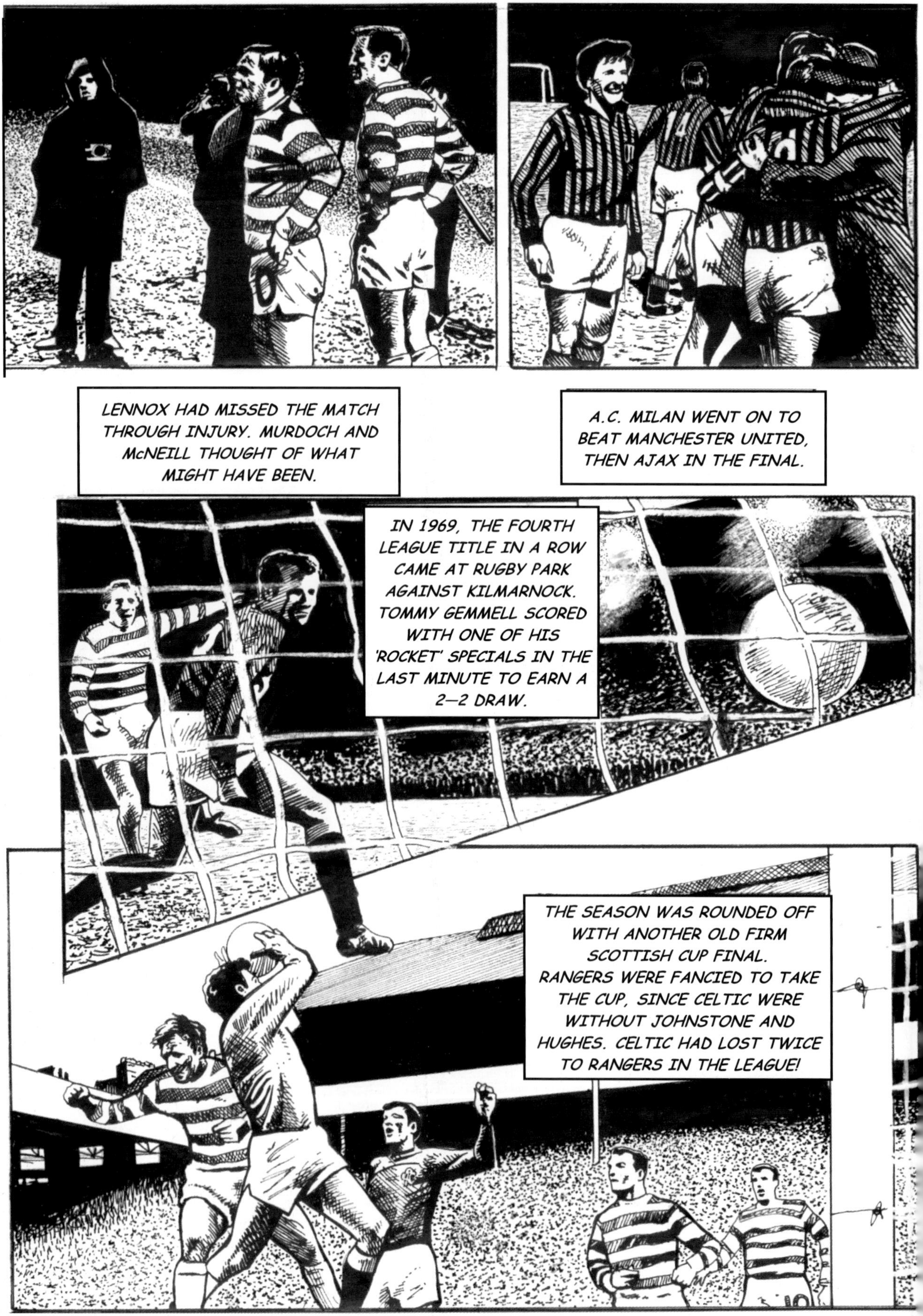
LENNOX HAD MISSED THE MATCH THROUGH INJURY. MURDOCH AND McNEILL THOUGHT OF WHAT MIGHT HAVE BEEN.
A.C. MILAN WENT ON TO BEAT MANCHESTER UNITED, THEN AJAX IN THE FINAL.
IN 1969, THE FOURTH LEAGUE TITLE IN A ROW CAME AT RUGBY PARK AGAINST KILMARNOCK. TOMMY GEMMELL SCORED WITH ONE OF HIS 'ROCKET' SPECIALS IN THE LAST MINUTE TO EARN A 2—2 DRAW.
THE SEASON WAS ROUNDED OFF WITH ANOTHER OLD FIRM SCOTTISH CUP FINAL. RANGERS WERE FANCIED TO TAKE THE CUP, SINCE CELTIC WERE WITHOUT JOHNSTONE AND HUGHES. CELTIC HAD LOST TWICE TO RANGERS IN THE LEAGUE!

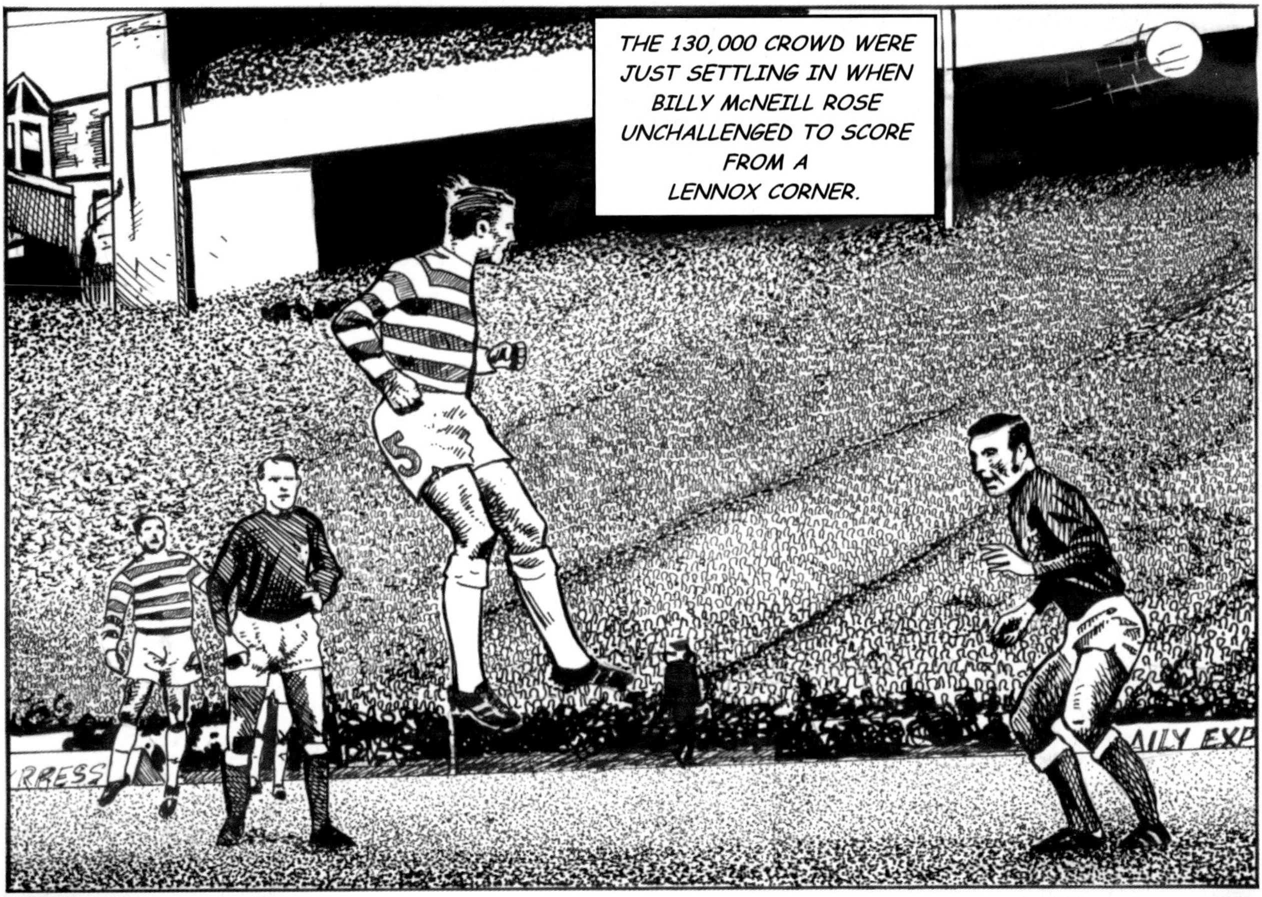
THE 130,000 CROWD WERE JUST SETTLING IN WHEN BILLY McNEILL ROSE UNCHALLENGED TO SCORE FROM A LENNOX CORNER.

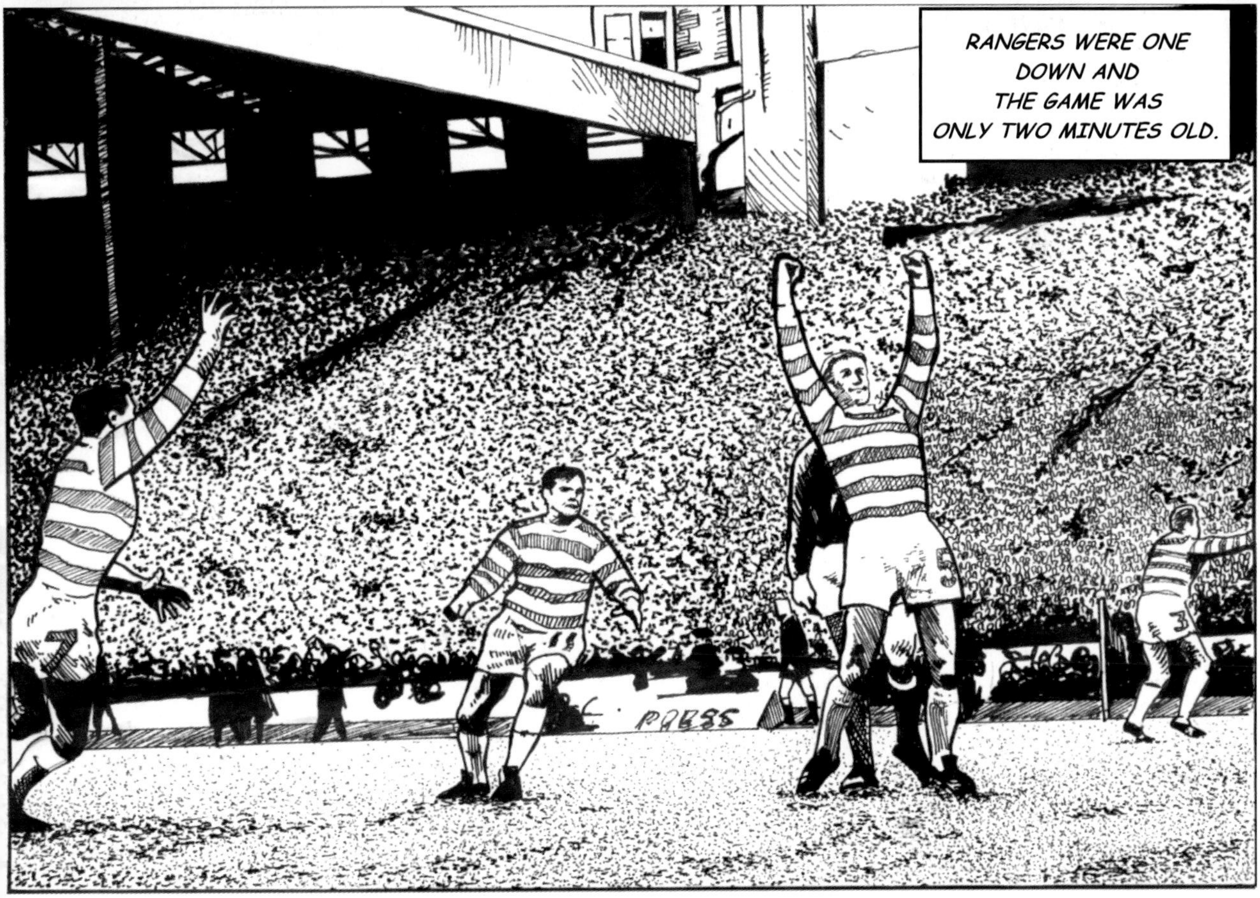
RANGERS WERE ONE DOWN AND THE GAME WAS ONLY TWO MINUTES OLD.

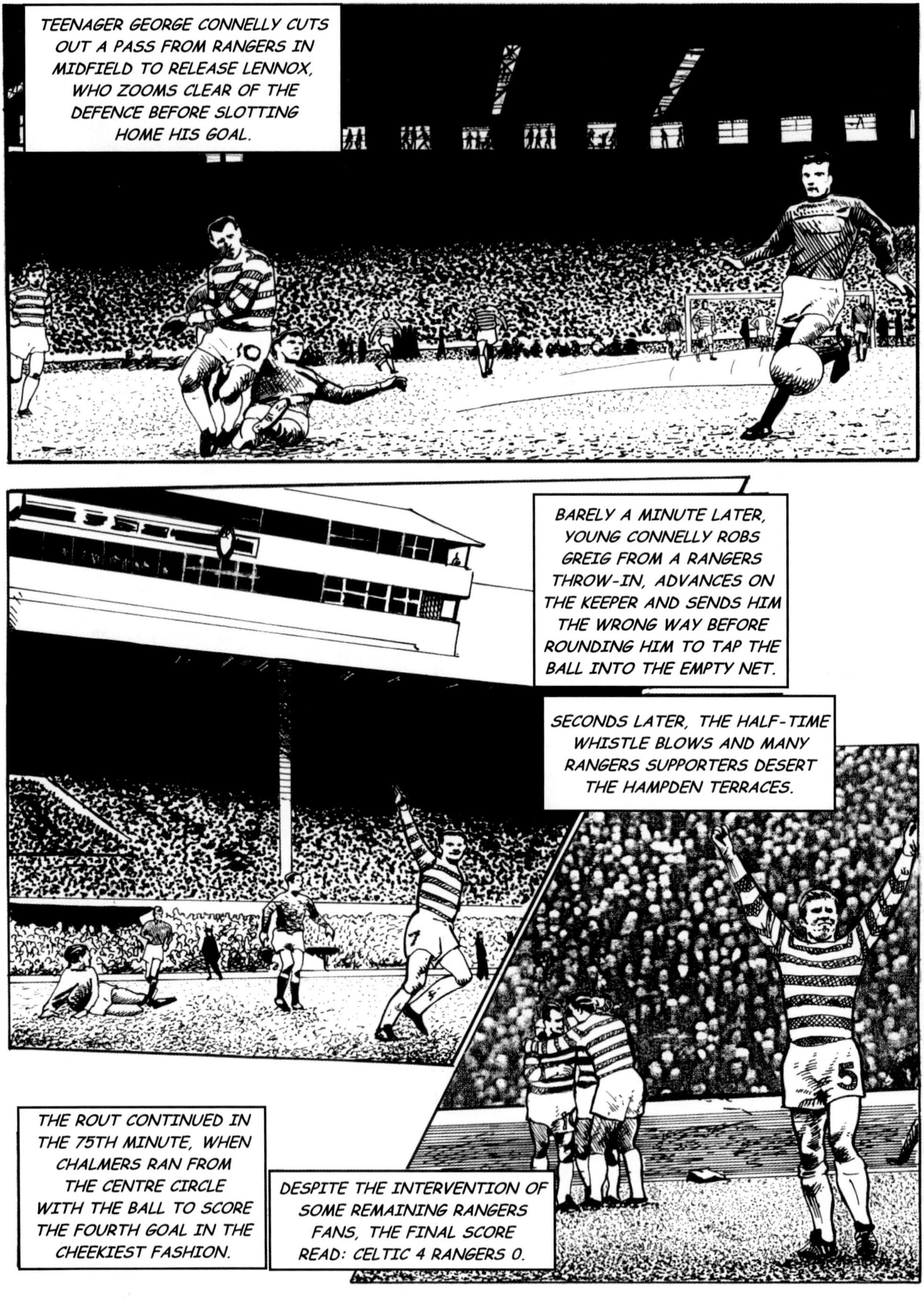
TEENAGER GEORGE CONNELLY CUTS OUT A PASS FROM RANGERS IN MIDFIELD TO RELEASE LENNOX, WHO ZOOMS CLEAR OF THE DEFENCE BEFORE SLOTTING HOME HIS GOAL.
BARELY A MINUTE LATER, YOUNG CONNELLY ROBS GREIG FROM A RANGERS THROW-IN, ADVANCES ON THE KEEPER AND SENDS HIM THE WRONG WAY BEFORE ROUNDING HIM TO TAP THE BALL INTO THE EMPTY NET.
SECONDS LATER, THE HALF-TIME WHISTLE BLOWS AND MANY RANGERS SUPPORTERS DESERT THE HAMPDEN TERRACES.
THE ROUT CONTINUED IN THE 75TH MINUTE, WHEN CHALMERS RAN FROM THE CENTRE CIRCLE WITH THE BALL TO SCORE THE FOURTH GOAL IN THE CHEEKIEST FASHION.
DESPITE THE INTERVENTION OF SOME REMAINING RANGERS FANS, THE FINAL SCORE READ: CELTIC 4 RANGERS 0.

1969 SAW THE RETIREMENT OF 'FAITHER' RONNIE SIMPSON. A RECURRING SHOULDER INJURY WAS SUSTAINED IN THE LEAGUE CUP SEMI-FINAL AGAINST AYR UNITED.

EVAN WILLIAMS SIGNED FROM WOLVES AND TOOK OVER FROM RONNIE SIMPSON IN GOAL.

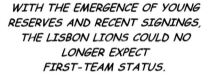

WITH THE EMERGENCE OF YOUNG RESERVES AND RECENT SIGNINGS, THE LISBON LIONS COULD NO LONGER EXPECT FIRST-TEAM STATUS.

THE VERSATILE HARRY HOOD SIGNED FROM CLYDE.

SKILFUL TOMMY CALLAGHAN SIGNED FROM DUNFERMLINE.

JIM BROGAN WAS A FINE LINK MAN FROM THE RESERVES.

GEORGE CONNELLY FROM THE RESERVES. IN MIDFIELD OR DEFENCE, HIS CLASS ALWAYS SHOWED.

DAVID HAY, AKA 'THE QUIET ASSASSIN', COULD FILL ANY POSITION IN MIDFIELD OR DEFENCE.

LOU MACARI, THE BUZZ BOMB OF THE FORWARD LINE.

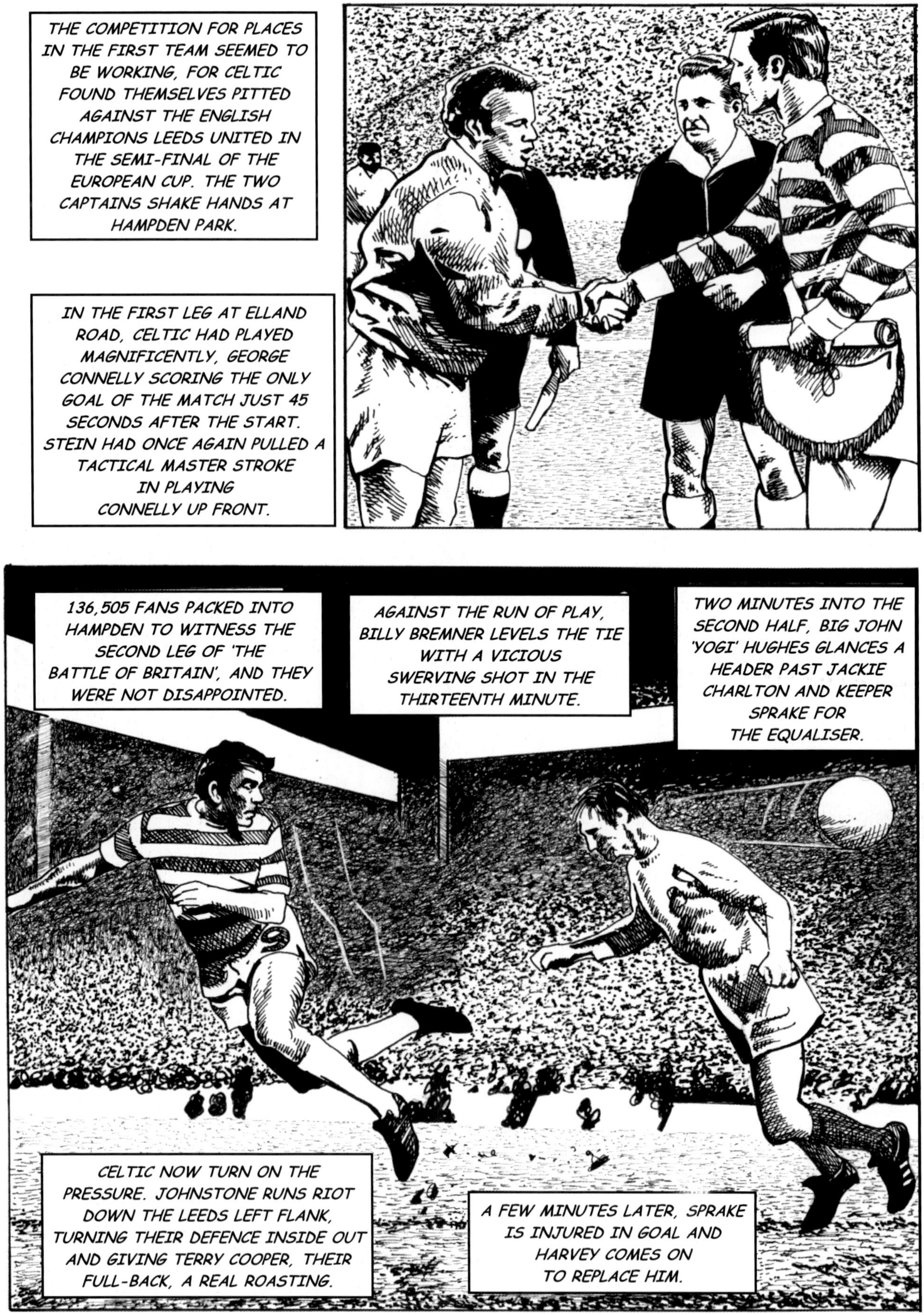
THE COMPETITION FOR PLACES IN THE FIRST TEAM SEEMED TO BE WORKING, FOR CELTIC FOUND THEMSELVES PITTED AGAINST THE ENGLISH CHAMPIONS LEEDS UNITED IN THE SEMI-FINAL OF THE EUROPEAN CUP. THE TWO CAPTAINS SHAKE HANDS AT HAMPDEN PARK.
IN THE FIRST LEG AT ELLAND ROAD, CELTIC HAD PLAYED MAGNIFICENTLY, GEORGE CONNELLY SCORING THE ONLY GOAL OF THE MATCH JUST 45 SECONDS AFTER THE START. STEIN HAD ONCE AGAIN PULLED A TACTICAL MASTER STROKE IN PLAYING CONNELLY UP FRONT.
136,505 FANS PACKED INTO HAMPDEN TO WITNESS THE SECOND LEG OF 'THE BATTLE OF BRITAIN', AND THEY WERE NOT DISAPPOINTED.
AGAINST THE RUN OF PLAY, BILLY BREMNER LEVELS THE TIE WITH A VICIOUS SWERVING SHOT IN THE THIRTEENTH MINUTE.
TWO MINUTES INTO THE SECOND HALF, BIG JOHN 'YOGI' HUGHES GLANCES A HEADER PAST JACKIE CHARLTON AND KEEPER SPRAKE FOR THE EQUALISER.
CELTIC NOW TURN ON THE PRESSURE. JOHNSTONE RUNS RIOT DOWN THE LEEDS LEFT FLANK, TURNING THEIR DEFENCE INSIDE OUT AND GIVING TERRY COOPER, THEIR FULL-BACK, A REAL ROASTING.
A FEW MINUTES LATER, SPRAKE IS INJURED IN GOAL AND HARVEY COMES ON TO REPLACE HIM.

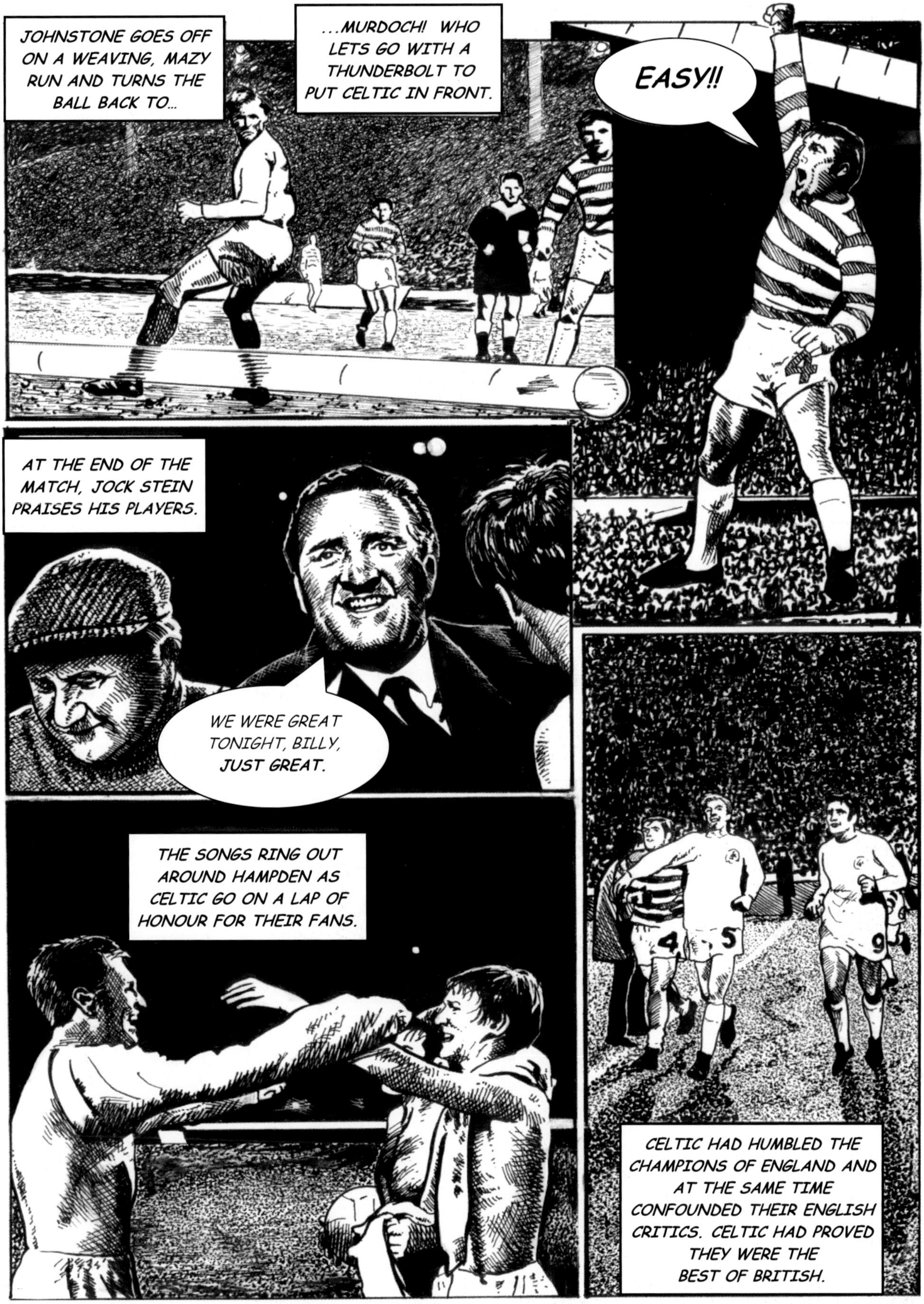

JOHNSTONE GOES OFF ON A WEAVING, MAZY RUN AND TURNS THE BALL BACK TO...
...MURDOCH! WHO LETS GO WITH A THUNDERBOLT TO PUT CELTIC IN FRONT.
EASY!!
AT THE END OF THE MATCH, JOCK STEIN PRAISES HIS PLAYERS.
WE WERE GREAT TONIGHT, BILLY, JUST GREAT.
THE SONGS RING OUT AROUND HAMPDEN AS CELTIC GO ON A LAP OF HONOUR FOR THEIR FANS.
CELTIC HAD HUMBLED THE CHAMPIONS OF ENGLAND AND AT THE SAME TIME CONFOUNDED THEIR ENGLISH CRITICS. CELTIC HAD PROVED THEY WERE THE BEST OF BRITISH.

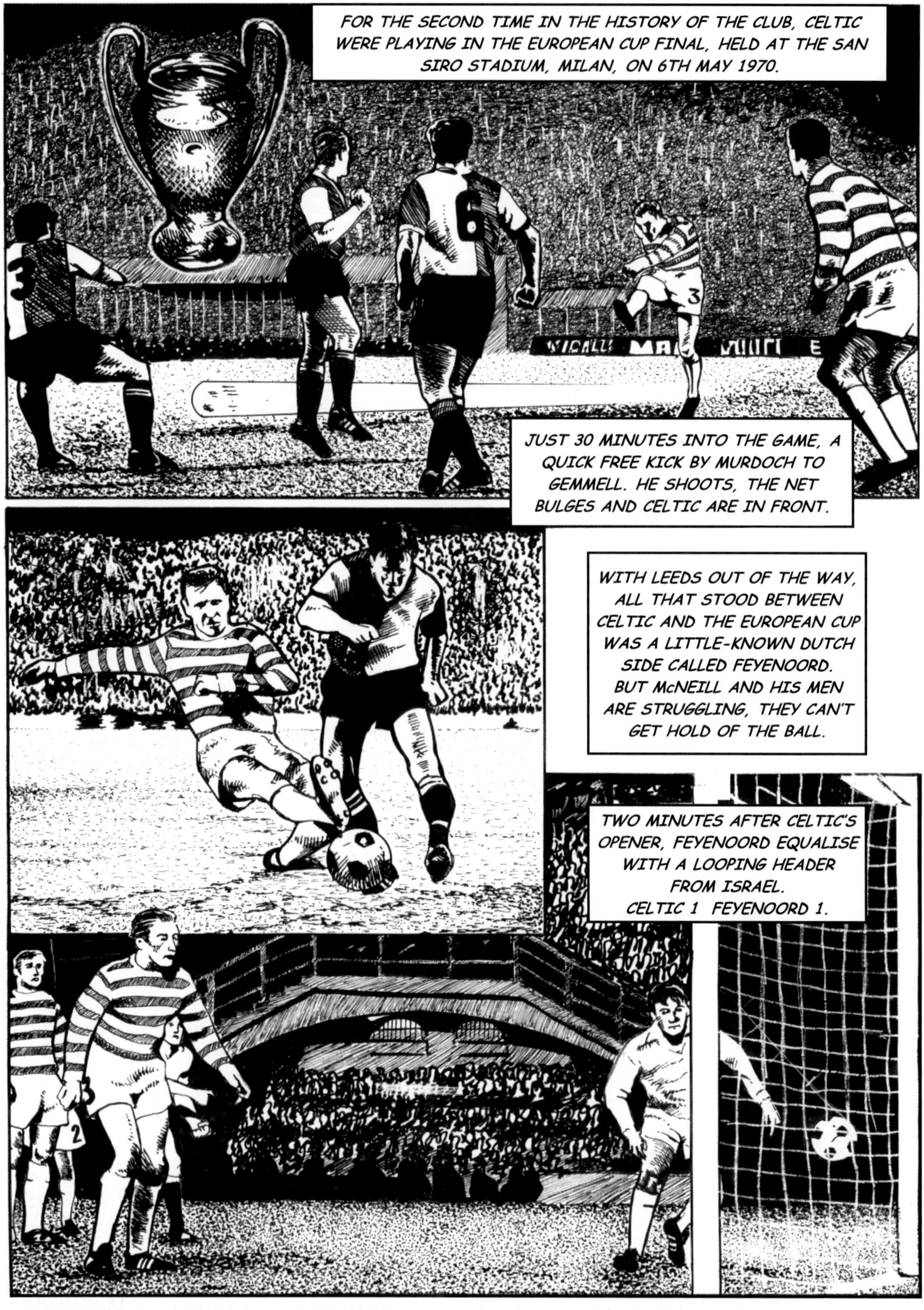
FOR THE SECOND TIME IN THE HISTORY OF THE CLUB, CELTIC WERE PLAYING IN THE EUROPEAN CUP FINAL, HELD AT THE SAN SIRO STADIUM, MILAN, ON 6TH MAY 1970.
JUST 30 MINUTES INTO THE GAME, A QUICK FREE KICK BY MURDOCH TO GEMMELL. HE SHOOTS, THE NET BULGES AND CELTIC ARE IN FRONT.
WITH LEEDS OUT OF THE WAY, ALL THAT STOOD BETWEEN CELTIC AND THE EUROPEAN CUP WAS A LITTLE-KNOWN DUTCH SIDE CALLED FEYENOORD. BUT McNEILL AND HIS MEN ARE STRUGGLING, THEY CAN'T GET HOLD OF THE BALL.
TWO MINUTES AFTER CELTIC'S OPENER, FEYENOORD EQUALISE WITH A LOOPING HEADER FROM ISRAEL.
CELTIC 1 FEYENOORD 1.

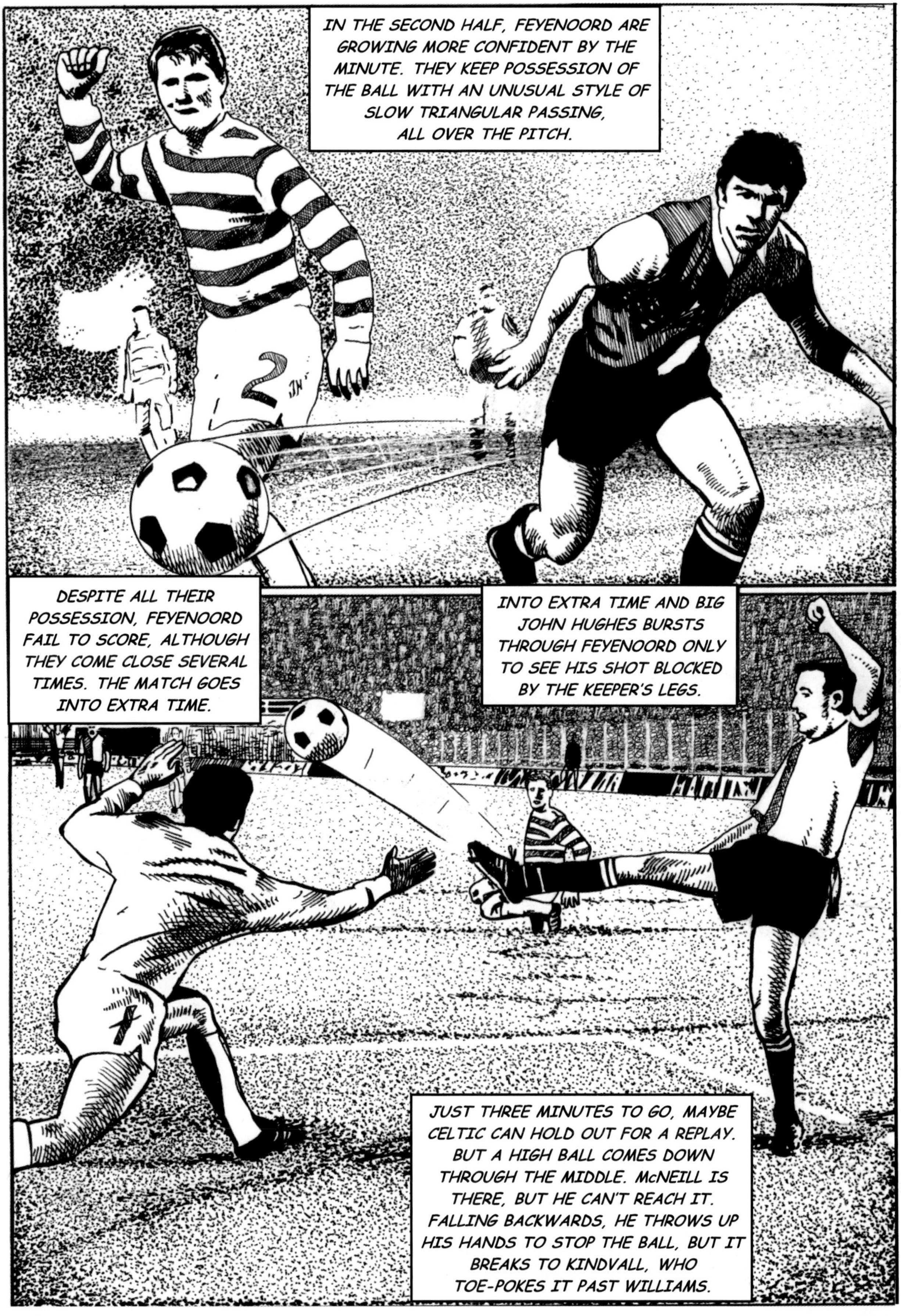
IN THE SECOND HALF, FEYENOORD ARE GROWING MORE CONFIDENT BY THE MINUTE. THEY KEEP POSSESSION OF THE BALL WITH AN UNUSUAL STYLE OF SLOW TRIANGULAR PASSING, ALL OVER THE PITCH.
DESPITE ALL THEIR POSSESSION, FEYENOORD FAIL TO SCORE, ALTHOUGH THEY COME CLOSE SEVERAL TIMES. THE MATCH GOES INTO EXTRA TIME.
INTO EXTRA TIME AND BIG JOHN HUGHES BURSTS THROUGH FEYENOORD ONLY TO SEE HIS SHOT BLOCKED BY THE KEEPER'S LEGS.
JUST THREE MINUTES TO GO, MAYBE CELTIC CAN HOLD OUT FOR A REPLAY. BUT A HIGH BALL COMES DOWN THROUGH THE MIDDLE. McNEILL IS THERE, BUT HE CAN'T REACH IT. FALLING BACKWARDS, HE THROWS UP HIS HANDS TO STOP THE BALL, BUT IT BREAKS TO KINDVALL, WHO TOE-POKES IT PAST WILLIAMS.

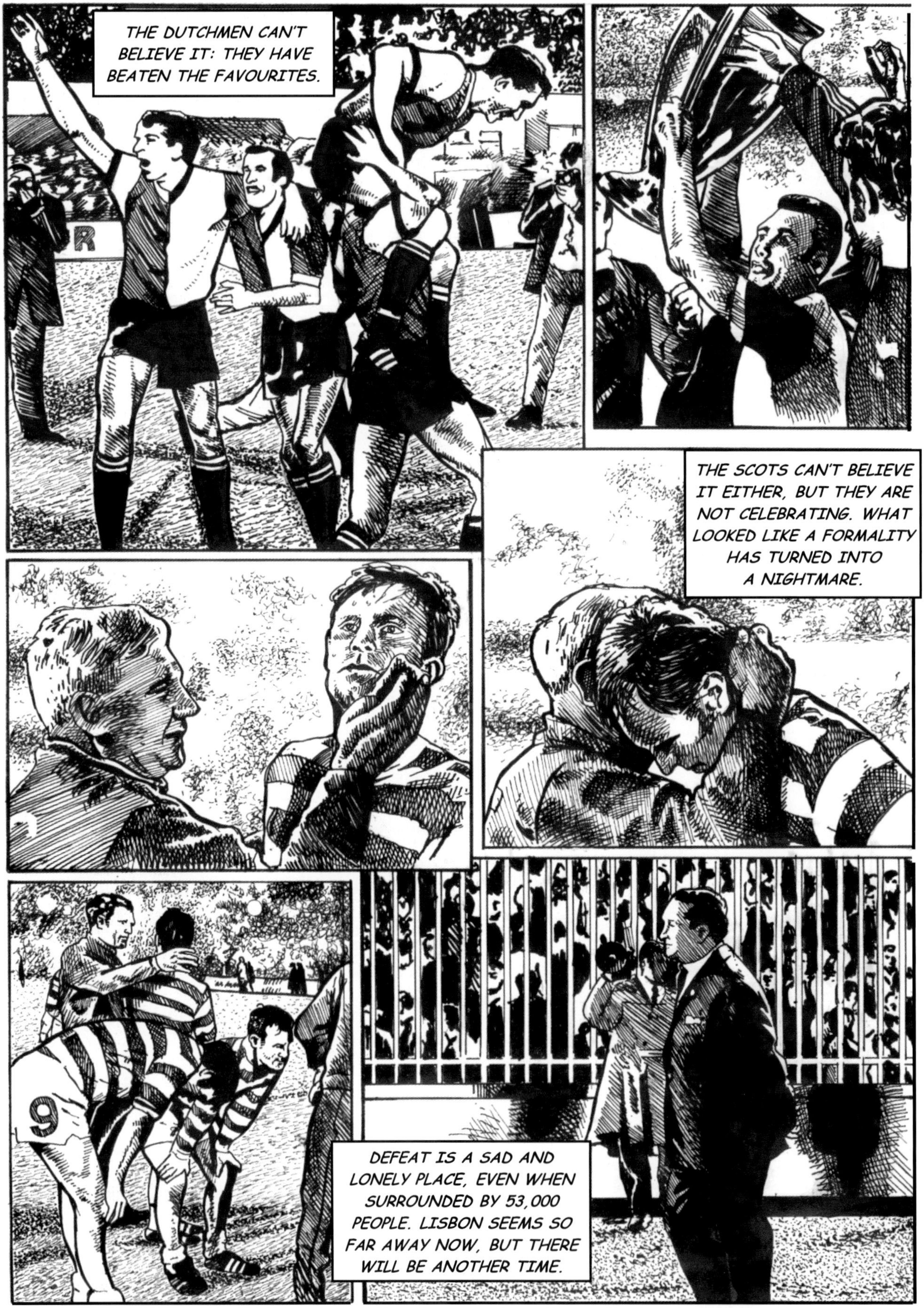
THE DUTCHMEN CAN'T BELIEVE IT: THEY HAVE BEATEN THE FAVOURITES.
THE SCOTS CAN'T BELIEVE IT EITHER, BUT THEY ARE NOT CELEBRATING. WHAT LOOKED LIKE A FORMALITY HAS TURNED INTO A NIGHTMARE.
DEFEAT IS A SAD AND LONELY PLACE, EVEN WHEN SURROUNDED BY 53,000 PEOPLE. LISBON SEEMS SO FAR AWAY NOW, BUT THERE WILL BE ANOTHER TIME.

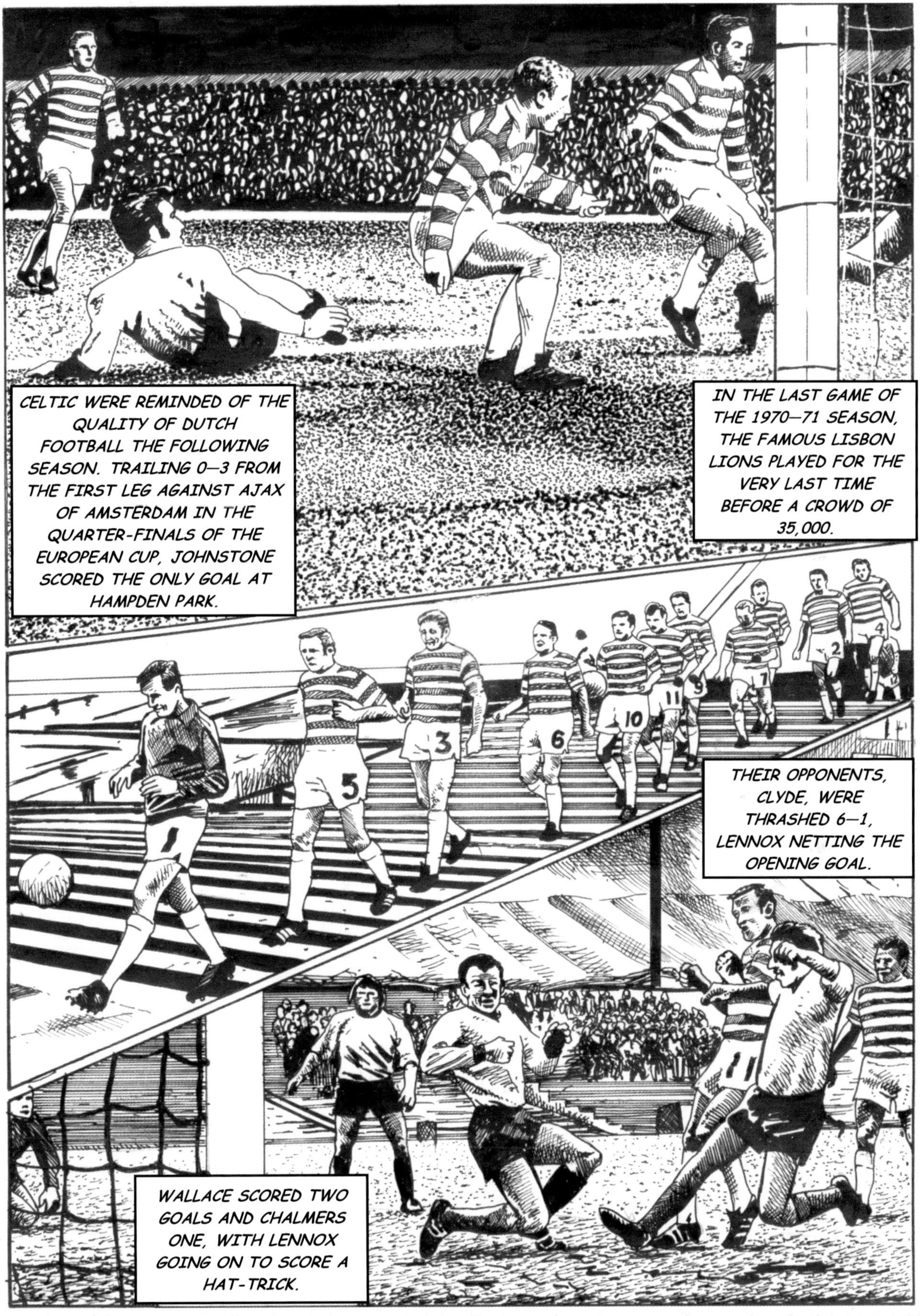
CELTIC WERE REMINDED OF THE QUALITY OF DUTCH FOOTBALL THE FOLLOWING SEASON. TRAILING 0—3 FROM THE FIRST LEG AGAINST AJAX OF AMSTERDAM IN THE QUARTER-FINALS OF THE EUROPEAN CUP, JOHNSTONE SCORED THE ONLY GOAL AT HAMPDEN PARK.
IN THE LAST GAME OF THE 1970—71 SEASON, THE FAMOUS LISBON LIONS PLAYED FOR THE VERY LAST TIME BEFORE A CROWD OF 35,000.
THEIR OPPONENTS, CLYDE, WERE THRASHED 6—1, LENNOX NETTING THE OPENING GOAL.
WALLACE SCORED TWO GOALS AND CHALMERS ONE, WITH LENNOX GOING ON TO SCORE A HAT-TRICK.

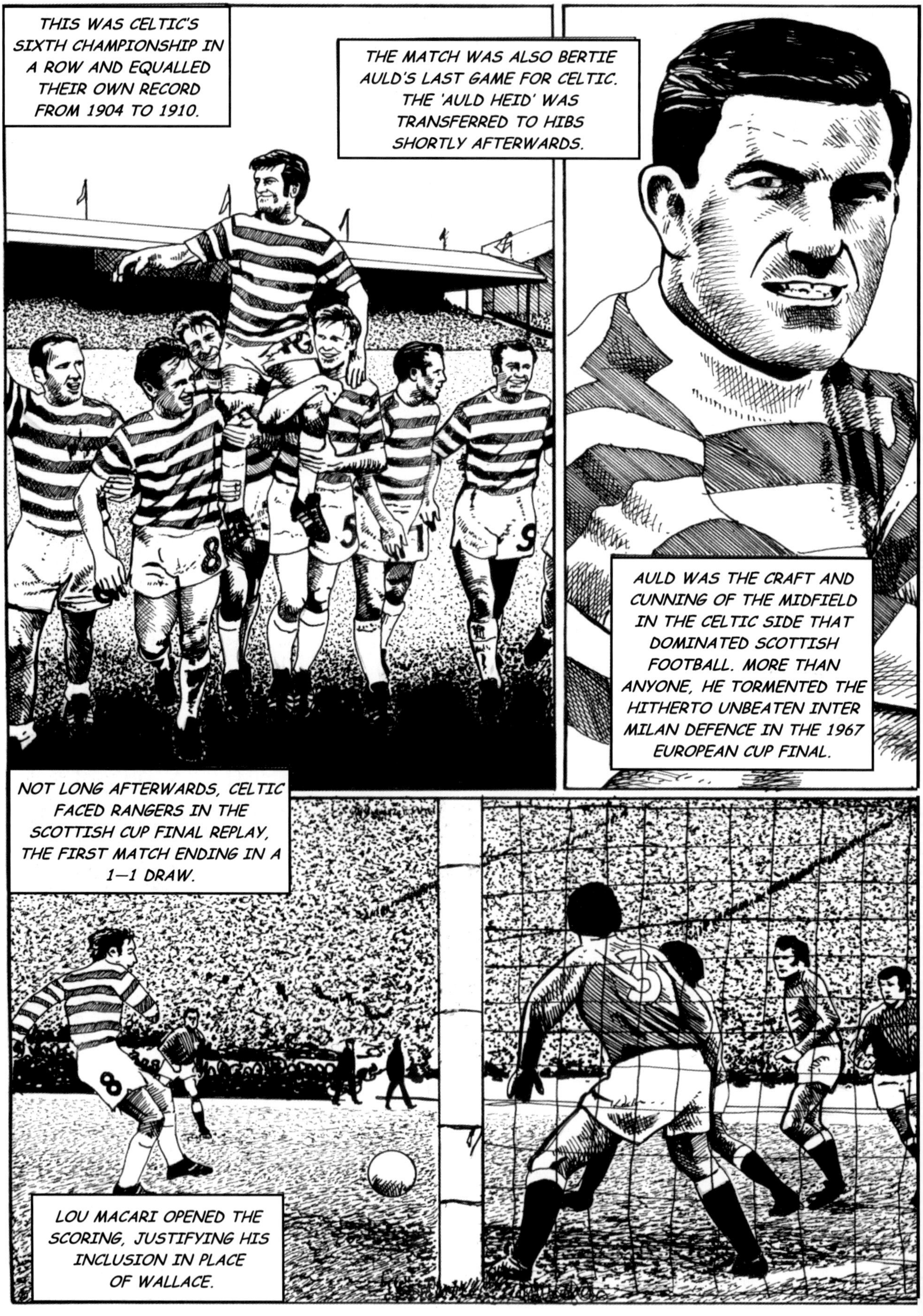
THIS WAS CELTIC'S SIXTH CHAMPIONSHIP IN A ROW AND EQUALLED THEIR OWN RECORD FROM 1904 TO 1910.
THE MATCH WAS ALSO BERTIE AULD'S LAST GAME FOR CELTIC. THE 'AULD HEID' WAS TRANSFERRED TO HIBS SHORTLY AFTERWARDS.
AULD WAS THE CRAFT AND CUNNING OF THE MIDFIELD IN THE CELTIC SIDE THAT DOMINATED SCOTTISH FOOTBALL. MORE THAN ANYONE, HE TORMENTED THE HITHERTO UNBEATEN INTER MILAN DEFENCE IN THE 1967 EUROPEAN CUP FINAL.
NOT LONG AFTERWARDS, CELTIC FACED RANGERS IN THE SCOTTISH CUP FINAL REPLAY, THE FIRST MATCH ENDING IN A 1—1 DRAW.
LOU MACARI OPENED THE SCORING, JUSTIFYING HIS INCLUSION IN PLACE OF WALLACE.

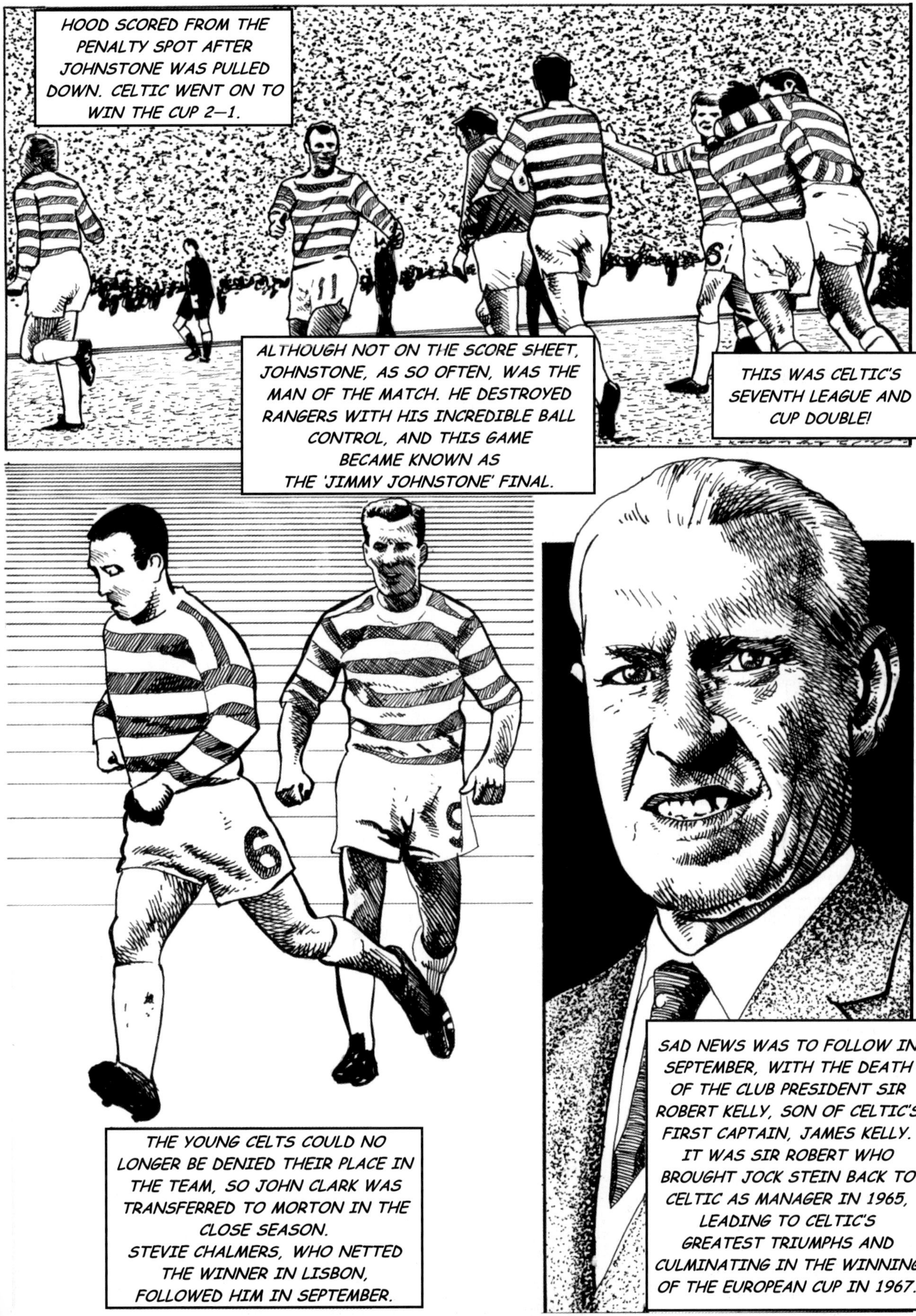
HOOD SCORED FROM THE PENALTY SPOT AFTER JOHNSTONE WAS PULLED DOWN. CELTIC WENT ON TO WIN THE CUP 2–1.
ALTHOUGH NOT ON THE SCORE SHEET, JOHNSTONE, AS SO OFTEN, WAS THE MAN OF THE MATCH. HE DESTROYED RANGERS WITH HIS INCREDIBLE BALL CONTROL, AND THIS GAME BECAME KNOWN AS THE 'JIMMY JOHNSTONE' FINAL.
THIS WAS CELTIC'S SEVENTH LEAGUE AND CUP DOUBLE!
THE YOUNG CELTS COULD NO LONGER BE DENIED THEIR PLACE IN THE TEAM, SO JOHN CLARK WAS TRANSFERRED TO MORTON IN THE CLOSE SEASON. STEVIE CHALMERS, WHO NETTED THE WINNER IN LISBON, FOLLOWED HIM IN SEPTEMBER.
SAD NEWS WAS TO FOLLOW IN SEPTEMBER, WITH THE DEATH OF THE CLUB PRESIDENT SIR ROBERT KELLY, SON OF CELTIC'S FIRST CAPTAIN, JAMES KELLY. IT WAS SIR ROBERT WHO BROUGHT JOCK STEIN BACK TO CELTIC AS MANAGER IN 1965, LEADING TO CELTIC'S GREATEST TRIUMPHS AND CULMINATING IN THE WINNING OF THE EUROPEAN CUP IN 1967.

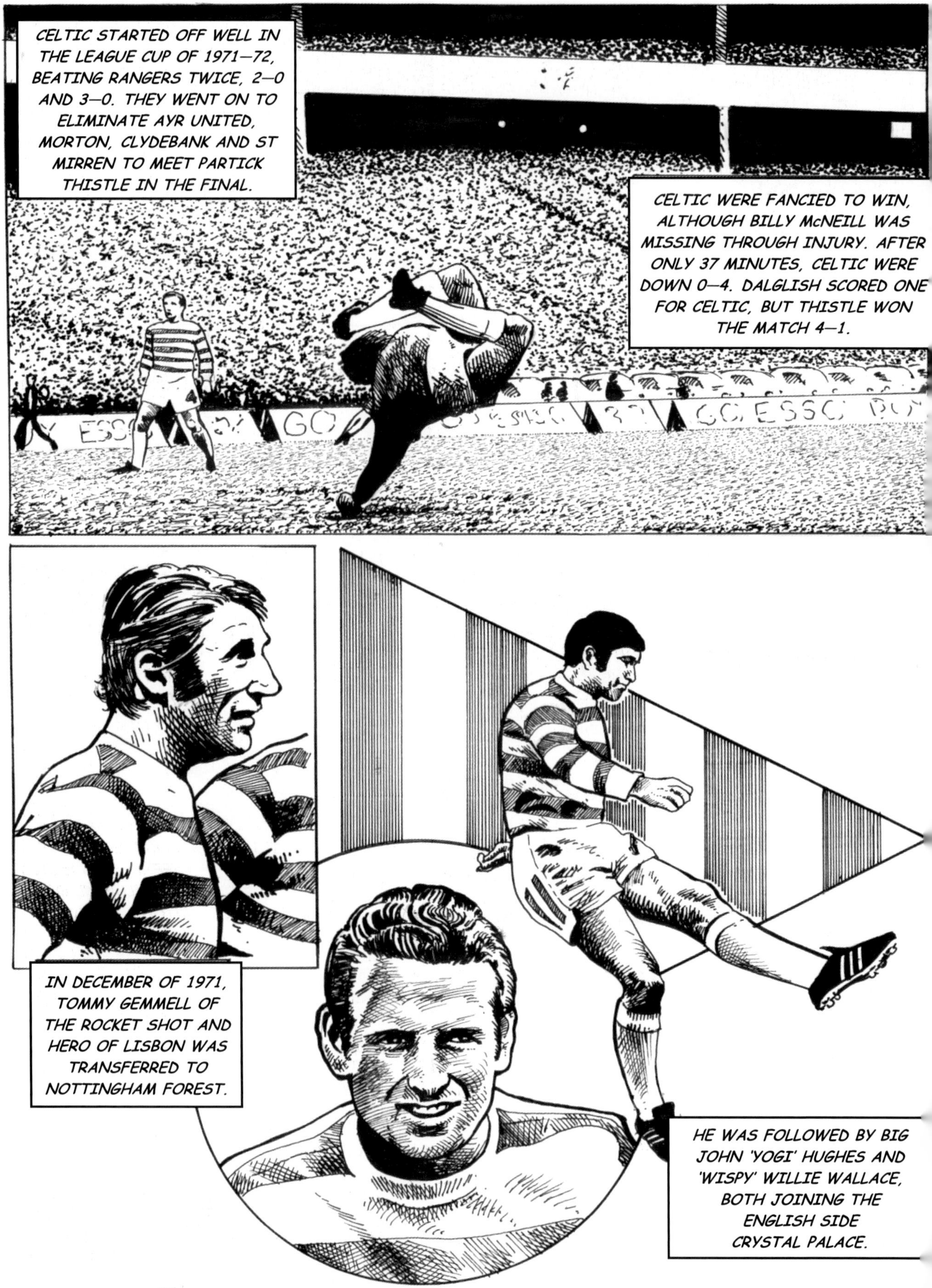
CELTIC STARTED OFF WELL IN THE LEAGUE CUP OF 1971–72, BEATING RANGERS TWICE, 2–0 AND 3–0. THEY WENT ON TO ELIMINATE AYR UNITED, MORTON, CLYDEBANK AND ST MIRREN TO MEET PARTICK THISTLE IN THE FINAL.
CELTIC WERE FANCIED TO WIN, ALTHOUGH BILLY McNEILL WAS MISSING THROUGH INJURY. AFTER ONLY 37 MINUTES, CELTIC WERE DOWN 0–4. DALGLISH SCORED ONE FOR CELTIC, BUT THISTLE WON THE MATCH 4–1.
IN DECEMBER OF 1971, TOMMY GEMMELL OF THE ROCKET SHOT AND HERO OF LISBON WAS TRANSFERRED TO NOTTINGHAM FOREST.
HE WAS FOLLOWED BY BIG JOHN 'YOGI' HUGHES AND 'WISPY' WILLIE WALLACE, BOTH JOINING THE ENGLISH SIDE CRYSTAL PALACE.

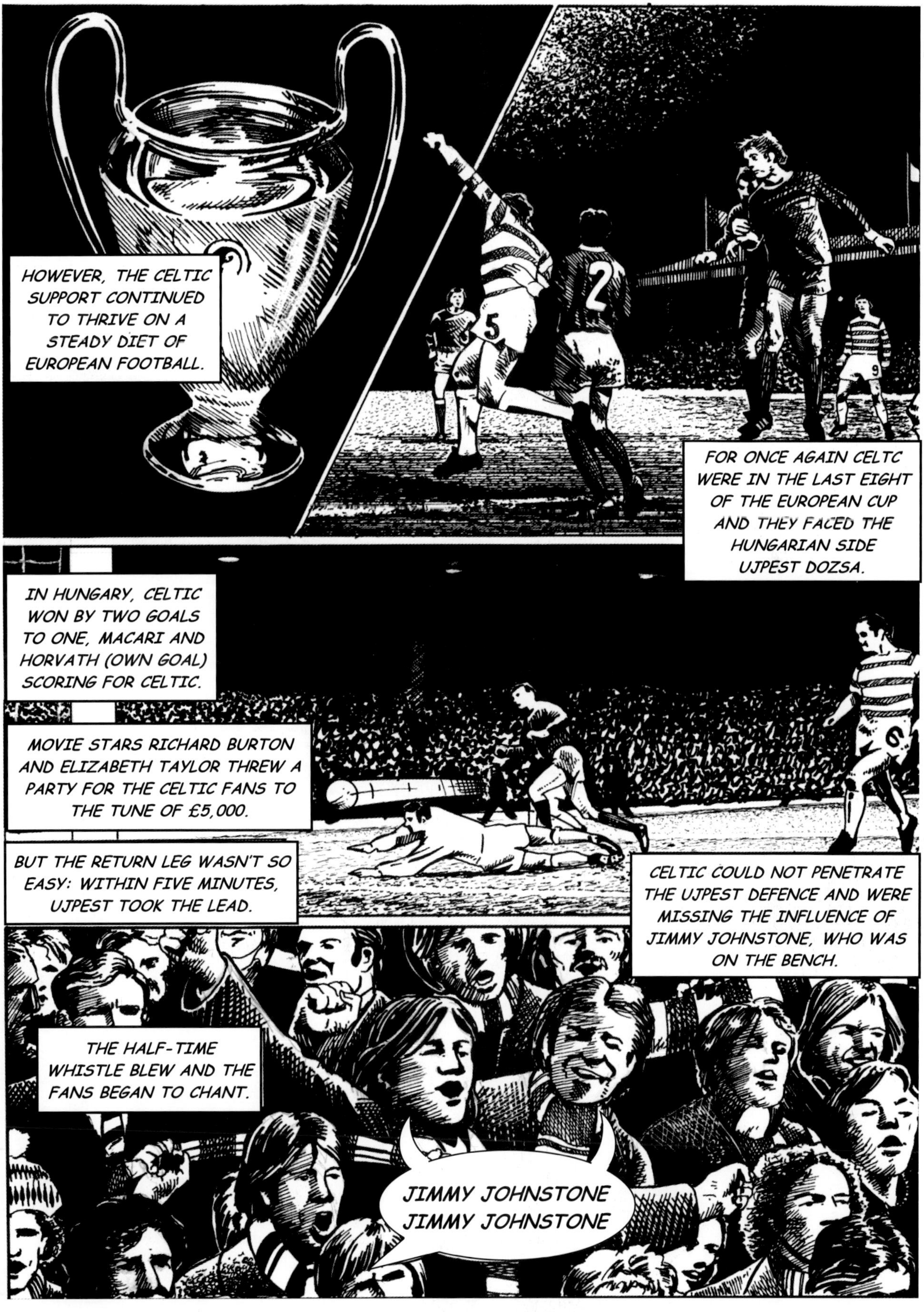
HOWEVER, THE CELTIC SUPPORT CONTINUED TO THRIVE ON A STEADY DIET OF EUROPEAN FOOTBALL.
FOR ONCE AGAIN CELTC WERE IN THE LAST EIGHT OF THE EUROPEAN CUP AND THEY FACED THE HUNGARIAN SIDE UJPEST DOZSA.
IN HUNGARY, CELTIC WON BY TWO GOALS TO ONE, MACARI AND HORVATH (OWN GOAL) SCORING FOR CELTIC.
MOVIE STARS RICHARD BURTON AND ELIZABETH TAYLOR THREW A PARTY FOR THE CELTIC FANS TO THE TUNE OF £5,000.
BUT THE RETURN LEG WASN'T SO EASY: WITHIN FIVE MINUTES, UJPEST TOOK THE LEAD.
CELTIC COULD NOT PENETRATE THE UJPEST DEFENCE AND WERE MISSING THE INFLUENCE OF JIMMY JOHNSTONE, WHO WAS ON THE BENCH.
THE HALF-TIME WHISTLE BLEW AND THE FANS BEGAN TO CHANT.
JIMMY JOHNSTONE JIMMY JOHNSTONE

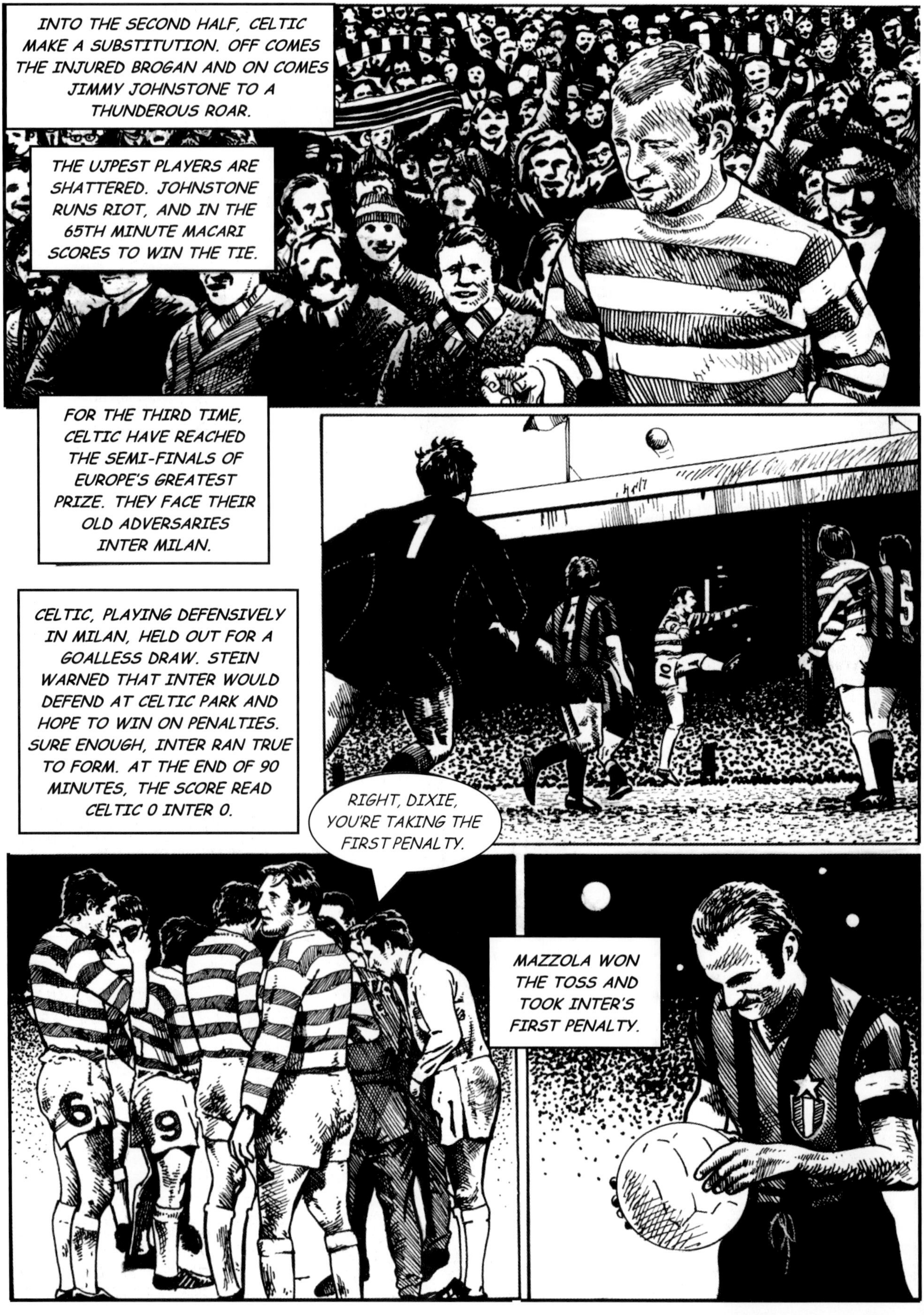
INTO THE SECOND HALF, CELTIC MAKE A SUBSTITUTION. OFF COMES THE INJURED BROGAN AND ON COMES JIMMY JOHNSTONE TO A THUNDEROUS ROAR.
THE UJPEST PLAYERS ARE SHATTERED. JOHNSTONE RUNS RIOT, AND IN THE 65TH MINUTE MACARI SCORES TO WIN THE TIE.
FOR THE THIRD TIME, CELTIC HAVE REACHED THE SEMI-FINALS OF EUROPE'S GREATEST PRIZE. THEY FACE THEIR OLD ADVERSARIES INTER MILAN.
CELTIC, PLAYING DEFENSIVELY IN MILAN, HELD OUT FOR A GOALLESS DRAW. STEIN WARNED THAT INTER WOULD DEFEND AT CELTIC PARK AND HOPE TO WIN ON PENALTIES. SURE ENOUGH, INTER RAN TRUE TO FORM. AT THE END OF 90 MINUTES, THE SCORE READ CELTIC 0 INTER 0.
RIGHT, DIXIE, YOU'RE TAKING THE FIRST PENALTY.
MAZZOLA WON THE TOSS AND TOOK INTER'S FIRST PENALTY.

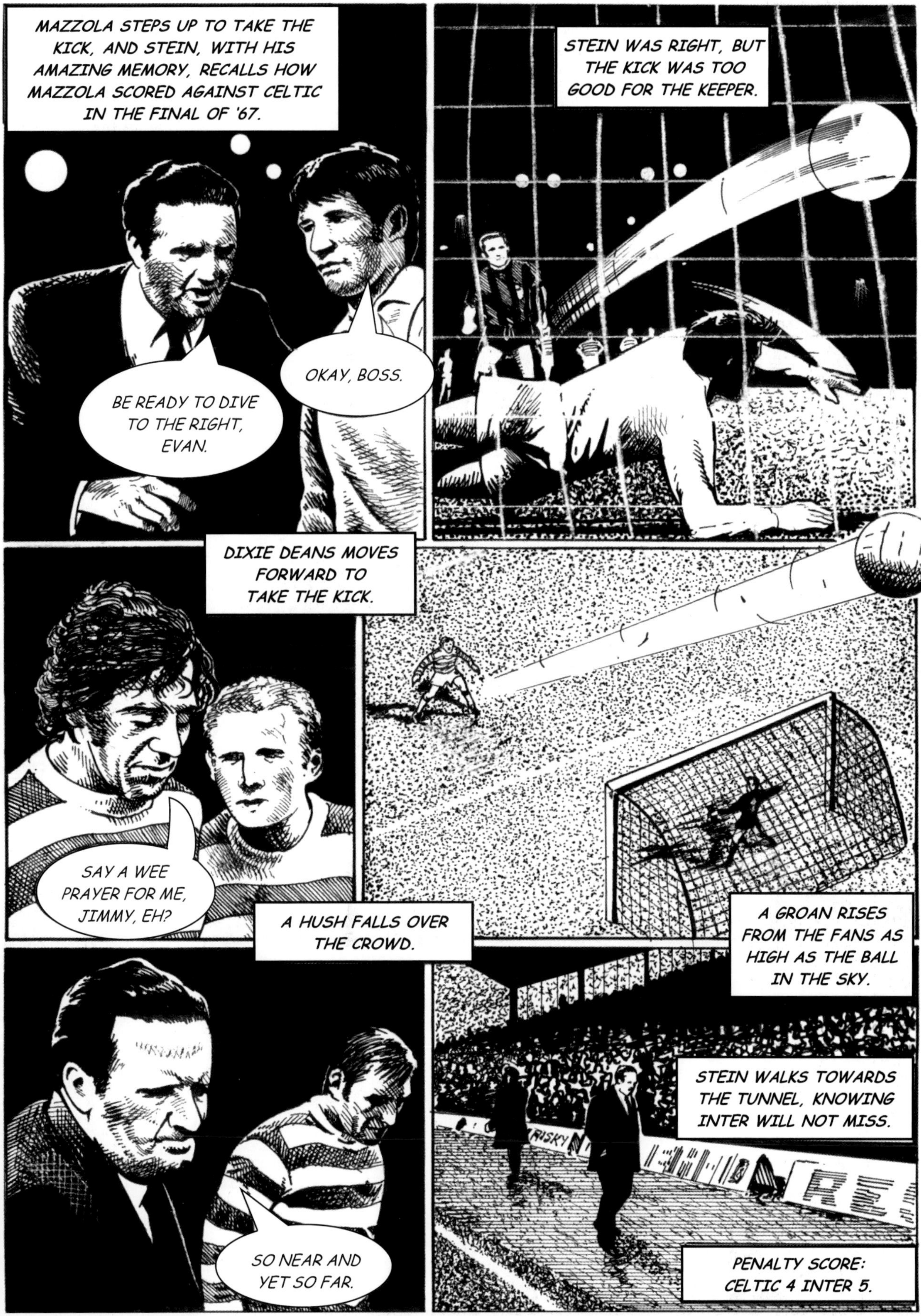
MAZZOLA STEPS UP TO TAKE THE KICK, AND STEIN, WITH HIS AMAZING MEMORY, RECALLS HOW MAZZOLA SCORED AGAINST CELTIC IN THE FINAL OF '67.
BE READY TO DIVE TO THE RIGHT, EVAN.
OKAY, BOSS.
STEIN WAS RIGHT, BUT THE KICK WAS TOO GOOD FOR THE KEEPER.
DIXIE DEANS MOVES FORWARD TO TAKE THE KICK.
SAY A WEE PRAYER FOR ME, JIMMY, EH?
A GROAN RISES FROM THE FANS AS HIGH AS THE BALL IN THE SKY.
A HUSH FALLS OVER THE CROWD.
SO NEAR AND YET SO FAR.
STEIN WALKS TOWARDS THE TUNNEL, KNOWING INTER WILL NOT MISS.
PENALTY SCORE: CELTIC 4 INTER 5.

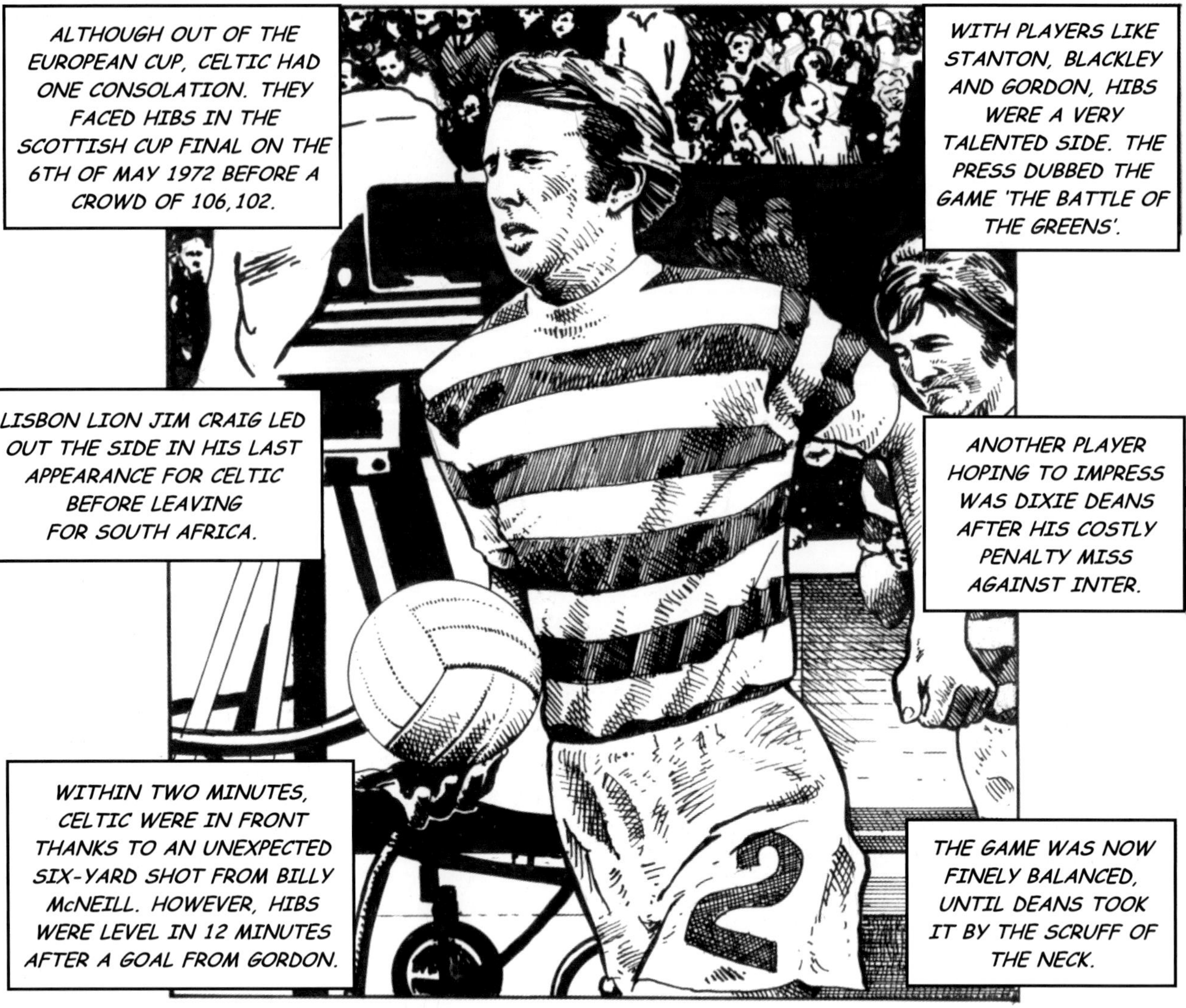
ALTHOUGH OUT OF THE EUROPEAN CUP, CELTIC HAD ONE CONSOLATION. THEY FACED HIBS IN THE SCOTTISH CUP FINAL ON THE 6TH OF MAY 1972 BEFORE A CROWD OF 106,102.
WITH PLAYERS LIKE STANTON, BLACKLEY AND GORDON, HIBS WERE A VERY TALENTED SIDE. THE PRESS DUBBED THE GAME 'THE BATTLE OF THE GREENS'.
LISBON LION JIM CRAIG LED OUT THE SIDE IN HIS LAST APPEARANCE FOR CELTIC BEFORE LEAVING FOR SOUTH AFRICA.
ANOTHER PLAYER HOPING TO IMPRESS WAS DIXIE DEANS AFTER HIS COSTLY PENALTY MISS AGAINST INTER.
WITHIN TWO MINUTES, CELTIC WERE IN FRONT THANKS TO AN UNEXPECTED SIX-YARD SHOT FROM BILLY McNEILL. HOWEVER, HIBS WERE LEVEL IN 12 MINUTES AFTER A GOAL FROM GORDON.
THE GAME WAS NOW FINELY BALANCED, UNTIL DEANS TOOK IT BY THE SCRUFF OF THE NECK.

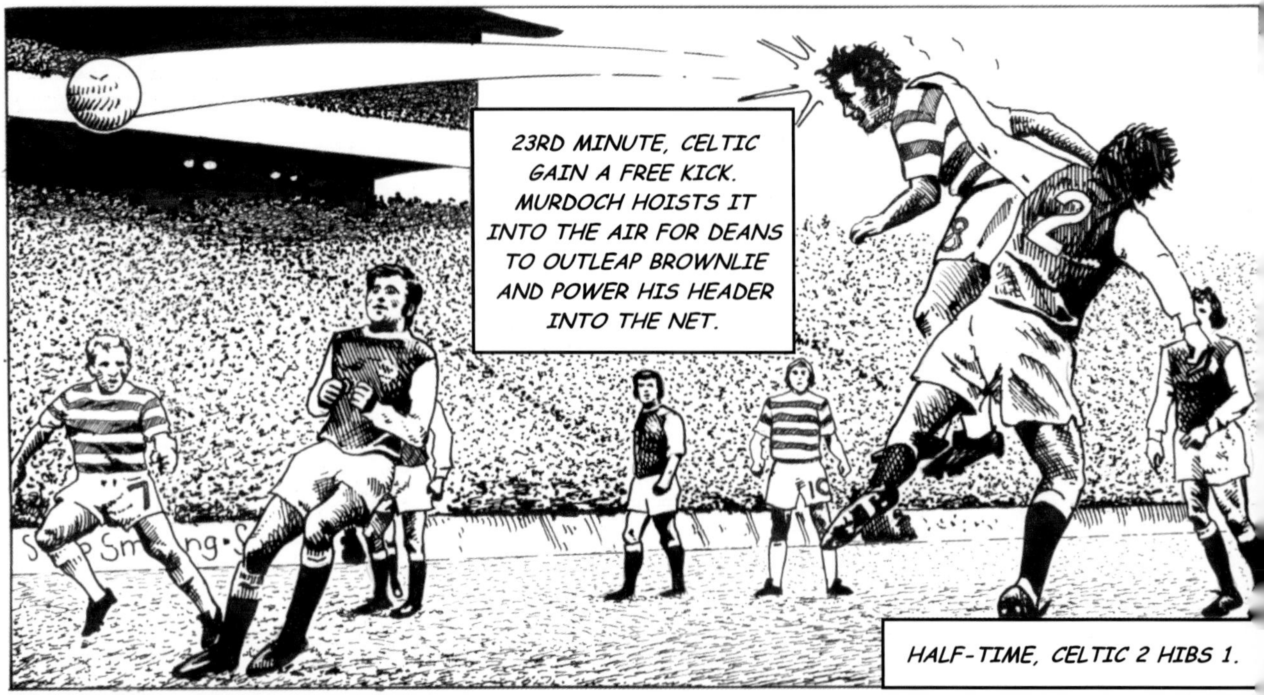
23RD MINUTE, CELTIC GAIN A FREE KICK. MURDOCH HOISTS IT INTO THE AIR FOR DEANS TO OUTLEAP BROWNLIE AND POWER HIS HEADER INTO THE NET.
HALF-TIME, CELTIC 2 HIBS 1.

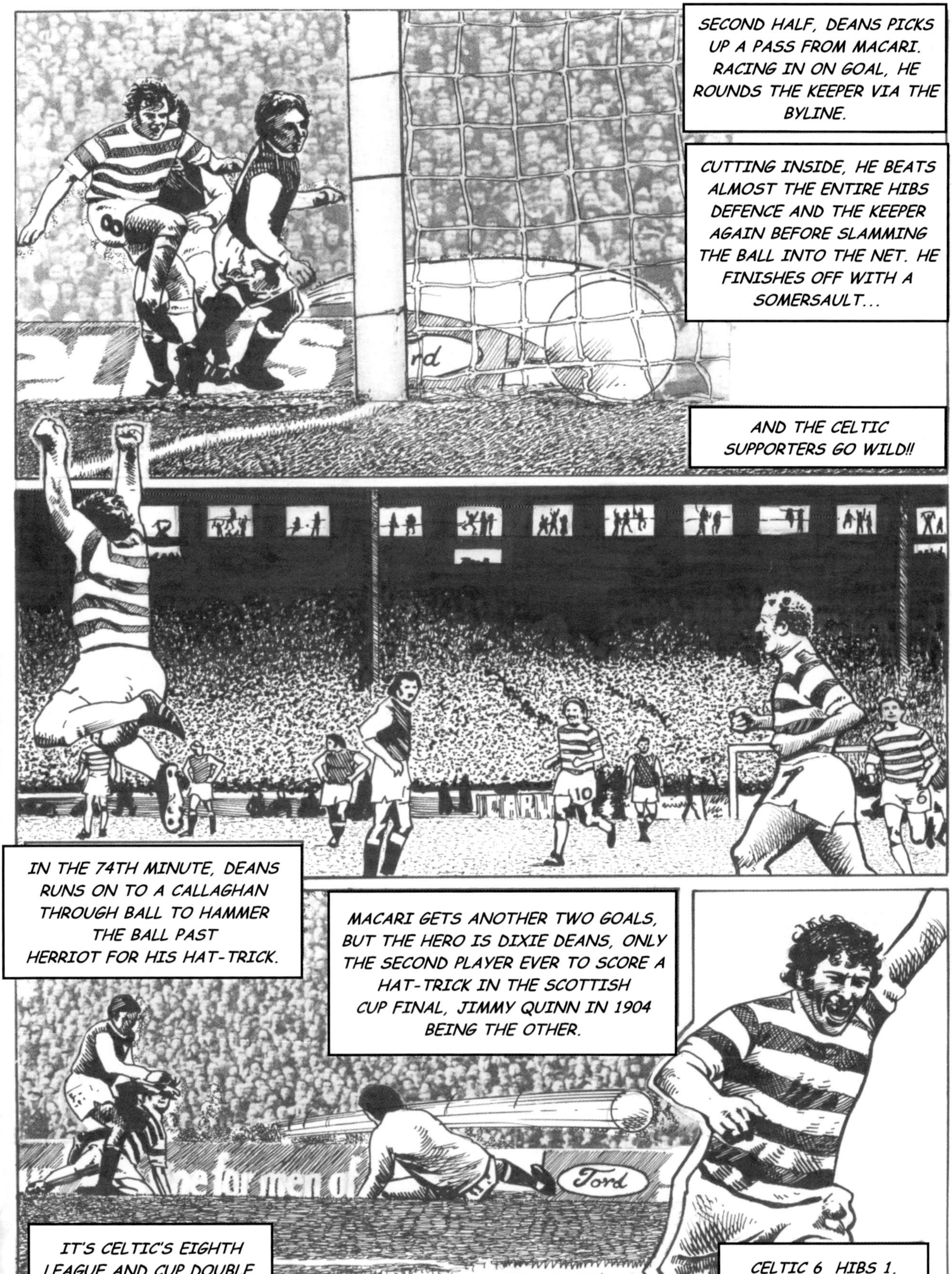
SECOND HALF, DEANS PICKS UP A PASS FROM MACARI. RACING IN ON GOAL, HE ROUNDS THE KEEPER VIA THE BYLINE.
CUTTING INSIDE, HE BEATS ALMOST THE ENTIRE HIBS DEFENCE AND THE KEEPER AGAIN BEFORE SLAMMING THE BALL INTO THE NET. HE FINISHES OFF WITH A SOMERSAULT...
AND THE CELTIC SUPPORTERS GO WILD!!
IN THE 74TH MINUTE, DEANS RUNS ON TO A CALLAGHAN THROUGH BALL TO HAMMER THE BALL PAST HERRIOT FOR HIS HAT-TRICK.
MACARI GETS ANOTHER TWO GOALS, BUT THE HERO IS DIXIE DEANS, ONLY THE SECOND PLAYER EVER TO SCORE A HAT-TRICK IN THE SCOTTISH CUP FINAL, JIMMY QUINN IN 1904 BEING THE OTHER.
Ford
IT'S CELTIC'S EIGHTH LEAGUE AND CUP DOUBLE.
CELTIC 6 HIBS 1.

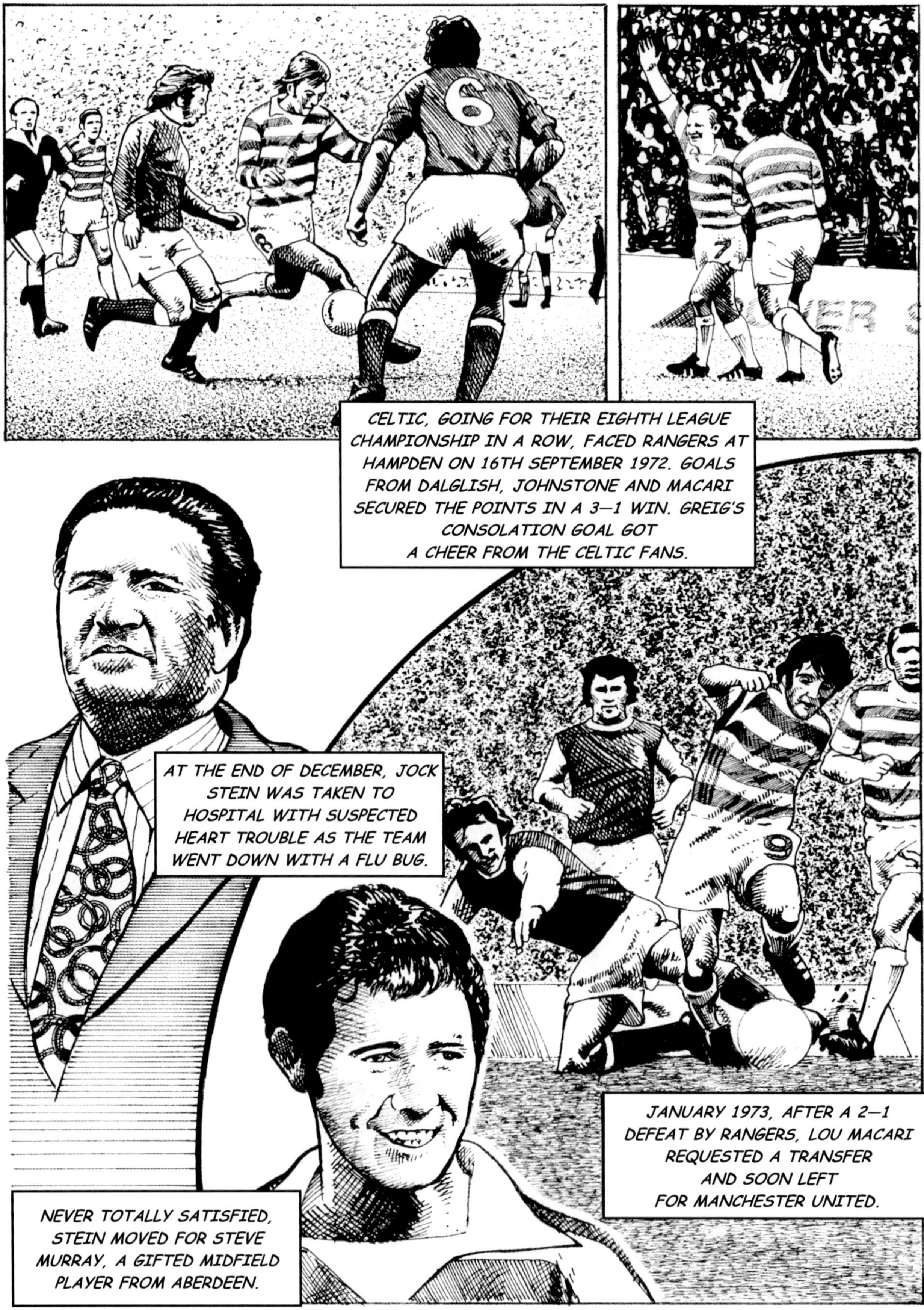
CELTIC, GOING FOR THEIR EIGHTH LEAGUE CHAMPIONSHIP IN A ROW, FACED RANGERS AT HAMPDEN ON 16TH SEPTEMBER 1972. GOALS FROM DALGLISH, JOHNSTONE AND MACARI SECURED THE POINTS IN A 3—1 WIN. GREIG'S CONSOLATION GOAL GOT A CHEER FROM THE CELTIC FANS.
AT THE END OF DECEMBER, JOCK STEIN WAS TAKEN TO HOSPITAL WITH SUSPECTED HEART TROUBLE AS THE TEAM WENT DOWN WITH A FLU BUG.
JANUARY 1973, AFTER A 2—1 DEFEAT BY RANGERS, LOU MACARI REQUESTED A TRANSFER AND SOON LEFT FOR MANCHESTER UNITED.
NEVER TOTALLY SATISFIED, STEIN MOVED FOR STEVE MURRAY, A GIFTED MIDFIELD PLAYER FROM ABERDEEN.

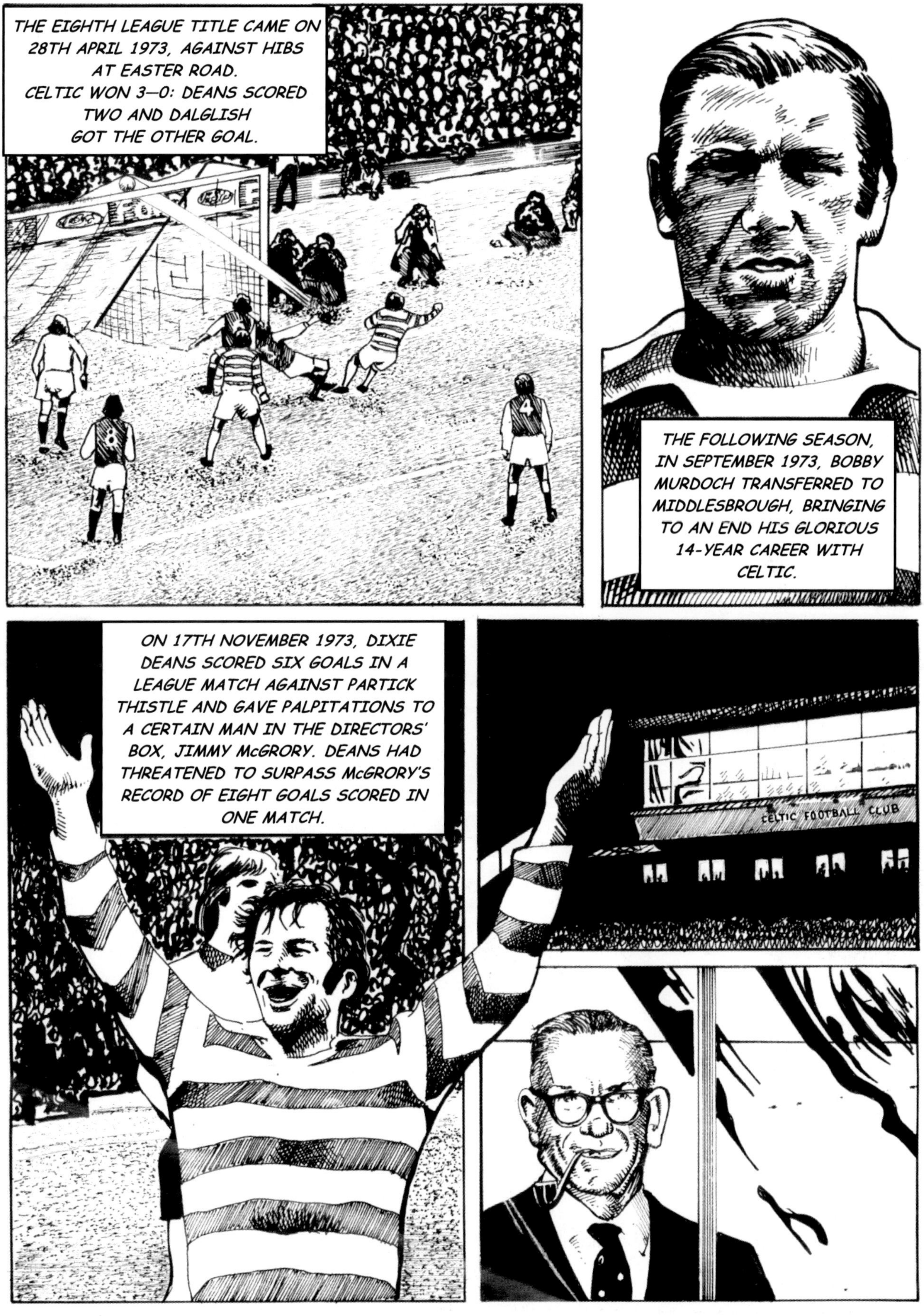

THE EIGHTH LEAGUE TITLE CAME ON 28TH APRIL 1973, AGAINST HIBS AT EASTER ROAD. CELTIC WON 3—0: DEANS SCORED TWO AND DALGLISH GOT THE OTHER GOAL.
THE FOLLOWING SEASON, IN SEPTEMBER 1973, BOBBY MURDOCH TRANSFERRED TO MIDDLESBROUGH, BRINGING TO AN END HIS GLORIOUS 14-YEAR CAREER WITH CELTIC.
ON 17TH NOVEMBER 1973, DIXIE DEANS SCORED SIX GOALS IN A LEAGUE MATCH AGAINST PARTICK THISTLE AND GAVE PALPITATIONS TO A CERTAIN MAN IN THE DIRECTORS' BOX, JIMMY McGRORY. DEANS HAD THREATENED TO SURPASS McGRORY'S RECORD OF EIGHT GOALS SCORED IN ONE MATCH.
CELTIC FOOTBALL CLUB

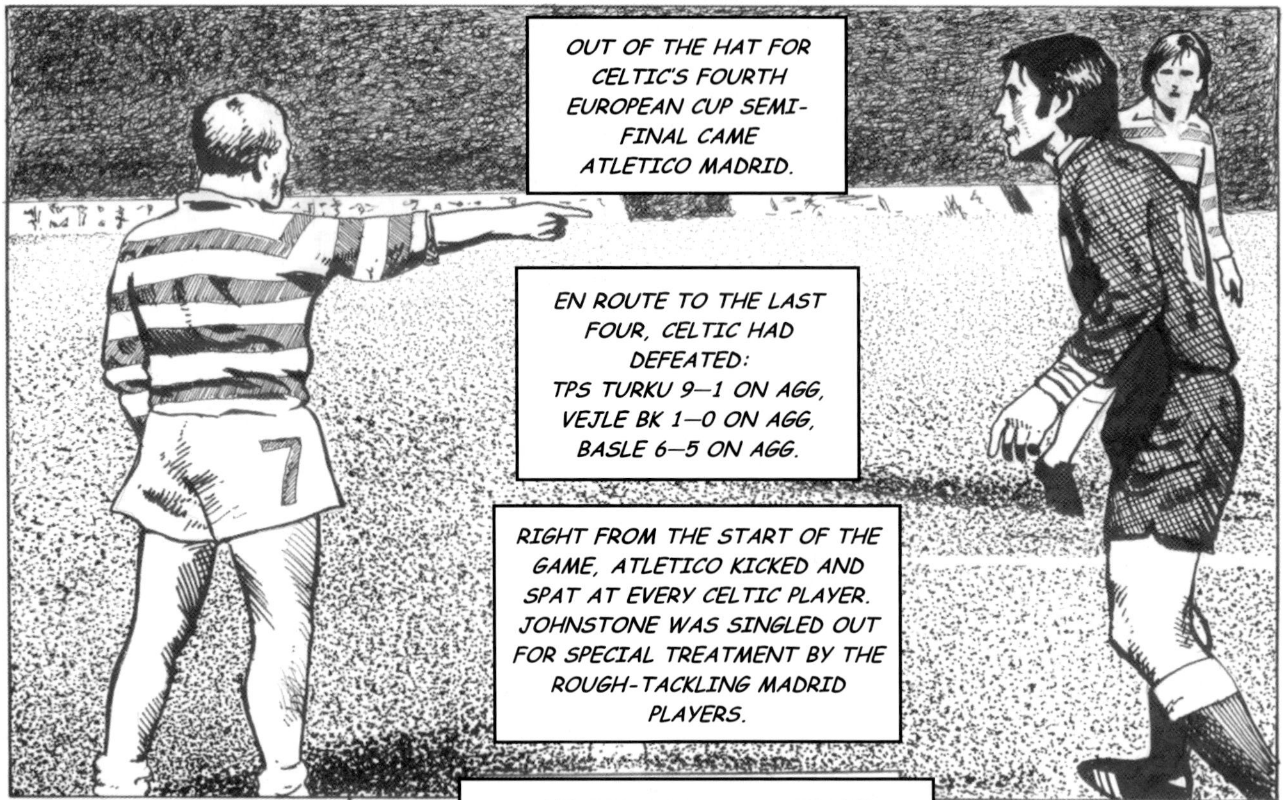
OUT OF THE HAT FOR CELTIC'S FOURTH EUROPEAN CUP SEMI-FINAL CAME ATLETICO MADRID.
EN ROUTE TO THE LAST FOUR, CELTIC HAD DEFEATED: TPS TURKU 9—1 ON AGG, VEJLE BK 1—0 ON AGG, BASLE 6—5 ON AGG.
RIGHT FROM THE START OF THE GAME, ATLETICO KICKED AND SPAT AT EVERY CELTIC PLAYER. JOHNSTONE WAS SINGLED OUT FOR SPECIAL TREATMENT BY THE ROUGH-TACKLING MADRID PLAYERS.

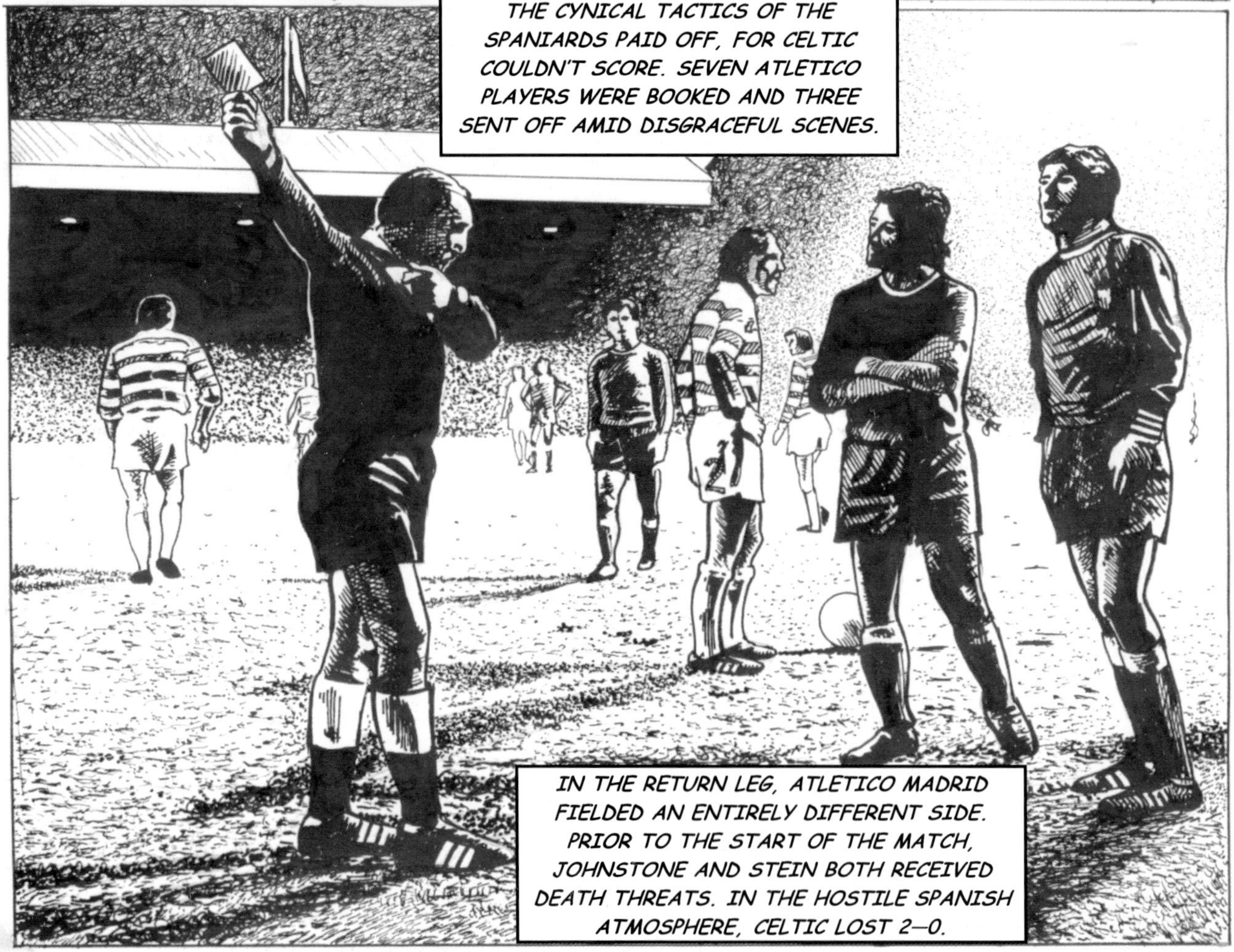
THE CYNICAL TACTICS OF THE SPANIARDS PAID OFF, FOR CELTIC COULDN'T SCORE. SEVEN ATLETICO PLAYERS WERE BOOKED AND THREE SENT OFF AMID DISGRACEFUL SCENES.
IN THE RETURN LEG, ATLETICO MADRID FIELDED AN ENTIRELY DIFFERENT SIDE. PRIOR TO THE START OF THE MATCH, JOHNSTONE AND STEIN BOTH RECEIVED DEATH THREATS. IN THE HOSTILE SPANISH ATMOSPHERE, CELTIC LOST 2—0.

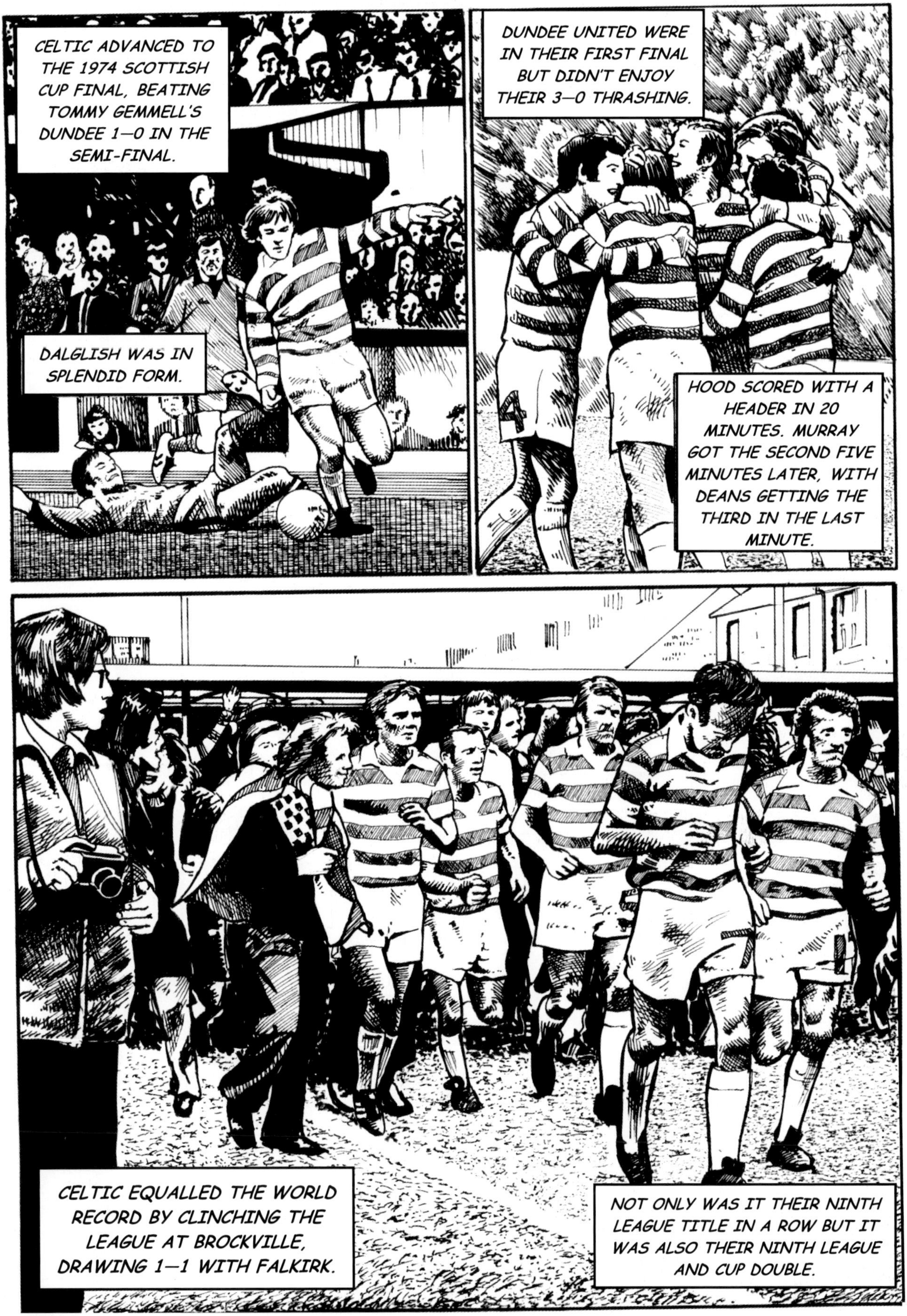
CELTIC ADVANCED TO THE 1974 SCOTTISH CUP FINAL, BEATING TOMMY GEMMELL'S DUNDEE 1—0 IN THE SEMI-FINAL.
DALGLISH WAS IN SPLENDID FORM.
DUNDEE UNITED WERE IN THEIR FIRST FINAL BUT DIDN'T ENJOY THEIR 3—0 THRASHING.
HOOD SCORED WITH A HEADER IN 20 MINUTES. MURRAY GOT THE SECOND FIVE MINUTES LATER, WITH DEANS GETTING THE THIRD IN THE LAST MINUTE.
CELTIC EQUALLED THE WORLD RECORD BY CLINCHING THE LEAGUE AT BROCKVILLE, DRAWING 1—1 WITH FALKIRK.
NOT ONLY WAS IT THEIR NINTH LEAGUE TITLE IN A ROW BUT IT WAS ALSO THEIR NINTH LEAGUE AND CUP DOUBLE.

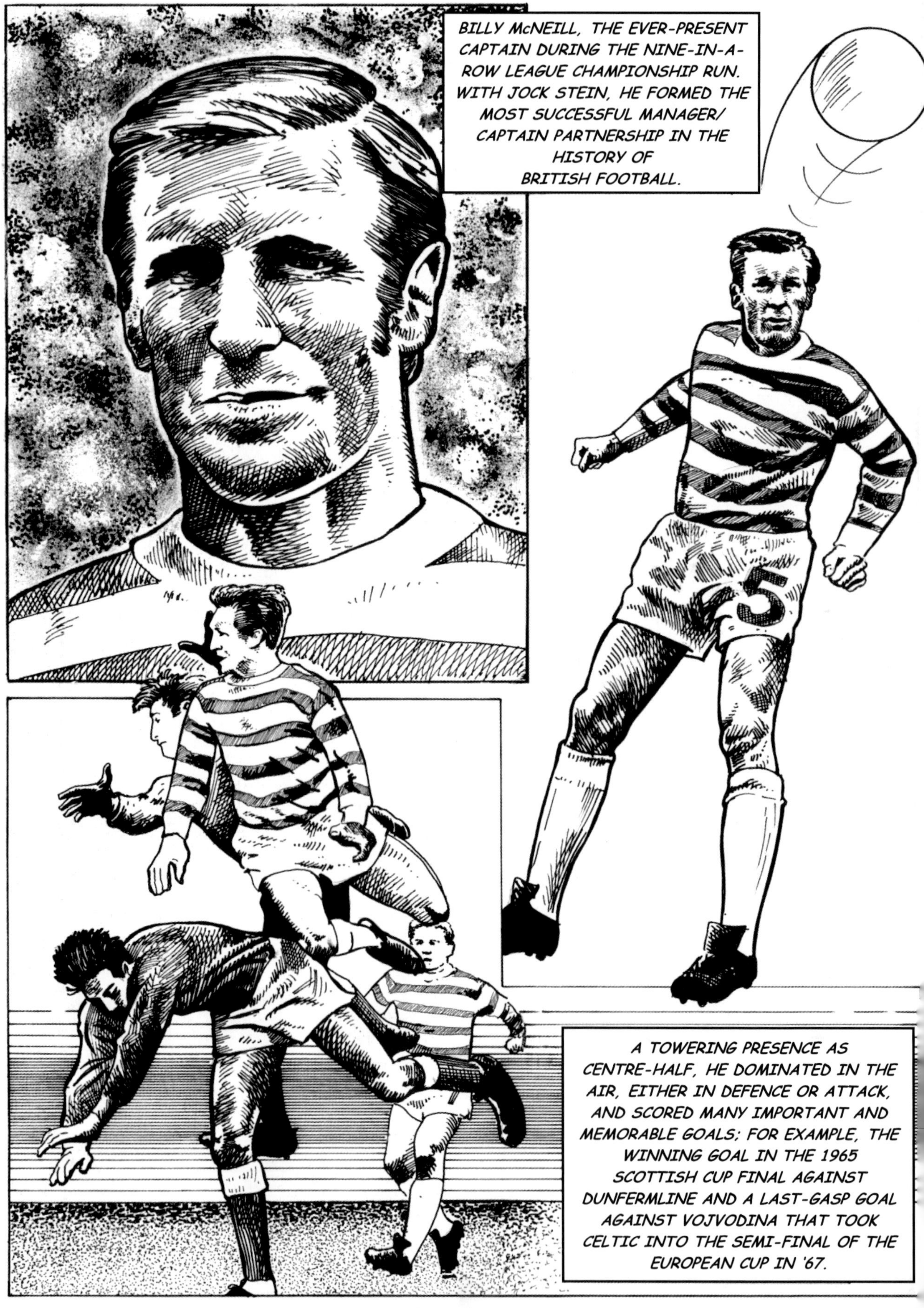
BILLY McNEILL, THE EVER-PRESENT CAPTAIN DURING THE NINE-IN-A-ROW LEAGUE CHAMPIONSHIP RUN. WITH JOCK STEIN, HE FORMED THE MOST SUCCESSFUL MANAGER/ CAPTAIN PARTNERSHIP IN THE HISTORY OF BRITISH FOOTBALL.
5
A TOWERING PRESENCE AS CENTRE-HALF, HE DOMINATED IN THE AIR, EITHER IN DEFENCE OR ATTACK, AND SCORED MANY IMPORTANT AND MEMORABLE GOALS; FOR EXAMPLE, THE WINNING GOAL IN THE 1965 SCOTTISH CUP FINAL AGAINST DUNFERMLINE AND A LAST-GASP GOAL AGAINST VOJVODINA THAT TOOK CELTIC INTO THE SEMI-FINAL OF THE EUROPEAN CUP IN '67.

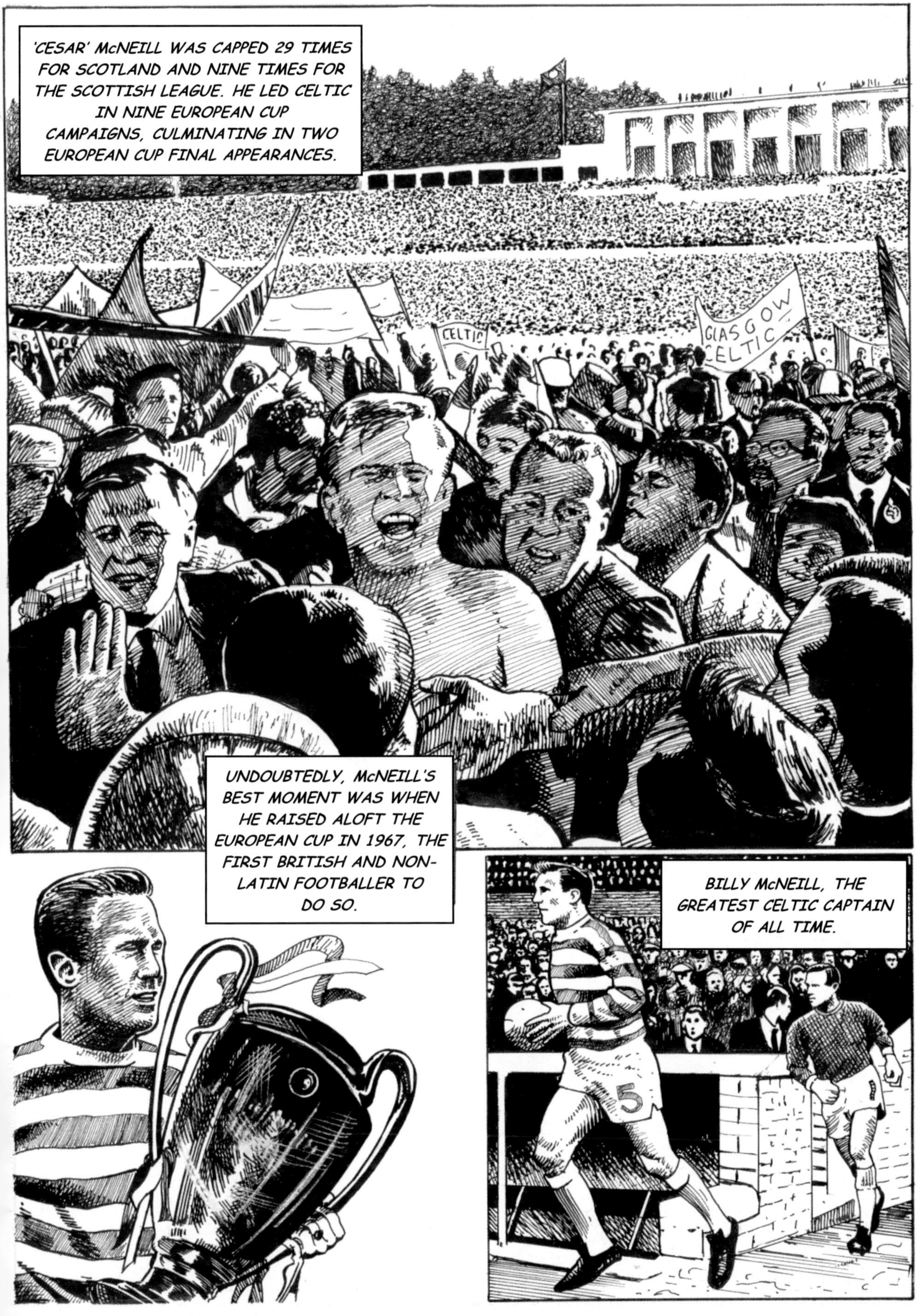
'CESAR' McNEILL WAS CAPPED 29 TIMES FOR SCOTLAND AND NINE TIMES FOR THE SCOTTISH LEAGUE. HE LED CELTIC IN NINE EUROPEAN CUP CAMPAIGNS, CULMINATING IN TWO EUROPEAN CUP FINAL APPEARANCES.
CELTIC
GLASGOW CELTIC
UNDOUBTEDLY, McNEILL'S BEST MOMENT WAS WHEN HE RAISED ALOFT THE EUROPEAN CUP IN 1967, THE FIRST BRITISH AND NON-LATIN FOOTBALLER TO DO SO.
BILLY McNEILL, THE GREATEST CELTIC CAPTAIN OF ALL TIME.
5

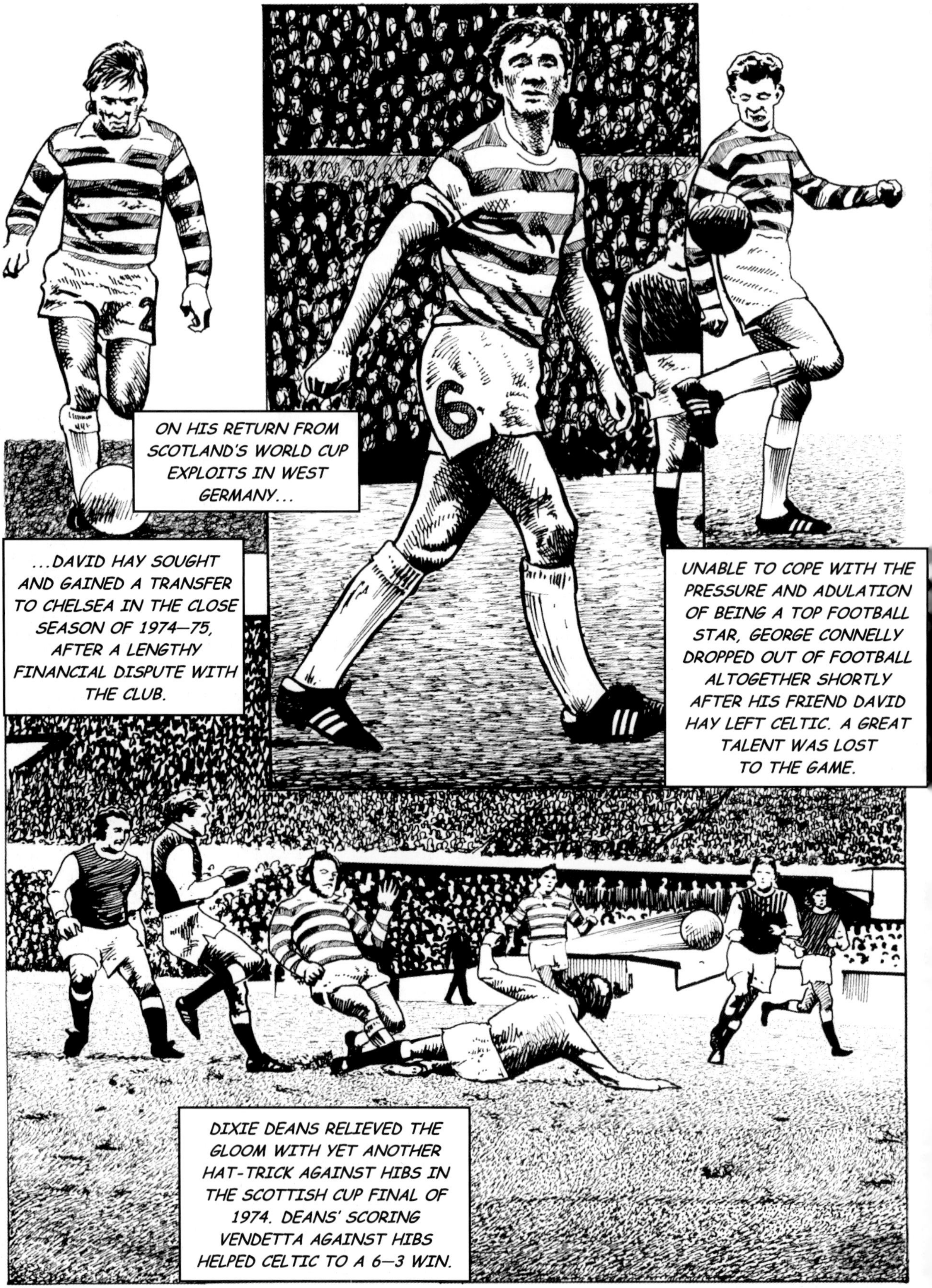
ON HIS RETURN FROM SCOTLAND'S WORLD CUP EXPLOITS IN WEST GERMANY...
...DAVID HAY SOUGHT AND GAINED A TRANSFER TO CHELSEA IN THE CLOSE SEASON OF 1974–75, AFTER A LENGTHY FINANCIAL DISPUTE WITH THE CLUB.
UNABLE TO COPE WITH THE PRESSURE AND ADULATION OF BEING A TOP FOOTBALL STAR, GEORGE CONNELLY DROPPED OUT OF FOOTBALL ALTOGETHER SHORTLY AFTER HIS FRIEND DAVID HAY LEFT CELTIC. A GREAT TALENT WAS LOST TO THE GAME.
DIXIE DEANS RELIEVED THE GLOOM WITH YET ANOTHER HAT-TRICK AGAINST HIBS IN THE SCOTTISH CUP FINAL OF 1974. DEANS' SCORING VENDETTA AGAINST HIBS HELPED CELTIC TO A 6–3 WIN.

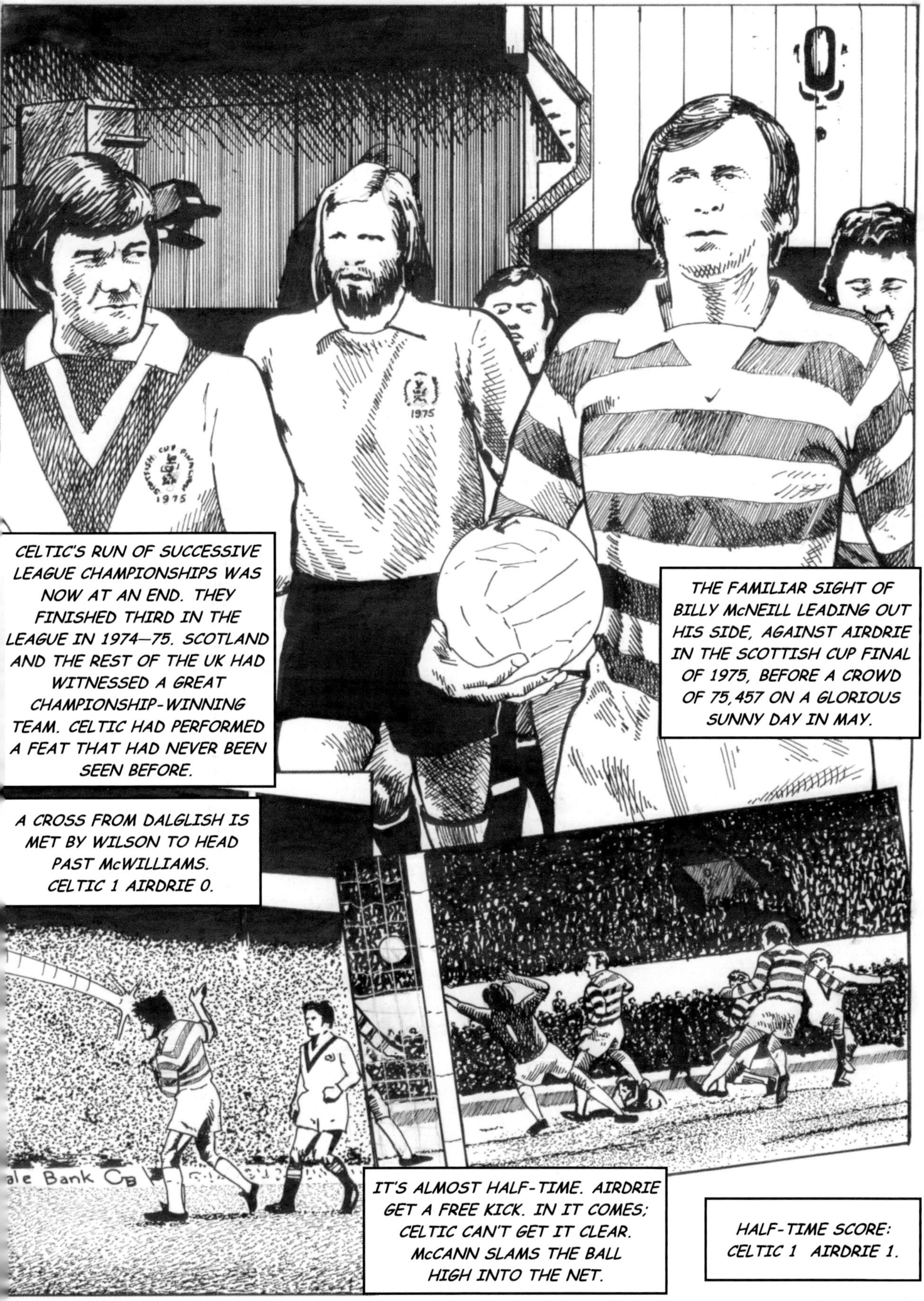
CELTIC'S RUN OF SUCCESSIVE LEAGUE CHAMPIONSHIPS WAS NOW AT AN END. THEY FINISHED THIRD IN THE LEAGUE IN 1974–75. SCOTLAND AND THE REST OF THE UK HAD WITNESSED A GREAT CHAMPIONSHIP-WINNING TEAM. CELTIC HAD PERFORMED A FEAT THAT HAD NEVER BEEN SEEN BEFORE.
THE FAMILIAR SIGHT OF BILLY McNEILL LEADING OUT HIS SIDE, AGAINST AIRDRIE IN THE SCOTTISH CUP FINAL OF 1975, BEFORE A CROWD OF 75,457 ON A GLORIOUS SUNNY DAY IN MAY.
A CROSS FROM DALGLISH IS MET BY WILSON TO HEAD PAST McWILLIAMS. CELTIC 1 AIRDRIE 0.
IT'S ALMOST HALF-TIME. AIRDRIE GET A FREE KICK. IN IT COMES; CELTIC CAN'T GET IT CLEAR. McCANN SLAMS THE BALL HIGH INTO THE NET.
HALF-TIME SCORE: CELTIC 1 AIRDRIE 1.

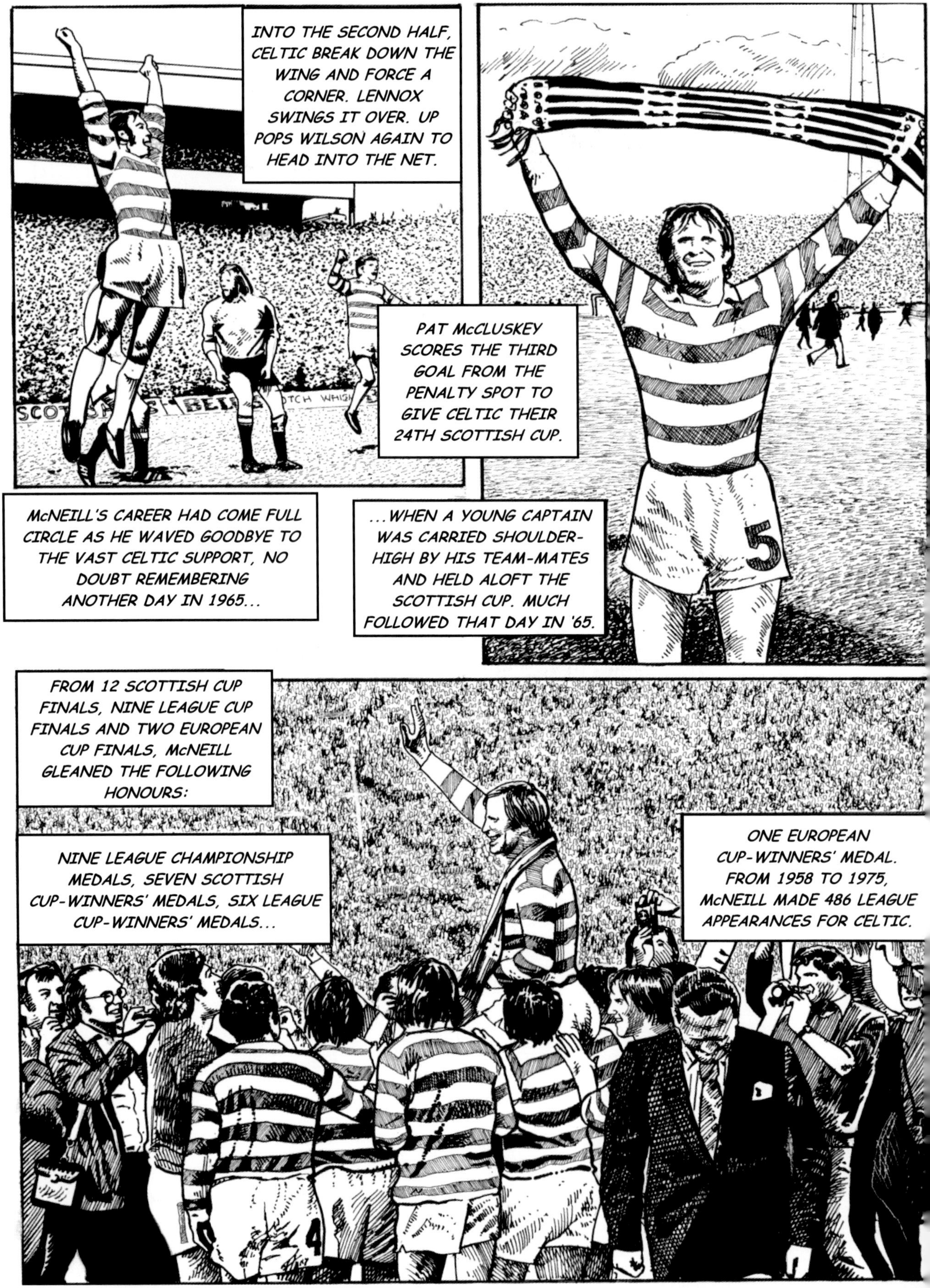
INTO THE SECOND HALF, CELTIC BREAK DOWN THE WING AND FORCE A CORNER. LENNOX SWINGS IT OVER. UP POPS WILSON AGAIN TO HEAD INTO THE NET.
PAT McCLUSKEY SCORES THE THIRD GOAL FROM THE PENALTY SPOT TO GIVE CELTIC THEIR 24TH SCOTTISH CUP.
McNEILL'S CAREER HAD COME FULL CIRCLE AS HE WAVED GOODBYE TO THE VAST CELTIC SUPPORT, NO DOUBT REMEMBERING ANOTHER DAY IN 1965...
...WHEN A YOUNG CAPTAIN WAS CARRIED SHOULDER-HIGH BY HIS TEAM-MATES AND HELD ALOFT THE SCOTTISH CUP. MUCH FOLLOWED THAT DAY IN '65.
5
FROM 12 SCOTTISH CUP FINALS, NINE LEAGUE CUP FINALS AND TWO EUROPEAN CUP FINALS, McNEILL GLEANED THE FOLLOWING HONOURS:
NINE LEAGUE CHAMPIONSHIP MEDALS, SEVEN SCOTTISH CUP-WINNERS' MEDALS, SIX LEAGUE CUP-WINNERS' MEDALS...
ONE EUROPEAN CUP-WINNERS' MEDAL. FROM 1958 TO 1975, McNEILL MADE 486 LEAGUE APPEARANCES FOR CELTIC.
4

chapter 7

the glory fades

'and the sweet silver song of a lark'

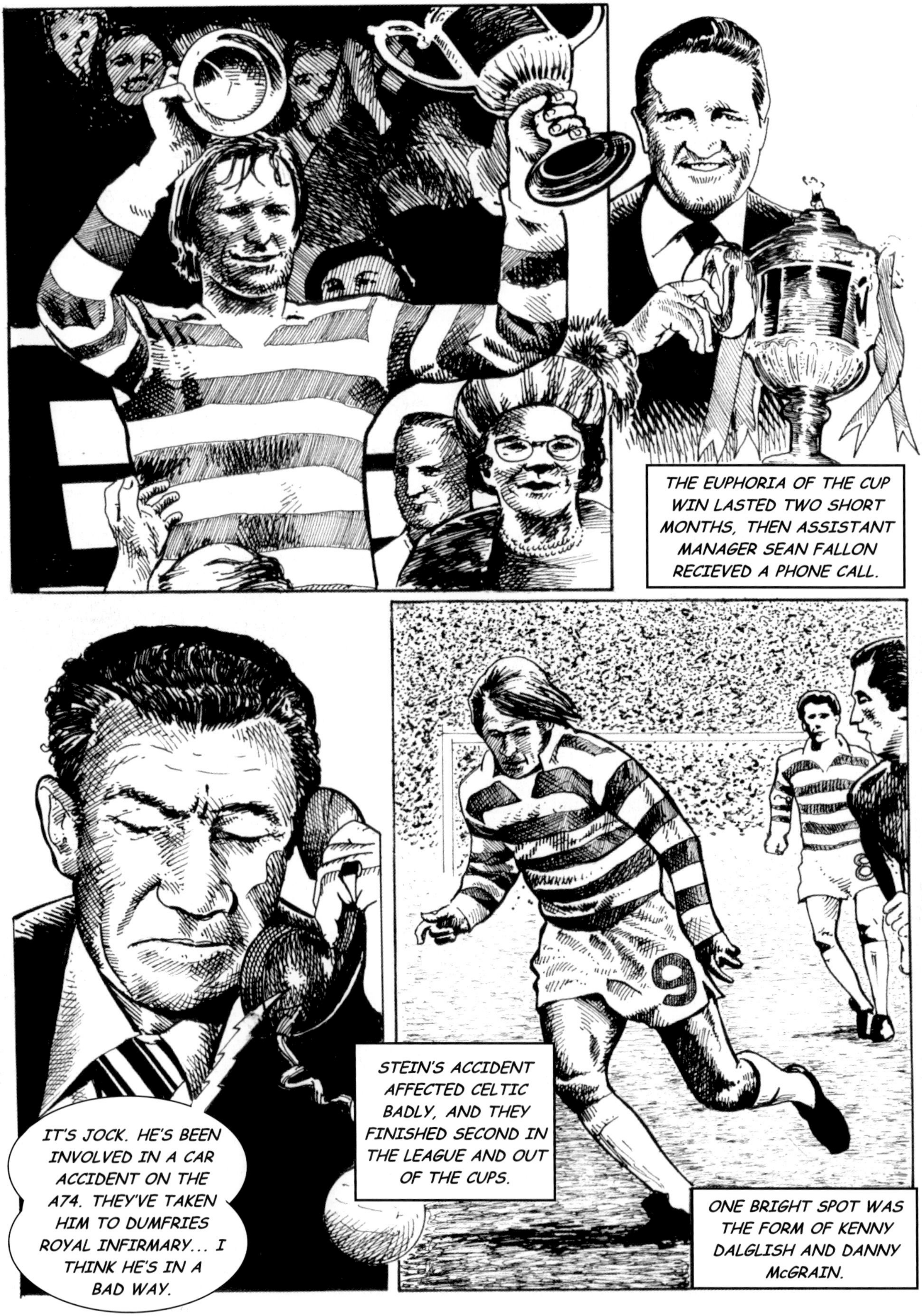
THE EUPHORIA OF THE CUP WIN LASTED TWO SHORT MONTHS, THEN ASSISTANT MANAGER SEAN FALLON RECIEVED A PHONE CALL.
IT'S JOCK. HE'S BEEN INVOLVED IN A CAR ACCIDENT ON THE A74. THEY'VE TAKEN HIM TO DUMFRIES ROYAL INFIRMARY... I THINK HE'S IN A BAD WAY.
STEIN'S ACCIDENT AFFECTED CELTIC BADLY, AND THEY FINISHED SECOND IN THE LEAGUE AND OUT OF THE CUPS.
ONE BRIGHT SPOT WAS THE FORM OF KENNY DALGLISH AND DANNY McGRAIN.

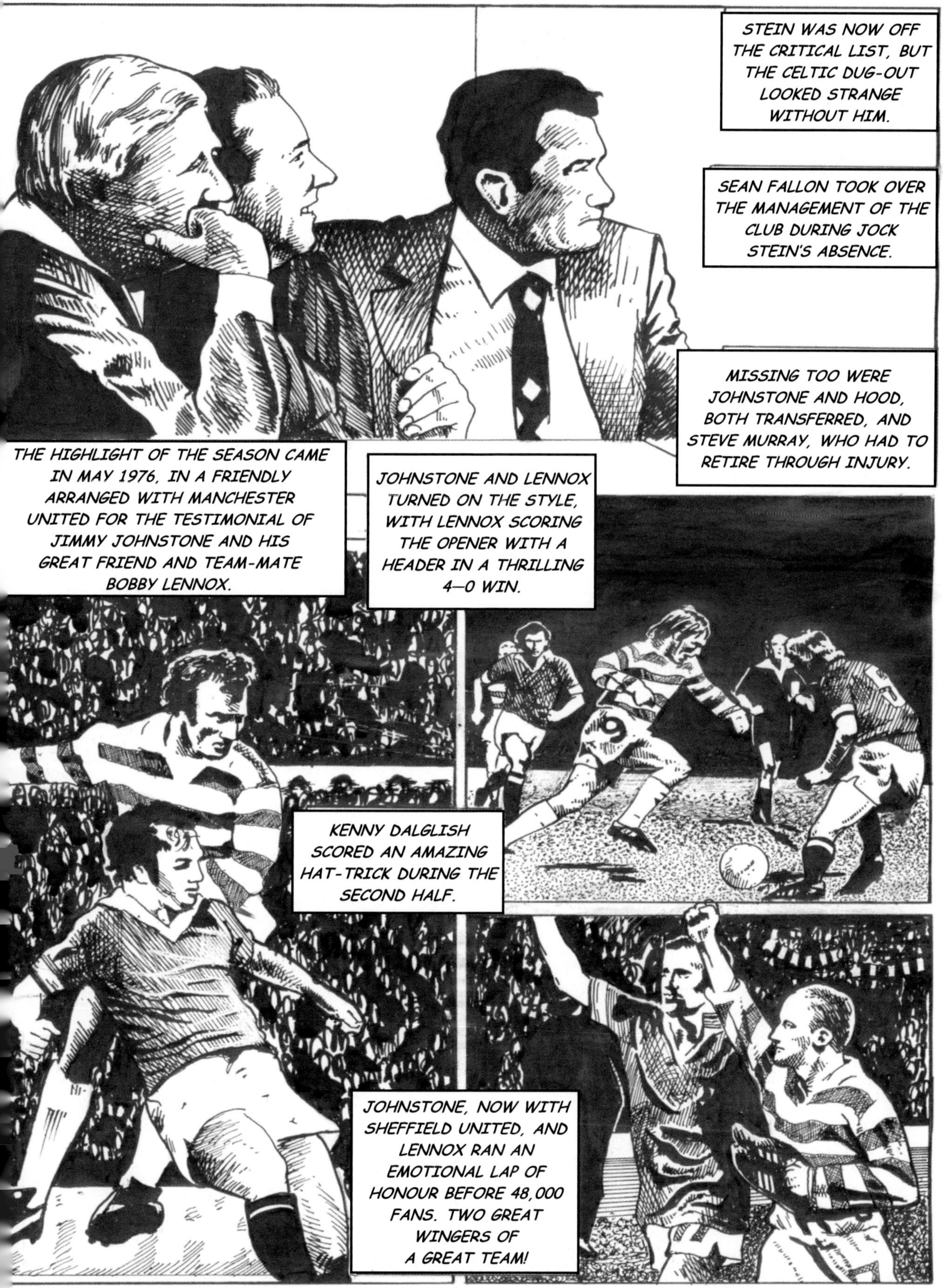
STEIN WAS NOW OFF THE CRITICAL LIST, BUT THE CELTIC DUG-OUT LOOKED STRANGE WITHOUT HIM.
SEAN FALLON TOOK OVER THE MANAGEMENT OF THE CLUB DURING JOCK STEIN'S ABSENCE.
MISSING TOO WERE JOHNSTONE AND HOOD, BOTH TRANSFERRED, AND STEVE MURRAY, WHO HAD TO RETIRE THROUGH INJURY.
THE HIGHLIGHT OF THE SEASON CAME IN MAY 1976, IN A FRIENDLY ARRANGED WITH MANCHESTER UNITED FOR THE TESTIMONIAL OF JIMMY JOHNSTONE AND HIS GREAT FRIEND AND TEAM-MATE BOBBY LENNOX.
JOHNSTONE AND LENNOX TURNED ON THE STYLE, WITH LENNOX SCORING THE OPENER WITH A HEADER IN A THRILLING 4—0 WIN.
KENNY DALGLISH SCORED AN AMAZING HAT-TRICK DURING THE SECOND HALF.
JOHNSTONE, NOW WITH SHEFFIELD UNITED, AND LENNOX RAN AN EMOTIONAL LAP OF HONOUR BEFORE 48,000 FANS. TWO GREAT WINGERS OF A GREAT TEAM!

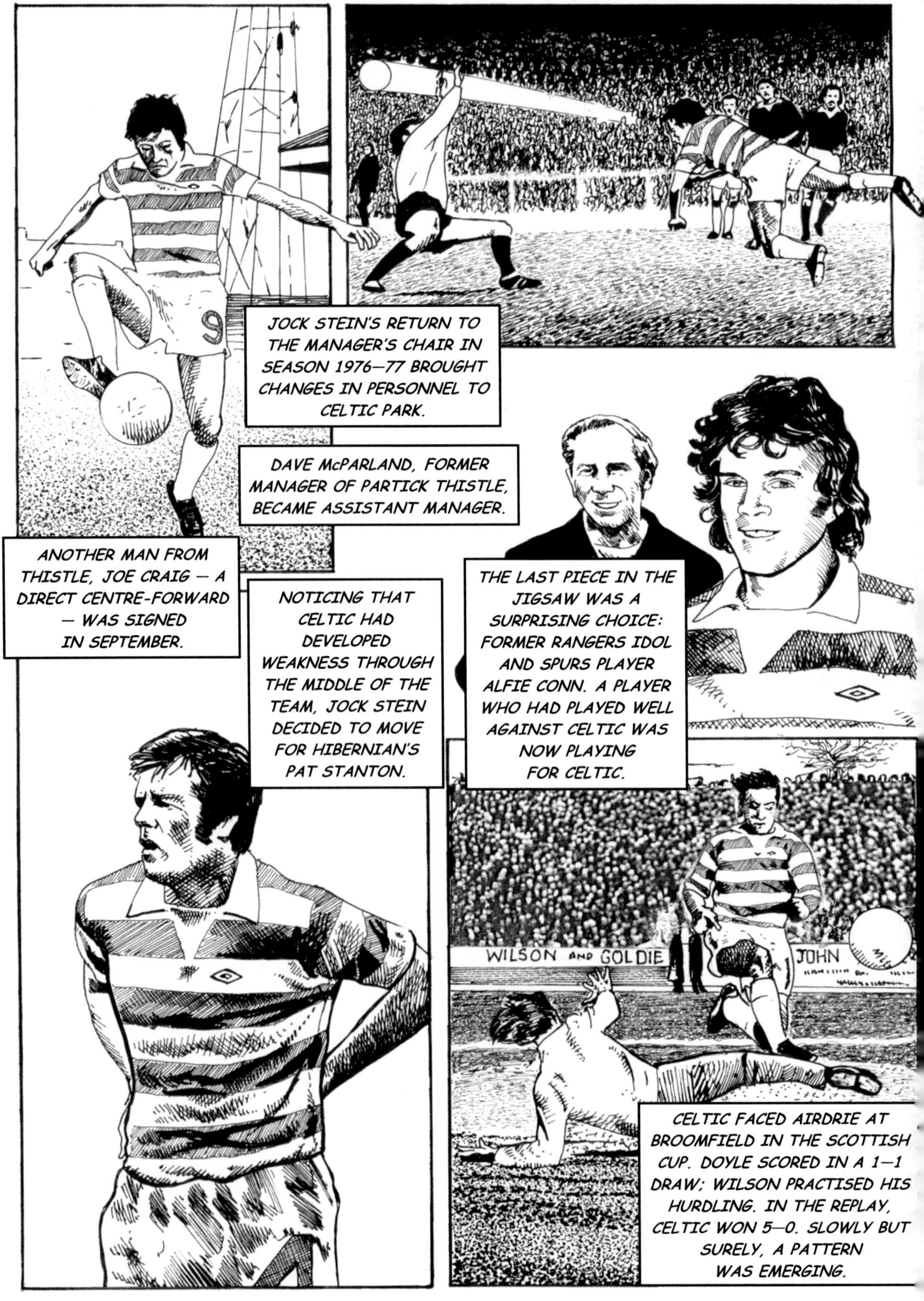
JOCK STEIN'S RETURN TO THE MANAGER'S CHAIR IN SEASON 1976–77 BROUGHT CHANGES IN PERSONNEL TO CELTIC PARK.
DAVE McPARLAND, FORMER MANAGER OF PARTICK THISTLE, BECAME ASSISTANT MANAGER.
ANOTHER MAN FROM THISTLE, JOE CRAIG — A DIRECT CENTRE-FORWARD — WAS SIGNED IN SEPTEMBER.
NOTICING THAT CELTIC HAD DEVELOPED WEAKNESS THROUGH THE MIDDLE OF THE TEAM, JOCK STEIN DECIDED TO MOVE FOR HIBERNIAN'S PAT STANTON.
THE LAST PIECE IN THE JIGSAW WAS A SURPRISING CHOICE: FORMER RANGERS IDOL AND SPURS PLAYER ALFIE CONN. A PLAYER WHO HAD PLAYED WELL AGAINST CELTIC WAS NOW PLAYING FOR CELTIC.
WILSON AND GOLDIE
JOHN
CELTIC FACED AIRDRIE AT BROOMFIELD IN THE SCOTTISH CUP. DOYLE SCORED IN A 1–1 DRAW; WILSON PRACTISED HIS HURDLING. IN THE REPLAY, CELTIC WON 5–0. SLOWLY BUT SURELY, A PATTERN WAS EMERGING.

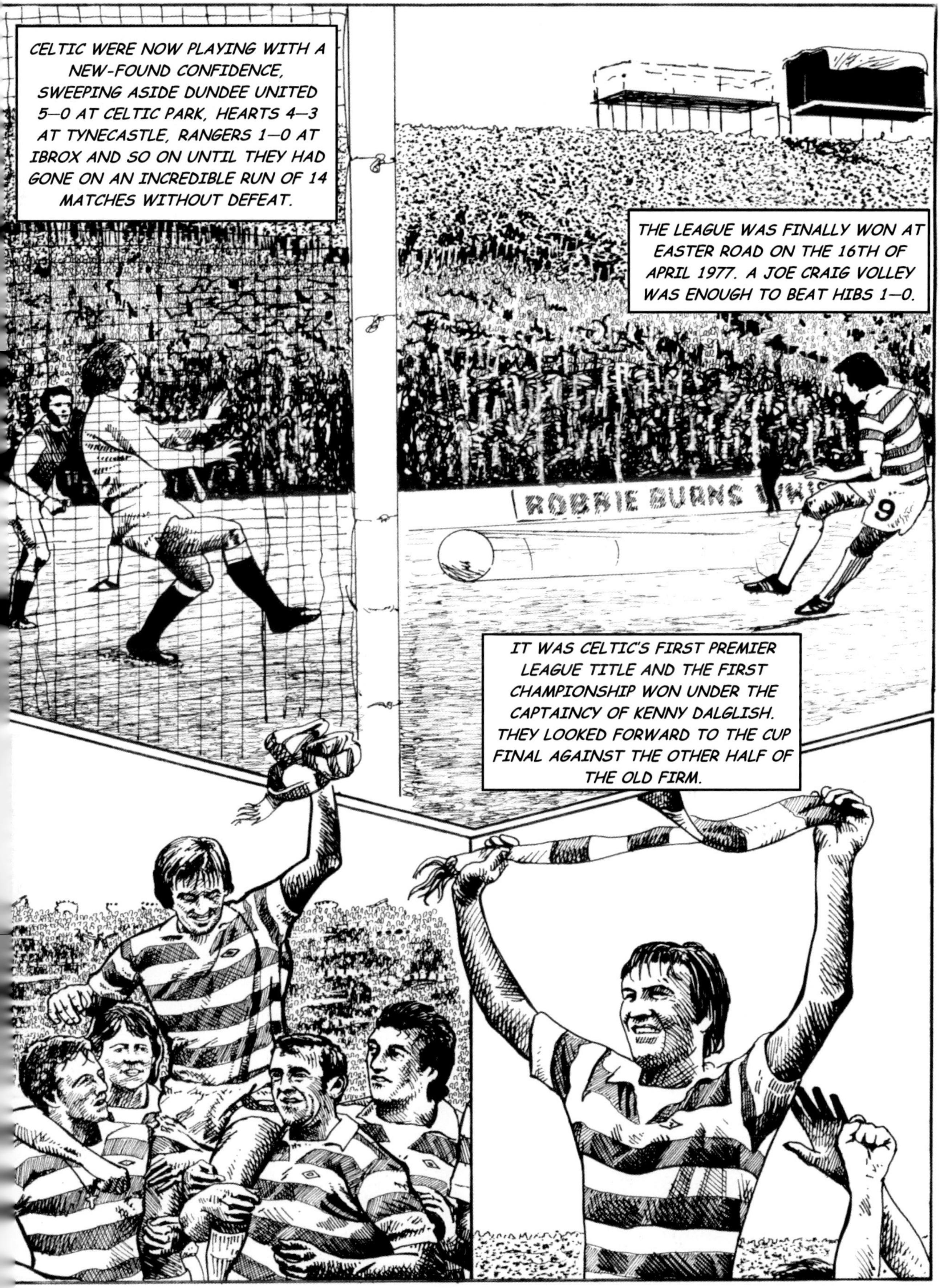
CELTIC WERE NOW PLAYING WITH A NEW-FOUND CONFIDENCE, SWEEPING ASIDE DUNDEE UNITED 5—0 AT CELTIC PARK, HEARTS 4—3 AT TYNECASTLE, RANGERS 1—0 AT IBROX AND SO ON UNTIL THEY HAD GONE ON AN INCREDIBLE RUN OF 14 MATCHES WITHOUT DEFEAT.
THE LEAGUE WAS FINALLY WON AT EASTER ROAD ON THE 16TH OF APRIL 1977. A JOE CRAIG VOLLEY WAS ENOUGH TO BEAT HIBS 1—0.
ROBBIE BURNS
9
IT WAS CELTIC'S FIRST PREMIER LEAGUE TITLE AND THE FIRST CHAMPIONSHIP WON UNDER THE CAPTAINCY OF KENNY DALGLISH. THEY LOOKED FORWARD TO THE CUP FINAL AGAINST THE OTHER HALF OF THE OLD FIRM.

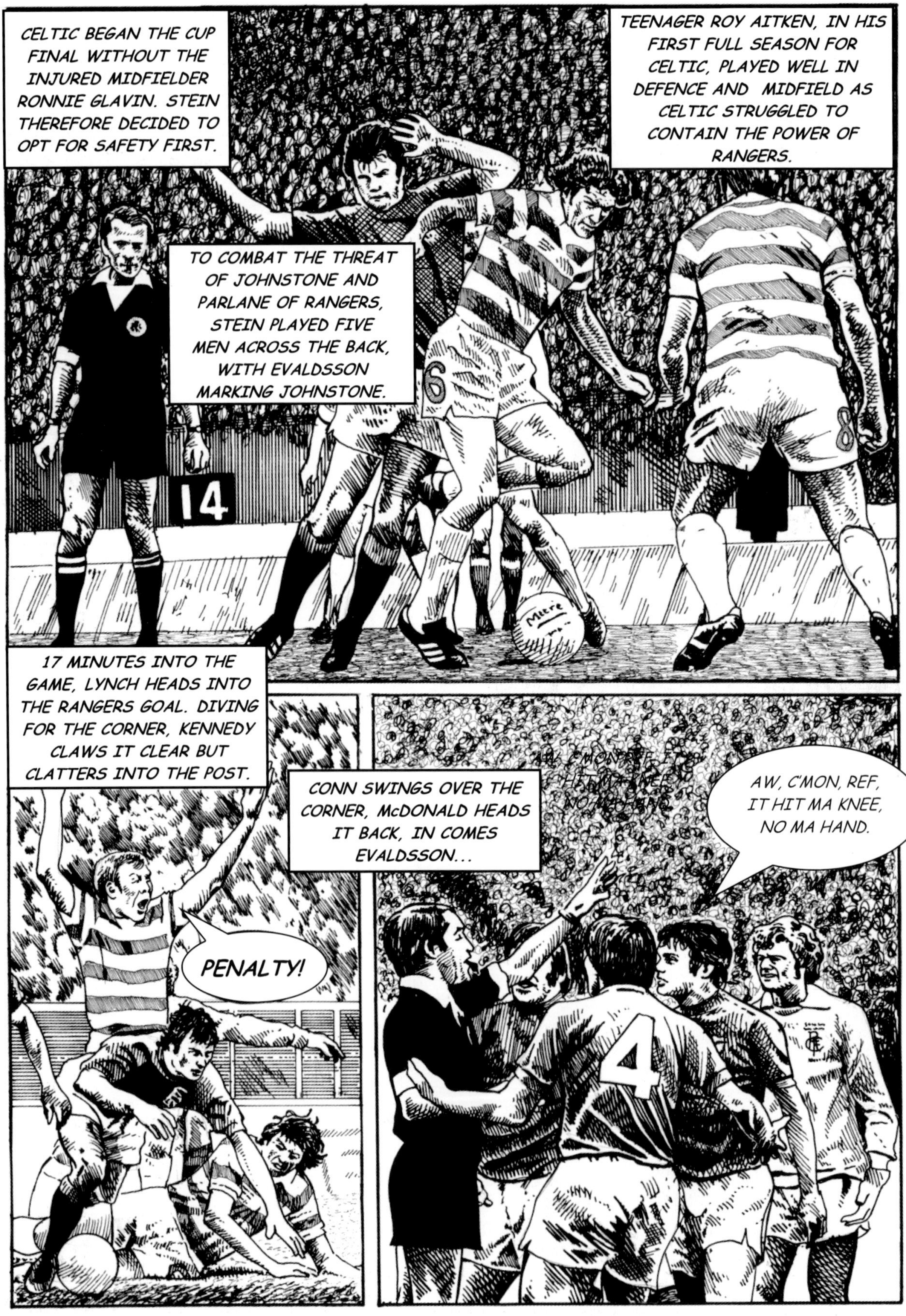
CELTIC BEGAN THE CUP FINAL WITHOUT THE INJURED MIDFIELDER RONNIE GLAVIN. STEIN THEREFORE DECIDED TO OPT FOR SAFETY FIRST.
TEENAGER ROY AITKEN, IN HIS FIRST FULL SEASON FOR CELTIC, PLAYED WELL IN DEFENCE AND MIDFIELD AS CELTIC STRUGGLED TO CONTAIN THE POWER OF RANGERS.
TO COMBAT THE THREAT OF JOHNSTONE AND PARLANE OF RANGERS, STEIN PLAYED FIVE MEN ACROSS THE BACK, WITH EVALDSSON MARKING JOHNSTONE.
14
17 MINUTES INTO THE GAME, LYNCH HEADS INTO THE RANGERS GOAL. DIVING FOR THE CORNER, KENNEDY CLAWS IT CLEAR BUT CLATTERS INTO THE POST.
PENALTY!
CONN SWINGS OVER THE CORNER, McDONALD HEADS IT BACK, IN COMES EVALDSSON...
AW, C'MON, REF, IT HIT MA KNEE, NO MA HAND.

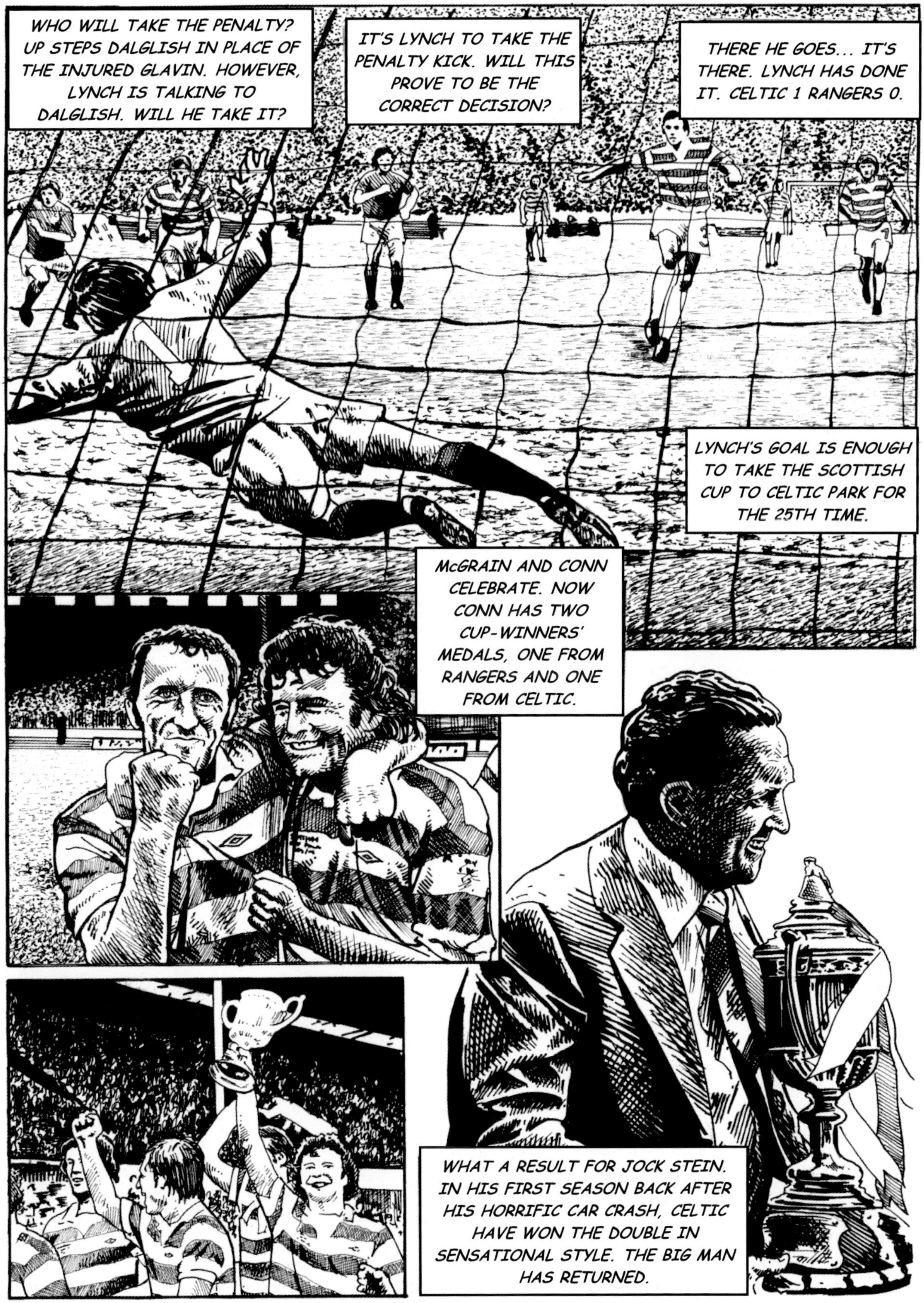
WHO WILL TAKE THE PENALTY? UP STEPS DALGLISH IN PLACE OF THE INJURED GLAVIN. HOWEVER, LYNCH IS TALKING TO DALGLISH. WILL HE TAKE IT?
IT'S LYNCH TO TAKE THE PENALTY KICK. WILL THIS PROVE TO BE THE CORRECT DECISION?
THERE HE GOES... IT'S THERE. LYNCH HAS DONE IT. CELTIC 1 RANGERS 0.
LYNCH'S GOAL IS ENOUGH TO TAKE THE SCOTTISH CUP TO CELTIC PARK FOR THE 25TH TIME.
McGRAIN AND CONN CELEBRATE. NOW CONN HAS TWO CUP-WINNERS' MEDALS, ONE FROM RANGERS AND ONE FROM CELTIC.
WHAT A RESULT FOR JOCK STEIN. IN HIS FIRST SEASON BACK AFTER HIS HORRIFIC CAR CRASH, CELTIC HAVE WON THE DOUBLE IN SENSATIONAL STYLE. THE BIG MAN HAS RETURNED.

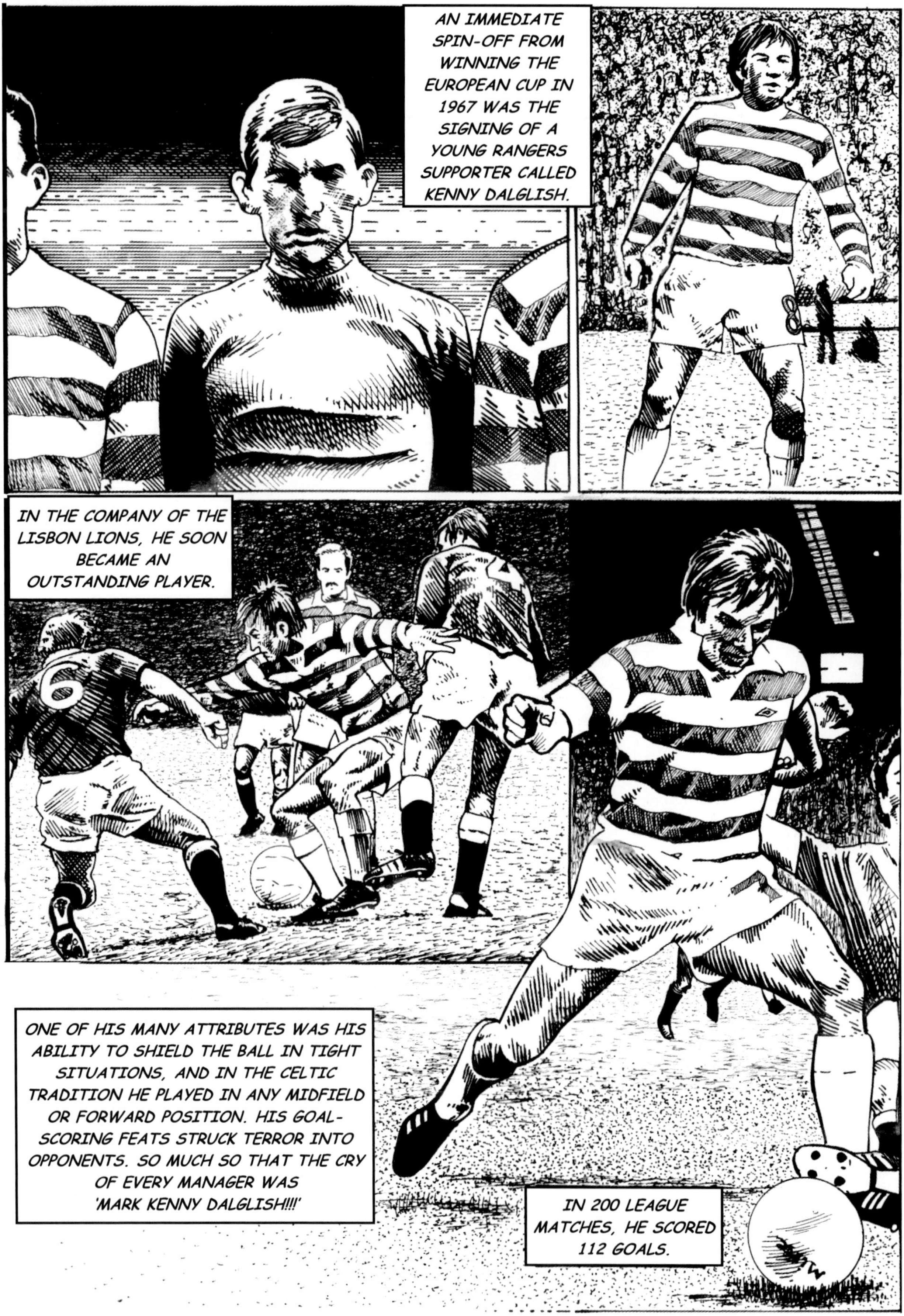
AN IMMEDIATE SPIN-OFF FROM WINNING THE EUROPEAN CUP IN 1967 WAS THE SIGNING OF A YOUNG RANGERS SUPPORTER CALLED KENNY DALGLISH.
IN THE COMPANY OF THE LISBON LIONS, HE SOON BECAME AN OUTSTANDING PLAYER.
ONE OF HIS MANY ATTRIBUTES WAS HIS ABILITY TO SHIELD THE BALL IN TIGHT SITUATIONS, AND IN THE CELTIC TRADITION HE PLAYED IN ANY MIDFIELD OR FORWARD POSITION. HIS GOAL-SCORING FEATS STRUCK TERROR INTO OPPONENTS. SO MUCH SO THAT THE CRY OF EVERY MANAGER WAS 'MARK KENNY DALGLISH!!!'
IN 200 LEAGUE MATCHES, HE SCORED 112 GOALS.

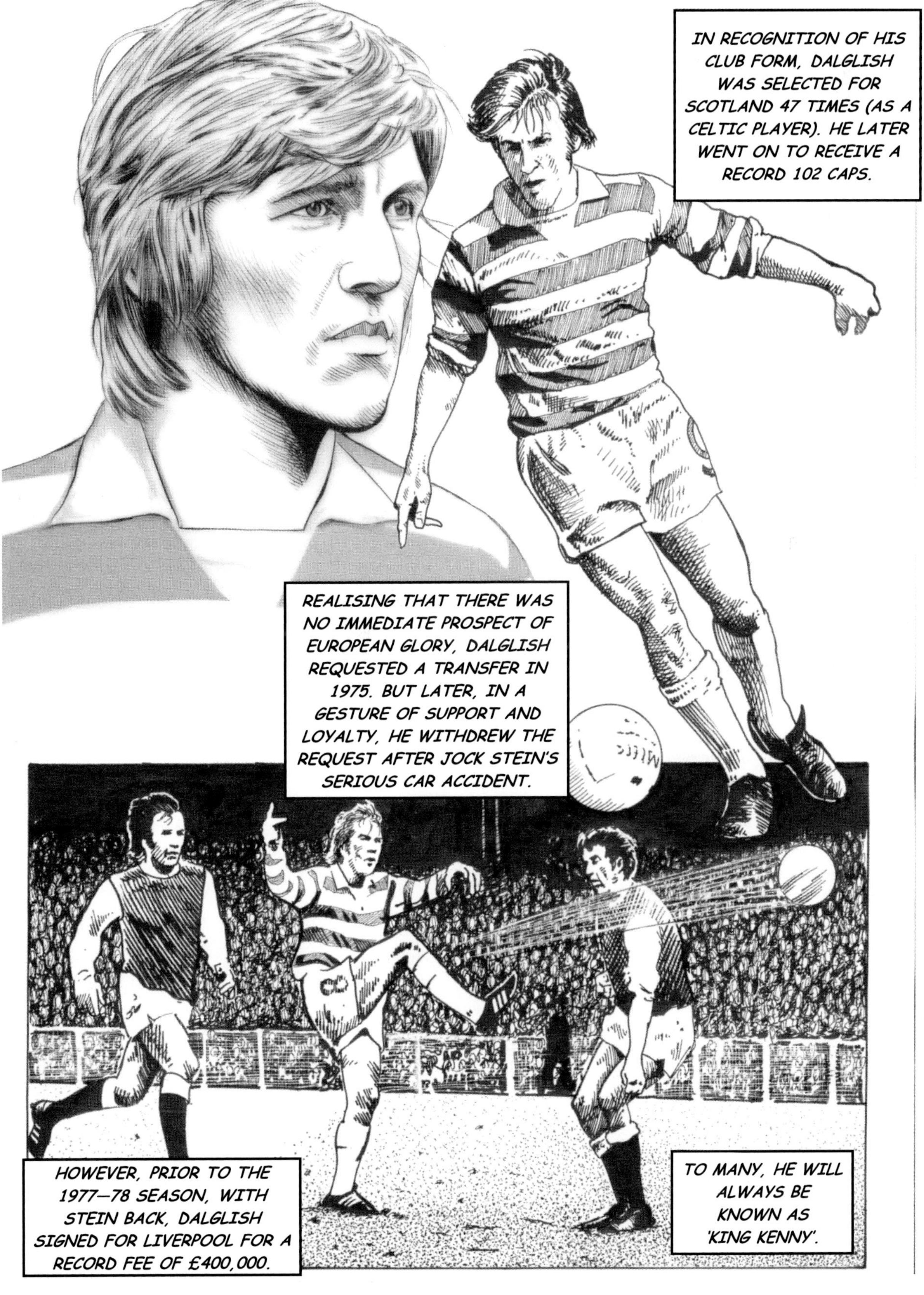
IN RECOGNITION OF HIS CLUB FORM, DALGLISH WAS SELECTED FOR SCOTLAND 47 TIMES (AS A CELTIC PLAYER). HE LATER WENT ON TO RECEIVE A RECORD 102 CAPS.
REALISING THAT THERE WAS NO IMMEDIATE PROSPECT OF EUROPEAN GLORY, DALGLISH REQUESTED A TRANSFER IN 1975. BUT LATER, IN A GESTURE OF SUPPORT AND LOYALTY, HE WITHDREW THE REQUEST AFTER JOCK STEIN'S SERIOUS CAR ACCIDENT.
HOWEVER, PRIOR TO THE 1977–78 SEASON, WITH STEIN BACK, DALGLISH SIGNED FOR LIVERPOOL FOR A RECORD FEE OF £400,000.
TO MANY, HE WILL ALWAYS BE KNOWN AS 'KING KENNY'.

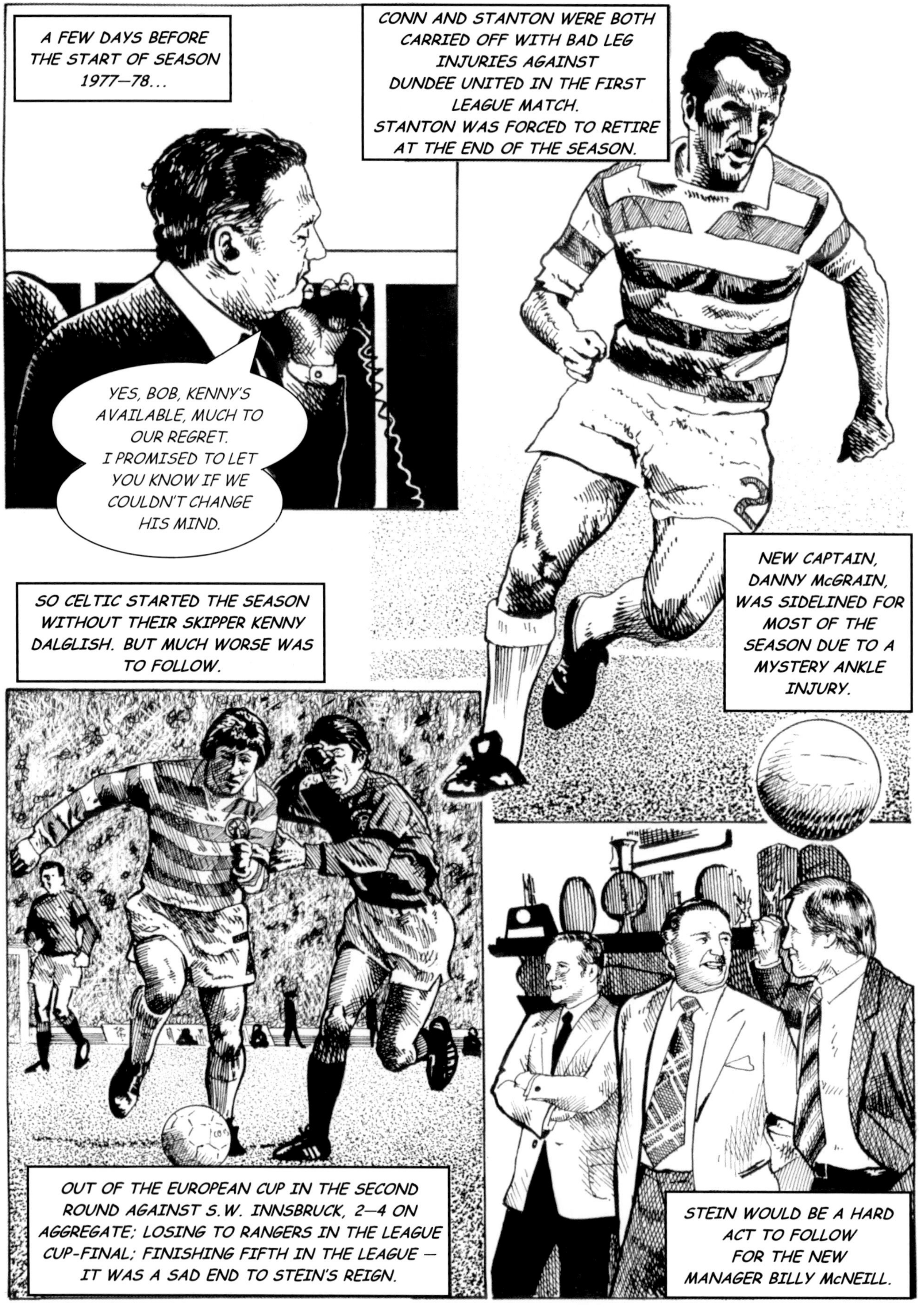
A FEW DAYS BEFORE THE START OF SEASON 1977–78...
CONN AND STANTON WERE BOTH CARRIED OFF WITH BAD LEG INJURIES AGAINST DUNDEE UNITED IN THE FIRST LEAGUE MATCH. STANTON WAS FORCED TO RETIRE AT THE END OF THE SEASON.
YES, BOB, KENNY'S AVAILABLE, MUCH TO OUR REGRET. I PROMISED TO LET YOU KNOW IF WE COULDN'T CHANGE HIS MIND.
NEW CAPTAIN, DANNY McGRAIN, WAS SIDELINED FOR MOST OF THE SEASON DUE TO A MYSTERY ANKLE INJURY.
SO CELTIC STARTED THE SEASON WITHOUT THEIR SKIPPER KENNY DALGLISH. BUT MUCH WORSE WAS TO FOLLOW.
OUT OF THE EUROPEAN CUP IN THE SECOND ROUND AGAINST S.W. INNSBRUCK, 2–4 ON AGGREGATE; LOSING TO RANGERS IN THE LEAGUE CUP-FINAL; FINISHING FIFTH IN THE LEAGUE – IT WAS A SAD END TO STEIN'S REIGN.
STEIN WOULD BE A HARD ACT TO FOLLOW FOR THE NEW MANAGER BILLY McNEILL.

chapter 8

cesar reigns

'walk on through the wind'

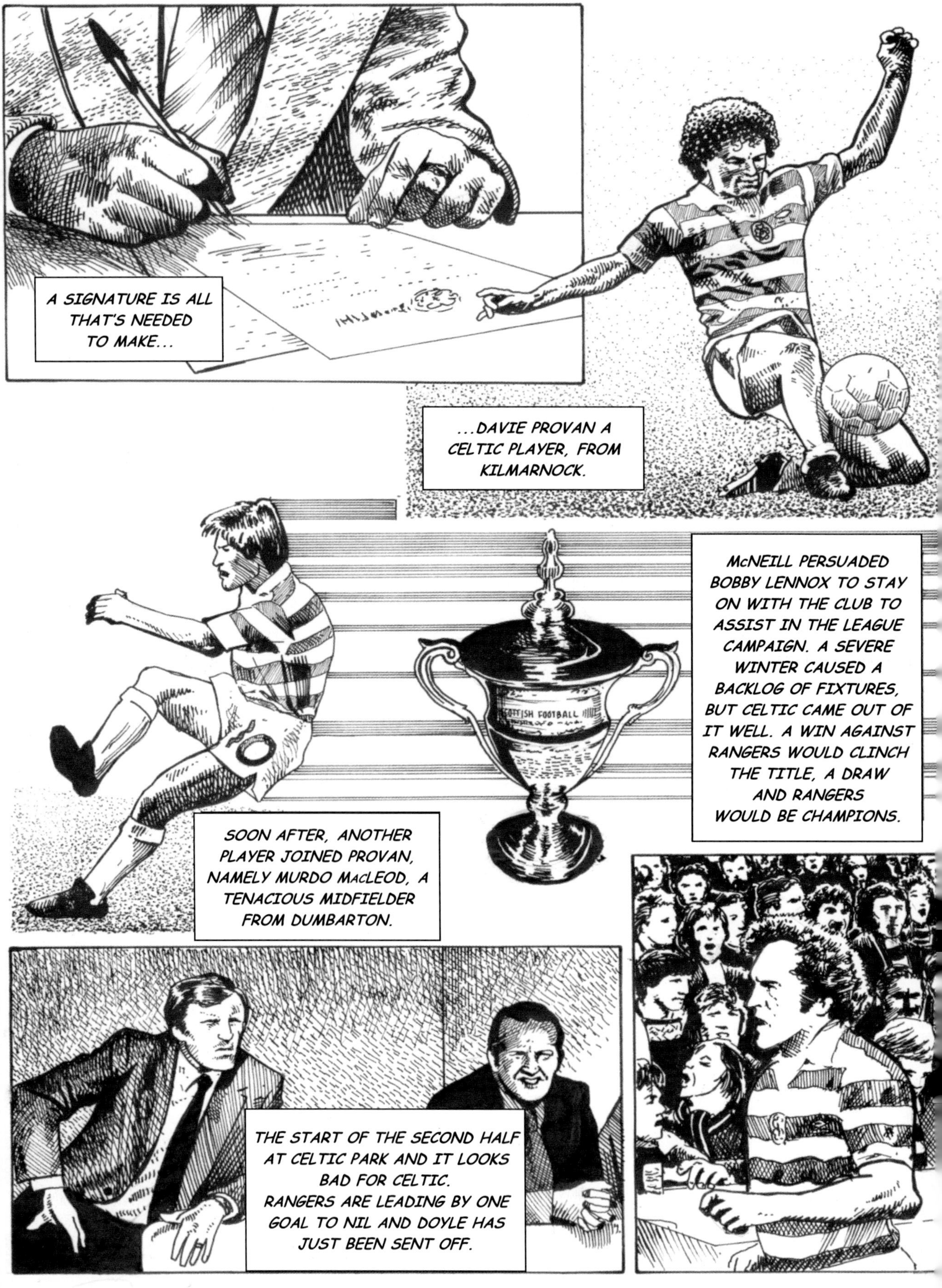

A SIGNATURE IS ALL THAT'S NEEDED TO MAKE...
...DAVIE PROVAN A CELTIC PLAYER, FROM KILMARNOCK.
SOON AFTER, ANOTHER PLAYER JOINED PROVAN, NAMELY MURDO MacLEOD, A TENACIOUS MIDFIELDER FROM DUMBARTON.
SCOTTISH FOOTBALL
McNEILL PERSUADED BOBBY LENNOX TO STAY ON WITH THE CLUB TO ASSIST IN THE LEAGUE CAMPAIGN. A SEVERE WINTER CAUSED A BACKLOG OF FIXTURES, BUT CELTIC CAME OUT OF IT WELL. A WIN AGAINST RANGERS WOULD CLINCH THE TITLE, A DRAW AND RANGERS WOULD BE CHAMPIONS.
THE START OF THE SECOND HALF AT CELTIC PARK AND IT LOOKS BAD FOR CELTIC.
RANGERS ARE LEADING BY ONE GOAL TO NIL AND DOYLE HAS JUST BEEN SENT OFF.

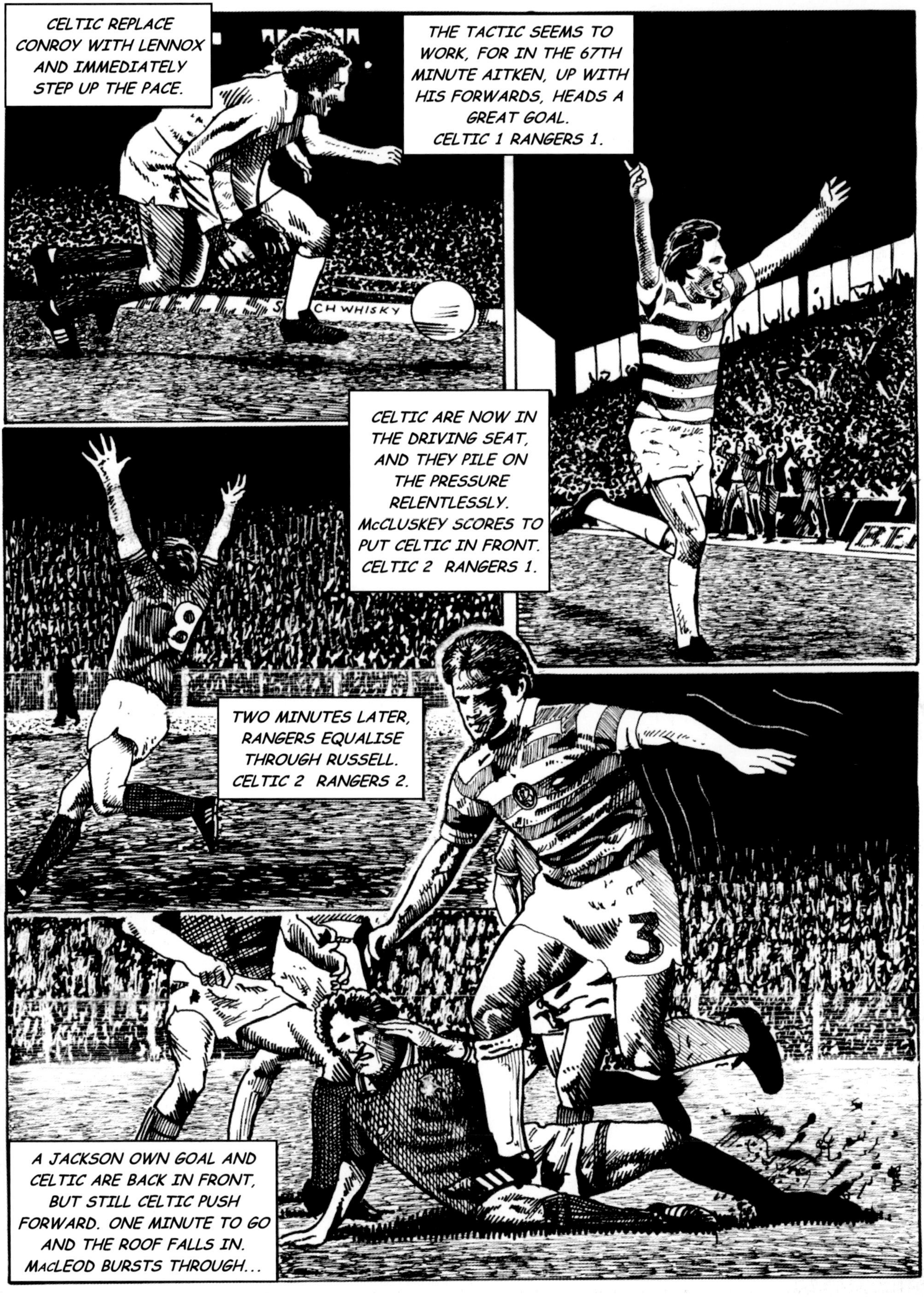
CELTIC REPLACE CONROY WITH LENNOX AND IMMEDIATELY STEP UP THE PACE.
THE TACTIC SEEMS TO WORK, FOR IN THE 67TH MINUTE AITKEN, UP WITH HIS FORWARDS, HEADS A GREAT GOAL. CELTIC 1 RANGERS 1.
CELTIC ARE NOW IN THE DRIVING SEAT, AND THEY PILE ON THE PRESSURE RELENTLESSLY. McCLUSKEY SCORES TO PUT CELTIC IN FRONT. CELTIC 2 RANGERS 1.
TWO MINUTES LATER, RANGERS EQUALISE THROUGH RUSSELL. CELTIC 2 RANGERS 2.
A JACKSON OWN GOAL AND CELTIC ARE BACK IN FRONT, BUT STILL CELTIC PUSH FORWARD. ONE MINUTE TO GO AND THE ROOF FALLS IN. MacLEOD BURSTS THROUGH...

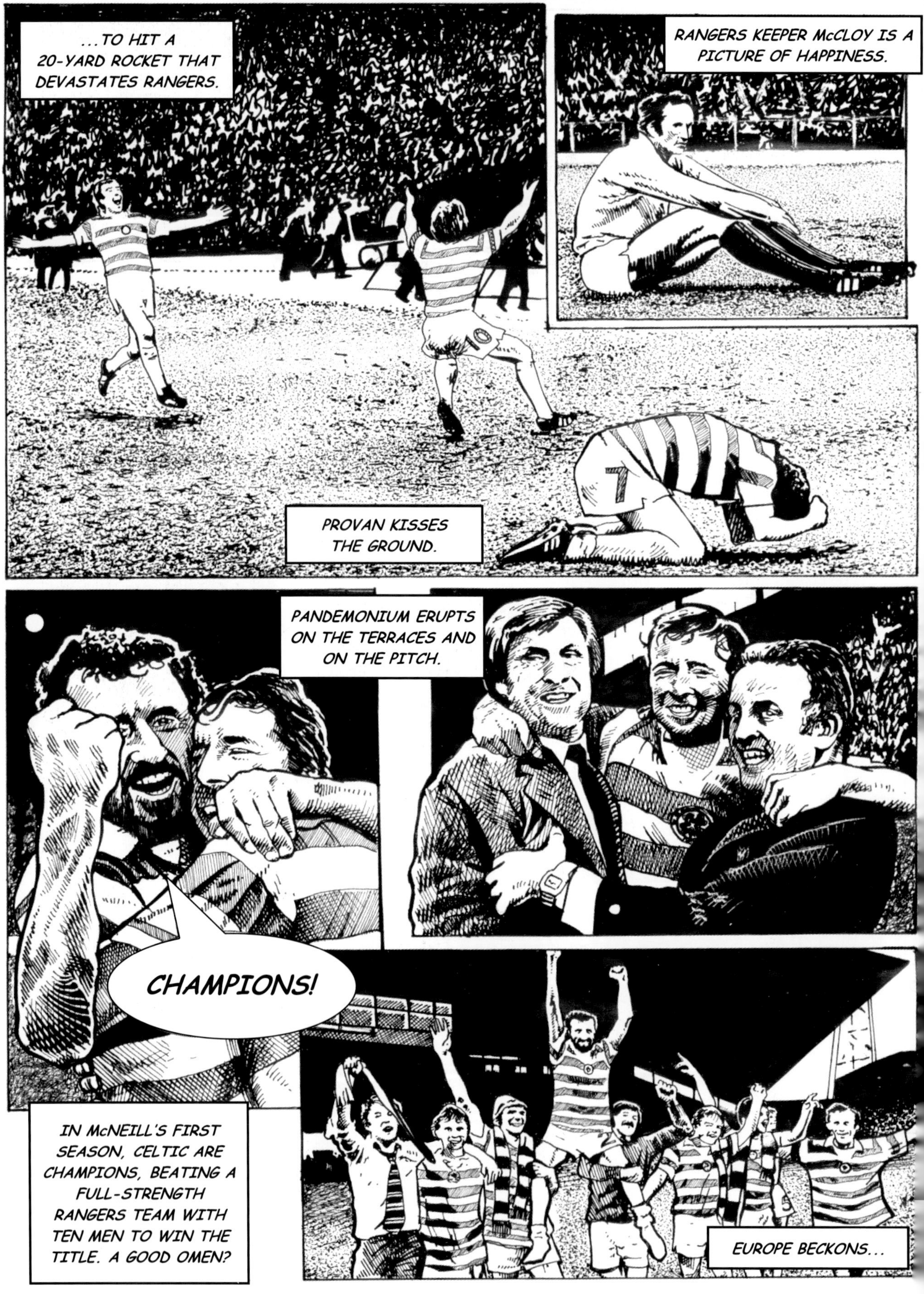
...TO HIT A 20-YARD ROCKET THAT DEVASTATES RANGERS.
RANGERS KEEPER McCLOY IS A PICTURE OF HAPPINESS.
PROVAN KISSES THE GROUND.
PANDEMONIUM ERUPTS ON THE TERRACES AND ON THE PITCH.
CHAMPIONS!
IN McNEILL'S FIRST SEASON, CELTIC ARE CHAMPIONS, BEATING A FULL-STRENGTH RANGERS TEAM WITH TEN MEN TO WIN THE TITLE. A GOOD OMEN?
EUROPE BECKONS...

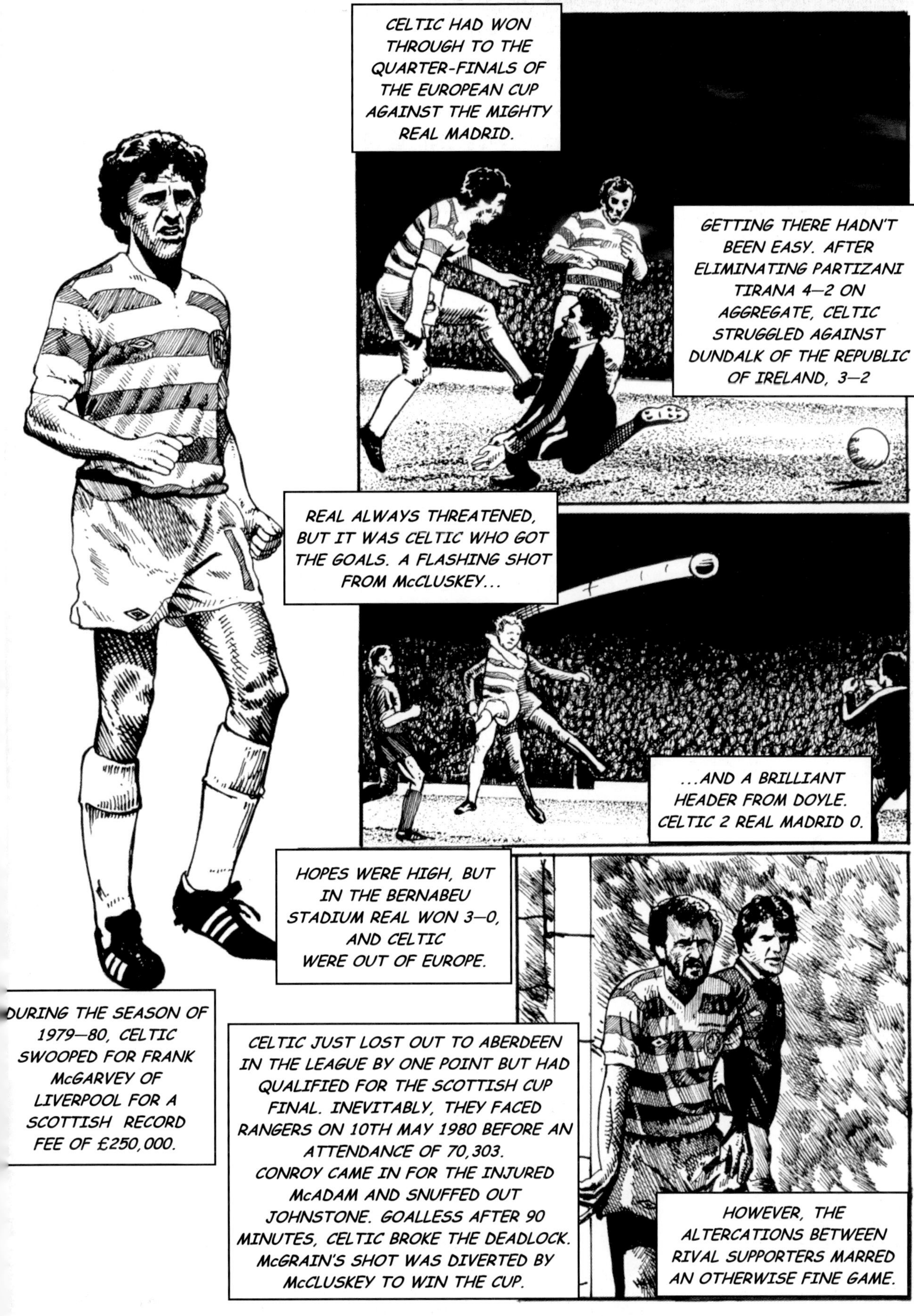

CELTIC HAD WON THROUGH TO THE QUARTER-FINALS OF THE EUROPEAN CUP AGAINST THE MIGHTY REAL MADRID.
GETTING THERE HADN'T BEEN EASY. AFTER ELIMINATING PARTIZANI TIRANA 4–2 ON AGGREGATE, CELTIC STRUGGLED AGAINST DUNDALK OF THE REPUBLIC OF IRELAND, 3–2
REAL ALWAYS THREATENED, BUT IT WAS CELTIC WHO GOT THE GOALS. A FLASHING SHOT FROM McCLUSKEY...
...AND A BRILLIANT HEADER FROM DOYLE. CELTIC 2 REAL MADRID 0.
HOPES WERE HIGH, BUT IN THE BERNABEU STADIUM REAL WON 3–0, AND CELTIC WERE OUT OF EUROPE.
DURING THE SEASON OF 1979–80, CELTIC SWOOPED FOR FRANK McGARVEY OF LIVERPOOL FOR A SCOTTISH RECORD FEE OF £250,000.
CELTIC JUST LOST OUT TO ABERDEEN IN THE LEAGUE BY ONE POINT BUT HAD QUALIFIED FOR THE SCOTTISH CUP FINAL. INEVITABLY, THEY FACED RANGERS ON 10TH MAY 1980 BEFORE AN ATTENDANCE OF 70,303. CONROY CAME IN FOR THE INJURED McADAM AND SNUFFED OUT JOHNSTONE. GOALLESS AFTER 90 MINUTES, CELTIC BROKE THE DEADLOCK. McGRAIN'S SHOT WAS DIVERTED BY McCLUSKEY TO WIN THE CUP.
HOWEVER, THE ALTERCATIONS BETWEEN RIVAL SUPPORTERS MARRED AN OTHERWISE FINE GAME.

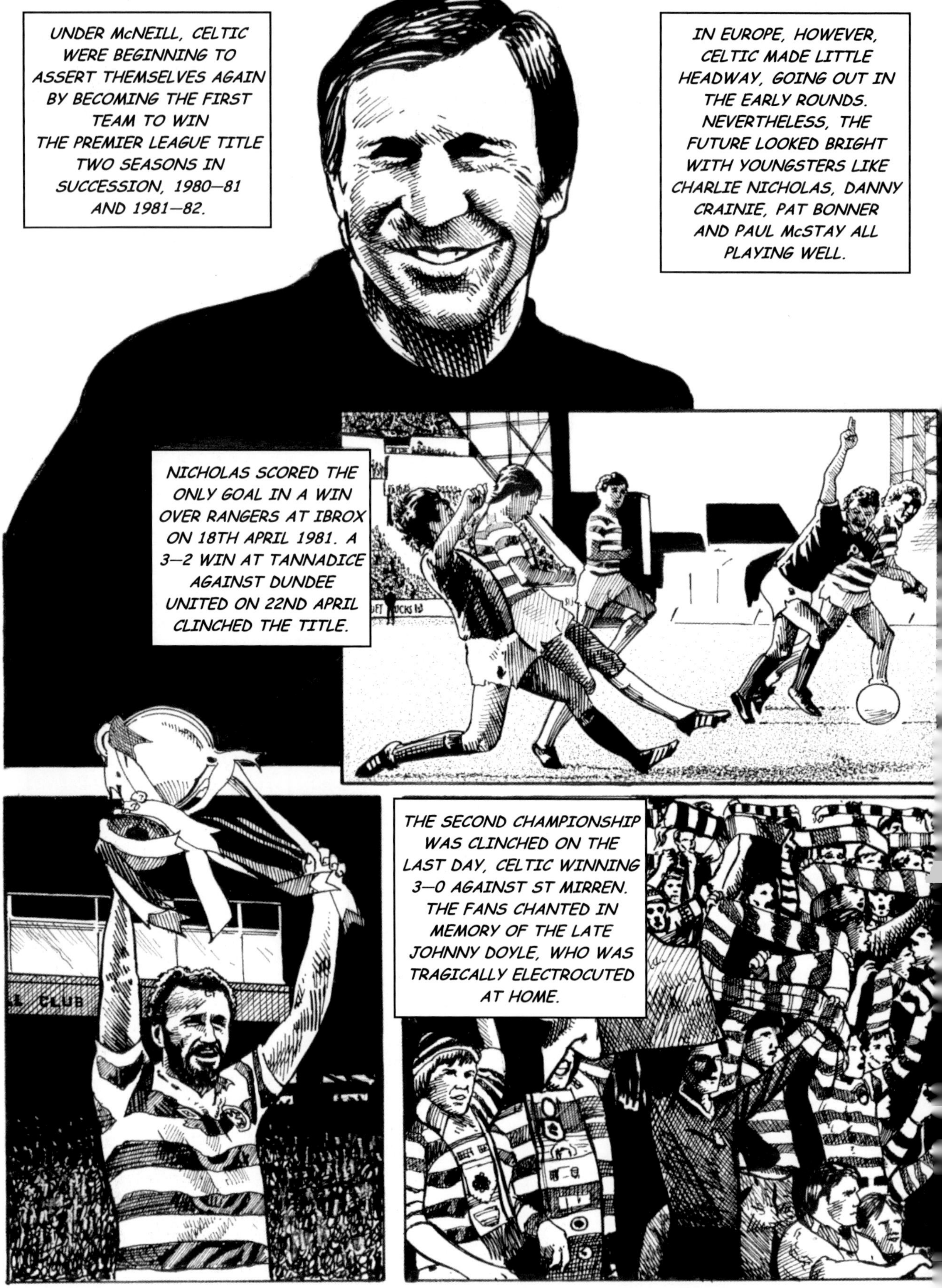
UNDER McNEILL, CELTIC WERE BEGINNING TO ASSERT THEMSELVES AGAIN BY BECOMING THE FIRST TEAM TO WIN THE PREMIER LEAGUE TITLE TWO SEASONS IN SUCCESSION, 1980–81 AND 1981–82.
IN EUROPE, HOWEVER, CELTIC MADE LITTLE HEADWAY, GOING OUT IN THE EARLY ROUNDS. NEVERTHELESS, THE FUTURE LOOKED BRIGHT WITH YOUNGSTERS LIKE CHARLIE NICHOLAS, DANNY CRAINIE, PAT BONNER AND PAUL McSTAY ALL PLAYING WELL.
NICHOLAS SCORED THE ONLY GOAL IN A WIN OVER RANGERS AT IBROX ON 18TH APRIL 1981. A 3–2 WIN AT TANNADICE AGAINST DUNDEE UNITED ON 22ND APRIL CLINCHED THE TITLE.
THE SECOND CHAMPIONSHIP WAS CLINCHED ON THE LAST DAY, CELTIC WINNING 3–0 AGAINST ST MIRREN. THE FANS CHANTED IN MEMORY OF THE LATE JOHNNY DOYLE, WHO WAS TRAGICALLY ELECTROCUTED AT HOME.

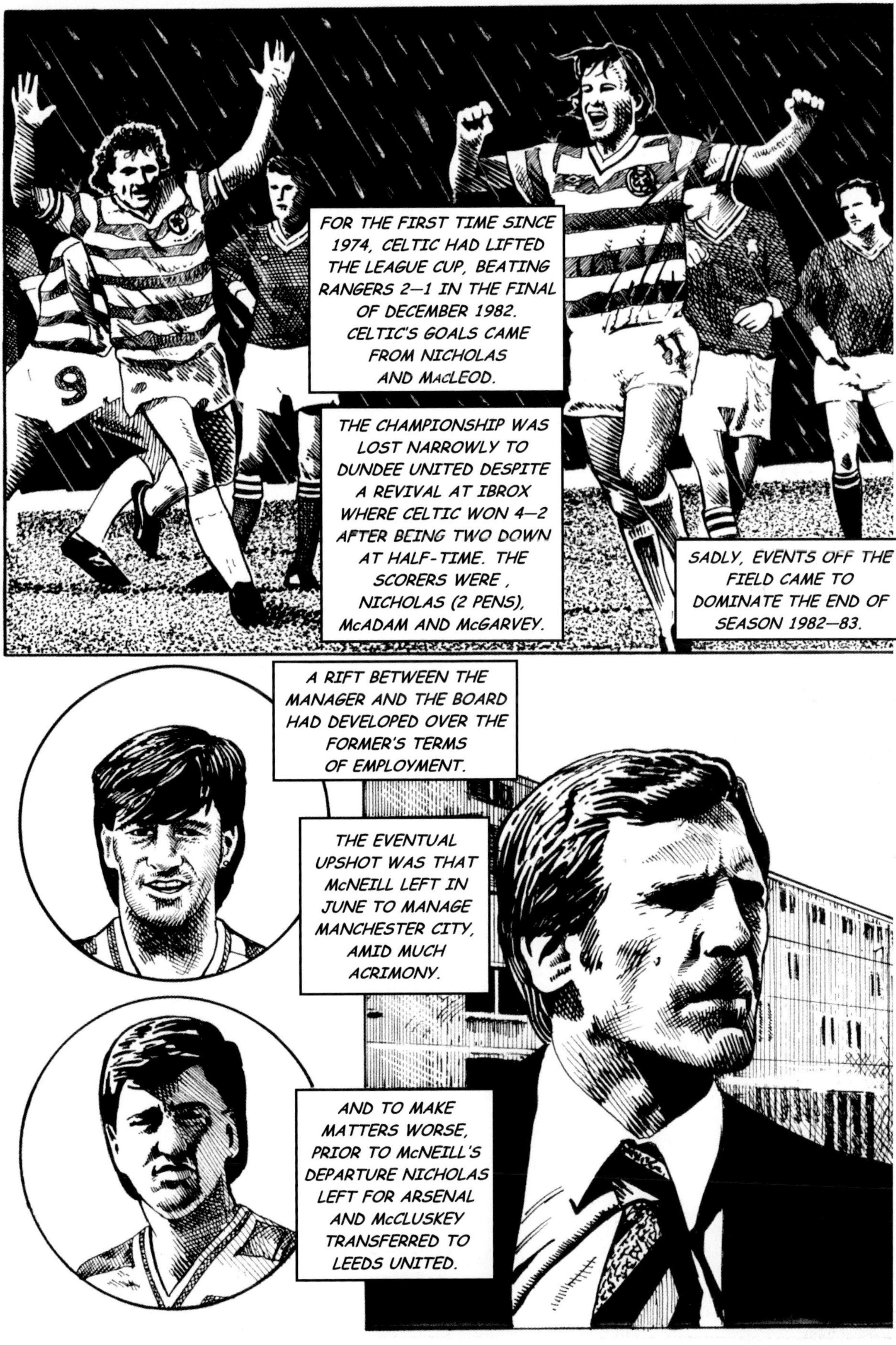
FOR THE FIRST TIME SINCE 1974, CELTIC HAD LIFTED THE LEAGUE CUP, BEATING RANGERS 2–1 IN THE FINAL OF DECEMBER 1982. CELTIC'S GOALS CAME FROM NICHOLAS AND MacLEOD.
THE CHAMPIONSHIP WAS LOST NARROWLY TO DUNDEE UNITED DESPITE A REVIVAL AT IBROX WHERE CELTIC WON 4–2 AFTER BEING TWO DOWN AT HALF-TIME. THE SCORERS WERE , NICHOLAS (2 PENS), McADAM AND McGARVEY.
SADLY, EVENTS OFF THE FIELD CAME TO DOMINATE THE END OF SEASON 1982–83.
A RIFT BETWEEN THE MANAGER AND THE BOARD HAD DEVELOPED OVER THE FORMER'S TERMS OF EMPLOYMENT.
THE EVENTUAL UPSHOT WAS THAT McNEILL LEFT IN JUNE TO MANAGE MANCHESTER CITY, AMID MUCH ACRIMONY.
AND TO MAKE MATTERS WORSE, PRIOR TO McNEILL'S DEPARTURE NICHOLAS LEFT FOR ARSENAL AND McCLUSKEY TRANSFERRED TO LEEDS UNITED.

chapter 9

making hay

'walk on through the rain'

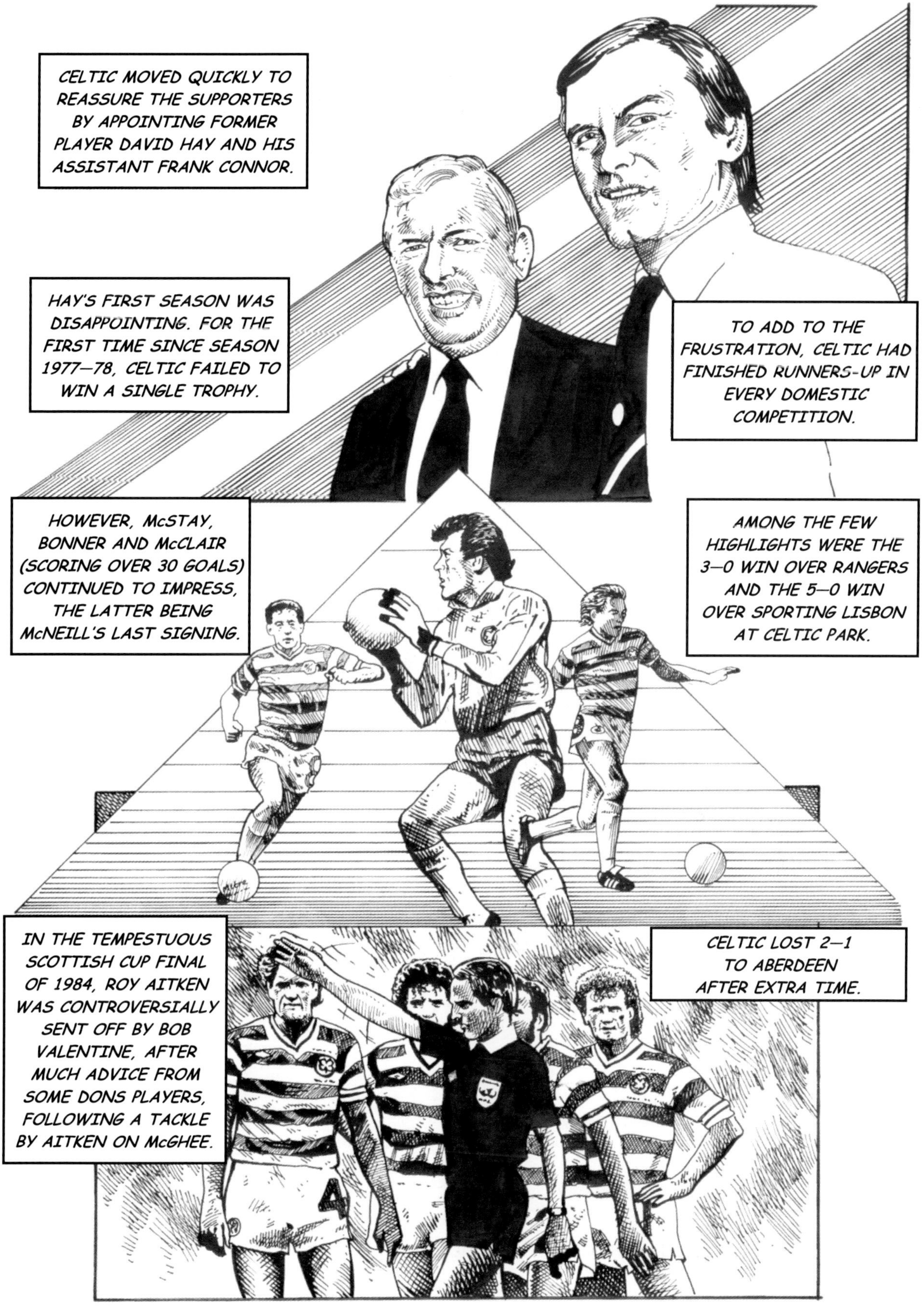
CELTIC MOVED QUICKLY TO REASSURE THE SUPPORTERS BY APPOINTING FORMER PLAYER DAVID HAY AND HIS ASSISTANT FRANK CONNOR.
HAY'S FIRST SEASON WAS DISAPPOINTING. FOR THE FIRST TIME SINCE SEASON 1977–78, CELTIC FAILED TO WIN A SINGLE TROPHY.
TO ADD TO THE FRUSTRATION, CELTIC HAD FINISHED RUNNERS-UP IN EVERY DOMESTIC COMPETITION.
HOWEVER, McSTAY, BONNER AND McCLAIR (SCORING OVER 30 GOALS) CONTINUED TO IMPRESS, THE LATTER BEING McNEILL'S LAST SIGNING.
AMONG THE FEW HIGHLIGHTS WERE THE 3–0 WIN OVER RANGERS AND THE 5–0 WIN OVER SPORTING LISBON AT CELTIC PARK.
IN THE TEMPESTUOUS SCOTTISH CUP FINAL OF 1984, ROY AITKEN WAS CONTROVERSIALLY SENT OFF BY BOB VALENTINE, AFTER MUCH ADVICE FROM SOME DONS PLAYERS, FOLLOWING A TACKLE BY AITKEN ON McGHEE.
CELTIC LOST 2–1 TO ABERDEEN AFTER EXTRA TIME.

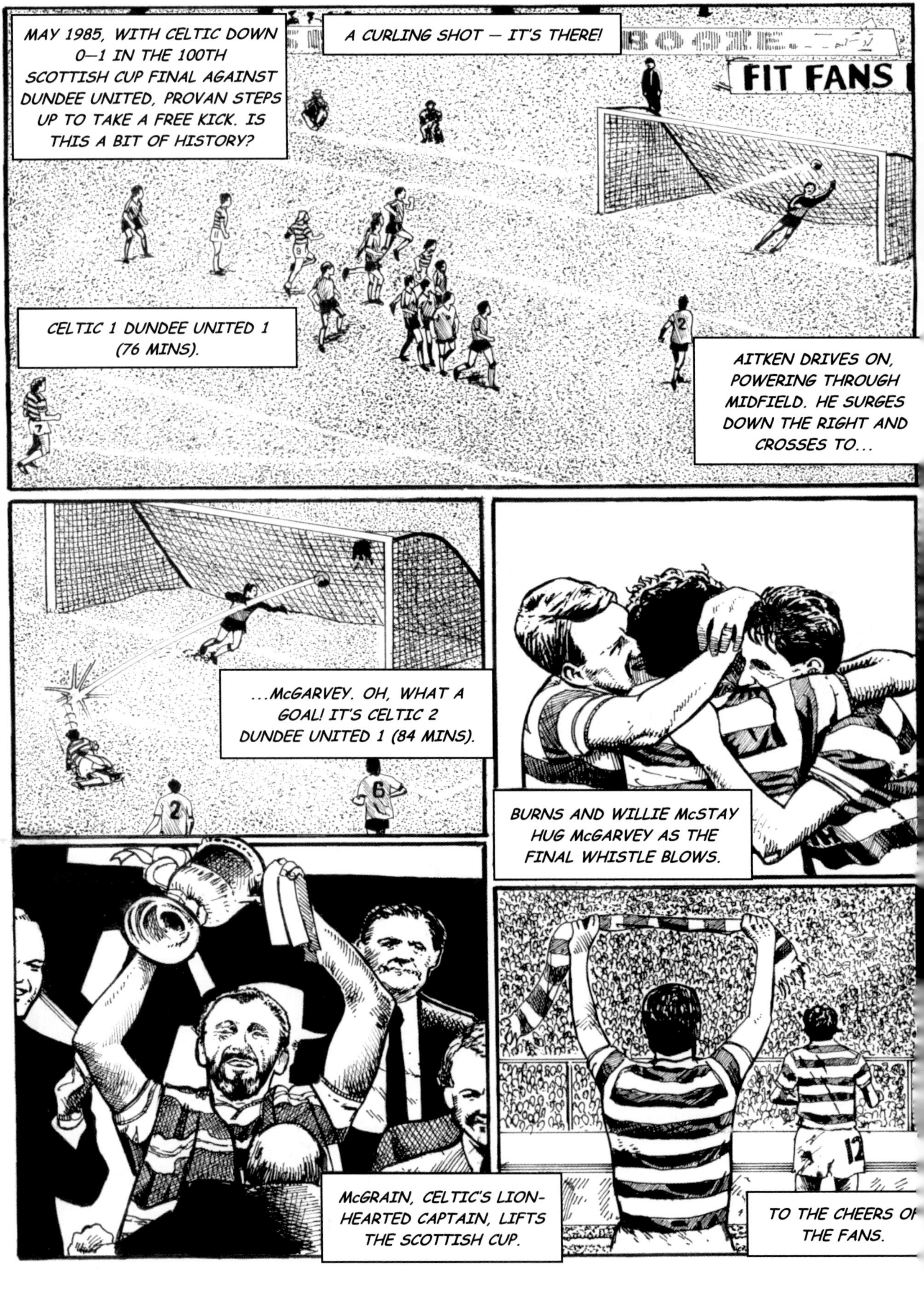
MAY 1985, WITH CELTIC DOWN 0–1 IN THE 100TH SCOTTISH CUP FINAL AGAINST DUNDEE UNITED, PROVAN STEPS UP TO TAKE A FREE KICK. IS THIS A BIT OF HISTORY?
A CURLING SHOT – IT'S THERE!
FIT FANS
CELTIC 1 DUNDEE UNITED 1 (76 MINS).
AITKEN DRIVES ON, POWERING THROUGH MIDFIELD. HE SURGES DOWN THE RIGHT AND CROSSES TO...
...McGARVEY. OH, WHAT A GOAL! IT'S CELTIC 2 DUNDEE UNITED 1 (84 MINS).
BURNS AND WILLIE McSTAY HUG McGARVEY AS THE FINAL WHISTLE BLOWS.
McGRAIN, CELTIC'S LION-HEARTED CAPTAIN, LIFTS THE SCOTTISH CUP.
TO THE CHEERS O
THE FANS.

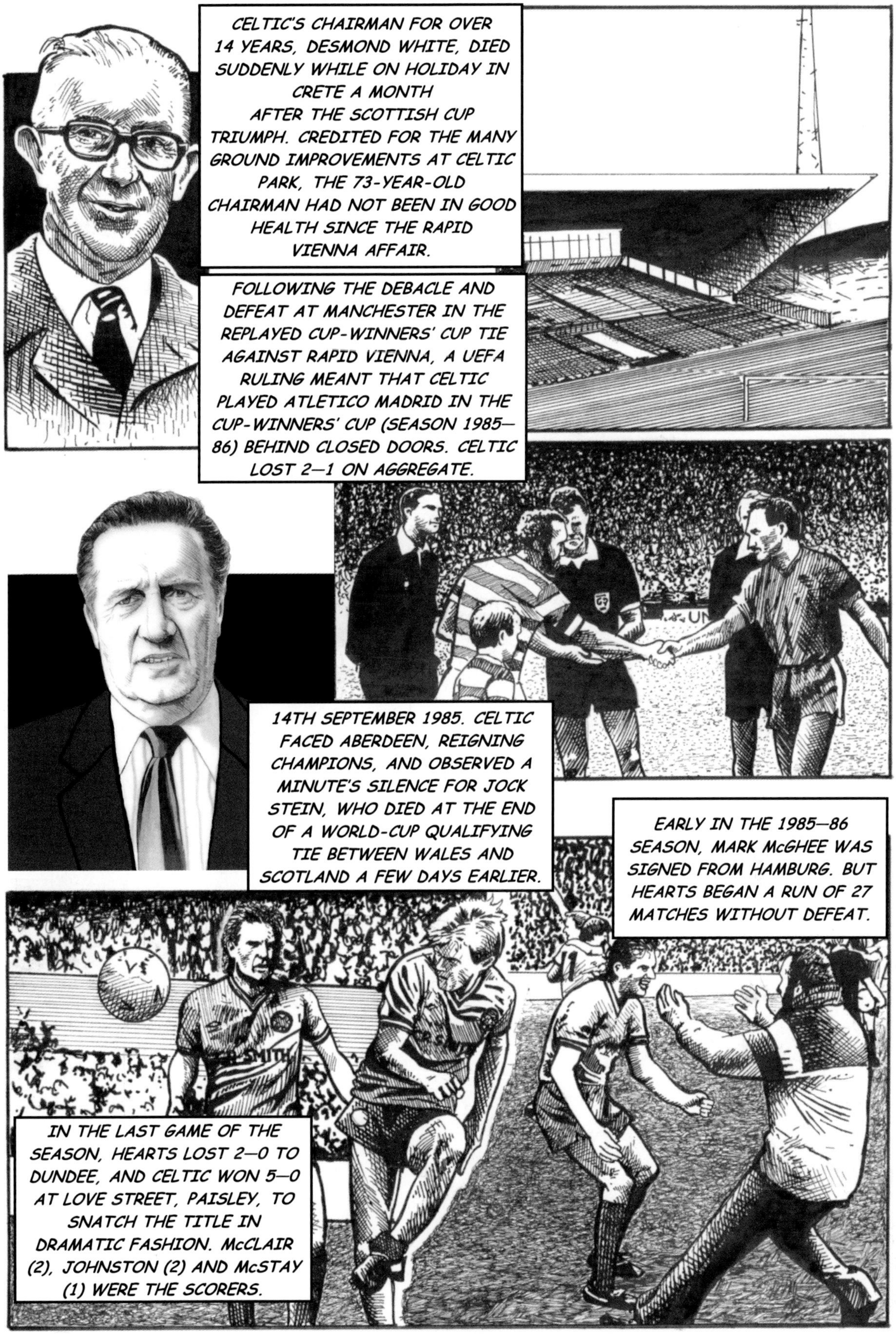
CELTIC'S CHAIRMAN FOR OVER 14 YEARS, DESMOND WHITE, DIED SUDDENLY WHILE ON HOLIDAY IN CRETE A MONTH AFTER THE SCOTTISH CUP TRIUMPH. CREDITED FOR THE MANY GROUND IMPROVEMENTS AT CELTIC PARK, THE 73-YEAR-OLD CHAIRMAN HAD NOT BEEN IN GOOD HEALTH SINCE THE RAPID VIENNA AFFAIR.
FOLLOWING THE DEBACLE AND DEFEAT AT MANCHESTER IN THE REPLAYED CUP-WINNERS' CUP TIE AGAINST RAPID VIENNA, A UEFA RULING MEANT THAT CELTIC PLAYED ATLETICO MADRID IN THE CUP-WINNERS' CUP (SEASON 1985–86) BEHIND CLOSED DOORS. CELTIC LOST 2–1 ON AGGREGATE.
14TH SEPTEMBER 1985. CELTIC FACED ABERDEEN, REIGNING CHAMPIONS, AND OBSERVED A MINUTE'S SILENCE FOR JOCK STEIN, WHO DIED AT THE END OF A WORLD-CUP QUALIFYING TIE BETWEEN WALES AND SCOTLAND A FEW DAYS EARLIER.
EARLY IN THE 1985–86 SEASON, MARK McGHEE WAS SIGNED FROM HAMBURG. BUT HEARTS BEGAN A RUN OF 27 MATCHES WITHOUT DEFEAT.
IN THE LAST GAME OF THE SEASON, HEARTS LOST 2–0 TO DUNDEE, AND CELTIC WON 5–0 AT LOVE STREET, PAISLEY, TO SNATCH THE TITLE IN DRAMATIC FASHION. McCLAIR (2), JOHNSTON (2) AND McSTAY (1) WERE THE SCORERS.

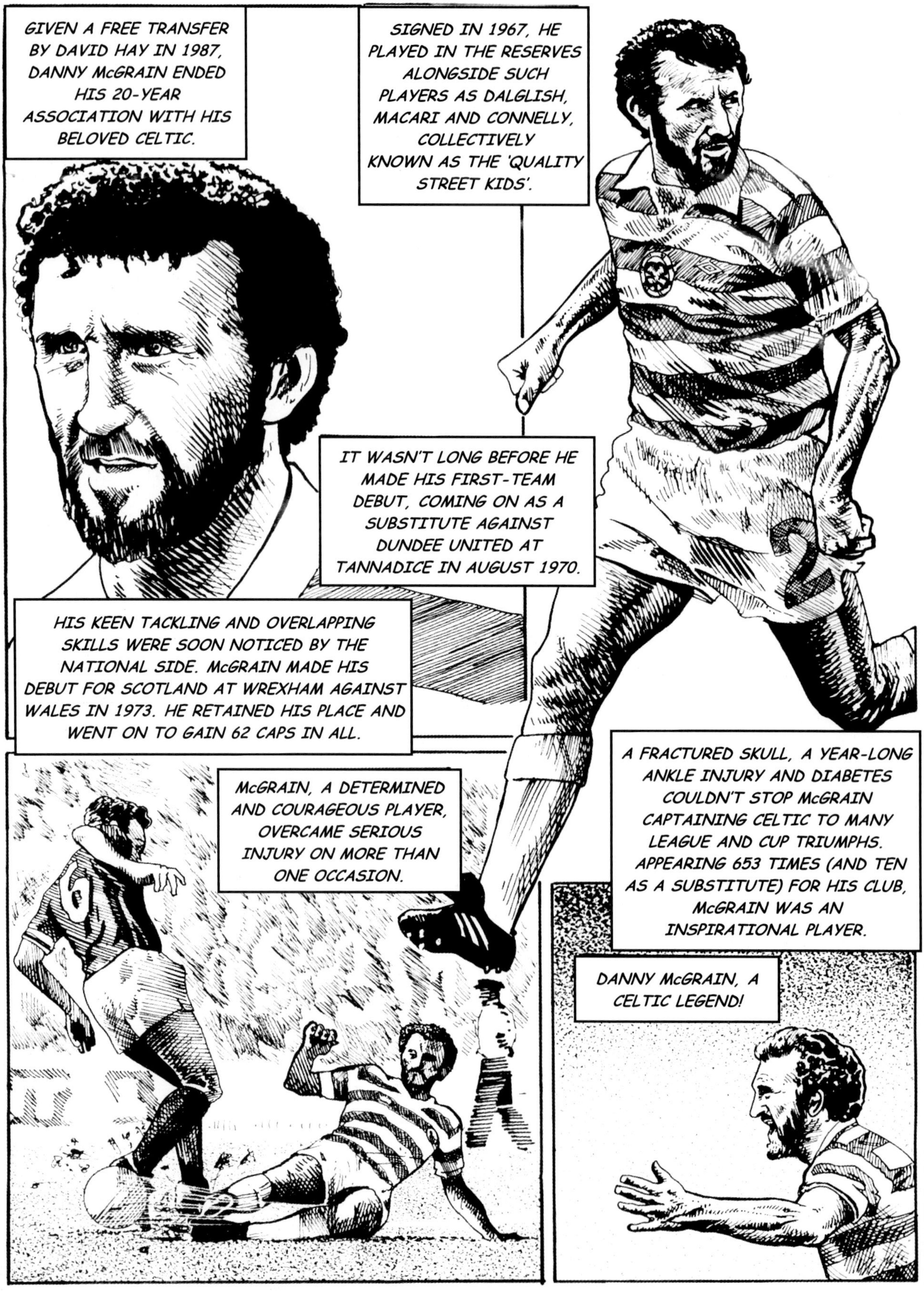
GIVEN A FREE TRANSFER BY DAVID HAY IN 1987, DANNY McGRAIN ENDED HIS 20-YEAR ASSOCIATION WITH HIS BELOVED CELTIC.
SIGNED IN 1967, HE PLAYED IN THE RESERVES ALONGSIDE SUCH PLAYERS AS DALGLISH, MACARI AND CONNELLY, COLLECTIVELY KNOWN AS THE 'QUALITY STREET KIDS'.
IT WASN'T LONG BEFORE HE MADE HIS FIRST-TEAM DEBUT, COMING ON AS A SUBSTITUTE AGAINST DUNDEE UNITED AT TANNADICE IN AUGUST 1970.
HIS KEEN TACKLING AND OVERLAPPING SKILLS WERE SOON NOTICED BY THE NATIONAL SIDE. McGRAIN MADE HIS DEBUT FOR SCOTLAND AT WREXHAM AGAINST WALES IN 1973. HE RETAINED HIS PLACE AND WENT ON TO GAIN 62 CAPS IN ALL.
McGRAIN, A DETERMINED AND COURAGEOUS PLAYER, OVERCAME SERIOUS INJURY ON MORE THAN ONE OCCASION.
A FRACTURED SKULL, A YEAR-LONG ANKLE INJURY AND DIABETES COULDN'T STOP McGRAIN CAPTAINING CELTIC TO MANY LEAGUE AND CUP TRIUMPHS. APPEARING 653 TIMES (AND TEN AS A SUBSTITUTE) FOR HIS CLUB, McGRAIN WAS AN INSPIRATIONAL PLAYER.
DANNY McGRAIN, A CELTIC LEGEND!

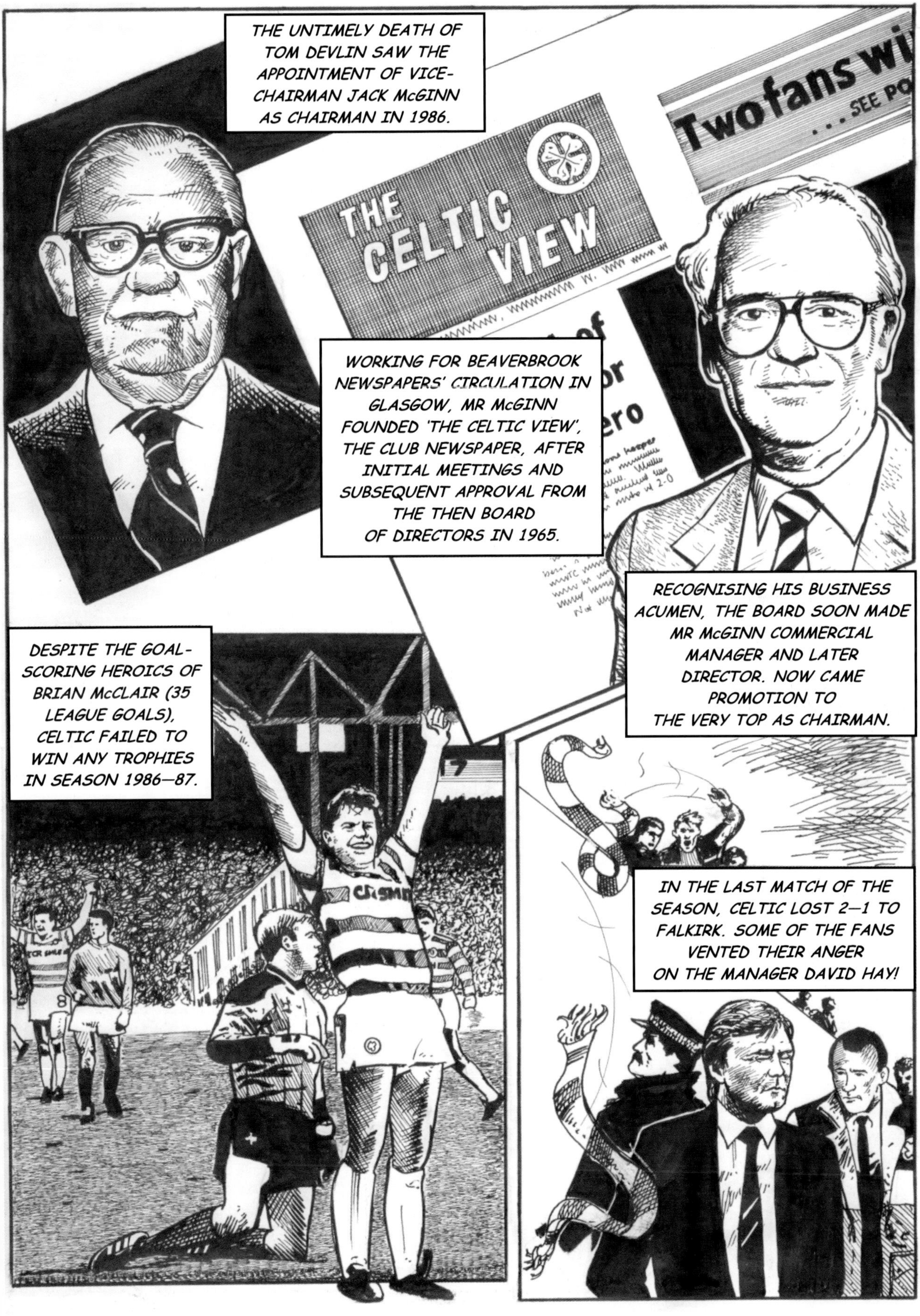
THE UNTIMELY DEATH OF TOM DEVLIN SAW THE APPOINTMENT OF VICE-CHAIRMAN JACK McGINN AS CHAIRMAN IN 1986.
THE CELTIC VIEW
WORKING FOR BEAVERBROOK NEWSPAPERS' CIRCULATION IN GLASGOW, MR McGINN FOUNDED 'THE CELTIC VIEW', THE CLUB NEWSPAPER, AFTER INITIAL MEETINGS AND SUBSEQUENT APPROVAL FROM THE THEN BOARD OF DIRECTORS IN 1965.
RECOGNISING HIS BUSINESS ACUMEN, THE BOARD SOON MADE MR McGINN COMMERCIAL MANAGER AND LATER DIRECTOR. NOW CAME PROMOTION TO THE VERY TOP AS CHAIRMAN.
DESPITE THE GOAL-SCORING HEROICS OF BRIAN McCLAIR (35 LEAGUE GOALS), CELTIC FAILED TO WIN ANY TROPHIES IN SEASON 1986—87.
IN THE LAST MATCH OF THE SEASON, CELTIC LOST 2—1 TO FALKIRK. SOME OF THE FANS VENTED THEIR ANGER ON THE MANAGER DAVID HAY!

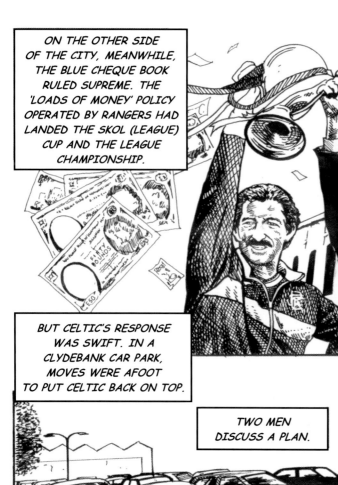

ON THE OTHER SIDE OF THE CITY, MEANWHILE, THE BLUE CHEQUE BOOK RULED SUPREME. THE 'LOADS OF MONEY' POLICY OPERATED BY RANGERS HAD LANDED THE SKOL (LEAGUE) CUP AND THE LEAGUE CHAMPIONSHIP.

BUT CELTIC'S RESPONSE WAS SWIFT. IN A CLYDEBANK CAR PARK, MOVES WERE AFOOT TO PUT CELTIC BACK ON TOP.

TWO MEN DISCUSS A PLAN.

SO THE BOARD WANT YOU BACK AT THE HELM. ARE YOU INTERESTED?

YES, JACK, I AM.

HAY IS INFORMED OF THE BOARD'S DECISION.

JUST 19 DAYS AFTER BEING SACKED BY ASTON VILLA, McNEILL BOUNCES BACK INTO PARADISE!

chapter 10

cesar's return

'tho' your dreams be tossed and blown'

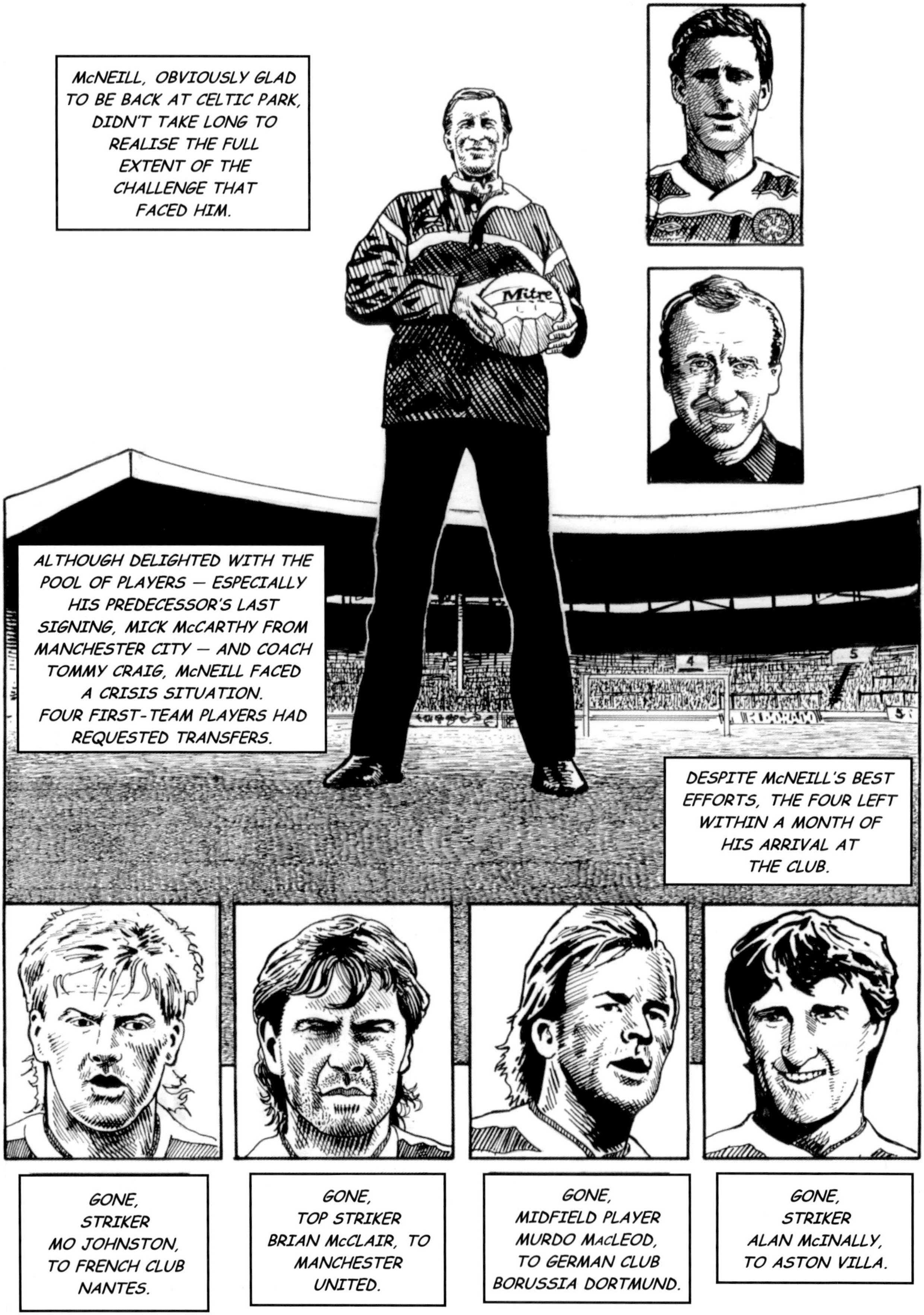
McNEILL, OBVIOUSLY GLAD TO BE BACK AT CELTIC PARK, DIDN'T TAKE LONG TO REALISE THE FULL EXTENT OF THE CHALLENGE THAT FACED HIM.
Mitre
ALTHOUGH DELIGHTED WITH THE POOL OF PLAYERS — ESPECIALLY HIS PREDECESSOR'S LAST SIGNING, MICK McCARTHY FROM MANCHESTER CITY — AND COACH TOMMY CRAIG, McNEILL FACED A CRISIS SITUATION. FOUR FIRST-TEAM PLAYERS HAD REQUESTED TRANSFERS.
DESPITE McNEILL'S BEST EFFORTS, THE FOUR LEFT WITHIN A MONTH OF HIS ARRIVAL AT THE CLUB.
GONE, STRIKER MO JOHNSTON, TO FRENCH CLUB NANTES.
GONE, TOP STRIKER BRIAN McCLAIR, TO MANCHESTER UNITED.
GONE, MIDFIELD PLAYER MURDO MacLEOD, TO GERMAN CLUB BORUSSIA DORTMUND.
GONE, STRIKER ALAN McINALLY, TO ASTON VILLA.

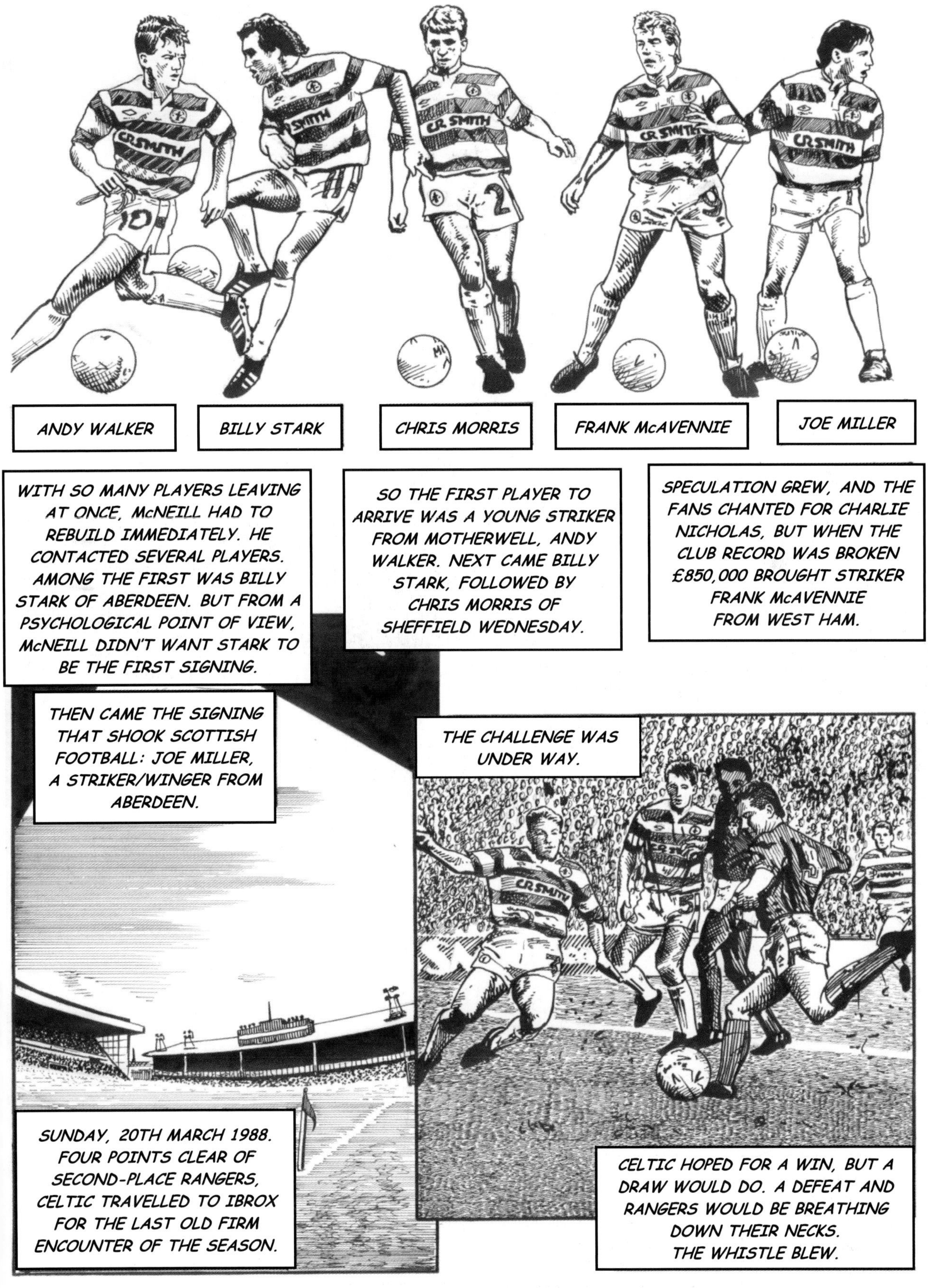

ANDY WALKER
BILLY STARK
CHRIS MORRIS
FRANK McAVENNIE
JOE MILLER
WITH SO MANY PLAYERS LEAVING AT ONCE, McNEILL HAD TO REBUILD IMMEDIATELY. HE CONTACTED SEVERAL PLAYERS. AMONG THE FIRST WAS BILLY STARK OF ABERDEEN. BUT FROM A PSYCHOLOGICAL POINT OF VIEW, McNEILL DIDN'T WANT STARK TO BE THE FIRST SIGNING.
SO THE FIRST PLAYER TO ARRIVE WAS A YOUNG STRIKER FROM MOTHERWELL, ANDY WALKER. NEXT CAME BILLY STARK, FOLLOWED BY CHRIS MORRIS OF SHEFFIELD WEDNESDAY.
SPECULATION GREW, AND THE FANS CHANTED FOR CHARLIE NICHOLAS, BUT WHEN THE CLUB RECORD WAS BROKEN £850,000 BROUGHT STRIKER FRANK McAVENNIE FROM WEST HAM.
THEN CAME THE SIGNING THAT SHOOK SCOTTISH FOOTBALL: JOE MILLER, A STRIKER/WINGER FROM ABERDEEN.
THE CHALLENGE WAS UNDER WAY.
SUNDAY, 20TH MARCH 1988. FOUR POINTS CLEAR OF SECOND-PLACE RANGERS, CELTIC TRAVELLED TO IBROX FOR THE LAST OLD FIRM ENCOUNTER OF THE SEASON.
CELTIC HOPED FOR A WIN, BUT A DRAW WOULD DO. A DEFEAT AND RANGERS WOULD BE BREATHING DOWN THEIR NECKS. THE WHISTLE BLEW.

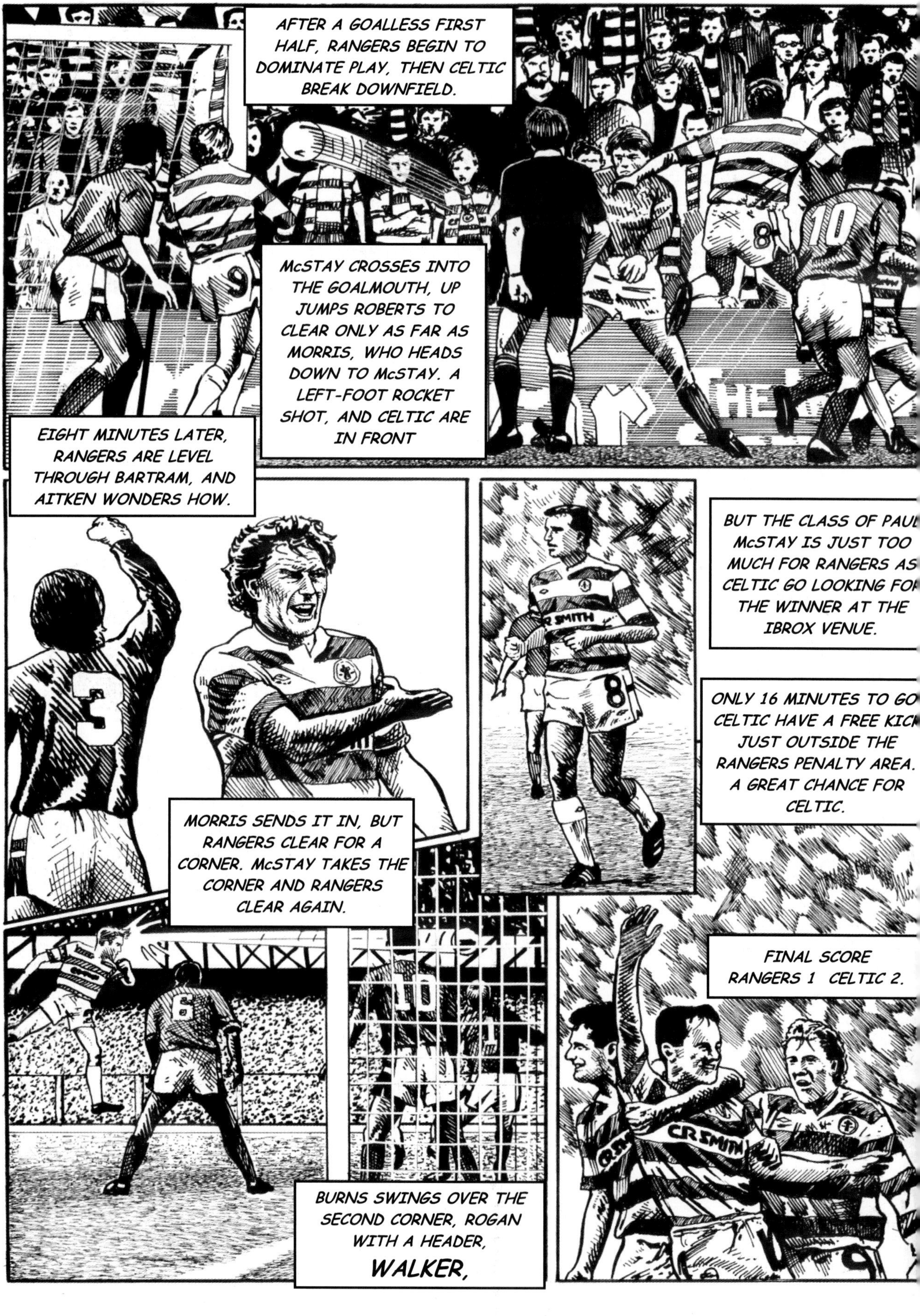
AFTER A GOALLESS FIRST HALF, RANGERS BEGIN TO DOMINATE PLAY, THEN CELTIC BREAK DOWNFIELD.
McSTAY CROSSES INTO THE GOALMOUTH, UP JUMPS ROBERTS TO CLEAR ONLY AS FAR AS MORRIS, WHO HEADS DOWN TO McSTAY. A LEFT-FOOT ROCKET SHOT, AND CELTIC ARE IN FRONT
EIGHT MINUTES LATER, RANGERS ARE LEVEL THROUGH BARTRAM, AND AITKEN WONDERS HOW.
BUT THE CLASS OF PAUL McSTAY IS JUST TOO MUCH FOR RANGERS AS CELTIC GO LOOKING FOR THE WINNER AT THE IBROX VENUE.
ONLY 16 MINUTES TO GO CELTIC HAVE A FREE KICK JUST OUTSIDE THE RANGERS PENALTY AREA. A GREAT CHANCE FOR CELTIC.
MORRIS SENDS IT IN, BUT RANGERS CLEAR FOR A CORNER. McSTAY TAKES THE CORNER AND RANGERS CLEAR AGAIN.
BURNS SWINGS OVER THE SECOND CORNER, ROGAN WITH A HEADER,
WALKER,
FINAL SCORE
RANGERS 1 CELTIC 2.

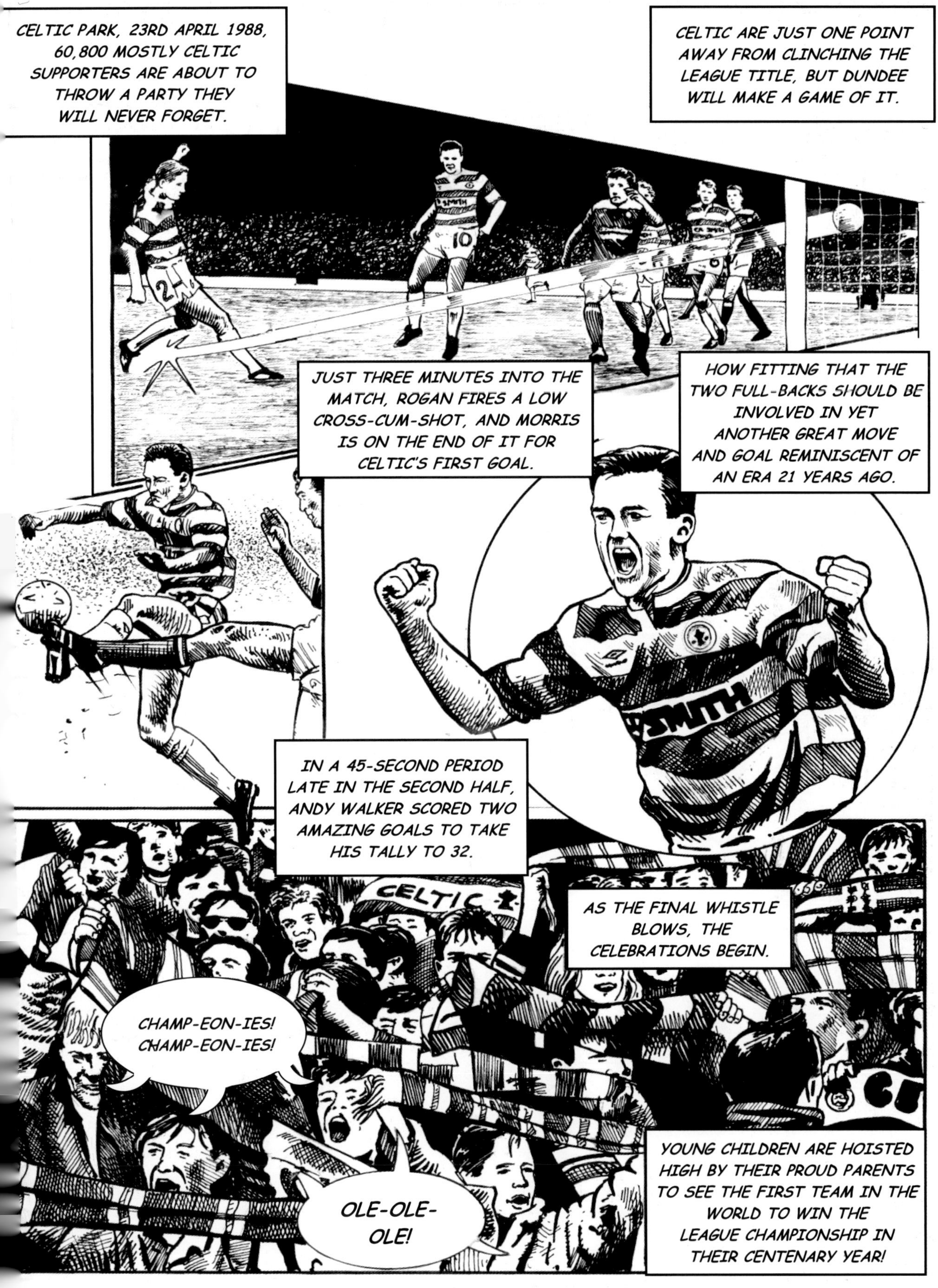
CELTIC PARK, 23RD APRIL 1988, 60,800 MOSTLY CELTIC SUPPORTERS ARE ABOUT TO THROW A PARTY THEY WILL NEVER FORGET.
CELTIC ARE JUST ONE POINT AWAY FROM CLINCHING THE LEAGUE TITLE, BUT DUNDEE WILL MAKE A GAME OF IT.
JUST THREE MINUTES INTO THE MATCH, ROGAN FIRES A LOW CROSS-CUM-SHOT, AND MORRIS IS ON THE END OF IT FOR CELTIC'S FIRST GOAL.
HOW FITTING THAT THE TWO FULL-BACKS SHOULD BE INVOLVED IN YET ANOTHER GREAT MOVE AND GOAL REMINISCENT OF AN ERA 21 YEARS AGO.
IN A 45-SECOND PERIOD LATE IN THE SECOND HALF, ANDY WALKER SCORED TWO AMAZING GOALS TO TAKE HIS TALLY TO 32.
AS THE FINAL WHISTLE BLOWS, THE CELEBRATIONS BEGIN.
CHAMP-EON-IES! CHAMP-EON-IES!
OLE-OLE-OLE!
YOUNG CHILDREN ARE HOISTED HIGH BY THEIR PROUD PARENTS TO SEE THE FIRST TEAM IN THE WORLD TO WIN THE LEAGUE CHAMPIONSHIP IN THEIR CENTENARY YEAR!

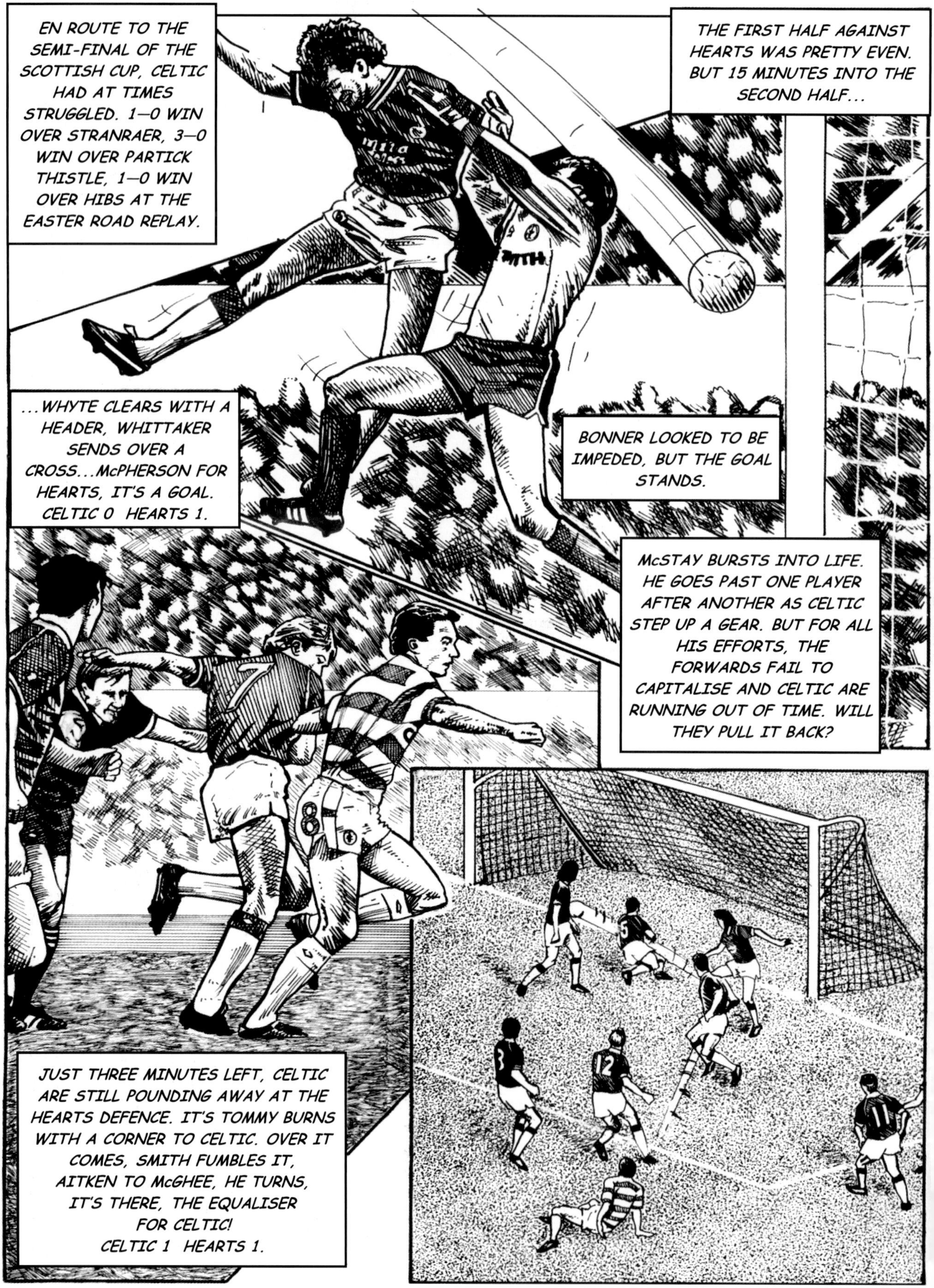
EN ROUTE TO THE SEMI-FINAL OF THE SCOTTISH CUP, CELTIC HAD AT TIMES STRUGGLED. 1–0 WIN OVER STRANRAER, 3–0 WIN OVER PARTICK THISTLE, 1–0 WIN OVER HIBS AT THE EASTER ROAD REPLAY.
THE FIRST HALF AGAINST HEARTS WAS PRETTY EVEN. BUT 15 MINUTES INTO THE SECOND HALF...
...WHYTE CLEARS WITH A HEADER, WHITTAKER SENDS OVER A CROSS...McPHERSON FOR HEARTS, IT'S A GOAL. CELTIC 0 HEARTS 1.
BONNER LOOKED TO BE IMPEDED, BUT THE GOAL STANDS.
McSTAY BURSTS INTO LIFE. HE GOES PAST ONE PLAYER AFTER ANOTHER AS CELTIC STEP UP A GEAR. BUT FOR ALL HIS EFFORTS, THE FORWARDS FAIL TO CAPITALISE AND CELTIC ARE RUNNING OUT OF TIME. WILL THEY PULL IT BACK?
JUST THREE MINUTES LEFT, CELTIC ARE STILL POUNDING AWAY AT THE HEARTS DEFENCE. IT'S TOMMY BURNS WITH A CORNER TO CELTIC. OVER IT COMES, SMITH FUMBLES IT, AITKEN TO McGHEE, HE TURNS, IT'S THERE, THE EQUALISER FOR CELTIC! CELTIC 1 HEARTS 1.

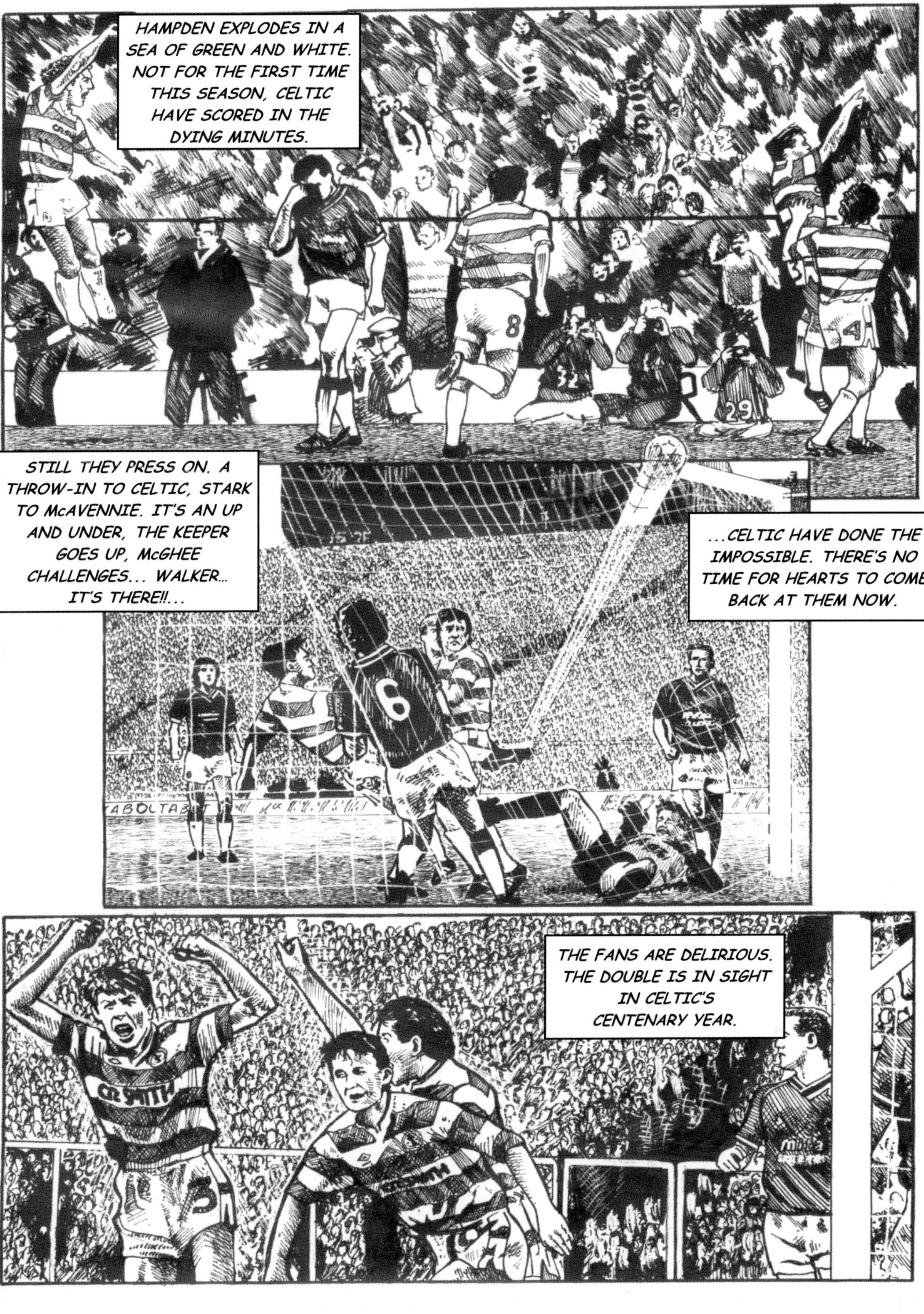
HAMPDEN EXPLODES IN A SEA OF GREEN AND WHITE. NOT FOR THE FIRST TIME THIS SEASON, CELTIC HAVE SCORED IN THE DYING MINUTES.
STILL THEY PRESS ON. A THROW-IN TO CELTIC, STARK TO McAVENNIE. IT'S AN UP AND UNDER, THE KEEPER GOES UP, McGHEE CHALLENGES... WALKER... IT'S THERE!!...
...CELTIC HAVE DONE THE IMPOSSIBLE. THERE'S NO TIME FOR HEARTS TO COME BACK AT THEM NOW.
THE FANS ARE DELIRIOUS. THE DOUBLE IS IN SIGHT IN CELTIC'S CENTENARY YEAR.

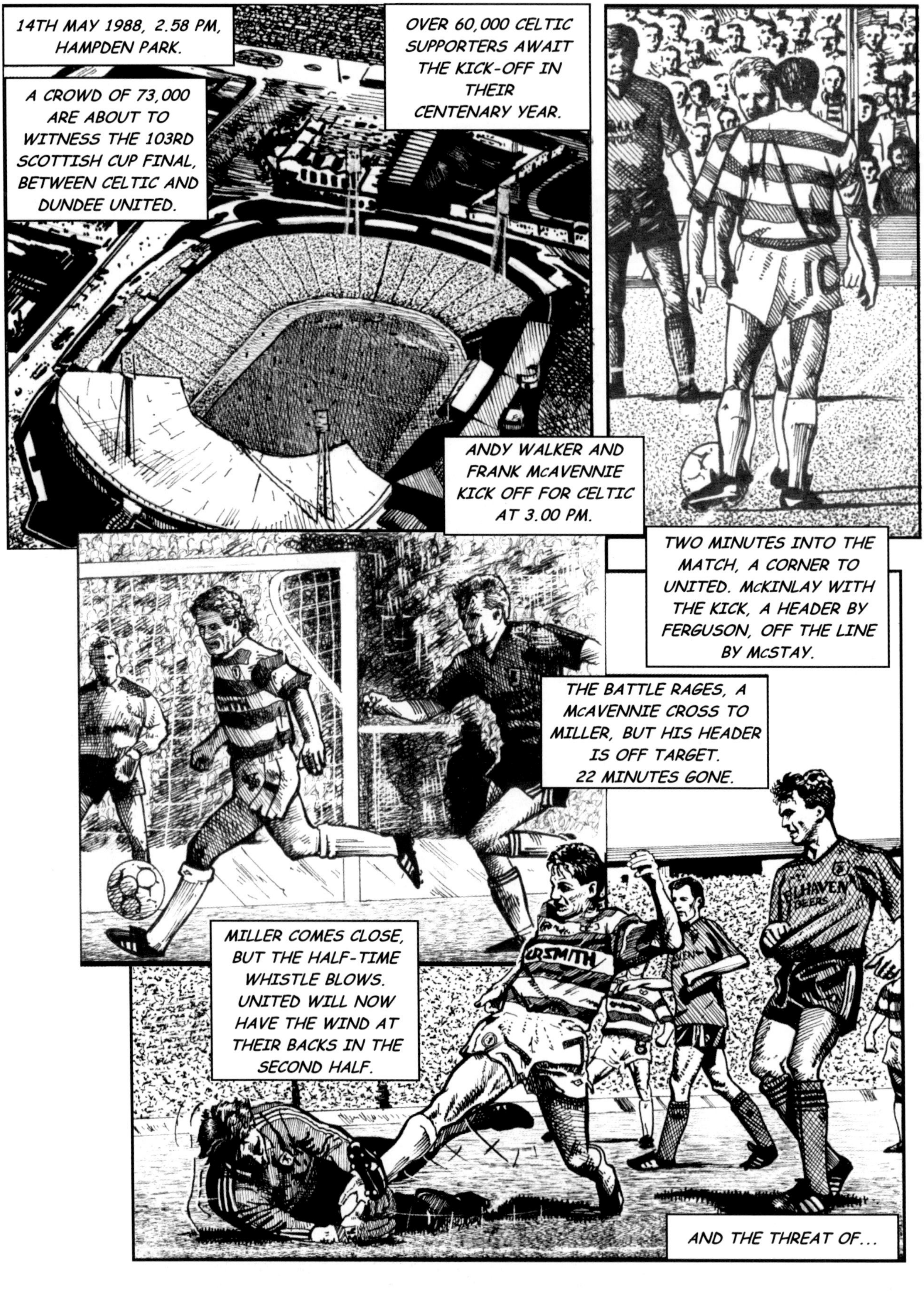
14TH MAY 1988, 2.58 PM, HAMPDEN PARK.
A CROWD OF 73,000 ARE ABOUT TO WITNESS THE 103RD SCOTTISH CUP FINAL, BETWEEN CELTIC AND DUNDEE UNITED.
OVER 60,000 CELTIC SUPPORTERS AWAIT THE KICK-OFF IN THEIR CENTENARY YEAR.
ANDY WALKER AND FRANK McAVENNIE KICK OFF FOR CELTIC AT 3.00 PM.
TWO MINUTES INTO THE MATCH, A CORNER TO UNITED. McKINLAY WITH THE KICK, A HEADER BY FERGUSON, OFF THE LINE BY McSTAY.
THE BATTLE RAGES, A McAVENNIE CROSS TO MILLER, BUT HIS HEADER IS OFF TARGET. 22 MINUTES GONE.
MILLER COMES CLOSE, BUT THE HALF-TIME WHISTLE BLOWS. UNITED WILL NOW HAVE THE WIND AT THEIR BACKS IN THE SECOND HALF.
AND THE THREAT OF...

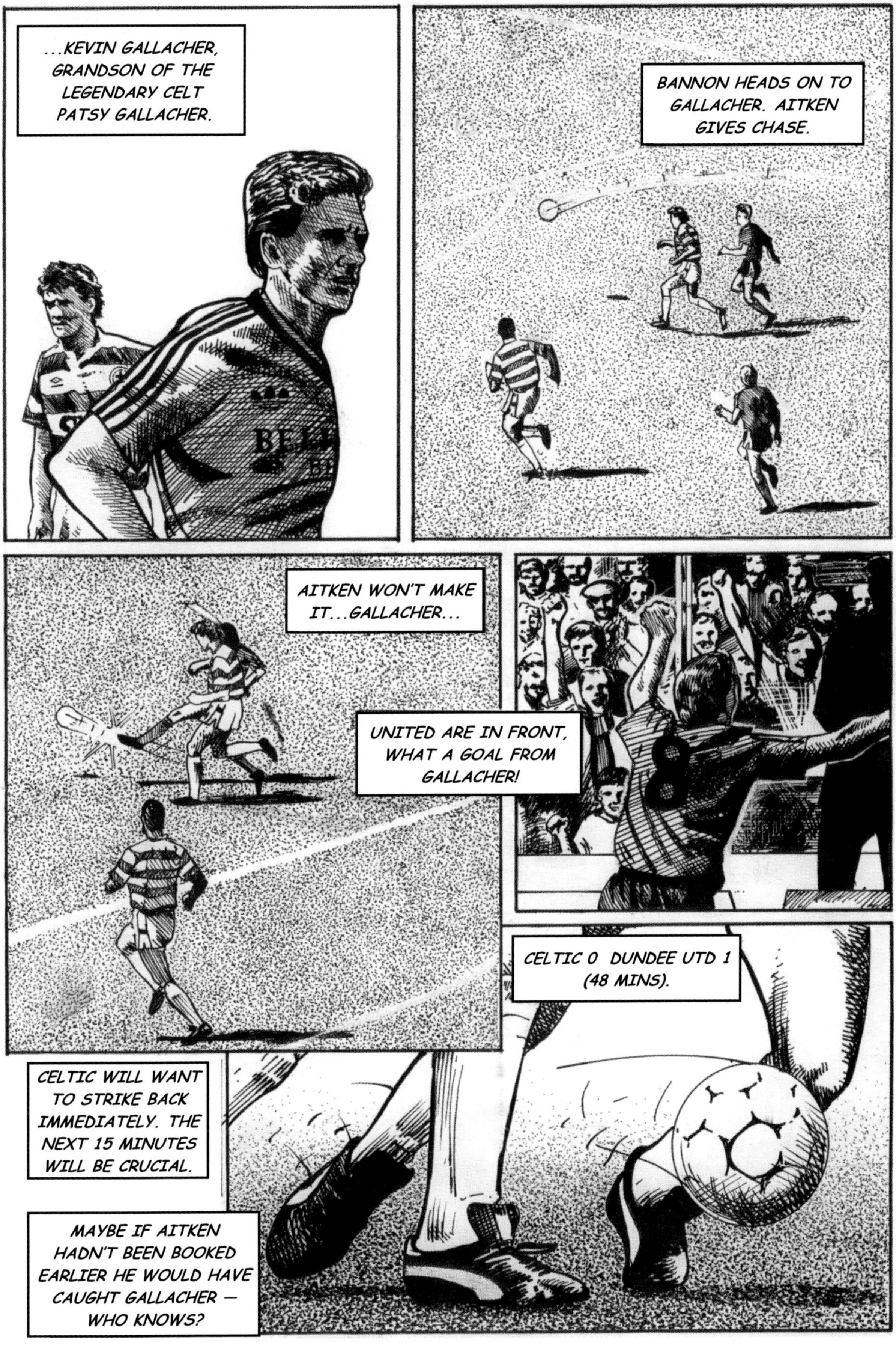
...KEVIN GALLACHER, GRANDSON OF THE LEGENDARY CELT PATSY GALLACHER.
BANNON HEADS ON TO GALLACHER. AITKEN GIVES CHASE.
AITKEN WON'T MAKE IT...GALLACHER...
UNITED ARE IN FRONT, WHAT A GOAL FROM GALLACHER!
CELTIC 0 DUNDEE UTD 1 (48 MINS).
CELTIC WILL WANT TO STRIKE BACK IMMEDIATELY. THE NEXT 15 MINUTES WILL BE CRUCIAL.
MAYBE IF AITKEN HADN'T BEEN BOOKED EARLIER HE WOULD HAVE CAUGHT GALLACHER — WHO KNOWS?

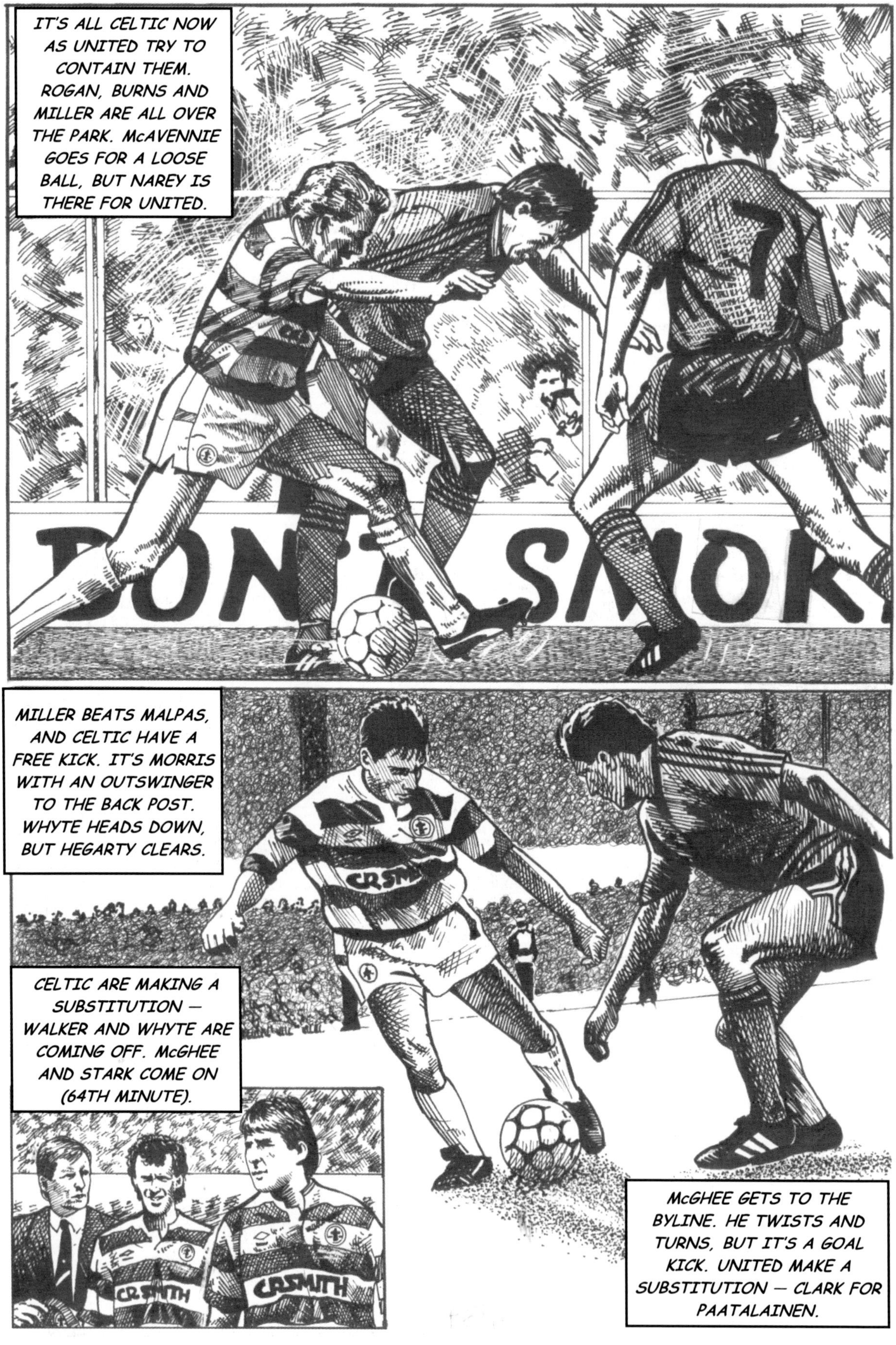
IT'S ALL CELTIC NOW AS UNITED TRY TO CONTAIN THEM. ROGAN, BURNS AND MILLER ARE ALL OVER THE PARK. McAVENNIE GOES FOR A LOOSE BALL, BUT NAREY IS THERE FOR UNITED.
MILLER BEATS MALPAS, AND CELTIC HAVE A FREE KICK. IT'S MORRIS WITH AN OUTSWINGER TO THE BACK POST. WHYTE HEADS DOWN, BUT HEGARTY CLEARS.
CELTIC ARE MAKING A SUBSTITUTION – WALKER AND WHYTE ARE COMING OFF. McGHEE AND STARK COME ON (64TH MINUTE).
McGHEE GETS TO THE BYLINE. HE TWISTS AND TURNS, BUT IT'S A GOAL KICK. UNITED MAKE A SUBSTITUTION – CLARK FOR PAATALAINEN.

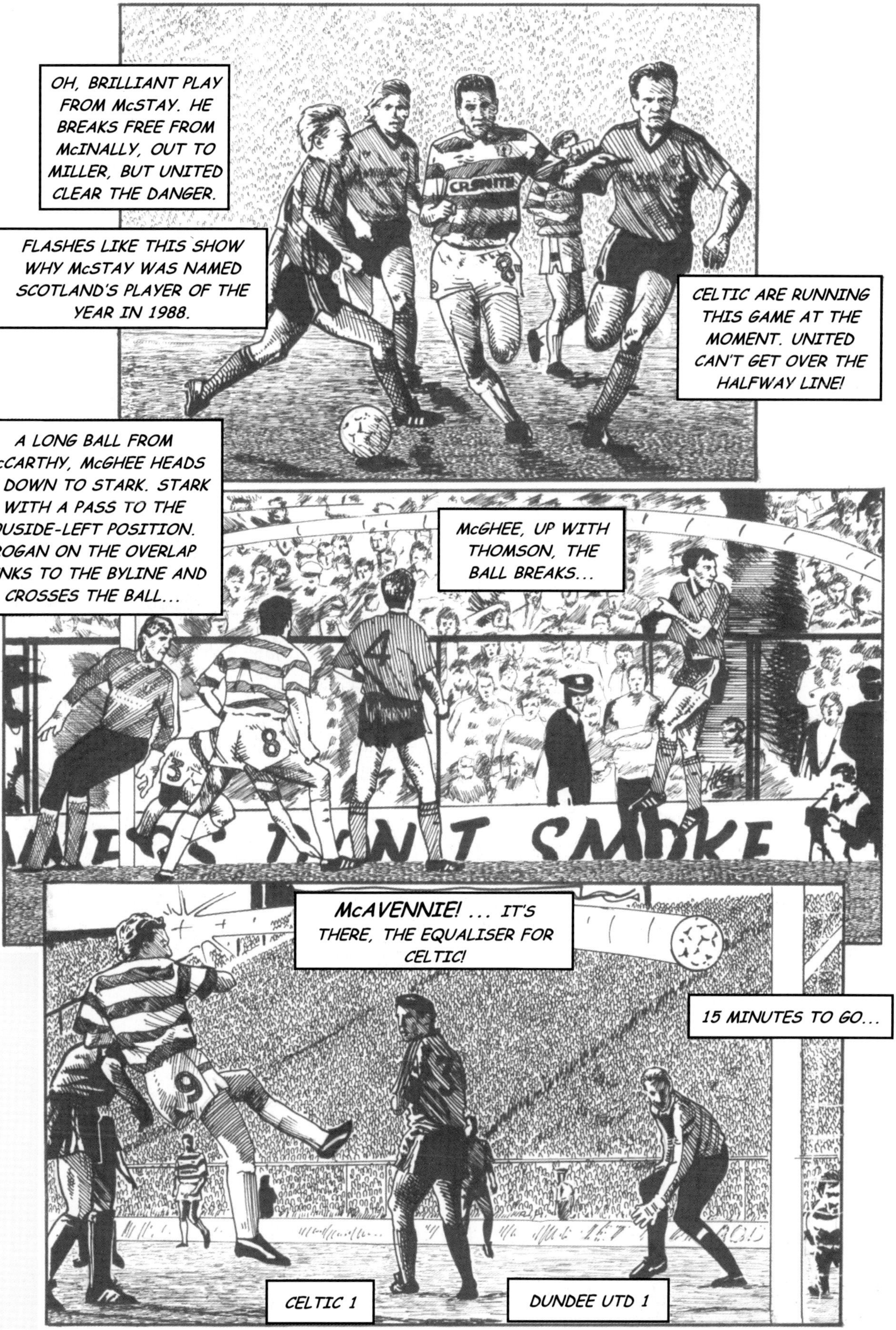
OH, BRILLIANT PLAY FROM McSTAY. HE BREAKS FREE FROM McINALLY, OUT TO MILLER, BUT UNITED CLEAR THE DANGER.
FLASHES LIKE THIS SHOW WHY McSTAY WAS NAMED SCOTLAND'S PLAYER OF THE YEAR IN 1988.
CELTIC ARE RUNNING THIS GAME AT THE MOMENT. UNITED CAN'T GET OVER THE HALFWAY LINE!
A LONG BALL FROM McCARTHY, McGHEE HEADS IT DOWN TO STARK. STARK WITH A PASS TO THE OUSIDE-LEFT POSITION. ROGAN ON THE OVERLAP JINKS TO THE BYLINE AND CROSSES THE BALL...
McGHEE, UP WITH THOMSON, THE BALL BREAKS...
McAVENNIE! ... IT'S THERE, THE EQUALISER FOR CELTIC!
15 MINUTES TO GO...
CELTIC 1
DUNDEE UTD 1

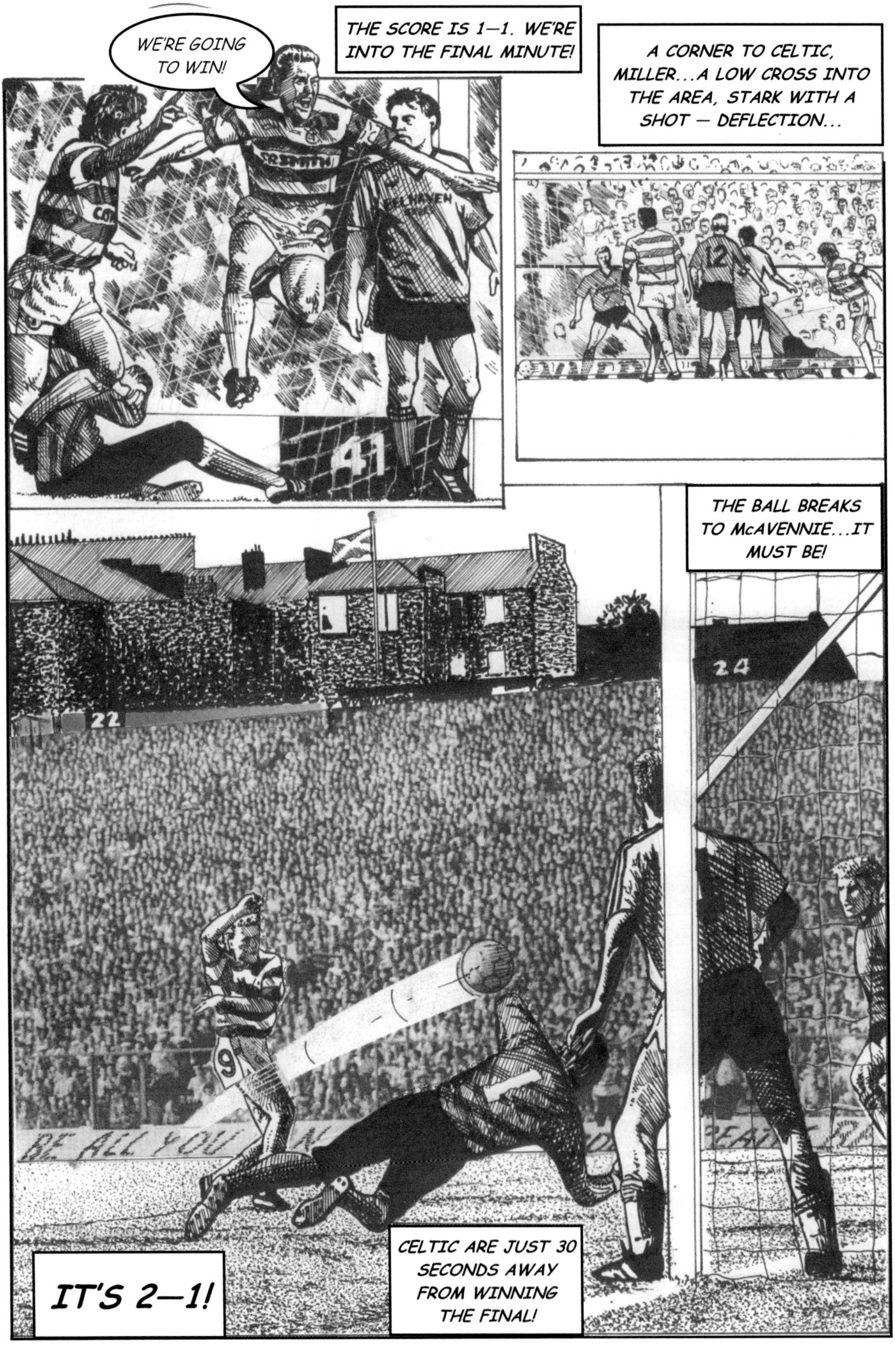
THE SCORE IS 1–1. WE'RE INTO THE FINAL MINUTE!
WE'RE GOING TO WIN!
A CORNER TO CELTIC, MILLER...A LOW CROSS INTO THE AREA, STARK WITH A SHOT – DEFLECTION...
THE BALL BREAKS TO McAVENNIE...IT MUST BE!
IT'S 2–1!
CELTIC ARE JUST 30 SECONDS AWAY FROM WINNING THE FINAL!

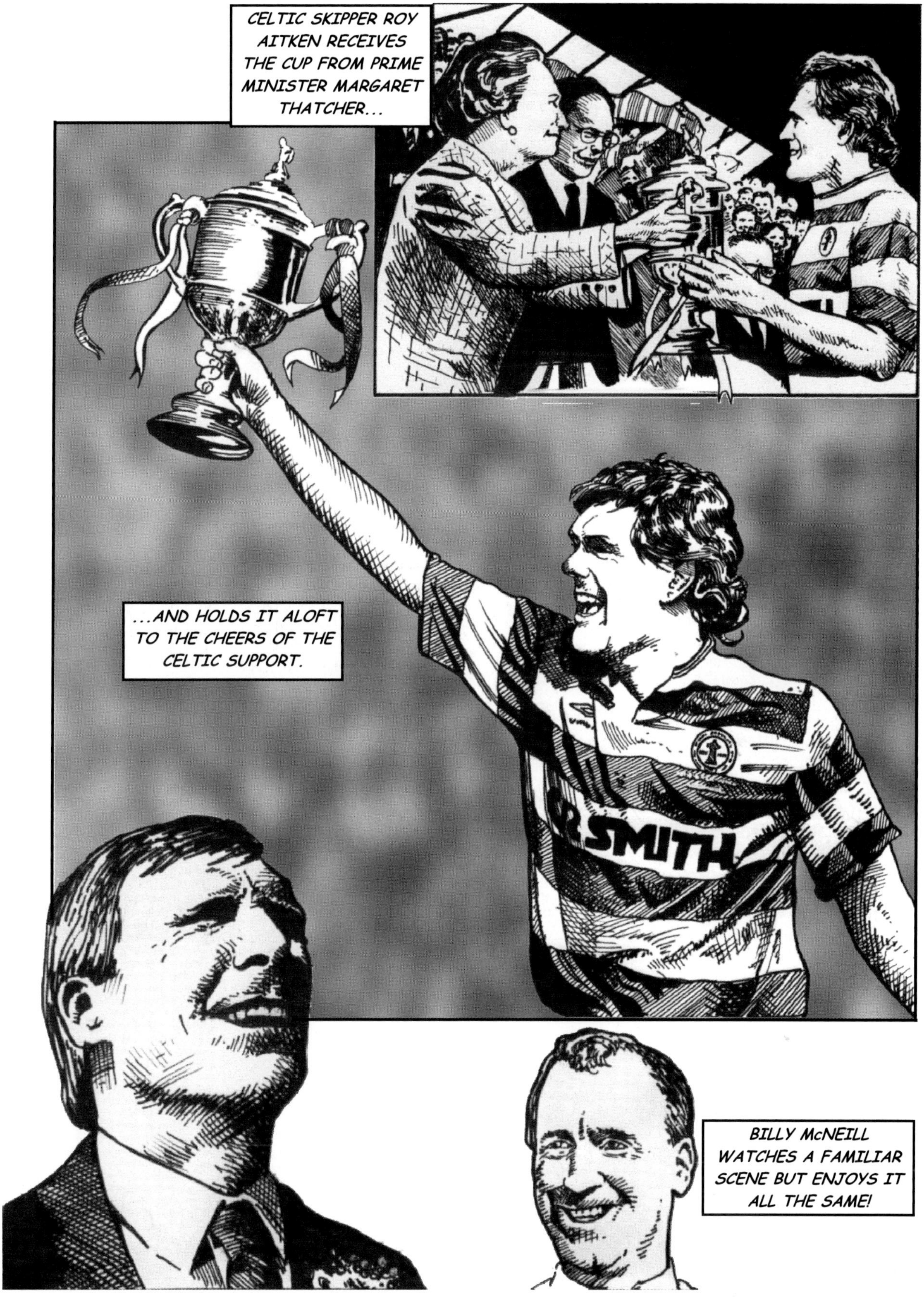
CELTIC SKIPPER ROY AITKEN RECEIVES THE CUP FROM PRIME MINISTER MARGARET THATCHER...
...AND HOLDS IT ALOFT TO THE CHEERS OF THE CELTIC SUPPORT.
BILLY McNEILL WATCHES A FAMILIAR SCENE BUT ENJOYS IT ALL THE SAME!

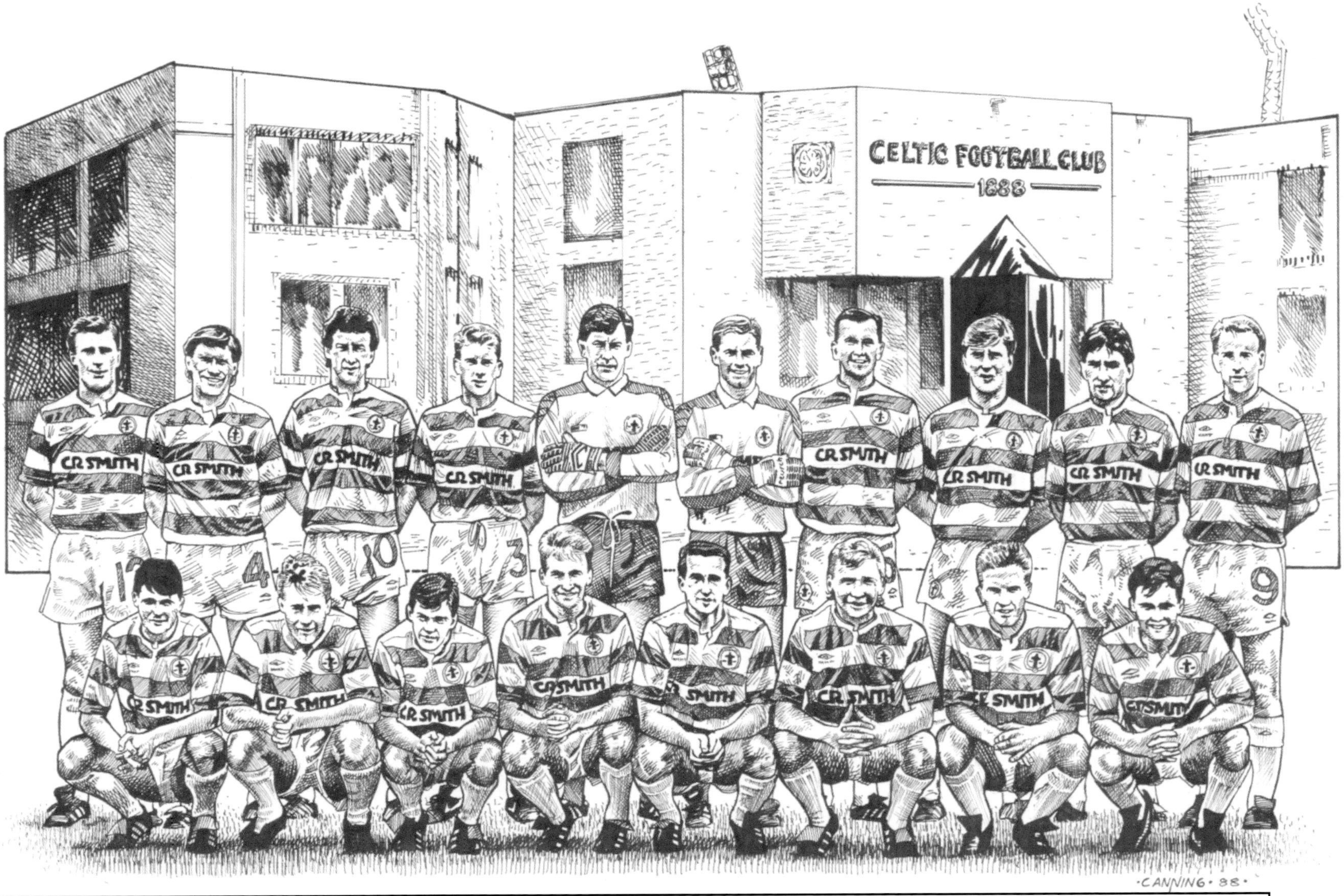
CELTIC FOOTBALL CLUB
1888
CANNING • 88 •

'THE CENTENARY DOUBLERS'

BACK ROW, L—R: M. McCARTHY, R. AITKEN (CAPT), W. STARK, D. WHYTE, P. BONNER, A. McKNIGHT, L. BAILLIE, A. ROGAN, M. McGHEE, T. BURNS.
FRONT ROW, L—R: O. ARCHDEACON, F. McAVENNIE, J. MILLER, C. MORRIS, P. McSTAY, P. GRANT, A. SHEPHERD, A. WALKER.

TOMMY COYNE JOINED CELTIC FROM DUNDEE IN MARCH 1989, SEEN BY SOME AS A REPLACEMENT FOR THE DEPARTING McAVENNIE. HOWEVER, BILLY McNEILL SAW IN HIM A DIFFERENT TYPE OF STRIKER AND WOULD TRY TO PAIR HIM WITH A COMPLEMENTARY PLAYER. FEW IN SCOTLAND COULD HAVE PREDICTED WHO WAS TO BE THE CHOICE OF PARTNER FOR COYNE.

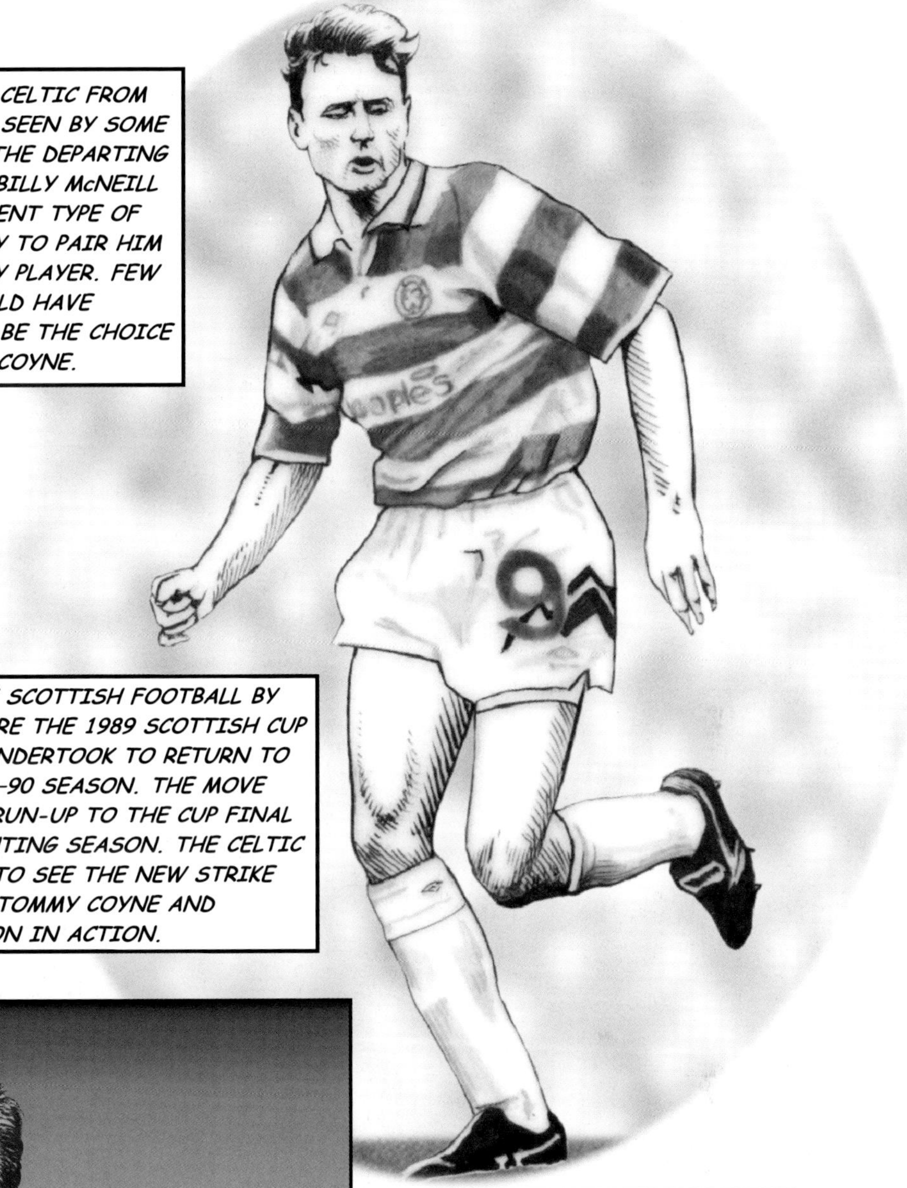

IN A MOVE THAT TOOK SCOTTISH FOOTBALL BY SURPRISE, SHORTLY BEFORE THE 1989 SCOTTISH CUP FINAL MO JOHNSTON UNDERTOOK TO RETURN TO CELTIC FOR THE 1989–90 SEASON. THE MOVE BUOYED CELTIC IN THE RUN-UP TO THE CUP FINAL FOLLOWING A DISAPPOINTING SEASON. THE CELTIC SUPPORT WERE EAGER TO SEE THE NEW STRIKE PARTNERSHIP OF TOMMY COYNE AND MO JOHNSTON IN ACTION.

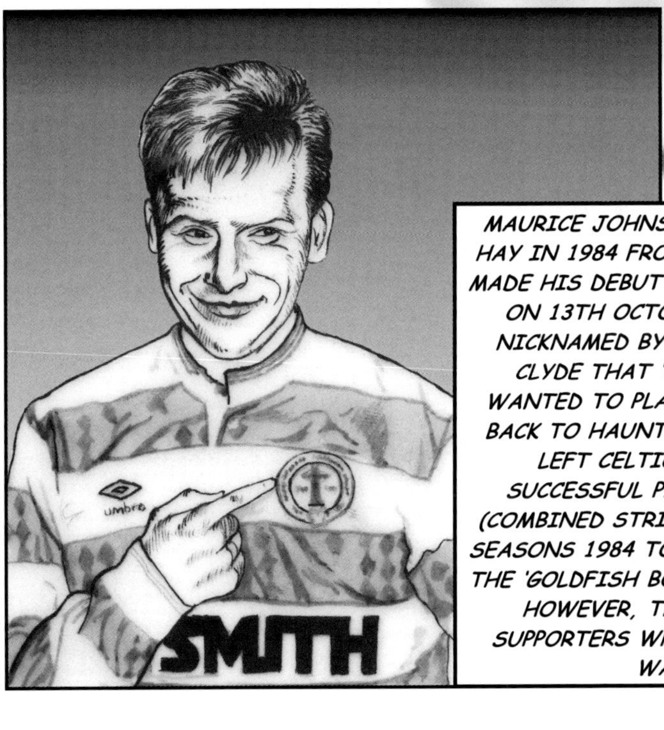
umbro
SMITH

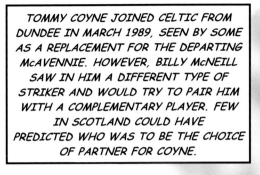

MAURICE JOHNSTON, ORIGINALLY SIGNED BY DAVIE HAY IN 1984 FROM WATFORD FOR A FEE OF £400,000, MADE HIS DEBUT AGAINST HIBERNIAN AT CELTIC PARK ON 13TH OCTOBER 1984. 'SUPER MO', AS HE WAS NICKNAMED BY CELTIC FANS, REVEALED ON RADIO CLYDE THAT 'CELTIC IS THE ONLY TEAM I EVER WANTED TO PLAY FOR'. THESE WORDS WOULD COME BACK TO HAUNT THE MERCURIAL STRIKER. WHEN HE LEFT CELTIC FOR NANTES IN 1987 AFTER A SUCCESSFUL PARTNERSHIP WITH BRIAN McCLAIR (COMBINED STRIKES OF 42, 49 AND 70 GOALS IN THE SEASONS 1984 TO 1987), HE SAID IT WAS BECAUSE OF THE 'GOLDFISH BOWL' OF FOOTBALL LIFE IN GLASGOW. HOWEVER, THIS WAS ALL FORGOTTEN BY THE SUPPORTERS WHEN IT WAS ANNOUNCED THAT 'MO' WAS BACK – OR WAS HE?

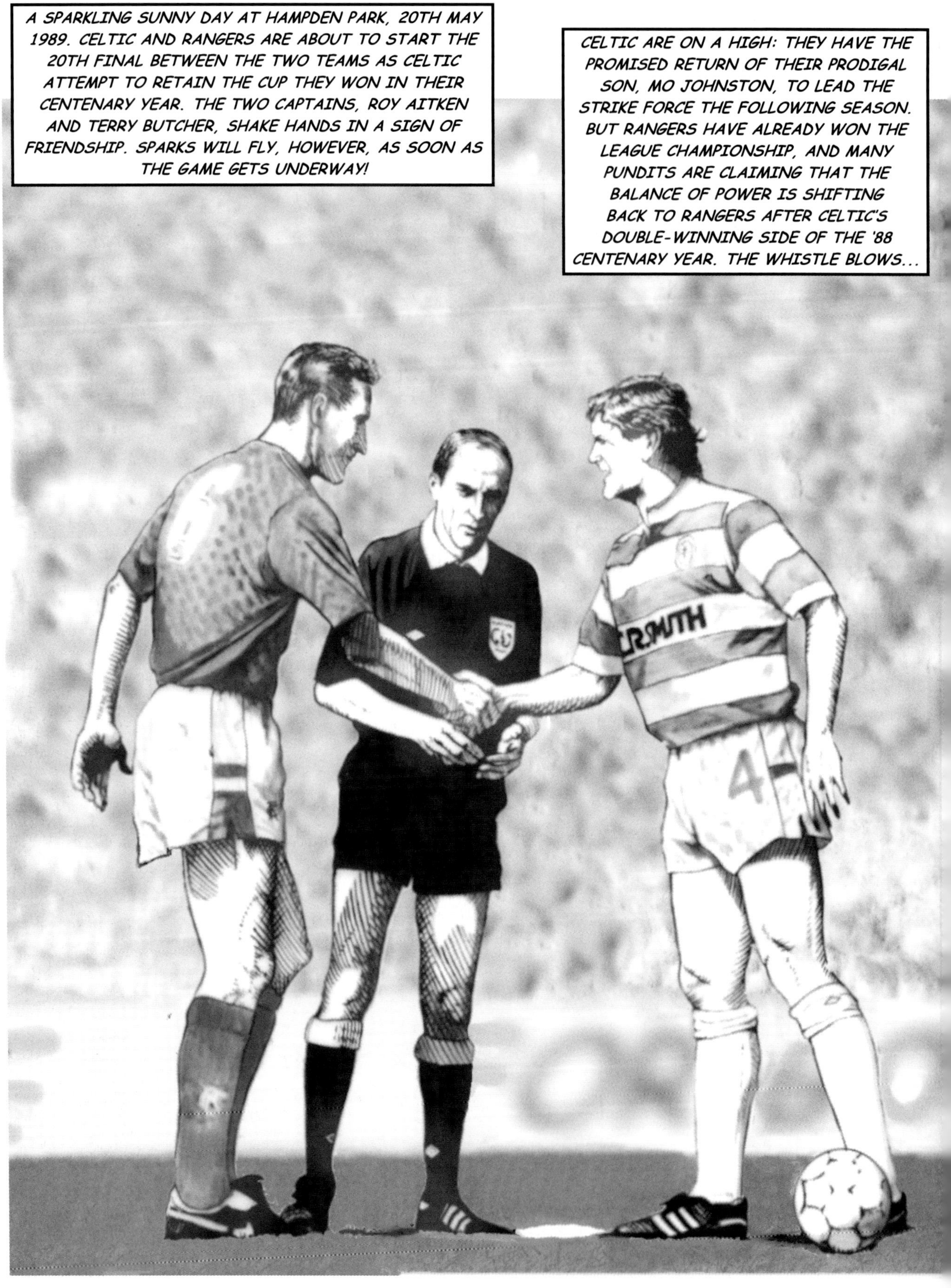
A SPARKLING SUNNY DAY AT HAMPDEN PARK, 20TH MAY 1989. CELTIC AND RANGERS ARE ABOUT TO START THE 20TH FINAL BETWEEN THE TWO TEAMS AS CELTIC ATTEMPT TO RETAIN THE CUP THEY WON IN THEIR CENTENARY YEAR. THE TWO CAPTAINS, ROY AITKEN AND TERRY BUTCHER, SHAKE HANDS IN A SIGN OF FRIENDSHIP. SPARKS WILL FLY, HOWEVER, AS SOON AS THE GAME GETS UNDERWAY!
CELTIC ARE ON A HIGH: THEY HAVE THE PROMISED RETURN OF THEIR PRODIGAL SON, MO JOHNSTON, TO LEAD THE STRIKE FORCE THE FOLLOWING SEASON. BUT RANGERS HAVE ALREADY WON THE LEAGUE CHAMPIONSHIP, AND MANY PUNDITS ARE CLAIMING THAT THE BALANCE OF POWER IS SHIFTING BACK TO RANGERS AFTER CELTIC'S DOUBLE-WINNING SIDE OF THE '88 CENTENARY YEAR. THE WHISTLE BLOWS...

RANGERS, ON THE VERGE OF SECURING THE DOMESTIC TREBLE, WERE DESPERATE TO WIN THE SCOTTISH CUP. CELTIC WERE ALSO ANXIOUS TO RETAIN THE TROPHY, AS THEY HAD ALREADY RELINQUISHED THE LEAGUE TO RANGERS.

THE MATCH ITSELF WAS A DOUR AFFAIR WITH BOTH SIDES CANCELLING EACH OTHER OUT, PARTICULARLY IN MIDFIELD, WHERE THE TACKLES WERE FIERCE AND COMBATIVE.

CELTIC'S PAUL McSTAY HAD TO GO OFF FOR TREATMENT (BUT RETURNED) AFTER A SERIES OF BAD CHALLENGES. TOMMY BURNS ALSO HAD TO PICK HIMSELF UP ON A FEW OCCASIONS AFTER ROBUST CHALLENGES. WITH BOTH DEFENCES ON TOP OF THE GAME, NEITHER GOALKEEPER HAD MUCH TO DO AND BOTH SETS OF STRIKERS WERE DENIED ANY CLEAR-CUT CHANCES.

HOWEVER, ONE LITTLE LAPSE FROM RANGERS WAS TO PROVE COSTLY AND AFFECT THE OUTCOME OF THE MATCH.

JUST BEFORE HALF-TIME, AITKEN CHALLENGES FOR THE BALL IN CELTIC'S HALF. THE BALL SEEMS TO COME OFF AITKEN AND GO OUT FOR A THROW-IN, BUT AITKEN TAKES THE THROW QUICKLY AND REFEREE BOB VALENTINE LETS IT GO CELTIC'S WAY!

FROM THE THROW-IN, GRANT CROSSES INTO THE PENALTY AREA. GOUGH HEADS CLEAR, BUT IT'S SHORT, AND BUTCHER AND McGHEE GO FOR IT. BUTCHER WINS AND PLAYS THE BALL TO STEVENS, WHOSE PASS BACK TO THE KEEPER IS SHORT. IN NIPS MILLER TO SLAM THE BALL PAST WOODS AND WIN THE CUP FOR CELTIC.

NOT ONLY WAS THIS THE LAST TIME ROY AITKEN HELD ALOFT A TROPHY WITH CELTIC, BUT IT WOULD ALSO BE THE LAST TROPHY CELTIC WOULD WIN FOR THE NEXT FIVE YEARS. AITKEN LEFT THE CLUB IN 1990.

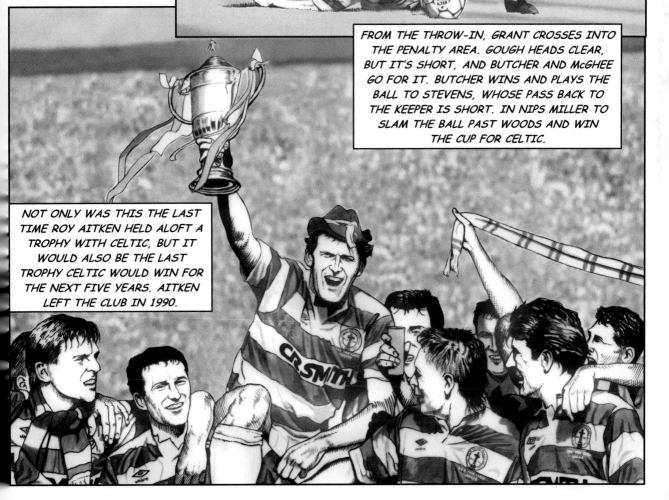

ROY AITKEN WAS BORN ON 24TH NOVEMBER 1958 IN IRVINE. HE WAS EDUCATED AT ST PETER'S PRIMARY SCHOOL, A PLACE THAT FUELLED HIS LOVE OF THE GAME, BEFORE GOING ON TO ST ANDREW'S ACADEMY IN SALTCOATS WHEN HE WAS 12. TWO YEARS LATER, ROY SIGNED AN S-FORM WITH HIS BOYHOOD HEROES CELTIC.

DURING HIS TIME AT SCHOOL, HE EXCELLED AT SPORTS, WINNING THE TITLE OF JUNIOR SPORTS CHAMPION AND THEN LATER WINNING THE SENIOR SPORTS CHAMPION TITLE WHILST STILL ONLY IN FOURTH YEAR.

BUT IT WAS AT CELTIC THAT HE TRULY EXCELLED. HE WAS NICKNAMED 'THE BEAR' BY THE SUPPORTERS DUE TO HIS LARGE FRAME AND COMMANDING PRESENCE. THE CHANT 'FEED THE BEAR' COULD BE HEARD ON A WEEKLY BASIS FROM THE TERRACES OF CELTIC PARK.

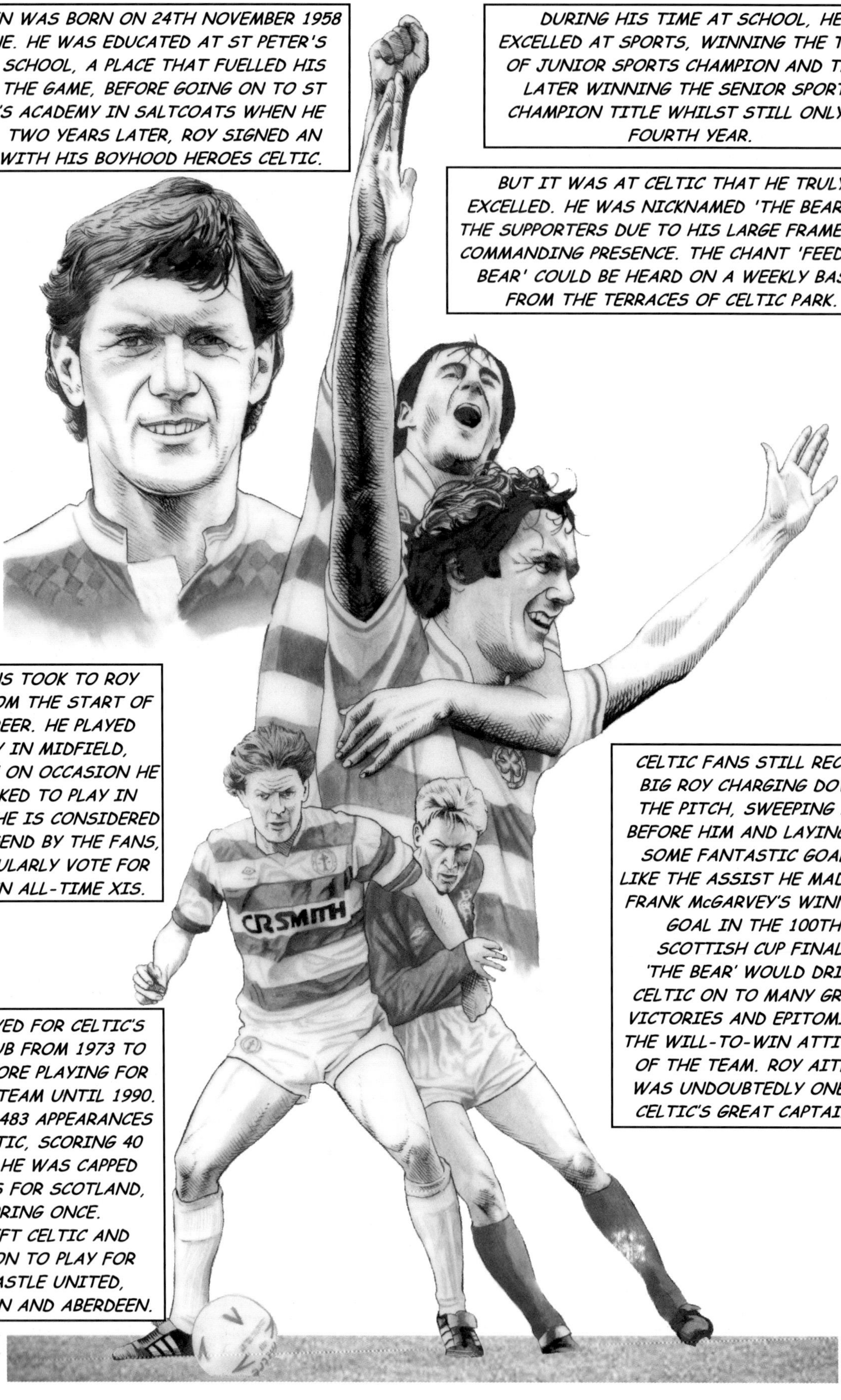
CRSMITH

THE FANS TOOK TO ROY RIGHT FROM THE START OF HIS CAREER. HE PLAYED MOSTLY IN MIDFIELD, ALTHOUGH ON OCCASION HE WAS ASKED TO PLAY IN DEFENCE. HE IS CONSIDERED A CLUB LEGEND BY THE FANS, WHO REGULARLY VOTE FOR AITKEN IN ALL-TIME XIS.

CELTIC FANS STILL RECALL BIG ROY CHARGING DOWN THE PITCH, SWEEPING ALL BEFORE HIM AND LAYING ON SOME FANTASTIC GOALS, LIKE THE ASSIST HE MADE TO FRANK McGARVEY'S WINNING GOAL IN THE 100TH SCOTTISH CUP FINAL. 'THE BEAR' WOULD DRIVE CELTIC ON TO MANY GREAT VICTORIES AND EPITOMISED THE WILL-TO-WIN ATTITUDE OF THE TEAM. ROY AITKEN WAS UNDOUBTEDLY ONE OF CELTIC'S GREAT CAPTAINS.

ROY PLAYED FOR CELTIC'S BOYS CLUB FROM 1973 TO 1976 BEFORE PLAYING FOR THE FULL TEAM UNTIL 1990. HE MADE 483 APPEARANCES FOR CELTIC, SCORING 40 GOALS. HE WAS CAPPED 57 TIMES FOR SCOTLAND, SCORING ONCE.
ROY LEFT CELTIC AND WENT ON TO PLAY FOR NEWCASTLE UNITED, ST MIRREN AND ABERDEEN.

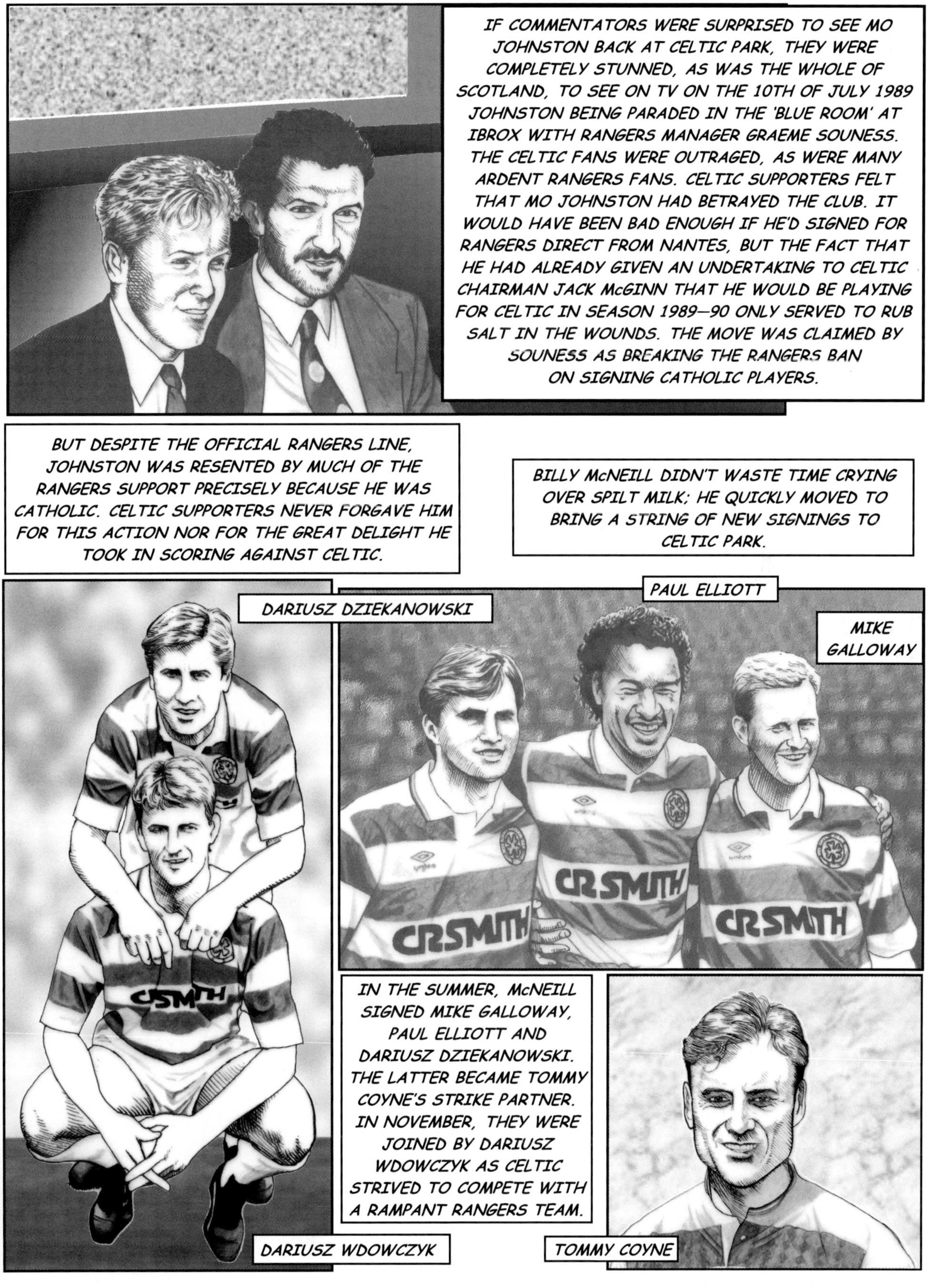
IF COMMENTATORS WERE SURPRISED TO SEE MO JOHNSTON BACK AT CELTIC PARK, THEY WERE COMPLETELY STUNNED, AS WAS THE WHOLE OF SCOTLAND, TO SEE ON TV ON THE 10TH OF JULY 1989 JOHNSTON BEING PARADED IN THE 'BLUE ROOM' AT IBROX WITH RANGERS MANAGER GRAEME SOUNESS. THE CELTIC FANS WERE OUTRAGED, AS WERE MANY ARDENT RANGERS FANS. CELTIC SUPPORTERS FELT THAT MO JOHNSTON HAD BETRAYED THE CLUB. IT WOULD HAVE BEEN BAD ENOUGH IF HE'D SIGNED FOR RANGERS DIRECT FROM NANTES, BUT THE FACT THAT HE HAD ALREADY GIVEN AN UNDERTAKING TO CELTIC CHAIRMAN JACK McGINN THAT HE WOULD BE PLAYING FOR CELTIC IN SEASON 1989–90 ONLY SERVED TO RUB SALT IN THE WOUNDS. THE MOVE WAS CLAIMED BY SOUNESS AS BREAKING THE RANGERS BAN ON SIGNING CATHOLIC PLAYERS.
BUT DESPITE THE OFFICIAL RANGERS LINE, JOHNSTON WAS RESENTED BY MUCH OF THE RANGERS SUPPORT PRECISELY BECAUSE HE WAS CATHOLIC. CELTIC SUPPORTERS NEVER FORGAVE HIM FOR THIS ACTION NOR FOR THE GREAT DELIGHT HE TOOK IN SCORING AGAINST CELTIC.
BILLY McNEILL DIDN'T WASTE TIME CRYING OVER SPILT MILK; HE QUICKLY MOVED TO BRING A STRING OF NEW SIGNINGS TO CELTIC PARK.
DARIUSZ DZIEKANOWSKI
DARIUSZ WDOWCZYK
PAUL ELLIOTT
MIKE GALLOWAY
CRSMITH
IN THE SUMMER, McNEILL SIGNED MIKE GALLOWAY, PAUL ELLIOTT AND DARIUSZ DZIEKANOWSKI. THE LATTER BECAME TOMMY COYNE'S STRIKE PARTNER. IN NOVEMBER, THEY WERE JOINED BY DARIUSZ WDOWCZYK AS CELTIC STRIVED TO COMPETE WITH A RAMPANT RANGERS TEAM.
TOMMY COYNE

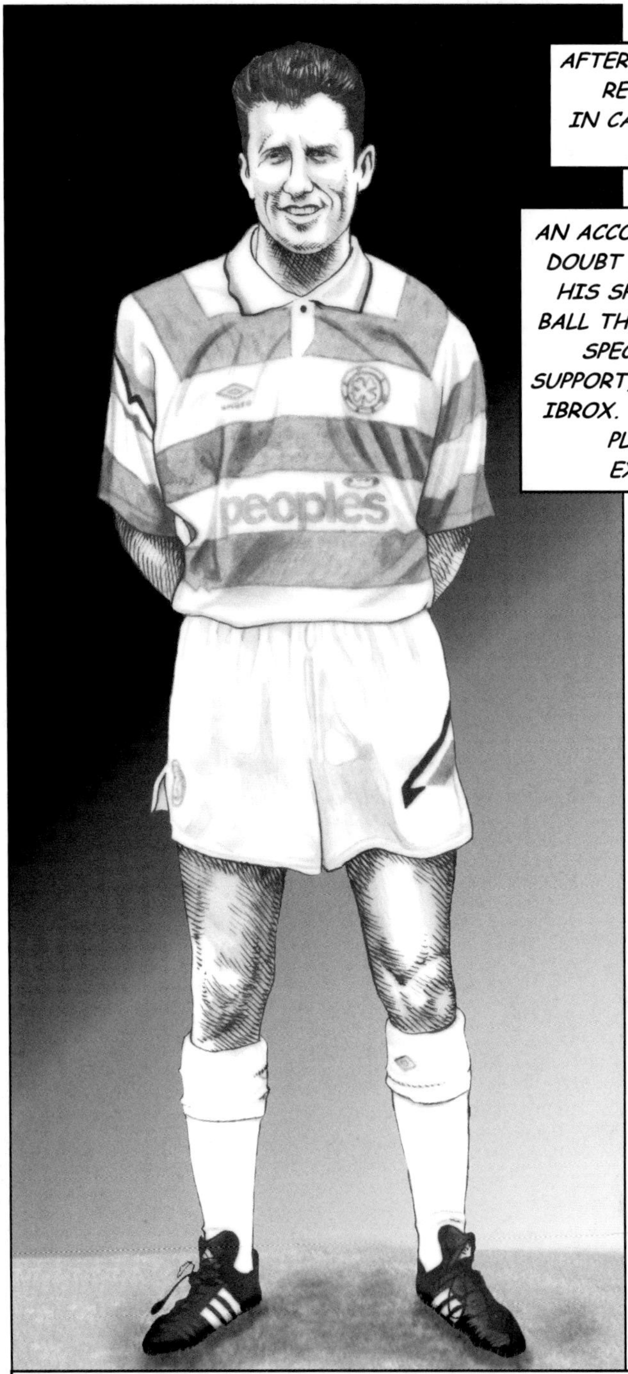
peoples

AFTER A BARREN 1989–90 SEASON, McNEILL RE-ENTERED THE TRANSFER MARKET. IN CAME JOHN COLLINS FROM HIBS FOR A RECORD FEE OF £1 MILLION.

AN ACCOMPLISHED MIDFIELD PLAYER, COLLINS WAS WITHOUT DOUBT A PLAYER WHO EXHIBITED REAL CLASS AND ABILITY. HIS SPECIALITY IN TAKING FREE KICKS AND BENDING THE BALL THROUGH SEEMINGLY IMPOSSIBLE ANGLES LED TO MANY SPECTACULAR GOALS, TO THE DELIGHT OF THE CELTIC SUPPORT, ESPECIALLY WHEN SCORED AGAINST THE TEAM FROM IBROX. COLLINS WAS ONE OF THE FEW TRULY WORLD-CLASS PLAYERS AT CELTIC PARK DURING A PERIOD WHEN EXCEPTIONAL TALENT WAS SCARCE AT THE CLUB.

THE CELTIC SUPPORT WERE GREATLY DISAPPOINTED, WHEN HE DECIDED TO LEAVE FOR MONACO IN 1996.

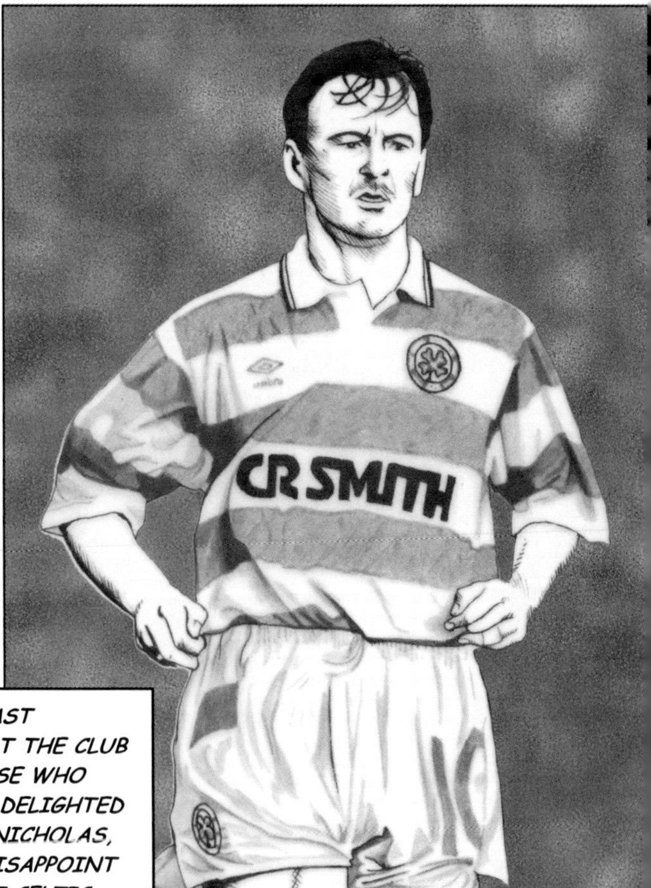
CR SMITH

CELTIC FAVOURITE CHARLIE NICHOLAS AT LAST RETURNED FROM ABERDEEN FOR HIS SECOND SPELL AT THE CLUB HE LOVED. THE CELTIC FANS, PARTICULARLY THOSE WHO REMEMBERED HIS DEBUT SEASON FOR CELTIC, WERE DELIGHTED AND HAD CHANTED HIS NAME AT MANY MATCHES. NICHOLAS, THOUGH LESS PRECOCIOUS THAN OF OLD, DIDN'T DISAPPOINT WITH HIS FINE PERFORMANCES. HE REMAINED AT CELTIC THROUGHOUT THE CLUB'S DARKEST SPELL IN RECENT TIMES. LOU MACARI GAVE NICHOLAS A FREE TRANSFER IN SEASON 1993–94, BUT TOMMY BURNS, WHO REPLACED MACARI IN 1994, BROUGHT NICHOLAS BACK FOR ONE FINAL SEASON. CHARLIE NICHOLAS ENDED HIS PLAYING CAREER AFTER A SHORT SPELL AT CLYDE.

THE SCOTTISH CUP QUARTER-FINALS, CELTIC V RANGERS, 17TH MARCH 1991. THIS MATCH WAS TO BECOME PART OF CELTIC FOLKLORE AND KNOWN AS 'THE ST PATRICK'S DAY MASSACRE'. RANGERS WERE GOING FOR THE TREBLE — THE UNTHINKABLE FOR CELTIC SUPPORTERS. CELTIC HAD TO WIN TO SAVE THEIR SEASON, AND THE MATCH HAPPENED TO BE ON THE FEAST DAY OF THE PATRON SAINT OF IRELAND — NO PRESSURE! CELTIC WERE ALSO DUE TO FACE RANGERS AT CELTIC PARK THE FOLLOWING WEEK IN THE LEAGUE — THE BLUE TOUCHPAPER WAS LIT!! THE FIREWORKS SOON BEGAN. SIX MINUTES INTO THE MATCH, A FREE KICK FROM WDOWCZYCK. THE BALL COMES INTO THE RANGERS HALF, UP JUMPS GOUGH, BUT TOMMY COYNE GETS THE VITAL TOUCH. THE BALL BREAKS TO CREANEY, WHO FIRES PAST WOODS. 1—0 TO CELTIC.

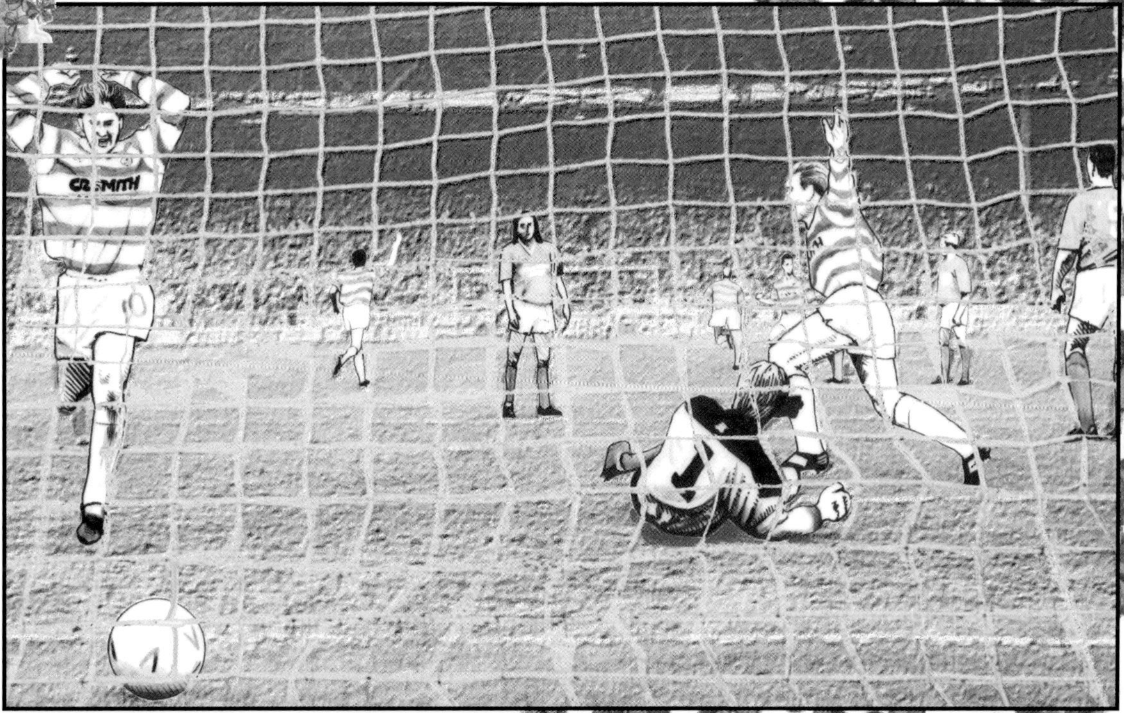
CR SMITH

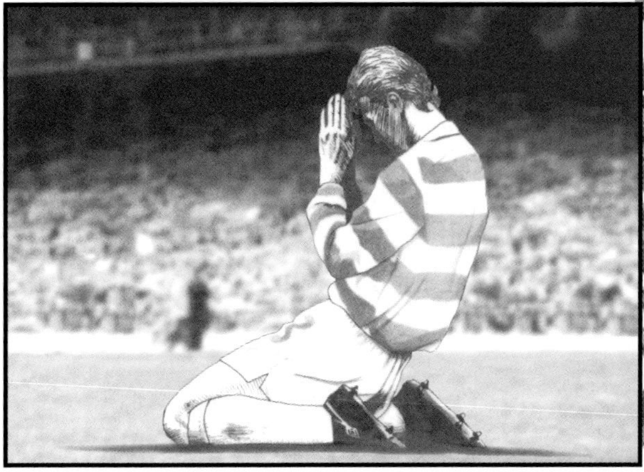

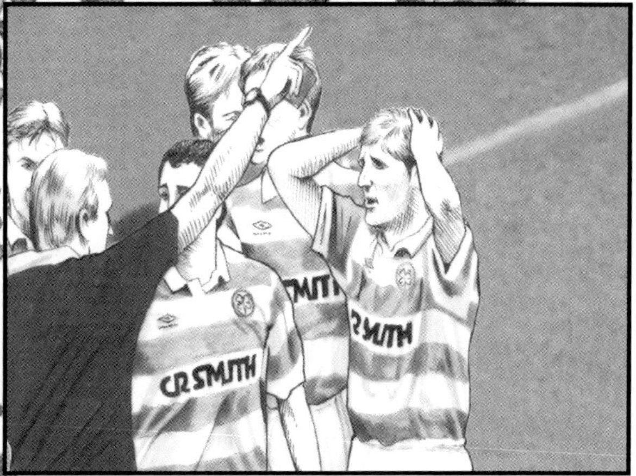
CR SMITH
CR SMITH
CR SMITH

RANGERS TRY TO RESPOND, BUT JUST BEFORE HALF-TIME, HURLOCK FOULS CREANEY 35 YARDS FROM GOAL. WDOWCZYCK TAKES AN ALMIGHTY RUN AT THE BALL, STRIKES IT, AND THE BALL ARCS OVER WOODS AFTER HURLOCK TRIES TO INTERCEPT IT. CELTIC 2 RANGERS 0. WDOWCZYCK FALLS DOWN ON HIS KNEES IN PRAYER. IN THE SECOND HALF, RANGERS THROW EVERYTHING AT CELTIC. GRANT HAULS JOHNSTON BACK AS HE HOMES IN ON GOAL, AND RANGERS GET A FREE KICK OUTSIDE THE BOX. JUST AS THE FREE KICK IS TAKEN, GRANT CHARGES OUT TOO SOON — A SECOND YELLOW CARD, AND HE'S SENT OFF BY REFEREE WADDELL. THE PACE QUICKENS FURTHER, AS DO THE RED CARDS.

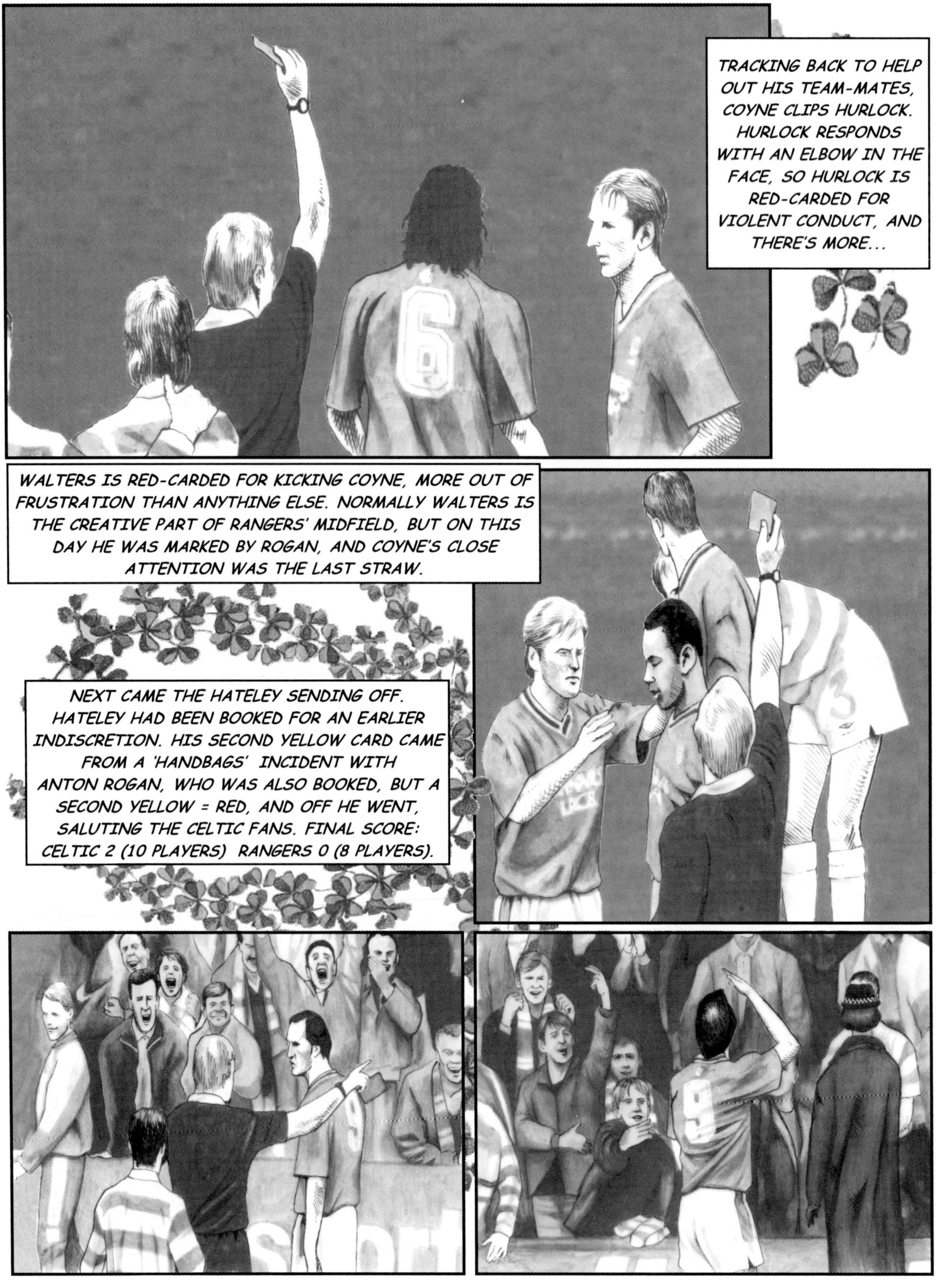
TRACKING BACK TO HELP OUT HIS TEAM-MATES, COYNE CLIPS HURLOCK. HURLOCK RESPONDS WITH AN ELBOW IN THE FACE, SO HURLOCK IS RED-CARDED FOR VIOLENT CONDUCT, AND THERE'S MORE...
WALTERS IS RED-CARDED FOR KICKING COYNE, MORE OUT OF FRUSTRATION THAN ANYTHING ELSE. NORMALLY WALTERS IS THE CREATIVE PART OF RANGERS' MIDFIELD, BUT ON THIS DAY HE WAS MARKED BY ROGAN, AND COYNE'S CLOSE ATTENTION WAS THE LAST STRAW.
NEXT CAME THE HATELEY SENDING OFF. HATELEY HAD BEEN BOOKED FOR AN EARLIER INDISCRETION. HIS SECOND YELLOW CARD CAME FROM A 'HANDBAGS' INCIDENT WITH ANTON ROGAN, WHO WAS ALSO BOOKED, BUT A SECOND YELLOW = RED, AND OFF HE WENT, SALUTING THE CELTIC FANS. FINAL SCORE: CELTIC 2 (10 PLAYERS) RANGERS 0 (8 PLAYERS).

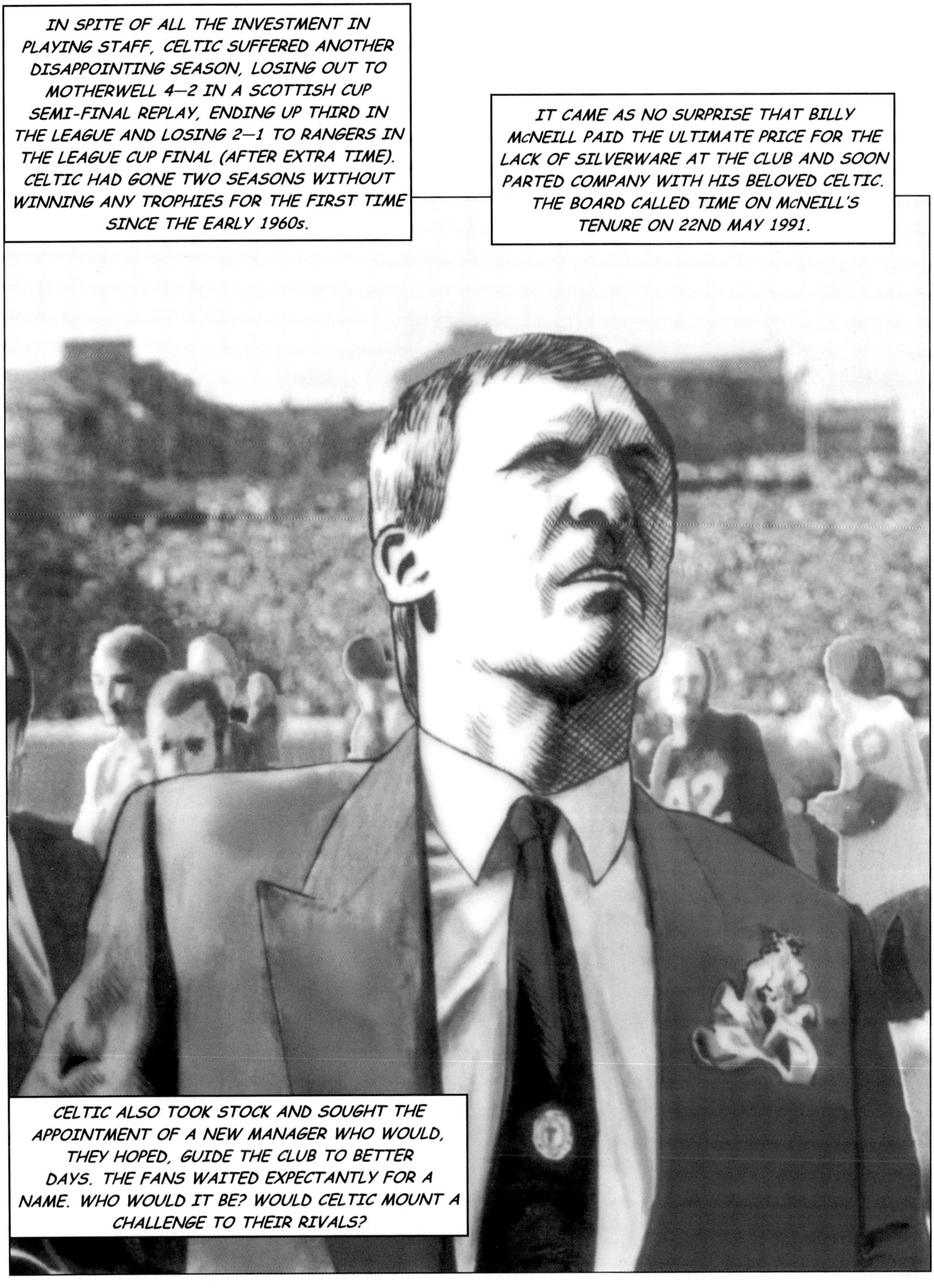
IN SPITE OF ALL THE INVESTMENT IN PLAYING STAFF, CELTIC SUFFERED ANOTHER DISAPPOINTING SEASON, LOSING OUT TO MOTHERWELL 4–2 IN A SCOTTISH CUP SEMI-FINAL REPLAY, ENDING UP THIRD IN THE LEAGUE AND LOSING 2–1 TO RANGERS IN THE LEAGUE CUP FINAL (AFTER EXTRA TIME). CELTIC HAD GONE TWO SEASONS WITHOUT WINNING ANY TROPHIES FOR THE FIRST TIME SINCE THE EARLY 1960s.
IT CAME AS NO SURPRISE THAT BILLY McNEILL PAID THE ULTIMATE PRICE FOR THE LACK OF SILVERWARE AT THE CLUB AND SOON PARTED COMPANY WITH HIS BELOVED CELTIC. THE BOARD CALLED TIME ON McNEILL'S TENURE ON 22ND MAY 1991.
CELTIC ALSO TOOK STOCK AND SOUGHT THE APPOINTMENT OF A NEW MANAGER WHO WOULD, THEY HOPED, GUIDE THE CLUB TO BETTER DAYS. THE FANS WAITED EXPECTANTLY FOR A NAME. WHO WOULD IT BE? WOULD CELTIC MOUNT A CHALLENGE TO THEIR RIVALS?

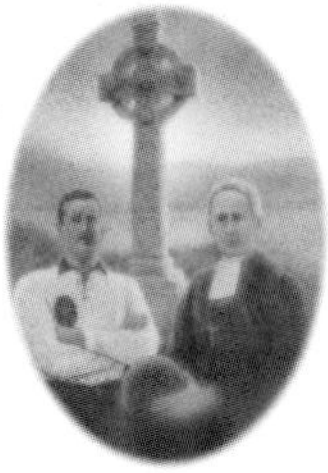

chapter 11

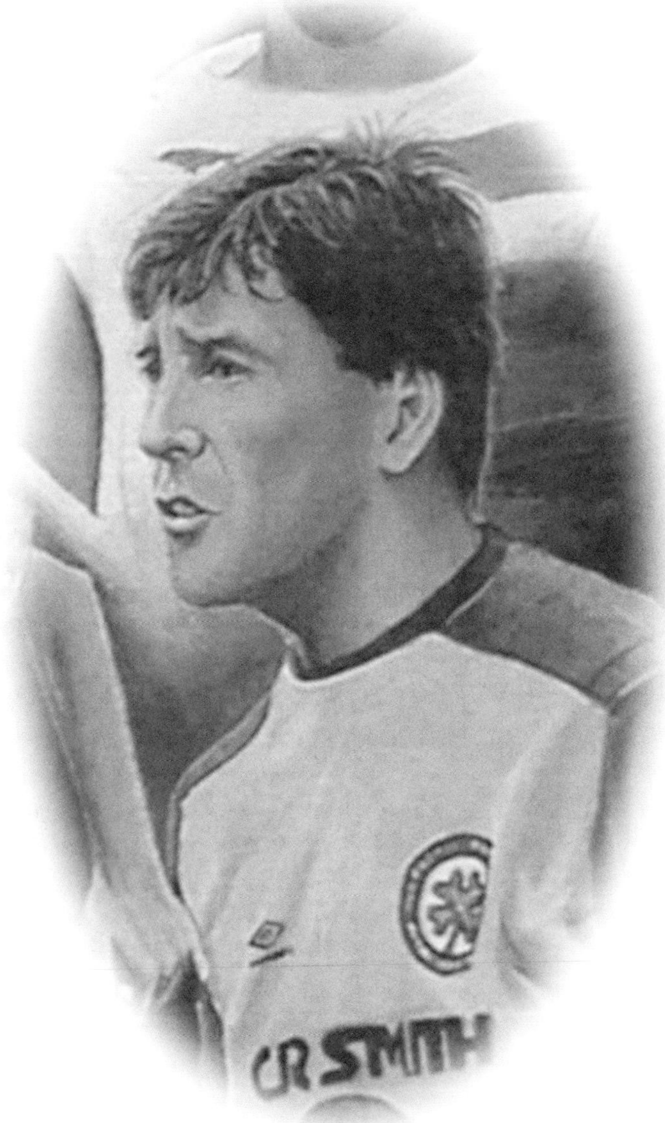
CR SMITH

the dark age

'walk on, walk on'

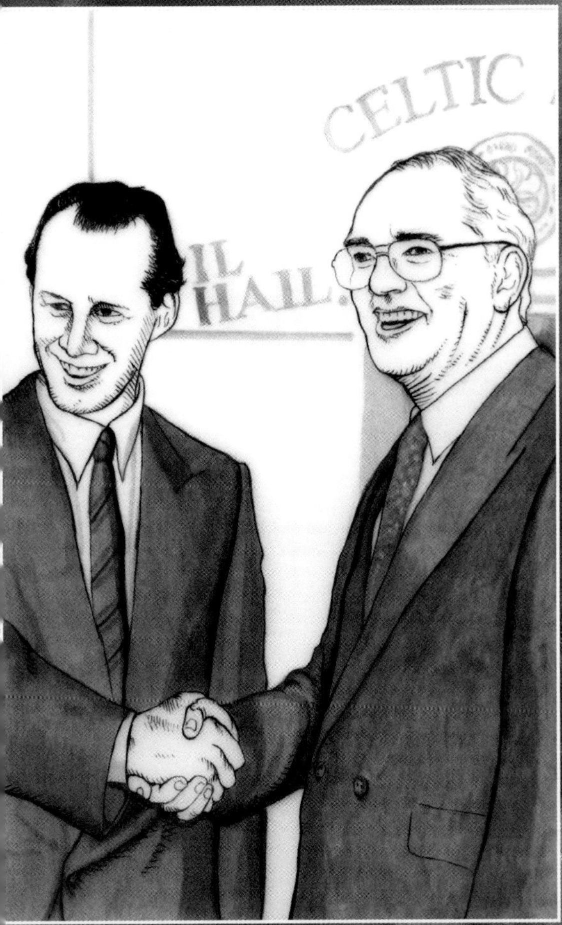

JACK McGINN, CHAIRMAN OF CELTIC, WELCOMES LIAM BRADY AS THE NEW MANAGER IN 1991, THE SUCCESSOR TO BILLY McNEILL. THE FORMER ARSENAL, JUVENTUS, SAMPDORIA, INTER MILAN, WEST HAM AND REPUBLIC OF IRELAND MIDFIELDER HAD LITTLE SUCCESS AT CELTIC IN TERMS OF RESULTS OR WINNING TROPHIES. MANY AGREED, THOUGH, THAT CELTIC PLAYED ATTRACTIVE ATTACKING FOOTBALL THAT WAS MOST ENJOYABLE TO WATCH, BUT RANGERS STILL ENJOYED DOMINANCE OF SCOTTISH FOOTBALL.

BRADY'S LEGACY WAS THOSE PLAYERS HE SIGNED FOR THE CLUB WHO WOULD GO ON TO BE STARS FOR CELTIC IN THE FUTURE.
CENTRE-HALF TONY MOWBRAY SHAKES HIS MANAGER'S HAND AS HE JOINS CELTIC FROM MIDDLESBROUGH FOR £1 MILLION. MOWBRAY, RECKONED TO BE MIDDLESBROUGH'S GREATEST EVER CAPTAIN, BECAME A CELTIC STALWART AND A FIRM FAVOURITE OF THE FANS.

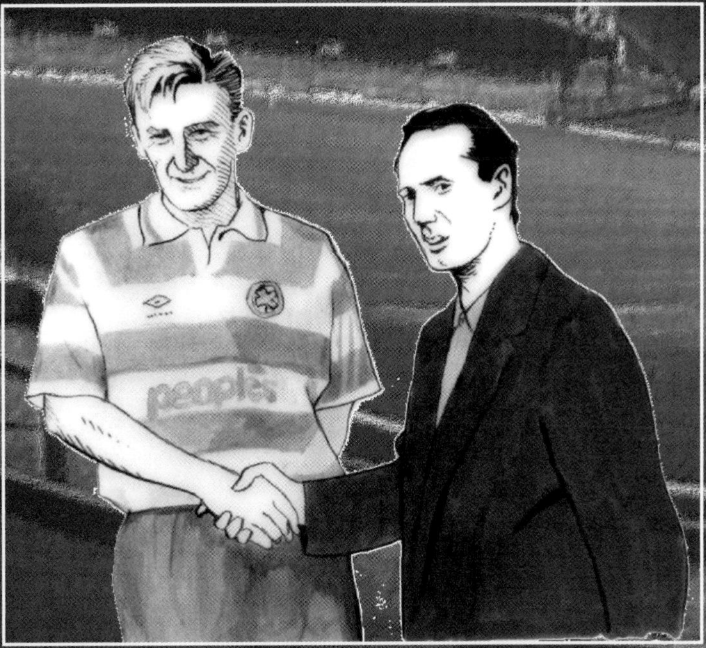
peoples

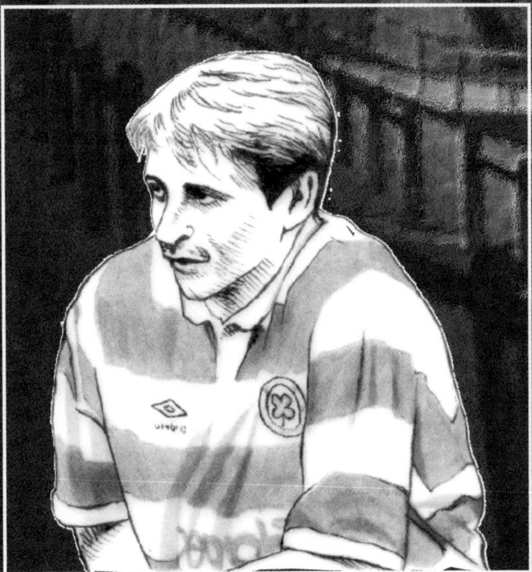

FROM CHELSEA CAME TOM BOYD, A DEFENDER OF SOME NOTE, IN A SWAP DEAL INVOLVING ANOTHER OF BRADY'S SIGNINGS – TONY CASCARINO. BOYD WOULD LATER BECOME CAPTAIN AND ONLY THE SECOND CELTIC CAPTAIN AFTER BILLY McNEILL TO WIN A SCOTTISH TREBLE.

AFTER JUST ONE AND A HALF SEASONS WITH NO SUCCESS, BRADY RESIGNED FROM CELTIC AS THE GLOOM AROUND CELTIC PARK DEEPENED.

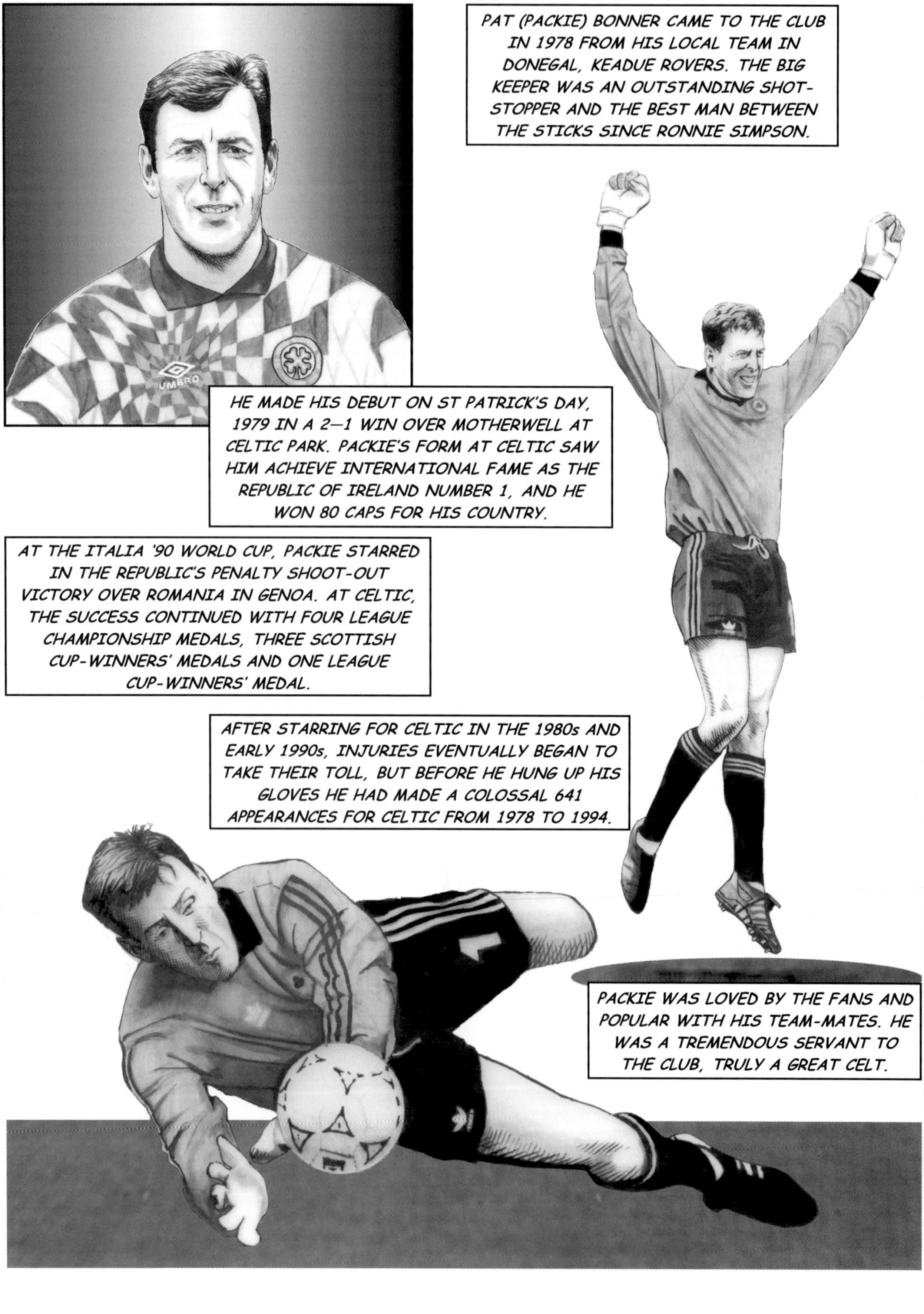
PAT (PACKIE) BONNER CAME TO THE CLUB IN 1978 FROM HIS LOCAL TEAM IN DONEGAL, KEADUE ROVERS. THE BIG KEEPER WAS AN OUTSTANDING SHOT-STOPPER AND THE BEST MAN BETWEEN THE STICKS SINCE RONNIE SIMPSON.
HE MADE HIS DEBUT ON ST PATRICK'S DAY, 1979 IN A 2–1 WIN OVER MOTHERWELL AT CELTIC PARK. PACKIE'S FORM AT CELTIC SAW HIM ACHIEVE INTERNATIONAL FAME AS THE REPUBLIC OF IRELAND NUMBER 1, AND HE WON 80 CAPS FOR HIS COUNTRY.
AT THE ITALIA '90 WORLD CUP, PACKIE STARRED IN THE REPUBLIC'S PENALTY SHOOT-OUT VICTORY OVER ROMANIA IN GENOA. AT CELTIC, THE SUCCESS CONTINUED WITH FOUR LEAGUE CHAMPIONSHIP MEDALS, THREE SCOTTISH CUP-WINNERS' MEDALS AND ONE LEAGUE CUP-WINNERS' MEDAL.
AFTER STARRING FOR CELTIC IN THE 1980s AND EARLY 1990s, INJURIES EVENTUALLY BEGAN TO TAKE THEIR TOLL, BUT BEFORE HE HUNG UP HIS GLOVES HE HAD MADE A COLOSSAL 641 APPEARANCES FOR CELTIC FROM 1978 TO 1994.
PACKIE WAS LOVED BY THE FANS AND POPULAR WITH HIS TEAM-MATES. HE WAS A TREMENDOUS SERVANT TO THE CLUB, TRULY A GREAT CELT.

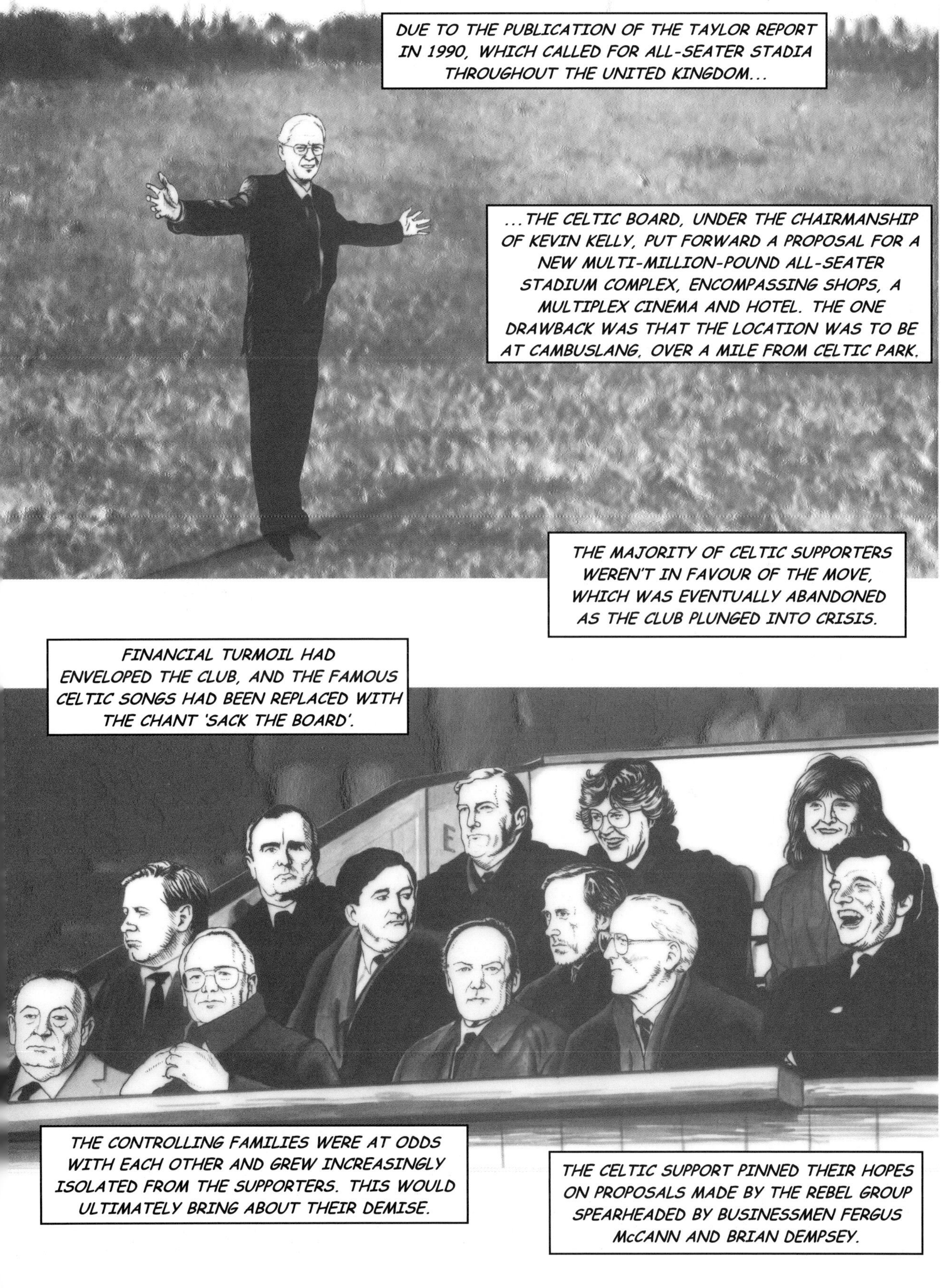
DUE TO THE PUBLICATION OF THE TAYLOR REPORT IN 1990, WHICH CALLED FOR ALL-SEATER STADIA THROUGHOUT THE UNITED KINGDOM...
...THE CELTIC BOARD, UNDER THE CHAIRMANSHIP OF KEVIN KELLY, PUT FORWARD A PROPOSAL FOR A NEW MULTI-MILLION-POUND ALL-SEATER STADIUM COMPLEX, ENCOMPASSING SHOPS, A MULTIPLEX CINEMA AND HOTEL. THE ONE DRAWBACK WAS THAT THE LOCATION WAS TO BE AT CAMBUSLANG, OVER A MILE FROM CELTIC PARK.
THE MAJORITY OF CELTIC SUPPORTERS WEREN'T IN FAVOUR OF THE MOVE, WHICH WAS EVENTUALLY ABANDONED AS THE CLUB PLUNGED INTO CRISIS.
FINANCIAL TURMOIL HAD ENVELOPED THE CLUB, AND THE FAMOUS CELTIC SONGS HAD BEEN REPLACED WITH THE CHANT 'SACK THE BOARD'.
THE CONTROLLING FAMILIES WERE AT ODDS WITH EACH OTHER AND GREW INCREASINGLY ISOLATED FROM THE SUPPORTERS. THIS WOULD ULTIMATELY BRING ABOUT THEIR DEMISE.
THE CELTIC SUPPORT PINNED THEIR HOPES ON PROPOSALS MADE BY THE REBEL GROUP SPEARHEADED BY BUSINESSMEN FERGUS McCANN AND BRIAN DEMPSEY.

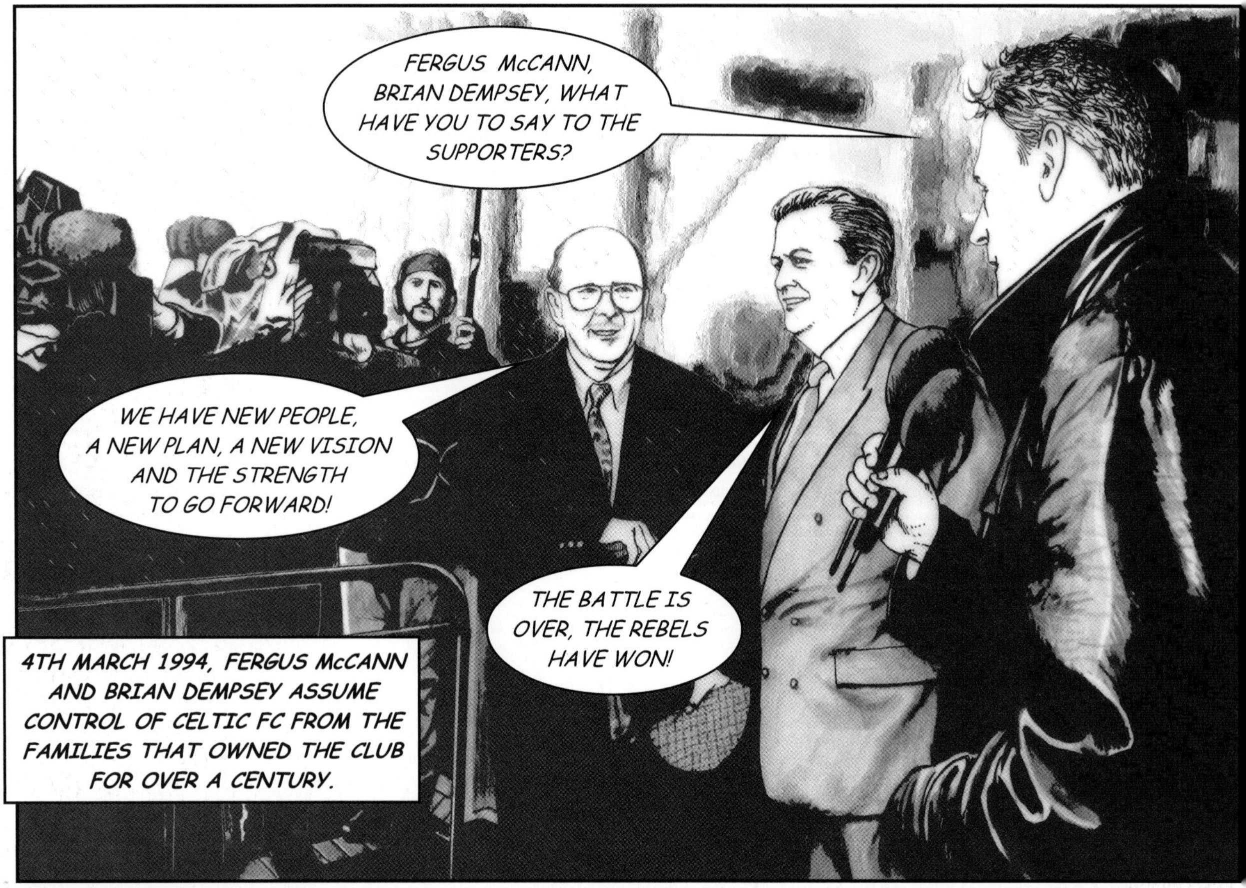
FERGUS McCANN, BRIAN DEMPSEY, WHAT HAVE YOU TO SAY TO THE SUPPORTERS?
WE HAVE NEW PEOPLE, A NEW PLAN, A NEW VISION AND THE STRENGTH TO GO FORWARD!
THE BATTLE IS OVER, THE REBELS HAVE WON!
4TH MARCH 1994, FERGUS McCANN AND BRIAN DEMPSEY ASSUME CONTROL OF CELTIC FC FROM THE FAMILIES THAT OWNED THE CLUB FOR OVER A CENTURY.

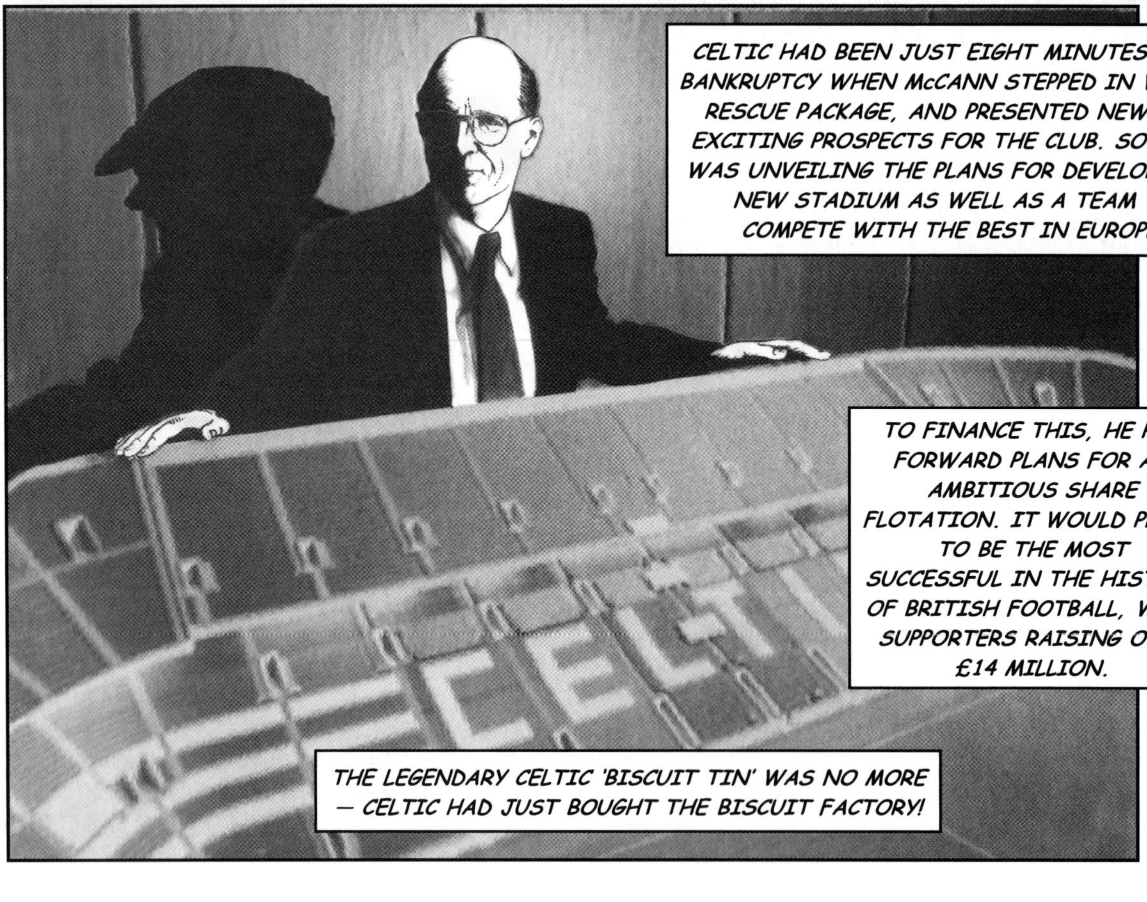
CELTIC HAD BEEN JUST EIGHT MINUTES FROM BANKRUPTCY WHEN McCANN STEPPED IN WITH A RESCUE PACKAGE, AND PRESENTED NEW AND EXCITING PROSPECTS FOR THE CLUB. SOON HE WAS UNVEILING THE PLANS FOR DEVELOPING A NEW STADIUM AS WELL AS A TEAM TO COMPETE WITH THE BEST IN EUROPE.
TO FINANCE THIS, HE PUT FORWARD PLANS FOR AN AMBITIOUS SHARE FLOTATION. IT WOULD PROVE TO BE THE MOST SUCCESSFUL IN THE HISTORY OF BRITISH FOOTBALL, WITH SUPPORTERS RAISING OVER £14 MILLION.
THE LEGENDARY CELTIC 'BISCUIT TIN' WAS NO MORE — CELTIC HAD JUST BOUGHT THE BISCUIT FACTORY!

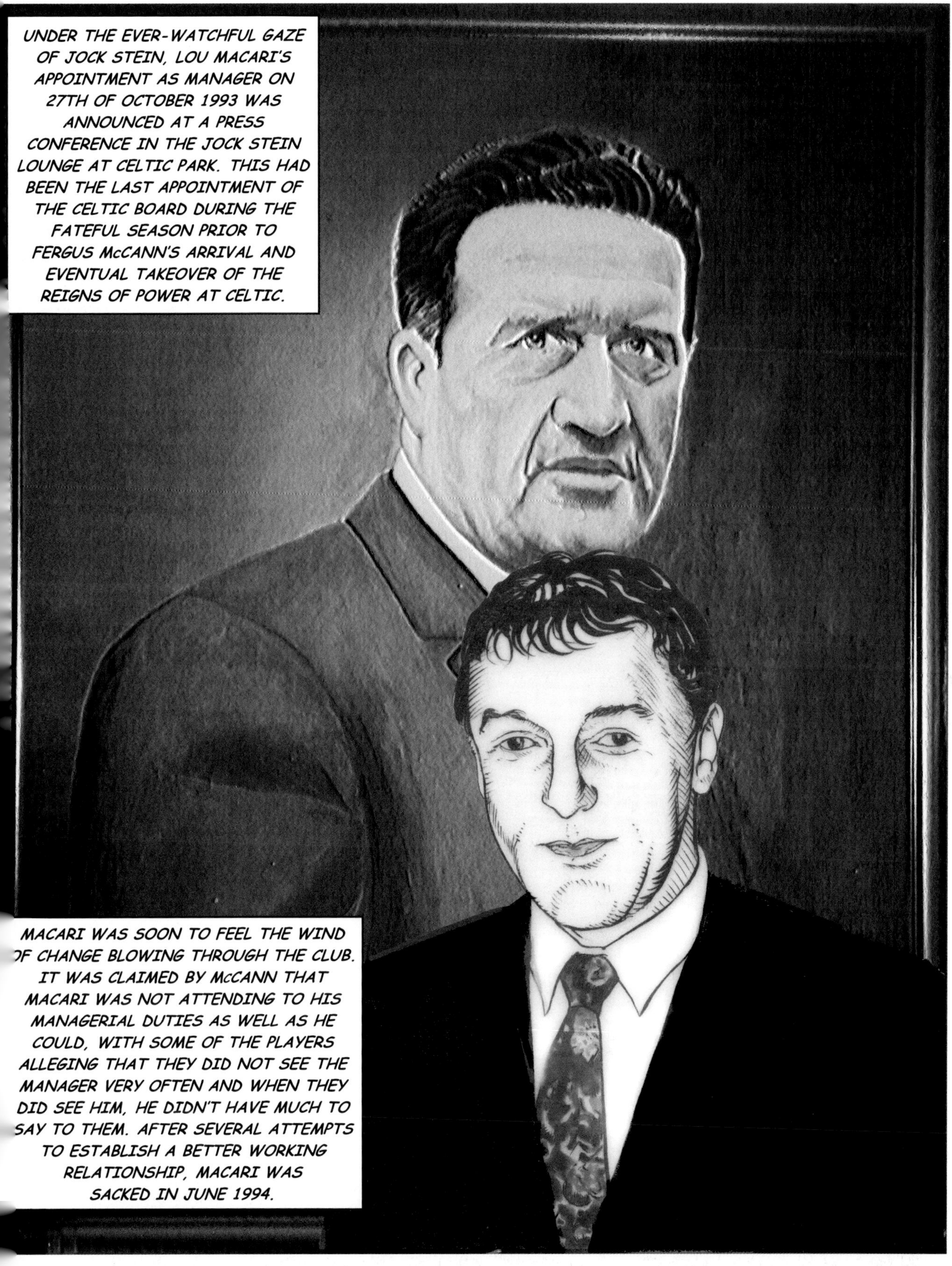
UNDER THE EVER-WATCHFUL GAZE OF JOCK STEIN, LOU MACARI'S APPOINTMENT AS MANAGER ON 27TH OF OCTOBER 1993 WAS ANNOUNCED AT A PRESS CONFERENCE IN THE JOCK STEIN LOUNGE AT CELTIC PARK. THIS HAD BEEN THE LAST APPOINTMENT OF THE CELTIC BOARD DURING THE FATEFUL SEASON PRIOR TO FERGUS McCANN'S ARRIVAL AND EVENTUAL TAKEOVER OF THE REIGNS OF POWER AT CELTIC.
MACARI WAS SOON TO FEEL THE WIND OF CHANGE BLOWING THROUGH THE CLUB. IT WAS CLAIMED BY McCANN THAT MACARI WAS NOT ATTENDING TO HIS MANAGERIAL DUTIES AS WELL AS HE COULD, WITH SOME OF THE PLAYERS ALLEGING THAT THEY DID NOT SEE THE MANAGER VERY OFTEN AND WHEN THEY DID SEE HIM, HE DIDN'T HAVE MUCH TO SAY TO THEM. AFTER SEVERAL ATTEMPTS TO ESTABLISH A BETTER WORKING RELATIONSHIP, MACARI WAS SACKED IN JUNE 1994.

chapter 12

return from exile

'with hope in your heart'

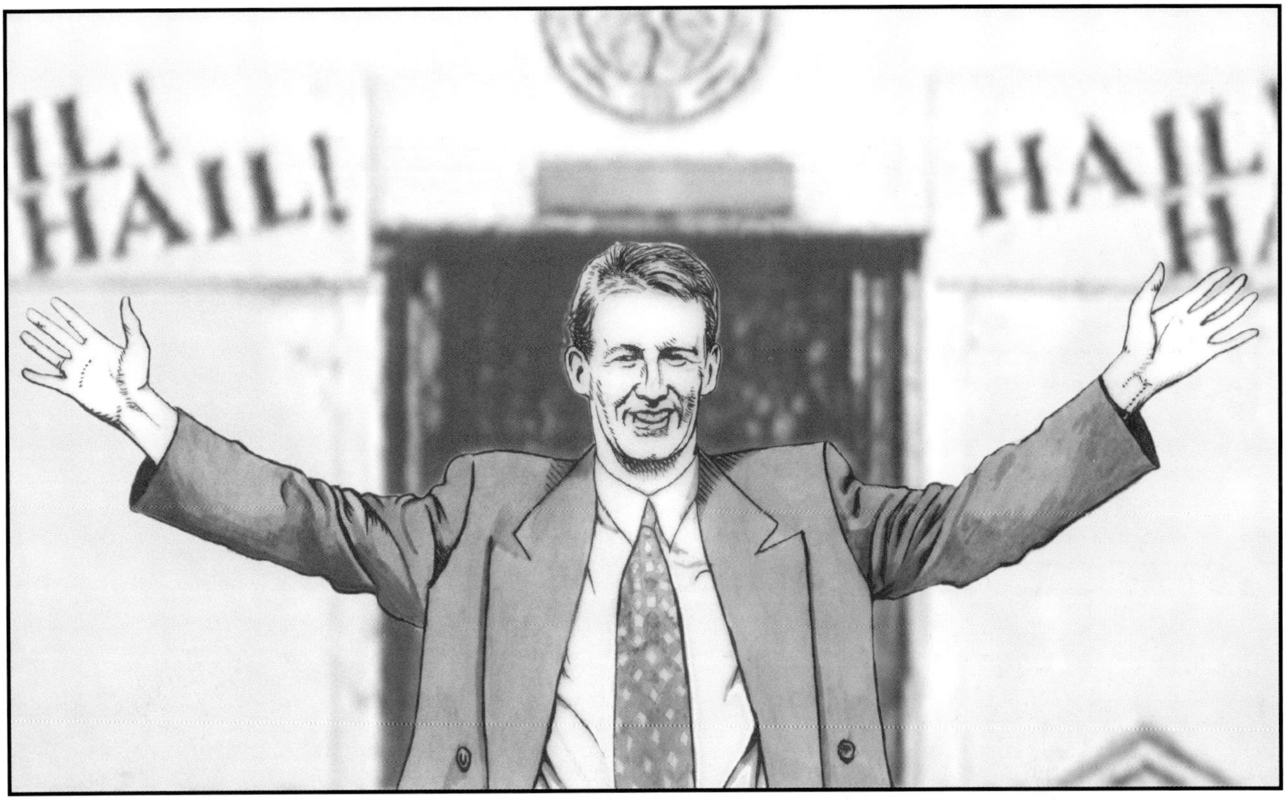
HAIL!

TOMMY BURNS WALKS THROUGH THE TUNNEL AT CELTIC PARK AS MANAGER ON 12TH JULY 1994. HIS RETURN TO HIS BELOVED CELTIC WAS NOT WITHOUT CONTROVERSY. CELTIC WERE ACCUSED OF 'TAPPING' BURNS WHILST HE WAS STILL MANAGER OF KILMARNOCK, AND THE CLUB WAS FINED HEAVILY AS A RESULT. BURNS HAD DONE WELL FOR KILMARNOCK BY GETTING THEM INTO THE PREMIER LEAGUE. HE ARRIVED AT CELTIC WITH HIS ASSISTANT BILLY STARK, WITH GREAT PLANS FOR REBUILDING THE CELTIC TEAM. IT WASN'T LONG BEFORE NEW PLAYERS BEGAN TO ARRIVE AT THE CLUB.

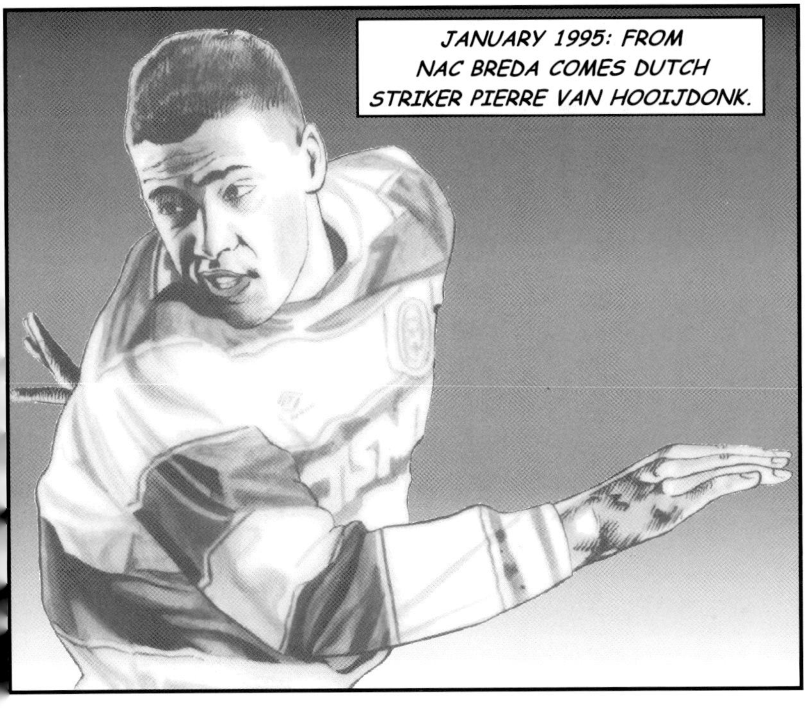
JANUARY 1995: FROM NAC BREDA COMES DUTCH STRIKER PIERRE VAN HOOIJDONK.

FULL-BACK TOSH McKINLAY SIGNED FROM HEARTS FOR £350,000.

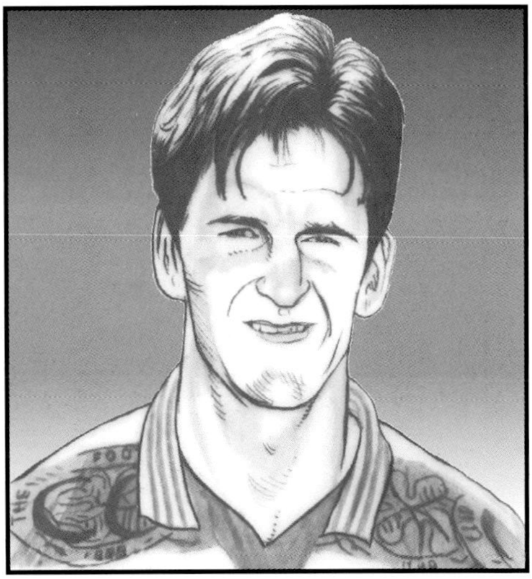

PHIL O'DONNELL, A RECORD SIGNING AT THE TIME FOR CELTIC AT £1.75 MILLION, TRANSFERRED FROM MOTHERWELL IN SEPTEMBER 1994. A WHOLE-HEARTED, STRONG-RUNNING AND DIRECT MIDFIELD PLAYER, O'DONNELL SCORED MANY IMPORTANT GOALS FOR CELTIC.

O'DONNELL SCORED TWICE ON HIS DEBUT AGAINST PARTICK THISTLE IN A 2–1 WIN.

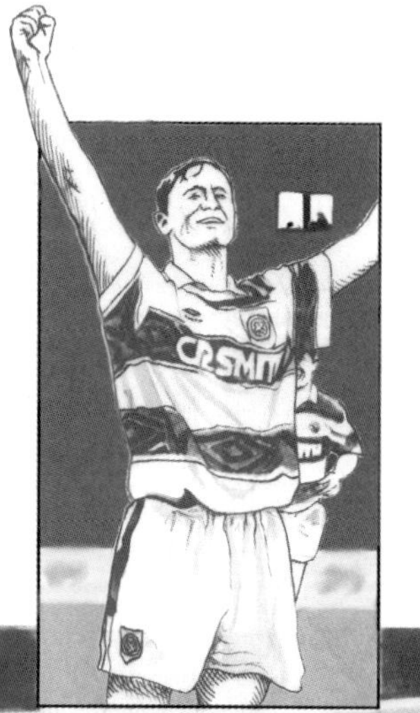

UNFORTUNATELY, HIS APPEARANCES FOR CELTIC WERE LIMITED DUE TO THE MANY INJURIES THAT HE SUFFERED AS A RESULT OF GIVING HIS ALL FOR THE CLUB. HE PLAYED FOR HIS COUNTRY IN 1994, WON A SCOTTISH CUP-WINNERS' MEDAL IN 1995 AND WON A LEAGUE CHAMPIONSHIP MEDAL WITH CELTIC IN 1998. PHIL O'DONNELL MADE 89 APPEARANCES FOR CELTIC AND SCORED 16 GOALS. IN 1999, HE LEFT FOR SHEFFIELD WEDNESDAY AND PLAYED THERE UNTIL 2003.

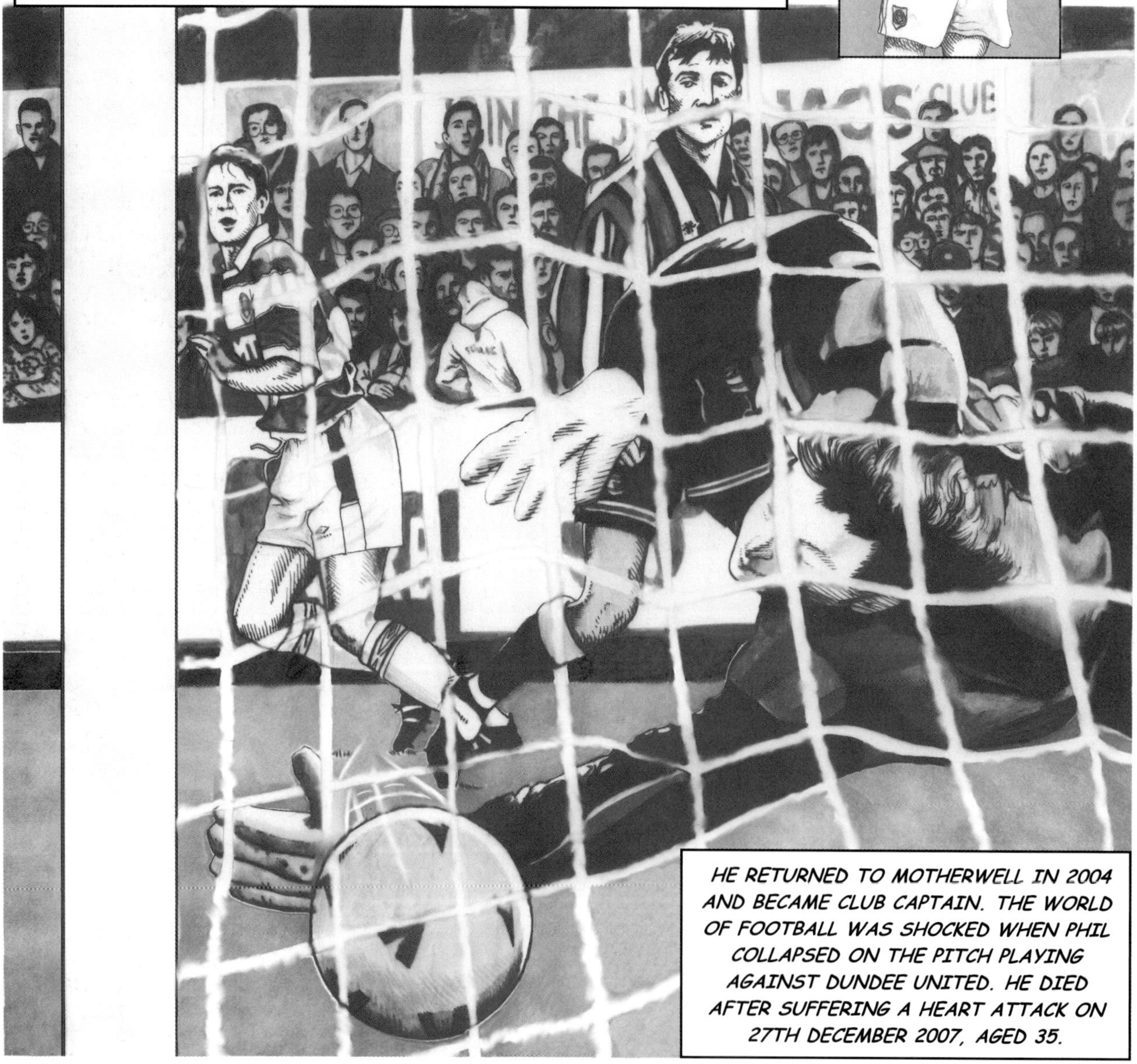
HE RETURNED TO MOTHERWELL IN 2004 AND BECAME CLUB CAPTAIN. THE WORLD OF FOOTBALL WAS SHOCKED WHEN PHIL COLLAPSED ON THE PITCH PLAYING AGAINST DUNDEE UNITED. HE DIED AFTER SUFFERING A HEART ATTACK ON 27TH DECEMBER 2007, AGED 35.

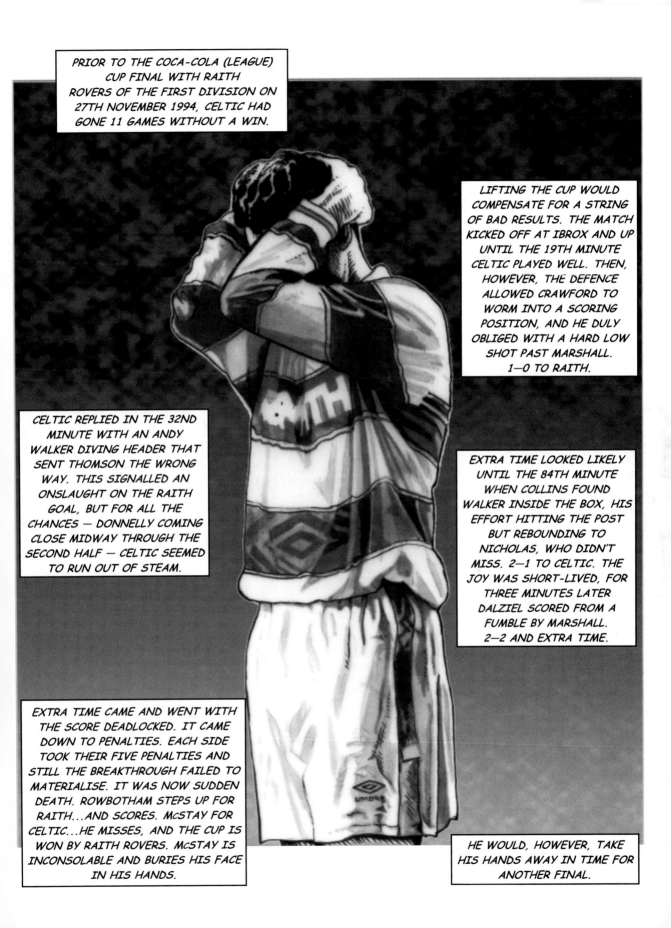

PRIOR TO THE COCA-COLA (LEAGUE) CUP FINAL WITH RAITH ROVERS OF THE FIRST DIVISION ON 27TH NOVEMBER 1994, CELTIC HAD GONE 11 GAMES WITHOUT A WIN.

LIFTING THE CUP WOULD COMPENSATE FOR A STRING OF BAD RESULTS. THE MATCH KICKED OFF AT IBROX AND UP UNTIL THE 19TH MINUTE CELTIC PLAYED WELL. THEN, HOWEVER, THE DEFENCE ALLOWED CRAWFORD TO WORM INTO A SCORING POSITION, AND HE DULY OBLIGED WITH A HARD LOW SHOT PAST MARSHALL. 1—0 TO RAITH.

CELTIC REPLIED IN THE 32ND MINUTE WITH AN ANDY WALKER DIVING HEADER THAT SENT THOMSON THE WRONG WAY. THIS SIGNALLED AN ONSLAUGHT ON THE RAITH GOAL, BUT FOR ALL THE CHANCES — DONNELLY COMING CLOSE MIDWAY THROUGH THE SECOND HALF — CELTIC SEEMED TO RUN OUT OF STEAM.

EXTRA TIME LOOKED LIKELY UNTIL THE 84TH MINUTE WHEN COLLINS FOUND WALKER INSIDE THE BOX, HIS EFFORT HITTING THE POST BUT REBOUNDING TO NICHOLAS, WHO DIDN'T MISS. 2—1 TO CELTIC. THE JOY WAS SHORT-LIVED, FOR THREE MINUTES LATER DALZIEL SCORED FROM A FUMBLE BY MARSHALL. 2—2 AND EXTRA TIME.

EXTRA TIME CAME AND WENT WITH THE SCORE DEADLOCKED. IT CAME DOWN TO PENALTIES. EACH SIDE TOOK THEIR FIVE PENALTIES AND STILL THE BREAKTHROUGH FAILED TO MATERIALISE. IT WAS NOW SUDDEN DEATH. ROWBOTHAM STEPS UP FOR RAITH...AND SCORES. McSTAY FOR CELTIC...HE MISSES, AND THE CUP IS WON BY RAITH ROVERS. McSTAY IS INCONSOLABLE AND BURIES HIS FACE IN HIS HANDS.

HE WOULD, HOWEVER, TAKE HIS HANDS AWAY IN TIME FOR ANOTHER FINAL.

THE SEASON HAD BEEN DIFFICULT FOR CELTIC, AS THE TEAM SPENT A YEAR IN EXILE AT HAMPDEN PARK. THE ATMOSPHERE AT HAMPDEN WAS NEVER THE BEST, AS THE TEAM AND FANS STRUGGLED TO SETTLE IN THEIR TEMPORARY HOME. THIS FACTOR PROBABLY CONTRIBUTED TO CELTIC'S INCONSISTENCY DURING 1994–95.

CELTIC FINISHED FOURTH IN THE LEAGUE WITH A POINTS TOTAL OF JUST 51, TWO POINTS BEHIND THIRD-PLACED HIBS AND THREE POINTS BEHIND SECOND-PLACED MOTHERWELL, BUT MORE EMPHATICALLY, CELTIC FINISHED 18 POINTS BEHIND LEAGUE CHAMPIONS RANGERS.

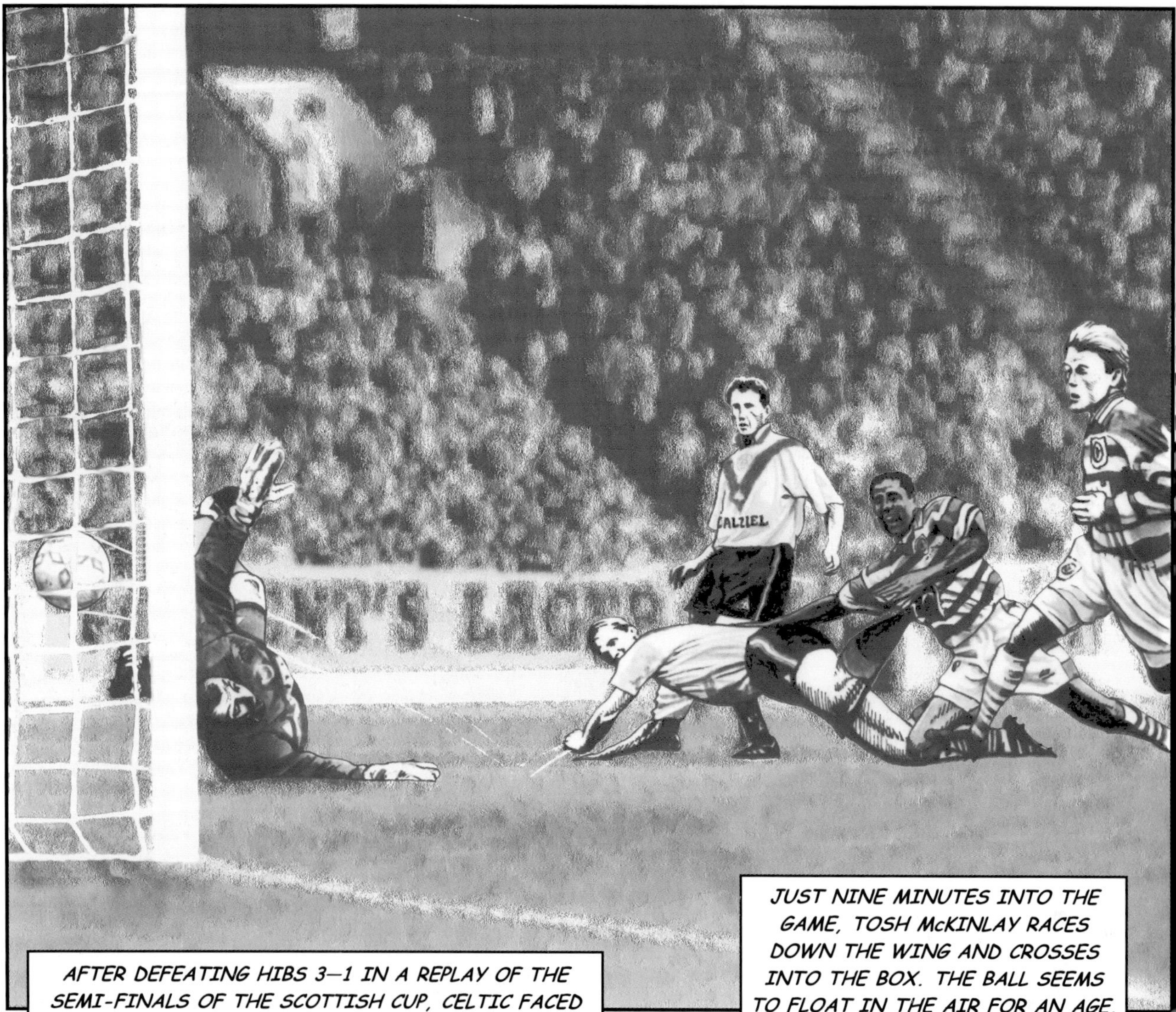

AFTER DEFEATING HIBS 3–1 IN A REPLAY OF THE SEMI-FINALS OF THE SCOTTISH CUP, CELTIC FACED AIRDRIE IN THE FINAL AT HAMPDEN PARK ON 27TH MAY 1995. IT HAD BEEN SIX LONG YEARS SINCE CELTIC HAD WON ANYTHING. COULD THIS BE THE MATCH THAT SEES TOMMY BURNS WIN HIS FIRST TROPHY AS MANAGER?

JUST NINE MINUTES INTO THE GAME, TOSH McKINLAY RACES DOWN THE WING AND CROSSES INTO THE BOX. THE BALL SEEMS TO FLOAT IN THE AIR FOR AN AGE. UP JUMPS VAN HOOIJDONK AND CONNECTS WITH AN ANGLED HEADER THAT BEATS KEEPER MARTIN. THE GIANT DUTCHMAN HAS SCORED FOR CELTIC AND TURNS TO CELEBRATE WITH HIS TEAM-MATES. THE FANS GO WILD.

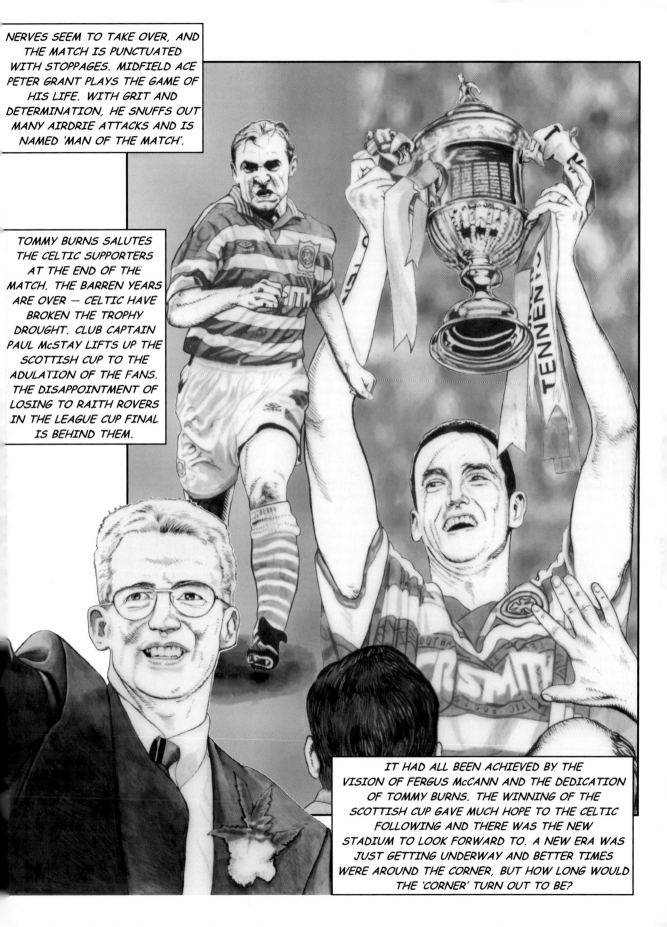

NERVES SEEM TO TAKE OVER, AND THE MATCH IS PUNCTUATED WITH STOPPAGES. MIDFIELD ACE PETER GRANT PLAYS THE GAME OF HIS LIFE. WITH GRIT AND DETERMINATION, HE SNUFFS OUT MANY AIRDRIE ATTACKS AND IS NAMED 'MAN OF THE MATCH'.

TOMMY BURNS SALUTES THE CELTIC SUPPORTERS AT THE END OF THE MATCH. THE BARREN YEARS ARE OVER — CELTIC HAVE BROKEN THE TROPHY DROUGHT. CLUB CAPTAIN PAUL McSTAY LIFTS UP THE SCOTTISH CUP TO THE ADULATION OF THE FANS. THE DISAPPOINTMENT OF LOSING TO RAITH ROVERS IN THE LEAGUE CUP FINAL IS BEHIND THEM.

IT HAD ALL BEEN ACHIEVED BY THE VISION OF FERGUS McCANN AND THE DEDICATION OF TOMMY BURNS. THE WINNING OF THE SCOTTISH CUP GAVE MUCH HOPE TO THE CELTIC FOLLOWING AND THERE WAS THE NEW STADIUM TO LOOK FORWARD TO. A NEW ERA WAS JUST GETTING UNDERWAY AND BETTER TIMES WERE AROUND THE CORNER, BUT HOW LONG WOULD THE 'CORNER' TURN OUT TO BE?

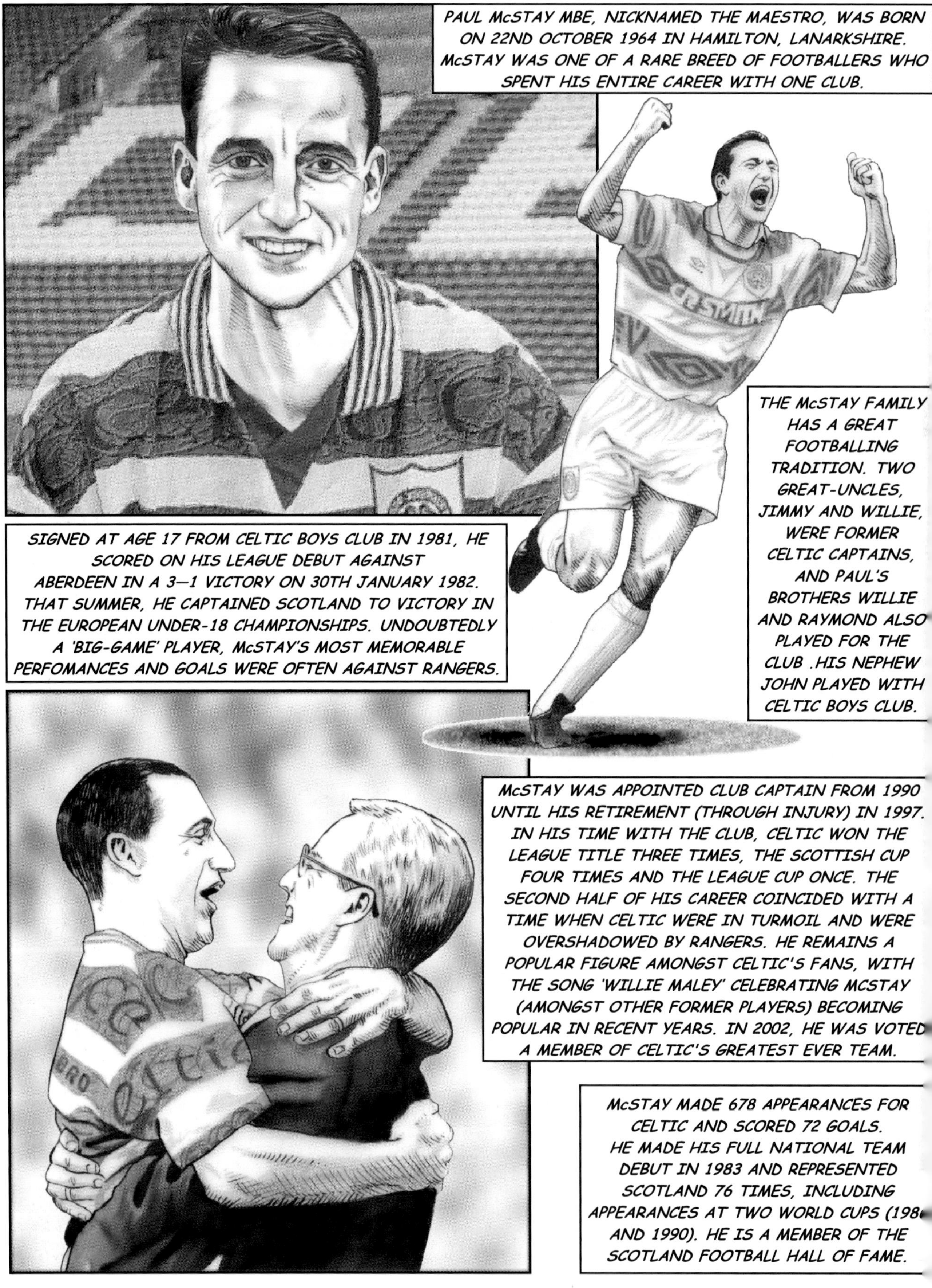
PAUL McSTAY MBE, NICKNAMED THE MAESTRO, WAS BORN ON 22ND OCTOBER 1964 IN HAMILTON, LANARKSHIRE. McSTAY WAS ONE OF A RARE BREED OF FOOTBALLERS WHO SPENT HIS ENTIRE CAREER WITH ONE CLUB.
CR SMITH
THE McSTAY FAMILY HAS A GREAT FOOTBALLING TRADITION. TWO GREAT-UNCLES, JIMMY AND WILLIE, WERE FORMER CELTIC CAPTAINS, AND PAUL'S BROTHERS WILLIE AND RAYMOND ALSO PLAYED FOR THE CLUB .HIS NEPHEW JOHN PLAYED WITH CELTIC BOYS CLUB.
SIGNED AT AGE 17 FROM CELTIC BOYS CLUB IN 1981, HE SCORED ON HIS LEAGUE DEBUT AGAINST ABERDEEN IN A 3—1 VICTORY ON 30TH JANUARY 1982. THAT SUMMER, HE CAPTAINED SCOTLAND TO VICTORY IN THE EUROPEAN UNDER-18 CHAMPIONSHIPS. UNDOUBTEDLY A 'BIG-GAME' PLAYER, McSTAY'S MOST MEMORABLE PERFOMANCES AND GOALS WERE OFTEN AGAINST RANGERS.
McSTAY WAS APPOINTED CLUB CAPTAIN FROM 1990 UNTIL HIS RETIREMENT (THROUGH INJURY) IN 1997. IN HIS TIME WITH THE CLUB, CELTIC WON THE LEAGUE TITLE THREE TIMES, THE SCOTTISH CUP FOUR TIMES AND THE LEAGUE CUP ONCE. THE SECOND HALF OF HIS CAREER COINCIDED WITH A TIME WHEN CELTIC WERE IN TURMOIL AND WERE OVERSHADOWED BY RANGERS. HE REMAINS A POPULAR FIGURE AMONGST CELTIC'S FANS, WITH THE SONG 'WILLIE MALEY' CELEBRATING MCSTAY (AMONGST OTHER FORMER PLAYERS) BECOMING POPULAR IN RECENT YEARS. IN 2002, HE WAS VOTED A MEMBER OF CELTIC'S GREATEST EVER TEAM.
McSTAY MADE 678 APPEARANCES FOR CELTIC AND SCORED 72 GOALS. HE MADE HIS FULL NATIONAL TEAM DEBUT IN 1983 AND REPRESENTED SCOTLAND 76 TIMES, INCLUDING APPEARANCES AT TWO WORLD CUPS (198 AND 1990). HE IS A MEMBER OF THE SCOTLAND FOOTBALL HALL OF FAME.

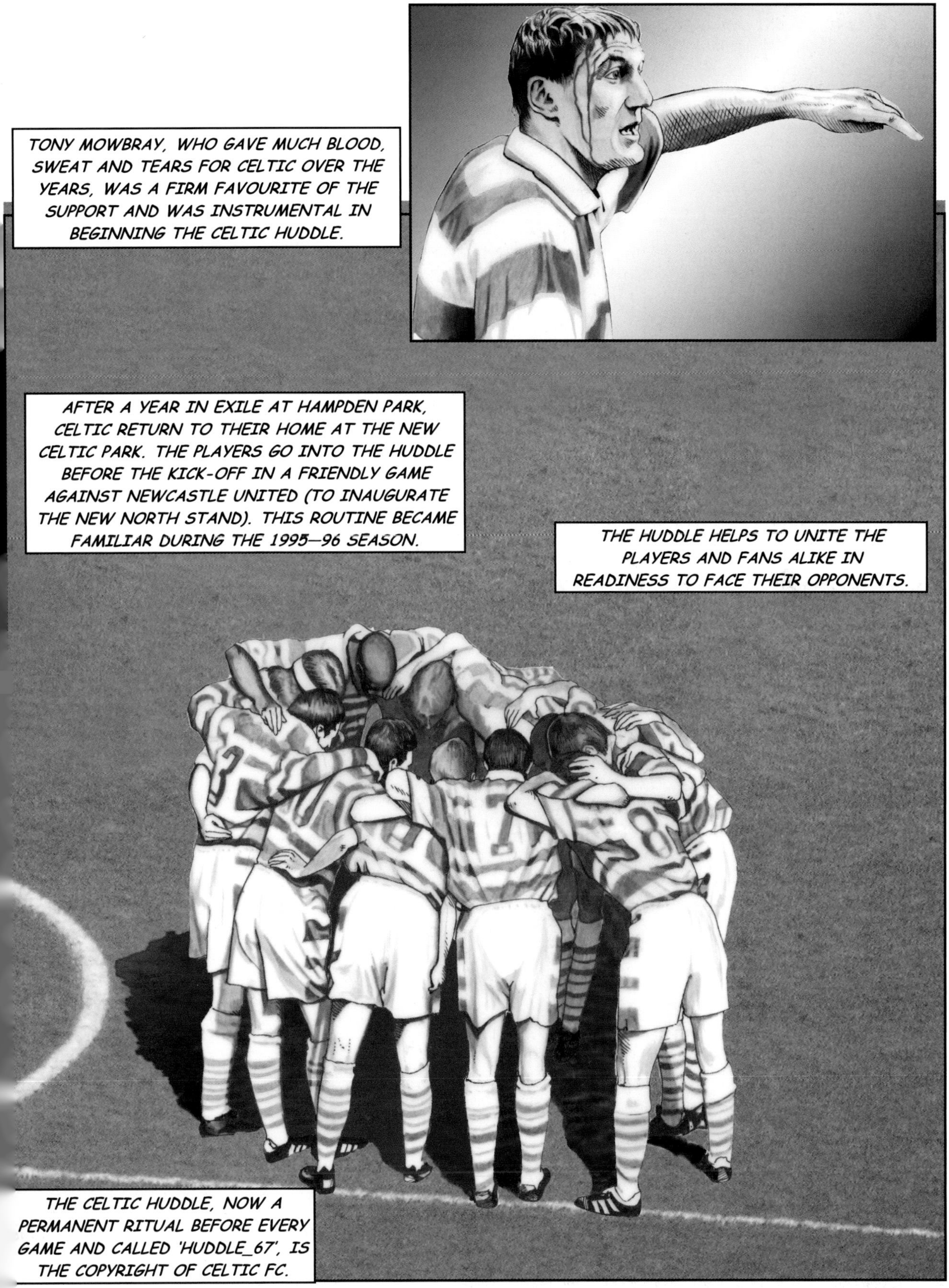
TONY MOWBRAY, WHO GAVE MUCH BLOOD, SWEAT AND TEARS FOR CELTIC OVER THE YEARS, WAS A FIRM FAVOURITE OF THE SUPPORT AND WAS INSTRUMENTAL IN BEGINNING THE CELTIC HUDDLE.
AFTER A YEAR IN EXILE AT HAMPDEN PARK, CELTIC RETURN TO THEIR HOME AT THE NEW CELTIC PARK. THE PLAYERS GO INTO THE HUDDLE BEFORE THE KICK-OFF IN A FRIENDLY GAME AGAINST NEWCASTLE UNITED (TO INAUGURATE THE NEW NORTH STAND). THIS ROUTINE BECAME FAMILIAR DURING THE 1995–96 SEASON.
THE HUDDLE HELPS TO UNITE THE PLAYERS AND FANS ALIKE IN READINESS TO FACE THEIR OPPONENTS.
THE CELTIC HUDDLE, NOW A PERMANENT RITUAL BEFORE EVERY GAME AND CALLED 'HUDDLE_67', IS THE COPYRIGHT OF CELTIC FC.

JACKIE McNAMARA WAS SIGNED FROM DUNFERMLINE ON 3RD OCTOBER 1995 FOR £600,000. HE IS THE SON OF JACKIE SNR, WHO ALSO PLAYED FOR CELTIC. JACKIE HAD EXCEPTIONAL PACE AND WAS GREAT IN DEFENCE.

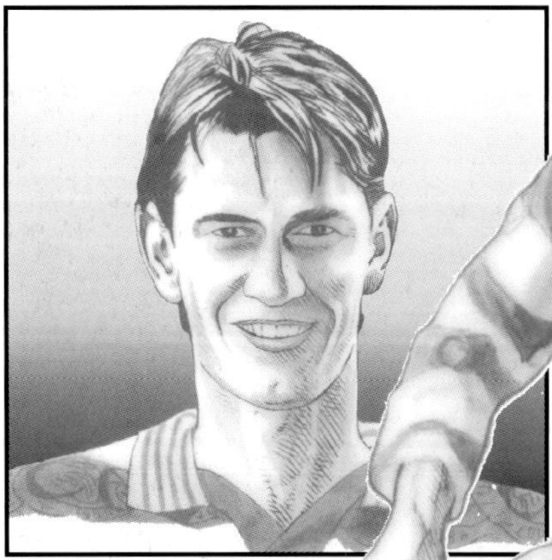

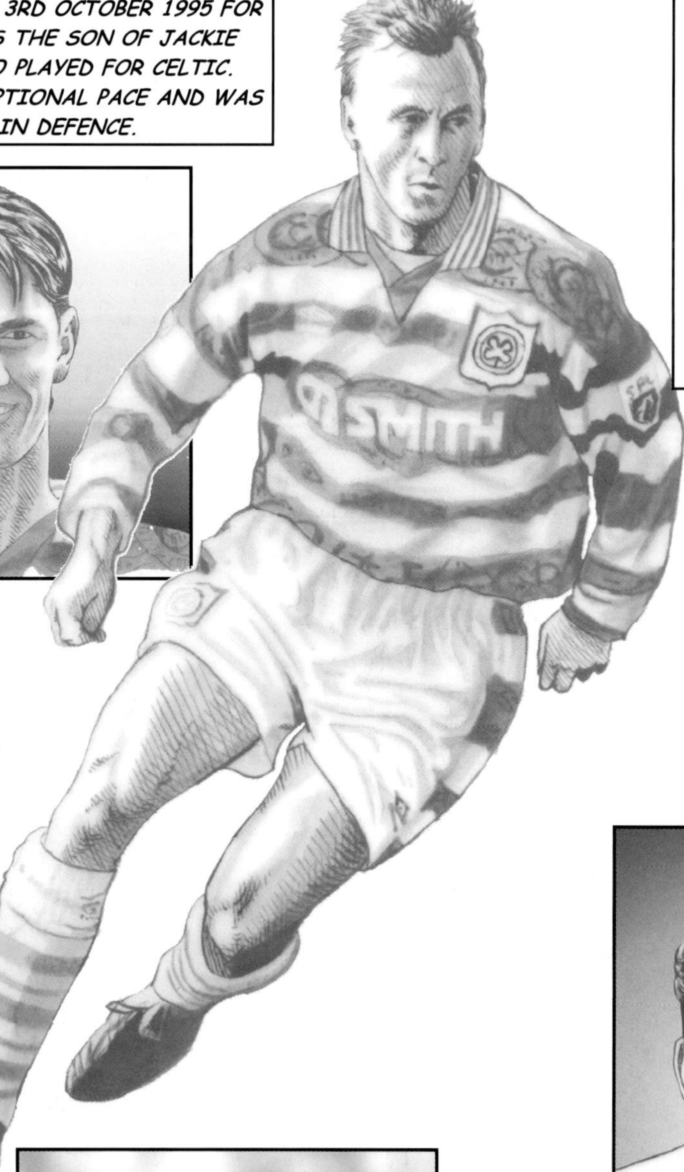

THE HOPE FOR THE FANS WAS NOT JUST IN WINNING THE SCOTTISH CUP OR THE NEW STADIUM. TOMMY BURNS WAS BRINGING FRESH TALENT TO CELTIC PARK. ANDREAS THOM ARRIVED FROM HERTHA BERLIN IN THE SUMMER OF 1995 FOR A RECORD FEE OF £2.2 MILLION. HE WAS A DIRECT AND SKILFUL FORWARD WITH BLISTERING PACE AND SOON BECAME A FAVOURITE AMONG THE FANS.

BOLTON WANDERERS PROVIDED ALAN STUBBS IN THE SPRING OF 1996. AN EXCELLENT CENTRE-BACK WHO COULD HIT 40-YARD PASSES WITH PIN-POINT ACCURACY, STUBBS WOULD BECOME A STALWART IN CELTIC'S REARGUARD.

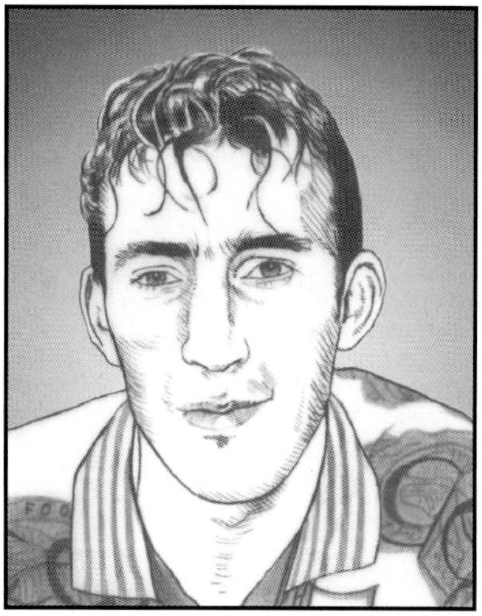

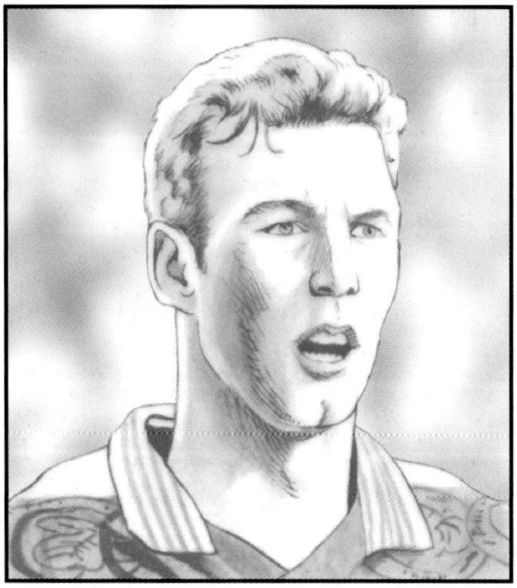

DANISH MIDFIELDER MORTEN WIEGHORST JOINED THE SIDE IN 1995 BUT COULD NOT HOLD DOWN A REGULAR FIRST-TEAM PLACE DUE TO INJURIES. HE WAS A PLAYER WHO WOULD PROVE INVALUABLE IN THE FUTURE.

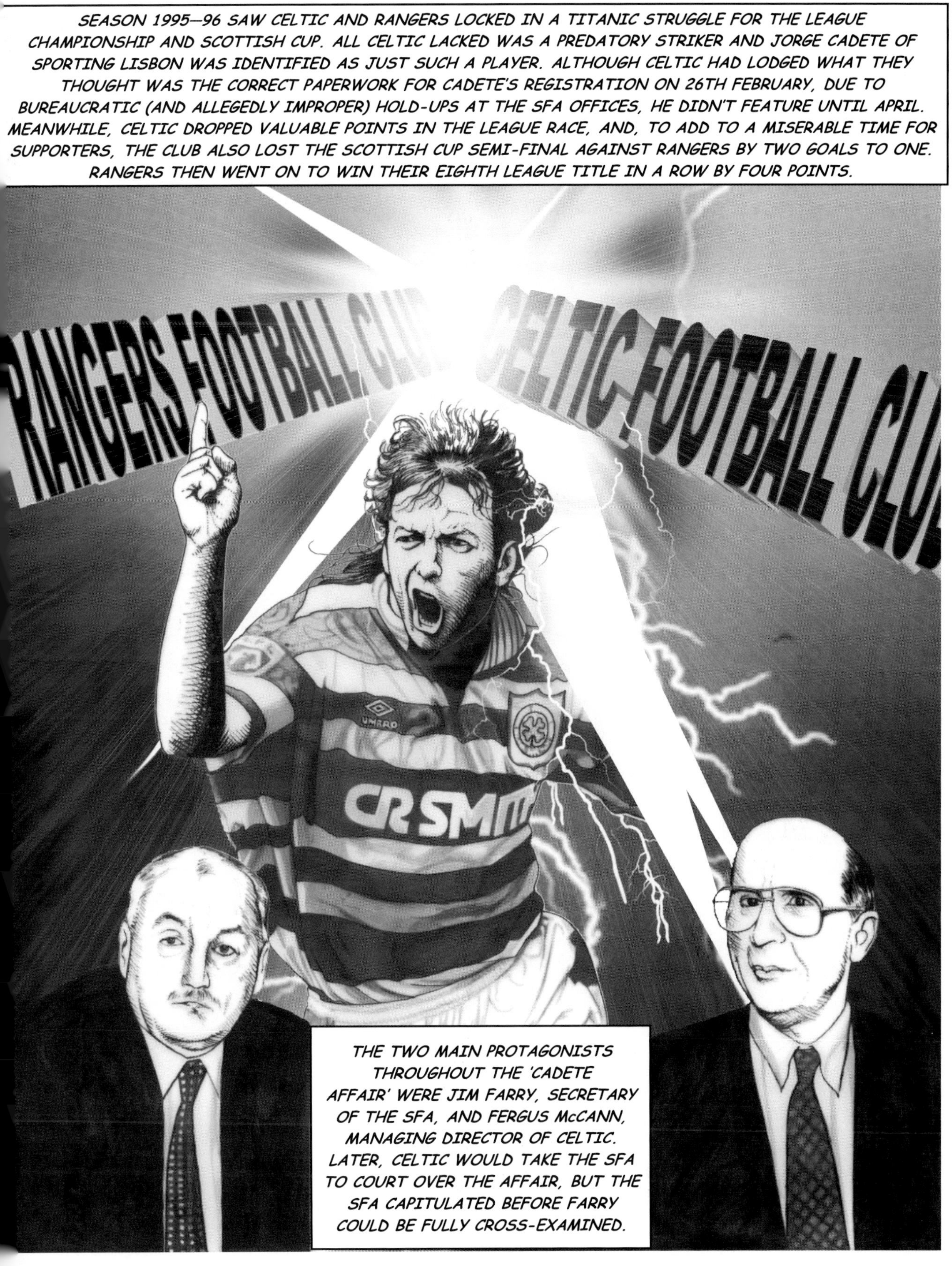
SEASON 1995–96 SAW CELTIC AND RANGERS LOCKED IN A TITANIC STRUGGLE FOR THE LEAGUE CHAMPIONSHIP AND SCOTTISH CUP. ALL CELTIC LACKED WAS A PREDATORY STRIKER AND JORGE CADETE OF SPORTING LISBON WAS IDENTIFIED AS JUST SUCH A PLAYER. ALTHOUGH CELTIC HAD LODGED WHAT THEY THOUGHT WAS THE CORRECT PAPERWORK FOR CADETE'S REGISTRATION ON 26TH FEBRUARY, DUE TO BUREAUCRATIC (AND ALLEGEDLY IMPROPER) HOLD-UPS AT THE SFA OFFICES, HE DIDN'T FEATURE UNTIL APRIL. MEANWHILE, CELTIC DROPPED VALUABLE POINTS IN THE LEAGUE RACE, AND, TO ADD TO A MISERABLE TIME FOR SUPPORTERS, THE CLUB ALSO LOST THE SCOTTISH CUP SEMI-FINAL AGAINST RANGERS BY TWO GOALS TO ONE. RANGERS THEN WENT ON TO WIN THEIR EIGHTH LEAGUE TITLE IN A ROW BY FOUR POINTS.
THE TWO MAIN PROTAGONISTS THROUGHOUT THE 'CADETE AFFAIR' WERE JIM FARRY, SECRETARY OF THE SFA, AND FERGUS McCANN, MANAGING DIRECTOR OF CELTIC. LATER, CELTIC WOULD TAKE THE SFA TO COURT OVER THE AFFAIR, BUT THE SFA CAPITULATED BEFORE FARRY COULD BE FULLY CROSS-EXAMINED.

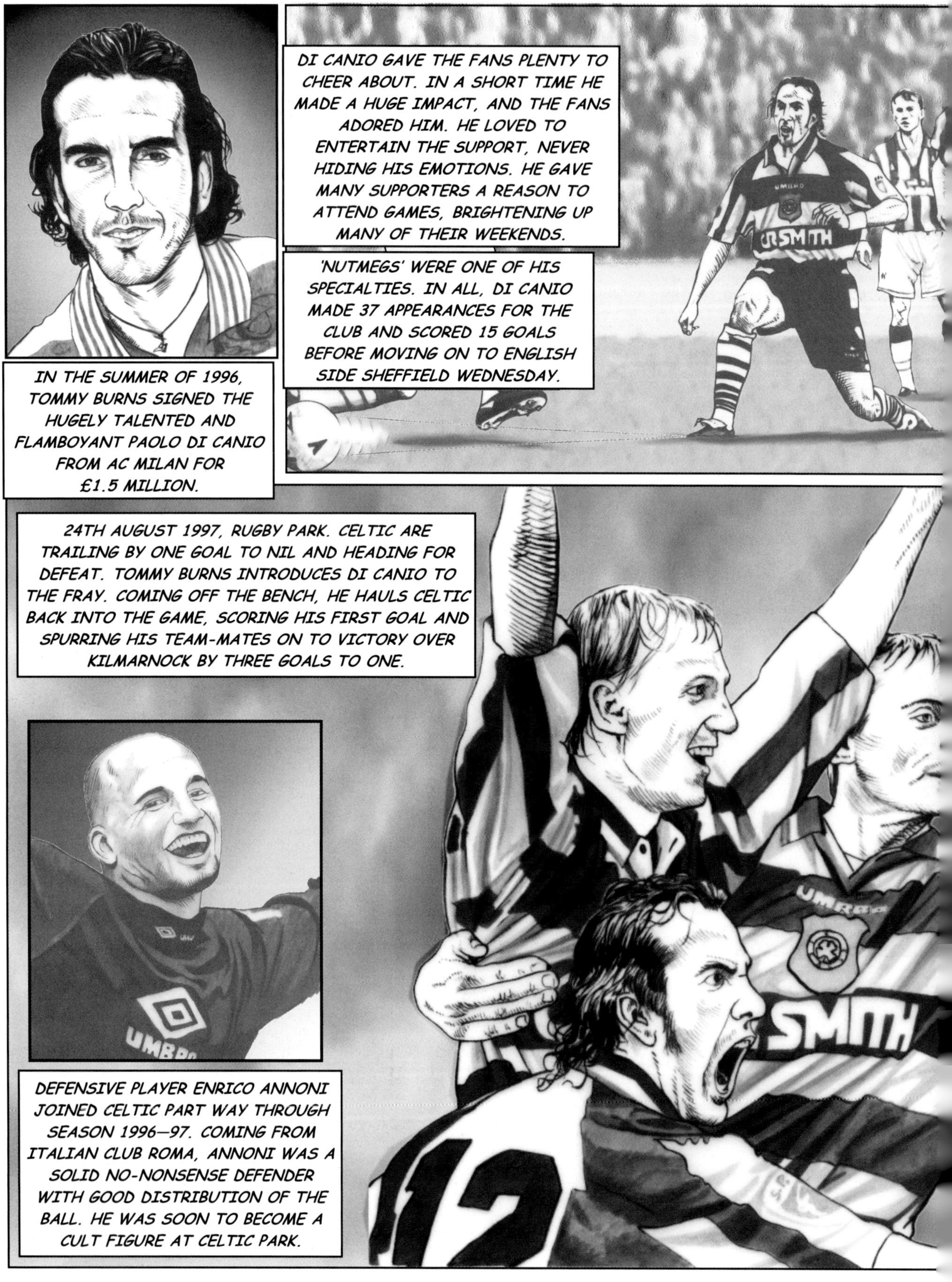
IN THE SUMMER OF 1996, TOMMY BURNS SIGNED THE HUGELY TALENTED AND FLAMBOYANT PAOLO DI CANIO FROM AC MILAN FOR £1.5 MILLION.
DI CANIO GAVE THE FANS PLENTY TO CHEER ABOUT. IN A SHORT TIME HE MADE A HUGE IMPACT, AND THE FANS ADORED HIM. HE LOVED TO ENTERTAIN THE SUPPORT, NEVER HIDING HIS EMOTIONS. HE GAVE MANY SUPPORTERS A REASON TO ATTEND GAMES, BRIGHTENING UP MANY OF THEIR WEEKENDS.
'NUTMEGS' WERE ONE OF HIS SPECIALTIES. IN ALL, DI CANIO MADE 37 APPEARANCES FOR THE CLUB AND SCORED 15 GOALS BEFORE MOVING ON TO ENGLISH SIDE SHEFFIELD WEDNESDAY.
24TH AUGUST 1997, RUGBY PARK. CELTIC ARE TRAILING BY ONE GOAL TO NIL AND HEADING FOR DEFEAT. TOMMY BURNS INTRODUCES DI CANIO TO THE FRAY. COMING OFF THE BENCH, HE HAULS CELTIC BACK INTO THE GAME, SCORING HIS FIRST GOAL AND SPURRING HIS TEAM-MATES ON TO VICTORY OVER KILMARNOCK BY THREE GOALS TO ONE.
DEFENSIVE PLAYER ENRICO ANNONI JOINED CELTIC PART WAY THROUGH SEASON 1996–97. COMING FROM ITALIAN CLUB ROMA, ANNONI WAS A SOLID NO-NONSENSE DEFENDER WITH GOOD DISTRIBUTION OF THE BALL. HE WAS SOON TO BECOME A CULT FIGURE AT CELTIC PARK.

ALTHOUGH HE ONLY PLAYED FOR ONE SEASON AT CELTIC, DI CANIO MADE A SIGNIFICANT CONTRIBUTION TO BURNS' REBUILDING PROGRAMME AT THE TIME. HE PROVIDED EXCITEMENT AND ENTERTAINMENT. A HALLMARK OF HIS PLAY WAS HIS QUICK STEP-OVERS AND THEATRICS TOWARDS REFEREES. DI CANIO AND CONTROVERSY WERE INSEPARABLE.

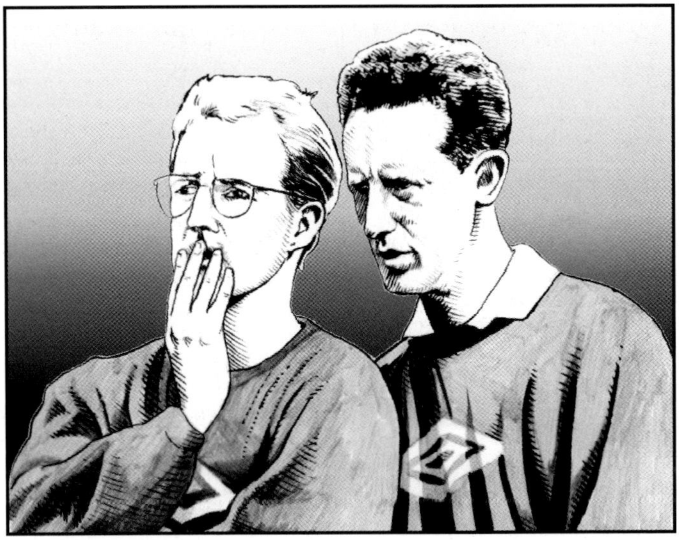

TOMMY BURNS AND BILLY STARK MOULDED CELTIC MORE INTO THE STYLE OF OLD, PLAYING A BRAND OF ENTERTAINING, ATTACKING FOOTBALL DURING SEASON 1996–97. WITH RANGERS ON THE VERGE OF MATCHING CELTIC'S NINE-IN-A-ROW LEAGUE CHAMPIONSHIPS, THE PRESSURE MOUNTED ON THE CELTIC MANAGEMENT TEAM.

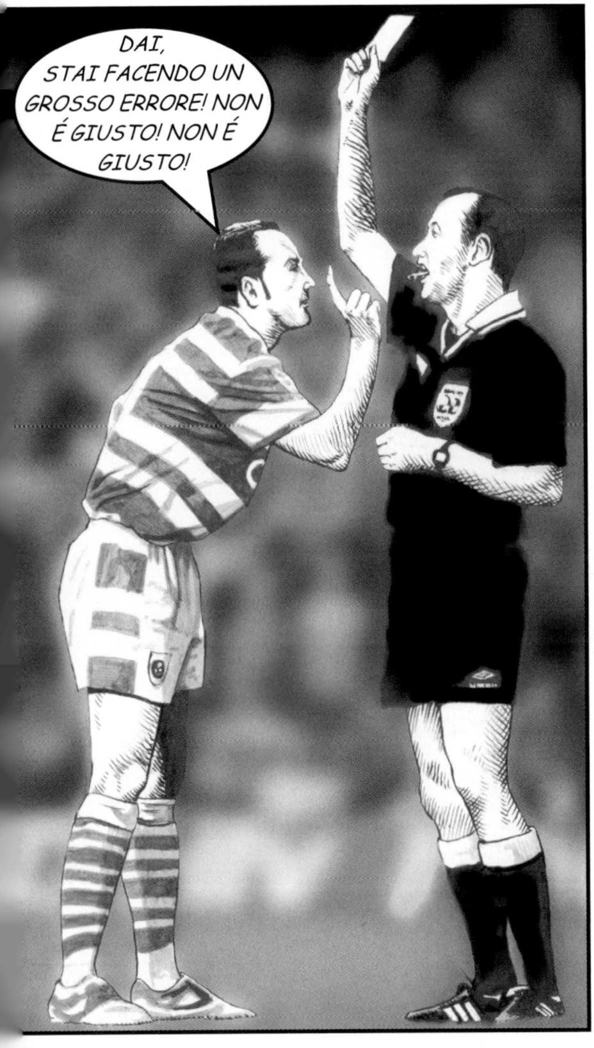
DAI, STAI FACENDO UN GROSSO ERRORE! NON É GIUSTO! NON É GIUSTO!

DESPITE SIGNING A NUMBER OF NEW PLAYERS, CELTIC WERE UNABLE TO STOP RANGERS WINNING THE LEAGUE CHAMPIONSHIP. A COMBINATION OF BAD LUCK, INCONSISTENT REFEREEING DECISIONS AND THE OUTSTANDING FORM OF RANGERS KEEPER ANDY GORAM CONSPIRED AGAINST CELTIC. TOMMY BURNS, AFTER BEING OFFERED A SIDEWAYS SHIFT TO YOUTH DEVELOPMENT, WHICH HE CONSIDERED A DEMOTION, RESIGNED.

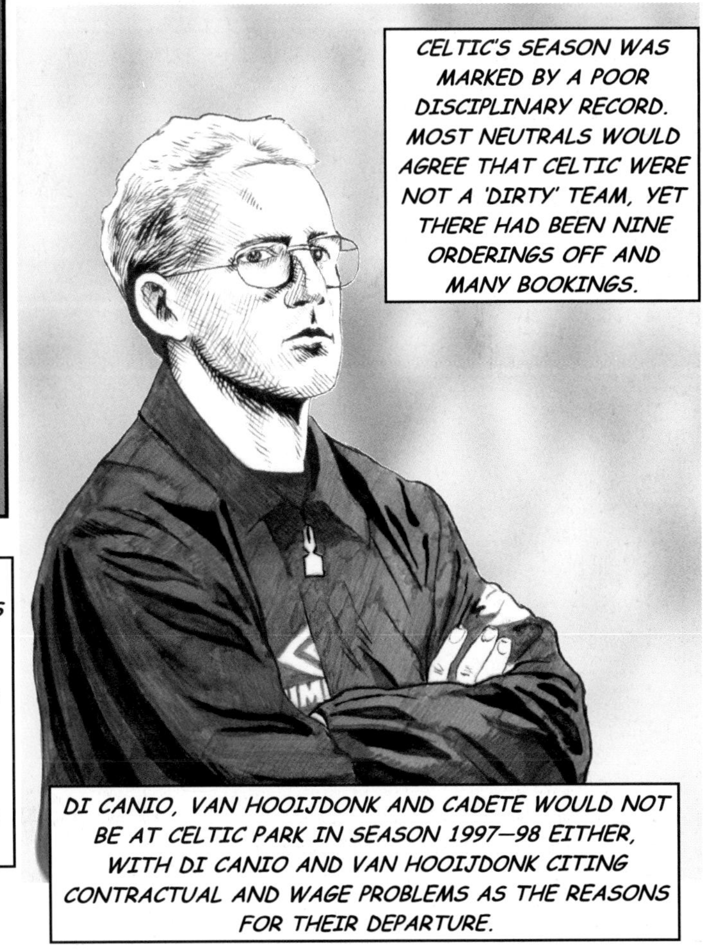
CELTIC'S SEASON WAS MARKED BY A POOR DISCIPLINARY RECORD. MOST NEUTRALS WOULD AGREE THAT CELTIC WERE NOT A 'DIRTY' TEAM, YET THERE HAD BEEN NINE ORDERINGS OFF AND MANY BOOKINGS.

DI CANIO, VAN HOOIJDONK AND CADETE WOULD NOT BE AT CELTIC PARK IN SEASON 1997–98 EITHER, WITH DI CANIO AND VAN HOOIJDONK CITING CONTRACTUAL AND WAGE PROBLEMS AS THE REASONS FOR THEIR DEPARTURE.

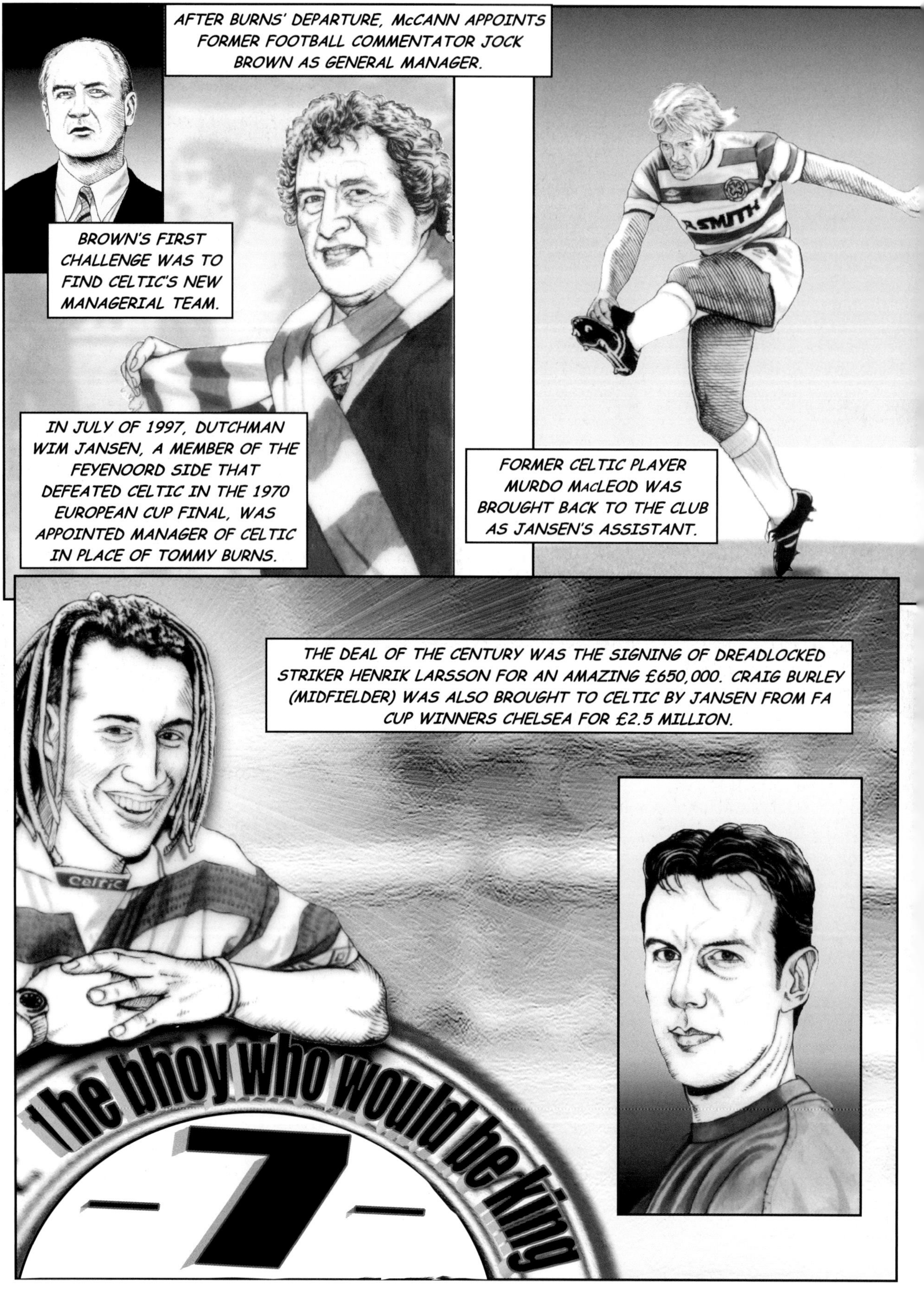
AFTER BURNS' DEPARTURE, McCANN APPOINTS FORMER FOOTBALL COMMENTATOR JOCK BROWN AS GENERAL MANAGER.
BROWN'S FIRST CHALLENGE WAS TO FIND CELTIC'S NEW MANAGERIAL TEAM.
IN JULY OF 1997, DUTCHMAN WIM JANSEN, A MEMBER OF THE FEYENOORD SIDE THAT DEFEATED CELTIC IN THE 1970 EUROPEAN CUP FINAL, WAS APPOINTED MANAGER OF CELTIC IN PLACE OF TOMMY BURNS.
FORMER CELTIC PLAYER MURDO MacLEOD WAS BROUGHT BACK TO THE CLUB AS JANSEN'S ASSISTANT.
THE DEAL OF THE CENTURY WAS THE SIGNING OF DREADLOCKED STRIKER HENRIK LARSSON FOR AN AMAZING £650,000. CRAIG BURLEY (MIDFIELDER) WAS ALSO BROUGHT TO CELTIC BY JANSEN FROM FA CUP WINNERS CHELSEA FOR £2.5 MILLION.
the bhoy who would be king
7

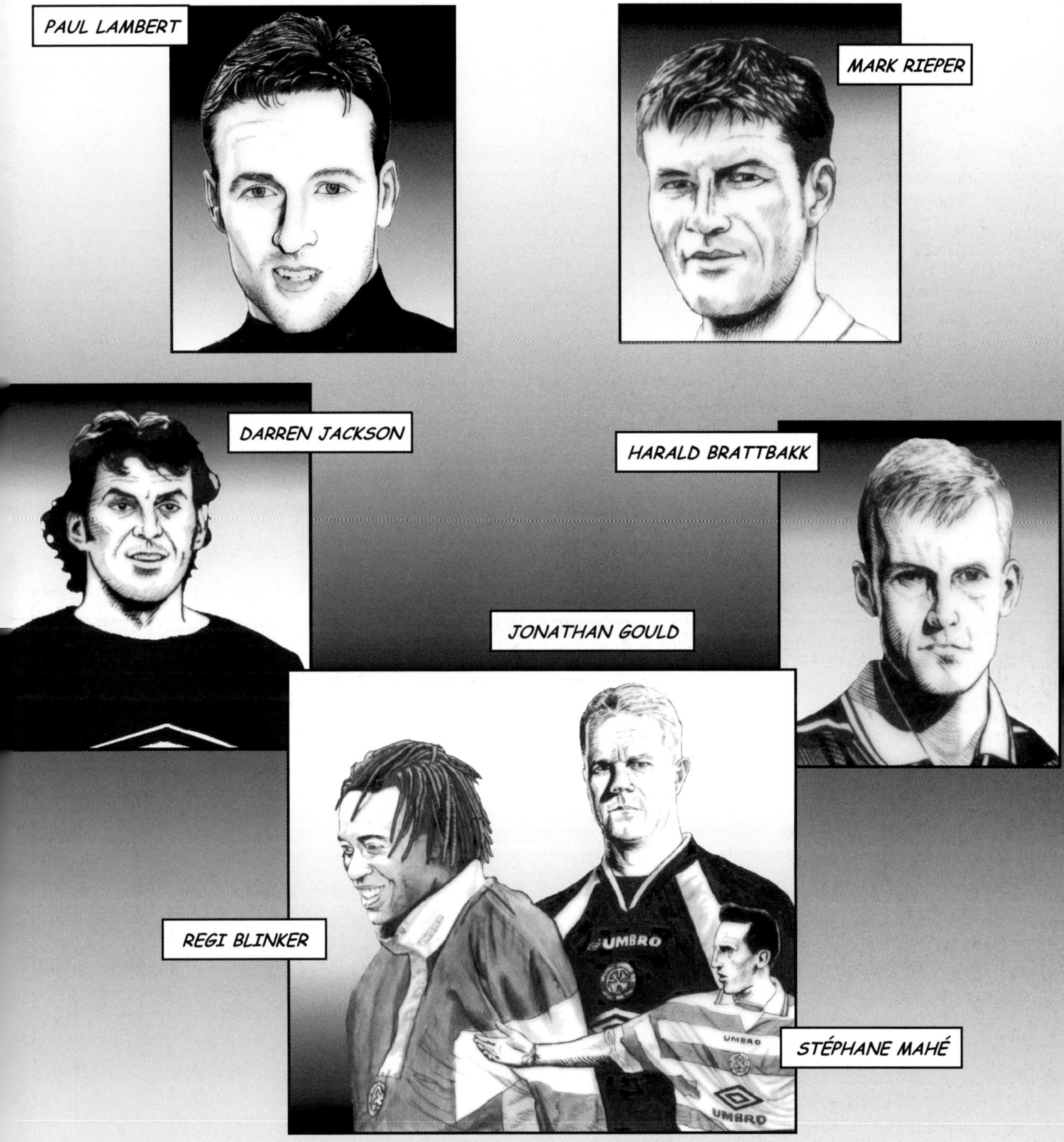
PAUL LAMBERT
MARK RIEPER
DARREN JACKSON
HARALD BRATTBAKK
JONATHAN GOULD
REGI BLINKER
STÉPHANE MAHÉ
UMBRO
UMBRO
UMBRO

WIM JANSEN CONTINUED TO REBUILD THE TEAM AND BROUGHT YET MORE PLAYERS TO THE CLUB, LIKE MIDFIELD ACE PAUL LAMBERT FROM BORUSSIA DORTMUND FOR A FEE OF £2 MILLION, MARK RIEPER, A CENTRAL DEFENDER FROM WEST HAM FOR AN UNDISCLOSED FEE, STRIKER HARALD BRATTBAKK FROM ROSENBORG FOR £2 MILLION AND STRIKER DARREN JACKSON FROM HIBS FOR £1.25 MILLION. PAOLO DI CANIO WAS TRADED FOR REGI BLINKER IN A £1.5 MILLION DEAL. KEEPER JONATHAN GOULD SIGNED AS SHORT-TERM COVER FOR STEWART KERR, WHILE FRENCH WING-BACK STÉPHANE MAHÉ ARRIVED FROM STADE RENNAIS FOR AN UNDISCLOSED FEE.

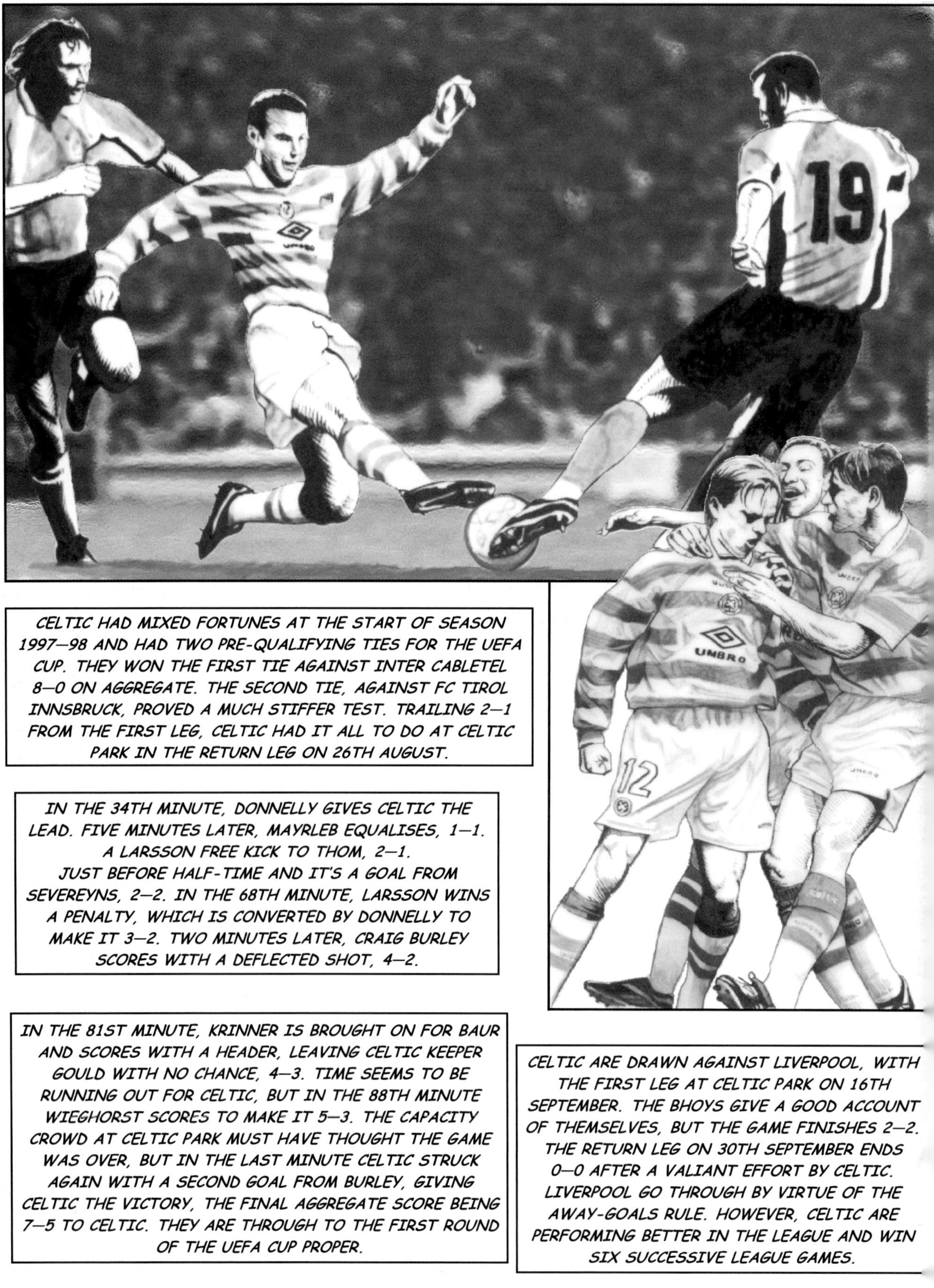

CELTIC HAD MIXED FORTUNES AT THE START OF SEASON 1997–98 AND HAD TWO PRE-QUALIFYING TIES FOR THE UEFA CUP. THEY WON THE FIRST TIE AGAINST INTER CABLETEL 8–0 ON AGGREGATE. THE SECOND TIE, AGAINST FC TIROL INNSBRUCK, PROVED A MUCH STIFFER TEST. TRAILING 2–1 FROM THE FIRST LEG, CELTIC HAD IT ALL TO DO AT CELTIC PARK IN THE RETURN LEG ON 26TH AUGUST.
IN THE 34TH MINUTE, DONNELLY GIVES CELTIC THE LEAD. FIVE MINUTES LATER, MAYRLEB EQUALISES, 1–1. A LARSSON FREE KICK TO THOM, 2–1. JUST BEFORE HALF-TIME AND IT'S A GOAL FROM SEVEREYNS, 2–2. IN THE 68TH MINUTE, LARSSON WINS A PENALTY, WHICH IS CONVERTED BY DONNELLY TO MAKE IT 3–2. TWO MINUTES LATER, CRAIG BURLEY SCORES WITH A DEFLECTED SHOT, 4–2.
IN THE 81ST MINUTE, KRINNER IS BROUGHT ON FOR BAUR AND SCORES WITH A HEADER, LEAVING CELTIC KEEPER GOULD WITH NO CHANCE, 4–3. TIME SEEMS TO BE RUNNING OUT FOR CELTIC, BUT IN THE 88TH MINUTE WIEGHORST SCORES TO MAKE IT 5–3. THE CAPACITY CROWD AT CELTIC PARK MUST HAVE THOUGHT THE GAME WAS OVER, BUT IN THE LAST MINUTE CELTIC STRUCK AGAIN WITH A SECOND GOAL FROM BURLEY, GIVING CELTIC THE VICTORY, THE FINAL AGGREGATE SCORE BEING 7–5 TO CELTIC. THEY ARE THROUGH TO THE FIRST ROUND OF THE UEFA CUP PROPER.
CELTIC ARE DRAWN AGAINST LIVERPOOL, WITH THE FIRST LEG AT CELTIC PARK ON 16TH SEPTEMBER. THE BHOYS GIVE A GOOD ACCOUNT OF THEMSELVES, BUT THE GAME FINISHES 2–2. THE RETURN LEG ON 30TH SEPTEMBER ENDS 0–0 AFTER A VALIANT EFFORT BY CELTIC. LIVERPOOL GO THROUGH BY VIRTUE OF THE AWAY-GOALS RULE. HOWEVER, CELTIC ARE PERFORMING BETTER IN THE LEAGUE AND WIN SIX SUCCESSIVE LEAGUE GAMES.

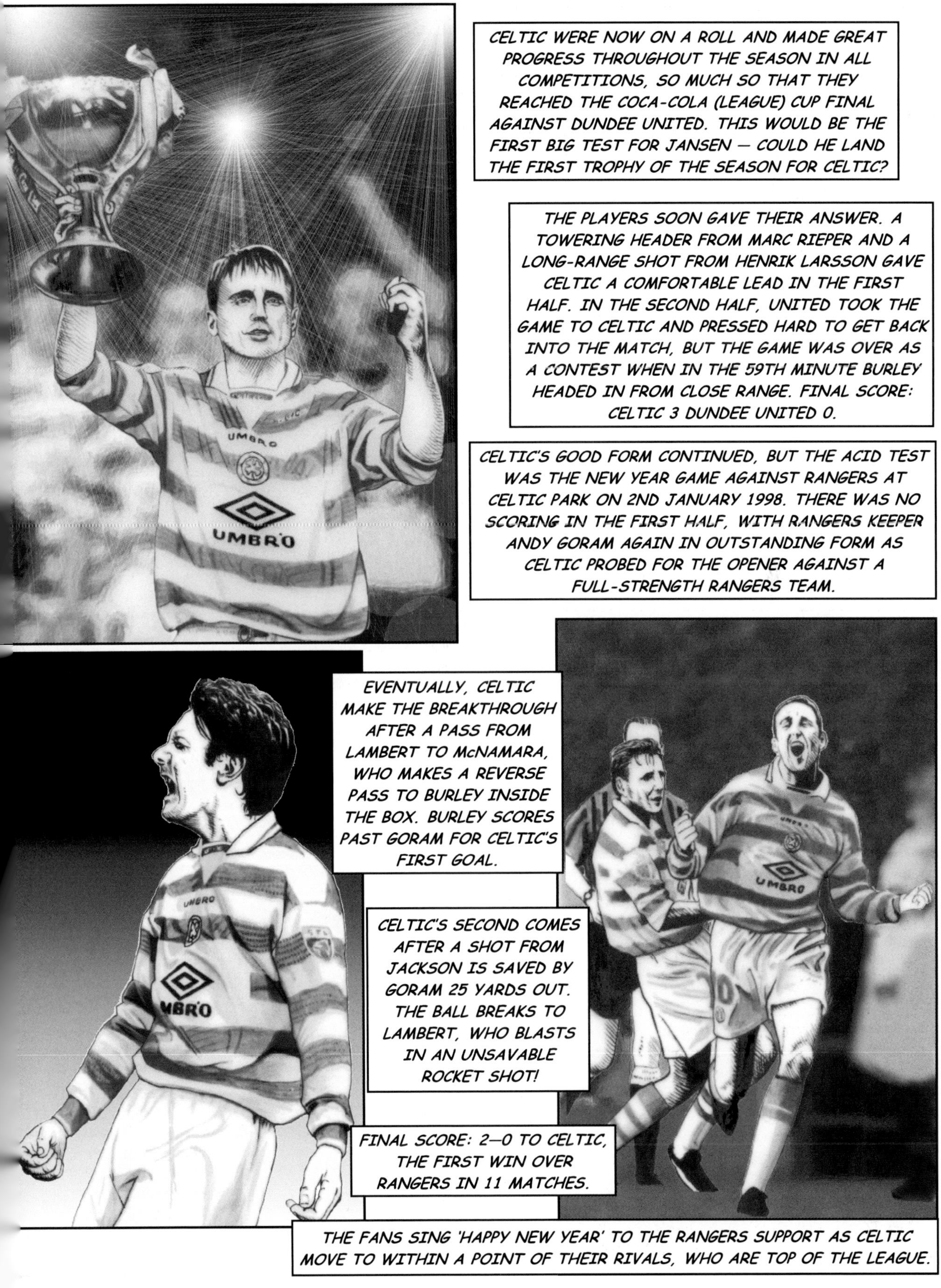
CELTIC WERE NOW ON A ROLL AND MADE GREAT PROGRESS THROUGHOUT THE SEASON IN ALL COMPETITIONS, SO MUCH SO THAT THEY REACHED THE COCA-COLA (LEAGUE) CUP FINAL AGAINST DUNDEE UNITED. THIS WOULD BE THE FIRST BIG TEST FOR JANSEN — COULD HE LAND THE FIRST TROPHY OF THE SEASON FOR CELTIC?
THE PLAYERS SOON GAVE THEIR ANSWER. A TOWERING HEADER FROM MARC RIEPER AND A LONG-RANGE SHOT FROM HENRIK LARSSON GAVE CELTIC A COMFORTABLE LEAD IN THE FIRST HALF. IN THE SECOND HALF, UNITED TOOK THE GAME TO CELTIC AND PRESSED HARD TO GET BACK INTO THE MATCH, BUT THE GAME WAS OVER AS A CONTEST WHEN IN THE 59TH MINUTE BURLEY HEADED IN FROM CLOSE RANGE. FINAL SCORE: CELTIC 3 DUNDEE UNITED 0.
CELTIC'S GOOD FORM CONTINUED, BUT THE ACID TEST WAS THE NEW YEAR GAME AGAINST RANGERS AT CELTIC PARK ON 2ND JANUARY 1998. THERE WAS NO SCORING IN THE FIRST HALF, WITH RANGERS KEEPER ANDY GORAM AGAIN IN OUTSTANDING FORM AS CELTIC PROBED FOR THE OPENER AGAINST A FULL-STRENGTH RANGERS TEAM.
EVENTUALLY, CELTIC MAKE THE BREAKTHROUGH AFTER A PASS FROM LAMBERT TO McNAMARA, WHO MAKES A REVERSE PASS TO BURLEY INSIDE THE BOX. BURLEY SCORES PAST GORAM FOR CELTIC'S FIRST GOAL.
CELTIC'S SECOND COMES AFTER A SHOT FROM JACKSON IS SAVED BY GORAM 25 YARDS OUT. THE BALL BREAKS TO LAMBERT, WHO BLASTS IN AN UNSAVABLE ROCKET SHOT!
FINAL SCORE: 2—0 TO CELTIC, THE FIRST WIN OVER RANGERS IN 11 MATCHES.
THE FANS SING 'HAPPY NEW YEAR' TO THE RANGERS SUPPORT AS CELTIC MOVE TO WITHIN A POINT OF THEIR RIVALS, WHO ARE TOP OF THE LEAGUE.

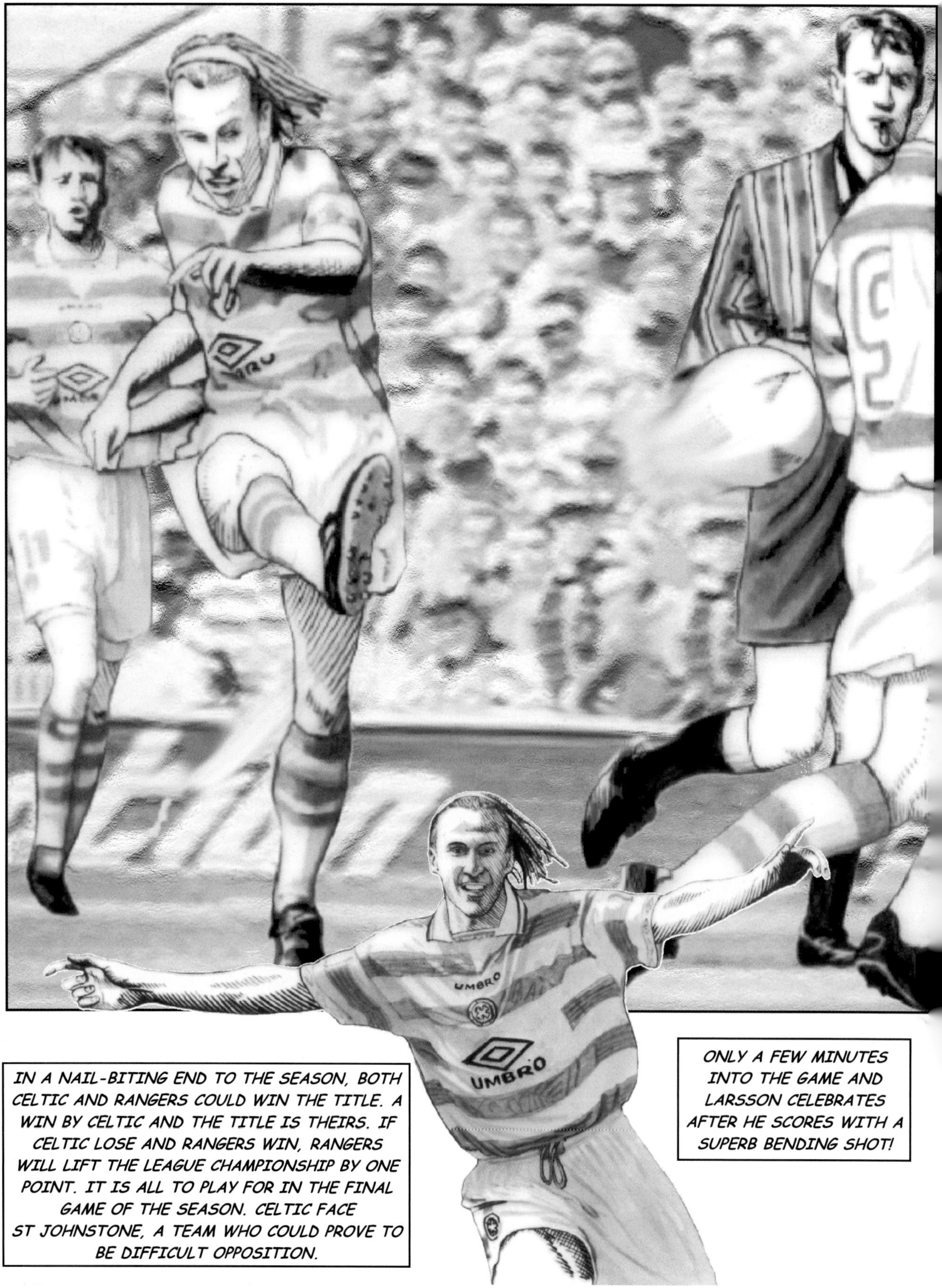
IN A NAIL-BITING END TO THE SEASON, BOTH CELTIC AND RANGERS COULD WIN THE TITLE. A WIN BY CELTIC AND THE TITLE IS THEIRS. IF CELTIC LOSE AND RANGERS WIN, RANGERS WILL LIFT THE LEAGUE CHAMPIONSHIP BY ONE POINT. IT IS ALL TO PLAY FOR IN THE FINAL GAME OF THE SEASON. CELTIC FACE ST JOHNSTONE, A TEAM WHO COULD PROVE TO BE DIFFICULT OPPOSITION.
ONLY A FEW MINUTES INTO THE GAME AND LARSSON CELEBRATES AFTER HE SCORES WITH A SUPERB BENDING SHOT!

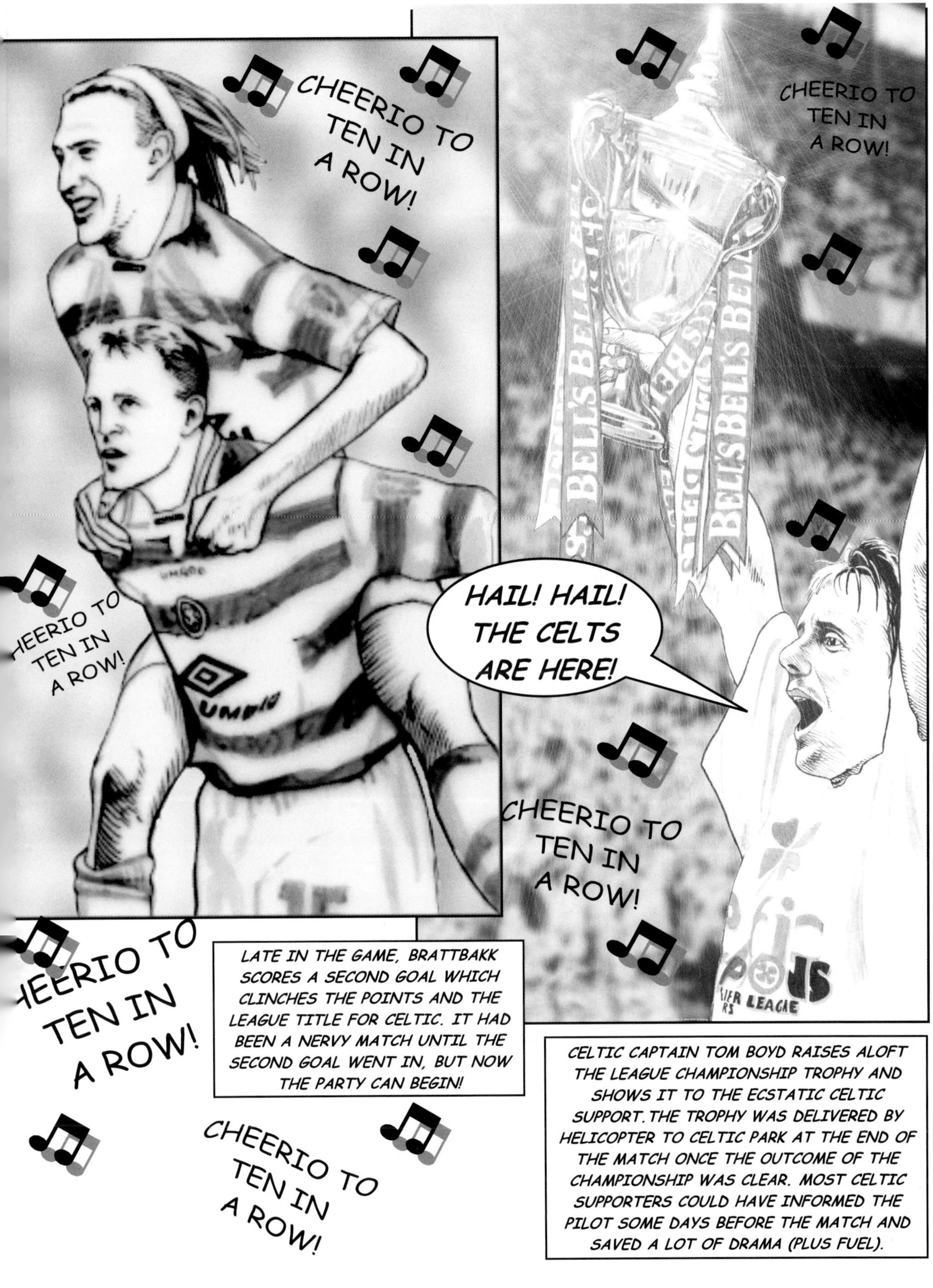
CHEERIO TO TEN IN A ROW!
HEERIO TO TEN IN A ROW!
HEERIO TO TEN IN A ROW!
LATE IN THE GAME, BRATTBAKK SCORES A SECOND GOAL WHICH CLINCHES THE POINTS AND THE LEAGUE TITLE FOR CELTIC. IT HAD BEEN A NERVY MATCH UNTIL THE SECOND GOAL WENT IN, BUT NOW THE PARTY CAN BEGIN!
CHEERIO TO TEN IN A ROW!
CHEERIO TO TEN IN A ROW!
HAIL! HAIL! THE CELTS ARE HERE!
CHEERIO TO TEN IN A ROW!
CELTIC CAPTAIN TOM BOYD RAISES ALOFT THE LEAGUE CHAMPIONSHIP TROPHY AND SHOWS IT TO THE ECSTATIC CELTIC SUPPORT. THE TROPHY WAS DELIVERED BY HELICOPTER TO CELTIC PARK AT THE END OF THE MATCH ONCE THE OUTCOME OF THE CHAMPIONSHIP WAS CLEAR. MOST CELTIC SUPPORTERS COULD HAVE INFORMED THE PILOT SOME DAYS BEFORE THE MATCH AND SAVED A LOT OF DRAMA (PLUS FUEL).

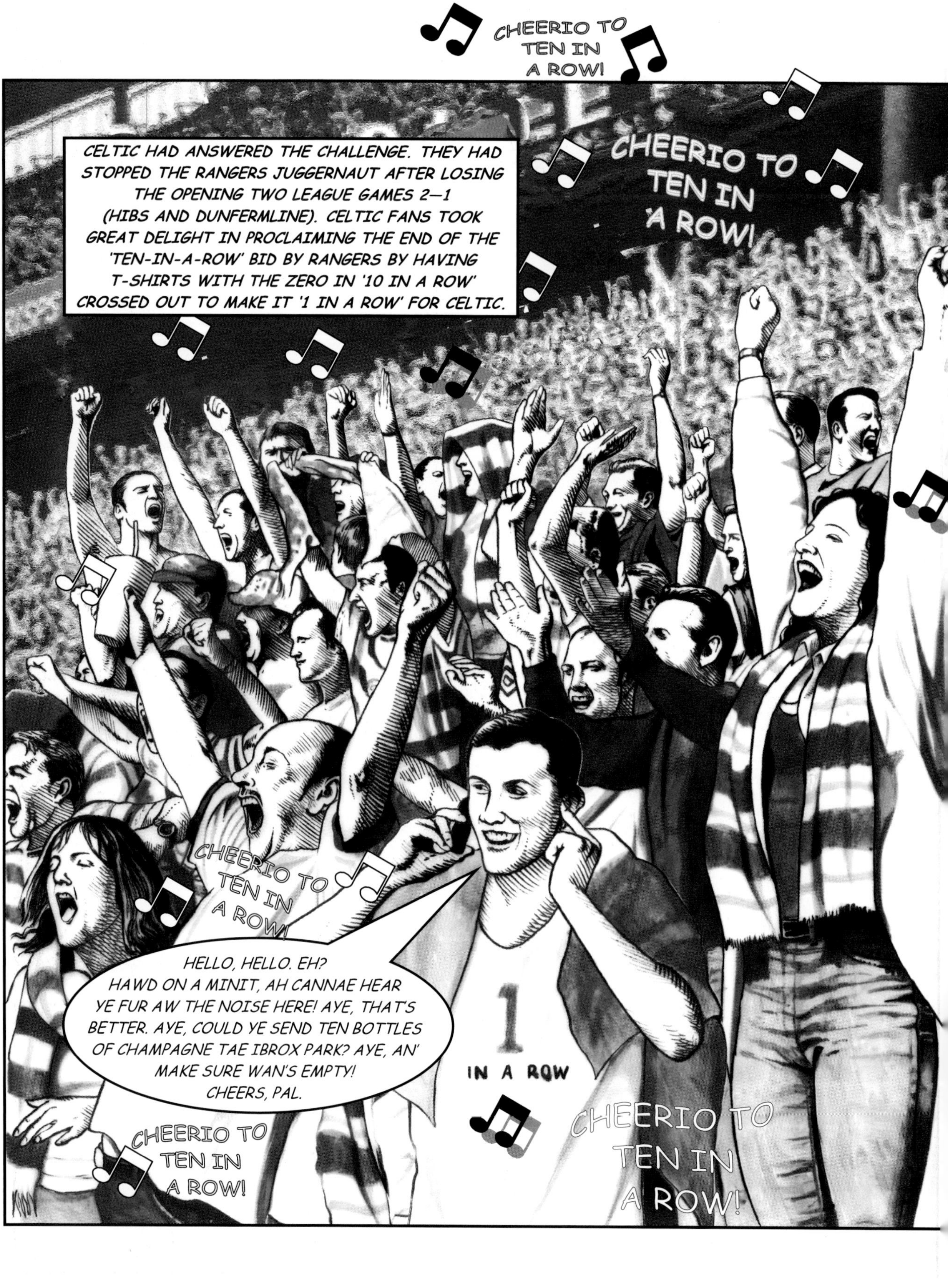
CHEERIO TO TEN IN A ROW!
CELTIC HAD ANSWERED THE CHALLENGE. THEY HAD STOPPED THE RANGERS JUGGERNAUT AFTER LOSING THE OPENING TWO LEAGUE GAMES 2–1 (HIBS AND DUNFERMLINE). CELTIC FANS TOOK GREAT DELIGHT IN PROCLAIMING THE END OF THE 'TEN-IN-A-ROW' BID BY RANGERS BY HAVING T-SHIRTS WITH THE ZERO IN '10 IN A ROW' CROSSED OUT TO MAKE IT '1 IN A ROW' FOR CELTIC.
CHEERIO TO TEN IN A ROW!
CHEERIO TO TEN IN A ROW!
HELLO, HELLO. EH? HAWD ON A MINIT, AH CANNAE HEAR YE FUR AW THE NOISE HERE! AYE, THAT'S BETTER. AYE, COULD YE SEND TEN BOTTLES OF CHAMPAGNE TAE IBROX PARK? AYE, AN' MAKE SURE WAN'S EMPTY! CHEERS, PAL.
1 IN A ROW
CHEERIO TO TEN IN A ROW!
CHEERIO TO TEN IN A ROW!

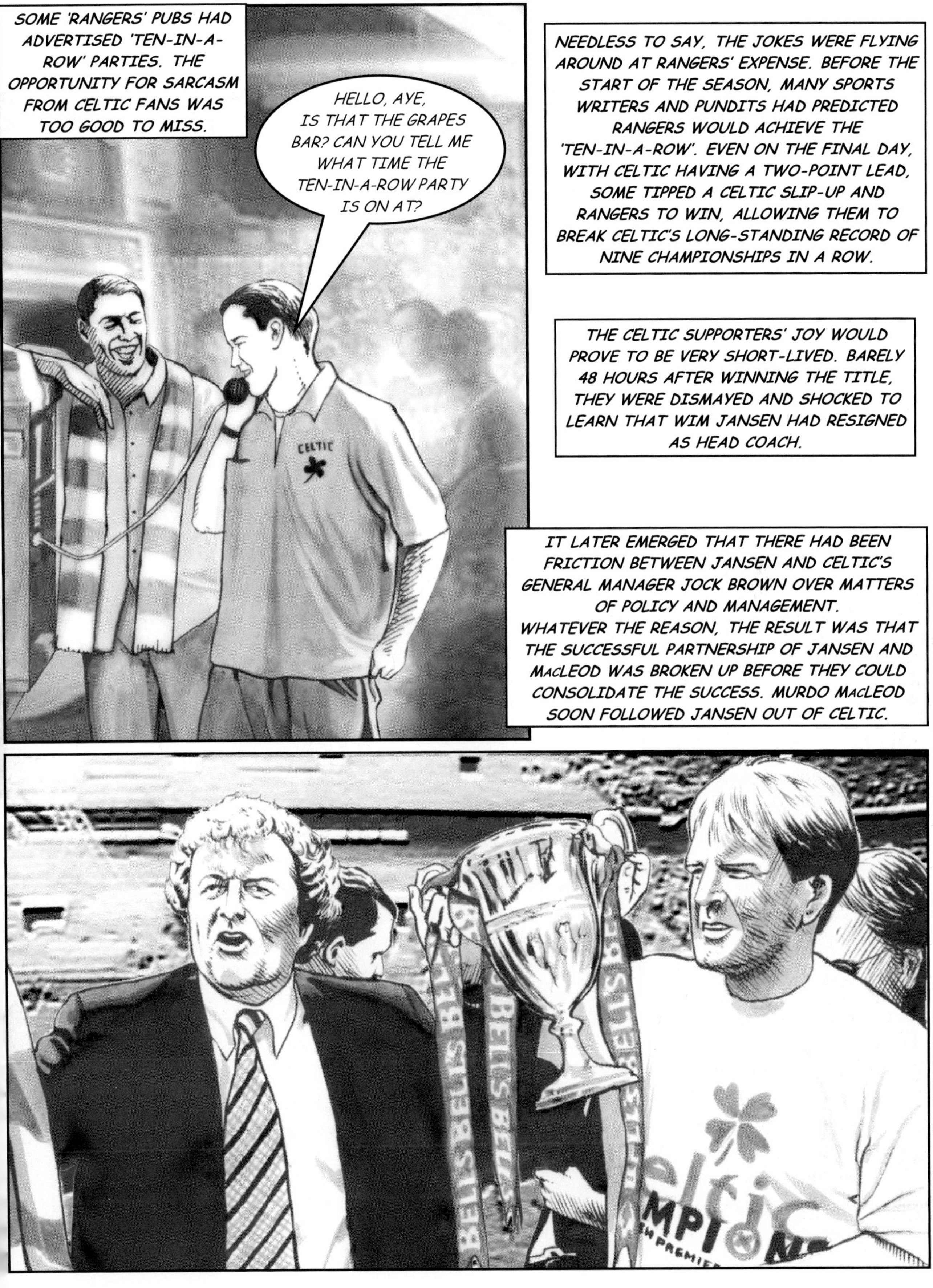
SOME 'RANGERS' PUBS HAD ADVERTISED 'TEN-IN-A-ROW' PARTIES. THE OPPORTUNITY FOR SARCASM FROM CELTIC FANS WAS TOO GOOD TO MISS.
HELLO, AYE, IS THAT THE GRAPES BAR? CAN YOU TELL ME WHAT TIME THE TEN-IN-A-ROW PARTY IS ON AT?
CELTIC
NEEDLESS TO SAY, THE JOKES WERE FLYING AROUND AT RANGERS' EXPENSE. BEFORE THE START OF THE SEASON, MANY SPORTS WRITERS AND PUNDITS HAD PREDICTED RANGERS WOULD ACHIEVE THE 'TEN-IN-A-ROW'. EVEN ON THE FINAL DAY, WITH CELTIC HAVING A TWO-POINT LEAD, SOME TIPPED A CELTIC SLIP-UP AND RANGERS TO WIN, ALLOWING THEM TO BREAK CELTIC'S LONG-STANDING RECORD OF NINE CHAMPIONSHIPS IN A ROW.
THE CELTIC SUPPORTERS' JOY WOULD PROVE TO BE VERY SHORT-LIVED. BARELY 48 HOURS AFTER WINNING THE TITLE, THEY WERE DISMAYED AND SHOCKED TO LEARN THAT WIM JANSEN HAD RESIGNED AS HEAD COACH.
IT LATER EMERGED THAT THERE HAD BEEN FRICTION BETWEEN JANSEN AND CELTIC'S GENERAL MANAGER JOCK BROWN OVER MATTERS OF POLICY AND MANAGEMENT.
WHATEVER THE REASON, THE RESULT WAS THAT THE SUCCESSFUL PARTNERSHIP OF JANSEN AND MacLEOD WAS BROKEN UP BEFORE THEY COULD CONSOLIDATE THE SUCCESS. MURDO MacLEOD SOON FOLLOWED JANSEN OUT OF CELTIC.

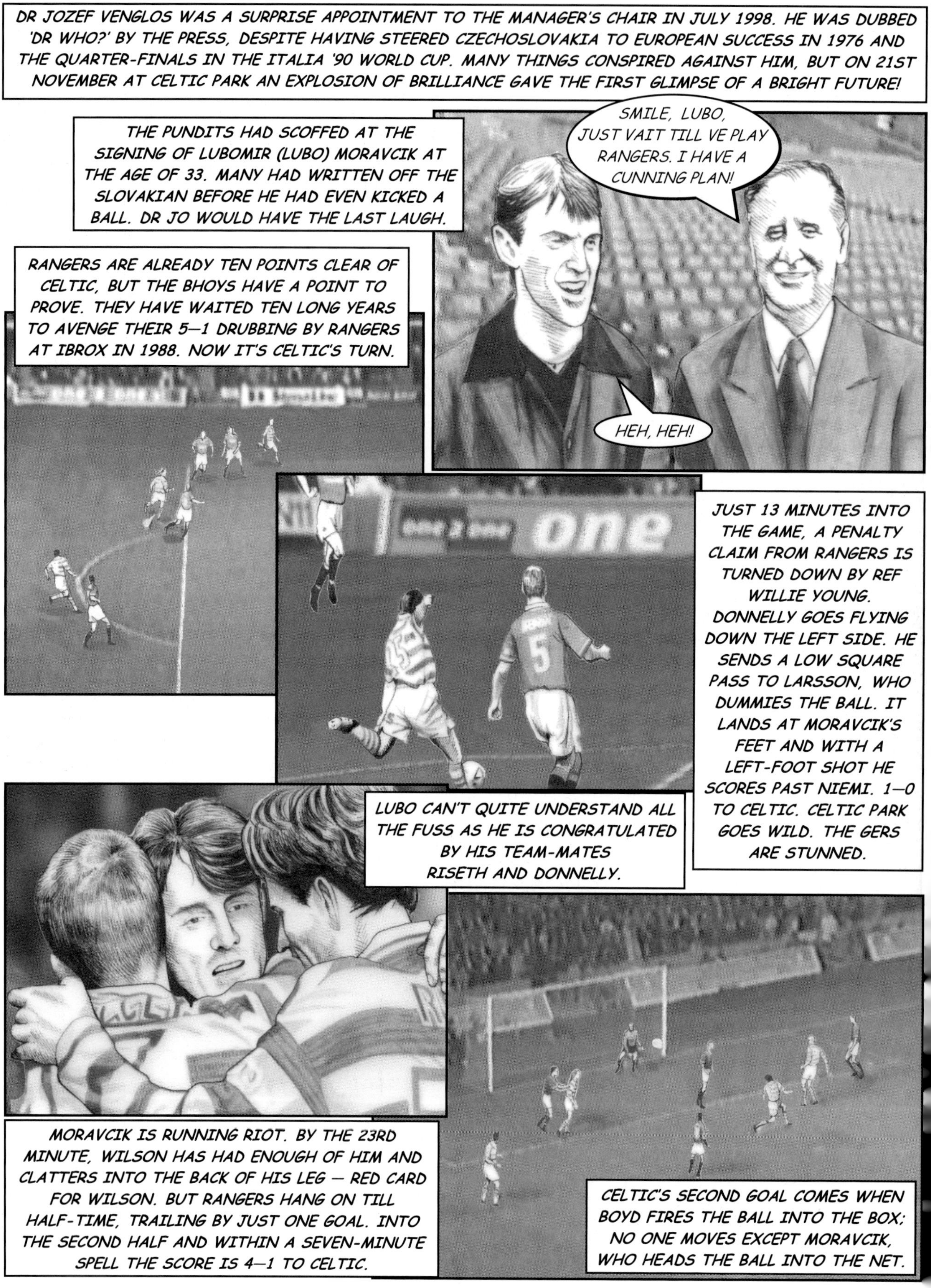
DR JOZEF VENGLOS WAS A SURPRISE APPOINTMENT TO THE MANAGER'S CHAIR IN JULY 1998. HE WAS DUBBED 'DR WHO?' BY THE PRESS, DESPITE HAVING STEERED CZECHOSLOVAKIA TO EUROPEAN SUCCESS IN 1976 AND THE QUARTER-FINALS IN THE ITALIA '90 WORLD CUP. MANY THINGS CONSPIRED AGAINST HIM, BUT ON 21ST NOVEMBER AT CELTIC PARK AN EXPLOSION OF BRILLIANCE GAVE THE FIRST GLIMPSE OF A BRIGHT FUTURE!
THE PUNDITS HAD SCOFFED AT THE SIGNING OF LUBOMIR (LUBO) MORAVCIK AT THE AGE OF 33. MANY HAD WRITTEN OFF THE SLOVAKIAN BEFORE HE HAD EVEN KICKED A BALL. DR JO WOULD HAVE THE LAST LAUGH.
SMILE, LUBO, JUST VAIT TILL VE PLAY RANGERS. I HAVE A CUNNING PLAN!
HEH, HEH!
RANGERS ARE ALREADY TEN POINTS CLEAR OF CELTIC, BUT THE BHOYS HAVE A POINT TO PROVE. THEY HAVE WAITED TEN LONG YEARS TO AVENGE THEIR 5—1 DRUBBING BY RANGERS AT IBROX IN 1988. NOW IT'S CELTIC'S TURN.
one
JUST 13 MINUTES INTO THE GAME, A PENALTY CLAIM FROM RANGERS IS TURNED DOWN BY REF WILLIE YOUNG. DONNELLY GOES FLYING DOWN THE LEFT SIDE. HE SENDS A LOW SQUARE PASS TO LARSSON, WHO DUMMIES THE BALL. IT LANDS AT MORAVCIK'S FEET AND WITH A LEFT-FOOT SHOT HE SCORES PAST NIEMI. 1—0 TO CELTIC. CELTIC PARK GOES WILD. THE GERS ARE STUNNED.
LUBO CAN'T QUITE UNDERSTAND ALL THE FUSS AS HE IS CONGRATULATED BY HIS TEAM-MATES RISETH AND DONNELLY.
MORAVCIK IS RUNNING RIOT. BY THE 23RD MINUTE, WILSON HAS HAD ENOUGH OF HIM AND CLATTERS INTO THE BACK OF HIS LEG — RED CARD FOR WILSON. BUT RANGERS HANG ON TILL HALF-TIME, TRAILING BY JUST ONE GOAL. INTO THE SECOND HALF AND WITHIN A SEVEN-MINUTE SPELL THE SCORE IS 4—1 TO CELTIC.
CELTIC'S SECOND GOAL COMES WHEN BOYD FIRES THE BALL INTO THE BOX; NO ONE MOVES EXCEPT MORAVCIK, WHO HEADS THE BALL INTO THE NET.

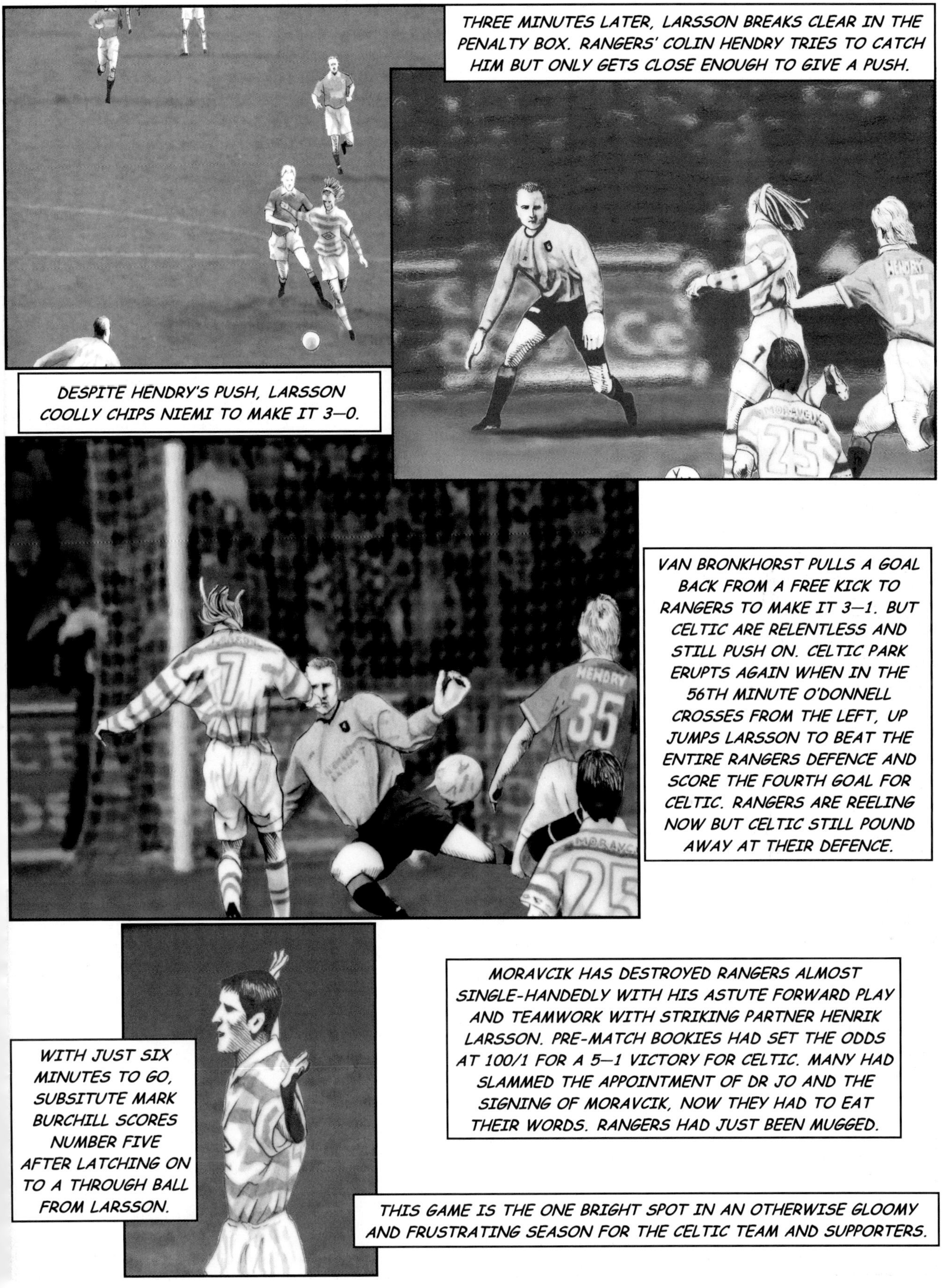
THREE MINUTES LATER, LARSSON BREAKS CLEAR IN THE PENALTY BOX. RANGERS' COLIN HENDRY TRIES TO CATCH HIM BUT ONLY GETS CLOSE ENOUGH TO GIVE A PUSH.
DESPITE HENDRY'S PUSH, LARSSON COOLLY CHIPS NIEMI TO MAKE IT 3—0.
VAN BRONKHORST PULLS A GOAL BACK FROM A FREE KICK TO RANGERS TO MAKE IT 3—1. BUT CELTIC ARE RELENTLESS AND STILL PUSH ON. CELTIC PARK ERUPTS AGAIN WHEN IN THE 56TH MINUTE O'DONNELL CROSSES FROM THE LEFT, UP JUMPS LARSSON TO BEAT THE ENTIRE RANGERS DEFENCE AND SCORE THE FOURTH GOAL FOR CELTIC. RANGERS ARE REELING NOW BUT CELTIC STILL POUND AWAY AT THEIR DEFENCE.
WITH JUST SIX MINUTES TO GO, SUBSITUTE MARK BURCHILL SCORES NUMBER FIVE AFTER LATCHING ON TO A THROUGH BALL FROM LARSSON.
MORAVCIK HAS DESTROYED RANGERS ALMOST SINGLE-HANDEDLY WITH HIS ASTUTE FORWARD PLAY AND TEAMWORK WITH STRIKING PARTNER HENRIK LARSSON. PRE-MATCH BOOKIES HAD SET THE ODDS AT 100/1 FOR A 5—1 VICTORY FOR CELTIC. MANY HAD SLAMMED THE APPOINTMENT OF DR JO AND THE SIGNING OF MORAVCIK, NOW THEY HAD TO EAT THEIR WORDS. RANGERS HAD JUST BEEN MUGGED.
THIS GAME IS THE ONE BRIGHT SPOT IN AN OTHERWISE GLOOMY AND FRUSTRATING SEASON FOR THE CELTIC TEAM AND SUPPORTERS.

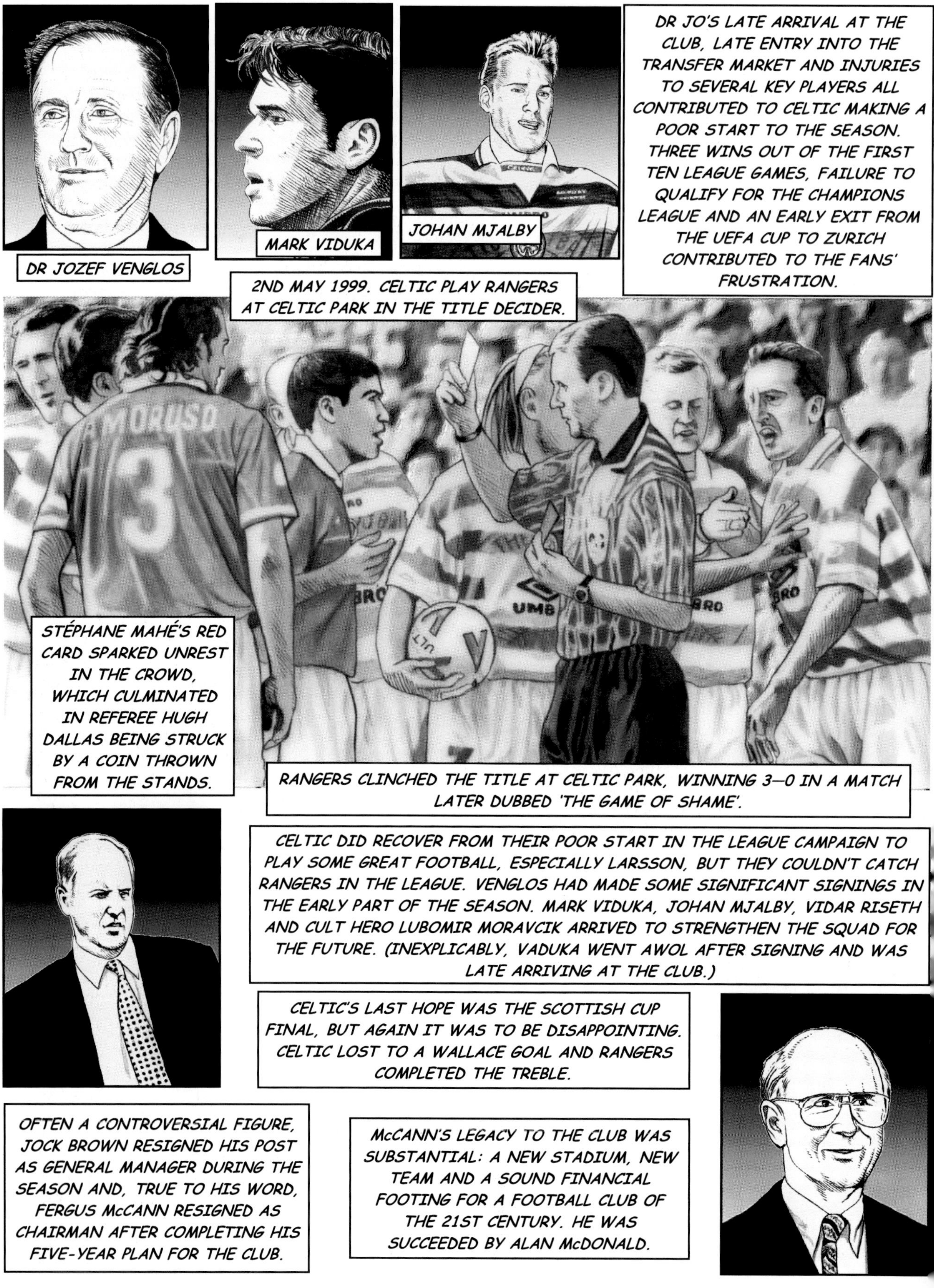
DR JOZEF VENGLOS
MARK VIDUKA
JOHAN MJALBY
DR JO'S LATE ARRIVAL AT THE CLUB, LATE ENTRY INTO THE TRANSFER MARKET AND INJURIES TO SEVERAL KEY PLAYERS ALL CONTRIBUTED TO CELTIC MAKING A POOR START TO THE SEASON. THREE WINS OUT OF THE FIRST TEN LEAGUE GAMES, FAILURE TO QUALIFY FOR THE CHAMPIONS LEAGUE AND AN EARLY EXIT FROM THE UEFA CUP TO ZURICH CONTRIBUTED TO THE FANS' FRUSTRATION.
2ND MAY 1999. CELTIC PLAY RANGERS AT CELTIC PARK IN THE TITLE DECIDER.
STÉPHANE MAHÉ'S RED CARD SPARKED UNREST IN THE CROWD, WHICH CULMINATED IN REFEREE HUGH DALLAS BEING STRUCK BY A COIN THROWN FROM THE STANDS.
RANGERS CLINCHED THE TITLE AT CELTIC PARK, WINNING 3—0 IN A MATCH LATER DUBBED 'THE GAME OF SHAME'.
CELTIC DID RECOVER FROM THEIR POOR START IN THE LEAGUE CAMPAIGN TO PLAY SOME GREAT FOOTBALL, ESPECIALLY LARSSON, BUT THEY COULDN'T CATCH RANGERS IN THE LEAGUE. VENGLOS HAD MADE SOME SIGNIFICANT SIGNINGS IN THE EARLY PART OF THE SEASON. MARK VIDUKA, JOHAN MJALBY, VIDAR RISETH AND CULT HERO LUBOMIR MORAVCIK ARRIVED TO STRENGTHEN THE SQUAD FOR THE FUTURE. (INEXPLICABLY, VADUKA WENT AWOL AFTER SIGNING AND WAS LATE ARRIVING AT THE CLUB.)
CELTIC'S LAST HOPE WAS THE SCOTTISH CUP FINAL, BUT AGAIN IT WAS TO BE DISAPPOINTING. CELTIC LOST TO A WALLACE GOAL AND RANGERS COMPLETED THE TREBLE.
OFTEN A CONTROVERSIAL FIGURE, JOCK BROWN RESIGNED HIS POST AS GENERAL MANAGER DURING THE SEASON AND, TRUE TO HIS WORD, FERGUS McCANN RESIGNED AS CHAIRMAN AFTER COMPLETING HIS FIVE-YEAR PLAN FOR THE CLUB.
McCANN'S LEGACY TO THE CLUB WAS SUBSTANTIAL: A NEW STADIUM, NEW TEAM AND A SOUND FINANCIAL FOOTING FOR A FOOTBALL CLUB OF THE 21ST CENTURY. HE WAS SUCCEEDED BY ALAN McDONALD.

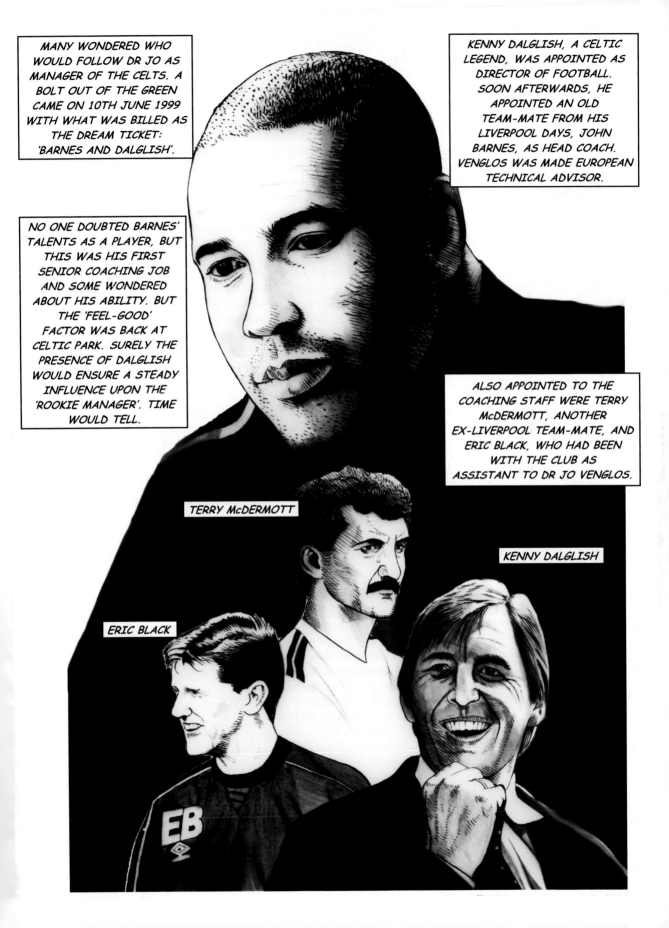

MANY WONDERED WHO WOULD FOLLOW DR JO AS MANAGER OF THE CELTS. A BOLT OUT OF THE GREEN CAME ON 10TH JUNE 1999 WITH WHAT WAS BILLED AS THE DREAM TICKET: 'BARNES AND DALGLISH'.

KENNY DALGLISH, A CELTIC LEGEND, WAS APPOINTED AS DIRECTOR OF FOOTBALL. SOON AFTERWARDS, HE APPOINTED AN OLD TEAM-MATE FROM HIS LIVERPOOL DAYS, JOHN BARNES, AS HEAD COACH. VENGLOS WAS MADE EUROPEAN TECHNICAL ADVISOR.

NO ONE DOUBTED BARNES' TALENTS AS A PLAYER, BUT THIS WAS HIS FIRST SENIOR COACHING JOB AND SOME WONDERED ABOUT HIS ABILITY. BUT THE 'FEEL-GOOD' FACTOR WAS BACK AT CELTIC PARK. SURELY THE PRESENCE OF DALGLISH WOULD ENSURE A STEADY INFLUENCE UPON THE 'ROOKIE MANAGER'. TIME WOULD TELL.

ALSO APPOINTED TO THE COACHING STAFF WERE TERRY McDERMOTT, ANOTHER EX-LIVERPOOL TEAM-MATE, AND ERIC BLACK, WHO HAD BEEN WITH THE CLUB AS ASSISTANT TO DR JO VENGLOS.

TERRY McDERMOTT

KENNY DALGLISH

ERIC BLACK

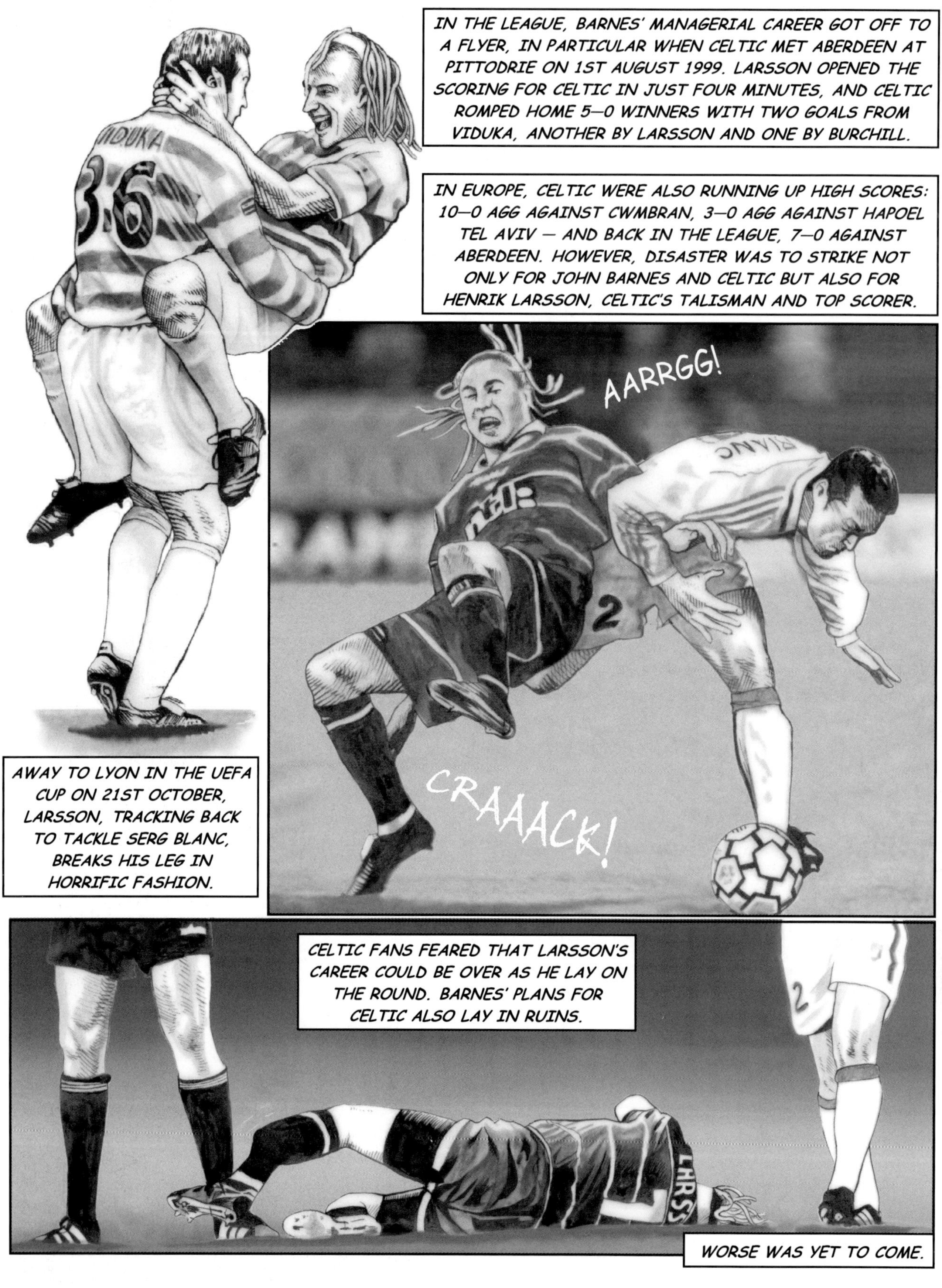
IN THE LEAGUE, BARNES' MANAGERIAL CAREER GOT OFF TO A FLYER, IN PARTICULAR WHEN CELTIC MET ABERDEEN AT PITTODRIE ON 1ST AUGUST 1999. LARSSON OPENED THE SCORING FOR CELTIC IN JUST FOUR MINUTES, AND CELTIC ROMPED HOME 5—0 WINNERS WITH TWO GOALS FROM VIDUKA, ANOTHER BY LARSSON AND ONE BY BURCHILL.
IN EUROPE, CELTIC WERE ALSO RUNNING UP HIGH SCORES: 10—0 AGG AGAINST CWMBRAN, 3—0 AGG AGAINST HAPOEL TEL AVIV — AND BACK IN THE LEAGUE, 7—0 AGAINST ABERDEEN. HOWEVER, DISASTER WAS TO STRIKE NOT ONLY FOR JOHN BARNES AND CELTIC BUT ALSO FOR HENRIK LARSSON, CELTIC'S TALISMAN AND TOP SCORER.
AARRGG!
CRAAACK!
AWAY TO LYON IN THE UEFA CUP ON 21ST OCTOBER, LARSSON, TRACKING BACK TO TACKLE SERG BLANC, BREAKS HIS LEG IN HORRIFIC FASHION.
CELTIC FANS FEARED THAT LARSSON'S CAREER COULD BE OVER AS HE LAY ON THE ROUND. BARNES' PLANS FOR CELTIC ALSO LAY IN RUINS.
WORSE WAS YET TO COME.

ON 5TH FEBRUARY, CELTIC LOST AT HOME TO HEARTS 3—2. BUT THE ROOF FELL IN JUST THREE DAYS LATER WHEN, IN THE THIRD ROUND OF THE SCOTTISH CUP AT CELTIC PARK, INVERNESS CALEY THISTLE DEFEATED CELTIC 3—1 AND PRODUCED ONE OF THE BIGGEST SHOCKS IN THE RECENT HISTORY OF SCOTTISH FOOTBALL.

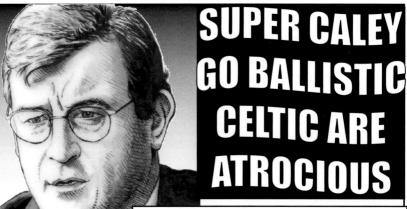

SUPER CALEY GO BALLISTIC CELTIC ARE ATROCIOUS

VIDUKA REFUSED TO GO BACK ON FOR THE SECOND HALF. BARNES HAD 'LOST THE DRESSING-ROOM' AND NOT LONG AFTERWARDS HE WOULD ALSO LOSE HIS JOB.

THE PRESS HAD A FIELD DAY, AS SUMMED UP IN THIS INFAMOUS NEWSPAPER HEADLINE THE DAY AFTER THE MATCH. CHIEF EXECUTIVE ALAN McDONALD MOVED QUICKLY TO LIMIT FURTHER DAMAGE TO THE CLUB.

ON 6TH FEBRUARY, DALGLISH WAS ASKED TO TAKE OVER AS CARETAKER MANAGER UNTIL THE END OF THE SEASON. HE APPOINTED TOMMY BURNS AS HIS ASSISTANT IN AN ATTEMPT TO TRY AND 'STEADY THE SHIP'. MANY HAD FELT THAT DALGLISH WAS NOT 'HANDS ON' ENOUGH DURING THE SHORT REIGN OF JOHN BARNES. NOW IT WAS DIFFERENT, AND COMING UP TO THE MONTH OF MARCH CELTIC WERE STILL IN WITH A SHOUT OF WINNING THE LEAGUE CHAMPIONSHIP. THE NEXT FEW RESULTS WOULD BE CRUCIAL.

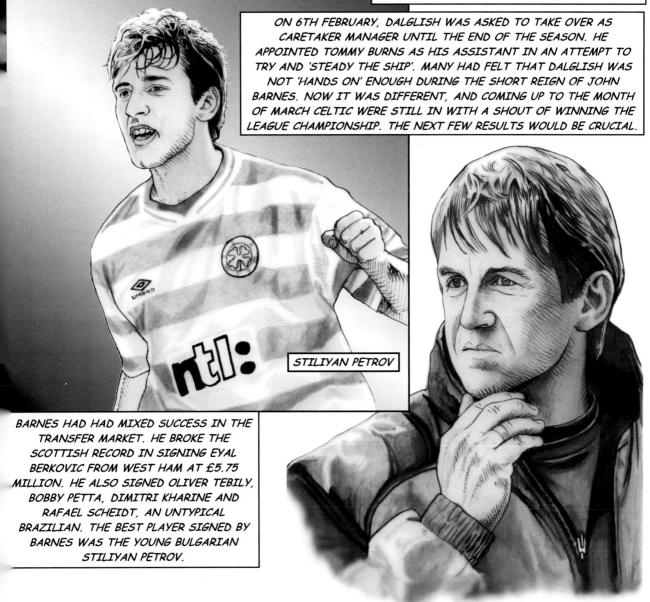

STILIYAN PETROV

BARNES HAD HAD MIXED SUCCESS IN THE TRANSFER MARKET. HE BROKE THE SCOTTISH RECORD IN SIGNING EYAL BERKOVIC FROM WEST HAM AT £5.75 MILLION. HE ALSO SIGNED OLIVER TEBILY, BOBBY PETTA, DIMITRI KHARINE AND RAFAEL SCHEIDT, AN UNTYPICAL BRAZILIAN. THE BEST PLAYER SIGNED BY BARNES WAS THE YOUNG BULGARIAN STILIYAN PETROV.

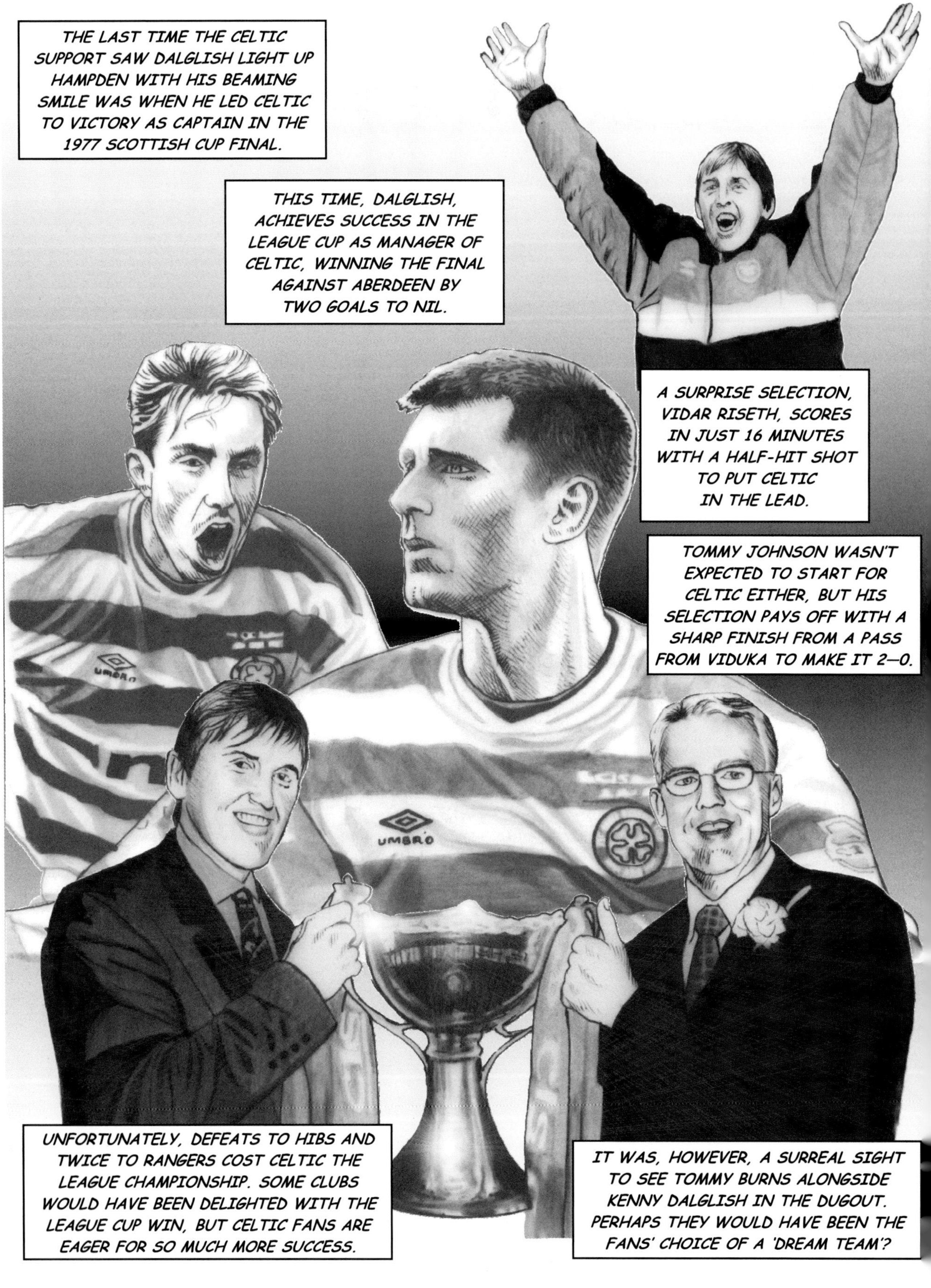
THE LAST TIME THE CELTIC SUPPORT SAW DALGLISH LIGHT UP HAMPDEN WITH HIS BEAMING SMILE WAS WHEN HE LED CELTIC TO VICTORY AS CAPTAIN IN THE 1977 SCOTTISH CUP FINAL.
THIS TIME, DALGLISH, ACHIEVES SUCCESS IN THE LEAGUE CUP AS MANAGER OF CELTIC, WINNING THE FINAL AGAINST ABERDEEN BY TWO GOALS TO NIL.
A SURPRISE SELECTION, VIDAR RISETH, SCORES IN JUST 16 MINUTES WITH A HALF-HIT SHOT TO PUT CELTIC IN THE LEAD.
TOMMY JOHNSON WASN'T EXPECTED TO START FOR CELTIC EITHER, BUT HIS SELECTION PAYS OFF WITH A SHARP FINISH FROM A PASS FROM VIDUKA TO MAKE IT 2–0.
UNFORTUNATELY, DEFEATS TO HIBS AND TWICE TO RANGERS COST CELTIC THE LEAGUE CHAMPIONSHIP. SOME CLUBS WOULD HAVE BEEN DELIGHTED WITH THE LEAGUE CUP WIN, BUT CELTIC FANS ARE EAGER FOR SO MUCH MORE SUCCESS.
IT WAS, HOWEVER, A SURREAL SIGHT TO SEE TOMMY BURNS ALONGSIDE KENNY DALGLISH IN THE DUGOUT. PERHAPS THEY WOULD HAVE BEEN THE FANS' CHOICE OF A 'DREAM TEAM'?

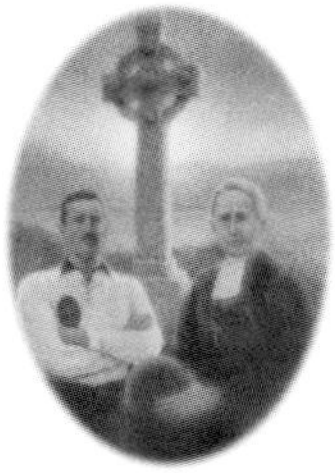

chapter 13

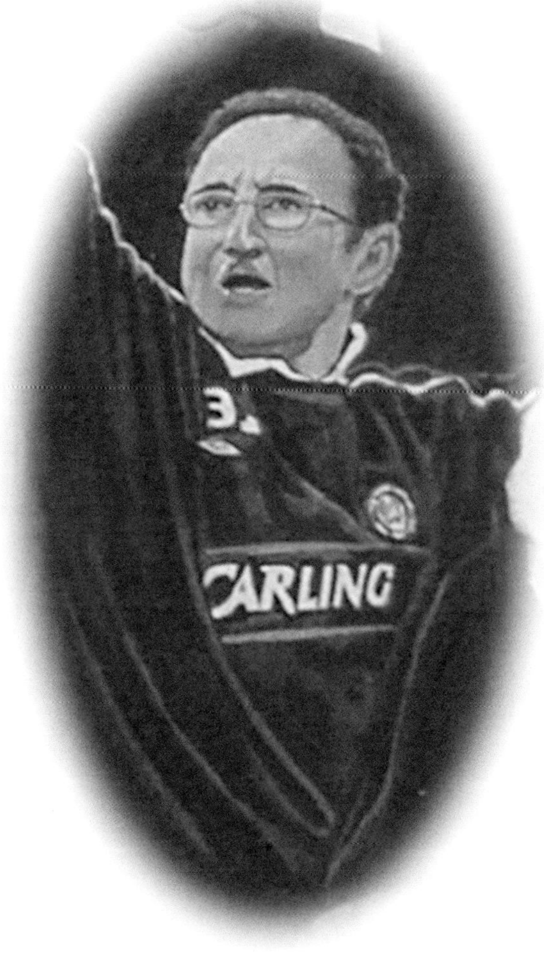

CARLING

a new springtime

'and you'll never walk alone'

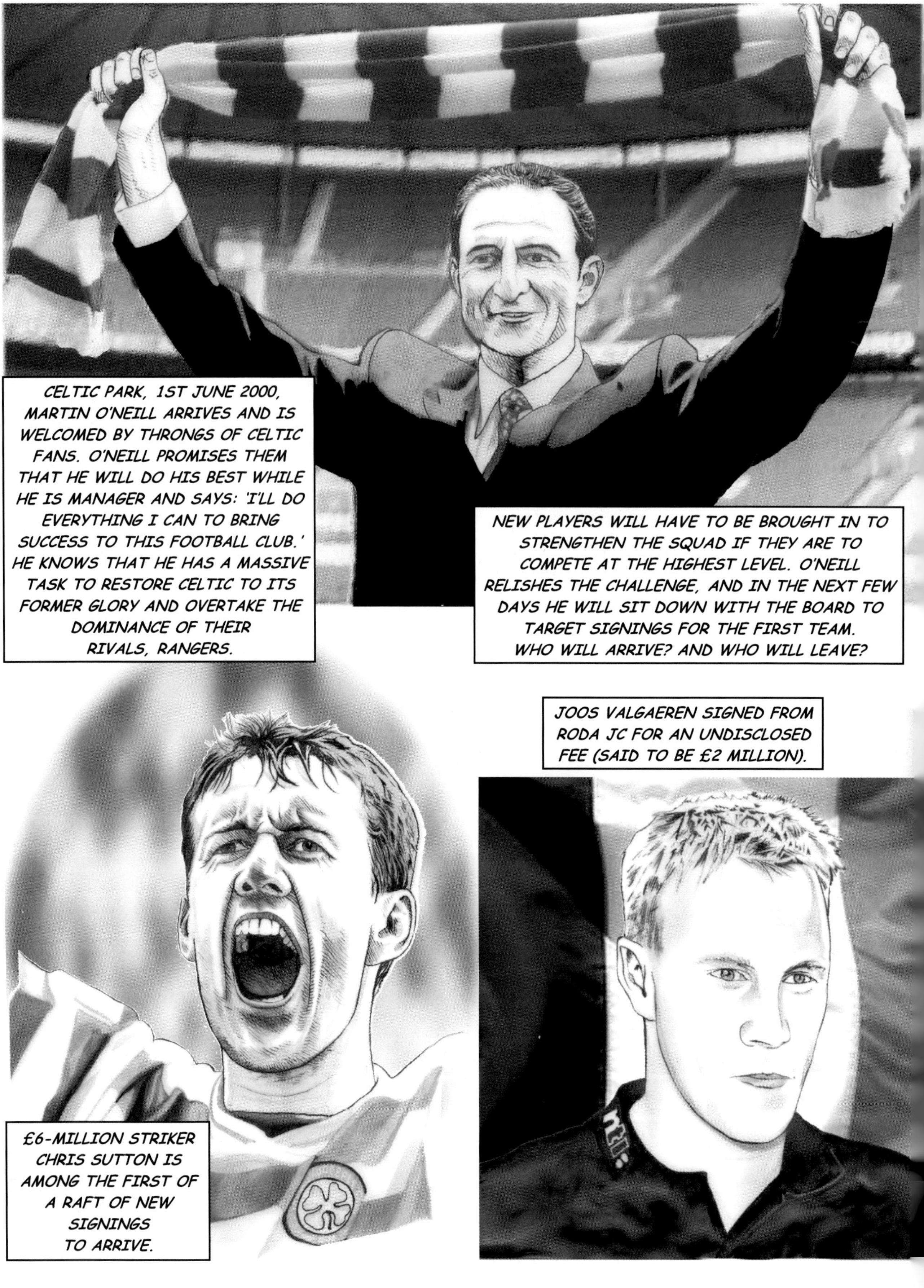
CELTIC PARK, 1ST JUNE 2000, MARTIN O'NEILL ARRIVES AND IS WELCOMED BY THRONGS OF CELTIC FANS. O'NEILL PROMISES THEM THAT HE WILL DO HIS BEST WHILE HE IS MANAGER AND SAYS: 'I'LL DO EVERYTHING I CAN TO BRING SUCCESS TO THIS FOOTBALL CLUB.' HE KNOWS THAT HE HAS A MASSIVE TASK TO RESTORE CELTIC TO ITS FORMER GLORY AND OVERTAKE THE DOMINANCE OF THEIR RIVALS, RANGERS.
NEW PLAYERS WILL HAVE TO BE BROUGHT IN TO STRENGTHEN THE SQUAD IF THEY ARE TO COMPETE AT THE HIGHEST LEVEL. O'NEILL RELISHES THE CHALLENGE, AND IN THE NEXT FEW DAYS HE WILL SIT DOWN WITH THE BOARD TO TARGET SIGNINGS FOR THE FIRST TEAM. WHO WILL ARRIVE? AND WHO WILL LEAVE?
£6-MILLION STRIKER CHRIS SUTTON IS AMONG THE FIRST OF A RAFT OF NEW SIGNINGS TO ARRIVE.
JOOS VALGAEREN SIGNED FROM RODA JC FOR AN UNDISCLOSED FEE (SAID TO BE £2 MILLION).

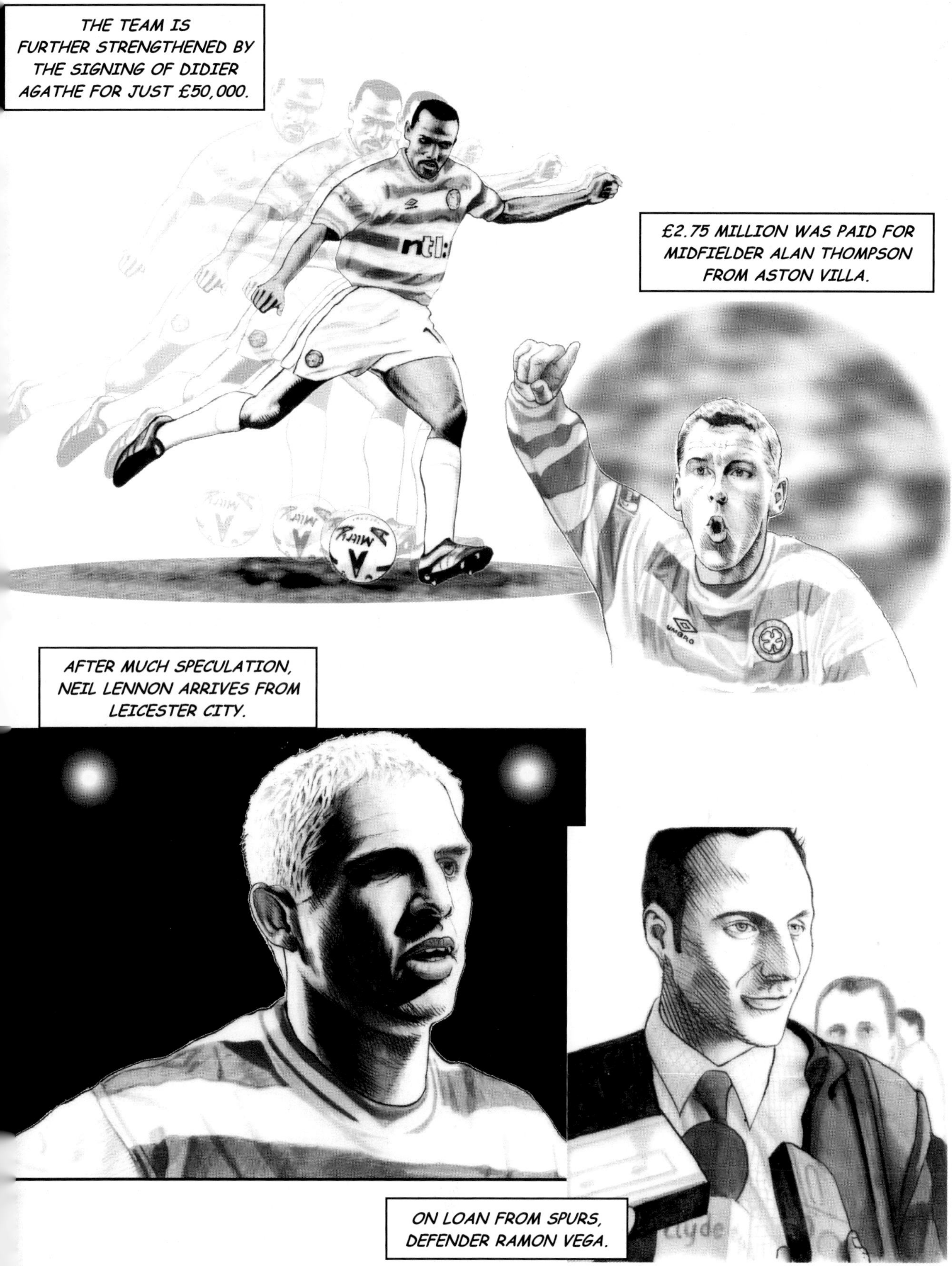
THE TEAM IS FURTHER STRENGTHENED BY THE SIGNING OF DIDIER AGATHE FOR JUST £50,000.
£2.75 MILLION WAS PAID FOR MIDFIELDER ALAN THOMPSON FROM ASTON VILLA.
AFTER MUCH SPECULATION, NEIL LENNON ARRIVES FROM LEICESTER CITY.
ON LOAN FROM SPURS, DEFENDER RAMON VEGA.

CELTIC PARK, 27TH AUGUST 2000. MARTIN O'NEILL'S FIRST SEASON. THE MATCH GETS UNDERWAY AGAINST WHAT O'NEILL HAD LABELLED 'THE BENCHMARK' OF SCOTTISH FOOTBALL, RANGERS. IN JUST 51 SECONDS, THE FASTEST GOAL EVER SCORED IN THE SPL IS SLOTTED HOME BY CHRIS SUTTON IN HIS OLD FIRM DEBUT. SUTTON ALMOST GOES INTO SHOCK AS HE RUNS TO CELEBRATE HIS SUDDEN STRIKE WITH ARMS OUTSTRETCHED. THE GOAL COULDN'T HAVE BEEN EASIER. A CORNER FROM MORAVCIK IS KNOCKED DOWN BY STUBBS TO LARSSON, WHO ATTEMPTS A SHOT THAT IS TAPPED IN BY SUTTON. 1–0 TO CELTIC.

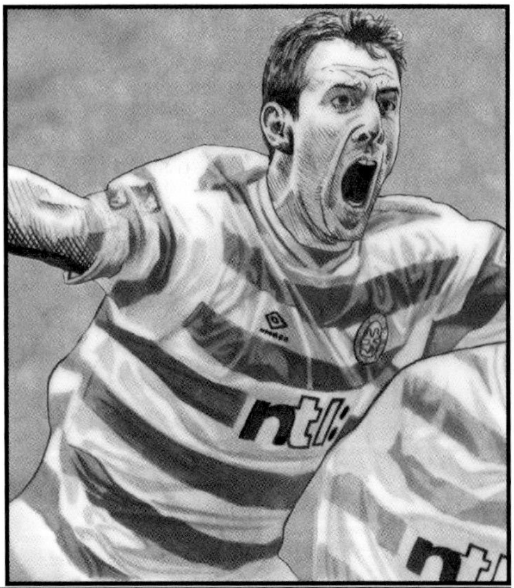
ntl:

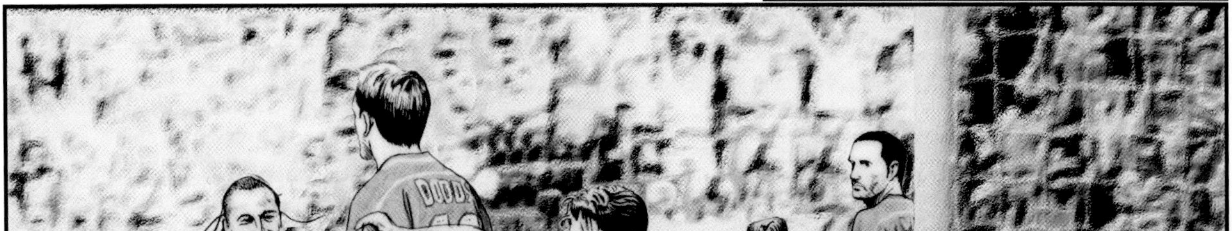
6
19
PHO
IOND

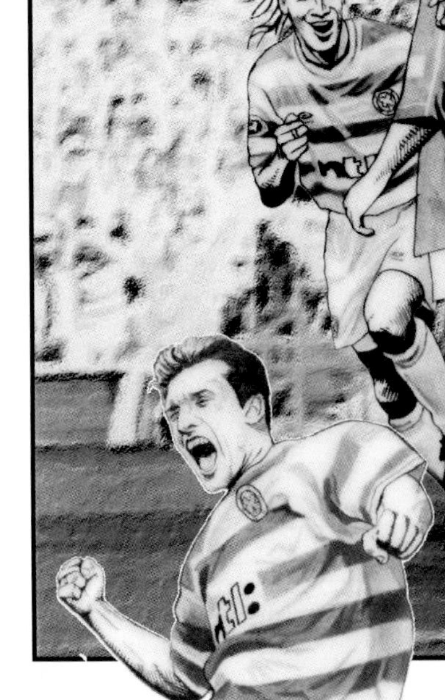
ntl:
19

AFTER 13 MINUTES, CELTIC WERE 3–0 UP. THE SECOND GOAL CAME FROM A POWERFUL PETROV HEADER. THE BULGARIAN MET THE BALL FROM A TRADEMARK DEADLY CORNER FROM MORAVCIK.

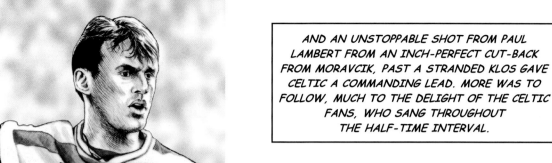

AND AN UNSTOPPABLE SHOT FROM PAUL LAMBERT FROM AN INCH-PERFECT CUT-BACK FROM MORAVCIK, PAST A STRANDED KLOS GAVE CELTIC A COMMANDING LEAD. MORE WAS TO FOLLOW, MUCH TO THE DELIGHT OF THE CELTIC FANS, WHO SANG THROUGHOUT THE HALF-TIME INTERVAL.

RICKSEN, AFTER A ROASTING FROM PETTA AND MORAVCIK, WAS SUBSTITUTED AFTER 20 MINUTES, BUT IT MADE NO DIFFERENCE TO THE PATTERN OF PLAY. NOT EVEN A GOAL FROM REYNA JUST BEFORE HALF-TIME COULD HOLD BACK THE CELTIC TIDE THAT WAS OVERWHELMING RANGERS.

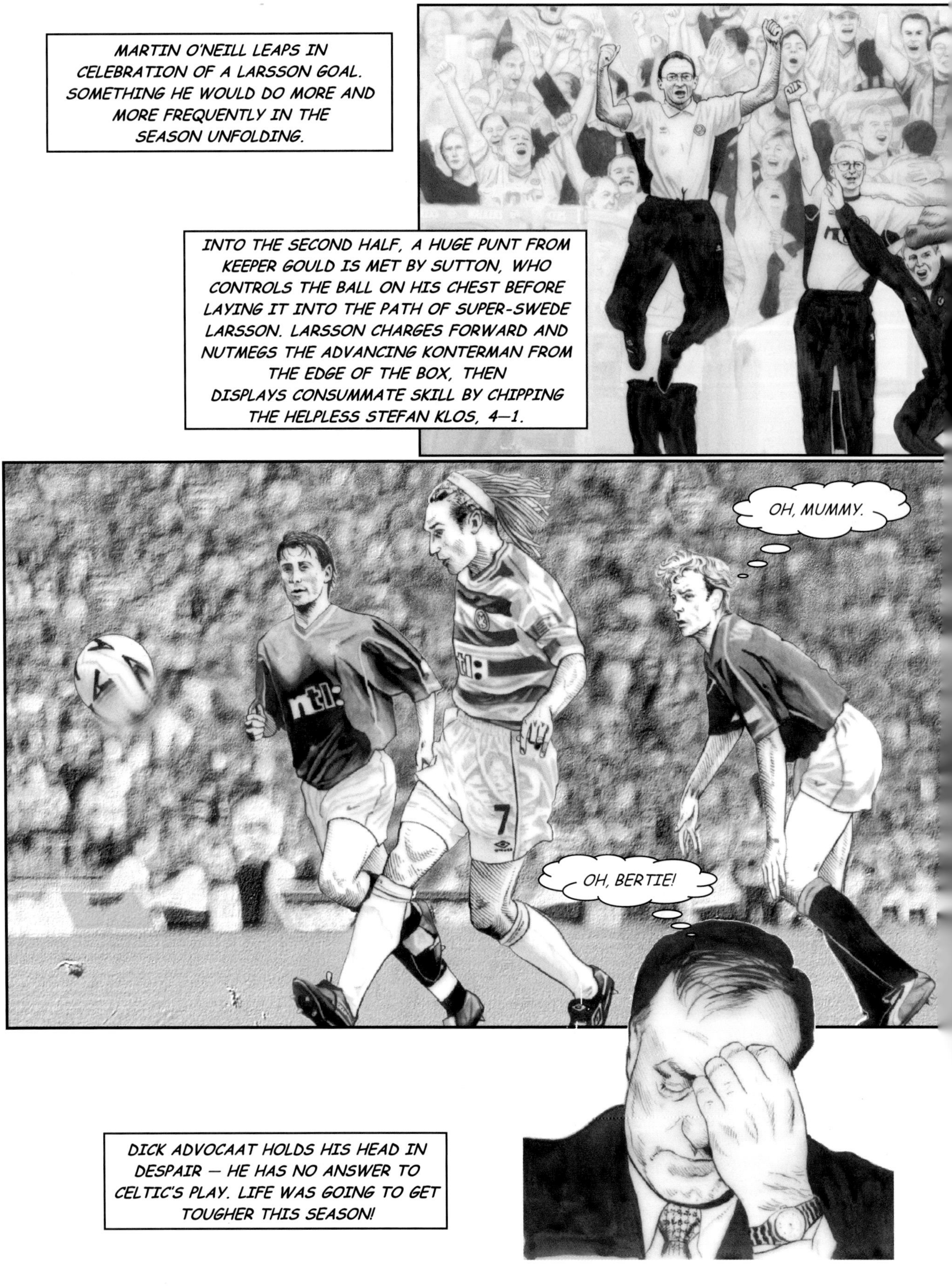
MARTIN O'NEILL LEAPS IN CELEBRATION OF A LARSSON GOAL. SOMETHING HE WOULD DO MORE AND MORE FREQUENTLY IN THE SEASON UNFOLDING.
INTO THE SECOND HALF, A HUGE PUNT FROM KEEPER GOULD IS MET BY SUTTON, WHO CONTROLS THE BALL ON HIS CHEST BEFORE LAYING IT INTO THE PATH OF SUPER-SWEDE LARSSON. LARSSON CHARGES FORWARD AND NUTMEGS THE ADVANCING KONTERMAN FROM THE EDGE OF THE BOX, THEN DISPLAYS CONSUMMATE SKILL BY CHIPPING THE HELPLESS STEFAN KLOS, 4—1.
OH, MUMMY.
OH, BERTIE!
DICK ADVOCAAT HOLDS HIS HEAD IN DESPAIR — HE HAS NO ANSWER TO CELTIC'S PLAY. LIFE WAS GOING TO GET TOUGHER THIS SEASON!

THE RETURN OF THE KING!

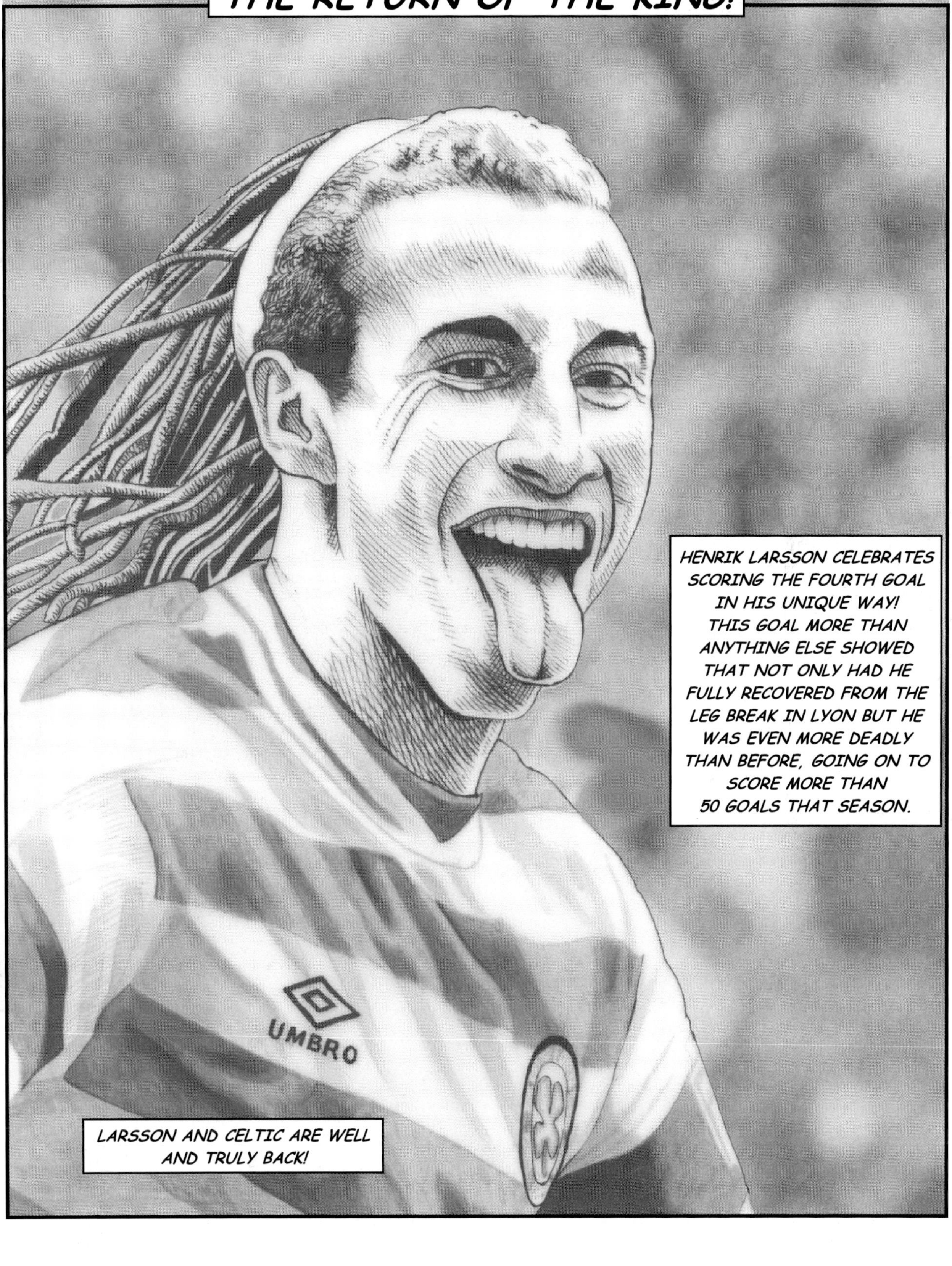
HENRIK LARSSON CELEBRATES SCORING THE FOURTH GOAL IN HIS UNIQUE WAY! THIS GOAL MORE THAN ANYTHING ELSE SHOWED THAT NOT ONLY HAD HE FULLY RECOVERED FROM THE LEG BREAK IN LYON BUT HE WAS EVEN MORE DEADLY THAN BEFORE, GOING ON TO SCORE MORE THAN 50 GOALS THAT SEASON.
UMBRO
LARSSON AND CELTIC ARE WELL AND TRULY BACK!

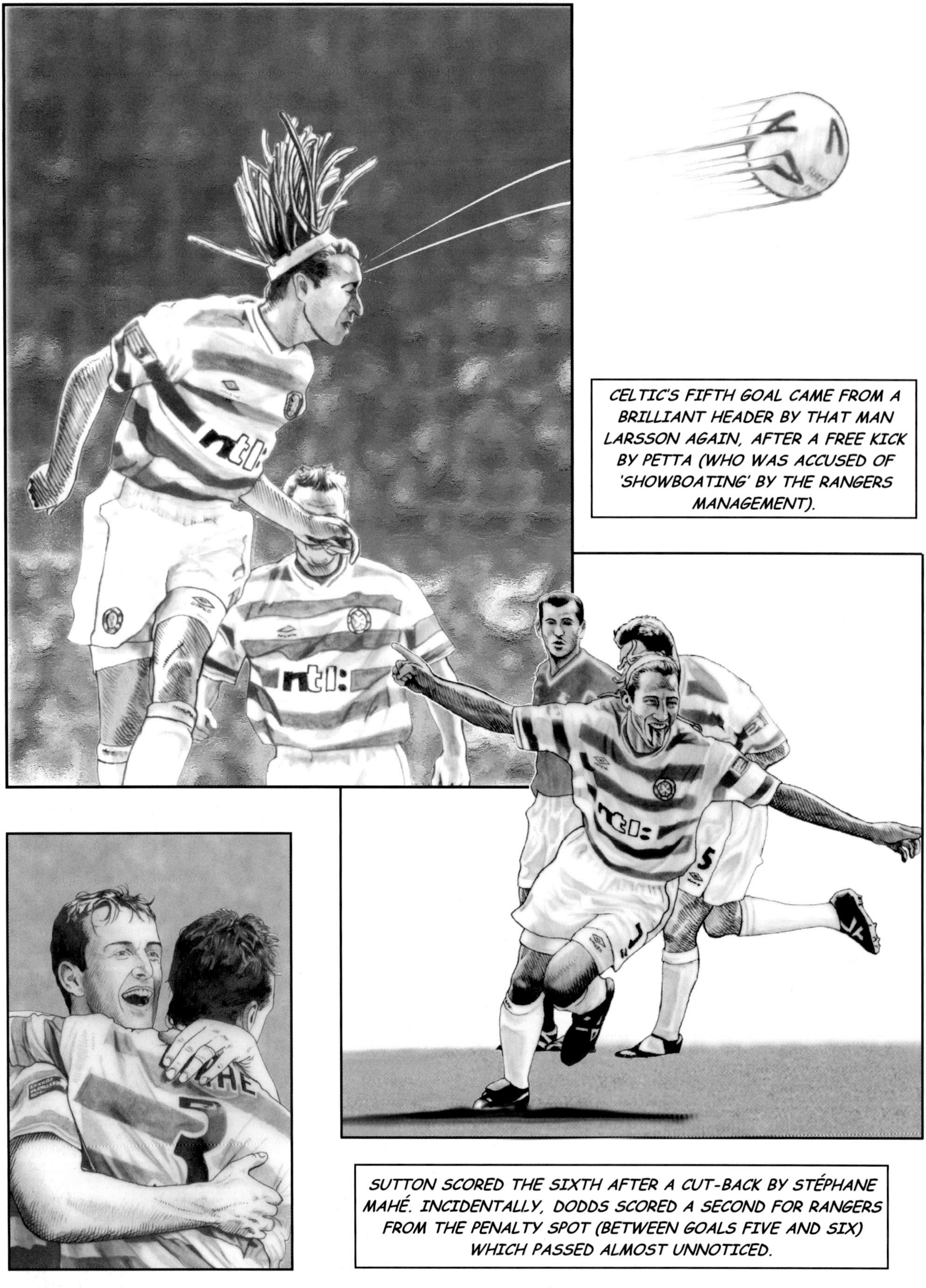
CELTIC'S FIFTH GOAL CAME FROM A BRILLIANT HEADER BY THAT MAN LARSSON AGAIN, AFTER A FREE KICK BY PETTA (WHO WAS ACCUSED OF 'SHOWBOATING' BY THE RANGERS MANAGEMENT).
SUTTON SCORED THE SIXTH AFTER A CUT-BACK BY STÉPHANE MAHÉ. INCIDENTALLY, DODDS SCORED A SECOND FOR RANGERS FROM THE PENALTY SPOT (BETWEEN GOALS FIVE AND SIX) WHICH PASSED ALMOST UNNOTICED.

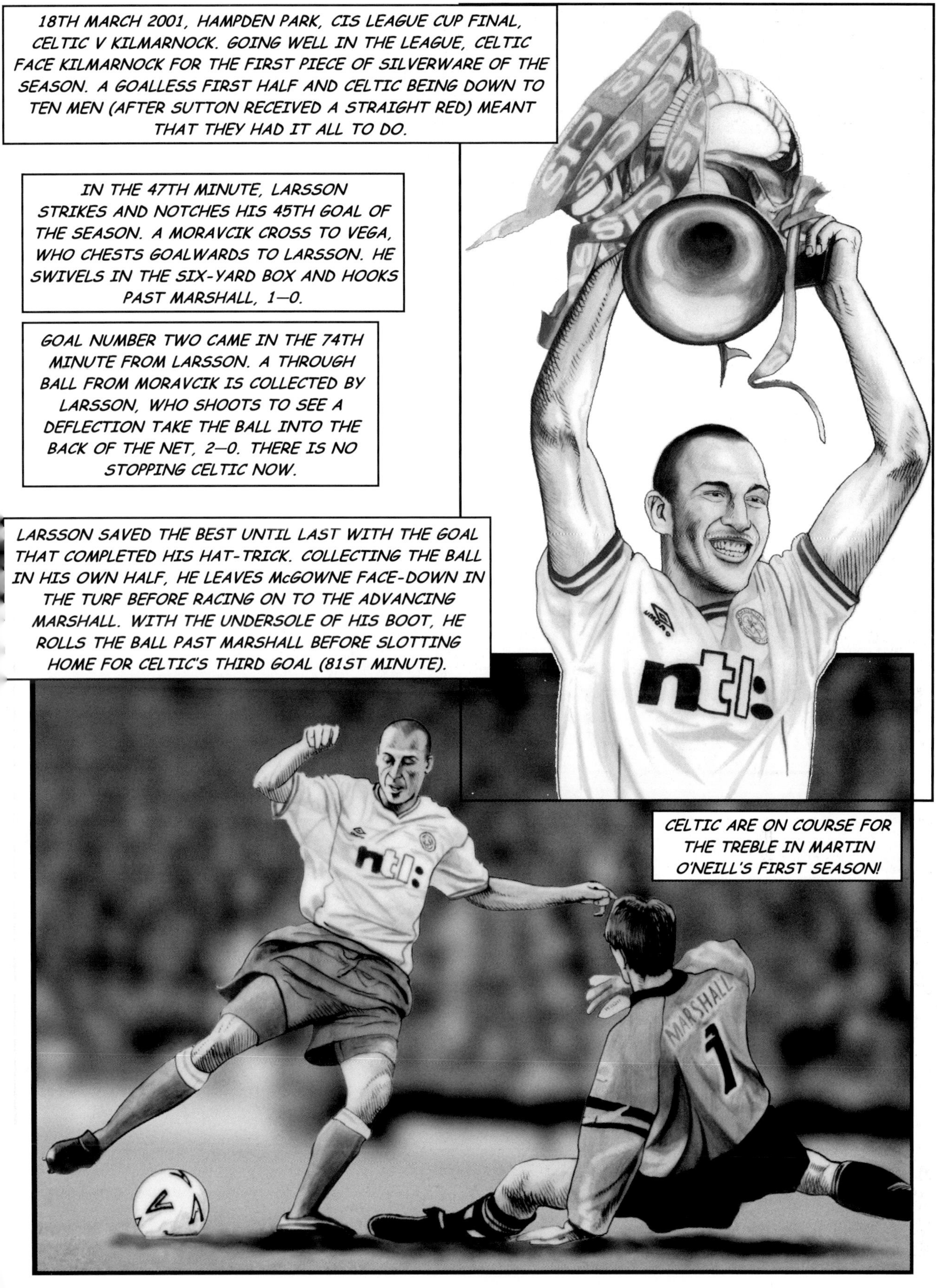
18TH MARCH 2001, HAMPDEN PARK, CIS LEAGUE CUP FINAL, CELTIC V KILMARNOCK. GOING WELL IN THE LEAGUE, CELTIC FACE KILMARNOCK FOR THE FIRST PIECE OF SILVERWARE OF THE SEASON. A GOALLESS FIRST HALF AND CELTIC BEING DOWN TO TEN MEN (AFTER SUTTON RECEIVED A STRAIGHT RED) MEANT THAT THEY HAD IT ALL TO DO.
IN THE 47TH MINUTE, LARSSON STRIKES AND NOTCHES HIS 45TH GOAL OF THE SEASON. A MORAVCIK CROSS TO VEGA, WHO CHESTS GOALWARDS TO LARSSON. HE SWIVELS IN THE SIX-YARD BOX AND HOOKS PAST MARSHALL, 1–0.
GOAL NUMBER TWO CAME IN THE 74TH MINUTE FROM LARSSON. A THROUGH BALL FROM MORAVCIK IS COLLECTED BY LARSSON, WHO SHOOTS TO SEE A DEFLECTION TAKE THE BALL INTO THE BACK OF THE NET, 2–0. THERE IS NO STOPPING CELTIC NOW.
ntl:
LARSSON SAVED THE BEST UNTIL LAST WITH THE GOAL THAT COMPLETED HIS HAT-TRICK. COLLECTING THE BALL IN HIS OWN HALF, HE LEAVES McGOWNE FACE-DOWN IN THE TURF BEFORE RACING ON TO THE ADVANCING MARSHALL. WITH THE UNDERSOLE OF HIS BOOT, HE ROLLS THE BALL PAST MARSHALL BEFORE SLOTTING HOME FOR CELTIC'S THIRD GOAL (81ST MINUTE).
CELTIC ARE ON COURSE FOR THE TREBLE IN MARTIN O'NEILL'S FIRST SEASON!
ntl:
MARSHALL
1

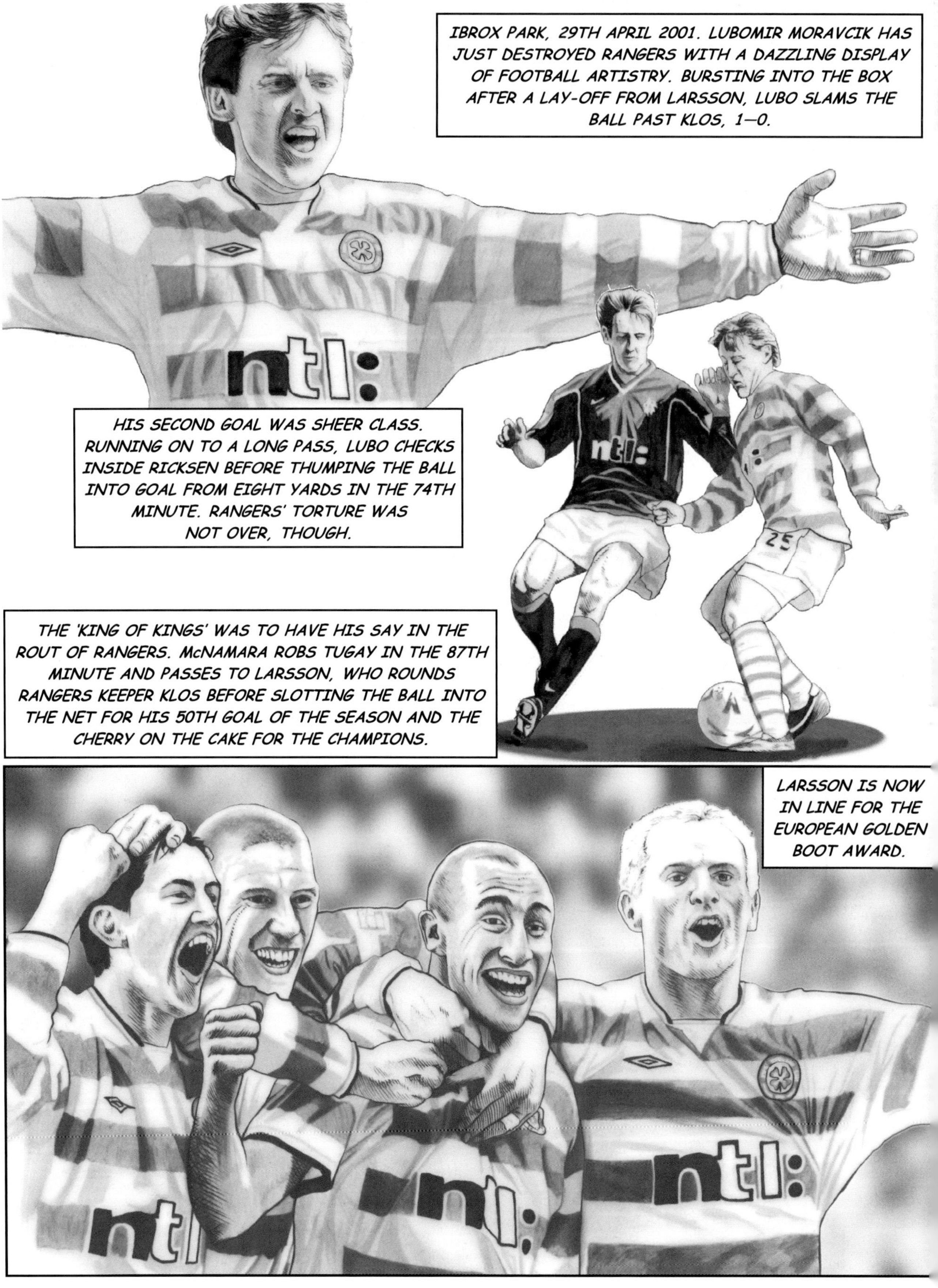
IBROX PARK, 29TH APRIL 2001. LUBOMIR MORAVCIK HAS JUST DESTROYED RANGERS WITH A DAZZLING DISPLAY OF FOOTBALL ARTISTRY. BURSTING INTO THE BOX AFTER A LAY-OFF FROM LARSSON, LUBO SLAMS THE BALL PAST KLOS, 1—0.
ntl:
HIS SECOND GOAL WAS SHEER CLASS. RUNNING ON TO A LONG PASS, LUBO CHECKS INSIDE RICKSEN BEFORE THUMPING THE BALL INTO GOAL FROM EIGHT YARDS IN THE 74TH MINUTE. RANGERS' TORTURE WAS NOT OVER, THOUGH.
ntl:
25
THE 'KING OF KINGS' WAS TO HAVE HIS SAY IN THE ROUT OF RANGERS. McNAMARA ROBS TUGAY IN THE 87TH MINUTE AND PASSES TO LARSSON, WHO ROUNDS RANGERS KEEPER KLOS BEFORE SLOTTING THE BALL INTO THE NET FOR HIS 50TH GOAL OF THE SEASON AND THE CHERRY ON THE CAKE FOR THE CHAMPIONS.
LARSSON IS NOW IN LINE FOR THE EUROPEAN GOLDEN BOOT AWARD.
ntl
ntl:
ntl:

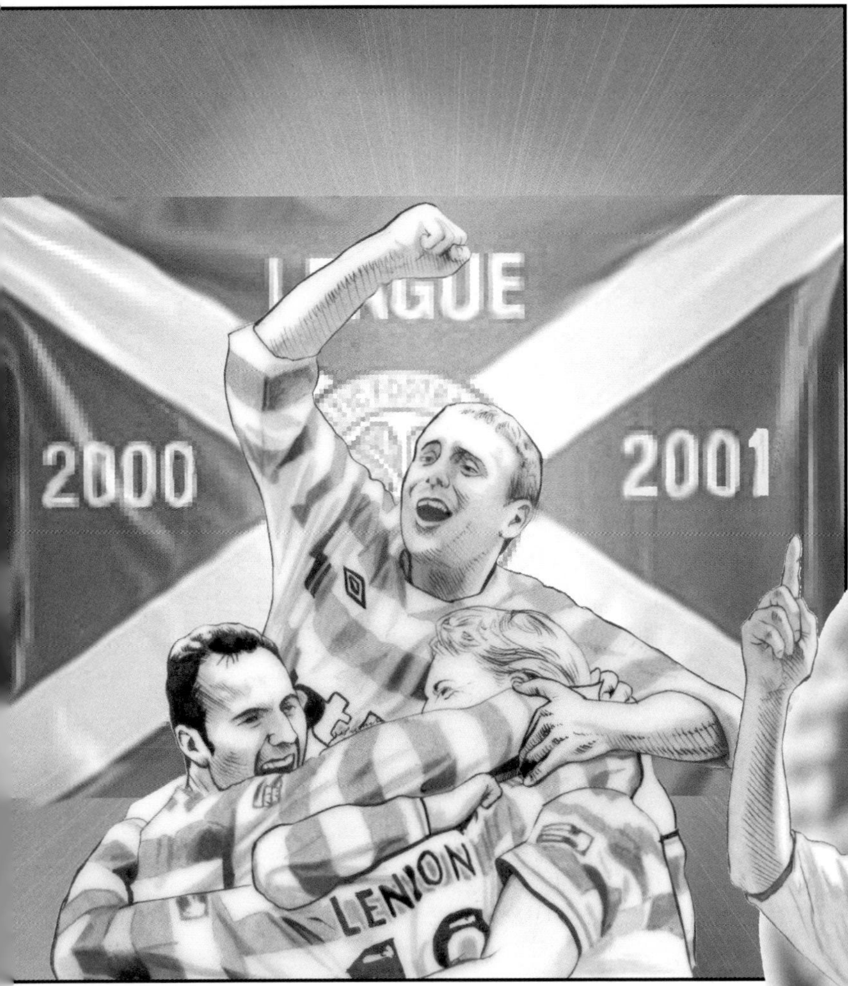
2000
2001
ON 26TH MAY 2001, McNAMARA OPENS THE SCORING FOR CELTIC IN THE 39TH MINUTE IN THE SCOTTISH CUP FINAL AGAINST HIBS. MORAVCIK HAD TO GO OFF DUE TO BURST STITCHES IN A LEG WOUND, BUT IT TURNED OUT WELL FOR CELTIC, AS 'WEE JACKIE' GOT THE OPENING GOAL. IT'S A TESTAMENT TO THE VERSATILITY OF McNAMARA THAT HE CAN PLAY ANYWHERE IN THE MIDFIELD OR DEFENCE. CELTIC ARE ON COURSE FOR THE TREBLE.

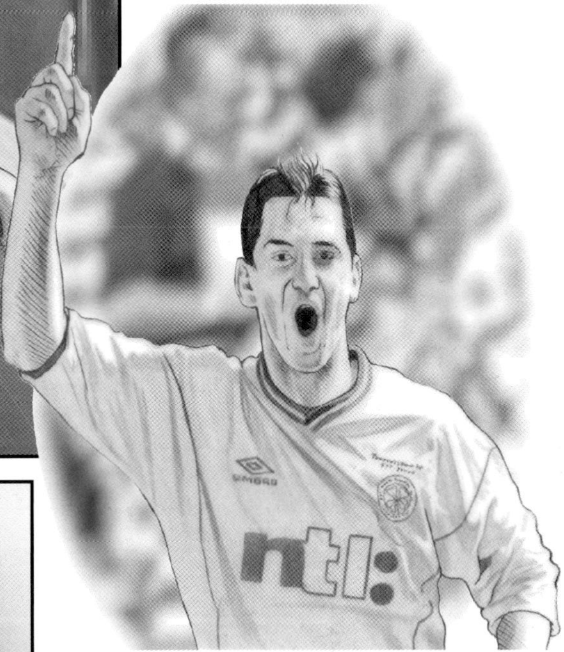
ntl:
LARSSON HAD A QUIET AND POOR FIRST HALF BY HIS VERY HIGH STANDARDS, BUT THINGS WOULD CHANGE IN THE SECOND HALF. DURING THE INTERVAL, LARSSON CHANGES HIS BOOTS, COMPLAINING THAT HE DID NOT HAVE ENOUGH GRIP ON THE PARK. JUST THREE MINUTES INTO THE SECOND HALF AND LARSSON POUNCES TO SCORE WITH A LEFT-FOOT SHOT, 2—0.

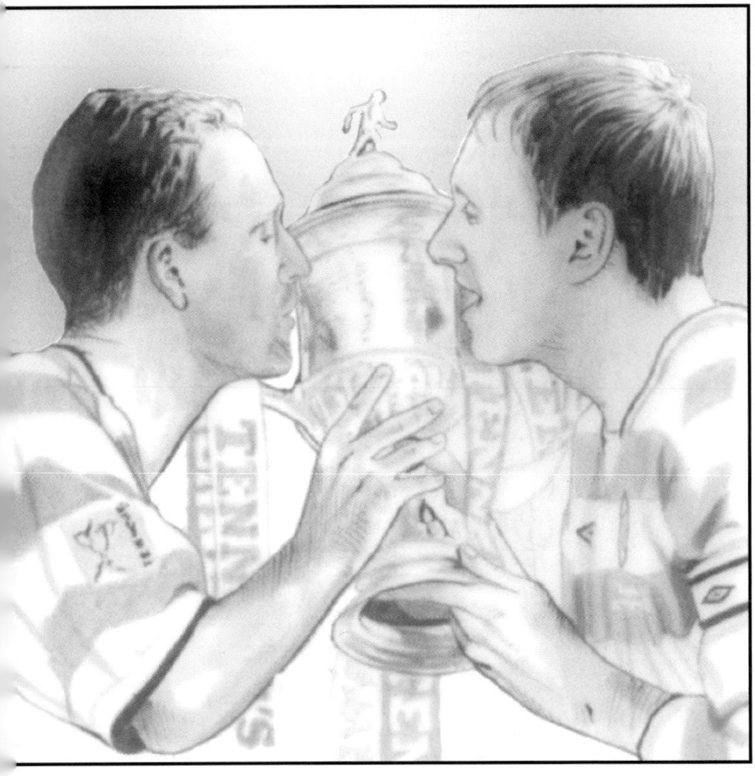
WITH JUST TEN MINUTES TO GO, LARSSON IS BROUGHT DOWN BY SMITH IN THE BOX. LARSSON CONVERTS THE PENALTY AND SCORES HIS 53RD GOAL OF THE SEASON. CELTIC SECURE THEIR FIRST TREBLE SINCE THE DAYS OF JOCK STEIN.

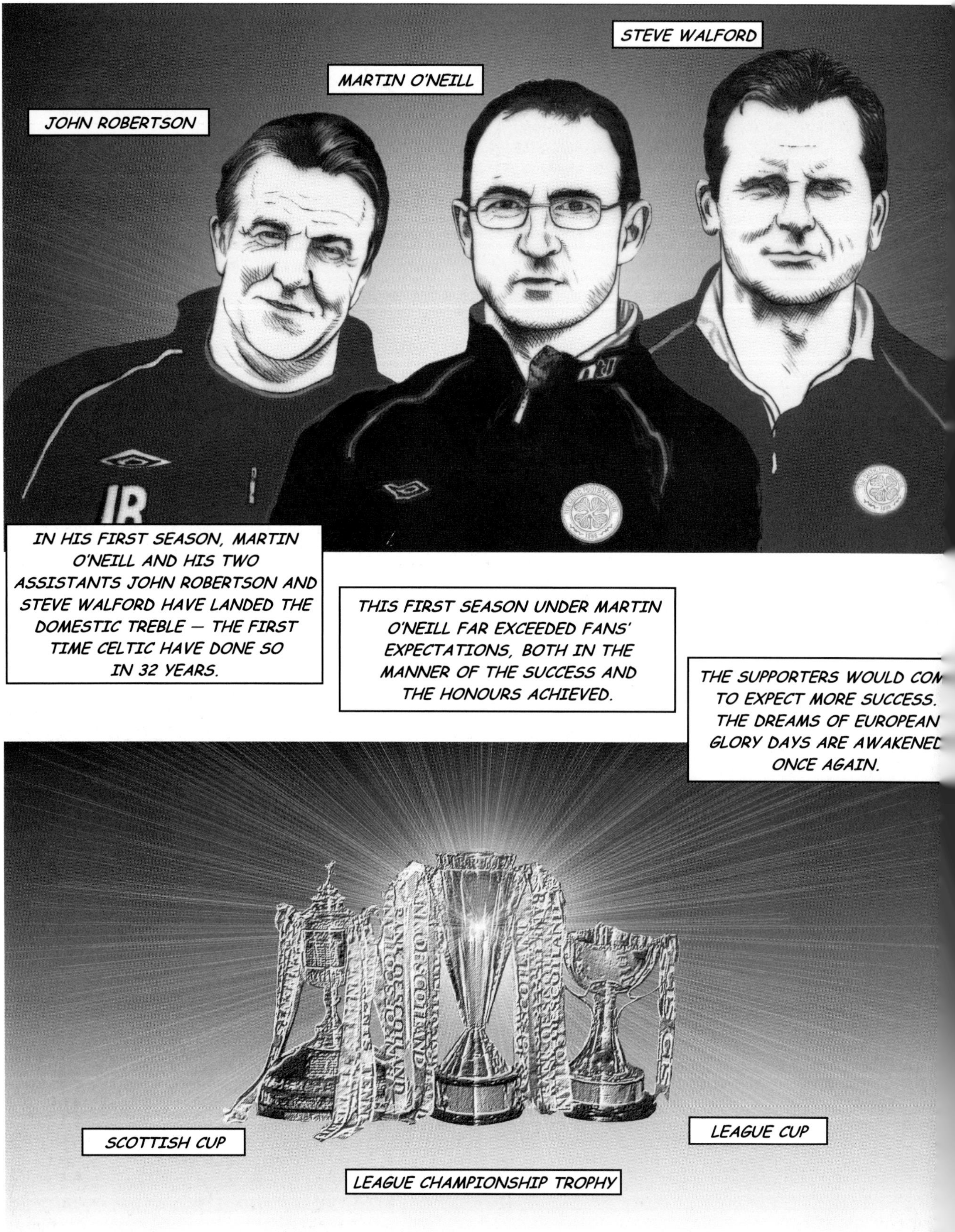

JOHN ROBERTSON
MARTIN O'NEILL
STEVE WALFORD
IN HIS FIRST SEASON, MARTIN O'NEILL AND HIS TWO ASSISTANTS JOHN ROBERTSON AND STEVE WALFORD HAVE LANDED THE DOMESTIC TREBLE – THE FIRST TIME CELTIC HAVE DONE SO IN 32 YEARS.
THIS FIRST SEASON UNDER MARTIN O'NEILL FAR EXCEEDED FANS' EXPECTATIONS, BOTH IN THE MANNER OF THE SUCCESS AND THE HONOURS ACHIEVED.
THE SUPPORTERS WOULD COM TO EXPECT MORE SUCCESS. THE DREAMS OF EUROPEAN GLORY DAYS ARE AWAKENE ONCE AGAIN.
SCOTTISH CUP
LEAGUE CHAMPIONSHIP TROPHY
LEAGUE CUP

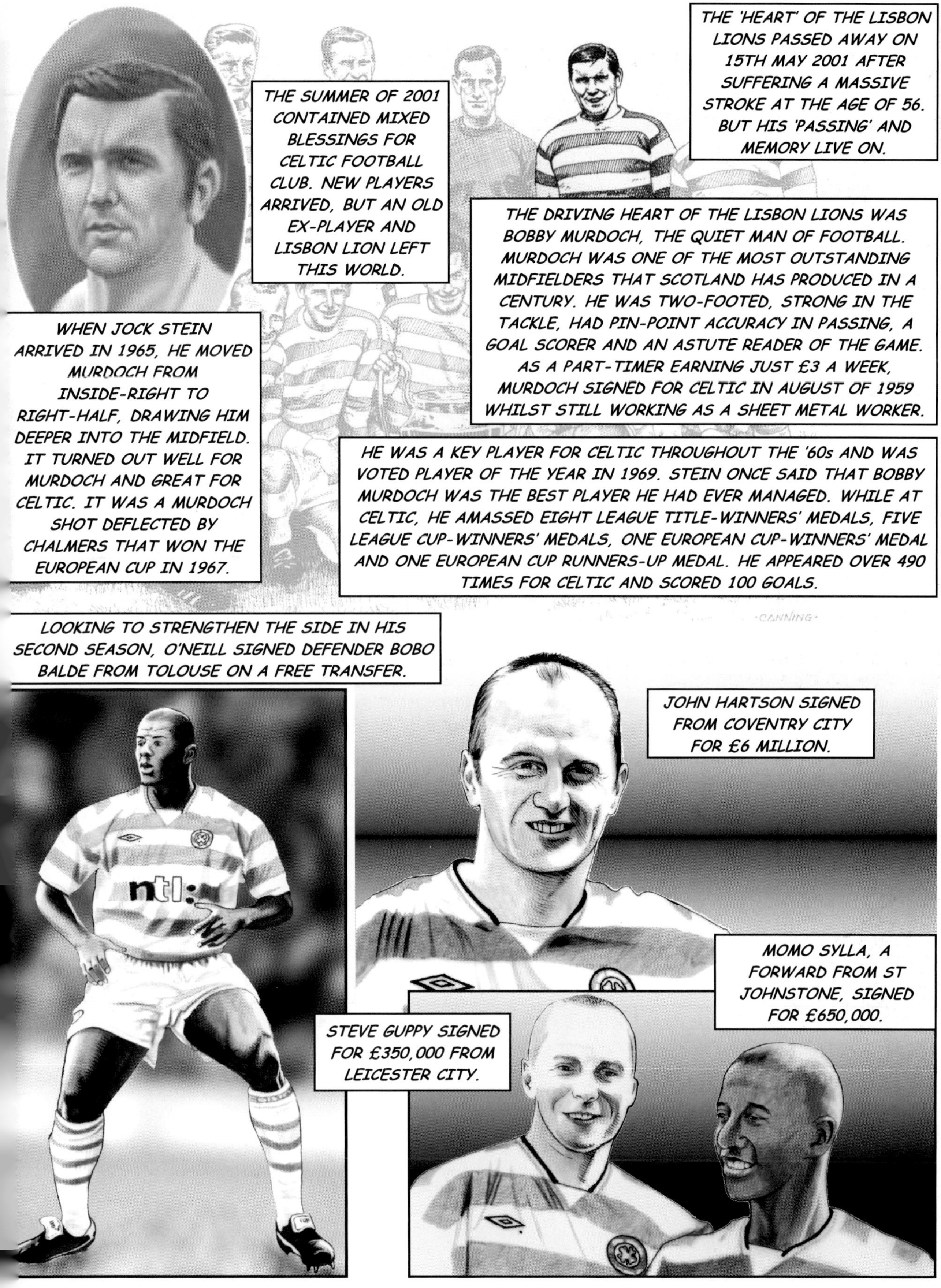
THE SUMMER OF 2001 CONTAINED MIXED BLESSINGS FOR CELTIC FOOTBALL CLUB. NEW PLAYERS ARRIVED, BUT AN OLD EX-PLAYER AND LISBON LION LEFT THIS WORLD.
THE 'HEART' OF THE LISBON LIONS PASSED AWAY ON 15TH MAY 2001 AFTER SUFFERING A MASSIVE STROKE AT THE AGE OF 56. BUT HIS 'PASSING' AND MEMORY LIVE ON.
THE DRIVING HEART OF THE LISBON LIONS WAS BOBBY MURDOCH, THE QUIET MAN OF FOOTBALL. MURDOCH WAS ONE OF THE MOST OUTSTANDING MIDFIELDERS THAT SCOTLAND HAS PRODUCED IN A CENTURY. HE WAS TWO-FOOTED, STRONG IN THE TACKLE, HAD PIN-POINT ACCURACY IN PASSING, A GOAL SCORER AND AN ASTUTE READER OF THE GAME. AS A PART-TIMER EARNING JUST £3 A WEEK, MURDOCH SIGNED FOR CELTIC IN AUGUST OF 1959 WHILST STILL WORKING AS A SHEET METAL WORKER.
WHEN JOCK STEIN ARRIVED IN 1965, HE MOVED MURDOCH FROM INSIDE-RIGHT TO RIGHT-HALF, DRAWING HIM DEEPER INTO THE MIDFIELD. IT TURNED OUT WELL FOR MURDOCH AND GREAT FOR CELTIC. IT WAS A MURDOCH SHOT DEFLECTED BY CHALMERS THAT WON THE EUROPEAN CUP IN 1967.
HE WAS A KEY PLAYER FOR CELTIC THROUGHOUT THE '60s AND WAS VOTED PLAYER OF THE YEAR IN 1969. STEIN ONCE SAID THAT BOBBY MURDOCH WAS THE BEST PLAYER HE HAD EVER MANAGED. WHILE AT CELTIC, HE AMASSED EIGHT LEAGUE TITLE-WINNERS' MEDALS, FIVE LEAGUE CUP-WINNERS' MEDALS, ONE EUROPEAN CUP-WINNERS' MEDAL AND ONE EUROPEAN CUP RUNNERS-UP MEDAL. HE APPEARED OVER 490 TIMES FOR CELTIC AND SCORED 100 GOALS.
·CANNING·
LOOKING TO STRENGTHEN THE SIDE IN HIS SECOND SEASON, O'NEILL SIGNED DEFENDER BOBO BALDE FROM TOLOUSE ON A FREE TRANSFER.
ntl:
JOHN HARTSON SIGNED FROM COVENTRY CITY FOR £6 MILLION.
MOMO SYLLA, A FORWARD FROM ST JOHNSTONE, SIGNED FOR £650,000.
STEVE GUPPY SIGNED FOR £350,000 FROM LEICESTER CITY.

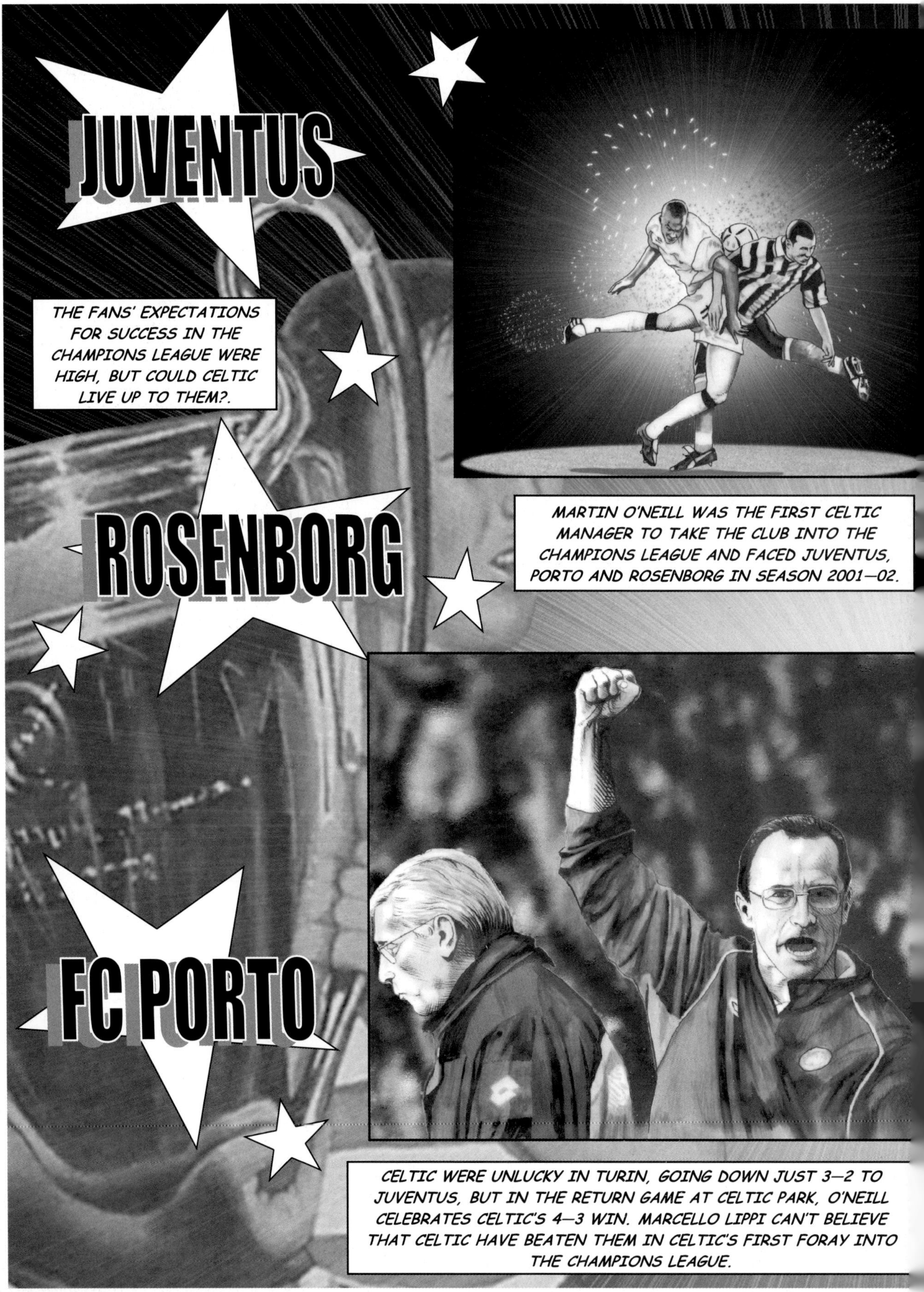
JUVENTUS
THE FANS' EXPECTATIONS FOR SUCCESS IN THE CHAMPIONS LEAGUE WERE HIGH, BUT COULD CELTIC LIVE UP TO THEM?.
ROSENBORG
MARTIN O'NEILL WAS THE FIRST CELTIC MANAGER TO TAKE THE CLUB INTO THE CHAMPIONS LEAGUE AND FACED JUVENTUS, PORTO AND ROSENBORG IN SEASON 2001–02.
FC PORTO
CELTIC WERE UNLUCKY IN TURIN, GOING DOWN JUST 3–2 TO JUVENTUS, BUT IN THE RETURN GAME AT CELTIC PARK, O'NEILL CELEBRATES CELTIC'S 4–3 WIN. MARCELLO LIPPI CAN'T BELIEVE THAT CELTIC HAVE BEATEN THEM IN CELTIC'S FIRST FORAY INTO THE CHAMPIONS LEAGUE.

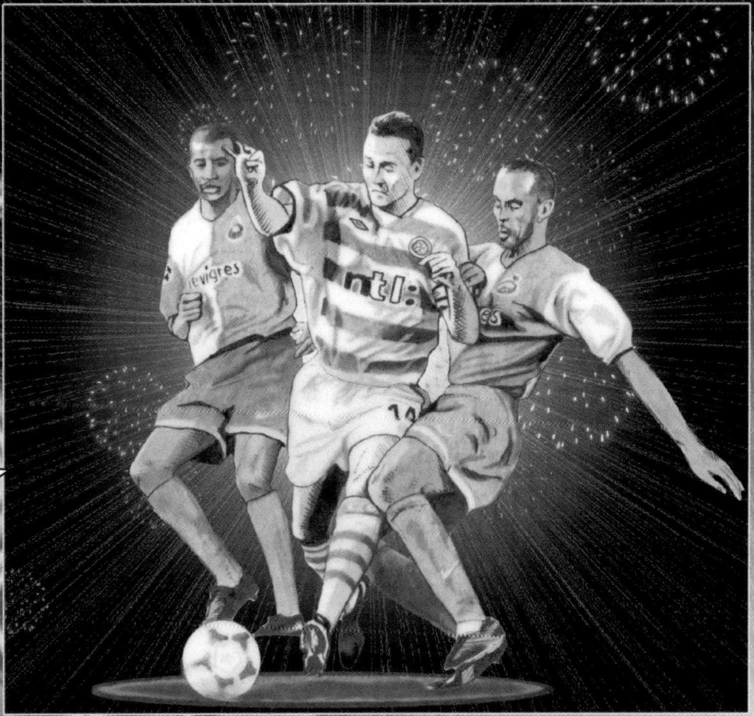

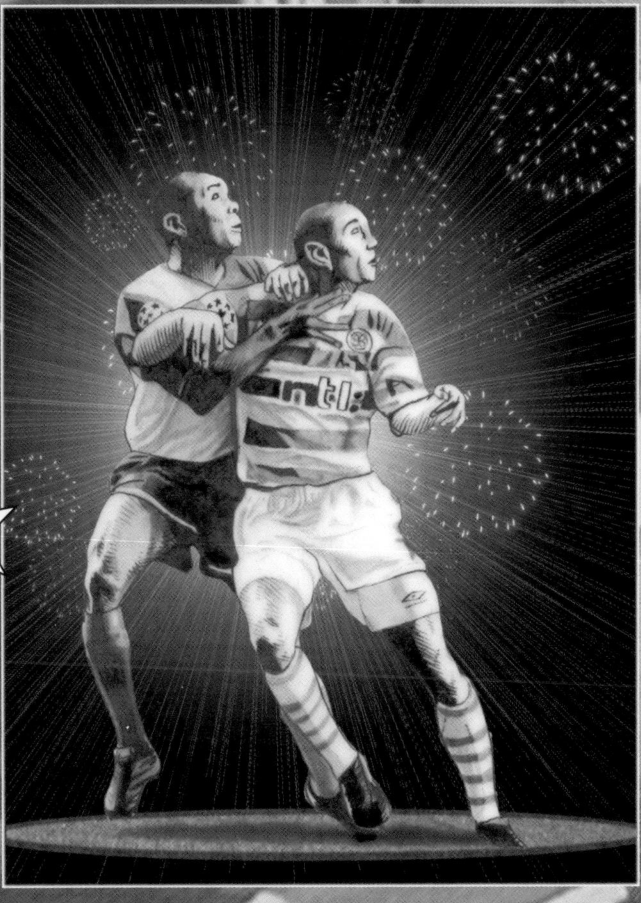

CELTIC DID WELL AT CELTIC PARK, WINNING ALL THEIR HOME GAMES, BUT THEY COULD NOT WIN AWAY FROM HOME OR EVEN MANAGE A DRAW. THIS WAS TO PROVE CRUCIAL. THE SCORES WERE:

<u>SEPTEMBER</u>

18TH: JUVENTUS 3—2 CELTIC
25TH: CELTIC 1—0 PORTO

<u>OCTOBER</u>

10TH: CELTIC 1—0 ROSENBORG
17TH: PORTO 3—0 CELTIC
23RD: ROSENBORG 2—0 CELTIC
31ST: CELTIC 4—3 JUVENTUS.

DESPITE FINISHING WITH A CREDITABLE NINE POINTS, CELTIC WENT OUT OF THE CHAMPIONS LEAGUE EVEN THOUGH SOME CLUBS HAD GONE THROUGH TO THE FINAL 16 WITH A LOWER POINTS TALLY. MARTIN O'NEILL HAD, HOWEVER, PUT CELTIC BACK ON THE EUROPEAN MAP AND THE FANS LOOKED FORWARD WITH EAGER ANTICIPATION TO THE FOLLOWING SEASON.

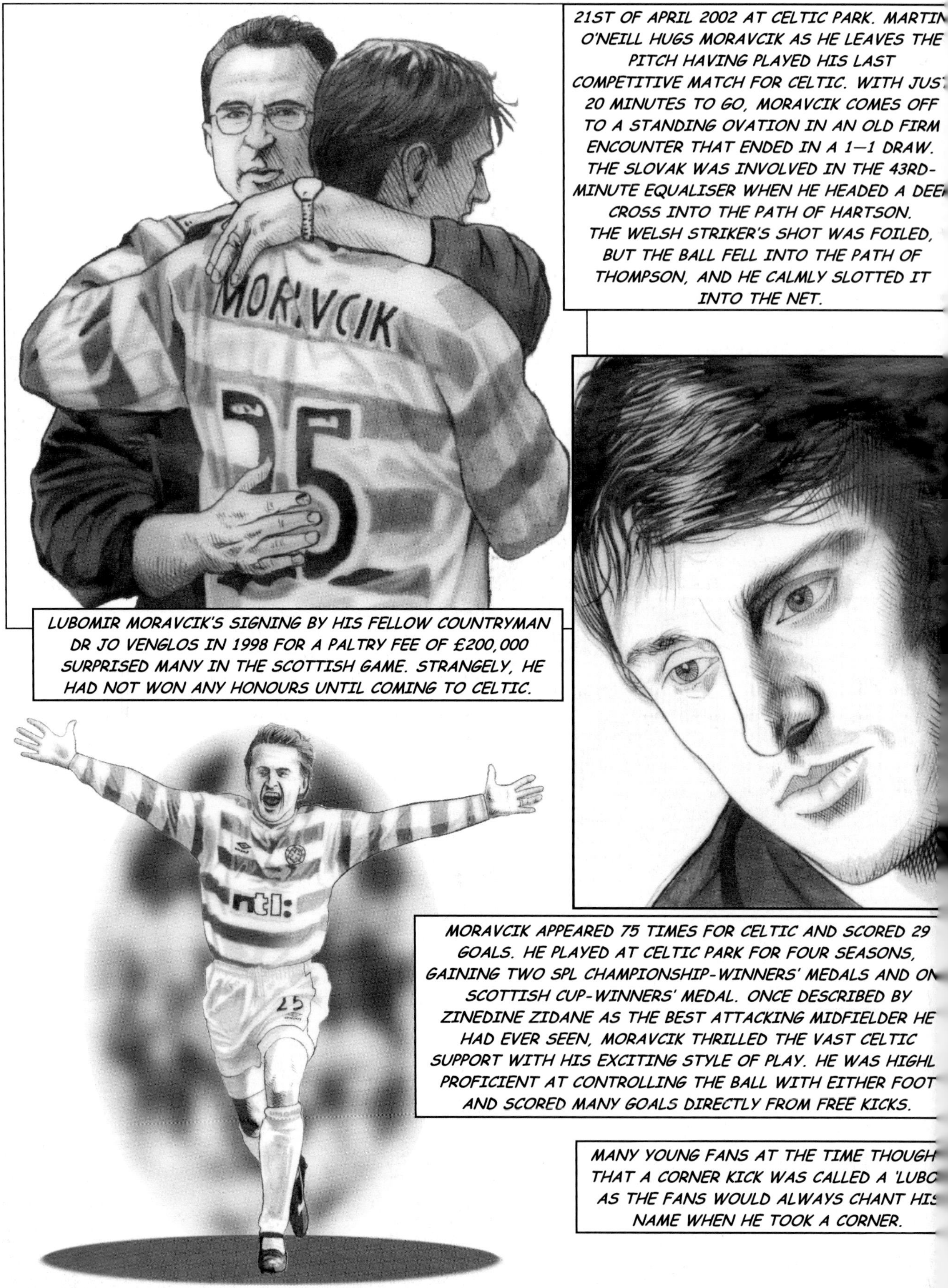
21ST OF APRIL 2002 AT CELTIC PARK. MARTIN O'NEILL HUGS MORAVCIK AS HE LEAVES THE PITCH HAVING PLAYED HIS LAST COMPETITIVE MATCH FOR CELTIC. WITH JUST 20 MINUTES TO GO, MORAVCIK COMES OFF TO A STANDING OVATION IN AN OLD FIRM ENCOUNTER THAT ENDED IN A 1—1 DRAW. THE SLOVAK WAS INVOLVED IN THE 43RD-MINUTE EQUALISER WHEN HE HEADED A DEEP CROSS INTO THE PATH OF HARTSON. THE WELSH STRIKER'S SHOT WAS FOILED, BUT THE BALL FELL INTO THE PATH OF THOMPSON, AND HE CALMLY SLOTTED IT INTO THE NET.
LUBOMIR MORAVCIK'S SIGNING BY HIS FELLOW COUNTRYMAN DR JO VENGLOS IN 1998 FOR A PALTRY FEE OF £200,000 SURPRISED MANY IN THE SCOTTISH GAME. STRANGELY, HE HAD NOT WON ANY HONOURS UNTIL COMING TO CELTIC.
MORAVCIK APPEARED 75 TIMES FOR CELTIC AND SCORED 29 GOALS. HE PLAYED AT CELTIC PARK FOR FOUR SEASONS, GAINING TWO SPL CHAMPIONSHIP-WINNERS' MEDALS AND ONE SCOTTISH CUP-WINNERS' MEDAL. ONCE DESCRIBED BY ZINEDINE ZIDANE AS THE BEST ATTACKING MIDFIELDER HE HAD EVER SEEN, MORAVCIK THRILLED THE VAST CELTIC SUPPORT WITH HIS EXCITING STYLE OF PLAY. HE WAS HIGHLY PROFICIENT AT CONTROLLING THE BALL WITH EITHER FOOT AND SCORED MANY GOALS DIRECTLY FROM FREE KICKS.
MANY YOUNG FANS AT THE TIME THOUGHT THAT A CORNER KICK WAS CALLED A 'LUBO' AS THE FANS WOULD ALWAYS CHANT HIS NAME WHEN HE TOOK A CORNER.

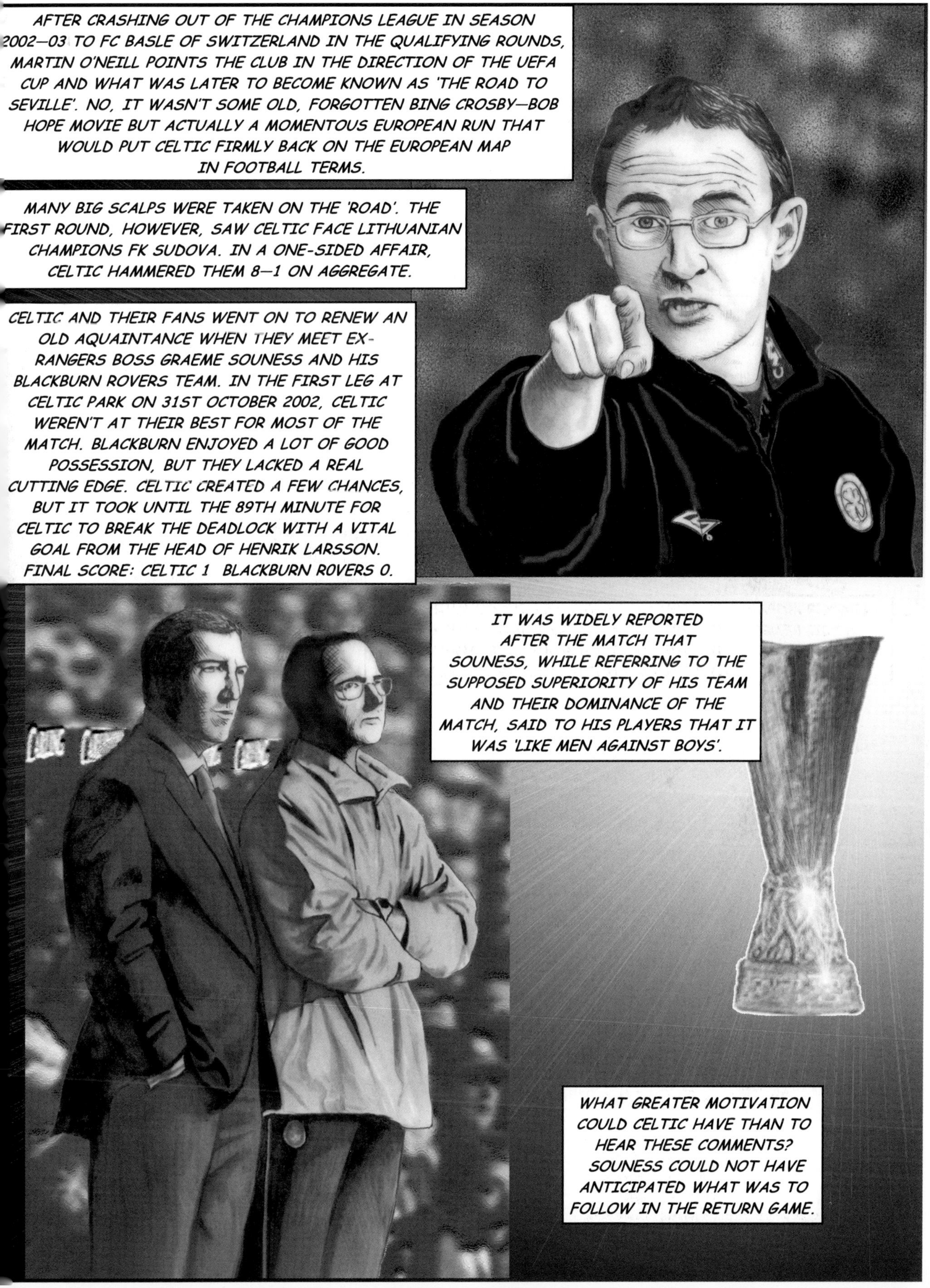
AFTER CRASHING OUT OF THE CHAMPIONS LEAGUE IN SEASON 2002–03 TO FC BASLE OF SWITZERLAND IN THE QUALIFYING ROUNDS, MARTIN O'NEILL POINTS THE CLUB IN THE DIRECTION OF THE UEFA CUP AND WHAT WAS LATER TO BECOME KNOWN AS 'THE ROAD TO SEVILLE'. NO, IT WASN'T SOME OLD, FORGOTTEN BING CROSBY–BOB HOPE MOVIE BUT ACTUALLY A MOMENTOUS EUROPEAN RUN THAT WOULD PUT CELTIC FIRMLY BACK ON THE EUROPEAN MAP IN FOOTBALL TERMS.
MANY BIG SCALPS WERE TAKEN ON THE 'ROAD'. THE FIRST ROUND, HOWEVER, SAW CELTIC FACE LITHUANIAN CHAMPIONS FK SUDOVA. IN A ONE-SIDED AFFAIR, CELTIC HAMMERED THEM 8–1 ON AGGREGATE.
CELTIC AND THEIR FANS WENT ON TO RENEW AN OLD AQUAINTANCE WHEN THEY MEET EX-RANGERS BOSS GRAEME SOUNESS AND HIS BLACKBURN ROVERS TEAM. IN THE FIRST LEG AT CELTIC PARK ON 31ST OCTOBER 2002, CELTIC WEREN'T AT THEIR BEST FOR MOST OF THE MATCH. BLACKBURN ENJOYED A LOT OF GOOD POSSESSION, BUT THEY LACKED A REAL CUTTING EDGE. CELTIC CREATED A FEW CHANCES, BUT IT TOOK UNTIL THE 89TH MINUTE FOR CELTIC TO BREAK THE DEADLOCK WITH A VITAL GOAL FROM THE HEAD OF HENRIK LARSSON. FINAL SCORE: CELTIC 1 BLACKBURN ROVERS 0.
IT WAS WIDELY REPORTED AFTER THE MATCH THAT SOUNESS, WHILE REFERRING TO THE SUPPOSED SUPERIORITY OF HIS TEAM AND THEIR DOMINANCE OF THE MATCH, SAID TO HIS PLAYERS THAT IT WAS 'LIKE MEN AGAINST BOYS'.
WHAT GREATER MOTIVATION COULD CELTIC HAVE THAN TO HEAR THESE COMMENTS? SOUNESS COULD NOT HAVE ANTICIPATED WHAT WAS TO FOLLOW IN THE RETURN GAME.

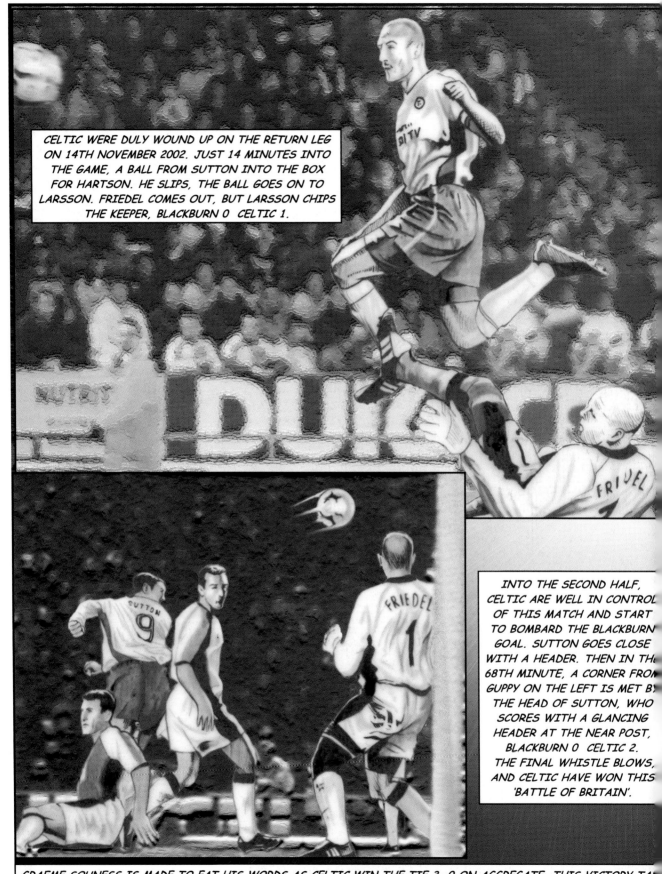

CELTIC WERE DULY WOUND UP ON THE RETURN LEG ON 14TH NOVEMBER 2002. JUST 14 MINUTES INTO THE GAME, A BALL FROM SUTTON INTO THE BOX FOR HARTSON. HE SLIPS, THE BALL GOES ON TO LARSSON. FRIEDEL COMES OUT, BUT LARSSON CHIPS THE KEEPER, BLACKBURN 0 CELTIC 1.

INTO THE SECOND HALF, CELTIC ARE WELL IN CONTROL OF THIS MATCH AND START TO BOMBARD THE BLACKBURN GOAL. SUTTON GOES CLOSE WITH A HEADER. THEN IN THE 68TH MINUTE, A CORNER FROM GUPPY ON THE LEFT IS MET BY THE HEAD OF SUTTON, WHO SCORES WITH A GLANCING HEADER AT THE NEAR POST, BLACKBURN 0 CELTIC 2. THE FINAL WHISTLE BLOWS, AND CELTIC HAVE WON THIS 'BATTLE OF BRITAIN'.

GRAEME SOUNESS IS MADE TO EAT HIS WORDS AS CELTIC WIN THE TIE 3—0 ON AGGREGATE. THIS VICTORY TAKES CELTIC INTO THE DRAW FOR THE THIRD ROUND, AND EUROPE BEGINS TO TAKE NOTICE OF MARTIN O'NEILL'S ME

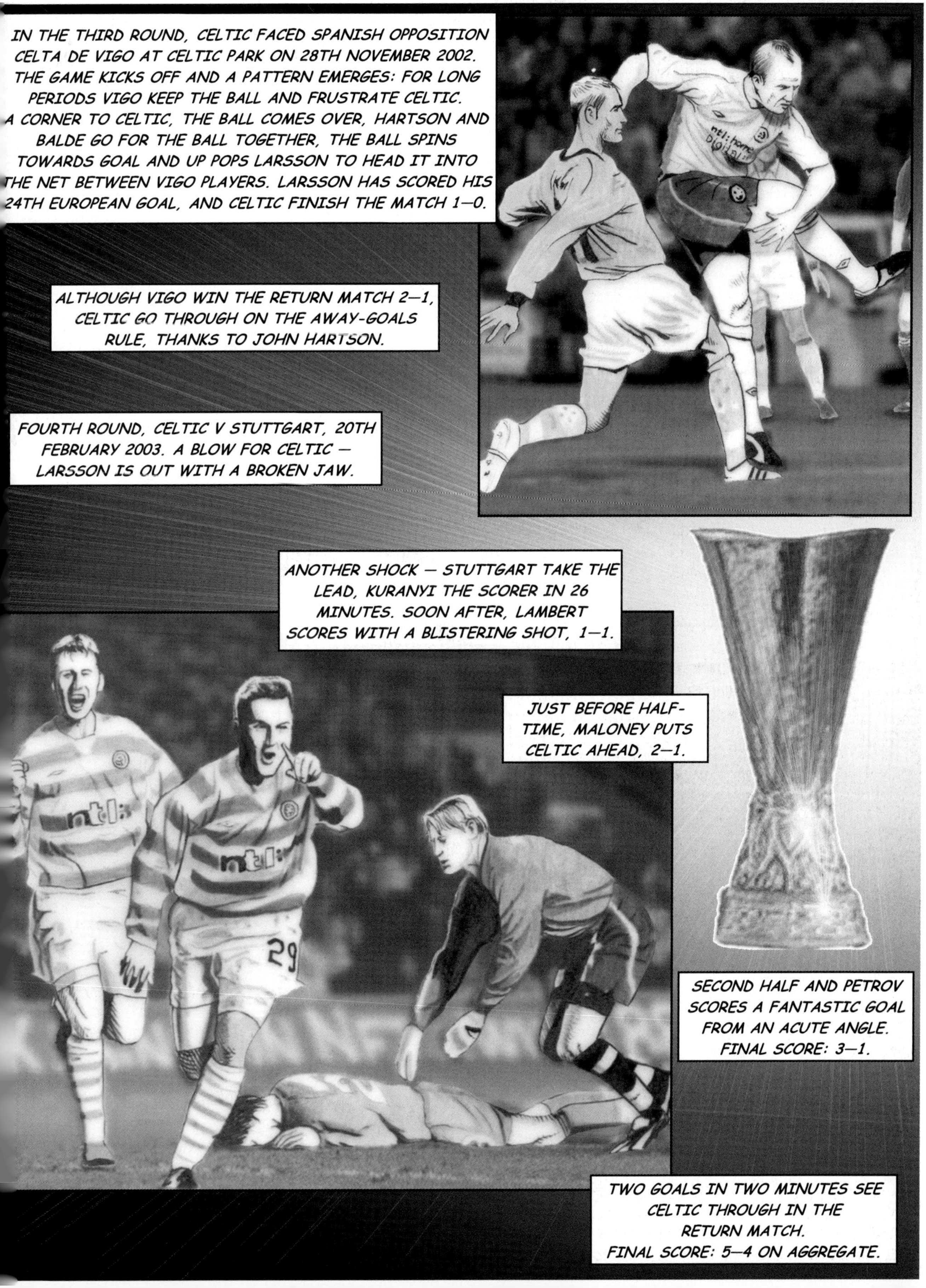
IN THE THIRD ROUND, CELTIC FACED SPANISH OPPOSITION CELTA DE VIGO AT CELTIC PARK ON 28TH NOVEMBER 2002. THE GAME KICKS OFF AND A PATTERN EMERGES: FOR LONG PERIODS VIGO KEEP THE BALL AND FRUSTRATE CELTIC. A CORNER TO CELTIC, THE BALL COMES OVER, HARTSON AND BALDE GO FOR THE BALL TOGETHER, THE BALL SPINS TOWARDS GOAL AND UP POPS LARSSON TO HEAD IT INTO THE NET BETWEEN VIGO PLAYERS. LARSSON HAS SCORED HIS 24TH EUROPEAN GOAL, AND CELTIC FINISH THE MATCH 1—0.
ALTHOUGH VIGO WIN THE RETURN MATCH 2—1, CELTIC GO THROUGH ON THE AWAY-GOALS RULE, THANKS TO JOHN HARTSON.
FOURTH ROUND, CELTIC V STUTTGART, 20TH FEBRUARY 2003. A BLOW FOR CELTIC — LARSSON IS OUT WITH A BROKEN JAW.
ANOTHER SHOCK — STUTTGART TAKE THE LEAD, KURANYI THE SCORER IN 26 MINUTES. SOON AFTER, LAMBERT SCORES WITH A BLISTERING SHOT, 1—1.
JUST BEFORE HALF-TIME, MALONEY PUTS CELTIC AHEAD, 2—1.
ntl:
ntl:
29
SECOND HALF AND PETROV SCORES A FANTASTIC GOAL FROM AN ACUTE ANGLE. FINAL SCORE: 3—1.
TWO GOALS IN TWO MINUTES SEE CELTIC THROUGH IN THE RETURN MATCH. FINAL SCORE: 5—4 ON AGGREGATE.

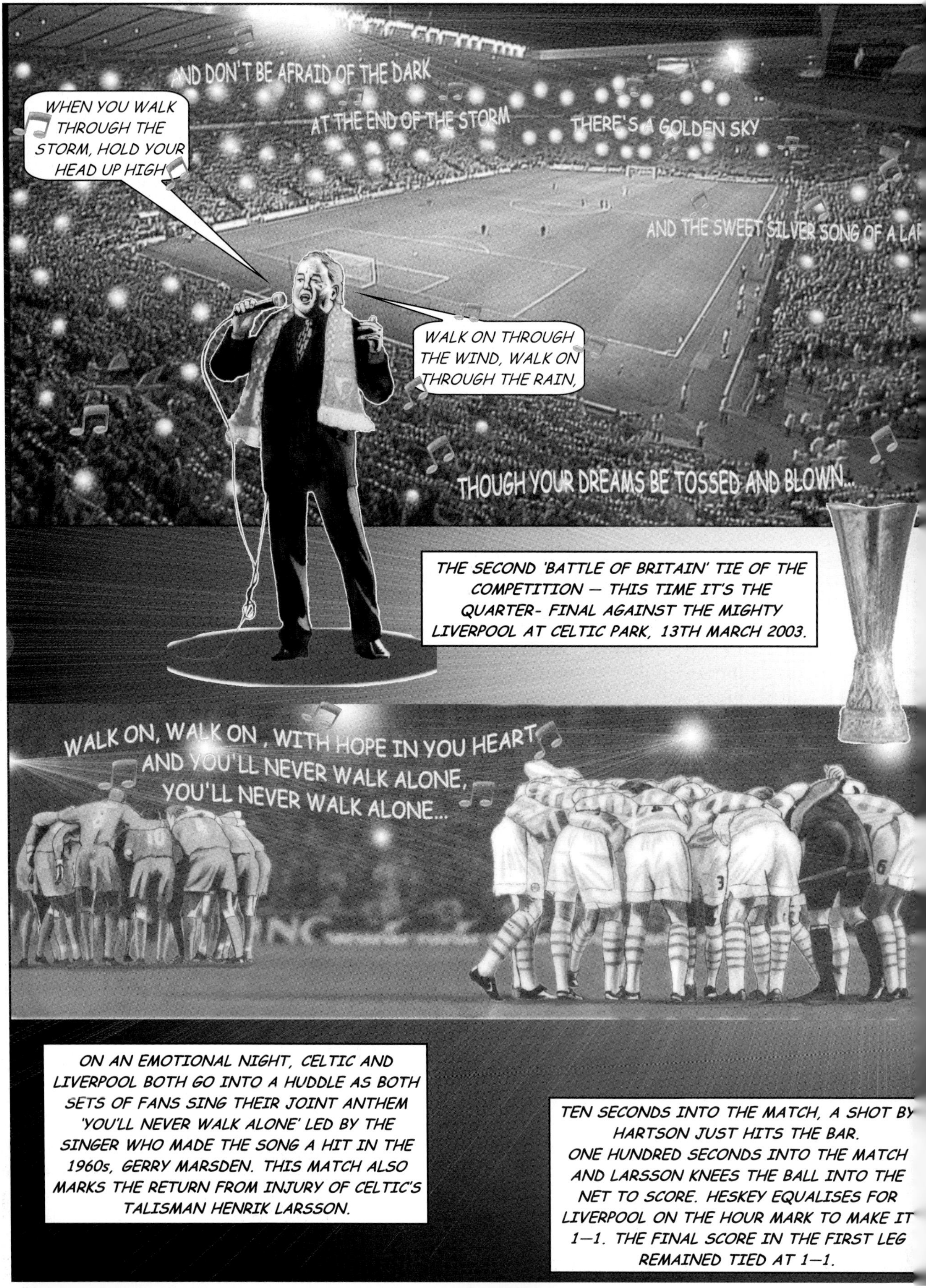

WHEN YOU WALK THROUGH THE STORM, HOLD YOUR HEAD UP HIGH
AND DON'T BE AFRAID OF THE DARK
AT THE END OF THE STORM
THERE'S A GOLDEN SKY
AND THE SWEET SILVER SONG OF A LA
WALK ON THROUGH THE WIND, WALK ON THROUGH THE RAIN,
THOUGH YOUR DREAMS BE TOSSED AND BLOWN...
THE SECOND 'BATTLE OF BRITAIN' TIE OF THE COMPETITION – THIS TIME IT'S THE QUARTER- FINAL AGAINST THE MIGHTY LIVERPOOL AT CELTIC PARK, 13TH MARCH 2003.
WALK ON, WALK ON , WITH HOPE IN YOU HEART
AND YOU'LL NEVER WALK ALONE,
YOU'LL NEVER WALK ALONE...
ON AN EMOTIONAL NIGHT, CELTIC AND LIVERPOOL BOTH GO INTO A HUDDLE AS BOTH SETS OF FANS SING THEIR JOINT ANTHEM 'YOU'LL NEVER WALK ALONE' LED BY THE SINGER WHO MADE THE SONG A HIT IN THE 1960s, GERRY MARSDEN. THIS MATCH ALSO MARKS THE RETURN FROM INJURY OF CELTIC'S TALISMAN HENRIK LARSSON.
TEN SECONDS INTO THE MATCH, A SHOT BY HARTSON JUST HITS THE BAR.
ONE HUNDRED SECONDS INTO THE MATCH AND LARSSON KNEES THE BALL INTO THE NET TO SCORE. HESKEY EQUALISES FOR LIVERPOOL ON THE HOUR MARK TO MAKE IT 1–1. THE FINAL SCORE IN THE FIRST LEG REMAINED TIED AT 1–1.

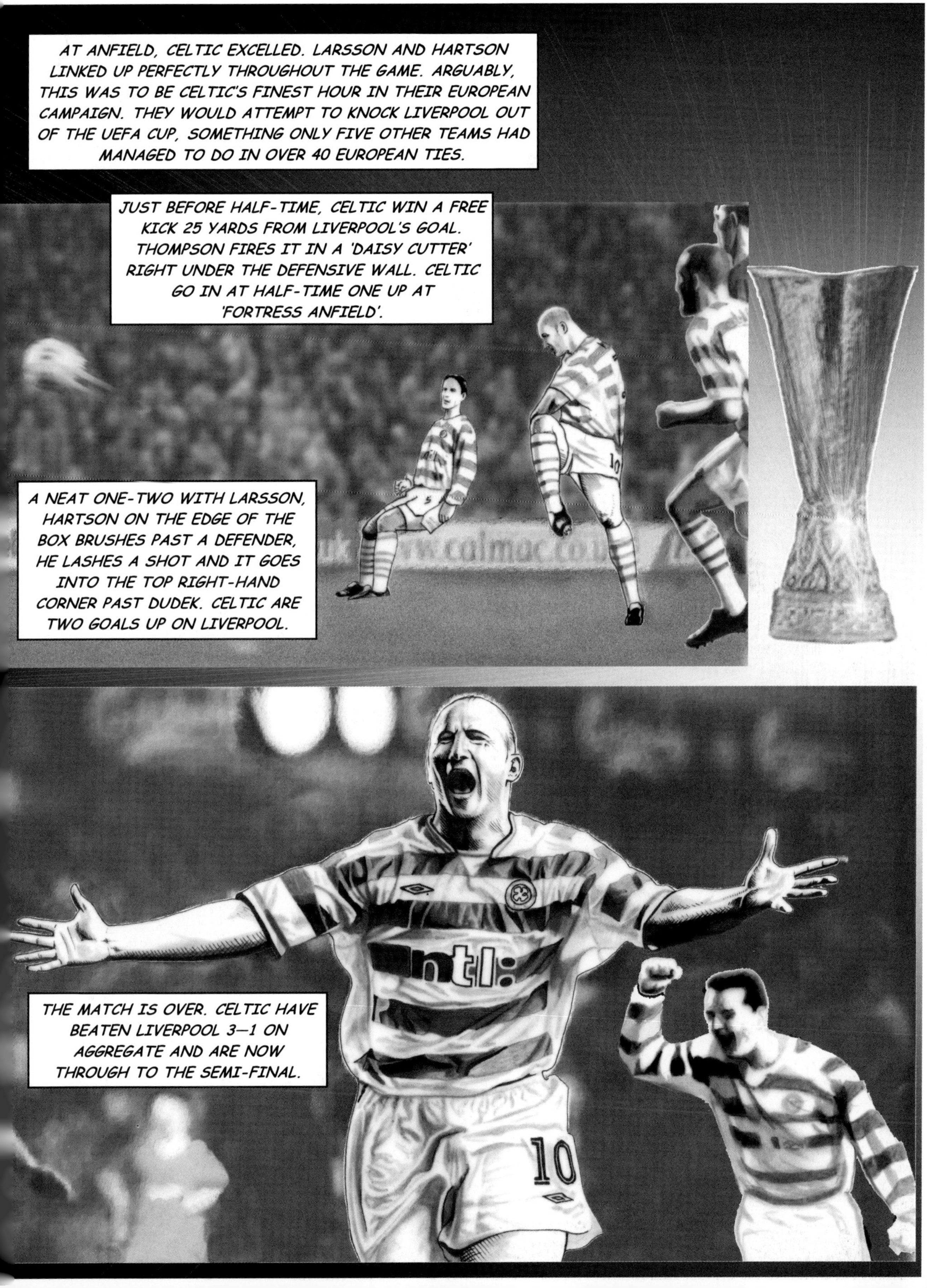
AT ANFIELD, CELTIC EXCELLED. LARSSON AND HARTSON LINKED UP PERFECTLY THROUGHOUT THE GAME. ARGUABLY, THIS WAS TO BE CELTIC'S FINEST HOUR IN THEIR EUROPEAN CAMPAIGN. THEY WOULD ATTEMPT TO KNOCK LIVERPOOL OUT OF THE UEFA CUP, SOMETHING ONLY FIVE OTHER TEAMS HAD MANAGED TO DO IN OVER 40 EUROPEAN TIES.
JUST BEFORE HALF-TIME, CELTIC WIN A FREE KICK 25 YARDS FROM LIVERPOOL'S GOAL. THOMPSON FIRES IT IN A 'DAISY CUTTER' RIGHT UNDER THE DEFENSIVE WALL. CELTIC GO IN AT HALF-TIME ONE UP AT 'FORTRESS ANFIELD'.
A NEAT ONE-TWO WITH LARSSON, HARTSON ON THE EDGE OF THE BOX BRUSHES PAST A DEFENDER, HE LASHES A SHOT AND IT GOES INTO THE TOP RIGHT-HAND CORNER PAST DUDEK. CELTIC ARE TWO GOALS UP ON LIVERPOOL.
THE MATCH IS OVER. CELTIC HAVE BEATEN LIVERPOOL 3—1 ON AGGREGATE AND ARE NOW THROUGH TO THE SEMI-FINAL.

AFTER A 1—1 DRAW AT CELTIC PARK ON 10TH APRIL 2003, CELTIC TRAVEL TO PORTUGAL FOR THE RETURN LEG OF THE SEMI-FINAL WITH BOAVISTA.

IN THE SECOND LEG ON 24TH APRIL, BOAVISTA CONTINUE THE NEGATIVE TACTICS EMPLOYED AGAINST CELTIC IN THE FIRST LEG AT CELTIC PARK, KNOWING THE DRAW WOULD TAKE THEM THROUGH AT CELTIC'S EXPENSE.

THE GAME IS A TENSE AFFAIR, WITH FEW CHANCES FOR CELTIC. THE FIRST HALF ENDS GOALLESS, TIME IS RUNNING OUT FOR CELTIC!

THE GAME ENTERS THE LAST 15 MINUTES STILL GOALLESS. IT BEGINS TO LOOK LIKE CELTIC ARE GOING TO RUE LARSSON'S PENALTY MISS AT CELTIC PARK!

THE 78TH MINUTE ARRIVES AND LARSSON STEPS UP TO REDEEM HIMSELF AND SEND CELTIC INTO THE FINAL. CELTIC ARE ON THE ATTACK, LARSSON FLICKS THE BALL TOWARDS HARTSON, BUT THE PASS IS BLOCKED. IT BREAKS TO LARSSON, WHO TAKES IT ON HIS LEFT FOOT AND DEFTLY CHIPS THE KEEPER. CELTIC ARE ONE GOAL UP, ENOUGH TO WIN THE GAME AND THE TIE.

THE CELTIC SUPPORT GO WILD WITH JOY. THE BHOYS HAVE DONE IT! CELTIC ARE IN THEIR FIRST EUROPEAN FINAL IN 33 YEARS! THE OPPONENTS FOR THE FINAL WILL BE F.C. PORTO FROM PORTUGAL, THE VENUE — SEVILLE IN SPAIN.

BEFORE THEN, THE FANS WOULD HAVE SOME FUN

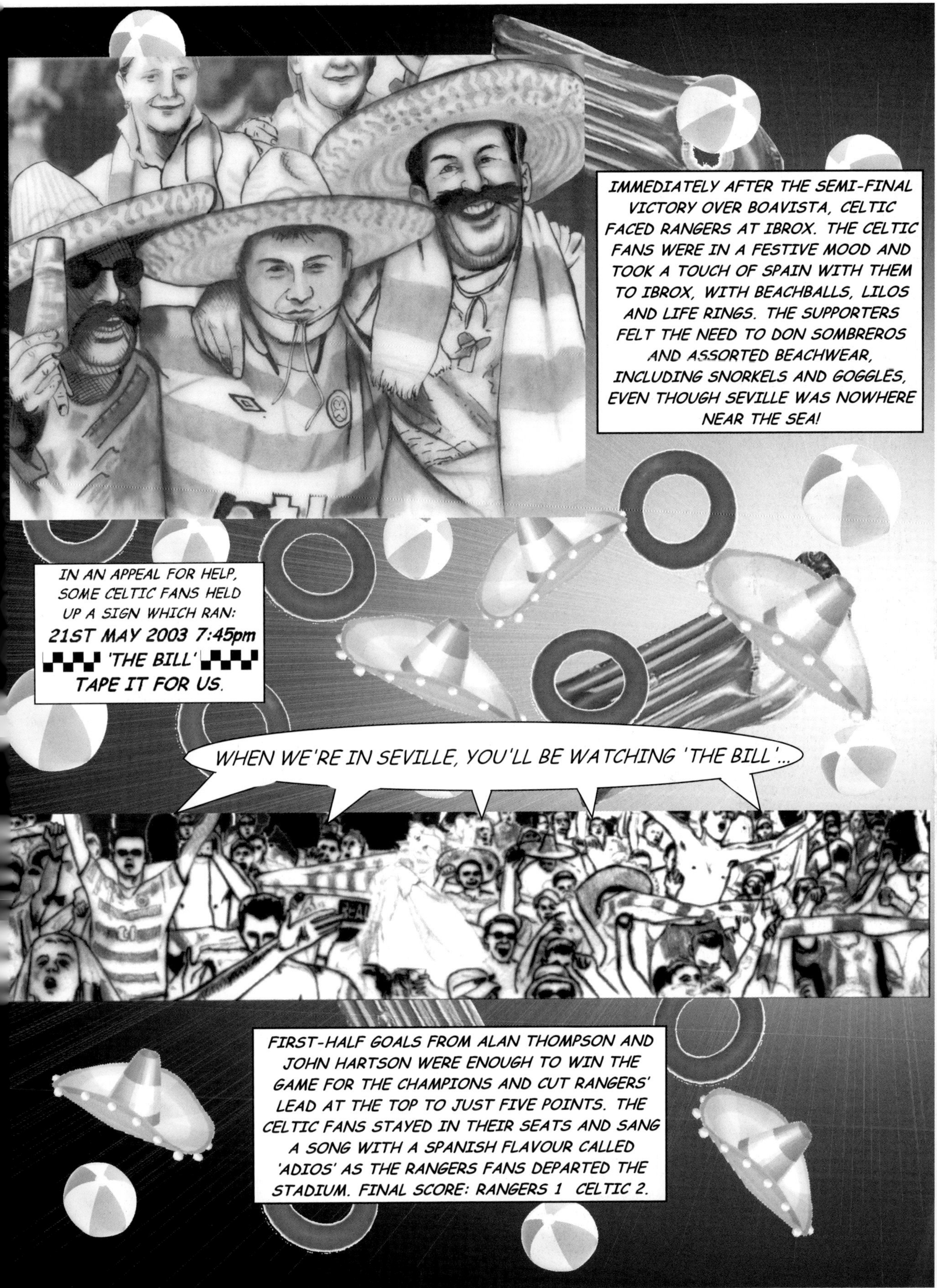
IMMEDIATELY AFTER THE SEMI-FINAL VICTORY OVER BOAVISTA, CELTIC FACED RANGERS AT IBROX. THE CELTIC FANS WERE IN A FESTIVE MOOD AND TOOK A TOUCH OF SPAIN WITH THEM TO IBROX, WITH BEACHBALLS, LILOS AND LIFE RINGS. THE SUPPORTERS FELT THE NEED TO DON SOMBREROS AND ASSORTED BEACHWEAR, INCLUDING SNORKELS AND GOGGLES, EVEN THOUGH SEVILLE WAS NOWHERE NEAR THE SEA!
IN AN APPEAL FOR HELP, SOME CELTIC FANS HELD UP A SIGN WHICH RAN:
21ST MAY 2003 7:45pm 'THE BILL' TAPE IT FOR US.
WHEN WE'RE IN SEVILLE, YOU'LL BE WATCHING 'THE BILL'...
FIRST-HALF GOALS FROM ALAN THOMPSON AND JOHN HARTSON WERE ENOUGH TO WIN THE GAME FOR THE CHAMPIONS AND CUT RANGERS' LEAD AT THE TOP TO JUST FIVE POINTS. THE CELTIC FANS STAYED IN THEIR SEATS AND SANG A SONG WITH A SPANISH FLAVOUR CALLED 'ADIOS' AS THE RANGERS FANS DEPARTED THE STADIUM. FINAL SCORE: RANGERS 1 CELTIC 2.

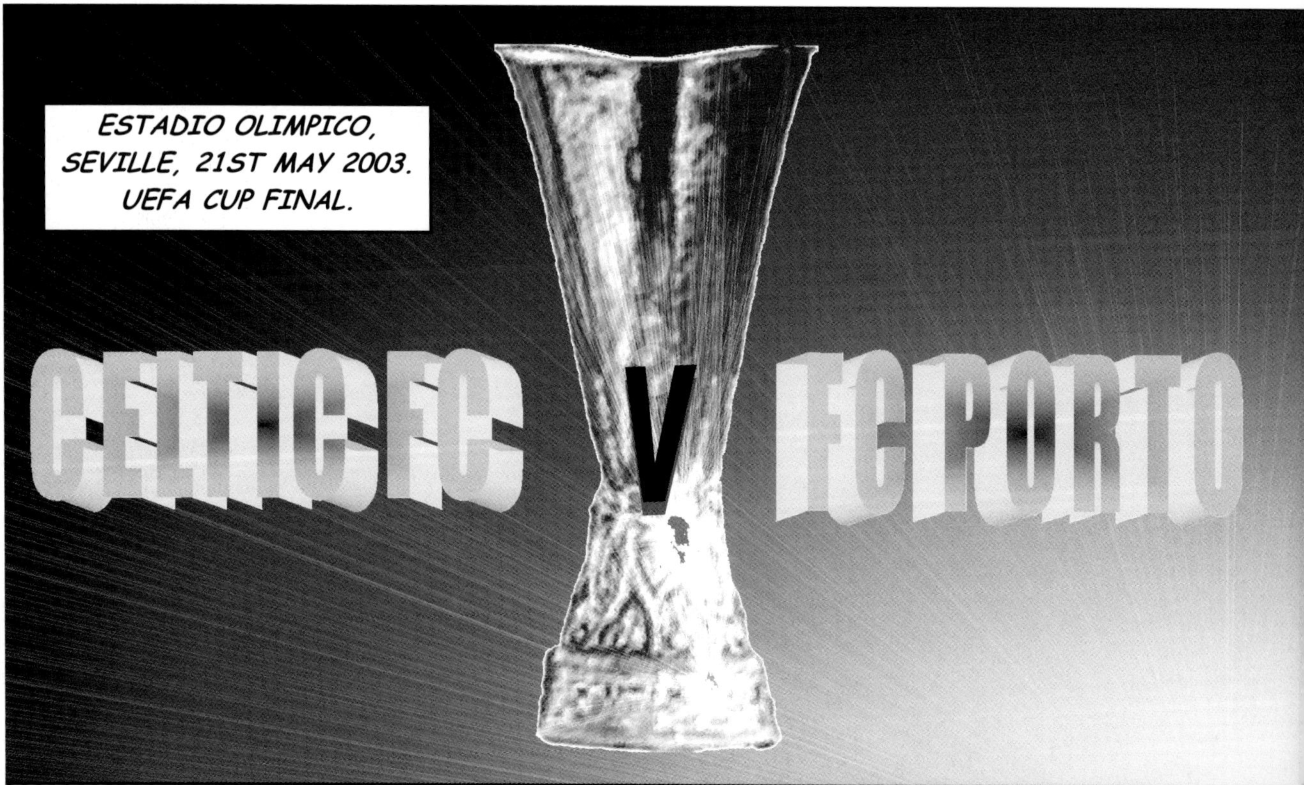
ESTADIO OLIMPICO, SEVILLE, 21ST MAY 2003. UEFA CUP FINAL.
CELTIC FC V FC PORTO

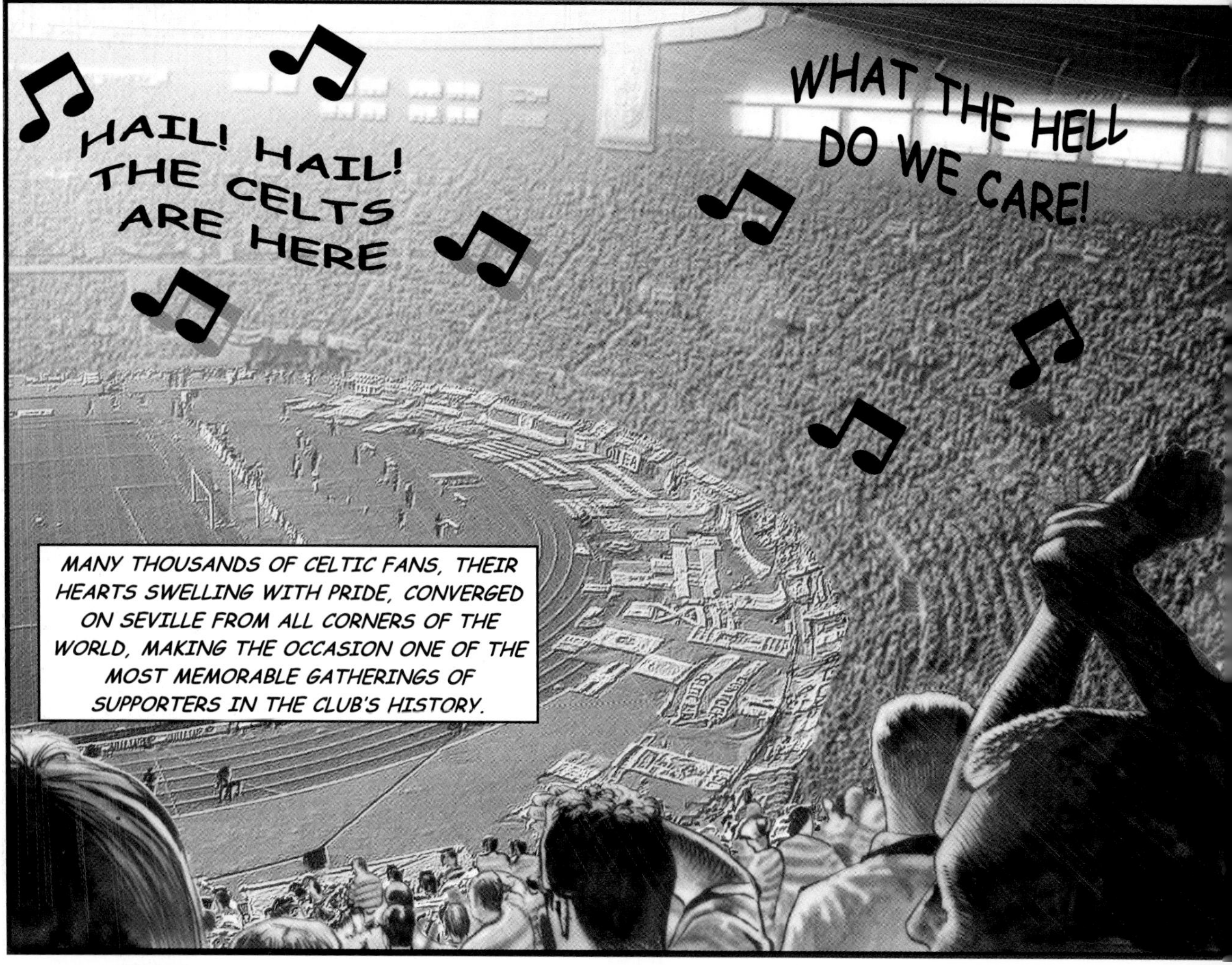
HAIL! HAIL! THE CELTS ARE HERE
WHAT THE HELL DO WE CARE!
MANY THOUSANDS OF CELTIC FANS, THEIR HEARTS SWELLING WITH PRIDE, CONVERGED ON SEVILLE FROM ALL CORNERS OF THE WORLD, MAKING THE OCCASION ONE OF THE MOST MEMORABLE GATHERINGS OF SUPPORTERS IN THE CLUB'S HISTORY.

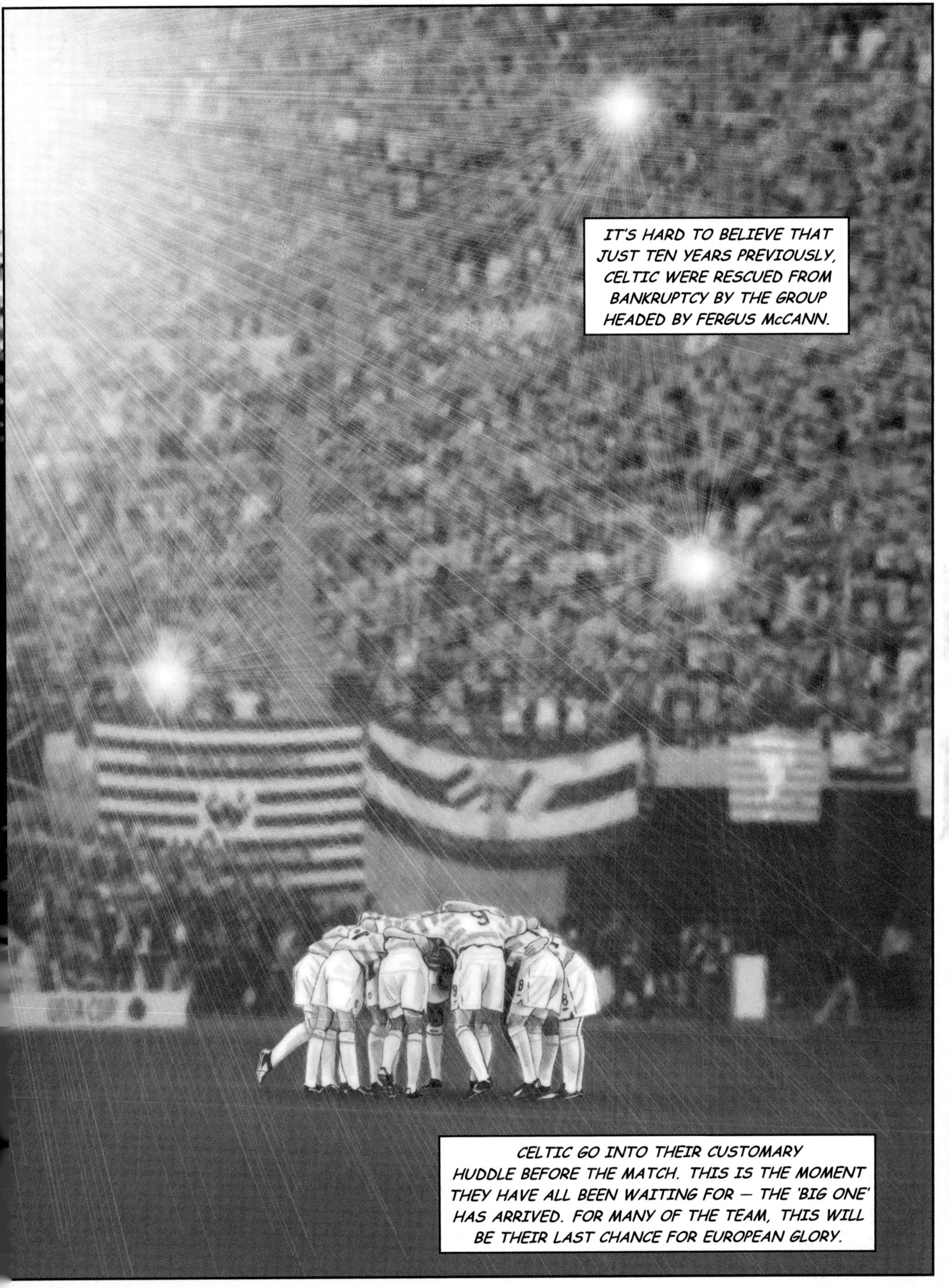
IT'S HARD TO BELIEVE THAT JUST TEN YEARS PREVIOUSLY, CELTIC WERE RESCUED FROM BANKRUPTCY BY THE GROUP HEADED BY FERGUS McCANN.
CELTIC GO INTO THEIR CUSTOMARY HUDDLE BEFORE THE MATCH. THIS IS THE MOMENT THEY HAVE ALL BEEN WAITING FOR – THE 'BIG ONE' HAS ARRIVED. FOR MANY OF THE TEAM, THIS WILL BE THEIR LAST CHANCE FOR EUROPEAN GLORY.

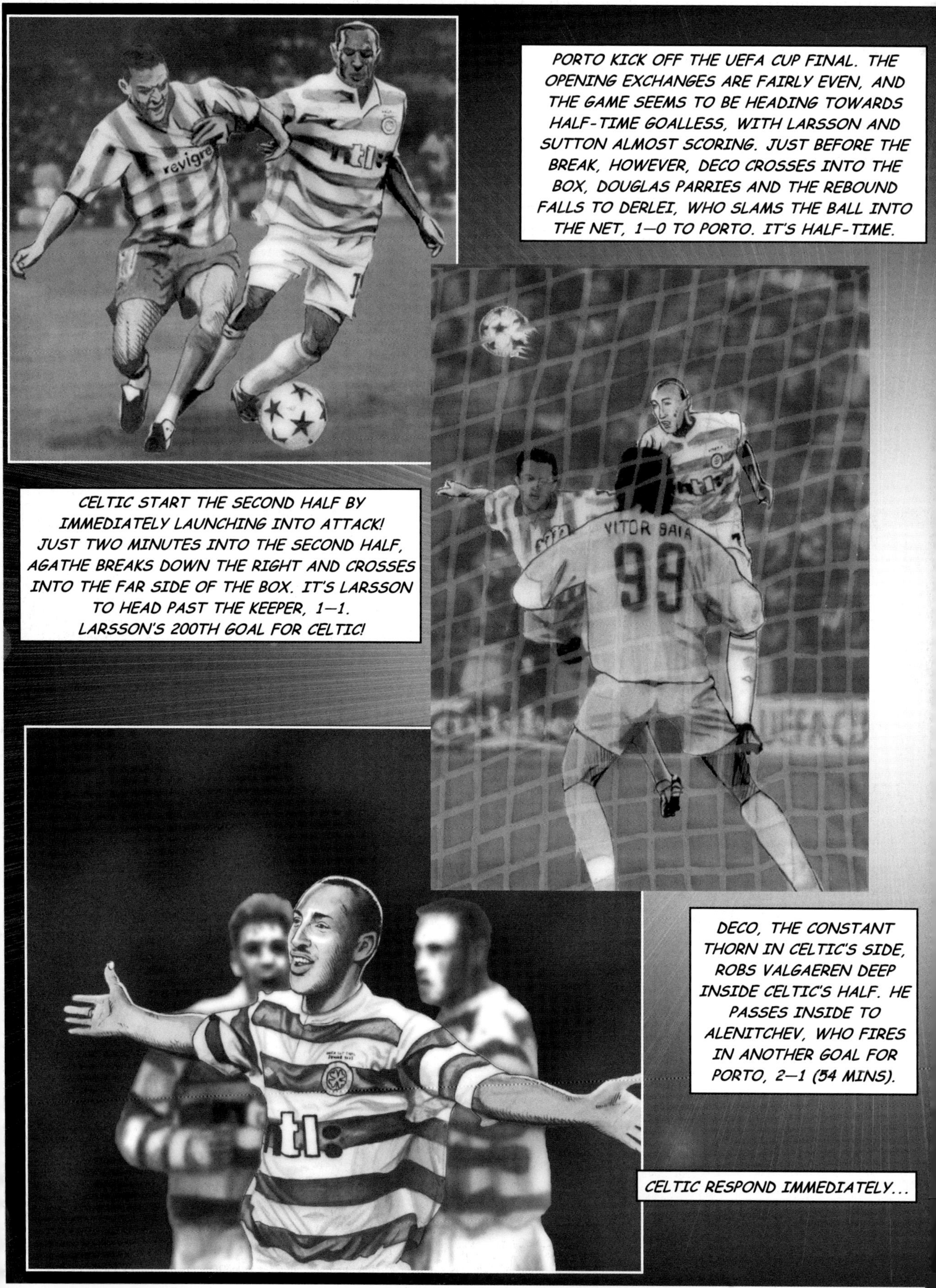
PORTO KICK OFF THE UEFA CUP FINAL. THE OPENING EXCHANGES ARE FAIRLY EVEN, AND THE GAME SEEMS TO BE HEADING TOWARDS HALF-TIME GOALLESS, WITH LARSSON AND SUTTON ALMOST SCORING. JUST BEFORE THE BREAK, HOWEVER, DECO CROSSES INTO THE BOX, DOUGLAS PARRIES AND THE REBOUND FALLS TO DERLEI, WHO SLAMS THE BALL INTO THE NET, 1—0 TO PORTO. IT'S HALF-TIME.
CELTIC START THE SECOND HALF BY IMMEDIATELY LAUNCHING INTO ATTACK! JUST TWO MINUTES INTO THE SECOND HALF, AGATHE BREAKS DOWN THE RIGHT AND CROSSES INTO THE FAR SIDE OF THE BOX. IT'S LARSSON TO HEAD PAST THE KEEPER, 1—1. LARSSON'S 200TH GOAL FOR CELTIC!
VITOR BAIA
99
DECO, THE CONSTANT THORN IN CELTIC'S SIDE, ROBS VALGAEREN DEEP INSIDE CELTIC'S HALF. HE PASSES INSIDE TO ALENITCHEV, WHO FIRES IN ANOTHER GOAL FOR PORTO, 2—1 (54 MINS).
CELTIC RESPOND IMMEDIATELY...

CORNER TO CELTIC. THOMPSON SWINGS IT OVER. IT'S LARSSON WITH A BULLET HEADER TO EQUALISE AGAIN!

THE SCORE REMAINS TIED AT 2–2 AT 90 MINUTES, SO THE GAME ENTERS EXTRA TIME. CELTIC ARE ON TOP, THOUGH, AND LOOK THE MORE LIKELY TEAM TO SCORE.

BUT DISASTER STRIKES WHEN BALDE IS SENT OFF FOR A BADLY TIMED TACKLE. WITH TEN MEN, CELTIC ARE NOW UP AGAINST IT BUT STILL MANAGE TO CREATE CHANCES.

MALONEY COMES ON FOR PETROV. HE BEATS TWO MEN AND CROSSES INTO THE BOX FOR LARSSON! BUT THE BALL IS CLEARED.

SECOND PERIOD OF EXTRA TIME, THE BALL COMES INTO CELTIC'S BOX, DOUGLAS FUMBLES, IT FALLS TO DERLEI, WHO SHOOTS PAST THE STRANDED KEEPER, 3–2 TO PORTO. CELTIC FIGHT BACK, TRYING TO EQUALISE AGAIN, BUT IT'S NOT TO BE THIS TIME AND ALL TOO SOON THE FULL-TIME WHISTLE BLOWS. IT'S ALL OVER!

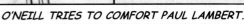

O'NEILL TRIES TO COMFORT PAUL LAMBERT.

THE SEASON'S DREAM HAS ENDED, BUT CELTIC ARE BACK IN THE EUROPEAN TOP FLIGHT ONCE MORE AND INTEND TO STAY!

NEIL LENNON IS DISTRAUGHT.

A SMALL CONSOLATION ARRIVES IN THE SHAPE OF THE AWARDS AND PRAISE GIVEN TO THE CELTIC SUPPORTERS FOR THEIR PART IN MAKING THE UEFA CUP FINAL A COLOURFUL OCCASION AND BEING SUCH A CREDIT TO THE CLUB.

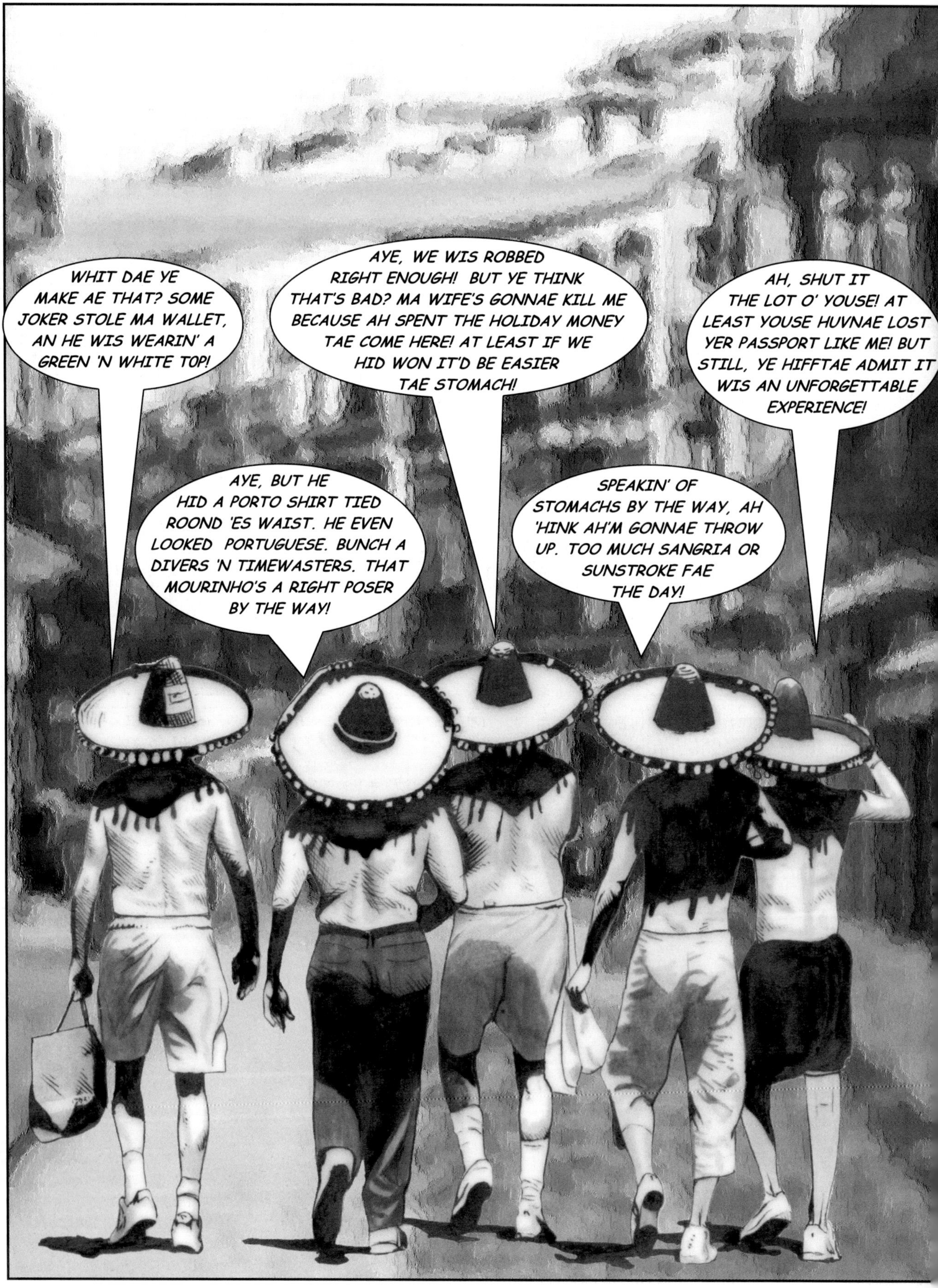
WHIT DAE YE MAKE AE THAT? SOME JOKER STOLE MA WALLET, AN HE WIS WEARIN' A GREEN 'N WHITE TOP!
AYE, BUT HE HID A PORTO SHIRT TIED ROOND 'ES WAIST. HE EVEN LOOKED PORTUGUESE. BUNCH A DIVERS 'N TIMEWASTERS. THAT MOURINHO'S A RIGHT POSER BY THE WAY!
AYE, WE WIS ROBBED RIGHT ENOUGH! BUT YE THINK THAT'S BAD? MA WIFE'S GONNAE KILL ME BECAUSE AH SPENT THE HOLIDAY MONEY TAE COME HERE! AT LEAST IF WE HID WON IT'D BE EASIER TAE STOMACH!
SPEAKIN' OF STOMACHS BY THE WAY, AH 'HINK AH'M GONNAE THROW UP. TOO MUCH SANGRIA OR SUNSTROKE FAE THE DAY!
AH, SHUT IT THE LOT O' YOUSE! AT LEAST YOUSE HUVNAE LOST YER PASSPORT LIKE ME! BUT STILL, YE HIFFTAE ADMIT IT WIS AN UNFORGETTABLE EXPERIENCE!

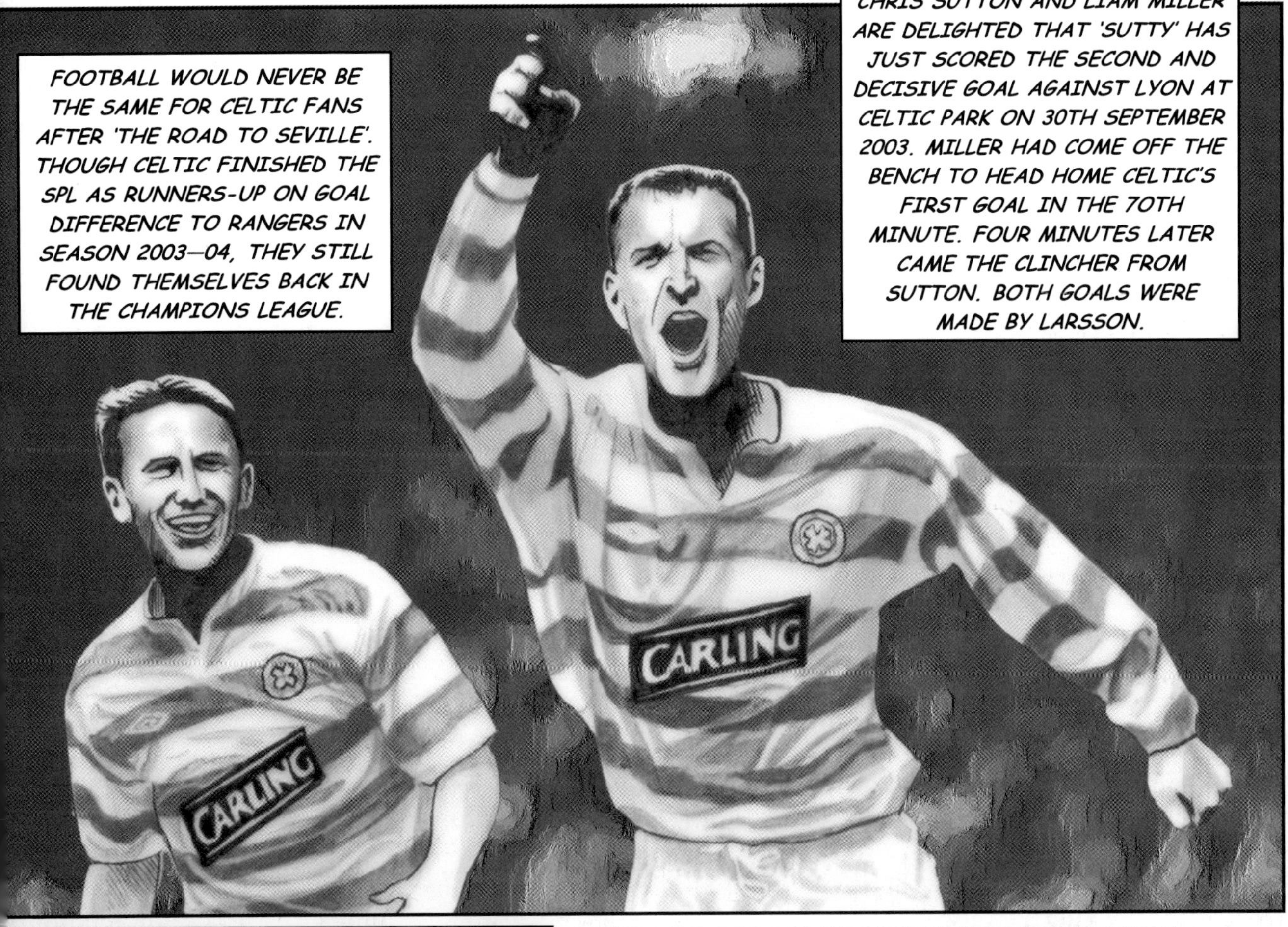
FOOTBALL WOULD NEVER BE THE SAME FOR CELTIC FANS AFTER 'THE ROAD TO SEVILLE'. THOUGH CELTIC FINISHED THE SPL AS RUNNERS-UP ON GOAL DIFFERENCE TO RANGERS IN SEASON 2003–04, THEY STILL FOUND THEMSELVES BACK IN THE CHAMPIONS LEAGUE.
CHRIS SUTTON AND LIAM MILLER ARE DELIGHTED THAT 'SUTTY' HAS JUST SCORED THE SECOND AND DECISIVE GOAL AGAINST LYON AT CELTIC PARK ON 30TH SEPTEMBER 2003. MILLER HAD COME OFF THE BENCH TO HEAD HOME CELTIC'S FIRST GOAL IN THE 70TH MINUTE. FOUR MINUTES LATER CAME THE CLINCHER FROM SUTTON. BOTH GOALS WERE MADE BY LARSSON.
CARLING
CARLING

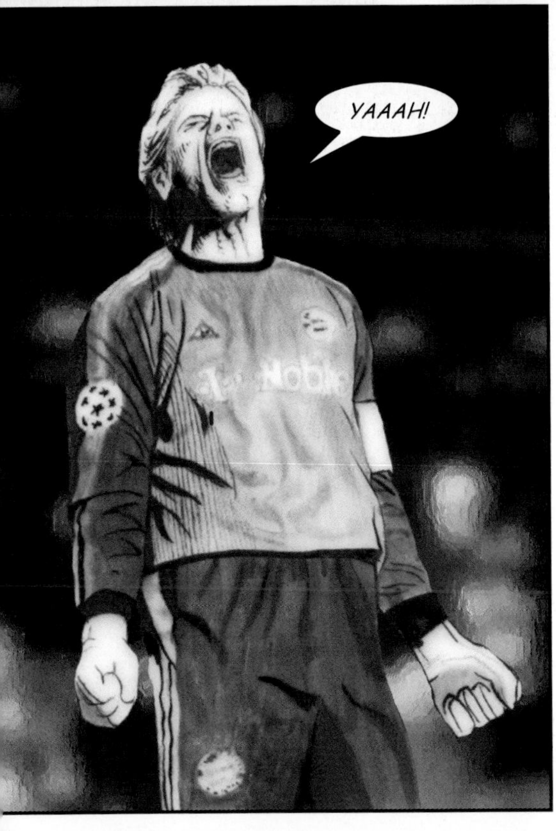
YAAAH!

OLIVER KAHN, KEEPER OF BAYERN MUNICH, IS BESIDE HIMSELF WITH JOY AFTER DRAWING WITH CELTIC 0–0 ON 25TH NOVEMBER 2003 AT CELTIC PARK IN THE CHAMPIONS LEAGUE. CELTIC'S RECORD WAS SO FORMIDABLE UNDER MARTIN O'NEILL THAT CELTIC USUALLY WON THEIR HOME GAMES IN THAT PARTICULAR COMPETITION. KAHN TREATED THE GOALLESS DRAW ALMOST LIKE A VICTORY. THE TRUTH WAS, HOWEVER, CELTIC'S RECORD THAT YEAR WAS DISAPPOINTING. HAD THEY WON AGAINST BAYERN, THEY WOULD HAVE QUALIFIED WITH TEN POINTS AND PIPPED BAYERN INSTEAD OF DROPPING OUT WITH ONLY SEVEN POINTS. STILL, THERE WAS THE UEFA CUP TO LOOK FORWARD TO, AND MEMORIES OF SEVILLE CAME FLOODING BACK.

<u>CHAMPIONS LEAGUE GROUP STAGE, GROUP A:</u>

17TH SEPTEMBER 2003: BAYERN MUNICH 2 CELTIC 1
30TH SEPTEMBER: CELTIC 2 OLYMPIQUE LYONNAIS 0
21ST OCTOBER: ANDERLECHT 1 CELTIC 0
5TH NOVEMBER: CELTIC 3 ANDERLECHT 1
25TH NOVEMBER: CELTIC 0 BAYERN MUNICH 0
10TH DECEMBER: OLYMPIQUE LYONNAIS 3 CELTIC 2

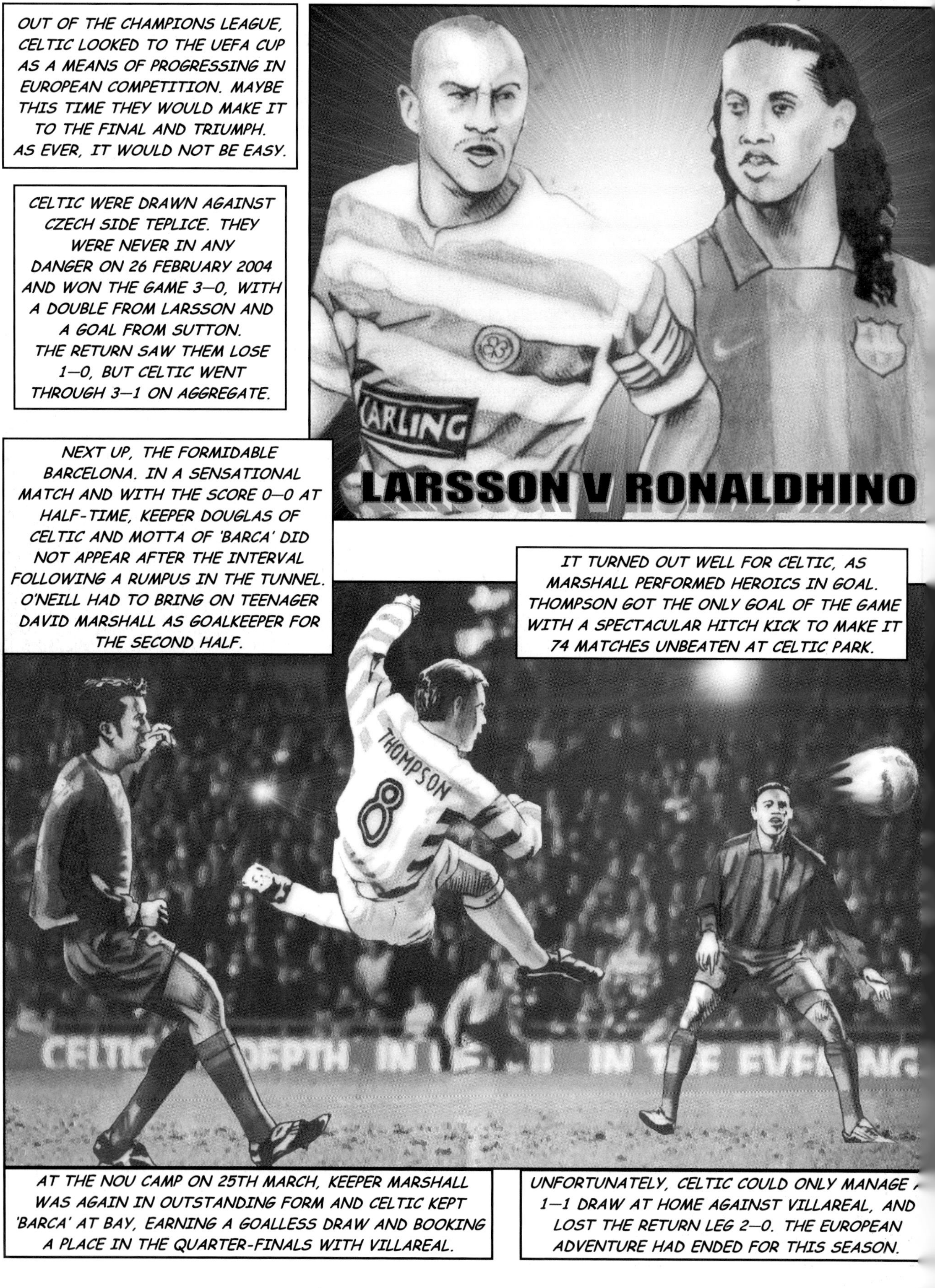
OUT OF THE CHAMPIONS LEAGUE, CELTIC LOOKED TO THE UEFA CUP AS A MEANS OF PROGRESSING IN EUROPEAN COMPETITION. MAYBE THIS TIME THEY WOULD MAKE IT TO THE FINAL AND TRIUMPH. AS EVER, IT WOULD NOT BE EASY.
CELTIC WERE DRAWN AGAINST CZECH SIDE TEPLICE. THEY WERE NEVER IN ANY DANGER ON 26 FEBRUARY 2004 AND WON THE GAME 3—0, WITH A DOUBLE FROM LARSSON AND A GOAL FROM SUTTON. THE RETURN SAW THEM LOSE 1—0, BUT CELTIC WENT THROUGH 3—1 ON AGGREGATE.
CARLING
LARSSON V RONALDHINO
NEXT UP, THE FORMIDABLE BARCELONA. IN A SENSATIONAL MATCH AND WITH THE SCORE 0—0 AT HALF-TIME, KEEPER DOUGLAS OF CELTIC AND MOTTA OF 'BARCA' DID NOT APPEAR AFTER THE INTERVAL FOLLOWING A RUMPUS IN THE TUNNEL. O'NEILL HAD TO BRING ON TEENAGER DAVID MARSHALL AS GOALKEEPER FOR THE SECOND HALF.
IT TURNED OUT WELL FOR CELTIC, AS MARSHALL PERFORMED HEROICS IN GOAL. THOMPSON GOT THE ONLY GOAL OF THE GAME WITH A SPECTACULAR HITCH KICK TO MAKE IT 74 MATCHES UNBEATEN AT CELTIC PARK.
THOMPSON
8
AT THE NOU CAMP ON 25TH MARCH, KEEPER MARSHALL WAS AGAIN IN OUTSTANDING FORM AND CELTIC KEPT 'BARCA' AT BAY, EARNING A GOALLESS DRAW AND BOOKING A PLACE IN THE QUARTER-FINALS WITH VILLAREAL.
UNFORTUNATELY, CELTIC COULD ONLY MANAGE A 1—1 DRAW AT HOME AGAINST VILLAREAL, AND LOST THE RETURN LEG 2—0. THE EUROPEAN ADVENTURE HAD ENDED FOR THIS SEASON.

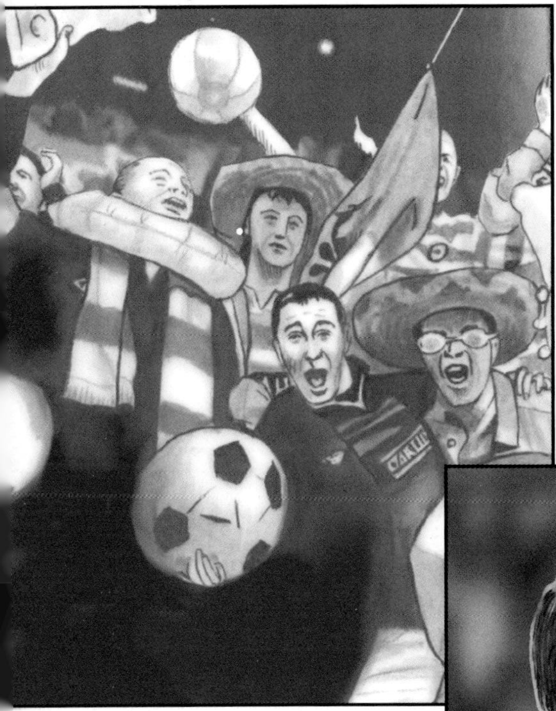

THE CELTIC FANS, IN PARTY MOOD AT IBROX ON 28TH MARCH 2004, DECIDED TO WEAR SOMBREROS AND THROW BEACH BALLS ABOUT. THE ATMOSPHERE HAD A DECIDEDLY SPANISH FEEL TO IT. MAYBE IT HAD SOMETHING TO DO WITH DEFEATING BARCELONA IN THE UEFA CUP?
LATER, THEY WOULD HAVE MORE TO CELEBRATE.

8TH MAY 2004. CHRIS SUTTON CELEBRATES AFTER SCORING THE WINNING GOAL AGAINST RANGERS WHICH SAW CELTIC COMPLETE THE 'GREEN & WHITE-WASH' OVER THEIR RIVALS, HAVING WON FIVE MATCHES IN A ROW, THE FIRST TIME THAT EITHER OLD FIRM CLUB HAD DONE SO.

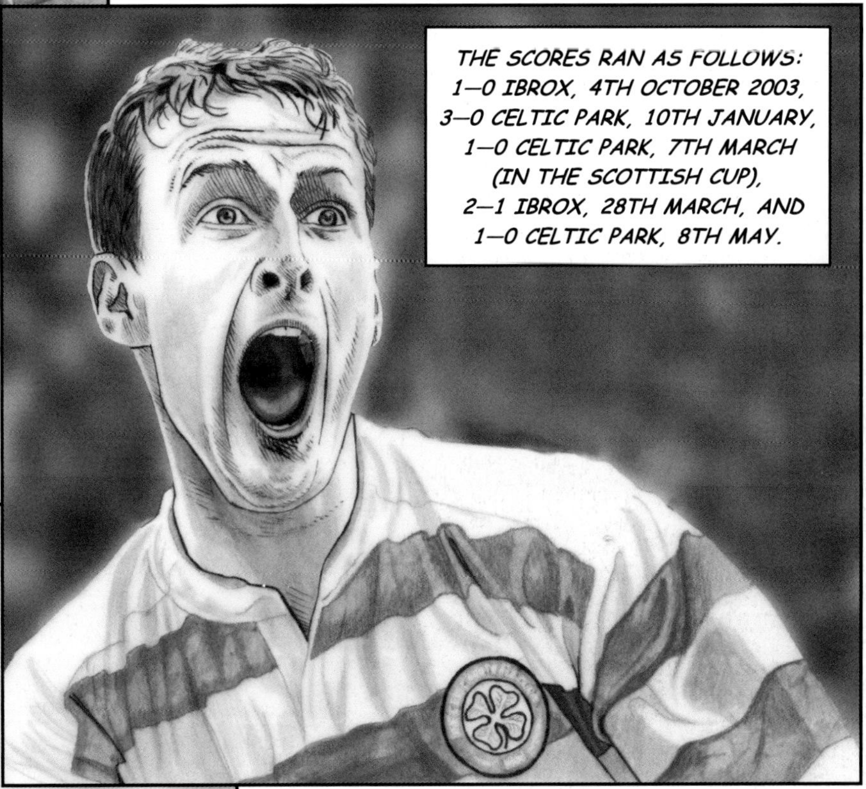
THE SCORES RAN AS FOLLOWS:
1—0 IBROX, 4TH OCTOBER 2003,
3—0 CELTIC PARK, 10TH JANUARY,
1—0 CELTIC PARK, 7TH MARCH
(IN THE SCOTTISH CUP),
2—1 IBROX, 28TH MARCH, AND
1—0 CELTIC PARK, 8TH MAY.

CELTIC HAD ALSO GONE ON A 25-MATCH UNBEATEN RUN TO SET AN ALL-TIME BRITISH RECORD. WHAT A SEASON!!

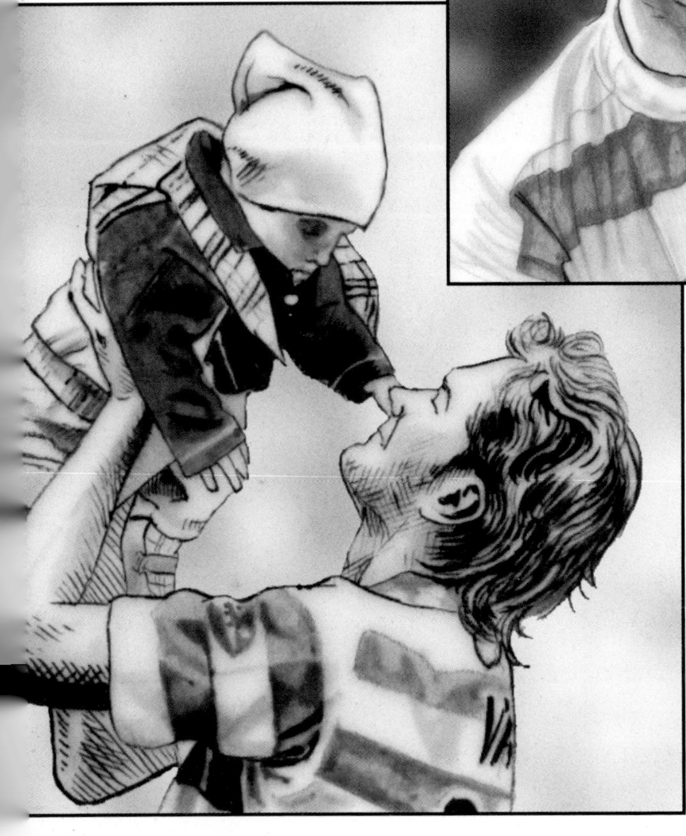

STAN VARGA SHOWS THAT HE CAN LIFT MORE THAN CUPS AND CHAMPIONSHIPS. CELTIC CLINCHED THE LEAGUE CHAMPIONSHIP AGAINST KILMARNOCK AT RUGBY PARK ON 18TH APRIL 2004, WINNING 1—0.

COMING NEXT... THE SCOTTISH CUP FINAL AGAINST DUNFERMLINE ON 22ND MAY 2004 AND HENRIK LARSSON'S LAST COMPETITIVE MATCH FOR CELTIC.

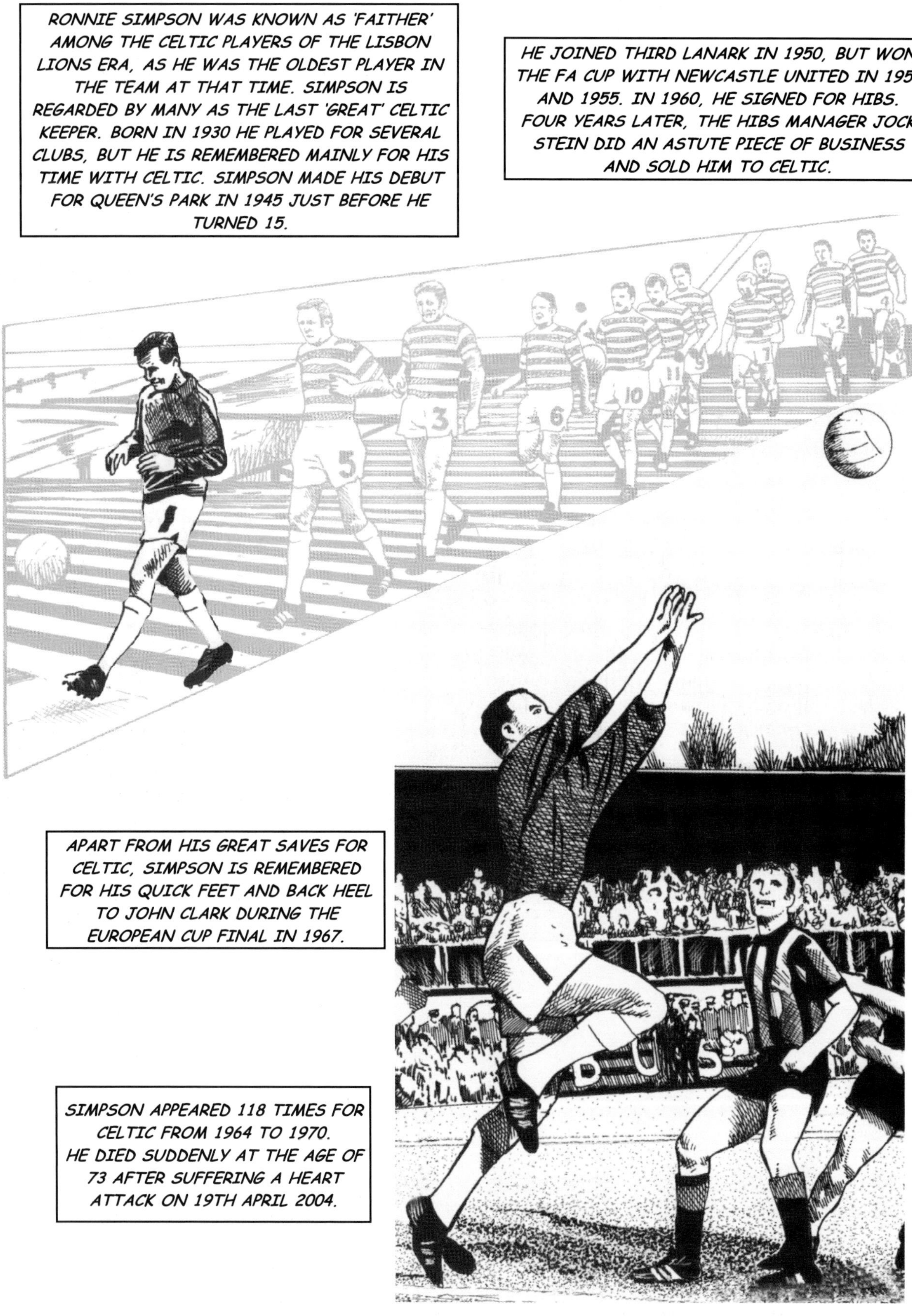
RONNIE SIMPSON WAS KNOWN AS 'FAITHER' AMONG THE CELTIC PLAYERS OF THE LISBON LIONS ERA, AS HE WAS THE OLDEST PLAYER IN THE TEAM AT THAT TIME. SIMPSON IS REGARDED BY MANY AS THE LAST 'GREAT' CELTIC KEEPER. BORN IN 1930 HE PLAYED FOR SEVERAL CLUBS, BUT HE IS REMEMBERED MAINLY FOR HIS TIME WITH CELTIC. SIMPSON MADE HIS DEBUT FOR QUEEN'S PARK IN 1945 JUST BEFORE HE TURNED 15.
HE JOINED THIRD LANARK IN 1950, BUT WON THE FA CUP WITH NEWCASTLE UNITED IN 1952 AND 1955. IN 1960, HE SIGNED FOR HIBS. FOUR YEARS LATER, THE HIBS MANAGER JOCK STEIN DID AN ASTUTE PIECE OF BUSINESS AND SOLD HIM TO CELTIC.
APART FROM HIS GREAT SAVES FOR CELTIC, SIMPSON IS REMEMBERED FOR HIS QUICK FEET AND BACK HEEL TO JOHN CLARK DURING THE EUROPEAN CUP FINAL IN 1967.
SIMPSON APPEARED 118 TIMES FOR CELTIC FROM 1964 TO 1970. HE DIED SUDDENLY AT THE AGE OF 73 AFTER SUFFERING A HEART ATTACK ON 19TH APRIL 2004.

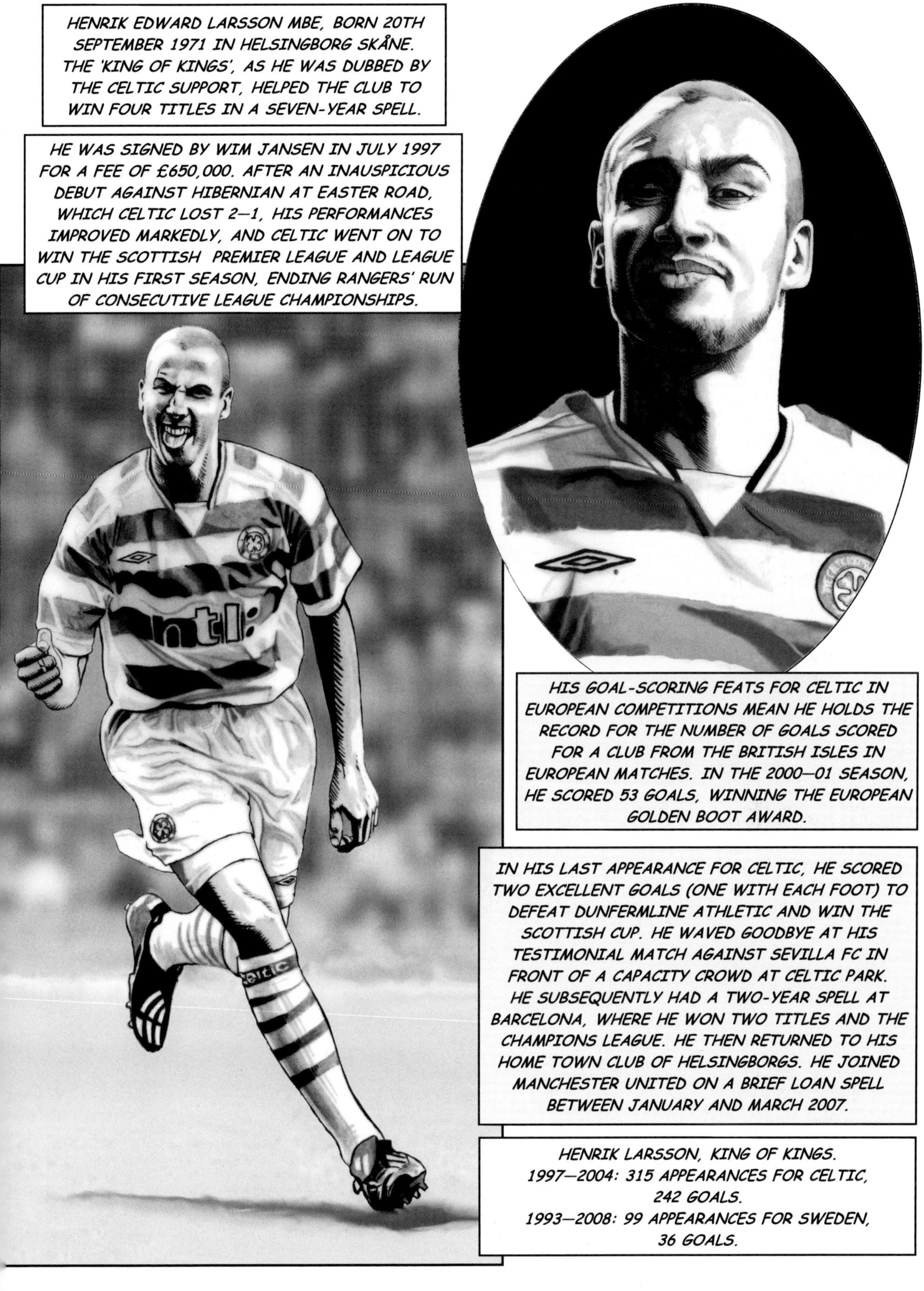
HENRIK EDWARD LARSSON MBE, BORN 20TH SEPTEMBER 1971 IN HELSINGBORG SKÅNE. THE 'KING OF KINGS', AS HE WAS DUBBED BY THE CELTIC SUPPORT, HELPED THE CLUB TO WIN FOUR TITLES IN A SEVEN-YEAR SPELL.
HE WAS SIGNED BY WIM JANSEN IN JULY 1997 FOR A FEE OF £650,000. AFTER AN INAUSPICIOUS DEBUT AGAINST HIBERNIAN AT EASTER ROAD, WHICH CELTIC LOST 2—1, HIS PERFORMANCES IMPROVED MARKEDLY, AND CELTIC WENT ON TO WIN THE SCOTTISH PREMIER LEAGUE AND LEAGUE CUP IN HIS FIRST SEASON, ENDING RANGERS' RUN OF CONSECUTIVE LEAGUE CHAMPIONSHIPS.
ntl:
HIS GOAL-SCORING FEATS FOR CELTIC IN EUROPEAN COMPETITIONS MEAN HE HOLDS THE RECORD FOR THE NUMBER OF GOALS SCORED FOR A CLUB FROM THE BRITISH ISLES IN EUROPEAN MATCHES. IN THE 2000—01 SEASON, HE SCORED 53 GOALS, WINNING THE EUROPEAN GOLDEN BOOT AWARD.
IN HIS LAST APPEARANCE FOR CELTIC, HE SCORED TWO EXCELLENT GOALS (ONE WITH EACH FOOT) TO DEFEAT DUNFERMLINE ATHLETIC AND WIN THE SCOTTISH CUP. HE WAVED GOODBYE AT HIS TESTIMONIAL MATCH AGAINST SEVILLA FC IN FRONT OF A CAPACITY CROWD AT CELTIC PARK. HE SUBSEQUENTLY HAD A TWO-YEAR SPELL AT BARCELONA, WHERE HE WON TWO TITLES AND THE CHAMPIONS LEAGUE. HE THEN RETURNED TO HIS HOME TOWN CLUB OF HELSINGBORGS. HE JOINED MANCHESTER UNITED ON A BRIEF LOAN SPELL BETWEEN JANUARY AND MARCH 2007.
HENRIK LARSSON, KING OF KINGS. 1997—2004: 315 APPEARANCES FOR CELTIC, 242 GOALS. 1993—2008: 99 APPEARANCES FOR SWEDEN, 36 GOALS.

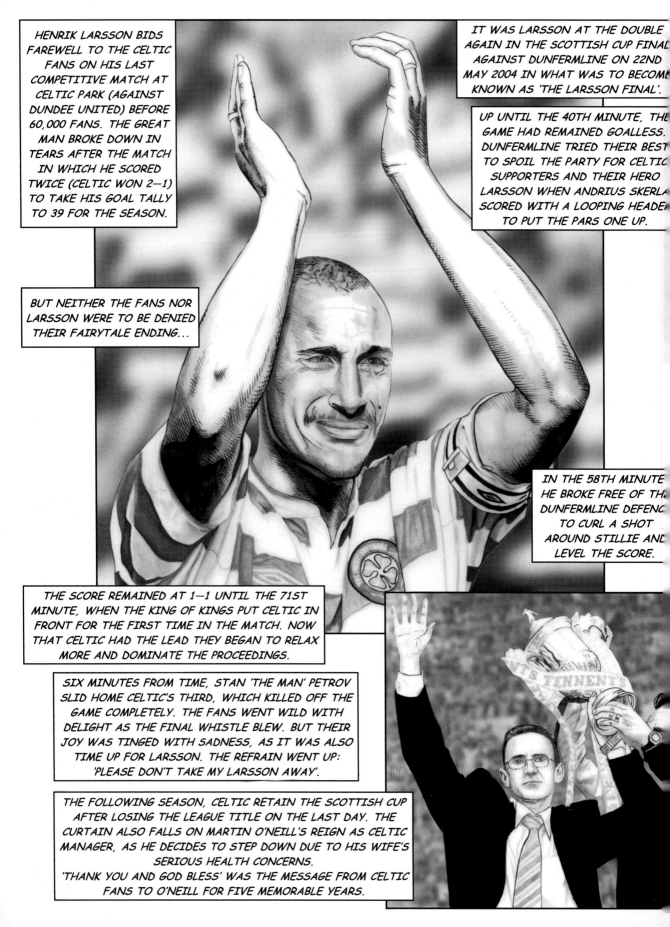

HENRIK LARSSON BIDS FAREWELL TO THE CELTIC FANS ON HIS LAST COMPETITIVE MATCH AT CELTIC PARK (AGAINST DUNDEE UNITED) BEFORE 60,000 FANS. THE GREAT MAN BROKE DOWN IN TEARS AFTER THE MATCH IN WHICH HE SCORED TWICE (CELTIC WON 2—1) TO TAKE HIS GOAL TALLY TO 39 FOR THE SEASON.

BUT NEITHER THE FANS NOR LARSSON WERE TO BE DENIED THEIR FAIRYTALE ENDING...

IT WAS LARSSON AT THE DOUBLE AGAIN IN THE SCOTTISH CUP FINAL AGAINST DUNFERMLINE ON 22ND MAY 2004 IN WHAT WAS TO BECOME KNOWN AS 'THE LARSSON FINAL'.

UP UNTIL THE 40TH MINUTE, THE GAME HAD REMAINED GOALLESS. DUNFERMLINE TRIED THEIR BEST TO SPOIL THE PARTY FOR CELTIC SUPPORTERS AND THEIR HERO LARSSON WHEN ANDRIUS SKERLA SCORED WITH A LOOPING HEADER TO PUT THE PARS ONE UP.

IN THE 58TH MINUTE HE BROKE FREE OF THE DUNFERMLINE DEFENCE TO CURL A SHOT AROUND STILLIE AND LEVEL THE SCORE.

THE SCORE REMAINED AT 1—1 UNTIL THE 71ST MINUTE, WHEN THE KING OF KINGS PUT CELTIC IN FRONT FOR THE FIRST TIME IN THE MATCH. NOW THAT CELTIC HAD THE LEAD THEY BEGAN TO RELAX MORE AND DOMINATE THE PROCEEDINGS.

SIX MINUTES FROM TIME, STAN 'THE MAN' PETROV SLID HOME CELTIC'S THIRD, WHICH KILLED OFF THE GAME COMPLETELY. THE FANS WENT WILD WITH DELIGHT AS THE FINAL WHISTLE BLEW. BUT THEIR JOY WAS TINGED WITH SADNESS, AS IT WAS ALSO TIME UP FOR LARSSON. THE REFRAIN WENT UP: 'PLEASE DON'T TAKE MY LARSSON AWAY'.

THE FOLLOWING SEASON, CELTIC RETAIN THE SCOTTISH CUP AFTER LOSING THE LEAGUE TITLE ON THE LAST DAY. THE CURTAIN ALSO FALLS ON MARTIN O'NEILL'S REIGN AS CELTIC MANAGER, AS HE DECIDES TO STEP DOWN DUE TO HIS WIFE'S SERIOUS HEALTH CONCERNS. 'THANK YOU AND GOD BLESS' WAS THE MESSAGE FROM CELTIC FANS TO O'NEILL FOR FIVE MEMORABLE YEARS.

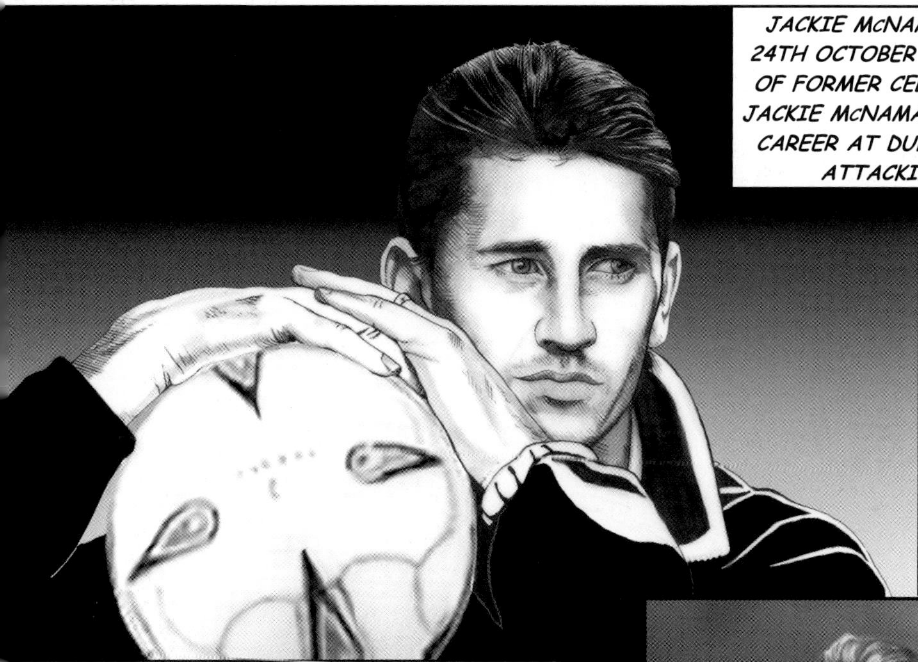

JACKIE McNAMARA (WEE JACKIE) — BORN 24TH OCTOBER 1973 IN GLASGOW. THE SON OF FORMER CELTIC AND HIBERNIAN PLAYER JACKIE McNAMARA SENIOR, HE STARTED HIS CAREER AT DUNFERMLINE ATHLETIC AS AN ATTACKING RIGHT WING-BACK.

JACKIE MOVED TO CELTIC FOR £650,000 IN 1995. HE MADE AN IMPRESSIVE START TO HIS CELTIC CAREER, BEING NAMED SCOTTISH PFA YOUNG PLAYER OF THE YEAR IN 1996. HE WON HIS FIRST TROPHY WITH THE CLUB IN THE 1997—98 SEASON WHEN CELTIC WON THE SCOTTISH PREMIER DIVISION, PREVENTING RANGERS WINNING TEN-IN-A-ROW.

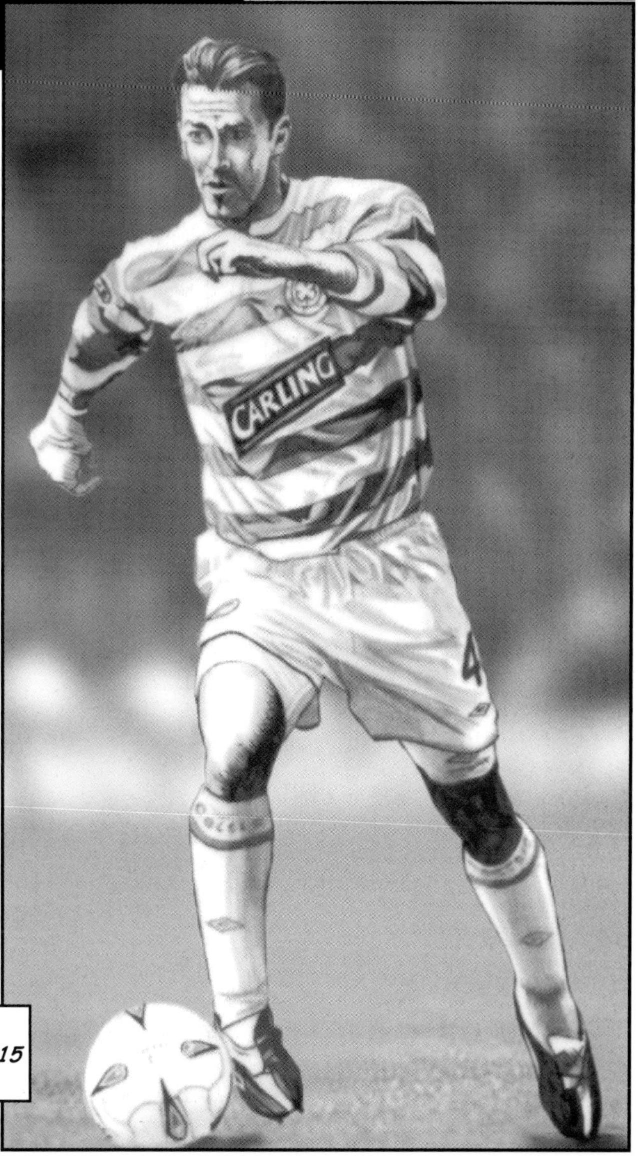
CARLING

IN HIS EARLY DAYS FOR CELTIC, McNAMARA HAD FORMED AN EXCITING PARTNERSHIP WITH SIMON DONNELLY ON THE RIGHT WING THAT THRILLED THE FANS. THE PAIR OF THEM USED TO TEAR INTO DEFENCES WITH PACE AND INCISIVE PLAY REMINISCENT OF THE EARLIER PARTNERSHIP ON THE RIGHT WING OF DALGLISH AND McGRAIN. LATER, McNAMARA PLAYED MAINLY IN DEFENCE AND OCCASIONALLY IN MIDFIELD.

JACKIE WAS A REGULAR IN THE CELTIC FIRST TEAM UNTIL THE ARRIVAL OF MARTIN O'NEILL IN THE 2000—01 SEASON, AFTER WHICH HE BECAME MORE OF A FRINGE PLAYER. BUT HE WOULD RE-ESTABLISH HIMSELF IN O'NEILL'S PLANS AND FEATURE MORE REGULARLY, BEING NAMED THE FOOTBALL WRITERS' PLAYER OF THE YEAR IN 2004. THE FOLLOWING YEAR, McNAMARA WAS NAMED CAPTAIN. HE PROVED HIMSELF A CONSISTENT AND RELIABLE PERFORMER FOR CELTIC, PLAYING ALMOST EVERY LEAGUE GAME IN THE 2004—05 SEASON.

TO REWARD HIS LOYALTY TO THE CLUB OVER THE 10 YEAR PERIOD, CELTIC PLAYED A TESTIMONIAL MATCH AGAINST THE REPUBLIC OF IRELAND ON THE 29TH MAY 2005. SOON AFTER MCNAMARA LEFT THE CLUB FOR WOLVERHAMPTON WANDERERS.

JACKIE McNAMARA MADE 289 APPEARANCES FOR CELTIC AND SCORED 15 GOALS. HE WON 33 SCOTLAND CAPS.

chapter 14

good things come in threes

'you'll never walk alone'

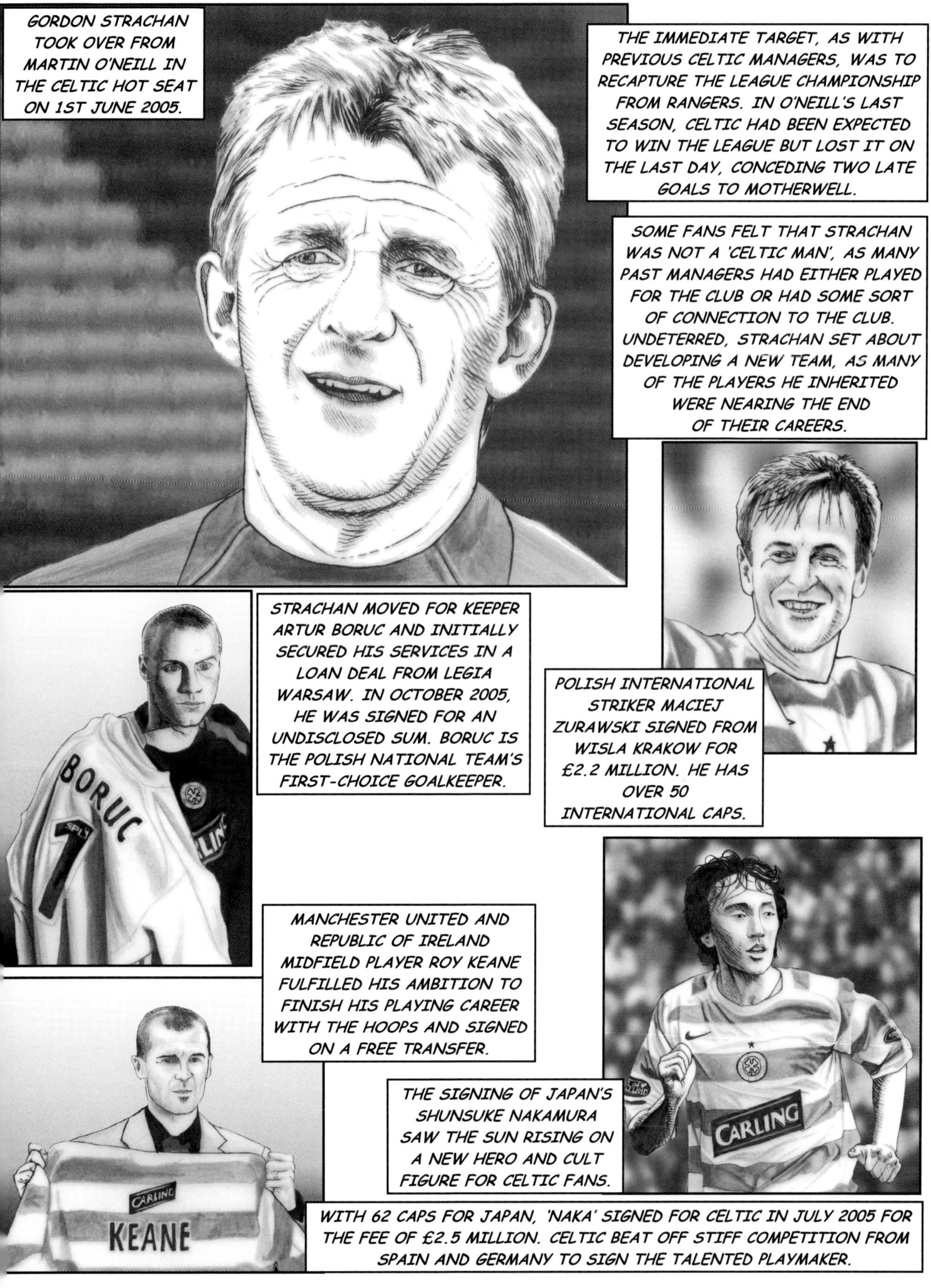
GORDON STRACHAN TOOK OVER FROM MARTIN O'NEILL IN THE CELTIC HOT SEAT ON 1ST JUNE 2005.
THE IMMEDIATE TARGET, AS WITH PREVIOUS CELTIC MANAGERS, WAS TO RECAPTURE THE LEAGUE CHAMPIONSHIP FROM RANGERS. IN O'NEILL'S LAST SEASON, CELTIC HAD BEEN EXPECTED TO WIN THE LEAGUE BUT LOST IT ON THE LAST DAY, CONCEDING TWO LATE GOALS TO MOTHERWELL.
SOME FANS FELT THAT STRACHAN WAS NOT A 'CELTIC MAN', AS MANY PAST MANAGERS HAD EITHER PLAYED FOR THE CLUB OR HAD SOME SORT OF CONNECTION TO THE CLUB. UNDETERRED, STRACHAN SET ABOUT DEVELOPING A NEW TEAM, AS MANY OF THE PLAYERS HE INHERITED WERE NEARING THE END OF THEIR CAREERS.
STRACHAN MOVED FOR KEEPER ARTUR BORUC AND INITIALLY SECURED HIS SERVICES IN A LOAN DEAL FROM LEGIA WARSAW. IN OCTOBER 2005, HE WAS SIGNED FOR AN UNDISCLOSED SUM. BORUC IS THE POLISH NATIONAL TEAM'S FIRST-CHOICE GOALKEEPER.
BORUC
POLISH INTERNATIONAL STRIKER MACIEJ ZURAWSKI SIGNED FROM WISLA KRAKOW FOR £2.2 MILLION. HE HAS OVER 50 INTERNATIONAL CAPS.
MANCHESTER UNITED AND REPUBLIC OF IRELAND MIDFIELD PLAYER ROY KEANE FULFILLED HIS AMBITION TO FINISH HIS PLAYING CAREER WITH THE HOOPS AND SIGNED ON A FREE TRANSFER.
CARLING
KEANE
CARLING
THE SIGNING OF JAPAN'S SHUNSUKE NAKAMURA SAW THE SUN RISING ON A NEW HERO AND CULT FIGURE FOR CELTIC FANS.
WITH 62 CAPS FOR JAPAN, 'NAKA' SIGNED FOR CELTIC IN JULY 2005 FOR THE FEE OF £2.5 MILLION. CELTIC BEAT OFF STIFF COMPETITION FROM SPAIN AND GERMANY TO SIGN THE TALENTED PLAYMAKER.

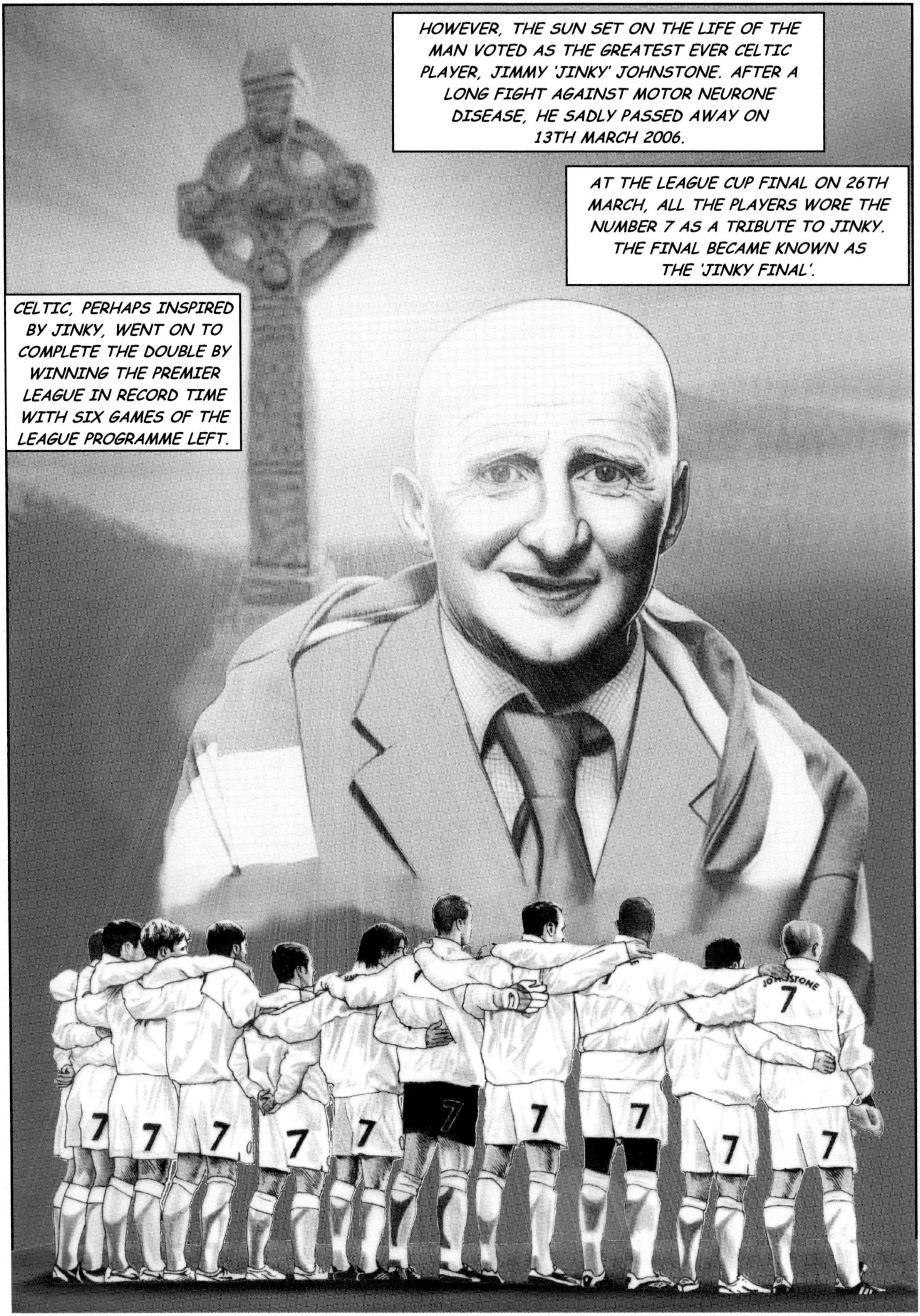
HOWEVER, THE SUN SET ON THE LIFE OF THE MAN VOTED AS THE GREATEST EVER CELTIC PLAYER, JIMMY 'JINKY' JOHNSTONE. AFTER A LONG FIGHT AGAINST MOTOR NEURONE DISEASE, HE SADLY PASSED AWAY ON 13TH MARCH 2006.
AT THE LEAGUE CUP FINAL ON 26TH MARCH, ALL THE PLAYERS WORE THE NUMBER 7 AS A TRIBUTE TO JINKY. THE FINAL BECAME KNOWN AS THE 'JINKY FINAL'.
CELTIC, PERHAPS INSPIRED BY JINKY, WENT ON TO COMPLETE THE DOUBLE BY WINNING THE PREMIER LEAGUE IN RECORD TIME WITH SIX GAMES OF THE LEAGUE PROGRAMME LEFT.
JOHNSTONE
7

DANISH INTERNATIONALIST AND ATTACKING MIDFIELDER THOMAS GRAVESEN CAME FROM REAL MADRID ON A THREE-YEAR DEAL FOR AN UNDISCLOSED SUM. GRAVESEN WAS BROUGHT IN TO ADD STEEL TO THE MIDFIELD. NEXT CAME A VERY SURPRISING SIGNING IN THE SHAPE OF EX-RANGERS AND WOLVES PLAYER KENNY MILLER, A STRIKER WHO WAS BEGINNING TO SHINE AT INTERNATIONAL LEVEL.

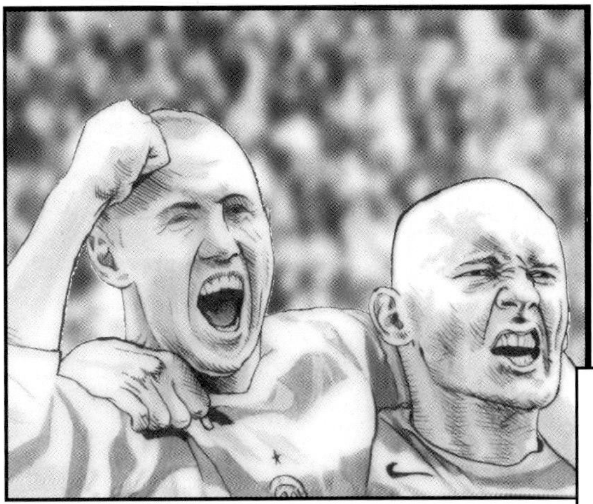

STRACHAN MANAGED TO PERSUADE GARY CALDWELL, INTERNATIONAL CENTRE-BACK FROM HIBS, TO SIGN A PRE-CONTRACT AGREEMENT WITH CELTIC ON 20TH JANUARY 2006. HE THEN SIGNED FOR CELTIC ON A FREE TRANSFER ON 1ST JUNE 2006. CALDWELL HAD BEEN OUTSTANDING FOR HIBS AND FOR SCOTLAND, HAVING BEEN CAPPED 20 TIMES.

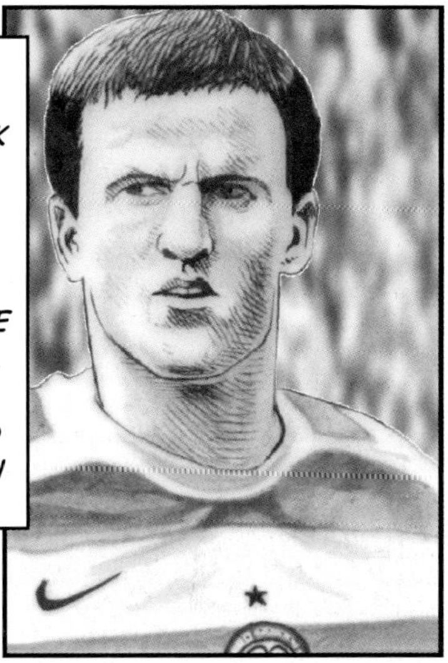

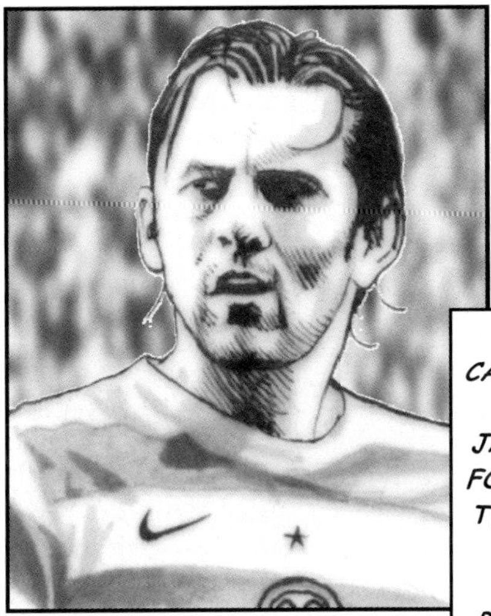

A CELTIC SUPPORTER FROM HEARTS CALLED PAUL HARTLEY SIGNED FOR THE CLUB ON THE LAST DAY OF THE JANUARY TRANSFER WINDOW IN 2007 FOR £1.1 MILLION. HARTLEY SIGNED A TWO-AND-A-HALF-YEAR CONTRACT. A SWASHBUCKLING MIDFIELDER, HARTLEY WAS A CONTROVERSIAL PLAYER FOR HEARTS WHEN HE PLAYED AGAINST CELTIC!

THE BIGGEST NAME IN DUTCH FOOTBALL SIGNED FROM PSV EINDHOVEN FOR £3.4 MILLION. JAN VENNEGOOR OF HESSELINK, A DUTCH INTERNATIONALIST WITH EIGHT CAPS, WAS CONTRACTED FOR THREE YEARS. THE DUTCHMAN' HAS BEEN BROUGHT IN AS A TARGET MAN, LAYING OFF BALLS TO HIS FELLOW FORWARDS.

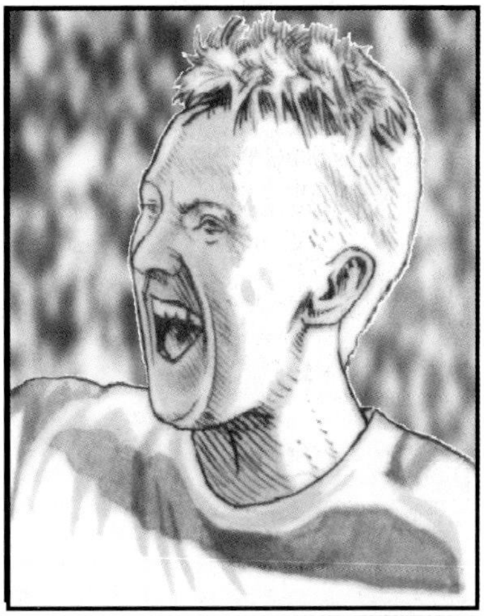

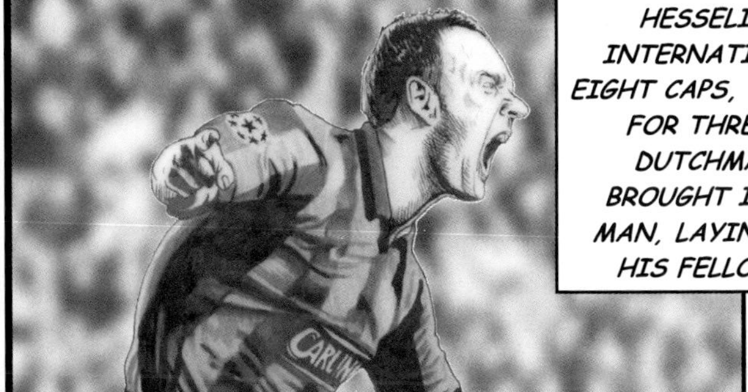

ANOTHER 'HIBEE' CAME TO CELTIC IN JUNE 2006 — DEREK RIORDAN, A PROMISING YOUNG FORWARD WITH A SWEET LEFT FOOT. HE SCORED 64 GOALS IN 146 APPEARANCES FOR HIBS AND WAS VOTED YOUNG PLAYER OF THE YEAR IN 2005.

CELTIC BEGAN SEASON 2006—07 AS CHAMPIONS ONCE AGAIN. 18TH AUGUST SAW A 2—0 WIN AT CELTIC PARK OVER ST MIRREN. GOALS FROM McMANUS AND PETROV SEALED THE POINTS. SUCH WAS THE FORM OF CELTIC THAT SOME BOOKMAKERS PAID OUT FOR CELTIC AS WINNERS OF THE SPL AS EARLY AS 4TH NOVEMBER, ONLY 13 GAMES INTO THE SEASON.
DURING THE JANUARY TRANSFER WINDOW, STEVEN PRESSLEY WAS SIGNED FROM HEARTS TO BOLSTER THE DEFENCE.

STEVEN PRESSLEY

RIGHT-BACK JEAN-JOËL PERRIER-DOUMBÉ CAME FROM RENNES, AND GOALKEEPER MARK BROWN ARRIVED FROM CALEY THISTLE. LEE NAYLOR, A LEFT-BACK, WAS SIGNED FROM WOLVES.

LEE NAYLOR

JEAN-JOËL PERRIER-DOUMBÉ

EVANDER SNO

OPPONENTS IN THE 1970 EUROPEAN CUP FINAL FEYENOORD PROVIDED MIDFIELD PLAYER EVANDER SNO, AND CHELSEA SOLD JIRI JAROSIK TO CELTIC FOR AN UNDISCLOSED SUM.

THE SEASON PROGRESSED WELL. AMONG THE HIGHLIGHTS WERE THE 2—0 WIN OVER RANGERS AT IBROX IN SEPTEMBER — GOALS BY NEW BOYS GRAVESEN AND MILLER; A 1—0 WIN OVER FC COPENHAGEN IN THE CHAMPIONS LEAGUE — MILLER ON THE SCORESHEET; AND A 3—0 WIN OVER BENFICA — MILLER (2) AND PEARSON THE SCORERS. FOR THE FIRST TIME, CELTIC MADE IT TO THE LAST 16 OF THE CHAMPIONS LEAGUE WHEN THEY DEFEATED MANCHESTER UNITED AT CELTIC PARK.
THE LEAGUE WAS CLINCHED WITH FOUR GAMES TO GO ON 22ND APRIL 2007 AND WITH 13 POINTS TO SPARE.
TO TOP OFF THE SEASON, CELTIC RENEWED THEIR ACQUAINTANCE WITH THE SCOTTISH CUP, DEFEATING DUNFERMLINE 1—0 IN THE FINAL ON 6TH MAY, DOUMBÉ SCORING IN THE 84TH MINUTE.

JIRI JAROSIK

MANCHESTER UNITED COME CALLING TO CELTIC PARK IN THE CHAMPIONS LEAGUE GROUP F ON 21ST NOVEMBER 2006. AT OLD TRAFFORD, CELTIC LOST NARROWLY, 3—2. THIS TIME, GORDON STRACHAN IS HOPING FOR THE SAME ENTERTAINMENT BUT A DIFFERENT RESULT. UNITED START WELL WITH PROLONGED PERIODS OF POSSESSION, BUT CELTIC GIVE NOTHING AWAY AT THE BACK AND LOOK VERY SOLID IN DEFENCE.

THE GAME IS LOCKED AT 0—0 UNTIL THE 80TH MINUTE. CELTIC GET A FREE KICK, BUT IT'S A LONG WAY OUT FROM GOAL, 30 YARDS AT LEAST.

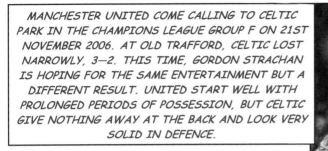

NAKAMURA AND MALONEY BOTH STEP UP. EITHER ONE CAN TAKE A LETHAL FREE KICK. IT'S NAKAMURA WITH A SHORT RUN UP. HE STRIKES THE BALL AND CURLS IT INTO THE TOP RIGHT-HAND CORNER OF THE NET. CELTIC 1 MAN UTD 0.

INTO THE LAST MINUTE, MALONEY HANDLES IN THE BOX — PENALTY TO UNITED, SAHA TO TAKE THE KICK. HE MAKES HIS RUN AND STRIKES THE BALL... IT'S **BORUC!!** HE DIVES TO HIS RIGHT AND PUSHES THE BALL AWAY. WHAT A SAVE!

THERE'S NO WAY BACK FOR UNITED NOW — CELTIC HAVE WON AND QUALIFIED FOR THE LAST 16 IN THE CHAMPIONS LEAGUE FOR THE FIRST TIME.

THE SEASON OF 2007–08 DID NOT BEGIN WELL. AT CELTIC PARK ON 5TH AUGUST, AN UNINSPIRING GOALLESS DRAW AGAINST KILMARNOCK DID NOTHING TO HINT AT THE DRAMA THAT WAS SUBSEQUENTLY TO UNFOLD.

THE MUCH-ADMIRED YOUNG TALENT SCOTT BROWN SIGNS FROM HIBS FOR A RECORD FEE BETWEEN SCOTTISH CLUBS OF £4.4 MILLION.

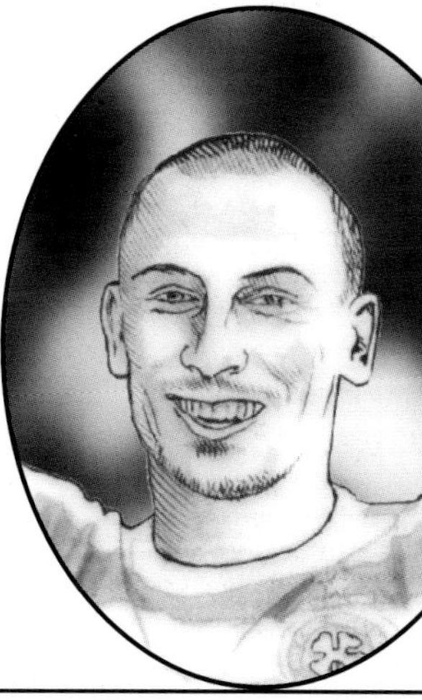

BROWN, HARTLEY AND McDONALD WERE THREE SIGNING TARGETS FOR RANGERS. HOWEVER, WITHIN FIVE MONTHS THEY HAD ALL SIGNED FOR CELTIC.

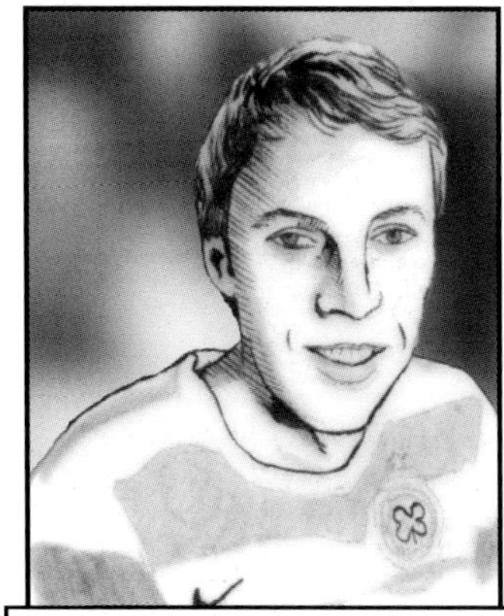

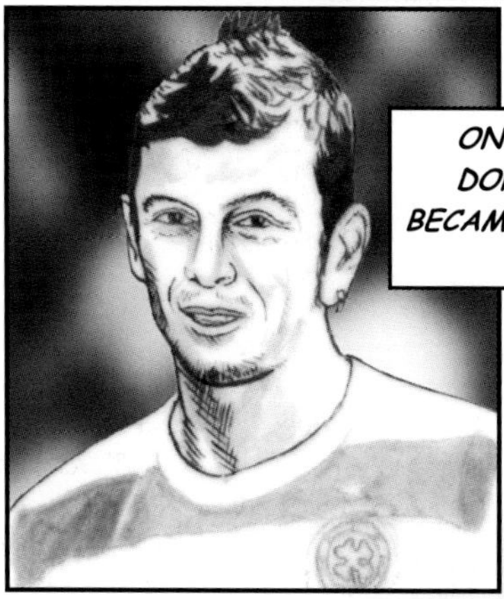

ON 29TH JUNE 2007, MIDFIELDER MASSIMO DONATI FROM ITALIAN GIANTS A.C. MILAN BECAME THE NEW NUMBER 18. CELTIC GAVE HIM A FOUR-YEAR CONTRACT.

GERMAN FULL-BACK ANDREAS HINKEL LEAVES SEVILLA TO JOIN CELTIC IN JANUARY 2008 ON A THREE-AND-A-HALF-YEAR DEAL. HINKEL HAS BEEN CAPPED 17 TIMES FOR HIS COUNTRY.

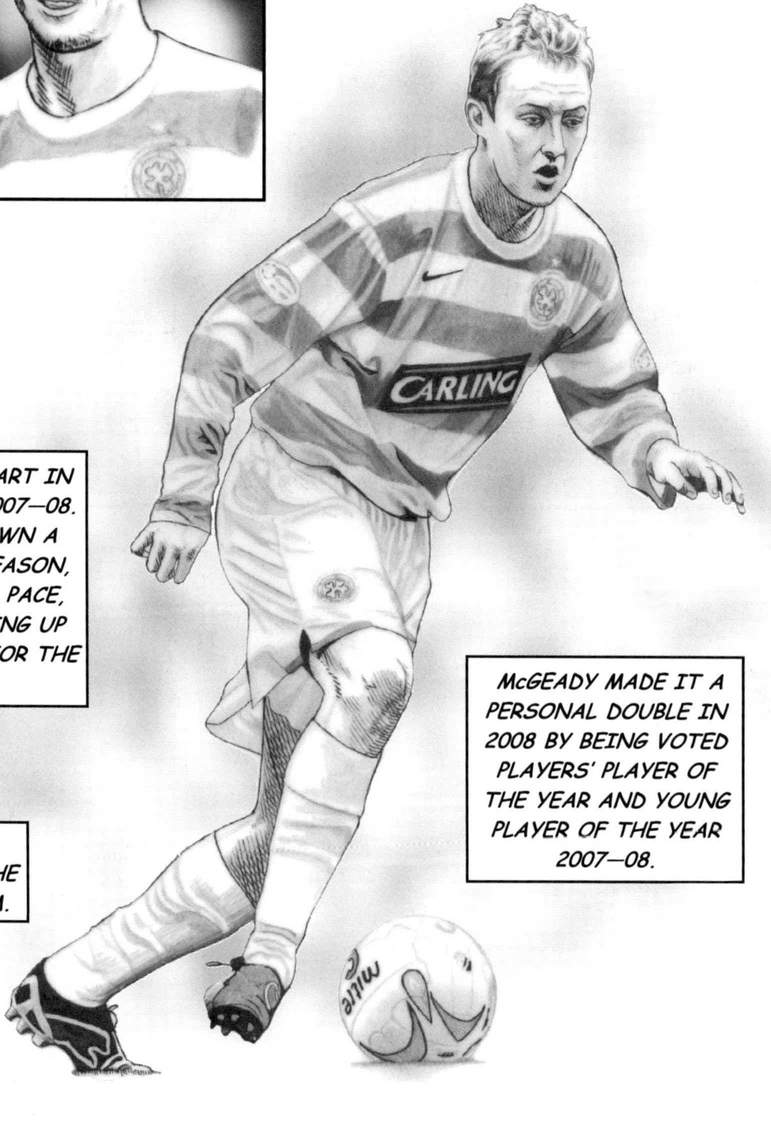
CARLING

AIDEN McGEADY PLAYED A MAJOR PART IN RETAINING THE TITLE IN SEASON 2007–08. THE YOUNG RISING STAR HAD SHOWN A GROWING MATURITY DURING THE SEASON, WITH HIS ELECTRIFYING SKILL AND PACE, ESPECIALLY DOWN THE LEFT, OPENING UP DEFENCES AND CREATING CHANCES FOR THE CELTIC STRIKERS.

McGEADY MADE IT A PERSONAL DOUBLE IN 2008 BY BEING VOTED PLAYERS' PLAYER OF THE YEAR AND YOUNG PLAYER OF THE YEAR 2007–08.

A PROTÉGÉ OF THE LATE TOMMY BURNS, McGEADY IS A PRODUCT OF THE CELTIC YOUTH-DEVELOPMENT SYSTEM.

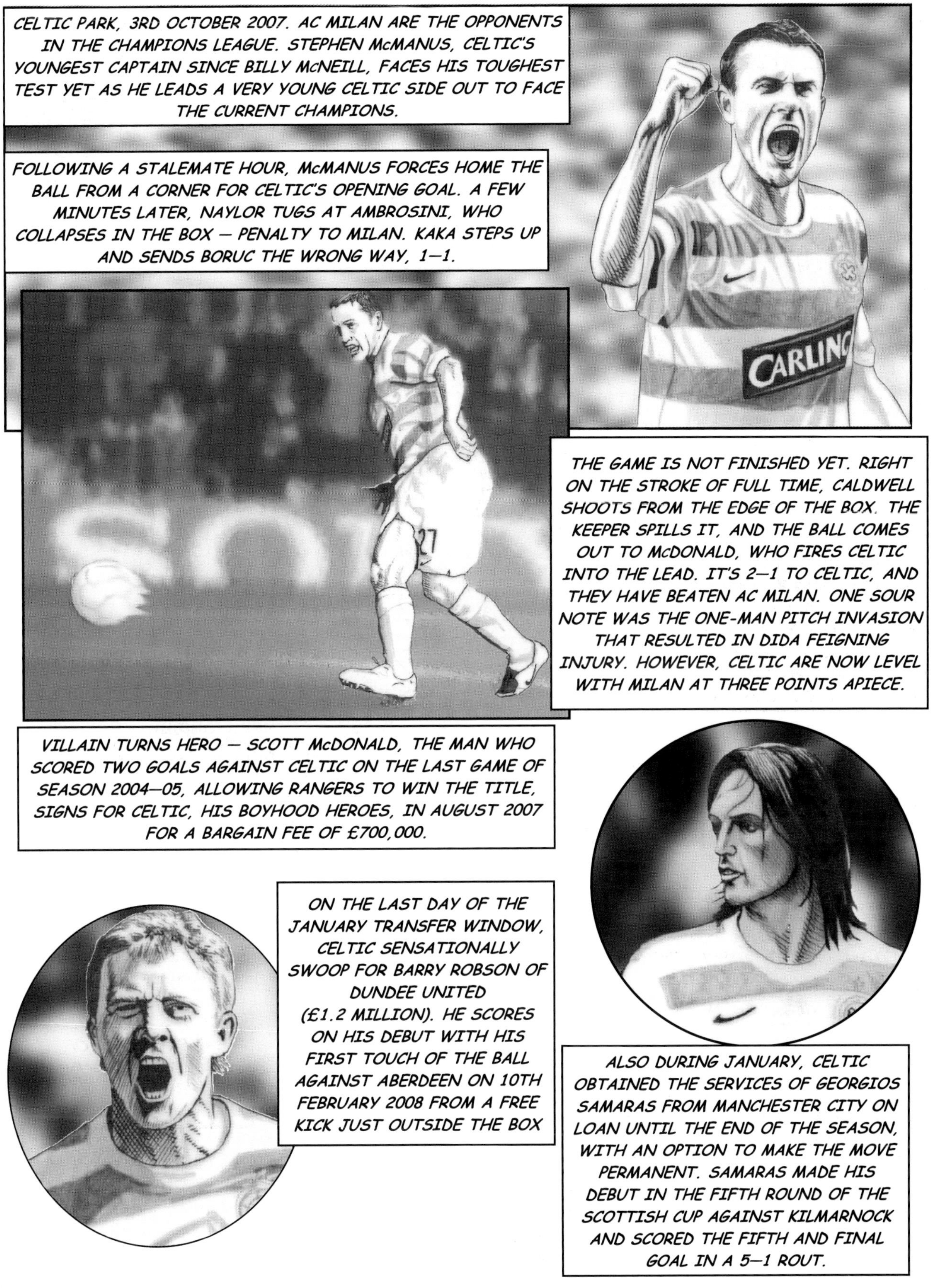
CELTIC PARK, 3RD OCTOBER 2007. AC MILAN ARE THE OPPONENTS IN THE CHAMPIONS LEAGUE. STEPHEN McMANUS, CELTIC'S YOUNGEST CAPTAIN SINCE BILLY McNEILL, FACES HIS TOUGHEST TEST YET AS HE LEADS A VERY YOUNG CELTIC SIDE OUT TO FACE THE CURRENT CHAMPIONS.
FOLLOWING A STALEMATE HOUR, McMANUS FORCES HOME THE BALL FROM A CORNER FOR CELTIC'S OPENING GOAL. A FEW MINUTES LATER, NAYLOR TUGS AT AMBROSINI, WHO COLLAPSES IN THE BOX – PENALTY TO MILAN. KAKA STEPS UP AND SENDS BORUC THE WRONG WAY, 1–1.
CARLING
27
THE GAME IS NOT FINISHED YET. RIGHT ON THE STROKE OF FULL TIME, CALDWELL SHOOTS FROM THE EDGE OF THE BOX. THE KEEPER SPILLS IT, AND THE BALL COMES OUT TO McDONALD, WHO FIRES CELTIC INTO THE LEAD. IT'S 2–1 TO CELTIC, AND THEY HAVE BEATEN AC MILAN. ONE SOUR NOTE WAS THE ONE-MAN PITCH INVASION THAT RESULTED IN DIDA FEIGNING INJURY. HOWEVER, CELTIC ARE NOW LEVEL WITH MILAN AT THREE POINTS APIECE.
VILLAIN TURNS HERO – SCOTT McDONALD, THE MAN WHO SCORED TWO GOALS AGAINST CELTIC ON THE LAST GAME OF SEASON 2004–05, ALLOWING RANGERS TO WIN THE TITLE, SIGNS FOR CELTIC, HIS BOYHOOD HEROES, IN AUGUST 2007 FOR A BARGAIN FEE OF £700,000.
ON THE LAST DAY OF THE JANUARY TRANSFER WINDOW, CELTIC SENSATIONALLY SWOOP FOR BARRY ROBSON OF DUNDEE UNITED (£1.2 MILLION). HE SCORES ON HIS DEBUT WITH HIS FIRST TOUCH OF THE BALL AGAINST ABERDEEN ON 10TH FEBRUARY 2008 FROM A FREE KICK JUST OUTSIDE THE BOX
ALSO DURING JANUARY, CELTIC OBTAINED THE SERVICES OF GEORGIOS SAMARAS FROM MANCHESTER CITY ON LOAN UNTIL THE END OF THE SEASON, WITH AN OPTION TO MAKE THE MOVE PERMANENT. SAMARAS MADE HIS DEBUT IN THE FIFTH ROUND OF THE SCOTTISH CUP AGAINST KILMARNOCK AND SCORED THE FIFTH AND FINAL GOAL IN A 5–1 ROUT.

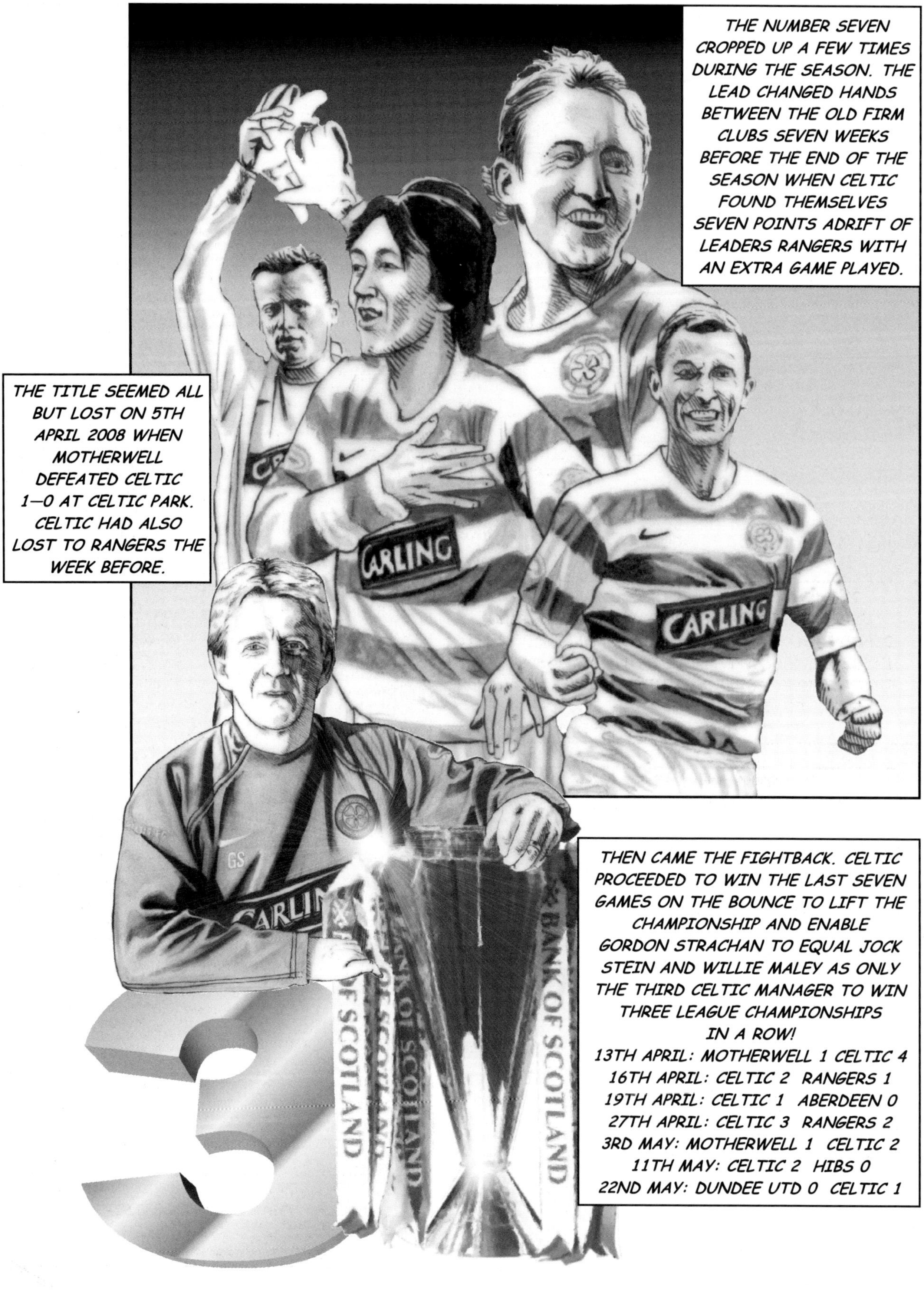
THE NUMBER SEVEN CROPPED UP A FEW TIMES DURING THE SEASON. THE LEAD CHANGED HANDS BETWEEN THE OLD FIRM CLUBS SEVEN WEEKS BEFORE THE END OF THE SEASON WHEN CELTIC FOUND THEMSELVES SEVEN POINTS ADRIFT OF LEADERS RANGERS WITH AN EXTRA GAME PLAYED.
THE TITLE SEEMED ALL BUT LOST ON 5TH APRIL 2008 WHEN MOTHERWELL DEFEATED CELTIC 1—0 AT CELTIC PARK. CELTIC HAD ALSO LOST TO RANGERS THE WEEK BEFORE.
CARLING
CARLING
GS
BANK OF SCOTLAND
BANK OF SCOTLAND
BANK OF SCOTLAND
THEN CAME THE FIGHTBACK. CELTIC PROCEEDED TO WIN THE LAST SEVEN GAMES ON THE BOUNCE TO LIFT THE CHAMPIONSHIP AND ENABLE GORDON STRACHAN TO EQUAL JOCK STEIN AND WILLIE MALEY AS ONLY THE THIRD CELTIC MANAGER TO WIN THREE LEAGUE CHAMPIONSHIPS IN A ROW!
13TH APRIL: MOTHERWELL 1 CELTIC 4
16TH APRIL: CELTIC 2 RANGERS 1
19TH APRIL: CELTIC 1 ABERDEEN 0
27TH APRIL: CELTIC 3 RANGERS 2
3RD MAY: MOTHERWELL 1 CELTIC 2
11TH MAY: CELTIC 2 HIBS 0
22ND MAY: DUNDEE UTD 0 CELTIC 1

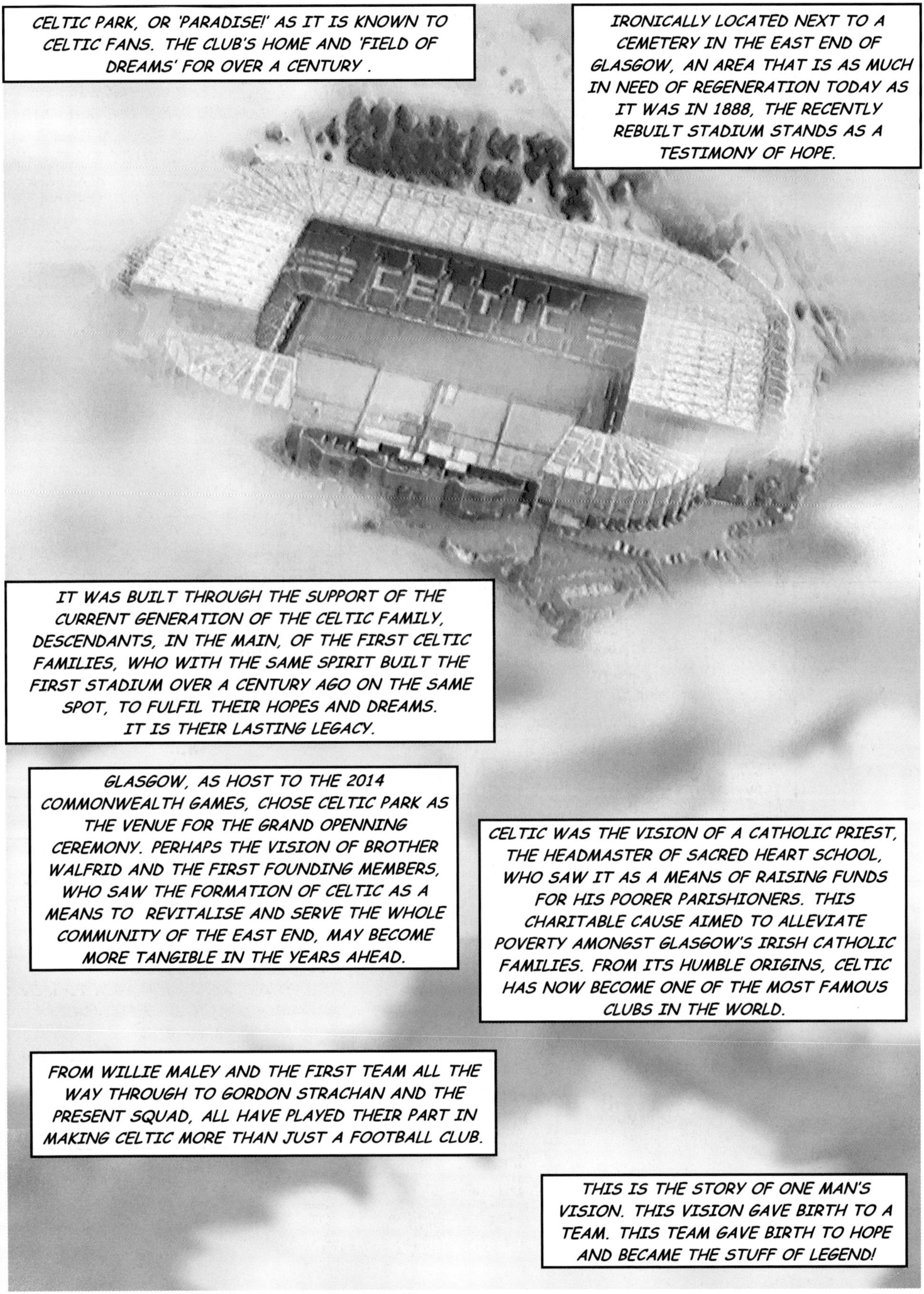
CELTIC PARK, OR 'PARADISE!' AS IT IS KNOWN TO CELTIC FANS. THE CLUB'S HOME AND 'FIELD OF DREAMS' FOR OVER A CENTURY .
IRONICALLY LOCATED NEXT TO A CEMETERY IN THE EAST END OF GLASGOW, AN AREA THAT IS AS MUCH IN NEED OF REGENERATION TODAY AS IT WAS IN 1888, THE RECENTLY REBUILT STADIUM STANDS AS A TESTIMONY OF HOPE.
CELTIC
IT WAS BUILT THROUGH THE SUPPORT OF THE CURRENT GENERATION OF THE CELTIC FAMILY, DESCENDANTS, IN THE MAIN, OF THE FIRST CELTIC FAMILIES, WHO WITH THE SAME SPIRIT BUILT THE FIRST STADIUM OVER A CENTURY AGO ON THE SAME SPOT, TO FULFIL THEIR HOPES AND DREAMS. IT IS THEIR LASTING LEGACY.
GLASGOW, AS HOST TO THE 2014 COMMONWEALTH GAMES, CHOSE CELTIC PARK AS THE VENUE FOR THE GRAND OPENNING CEREMONY. PERHAPS THE VISION OF BROTHER WALFRID AND THE FIRST FOUNDING MEMBERS, WHO SAW THE FORMATION OF CELTIC AS A MEANS TO REVITALISE AND SERVE THE WHOLE COMMUNITY OF THE EAST END, MAY BECOME MORE TANGIBLE IN THE YEARS AHEAD.
CELTIC WAS THE VISION OF A CATHOLIC PRIEST, THE HEADMASTER OF SACRED HEART SCHOOL, WHO SAW IT AS A MEANS OF RAISING FUNDS FOR HIS POORER PARISHIONERS. THIS CHARITABLE CAUSE AIMED TO ALLEVIATE POVERTY AMONGST GLASGOW'S IRISH CATHOLIC FAMILIES. FROM ITS HUMBLE ORIGINS, CELTIC HAS NOW BECOME ONE OF THE MOST FAMOUS CLUBS IN THE WORLD.
FROM WILLIE MALEY AND THE FIRST TEAM ALL THE WAY THROUGH TO GORDON STRACHAN AND THE PRESENT SQUAD, ALL HAVE PLAYED THEIR PART IN MAKING CELTIC MORE THAN JUST A FOOTBALL CLUB.
THIS IS THE STORY OF ONE MAN'S VISION. THIS VISION GAVE BIRTH TO A TEAM. THIS TEAM GAVE BIRTH TO HOPE AND BECAME THE STUFF OF LEGEND!